CONSTRUCTING SEXUALITIES

CONSTRUCTING SEXUALITIES
READINGS IN SEXUALITY, GENDER, AND CULTURE

Edited by

Suzanne LaFont

The City University of New York
Kingsborough Community College

Prentice
Hall

Upper Saddle River, New Jersey 07458

Library of Congress Cataloging-in-Publication Data

Constructing sexualities: readings in sexuality, gender, and culture / edited by Suzanne LaFont.
　　　p. cm.
　　Includes bibliographical references and index.
　　ISBN 0-13-009661-X (pbk.)
　　1. Sex role.　2. Sex differences.　3. Sex customs.　4. Gender identity.　I. LaFont, Suzanne,
(date)

GN479.65.C66 2003
305.3—dc21

2002074861

AVP/Publisher: Nancy Roberts
Editorial Assistant: Lee Peterson
Editorial/production supervision and interior design: Mary Araneo
Senior Marketing Manager: Amy Speckman
Prepress and Manufacturing Buyer: Ben Smith
Cover Art Director: Jayne Conte
Cover Designer: Bruce Kenselaar
Cover art: Jose Ortega/Stock Illustration Source, Inc.

This book was set in 10/11 New Baskerville by TSI Graphics.
The cover was printed by Phoenix Color Corp.

© 2003 by Pearson Education, Inc.
Upper Saddle River, New Jersey 07458

Printed in the United States of America

10　9　8　7　6　5　4

ISBN 0-13-009661-X

Pearson Education LTD., London
Pearson Education Australia PTY, Limited, Sydney
Pearson Education Singapore, Pte. Ltd
Pearson Education North Asia Ltd, Hong Kong
Pearson Education Canada, Ltd., Toronto
Pearson Educación de Mexico, S.A. de C.V.
Pearson Education—Japan, Tokyo
Pearson Education Malaysia, Pte. Ltd
Pearson Education, Upper Saddle River, New Jersey

This reader is dedicated
to the gender rebels of the world,
past and present.

CONTENTS

PART THREE

SEXUAL POTENTIALITIES:
LESSONS FROM EARLY ETHNOGRAPHIES   66

PART FOUR

RITES OF PASSAGE AND GENITAL MUTILATION   115

PART FIVE

MARRIAGE AND LOVE   134

PART SIX

CONSTRUCTING AND DECONSTRUCTING BODIES   162

PART ELEVEN

THE RIGHT TO SAY NO, THE RIGHT TO SAY YES: GENDER, SEXUALITIES, AND SELF-DETERMINATION 329

PART TWELVE

THE FUTURE OF SEXUALITIES 358

PREFACE

The average person, if there is such an animal, will probably have 100s, if not 1,000s, of sexual encounters in the course of his or her life. All of that sexual activity will result, on average, in two children. The point is that most human sexual behavior is not about reproducing, and in fact, most of us will spend a considerable amount of time and energy making sure that our sexual encounters do not lead to children. Despite this, until recently most discussions about gender and sexualities focused on reproduction. No one is denying that there is a link between sex and reproduction, yet social and physical scientists are still struggling with its role as the motivation for gender roles and sex acts. Explanations put forth by biologists, psychologists, sociologist, sexologists, and anthropologists differ and even pit one discipline against the other. Hence, questions about the roles of sexuality and gender have generated some of the most contested hypotheses in the sciences.

On one side of the debate, some sociobiologists reduce human sexuality to reproduction, looking for the sexual "whys" in how a behavior increases our reproductive success. Their views are very seductive and support the widely held belief that reproduction is the "true" purpose of sex and that gender has been "naturally" shaped to complement reproductive roles. Working under these assumptions, forms of sexual behavior that fall outside of what could be reproductive (even if reproduction is not desired) are then *ipso facto* unnatural.

On the other side of the debate, social construction theorists call for a revision in some of the evolutionary theories that make claims about gender behavior and sexuality. They question the widely held assumptions about an innate sexual drive (libido) and innate programming channeling sexual desire towards members of the opposite sex (sexual orientation). They suggest that beliefs about sexualities should be understood as hypotheses, not scientific truths. These "facts" have not, after all, been proven through the scientific method. Social constructionists argue that understanding precultural human sexualities may not be possible because of the intensive cultural intervention that begins at birth. The book is not closed on these debates, rather, the most exciting work has probably yet to be done, advances in research continuously add to our knowledge.

Both schools of thought agree that no culture in the world treats sex as a physical act without meaning. Unlike other animals who mate and engage in sex acts without societal, parental, ideological, and legal influences, humans experience socialization that comes with a host of messages about sex, gender, and sexualities. That is why dog sex is more or less dog sex. It does not matter whether it involves Poodles or Great Danes (or a coupling of the two), basically the same thing is going to happen. Among humans, on the other hand, we find an immense amount of variation. The range of human sexual potentialities is best discerned by the ethnographic records, but even that data does not give us the whole story.

To fully understand what sex and gender mean to humans, a three part investigation is necessary. Primate modeling is useful because of our close connection with primates. They are used extensively in evolutionary studies as pre-hominid prototypes. Primates, unlike us, do not mind being observed. They lack the moral/privacy/honest issues that interfere with sexuality and gender research among humans. Secondly, history is important to sexuality/gender research because it demonstrates how ideas about sexualities have changed over time. Changes in sexual and gender behavior support the idea that there is a fixed, biological basis for such behavior. Finally, cross-cultural studies of sexualities suggest that we cannot really talk about much sexual behavior in terms of human universals. For example, in some societies women should be virgins when they marry, while in others they need to prove their fertility prior to marriage by having children. Such ethnographic data supports the idea that sexualities and gender are plastic and can be shaped through the socialization process.

Today, gay rights, transgendered movements, intersexed awareness, female genital mutilation, male circumcision, AIDS, sex tourism, and the sex.com explosion on the Internet have forced sexualities and gender into the forefront of popular and academic discourse. The goal of the collection of readings presented in *Constructing Sexualities* is to introduce students to these issues, encourage critical thinking on a variety of sexuality and gender topics, and reveal how ideas, beliefs, and ideals of gender and sexualities are constructed by culture. The reader is a collection of articles, classic and current, with topics including variations in sexual and gender ideologies, expressions of sexualities, gender diversity, and global issues. It adopts an interdisciplinary approach, including works by anthropologists, psychologists, activists, biologists, physicians, historians, and sociologists.

I have tried to choose readings that are student-friendly, light on technical language, and understandable to nonspecialists. Some readings were chosen because they are classics and/or the author was/is an important scholar in the field of Sexuality, Gender, and Culture (SGC). Still other articles were included because they or their theoretical perspective has played/plays an important role in the study of SGC.

One of the difficulties I encountered while organizing the articles was the task of dividing the readings into topic sections. While some articles fit fairly neatly into the section's "subject," others transcend subject sections and defy compartmentalization. In making subject division decisions, I tried to arrange the material in a way that would be best suited for students and teachers alike.

This reader is about critical thought. It is about deconstructing our ideas about facts, scientific objectivity, and neutrality. I am committed to providing students with a broad range of topics. Doing this enhanced the reader, but it also made my job much more difficult. Consequently, some important readings and web sites have unintentionally been omitted.

Ultimately the purpose of the readings is to provide students with materials that will aid them in formulating their own thoughts of sexualities, gender, and culture. It is more about asking the questions than providing the answers.

In class or while talking to friends or family, take the gender, sexualities, culture challenge:

Find an example of gender behavior that is not related to sexuality.
Find an example of sexuality that is not related to gender.
Find an example of sexuality that is not related to culture.
Find an example of gender that is not related to culture.

Thoughts and discussions relating to this simple (actually not so simple) exercise can serve as a good start on students' exploration of this immensely important aspect of their lives.

NOTE ON RESEARCHING SEXUALITIES ON THE INTERNET

Throughout the reader, web site addresses have been provided to aid students who are interested in exploring a subject in more depth than is possible in a general reader. Anyone who searches the net for just about anything will stumble across sites with sex-related material. In particular, when searching for web sites relating to sexuality and gender, you are likely to encounter pornographic pop-ups and/or links to pornographic web sites. Simply modifying a search, for example, adding an "academic" word such as gender or culture, tends to minimize the "porn" effect. Students should be made aware of the sexual content they may encounter on the internet, and they should be instructed on how to avoid the bulk of it. If such exposure makes them uncomfortable, their assignments should be changed to meet their personal, moral, religious, or psychological needs.

Please address any comments or suggestions to constructingsexualities@hotmail.com

Suzanne LaFont

ACKNOWLEDGMENTS

Several people have helped to make this reader a reality. The utmost thanks goes to William Burger, his unwavering support was the cornerstone for this project. Susan Farell, Ilsa Glazer, Nathaniel Gould, Karl Heider, Gilbert Herdt, Lynn Manners, Serena Nanda, David Valentine all deserve thanks for their support, assistance, and suggestions. Anders Peltomaa and Eric Kaplan helped in too many ways to list and have both earned a lifetime of my gratitude. I am also grateful to all the authors whose wonderful research and writing inspired the idea of this reader and made it possible. I would like to thank the anonymous reviewers for their comments and suggestions. Last but not least, I would like to thank all the people at Prentice Hall who helped bring this project to fruition. Nancy Roberts provided much appreciated enthusiasm and support. Lee Peterson was patient and helpful. And Mary Araneo enhanced the final product with her eye for detail.

Suzanne LaFont

CONSTRUCTING SEXUALITIES

◨ PART ONE ◨

RESEARCHING SEXUALITIES AND GENDER

READINGS IN THIS PART

INTRODUCTION TO THE SUBJECT AND READINGS

The vibrator, one of the first electrical appliances, was developed in the 1880s to aid doctors in external pelvic massage. At the time, stimulating women's genitals was an accepted and well-established treatment for female hysteria and congestion of the genitalia, but was considered an uninteresting and time-consuming procedure. The vibrator produced wonderful results (efficient, practical, and fast). Doctors reported that women were so satisfied with the improved massage, that some returned frequently enough to be called "cash cows." Vibrators were seen as so nonsexual that they were soon marketed for home use in respectable ladies' journals. In 1918, Sears advertised vibrators as "Aids that every woman appreciates." (Maines 1999:105).

We may be amused by the image of Victorian women visiting their doctors for genital massage or leafing through the Sears catalogue considering the benefits of one vibrator in comparison to another. Transcending the anecdote, this moment in the history of sexuality introduces several of the issues that will be discussed in this section and throughout the reader. It demonstrates how ideas and knowledge of sexualities have dramatically changed over time. It reveals the errors of medical professionals and scientists—highlighting how little was known about women's sexualities and sexual response and how that knowledge was shaped by ideas about the role of women. Doctors performed medical procedures considered scientific, moral, and ethical, that would today be considered quackery, *im*moral, and *un*ethical.

The history of the vibrator prompts several questions. If sexuality is a fixed, natural force in our lives, why have our ideas about it changed over time? What makes something sexual? It is possible to have a science of sexualities that is neutral and objective? What is the relationship between gender and sexualities? We will learn that sexualities and gender are more interconnected and interrelated than most of us ever imagined. Throughout this reader you will find that you may start with sexuality but cannot go far without bumping directly into gender and less obviously, into culture.

This is well illustrated by the history of vibrators which has come full circle. In the 1880s, male doctors controlled not only the vibrator, but ideas and information about women's sexualities. This gendered interaction paralleled (while shaping and reflecting) sexualities and gender in the U.S. culture. Men controlled, or attempted to control women and women's sexualities. As the image of the vibrator changed, and it began its career as a sex toy for women's sexual gratification, this once heralded medical technology fell off the respectability wagon. The sale of vibrators has been banned, predominately by male legislators, in Alabama, Georgia, and Texas. Enhancements for male sexual pleasure have not met with the same resistance. Viagra is not only widely available and endorsed but also covered by many insurance plans that do not cover birth-control pills. Such developments demonstrate that sexuality, gender, and culture are not fixed, neutral entities, but ideas, notions, and "science" worth fighting over.

The articles in this section reveal the need to revise many of our ideas about sexualities, gender, and their relationship to science. Jennifer Harding's article, *Investigating Sex: Essentialism and Constructionism,* addresses the two major perspectives currently debated by sexual/gender researchers. The essentialism/constructionism debate relates to the older nature/nurture arguments that have pitted physical scientists against social scientists for many years. A model of the basic difference is offered below.

Nature	*Nurture*
biology	culture
essentialism	constructionism
natural science produces truths	ideas about "natural" are shaped by culture

Harding argues that regarding sexual behavior and sexualities, scientists on the nature side of the debate usually promote the idea that humans have an innate drive to have sexual relations and reproduce. They believe that it is possible to trace the origins of gender and sexual behavior by explaining how aspects of our behavior function to maximize reproductive success. Constructionists, on the other hand, see gender and sexualities as a discourse—culture shapes and reflects beliefs and behavior while at the same time being shaped by them.

Anne Fausto-Sterling, herself a biologist, brings us to the next step in understanding the links between sexualities, gender, and culture. Rising above the nature vs. nurture argument, Fausto-Sterling formulated the idea of developmental systems theory. "Developmental systems theorists deny that there are fundamentally two kinds of processes, one guided by genes, hormones and brain cells (i.e., nature), the other by the environment, experience, learning, or inchoate social forces (i.e., nurture)." pp. 20–21.

Emily Martin's article *The Egg and the Sperm: How Science has Constructed a Romance Based on Stereotypical Male-Female Roles* tears down the sacred walls of science by deconstructing the description and language of conception. She exposes the sexism behind the familiar image of strong sperms swimming aggressively hoping to penetrate passive eggs and concludes that science has created a conception scenario in which sperms behave masculinely and eggs behave femininely. In reality, the zona or surface of the egg that the sperm "penetrates" can be seen as a sperm catcher; rather than laying "waiting to be penetrated," the egg *selects* an appropriate mate.

Martin convincingly demonstrated that the science of human reproduction is gendered. She forces us to reexamine the core of our beliefs about sexualities and gender (and just about everything else). The foundation of our theories, ideas, and beliefs no longer provides a comfortable and safe retreat—and once that door is opened it can never be closed again.

Ruth Benedict's article, *Sex in Primitive Society,* a short piece on sexuality in small nonmodern cultures, concludes this section. The reasons for the inclusion of this article are twofold: (1) Ruth Benedict was a pioneer in the study of sexuality in the social science, and (2) her article illustrates how, in 1937, scientists understood the relationship between culture and sexuality. Benedict uses the ethnographic record to address what Dr. Wortis termed "crimes against nature." This phrase, used even today to describe sex offenses, raises many questions. When it comes to sexual behavior, what is natural? Articles in upcoming sections will reveal that if we use animal sexual behavior as a gauge of naturalness, then the wildest sexual exploits of humans seem mundane.

Benedict was clearly progressive and outspoken about sexuality at a time when most ethnographies presented cultures as asexual. She argues that culture influences sexual behavior and cannot be studied in isolation of "familial, political, economic and religious institutions." Benedict employed the model of sexuality called the "cultural influence model." This model recognizes variations in sexual behavior and attitudes cross-culturally and was widely accepted. Although outdated, it is still used today. Importantly, it laid the groundwork for social constructionism; thus, the first three articles would not have been possible without anthropological rebels such as Ruth Benedict.

TERMS AND CONCEPTS

biological imperative
cross-cultural comparison
cultural influence model
deconstructing
developmental system theory (DST)
empirical research
essentialism

libido
naturalist approach
paradigm
sexology
social constructionism theory
Victorian Era

IMPORTANT RESEARCHERS

Brief biographical information about these researchers can be found in the glossary.

Sigmund Freud
Richard von Krafft-Ebing
Havelock Ellis
Magnus Hirshfield

Alfred Kinsey
Masters and Johnson
Michel Foucault

CRITICAL THINKING AND QUESTIONS TO CONSIDER

1. Summarize the essentialist perspective and the constructionist perspective as described by Harding. Which perspective most closely describes your own ideas about sexualities?
2. Using Harding's article, describe Foucault's contribution to our understanding of sexualities.
3. According to Martin, in what ways have scientists gendered sperms and eggs? Do these gendered characteristics accurately describe the behavior of eggs and sperms?
4. Will revisionist accounts of reproduction/fertilization, as advocated by Martin, lead to a revision of ideas concerning female and male sexualities? Why? Or why not?
5. Draw a parallel between the classical description of female eggs and stereotypical accounts of women's sexual response. Do the same for sperm and men's sexual response.
6. Describe Fausto-Sterling's "development systems theory." How does this theory transcend the nature v. nurture debate?
7. According to Fausto-Sterling, what is the pitfall of the Euro-Americans' use of dualism?
8. Benedict argues that sex crimes are virtually nonexistent in "primitive society." List some of the reasons that she gives for the lack of sex crimes.
9. Would Benedict best be described as an essentialist or as a constructionist? Support your answer with examples from her article.
10. Where would you place yourself on the essentialist/constructionist continuum? Explain the reason for your placement choice.

All biology ——————————————all cultural

FURTHER READINGS

Caplan, Pat (ed.). 1987. *The Cultural Construction of Sexuality*. New York: Routledge.

Bland, Lucy, and Laura Doan (eds.). 1998. *Sexology Uncensored: The Documents of Sexual Science*. Chicago: The University of Chicago Press.

———. 1998. *Sexology in Culture: Labelling Bodies and Desires*. Chicago: The University of Chicago Press.

Bullough, Vern L. 1994. *Science in the Bedroom: A History of Sex Research*. New York: Basic Books.

Fausto-Sterling, Anne. 2000. *Sexing the Body: How Biologists Construct Human Sexuality*. New York: Basic Books.

Foucault, Michel. 1978. *The History of Sexuality, Volume I: An Introduction*. New York: Random Books.

Francouer, Robert T. (ed.). 1997. *The International Encyclopedia of Sexuality*, Vol. 1–3. New York: Continuum Publishing.

Harding, Jennifer. 1998. *Sex Acts: Practices of Femininity and Masculinity*. London: Sage Publications.

Maines, Rachel P. 1999. *The Technology of Orgasm: Hysteria, the Vibrator, and Women's Sexual Satisfaction*. Baltimore: Johns Hopkins University Press.

Michael, Robert T., John H. Gagnon, Edward O. Laumann, and Gina Kolata. 1994. *Sex in America: A Definitive Survey*. Boston: Warner Books.

Ortner, Sherry B., and Harriet Whitehead (eds.). 1981. *Sexual Meanings: The Cultural Construction of Gender and Sexuality*. New York: Cambridge University Press.

Vance, Carol S. 1991. Anthropology rediscovers sexuality: A theoretical comment. *Social Science and Medicine*, 33(8) 875–884.

Weston, Kath. 1998. *Long Slow Burn: Sexuality and Social Science*. New York: Routledge.

RELATED WEBSITES

Human Sexuality Collection at Cornell University Library
http://rmc.library.cornell.edu/HSC/default.htm

IASSCS (The International Association for the Study of Sexuality, Culture and Society)
www.miid.net/diversity/iss2.htm

The Kinsey Institute
www.indiana.edu/~kinsey/index.html

Magnus Hirshfeld Archive for Sexology
www2.hu-berlin.de/sexology/GESUND/ARCHIV/TESTHOM2.HTM

Netherlands Institute of Social Sexological Research
www.nisso.nl

On-Line Encyclopedia of Sex (The Sinclair Intimacy Institute)
www.sexualitydata.com/sex_data/index.html

Sexuality The Study for the Scientific Study of Sexuality
www.sexscience.org

World Association for Sexology
www.tc.ymn.edu/~colem001/was

1

Investigating Sex
Essentialism and Constructionism

Jennifer Harding
London Guildhall University

Sexuality is highly contested. Its contestability opens the way for numerous strategies aimed at defining, explaining, and hence regulating, what 'the sexual' comprises.

Researchers have adopted different ways of thinking about, investigating and explaining 'the sexual'. The distinction most commonly made is between 'essentialist' and 'constructionist' approaches. Put another way, a distinction can be made between the perception that sexuality is a 'biological' phenomenon and the perception that it is a 'social' phenomenon.

Lynne Segal (1994) identifies three dominant paradigms in the history of Western approaches to sexual matters—the spiritual, the biological and the social.[1] According to Segal, in pre-industrial European societies, the regulation of sexual behaviour was primarily a spiritual and religious affair (Segal, 1994: 72). However, 'the sexual became synonymous with

Source: Investigating sex: Essentialism and constructionism. In *Sex Acts*, by Jennifer Harding. London: Sage Publications, 1998, pp. 8–22. © 1998 Sage Publications Ltd. Reprinted by permission of the publisher.

the biological' with the birth of the scientific study of sex and the usurpation of authority by doctors and scientists to speak of sexual normality and deviance. Scientific explanations of sex and sexuality have proved especially powerful and enduring. However, scientific paradigms have been seriously challenged, though not dismissed, in recent decades by the perception that nature and biology are social constructions and the notion that 'our experiences of the body and its desires are produced externally through the range of social discourses and institutions which describe and manipulate them' (Segal, 1994: 73).

A new way of thinking about sex does not completely replace a previous one, and different paradigms may coexist. Indeed, biological discourse—deploying scientific method and essentialist premises—has dominated perceptions of the body and sex/uality throughout the twentieth century. The uptake of a constructionist perspective in the social sciences has not meant the abandonment of the scientific study of sex in disciplines like psychology.

'Essentialism' entails the belief that sexuality is purely a natural phenomenon, outside of culture and society, made up of fixed and inherent drives, and that nature and these drives dictate our sexual identities (Weeks, 1995). Sexuality is thus viewed as an instinctual, driving and potentially overwhelming force, which exerts an influence both on the individual and on culture. Essentialists tend to subscribe to the belief that sexual instinct, rightly or wrongly, is held in check by social, moral, medical mechanisms (Weeks, 1985). The individual is the subject of investigation and of necessary (for society to be possible) repressions. An essentialist model of sexuality unites different shades of political opinion, including that aimed at controlling (on the moral right) and liberating (on the left) sexuality (Weeks, 1989).

'Constructionism' entails the belief that sexuality has no inherent essence but must be understood as configuration of cultural meanings which are themselves generated within matrices of social (power) relations (Gagnon and Parker, 1995; Segal, 1994; Weeks, 1995). Cultural institutions (like marriage and patriarchy), norms, practices and relations are the objects of study. Constructionist approaches have been explicitly concerned with power and politics—that is, the ways in which the construction of the sexual has the effect of privileging some sexual forms and denigrating others. However, ideas about the ways in which power 'works' through sexuality and constructs sexual identities and practices vary a great deal.

Essentialism and constructionism are not single political/theoretical positionings. Each is an 'umbrella' term which spans many differences in research agendas, perspectives and methodologies. The terms are themselves historically specific products of particular cultural, political and historical contexts. However, they can be contrasted in terms of a few broad assumptions about what the sexual comprises and how it is constituted.

SEXOLOGY AND ESSENTIALISM

'Sexology' is a term used to describe a range of historically specific endeavours directed at the 'scientific' study of sex. Gagnon and Parker (1995) describe what they call a 'sexological period', dating from 1890 to 1980, in which sex researchers and activists attempted to bring sexuality under the control of 'science'.

Sexologists in the late nineteenth century and early twentieth century were eager to reform sexuality, to oppose what were seen as repressive and restrictive doctrines and practices of the Victorian era (Gagnon and Parker, 1995: 5).[2] Sexological views were seen by the radicals and reformers of the time as liberating.

'Sexology' does not refer to a unified discipline or theoretical perspective. The generic term *science* tends to imply a closed and monolithic domain of knowledge, but this obscures the diversity of methods, problems and complexities addressed by different inquiries (Harding, S., 1986). Sexologists have used a variety of methods in the study of sexuality—from the clinical interview and life history up to the 1930s, to survey questionnaires and field studies of the 1940s to 1960s, laboratory observation and experimentation, in the 1960s and 1970s and ethnographic approaches in the 1970s (Gagnon and Parker, 1995: 6).

One approach is aimed at *describing* the diversity of existing sexual practices and preferences and concentrates on the collection of empirical data. Weeks describes this approach as 'naturalist', since it aims to describe, classify and categorise 'sexual forms that exist "in nature"' (Weeks, 1989: 2). A naturalist approach is typified in the late nineteenth-century sexological work of Havelock Ellis and has been evident in many large surveys of sexual attitudes and behaviours conducted since then.

For example, the scientific study of sex has been extended by the statistical analyses of the sexual behaviour of 12,000 white Americans based on detailed interviews produced by Albert Kinsey (Segal, 1994: 88); by surveys of 15,000 men's and women's experiences of sex conducted by Shere Hite between 1972 and 1986 (Hite, 1994); and, in 1994, by the publication of a report of a national survey of sexual attitudes and lifestyles of the British population based on statistical analysis of the interview responses of almost 20,000 randomly selected (to represent the views of the whole population) Britons (Wellings et al., 1994). Other descriptive work includes the ethnographic field work of social anthropologists. Many of these researchers (in particular Ellis and Kinsey) presented their data on the existence of diverse sexual forms and practices as evidence that they existed 'in nature' and were, therefore, not to be considered abnormal. Lynne Segal claims that Kinsey considered that which is natural to be healthy (learning from other mammals) (Segal, 1994: 88) and that 'his dogged determinism to disclose the variability and fluidity of sexual behaviour provided an important weapon for sexual minorities who, like Kinsey himself, wanted to abolish the distinction between "normal" and "abnormal" sexuality and insist that sexual conventions should encompass sexual realities' (Segal, 1994: 89).[3] Masters and Johnson studied what they called the human sexual response, defined as a distinctively physiological response, in an experimental study. They recorded 'the bodily contractions, secretions, pulse rates and tissue colour changes occurring during more than 10,000 male and female orgasms, produced in the laboratory by 694 white, middle-class heterosexual men and women' and defined women's sexual capacity as greater and more varied than men's (Segal, 1994: 93). These studies have produced a great deal of information but little explanation of the variations reported in sexual forms and how attitudes change. Other sexological studies of sexuality (usually derived from psychodynamic or neo-Freudian theory) have produced theories to explain the development of specific sexual forms, but have prioritised theoretical constructs over the collection of 'empirical evidence' (Weeks, 1989: 2).

Sexologists, despite considerable differences, have in common a commitment to producing a 'science of sex', and share several concerns and beliefs about sex. In particular, they subscribe to the idea that sex has an ultimately discoverable *essence*, insisting on the privileged role of sex in expressing 'the natural' and constituting 'sexuality as an "eternal duel"

of the "unruly energy" and the constraints of "society"' (Weeks, 1985: 11). Sexologists agreed that 'sex was a natural force that existed in opposition to civilisation, culture or society' (Gagnon and Parker, 1995: 7). Cultures and societies were seen as responding to, rather than shaping, the sexual impulse. Thus, 'the individual and the drive were prior to the social or cultural order,' (ibid.), and sexuality was a powerful and profound force. However, they were divided on whether the sex drive was 'a virtuous force warped by a negative civilisation (see Masters and Johnson, Kinsey, Mead, Ellis) or a negative force that required social control (see Freud and most of his followers)' (ibid.).

Even though sexologists were adamant in their attempts to 'explain the biological imperative of sex', they did acknowledge that social control and regulation varied within and across different cultures. They recognised 'different rules of marriage, monogamy, taboos against incest and responses to non-procreative sex even as they sought to naturalise them' (Weeks, 1985: 97). Sexologists held differing views with regard to how, and the degree to which, the expression of sexual instinct should be patrolled by social and cultural mechanisms and the possible consequences of particular social interventions (Wood, 1985: 157). The conduct of individuals was the focus of research because the drive was embedded in the individual.

Importantly, science, because of its claims to objectivity and impartiality, was seen to make the study of sex 'respectable' (whereas otherwise it had seemed distasteful). The scientific study of sex was justified by the belief that science was capable of producing 'an unbiased version of sexuality' which if understood and applied would reduce ignorance about sex and lead to 'human betterment' (Gagnon and Parker, 1995: 7). Sexologists shared a belief in 'the privileged character of positive scientific knowledge', which was seen as trans-cultural and trans-historical. Admittedly, there might be 'variations in cultural practices', but 'the underlying nature of sexuality remains the same in all times and places' (Gagnon and Parker, 1995: 7–8).

Nearly all theorists of 'the sexological period' believed that there were fundamental differences between the sexuality of men and of women—'differences that followed upon the natural differences between the feminine and the masculine':

> As a corollary of these beliefs . . . theories of sexuality were normatively dominated by notions of men's sexuality and by heterosexual images and practices. (Gagnon and Parker, 1995: 7)

Sexual instinct was invested with a biologically ordained *aim* (intercourse) and *object* (usually a person of the opposite sex) (Wood, 1985). According to Segal, early sexologists 'saw male and female sexuality as fundamentally opposed: the one aggressive and forceful, the other responsive and maternal' (Segal, 1994: 76). Early sex researchers helped to affirm 'male domination as biological necessity, portraying "the sex act", understood as heterosexual genital engagement, as its exemplary moment' (Segal, 1994: 79).

These ideas were not uncontested. Whilst nineteenth-century feminists had been primarily concerned with 'protecting women from the dangers of male sexuality—disgrace, forced sex and unwanted pregnancy', many resisted the repressive culture of the time (Segal, 1994: 83). In the early part of the twentieth century, feminists like Stella Browne and Olive Schreiner argued for women's rights to the fulfilment of their sexuality on its own terms, which was seen as different from men's, and in this way helped to articulate new positions of desiring subjectivity for women (Browne, 1915; Rowbotham, 1977a: 87–90; Weeks, 1989: 167).

There has been a gradual shift in emphasis in twentieth-century sexological discourse away from sexual difference and towards sameness. There has been increasing recognition of women's, as well as men's, capacity for sexual pleasure and a commitment to the idea that women could and should experience such pleasure. However, this is not to say that women's and men's sexual pleasures were seen as equivalent or that imbalances in the power relations of heterosexuality were being addressed:

> whether feminists demanded or decried the expression of women's desire for sex with men,

metaphors of male conquest and female submission have remained, to this day, tied in with conceptions of heterosexuality. (Segal, 1994: 85)

Sexological discourse has been extremely influential in defining and explaining 'the sexual'. Sexology has achieved a privileged status, based on its claims to scientific and political rationality, and, consequently, has influenced many other social activities and institutions, including the law, medicine and social welfare agencies. The definitions produced within sexological discourse have had 'major effects in shaping our concepts of male and female sexuality, in demarcating the boundaries of the normal and abnormal, in defining the homosexual and other sexual "deviants"' (Weeks, 1985: 91).

However, the objectivity and impartiality claimed by sexologists have been challenged by the assertions that these definitions are themselves highly political and that sexological discourse has always been deeply entangled with other contemporary discourses: in particular, discourses on gender, race, class and nationality.

CHALLENGES TO ESSENTIALISM

Essentialist accounts of sexuality, in which sexuality is seen as biologically given and socially repressed, have been challenged from several different theoretical perspectives within the last few decades.

Jeffrey Weeks (1989) suggests that the main theoretical challenges have been: 'the interactionist', 'the psychoanalytical' and 'the discursive' (Weeks, 1989: 3).[4] According to Weeks, despite their use of very different theoretical approaches, these challenges converge on several important themes. In particular, all of these approaches reject the idea that the sexual is an autonomous and rebellious realm which the social controls. From an interactionist perspective, it is suggested that 'nothing is intrinsically sexual' and 'anything can be sexualised' (Weeks, 1989: 3). In Lacan's reinterpretation of Freud, sexuality is constituted in language. In Foucault's writing, sexuality is 'the name that can be given to a historical construct' (ibid.: 4). Anti-essentialist critiques are also linked by 'a recognition of the social and historical sources of sexual definitions' (ibid.).[5]

'Interests' have been crucial in the evolution of anti-essentialist approaches. Gagnon and Parker argue that by the 1960s

> it was clear that the sexological paradigm was in serious trouble, particularly at the level of explanation. . . . The important criticisms came from social scientists within sex research and from activist groups who were attempting to reconstruct central features of the paradigm that were prejudicial to their interests. (1995: 8)

Critics of sexology challenged 'both the universalist conception of the sexual as well as the privileged status of scientific inquiry' (ibid.). They argued that science was not unbiased.

Critical studies of science[6] and different feminist research programmes[7] have proliferated in recent decades to demonstrate the ways in which science can be considered 'biased'.

Sexologists' belief in the neutral, transcultural and trans-historical character of scientific knowledge was countered with the claim that sexological knowledge was historically and culturally specific and also highly political in its generation and application. The concepts deployed in sexological discourse (for example, conceptions of the individual and the purpose of sexuality) reflected the uneven relations of gender, race and class. Further, it was argued that science did not reveal the truth about a naturally occurring sexuality 'out there'; instead it helped to construct it through the knowledge it produced, which legitimised some sexual practices and denigrated others.[8] That is, cultural notions about the proper roles and functions of men and women have influenced scientific understandings of sex and sexuality (Jacobus et al., 1990; Martin, 1989, 1990; Poovey, 1990).

Many of the key categories used in sexology to describe and classify aspects of sexual life (like homosexuality, masculinity and fem-

ininity) have been shown not to be universal but highly localised (Gagnon and Parker, 1995: 11). Categories like 'sex', 'the body' and 'nature', the taken-for-granted transcultural and trans-historical bedrock of sexological research, have been deconstructed to show how they are the product, not the cause of contemporary cultural preoccupations. For example, it is widely believed in scientific and popular cultures that sex is a universal, ahistorical attribute of the body, and the basis of social and sexual behaviour. However, 'the sexed body' has been shown to be a changing idea in history, culture and discourse.[9] Historians have demonstrated that sex has been differently conceptualised by scientists at different historical moments and that their conceptualisations have reflected the contemporary social organisation of gender (Jacobus et al., 1990; Laqueur, 1990; Martin, 1989; Oudshoorn, 1994; Schiebinger, 1986). Scientists' conceptions of sex had the effect of 'naturalising' gender relations—that is, giving the impression that they were determined by an underlying 'nature' and so were inevitable. This was the result of scientists' claim that they could describe and explain 'nature' as it really was and represent nature as a force directing the world, to which the social responds. Scientists' descriptions of 'sex' were assumed to be an accurate record of that which existed in nature and dictated the social dimensions of gender. Not surprisingly, 'nature' has increasingly become the object of deconstruction.

The idea that sexuality is a 'natural' force, deriving from our biological being, has been extremely powerful in popular and scientific discourse and continues to be influential. Deployed as a key category in sexology, 'nature' has considerable rhetorical and persuasive power. It must then be asked: To what precisely do 'nature' and 'natural' refer?

'Nature' can be viewed as an idea in history whose meanings have changed over time. The idea that biological sex research is more basic than other approaches, because it examines something closer to nature and pre-social (and therefore more generalisable) can be traced to constructions of nature which served Enlightenment politics (Tiefer, 1995: 38).

Since the inception of what is often called 'The Enlightenment Project',[10] the natural world has been construed as the ideal object of intellectual endeavour and as the source of knowledge. The exercise of reason has been seen as the best way of producing an objective, reliable and universal foundation for knowledge (Flax, 1990: 41). It was thought that the knowledge produced through the correct use of reason would be 'true'. Science achieved a special significance and authority in modern societies because it was seen to exemplify the right use of reason, to enable a more rigorous and comprehensive commitment to the principles of objectivity, impartiality and independence, and to be impartial in method and content (Flax, 1990; Hall et al., 1992). Reason itself, considered to possess transcendental and universal qualities, was thought to exist 'independently of the self's contingent existence (e.g. bodily, historical, and social experiences do not affect reason's structure or its capacity to produce atemporal knowledge)' (Flax, 1990: 41). Thus, scientists claim to discover facts about 'nature' which are disinterested and true and, in doing so, to exert control over it (nature). The capacity of scientific discourse to effect such mastery relies upon and embodies a binary logic, comprising a series of conceptual dichotomies—culture vs. nature, mind vs. body, reason vs. emotion, objectivity vs. subjectivity—in which the former terms must dominate the latter (Harding, S., 1986: 23). Some feminists have claimed that the former (dominating categories) are systematically associated with the masculine and the latter (subordinated categories) with the feminine.

Nature, according to Raymond Williams, is possibly the 'most complex word' in the English language (Williams, 1976: 184).[11] Williams traces the historical development of the word, discussing three uses of the word 'nature'. The first meaning, from the thirteenth century, is 'the essential quality and character *of* something'; the second, from the fourteenth century, is 'the inherent force which directs either the world or human beings or both'; the third, the seventeenth century, is 'the material world itself, taken as including or not including human beings'. The latter use has

retained currency and nature is used to mean the countryside ('the "unspoiled" places, plants and creatures other than man') in distinguishing between town and country (Williams, 1976: 186).

In *Sex Is Not a Natural Act*, Leonore Tiefer examines Williams's history of the meanings of nature in relation to sexological research. She argues that 'the term *nature* is often used in sexology for its rhetorical power'. By emphasizing that something is *in nature*, a sense of solidity and validity is conferred. This use calls on nature *in contrast with culture*, implying that anything human-made is 'false', whereas something outside of human culture is 'true'. 'Sexual nature', Tiefer writes, sounds 'like something solid and valid, not human-made' (Tiefer, 1995: 32, 33).

DECONSTRUCTION/RECONSTRUCTION

Constructionism meant, among other things, that it was theoretically possible to deconstruct and reconstruct popular and scientific conceptions of sexuality.

Within the framework of what Weeks calls the 'new social histories', sexuality was understood as a variable category of experience and was constituted in relation to, and in interaction with, other historically and culturally variable social practices (legal, biomedical, religious, economic) and relations (class, race and gender). These practices and relations also helped to generate categories and concepts which organise sexuality and define grids of tolerance and intolerance towards, for example, teenage pregnancy and sex outside of marriage, openly declared homosexuality, prostitution and children's sexual knowledge. (In)tolerance is based on definitions of what is considered healthy and unhealthy, normal and abnormal, appropriate and inappropriate in sexual life formulated within the same practices and relations (Weeks, 1985: 7).

The 'naturalness' of contemporary sexuality, gender roles and sexual attitudes was also undermined by the radical movements of the 1970s (in particular the women's movement and the lesbian and gay movement) (Segal, 1994; Weeks, 1985). If sex felt individual and private, individuality and privacy were *ideas* which also incorporated the roles, definitions, symbols and meanings of the worlds in which they were constructed: they were culturally and historically contingent.

'The personal is the political' was the feminist slogan which encapsulated this insight. Feminists argued that prevailing patterns of subordination and domination in society at large were reproduced in the most intimate sphere of private life, that of sexual relations. Moreover, these relations were sustained by *social* definitions of female sexuality disguised as descriptions of 'essential' female sexuality. Most importantly, feminists have revealed the interconnections of power and sexuality and therefore made sexual politics a central aspect of everyday life and the social and political relations which organise it (Weeks, 1985; Wood, 1985).

The critical contribution of feminist studies to sex research was, according to Gagnon and Parker, 'the recognition that gender was a larger frame through which sexuality in Western societies should be interpreted' (1995: 8). Feminist studies drew attention to the 'facts' that men did most of the research on sex, that the sexuality of men was taken to be the norm (against which all else was compared), that sexual practices of women and men were determined by inequalities in power, and that the relation of gender to sexuality was not fixed (1995: 8–9).

Lesbian and gay studies drew attention to variable and complex relations between identity and behaviour and showed that categories like '"homosexual", "bisexual", and "heterosexual", "gay", "queer", and "clone" are all social constructs which are ambiguously tied to behaviour' (Gagnon and Parker, 1995a). These insights also have implications for race, gender and class issues 'in which public performances are often tied to private identities' (Gagnon and Parker, 1995a). . . .

Lesbian and gay critiques of sexology have shown 'the increased importance of self-identified lesbian and gay researchers in doing research on lesbian and gay issues' (Gagnon and Parker, 1995: 9). Gays had previously been excluded from studying gays on the grounds of likely bias, whilst it was not recognised that heterosexuals would be biased (more so perhaps because of homophobia). The emergence of gay researchers implied a significant critique 'both of the positivist ideal of unbiased research and of the idea that same-gender sexual practices are abnormal' (Gagnon and Parker, 1995: 10). Ironically, the consequences of these developments may be more conservative than radical.

Women's studies and lesbian and gay studies have carved out new fields of study and have been successful because men and heterosexuals have given over this territory. In doing so, these dominant groups have been able to avoid in part 'an analysis of men as gendered creatures as well as an analysis of the socially constructed nature of contemporary heterosexuality' (Gagnon and Parker, 1995: 10). A continued focus on the gender/sexualities of non-dominant groups (even though women and gays may be the researchers) makes these into problems and leaves the masculine and heterosexual undeconstructed as the norm.

Social constructionists held that sexuality was not 'based on internal drives, but was elicited in specific historical and social circumstances' (Gagnon and Parker, 1995: 8). The constructionist view was that we can only understand sexuality through the cultural meanings which construct it (Weeks, 1995). This approach does not assume that biology is unimportant, nor that individuals are simply blank sheets on which society writes its cultural messages. According to Weeks, it is not a question of whether, for example, homosexuality is inborn or learned, but of the meanings that a particular culture 'gives to homosexual behaviour, however it may be caused, and what are the effects of those particular meanings on the ways in which individuals organise their lives' (Weeks, 1995: 34). Weeks suggests that this is a historical and a highly political question—one, which concerns *not* the true nature of identities but identities' political relevance. Thus, Weeks argues that where it is commonly believed that sexuality is the least changeable amongst social phenomena, this is an effect of ideology which makes 'us believe that what is socially created, and therefore subject to change, is really natural, and therefore immutable' (ibid.).

SETTING THE SCENE FOR *SEX ACTS*

Deconstruction is never complete. The logic of constructionism is that all knowledge production is political in the sense that it is intimately bound up with power relations. Constructionists' researchs and explanations are also constructed.

Feminist, lesbian and gay studies of sexuality have undoubtedly posed important and interesting challenges to the orthodoxies of sexological discourse. Because of the theoretical/political underpinnings of this work, Gagnon and Parker argue, it has tended to be historical, since 'it is difficult to be constructionist when engaged in social resistance since constructionism emphasises the temporary character of both oppressors and revolutionaries' (Gagnon and Parker, 1995: 10). One effect of this has been to formulate identities and sexualities as self-evident categories to be liberated from previous constraints and oppressions and, simultaneously, to tend towards essentialising such sexual identities. As a way of 'getting at' the present and the contingencies of identity categories, I pitch my analysis of sexuality at the level of discourse.

In *Sex Acts* I view sexuality *as* discourse. Several points motivate this approach. Firstly, the 'hold' that science appears to have on 'truth', and the widespread popular appeal of this and the security it provides, is deeply entrenched in modern Western cultures. By viewing science as one of a number of plausible discourses, which are culturally and historically located, it is possible to thoroughly question (rather than simply reproduce and reinforce) its terms of reference. It is possible to reveal some of the cultural meanings underpinning scientific statements and open the way for producing alternative (possibly less constraining) meanings.

Secondly, whilst some anti-essentialist approaches developed by theorists/activists in response to aspects of the sexological paradigm prejudicial to their 'interests' have given rise to the description and celebration (rather than denigration) of sexualities these have not been subjected to the same level of critique. That is, these (newly 'liberated') sexualities have not always been viewed as also historically contingent. My point here is that sexuality can never be separated from power, so there can be no truly free or liberated sexuality—just new configurations of 'the sexual' within power relations which also cannot help but regulate subjects (albeit in different ways). This is not to say that some forms of regulation might not be preferable to others and less constraining for some. A focus on sexuality as discourse requires that the political discourses of particular self-identified collectivities (feminist, lesbian, gay) also be scrutinised to reveal the ways in which they construct sexual identities in specific historical and cultural circumstances.

Thirdly, ideas about sexuality are complex and hybrid: they do not necessarily belong to one paradigm or another but circulate and are borrowed and modified, whether consciously or unconsciously, by different researchers/activists. Analysis of discourse—involving a detailed examination of what gets said, by whom and from where—is one way of working beyond the limits of specific disciplines to discover how specific ideas come about and their effects (deconstruction) and to think about other ways in which sex might be put into words, and for which purposes (reconstruction).

Working at the level of discourse, as Foucault (1986) conceptualises it, will facilitate my looking at the ways in which sexualities are shaped and organised in the 1990s. This approach provides an effective means of deconstructing powerful ideas and theories—those of science and those of political 'identity politics'.

FOUCAULT, SEX AND DISCOURSE

In *The History of Sexuality* (1981), Foucault discusses the relations between sex, power and discourse. Sexuality, for Foucault, is historically and discursively constructed within relations of power. There is no essential human quality (sexuality) to be repressed or liberated. Rather, there are ideas about sexuality which are put into words—discourses.[12] Weeks reads this as meaning that 'the sexual only exists in and through the modes of its organisation and representation' (1985: 10)—that is, through aesthetic, scientific, historical and political discourses. Sexuality has no reality outside of these discourses, which claimed merely to describe it but actually construct it. The history of sexuality in the West is actually the history of discourses on sexuality. Sexuality is then the endpoint of discourses which attempt to define it, analyse it, control it, emancipate it (Weeks, 1989).

Foucault argues that sex has been volubly and excessively spoken about in modern societies since the seventeenth century, as part of the processes of modern power (Foucault, 1981). Contrary to popular belief, the Victorian era was not a time of repression of sexuality in the West, which could then be liberated in the twentieth century. Instead, Foucault argues, far from being repressed or restricted, discourse on sex has been 'subjected to a mechanism of increasing excitement' (1981: 12). The explosion of discourses on sex can be seen as part of a complex extension of social control over the individual through the apparatus of sexuality (Weeks, 1989). Discourses have issued from a variety of institutions (medical, religious, legal, psychiatric, educational) and these discourses have *constructed* sexuality (as residing in organs, endowed with instincts, leading a separate life in the inner recesses of the individual).

Modern societies have been inclined to define the relation between sex and power as one of repression, whereby sex is considered in need of liberation. This definition may be particularly gratifying because if sex is repressed and condemned to silence, then the mere act of speaking about it has 'the appearance of a deliberate transgression' (Foucault, 1981: 7). Someone who talks about sex in this way appears to be 'outside the reach of power' and is conscious of defying power (ibid.). Contemporary representations of sexualities may be transgressive,

because they dare to speak out about sex and name its unacceptable—adulterous, criminal, perverse forms. In this sense, someone who, for example, 'comes out' or attempts to 'out' someone else is exercising a degree of power. They may also help to constitute and reinforce a boundary between public and private domains, even as they appear to erase it.

According to Weeks, what is ultimately significant in Foucault's work is his 'recognition of the constant struggles within the definition of sexuality'. Thus, he rejects the concept of 'liberation' and maintains that sexual radicalism should not try to free a repressed essence but to consciously intervene 'at the level of the definition of appropriate sexual behaviour' (Weeks, 1989: 10).

ANALYSIS OF DISCOURSE

'Discourse analysis' refers to a method of investigating the social construction of phenomena, including ideas, practices and domains of knowledge. According to Foucault, 'discourse' constitutes social phenomena (Foucault, 1979, 1981, 1986). Discourses are *practices*, rather than structures or superstructures, that are lived, acted out and spoken by individuals. Discourses operate as fields of fluid and mobile 'relations' and 'interrelations' which produce and transmit knowledge and power relations (Foucault, 1979, 1986).

In Foucault's texts, power and knowledge directly imply one another. Thus, 'there is no power relation without the correlative constitution of a field of knowledge, nor any knowledge, that does not presuppose and constitute at the same time power relations' (Foucault, 1979: 27). Knowledge does not derive from some subject of knowledge but from the power relations, the processes and struggles, that traverse and invest it. The important point about Foucault's concept of power is that it is not a property but a strategy that is exercised from 'innumerable points in the interplay of non egalitarian and mobile relations' (Foucault, 1981: 94) and is met with a 'multiplicity of points of resistance' (ibid.: 95). In this way, Foucault conceptualises power as positive (meaning that it is creative), rather than negative (meaning that it is constraining).

Discourses, according to Foucault (1986) are comprised of statements which must be spoken from somewhere and by someone, and this speaking entails the *bringing into being* and positioning of a subject and assignment of a 'subject position'. The idea of 'subject positions' located within the historical contingencies of a specific discourse, spoken from a particular time and place, replaces the idea of a hegemonic knowing subject or coherent subjectivity which exists before and across discourses. Within this framework, emphasis is placed on examining particular statements to ascertain who is speaking from where, of what, and how it is possible to create new statements, subjects and speaking positions. For any individual, subjectivity is not coherent nor complete but must be repeatedly (re)signified in and through discourse, involving the assignment and adoption of different positions of subjectivity.

The objects of discourse and discourse itself emerge in the same process (Foucault, 1986: 45). Discourses systematically form and order, within relations of power, the objects of which they speak. This conceptualisation does not involve denying a prediscursive existence for the subject nor for the objects of discourse. Rather, whether or not object and subjects exist outside of discourse, they are constituted as such within discourse (Laclau and Mouffe, 1985: 108). Within this framework, even their prediscursive existence is produced in discourse.[13]

In the following chapters, I emphasise the productive and organising functions of discourse in order to show how sex/ualities are made and might be remade, and how specific discursive constructions of 'the sexual' create some sexual subject positions and foreclose others. I look at how different (sometimes conflicting) discourses intersect to address and 'position' sexual subjects and the ways in which these 'positionings' may be resisted. This approach opens up more room for manoeuvre (theoretically/politically speaking) than one which is based on the idea of a repressed/liberated sexuality.

NOTES

1. 'A paradigm is composed of an interrelated set of accepted explanations, methods and observations' (Gagnon and Parker, 1995: 8).

2. According to Gagnon and Parker, the following were key names in sexology: Freud and his followers, Ellis, Hirshfield, Malinowski, Stopes, Sanger, Guyon, Reich, Mead, Kinsey and his associates, and Masters and Johnson (Gagnon and Parker, 1995: 5).

3. 'For example, he reported that at least 37% of the thousands of American males he interviewed had some homosexual experience' (Segal, 1994: 89).

4. According to Weeks (1989) 'the interactionist' is associated with the work of Gagnon and Simon and Plummer. See Gagnon and Simon, 1973. 'The psychoanalytical' is associated with Jacques Lacan's reinterpretation of Freud and has subsequently been taken up by feminists like Juliet Mitchell. See Mitchell, 1975 and also Mitchell and Rose, 1982. 'The discursive' is primarily associated with the work of Michel Foucault and especially *The History of Sexuality. Volume One* (Foucault, 1981).

5. See Weeks (1989: 4–6) for a fuller discussion of the key differences between these challenges to essentialist views.

6. These include studies of/in science, the history of science, the philosophy of science and feminist critiques of science. Critiques are extremely diverse, employing different methods, conceptualising different problems and coming up with different conclusions. . . .

7. Sandra Harding (1986) distinguishes five research programmes aimed at challenging 'gender bias' in science: (1) 'equity studies' examining the barriers to women's participation in science; (2) 'studies of the uses and abuses of biology, the social sciences and their technologies' which have revealed 'the ways in which science is used in the services of sexist, racist, homophobic and classist social projects' (e.g. reproductive policies, medical cures for homosexuals) (Harding, S., 1986: 21) (the assumption here is that there can be a value-free science, pure scientific research that can be distinguished from the social uses of science); (3) usual science as 'bad science', based on the idea that the selection and definition of problematics have been skewed towards men's problems (not women's) and explanations of men's gender desires and needs, i.e. the design and interpretation of research is masculine biased (as if it could be other than value laden) (Harding, S., 1986: 22); (4) 'reading science as text' (using techniques of

literary criticism, historical interpretation and psychoanalysis)—this is directed at revealing 'the social meanings—the hidden semiotic and structural agendas—of purportedly value-neutral claims and practices' (ibid.: 23). This includes drawing out 'metaphors of gender politics' and viewing the 'rigid series of dichotomies in science and epistemology' ('objectivity vs. subjectivity, the scientist as the knowing subject vs. the object of his inquiry, reason vs. the emotions, mind vs. body', in which 'the former has been associated with masculinity and the latter with femininity' and it has been claimed that 'human progress requires the former to achieve domination of the latter': ibid.) *not* as 'a reflection of the progressive character of scientific inquiry', rather, as 'inextricably connected with specifically masculine—perhaps uniquely Western and bourgeois—needs and desires' (ibid.); (5) 'feminist epistemological inquiries' which form a basis for understanding how 'beliefs are grounded in social experiences, and of what kind of experience ground the beliefs we honor as knowledge' (ibid.: 24).

8. Nelly Oudshoorn (among others) states very clearly the view that, rather than discovering facts about reality 'out there', scientists are engaged in the collective creation of statements constituting reality (Oudshoorn, 1994).

9. See Chapter 3 for a fuller discussion of this.

10. 'The Enlightenment Project' refers to an intellectual and philosophical movement originating in the eighteenth century and comprising clusters of assumptions and expectations, sets of ideas and themes, that occurred 'at the threshold of typically modern Western society' (McLennan, G., 1992).

11. 'Any full history of the uses of *nature* would be a history of a large part of human thought' (Williams, 1976: 186). 'Nature' conveys many of the variations in human thought over time and all its meanings are in use, often together (ibid.: 189).

12. Foucault is interested in the way in which 'sex is put into discourse' and 'the discourses it permeates in order to reach the most tenuous and individual modes of behaviour' and how it 'penetrates and controls everyday pleasure', all of which constitute 'polymorphous techniques of power' (Foucault, 1981: 11).

13. This does not necessarily involve a rejection of those critiques which address 'the subject' as a prediscursive entity, but may in some ways complement this significant field of inquiry. I am thinking particularly of feminist psychoanalytic critiques of, and attempts to destabilise, the (masculine) subject: including those based in object relations (Chodorow, 1978; Dinnerstein, 1978); and those which, in very different ways, take Lacanian psy-

choanalytic theory as a point of departure (Mitchell, 1975; Rose, 1986; Kristeva, 1982, 1986; Irigaray, 1985, 1988); and also French feminists' *écriture feminine* (Marks and de Courtivron, 1981). See also Judith Butler (1990b) for a discussion of how many feminist attempts at destabilising the (masculine) subject tend, nevertheless, to effect 'a false stabilisation of the category of women' (Butler, 1990b: 329).

BIBLIOGRAPHY

Browne, S. 1915. The sexual variety and variability among women and their bearing upon social reconstruction, in Rowbotham 1977.

Chodorow, N. 1978. *The Reproduction of Mothering: Psycholanalysis and the Sociology of Gender*. Berkeley: University of California Press.

Dinnerstein, D. 1978. *The Rocking of the Cradle and the Ruling of the World*. London: Souvenir Press.

Flax, J. 1990. Postmodernism and gender relations in feminist theory, in Nicholson, L. (ed.). *Feminism/Postmodernism*. New York and London: Rutledge.

Foucault, M. 1979. *Discipline and Punish. The Birth of the Prison*. New York: Vintage Books.

———. 1981. *The History of Sexuality. Volume One. An Introduction*. Harmondsworth, Middlesex: Penguin Books.

———. 1986. *The Archaeology of Knowledge*. London: Tavistock.

Gagnon, J. H., and R. G. Parker. 1995. Conceiving sexuality, in Parker and Gagnon 1995.

Hall, S., D. Held, and T. McGrew (eds.). 1992. *Modernity and its Futures*. Cambridge: Polity Press.

Harding, S. 1986. *The Science Question in Feminism*. Milton Keynes: Open University Press.

Hite, S. 1994. *Women as Revolutionary Agents of Change. The Hite Reports: Sexuality, Love and Emotion*. London: Hodder and Stoughton.

Jacobus, M., E. Keller, and S. Shuttleworth (eds.). 1990. *Body/Politics. Women and the Discourses of Science*. New York and London: Routledge.

Laclau, E., and C. Mouffe. 1985. *Hegemony and Socialist Strategy: Towards a Radical Democratic Politics*. London: Verso.

Laqueur, T. 1990. *Making Sex: Body and Gender from the Greeks to Freud*. Cambridge, MA and London: Harvard University Press.

McLennan, G. 1992. The Enlightenment Project revisited, in Hall et al. 1992.

Martin, E. 1989. *The Woman in the Body. A Cultural Analysis of Reproduction*. Milton Keynes: Open University Press.

————. 1990. Science and women's bodies: Forms of anthropological knowledge, in Jacobus et al. 1990.

Mitchell, J. 1975. *Psychoanalysis and Feminism*. Harmondsworth, Middlesex: Penguin Books.

Mitchell, J., and J. Rose (eds.). 1982. *Feminine Sexuality. Jacques Lacan and the École freudienne*. London: Macmillan Press.

Oudshoorn, N. 1994. *Beyond the Natural Body. An Archaeology of Sex Hormones*. London and New York: Routledge.

Parker, R. G., and J. H. Gagnon (eds.). 1995. *Conceiving Sexuality. Approaches to Sex Research in a Postmodern World*. New York and London: Routledge.

Poovey, M. 1990. Speaking of the body: Mid-Victorian constructions of female desire, in Jacobus et al. 1990.

Rose, J. 1986. *Sexuality in the Field of Vision*. London: Verso.

Rowbotham, S. 1977. *A New World for Women. Stella Browne: Socialist Feminist*. London: Pluto Press.

Schiebinger, L. 1986. Skeletons in the closet: The first illustrations of the female skeleton in nineteenth century anatomy, *Representations*, 14:42–83.

Segal, L. 1994. *Straight Sex: The Politics of Pleasure*. London: Virago.

Tiefer, L. 1995. *Sex Is Not a Natural Act and Other Essays*. Boulder, CO, San Francisco, and Oxford: Westview Press.

Weeks, J. 1985. *Sexuality and Its Discontents*. London and New York: Routledge.

————. 1989. *Sex, Politics and Society. The Regulation of Sexuality since 1800*. London and New York: Longman.

————. 1995. History, desire, and identities, in Parker and Gagnon 1995.

Wellings, K., J. Field, A. M. Johnson, and J. Wadsworth. 1994. *Sexual Behaviour in Britain. The National Survey of Sexual Attitudes and Lifestyles*. Harmondsworth, Middlesex: Penguin Books.

Williams, R. 1976. *Keywords*. London: Fontana.

Wood, N. 1985. Foucault on the history of sexuality: An introduction, in V. Beechey and J. Donald (eds.). *Subjectivity and Social Relations*. Milton Keynes: Open University Press.

2
Sexing the Body
How Biologists Construct Human Sexuality

Anne Fausto-Sterling
Brown University

Abstract

This article is a version of Chapter One: Sexing the Body: Gender Politics and the Construction of Sexuality. In it is argued that science is often thought of as being beyond the reach of social and political debates. In fact, it is precisely such debates that have dictated the course of scientific research, ranging from the very questions scientists pose to the experimental methods they employ. And this is highly pertinent to the ongoing debate concerning the biological versus social nature of gender and sexuality. In most public and in most scientific discussions, sex and nature, are thought to be real, while gender and culture are seen as constructed. But these are

Source: From *Sexing the Body: How Biologists Construct Human Sexuality,* by Anne Fausto-Sterling (as reprinted in *The International Journal of Transgenderism*). New York: Basic Books. Copyright © 2000 by Basic Books, a member of the Perseus Book Group. Reprinted by permission of Basic Books, a member of Perseus Books, L.L.C.

false dichotomies. In fact, it is argued, there is a complex and subtle interaction that exists between the biological and the social/political that must be understood and reexamined.

In *The Tempest*, Shakespeare's Prospero denounces Caliban as, "A devil, a born devil, one whose nature nurture can never stick . . ." This passage of *The Tempest* makes clear that questions of nature and nurture have troubled European culture for some time. Euro-American ways of understanding how the world works depend heavily on the use of dualisms—pairs of opposing concepts, objects or belief systems. Let me consider today three related pairs—sex/gender, nature/nurture and real/constructed. We usually employ dualisms in some form of hierarchical argument. Prospero complains that nature controls Caliban's behavior and that his, Prospero's, "pains humanely taken" (to civilize Caliban) are to no avail. Humane nurture can't conquer the devil's nature. Today, I will argue that intellectual questions cannot be resolved nor social progress made by reverting to Prospero's complaint. In the creation of biological knowledge about human sexuality, I look to cut through the Gordian knot of dualistic thought. I propose instead of nature vs. nurture or real vs. constructed, that sexuality is a somatic fact created by a cultural effect.

Ultimately, the sex/gender dualism limits feminist and other forms of analysis. The term 'gender,' placed in a dichotomy, necessarily excludes biology. Thinking critically about biology remains impossible because of the real/constructed divide (sometimes formulated as a division between nature and culture), in which many map the knowledge of the real onto the domain of science while equating the constructed with the cultural. Dichotomous formulations from feminists and non-feminists alike conspire to make a socio-cultural analysis of the body seem impossible.

Some feminist theorists, especially during the last decade, have tried—with varying degrees of success—to create a non-dualistic account of the body. Feminist philosopher Judith Butler, for example, tries to reclaim the material body for feminist thought. Why, she wonders, has the idea of materiality come to signify that which is irreducible, that which can support construction but cannot, itself be constructed. We have, Butler says, (and I agree) to talk about the material body. There are hormones, genes, prostates, uteri and other body parts and physiologies that we use to differentiate male from female, that become part of the ground from which varieties of sexual experience and desire emerge. Furthermore, variations in each of these aspects of physiology profoundly affect an individual's experience of gender and sexuality. But every time we try to return to the body as something which exists prior to socialization, prior to discourse about male and female, Butler writes, "we discover that matter is fully sedimented with discourses on sex and sexuality that prefigure and constrain the uses to which that term can be put."

Western notions of matter and bodily materiality, Butler argues, have been constructed through a "gendered matrix". Classical philosophers associated femininity with materiality. Consider, for example, the origins of the word "matter" from mater and matrix referring to the womb and problems of reproduction. In both Greek and Latin, according to Butler, matter was not understood to be a blank slate awaiting the application of external meaning.

"The matrix is a . . . formative principle which inaugurates and informs a development of some organism or object . . . for Aristotle, 'matter is potentiality, form actuality.' . . . In reproduction women are said to contribute the matter, men the form." As Butler notes, the title of her book, Bodies that Matter, is a deeply intentional pun. To be material is to speak about the process of materialization. And if viewpoints about sex and sexuality are already embedded in our philosophical concepts of how matter forms into bodies, the matter of bodies cannot form a neutral, pre-existing ground from which to understand the origins of sexual difference. This, then, is our dilemma: since matter already contains notions of gender and sexuality, it cannot be a neutral recourse on which to build "scientific" or "objective" theories of sexual development and differentiation. At the same time, we have to acknowledge and use aspects of materiality that "pertain to the body." "The domains of biology, anatomy, physiology, hormonal and chemical composition, illness, age, weight, metabolism, life and death" cannot "be denied." In other words, to talk about human sexuality requires a notion of the material. Yet the idea of the material comes to us already tainted, containing within it pre-existing ideas about sexual difference. Butler suggests that we must look at the body as a system that simultaneously produces and is produced by social meanings, just as any biological organism always results from the combined and simultaneous actions of nature and nurture.

Unlike Butler, feminist philosopher Elizabeth Grosz allows some biological processes a status that pre-exists their meaning. She believes that biological instincts or drives provide a kind of raw material for the development of sexuality. But raw materials are never enough. They must be provided with a set of meanings, "a network of desires which" organize the meanings and consciousness of the child's bodily functions. This claim becomes clear if one follows the stories of so-called "wild children" raised without human constraints or the inculcation of meaning. Such children acquire neither language nor sexual drive. Thus while their bodies provided the raw materials, without a human social setting, the clay could not be molded into recognizable psychic form. Without human sociality, human sexuality cannot develop. Grosz tries to understand how human sociality and meaning that clearly originate outside the body, end up incorporated into its physiological, demeanor, and both unconscious and conscious behaviors. Some concrete examples illustrate the problem: consider a tiny gray-haired woman, well into her 9th decade, peering into the mirror at her wrinkled face. "Who IS that woman in the mirror?" she wonders. Her mind's image of her body does not synchronize with the mirror's reflection. Her daughter, now in her mid-fifties, tries to remember that unless she thinks about using her leg muscles instead of her knee joint, going up and down the stairs will be quite painful. (Eventually she will acquire a new kinesic habit and dispense with conscious thought about the matter.) Both women are working at readjusting the visual and kinesic components of their body image, formed on the basis of past information, but always a bit out of date with the current physical body. How do such readjustments occur, and how do our earliest body images form in the first place? To discuss this problem we need the concept of the psyche—a place where two-way translations between the mind and the body take place—a United Nations, as it were, of bodies and experiences. In *Volatile Bodies* Elizabeth Grosz thinks out loud about how the body and the mind come into being together. To facilitate her project she uses the image of a Mobius strip as a metaphor for the psyche. The Mobius strip is a topological puzzle, a flat ribbon, twisted once and then attached end to end to form a circular twisted surface. One can trace the surface, for example, by imagining an ant walking along it. At the beginning of the circular journey, the ant is clearly on the outside. But as it traverses the twisted ribbon, without ever lifting its legs from the plane, it ends up on the inside surface. Grosz proposes that we think of the body—the brain, muscles, sex organs, hormones and more—as comprising the inside of the Mobius strip. Culture and experience, would constitute the outside surface. But, as the image suggests, the inside and outside are continuous and one can move from one space to the other without ever lifting one's feet off the ground.

Grosz envisions that bodies create psyches by using the libido as a marker pen to trace a path from biological processes to an interior structure of desire. It falls to a different arena of scholarship to study the "outside" of the strip, a more obviously social surface marked by "pedagogical, juridical, medical, and economic texts, laws and practices" in order to "carve out a social subject . . . capable of labor, or production and manipulation, a subject capable of acting as a subject . . .". Thus Grosz also rejects a nature vs. nurture model of human development. While acknowledging that we do not understand the range and limits of the body's pliability, she insists that we cannot merely "subtract the environment, culture, history" and end up with "nature or biology." This is where a lot of feminist constructed work happens.

BEYOND DUALISMS

Grosz postulates innate drives that become organized by physical experience into somatic feelings that translate into what we call emotions. Taking the innate at face value, however, still leaves us with an unexplained residue of nature. Humans are biological and thus in some sense natural beings AND social, and thus in some sense artificial, or, if you will, constructed entities. Can we devise a way of seeing ourselves, as we develop from fertilization to old age, as simultaneously natural and unnatural? During the past decade an exciting vision has emerged which I have loosely grouped under the rubric of developmental systems theory, or DST. What do we gain by choosing DST as an analytic framework? Developmental systems theorists deny that there are fundamentally two kinds of processes, one guided by genes, hormones and brain cells (i.e. nature), the other by the environment, experience, learning or inchoate social forces (i.e. nurture).

How, specifically, can DST help us break away from dualistic thought processes? Consider a goat born with no front legs. During its lifetime it managed to hop around on its hind limbs. An anatomist who studied the goat after it died found that it had an S-shaped spine (as do humans) "thickened bones, modified muscle insertions, and other correlates of moving on two legs." This (and every goat's) skeletal system developed as part of its manner of walking. Neither its genes, nor its environment determined its anatomy. Only the ensemble had such power. Many developmental physiologists recognize this principle. As one biologist writes, "Enstructuring occurs during the enactment of individual life histories." A few years ago, when neuroscientist Simon LeVay reported that the brain structures of gay and heterosexual men differed (and that this mirrored a more general sex difference between straight men and women), he became the center of a firestorm. Although an instant hero among many gay males, he was at odds with a rather mixed group. On the one hand feminists such as myself disliked his unquestioning use of gender dichotomies which have in the past never worked to further equality for women. On the other, members of the Christian right hated his work because they believe that homosexuality is a sin which individuals can choose to reject. LeVay's, and later geneticist Dean Hamer's, work suggested to them that homosexuality was inborn or innate. The language of the public debate quickly became polarized. Both sides contrasted words such as genetic, biological, inborn, innate, and unchanging with ones such as environmental, acquired, constructed and choice.

The ease with which such debates evoke the nature/nurture divide is a consequence of the poverty of a non-systems approach. Politically, the nature/nurture framework holds enormous dangers. Although some hope that a belief in the nature side of things will lead to greater tolerance, past history suggests that the opposite is also possible. Even the scientific architects of the nature argument recognize the dangers. In an extraordinary passage in the pages of *Science*, Dean Hamer and his collaborators indicated their concern. "It would be fundamentally unethical to use such information to try to assess or alter a person's current or future sexual orientation . . . Rather, scientists, educators, policy-makers and the public should work together to ensure that such research is used to benefit all members of society." Feminist psychologist and critical theorist Elisabeth Wilson uses the hubbub over LeVay's work to make some important points about systems theory. Many feminist, queer and critical theorists work by deliberately displacing biology, hence opening the body to social and cultural shaping. This, however, is the wrong move to make. Wilson writes: "What may be politically and critically contentious in LeVay's hypothesis is not the conjunction neurology-sexuality per se, but the particular manner in which such a conjunction is enacted." An effective political response, she continues, doesn't have to separate the study of sexuality from the neurosciences. Instead, Wilson, who wants us to develop a theory of mind and body—an account of psyche that joins libido to body—suggests that we feminists incorporate into our world view an account of how the brain works that is, broadly speaking, called connectionism.

The old fashioned approach to understanding the brain was anatomical. Function could be located in particular parts of the brain. Ultimately function and anatomy were one. This idea underlies the uproar over LeVay's work. Many scientists believe that a structural difference represents the brain location for measured behavioral differences. In contrast, connectionist models argue that function emerges from the complexity and strength of many neural connections acting at once. The system has some important characteristics: (1) the responses are often non linear, (2) the networks can be "trained" to respond in particular ways, (3) the nature of the response is not easily predictable, and (4) information is not located anywhere, rather it is the net result of the many different connections and their differing strengths.

The tenets of some connectionist theory provide interesting starting points for understanding human sexual development. Because connectionist networks, for example, are usually non linear, small changes can produce large effects. One implication for studying sexuality: we could easily be looking in the wrong places and on the wrong scale for aspects of the environment which shape human development. Furthermore, a single behavior may have many underlying causes: events that happen at different times in development. I suspect that sexualities which we label as homosexual, heterosexual, bisexual, and transgender are really not good categories at all, and are best understood only in terms of unique individual developmental events. Thus, I agree with those connectionists who argue that "the developmental process itself lies at the heart of knowledge acquisition . . . Development is a process of emergence."

In most public and in most scientific discussions, sex and nature, are thought to be real, while gender and culture are seen as constructed. But these are false dichotomies. Sometimes, for example, sex is, literally, constructed. In the case of intersexuality, surgeons remove parts and use plastic to create "appropriate" genitalia for people born with body parts that are not easily identifiable as male or female. Physicians believe that their expertise enables them to "hear" nature telling them the truth about what sex their patient ought to be. Alas, their truths come from the social arena and are reinforced, in part, by the medical tradition of rendering intersexual births invisible.

Let me sum up: when we examine the construction of sexuality starting with structures visible on the body's exterior surface and ending with behaviors and motivations—that is

with activities and forces which are patently invisible—inferred only from their outcome, but presumed to be located deep within the body's interior, we find that behaviors are generally social activities, expressed in interaction with distinctly separate objects and beings. Thus, as we move from genitalia on the outside, to the invisible psyche, we find ourselves, suddenly, walking along the surface of a Mobius strip back towards, and beyond, the body's exterior. Only if we conceptualize sexuality as part of a developmental system which reaches from our cultural and social history to the cells in our bodies can we learn how we move from outside to inside and back out again, without ever lifting our feet from the strip's surface.

REFERENCES

Butler, Judith. 1993. *Bodies That Matter: On the Discursive Limits of "Sex."* London: Routledge.

Grosz, Elizabeth A. 1994. *Volatile Bodies: Toward A Corporeal Feminism.* Bloomington, IN: University Press.

Hamer, Dean H., and Peter Copeland. 1994. *The Science of Desire: The Search for the Gay Gene and the Biology of Behavior.* New York: Simon & Schuster.

LeVay, Simon. 1991. A difference in hypothalamic structure between heterosexual and homosexual men. *Science* 253: 1034–1037.

LeVay, Simon. 1996. *Queer Science: The Use and Abuse of Research into Homosexuality.* Cambridge, MA: MIT Press.

Wilson, Elizabeth A. 1998. *Neural Geographies: Feminism and the Microstructure of Cognition.* New York: Routledge.

3

The Egg and the Sperm
How Science Has Constructed a Romance Based on Stereotypical Male-Female Roles

Emily Martin
Johns Hopkins University

The theory of the human body is always a part of a world-picture. . . . The theory of the human body is always a part of a *fantasy*. [JAMES HILLMAN, *The Myth of Analysis*][1]

As an anthropologist, I am intrigued by the possibility that culture shapes how biological scientists describe what they discover about the natural world. If this were so, we would be learning about more than the natural world in high school biology class; we would be learning about cultural beliefs and practices as if they were part of nature. In the course of my research I realized that the picture of egg and sperm drawn in popular as well as scientific accounts of reproductive biology relies on stereotypes central to our cultural definitions of male and female. The stereotypes imply not only that female bio-

Source: The egg and the sperm: How science has constructed a romance based on stereotypical male-female roles, by Emily Martin. In *Signs*, 1991, vol. 16, no. 3, pp. 485–501. © 1991 The University of Chicago Press. Reprinted by permission of the publisher.

logical processes are less worthy than their male counterparts but also that women are less worthy than men. Part of my goal in writing this article is to shine a bright light on the gender stereotypes hidden within the scientific language of biology. Exposed in such a light, I hope they will lose much of their power to harm us.

EGG AND SPERM: A SCIENTIFIC FAIRY TALE

At a fundamental level, all major scientific textbooks depict male and female reproductive organs as systems for the production of valuable substances, such as eggs and sperm.[2] In the case of women, the monthly cycle is described as being designed to produce eggs and prepare a suitable place for them to be fertilized and grown—all to the end of making babies. But the enthusiasm ends there. By extolling the female cycle as a productive enterprise, menstruation must necessarily be viewed as a failure. Medical texts describe menstruation as the "debris" of the uterine

23

lining, the result of necrosis, or death of tissue. The descriptions imply that a system has gone awry, making products of no use, not to specification, unsalable, wasted, scrap. An illustration in a widely used medical text shows menstruation as a chaotic disintegration of form, complementing the many texts that describe it as "ceasing," "dying," "losing," "denuding," "expelling."[3]

Male reproductive physiology is evaluated quite differently. One of the texts that sees menstruation as failed production employs a sort of breathless prose when it describes the maturation of sperm: "The mechanisms which guide the remarkable cellular transformation from spermatid to mature sperm remain uncertain. . . . Perhaps the most amazing characteristic of spermatogenesis is its sheer magnitude: the normal human male may manufacture several hundred million sperm per day."[4] In the classic text *Medical Physiology,* edited by Vernon Mountcastle, the male/female, productive/destructive comparison is more explicit: "Whereas the female *sheds* only a single gamete each month, the seminiferous tubules *produce* hundreds of millions of sperm each day" (emphasis mine).[5] The female author of another text marvels at the length of the microscopic seminiferous tubules, which, if uncoiled and placed end to end, "would span almost one-third of a mile!" She writes, "In an adult male these structures produce millions of sperm cells each day." Later she asks, "How is this feat accomplished?"[6] None of these texts expresses such intense enthusiasm for any female processes. It is surely no accident that the "remarkable" process of making sperm involves precisely what, in the medical view, menstruation does not: production of something deemed valuable.[7]

One could argue that menstruation and spermatogenesis are not analogous processes and, therefore, should not be expected to elicit the same kind of response. The proper female analogy to spermatogenesis, biologically, is ovulation. Yet ovulation does not merit enthusiasm in these texts either. Textbook descriptions stress that all of the ovarian follicles containing ova are already present at birth. Far from being *produced,* as

sperm are, they merely sit on the shelf, slowly degenerating and aging like overstocked inventory: "At birth, normal human ovaries contain an estimated one million follicles [each], and no new ones appear after birth. Thus, in marked contrast to the male, the newborn female already has all the germ cells she will ever have. Only a few, perhaps 400, are destined to reach full maturity during her active productive life. All the others degenerate at some point in their development so that few, if any, remain by the time she reaches menopause at approximately 50 years of age."[8] Note the "marked contrast" that this description sets up between male and female: the male, who continuously produces fresh germ cells, and the female, who has stockpiled germ cells by birth and is faced with their degeneration.

Nor are the female organs spared such vivid descriptions. One scientist writes in a newspaper article that a woman's ovaries become old and worn out from ripening eggs every month, even though the woman herself is still relatively young: "When you look through a laparoscope . . . at an ovary that has been through hundreds of cycles, even in a superbly healthy American female, you see a scarred, battered organ."[9]

To avoid the negative connotations that some people associate with the female reproductive system, scientists could begin to describe male and female processes as homologous. They might credit females with "producing" mature ova one at a time, as they're needed each month, and describe males as having to face problems of degenerating germ cells. This degeneration would occur throughout life among spermatogonia, the undifferentiated germ cells in the testes that are the long-lived, dormant precursors of sperm.

But the texts have an almost dogged insistence on casting female processes in a negative light. The texts celebrate sperm production because it is continuous from puberty to senescence, while they portray egg production as inferior because it is finished at birth. This makes the female seem unproductive, but some texts will also insist that it is she who is wasteful.[10] In a section heading for *Molecular*

Biology of the Cell, a best-selling text, we are told that "Oogenesis is wasteful." The text goes on to emphasize that of the seven million oogonia, or egg germ cells, in the female embryo, most degenerate in the ovary. Of those that do go on to become oocytes, or eggs, many also degenerate, so that at birth only two million eggs remain in the ovaries. Degeneration continues throughout a woman's life: by puberty 300,000 eggs remain, and only a few are present by menopause. "During the 40 or so years of a woman's reproductive life, only 400 to 500 eggs will have been released," the authors write. "All the rest will have degenerated. It is still a mystery why so many eggs are formed only to die in the ovaries."[11]

The real mystery is why the male's vast production of sperm is not seen as wasteful.[12] Assuming that a man "produces" 100 million (10^8) sperm per day (a conservative estimate) during an average reproductive life of sixty years, he would produce well over two trillion sperm in his lifetime. Assuming that a woman "ripens" one egg per lunar month, or thirteen per year, over the course of her forty-year reproductive life, she would total five hundred eggs in her lifetime. But the word "waste" implies an excess, too much produced. Assuming two or three offspring, for every baby a woman produces, she wastes only around two hundred eggs. For every baby a man produces, he wastes more than one trillion (10^{12}) sperm.

How is it that positive images are denied to the bodies of women? A look at language—in this case, scientific language—provides the first clue. Take the egg and the sperm.[13] It is remarkable how "femininely" the egg behaves and how "masculinely" the sperm.[14] The egg is seen as large and passive.[15] It does not *move* or *journey,* but passively "is transported," "is swept,"[16] or even "drifts"[17] along the fallopian tube. In utter contrast, sperm are small, "streamlined,"[18] and invariably active. They "deliver" their genes to the egg, "activate the developmental program of the egg,"[19] and have a "velocity" that is often remarked upon.[20] Their tails are "strong" and efficiently powered.[21] Together with the forces of ejaculation, they can "propel the semen into the deepest recesses of the vagina."[22] For this they need "energy," "fuel,"[23] so that with a "whiplashlike motion and strong lurches"[24] they can "burrow through the egg coat"[25] and "penetrate" it.[26]

At its extreme, the age-old relationship of the egg and the sperm takes on a royal or religious patina. The egg coat, its protective barrier, is sometimes called its "vestments," a term usually reserved for sacred, religious dress. The egg is said to have a "corona,"[27] a crown, and to be accompanied by "attendant cells."[28] It is holy, set apart and above, the queen to the sperm's king. The egg is also passive, which means it must depend on sperm for rescue. Gerald Schatten and Helen Schatten liken the egg's role to that of Sleeping Beauty: "a dormant bride awaiting her mate's magic kiss, which instills the spirit that brings her to life."[29] Sperm, by contrast, have a "mission,"[30] which is to "move through the female genital tract in quest of the ovum."[31] One popular account has it that the sperm carry out a "perilous journey" into the "warm darkness," where some fall away "exhausted." "Survivors" "assault" the egg, the successful candidates "surrounding the prize."[32] Part of the urgency of this journey, in more scientific terms, is that "once released from the supportive environment of the ovary, an egg will die within hours unless rescued by a sperm."[33] The wording stresses the fragility and dependency of the egg, even though the same text acknowledges elsewhere that sperm also live for only a few hours.[34]

In 1948, in a book remarkable for its early insights into these matters, Ruth Herschberger argued that female reproductive organs are seen as biologically interdependent, while male organs are viewed as autonomous, operating independently and in isolation:

> At present the functional is stressed only in connection with women: it is in them that ovaries, tubes, uterus, and vagina have endless interdependence. In the male, reproduction would seem to involve "organs" only.
>
> Yet the sperm, just as much as the egg, is dependent on a great many related processes. There are secretions which mitigate the urine in the urethra before ejaculation, to protect the sperm. There is the reflex shutting off of the

bladder connection, the provision of prostatic secretions, and various types of muscular propulsion. The sperm is no more independent of its milieu than the egg, and yet from a wish that it were, biologists have lent their support to the notion that the human female, beginning with the egg, is congenitally more dependent than the male.[35]

Bringing out another aspect of the sperm's autonomy, an article in the journal *Cell* has the sperm making an "existential decision" to penetrate the egg: "Sperm are cells with a limited behavioral repertoire, one that is directed toward fertilizing eggs. To execute the decision to abandon the haploid state, sperm swim to an egg and there acquire the ability to effect membrane fusion."[36] Is this a corporate manager's version of the sperm's activities— "executing decisions" while fraught with dismay over difficult options that bring with them very high risk?

There is another way that sperm, despite their small size, can be made to loom in importance over the egg. In a collection of scientific papers, an electron micrograph of an enormous egg and tiny sperm is titled "A Portrait of the Sperm."[37] This is a little like showing a photo of a dog and calling it a picture of the fleas. Granted, microscopic sperm are harder to photograph than eggs, which are just large enough to see with the naked eye. But surely the use of the term "portrait," a word associated with the powerful and wealthy, is significant. Eggs have only micrographs or pictures, not portraits.

One depiction of sperm as weak and timid, instead of strong and powerful—the only such representation in western civilization, so far as I know—occurs in Woody Allen's movie *Everything You Always Wanted To Know About Sex* * *But Were Afraid to Ask*. Allen, playing the part of an apprehensive sperm inside a man's testicles, is scared of the man's approaching orgasm. He is reluctant to launch himself into the darkness, afraid of contraceptive devices, afraid of winding up on the ceiling if the man masturbates.

The more common picture—egg as damsel in distress, shielded only by her sacred garments; sperm as heroic warrior to the rescue—cannot be proved to be dictated by the biology of these events. While the "facts" of biology may not *always* be constructed in cultural terms, I would argue that in this case they are. The degree of metaphorical content in these descriptions, the extent to which differences between egg and sperm are emphasized, and the parallels between cultural stereotypes of male and female behavior and the character of egg and sperm all point to this conclusion.

NEW RESEARCH, OLD IMAGERY

As new understandings of egg and sperm emerge, textbook gender imagery is being revised. But the new research, far from escaping the stereotypical representations of egg and sperm, simply replicates elements of textbook gender imagery in a different form. The persistence of this imagery calls to mind what Ludwik Fleck termed "the self-contained" nature of scientific thought. As he described it, "the interaction between what is already known, what remains to be learned, and those who are to apprehend it, go to ensure harmony within the system. But at the same time they also preserve the harmony of illusions, which is quite secure within the confines of a given thought style."[38] We need to understand the way in which the cultural content in scientific descriptions changes as biological discoveries unfold, and whether that cultural content is solidly entrenched or easily changed.

In all of the texts quoted above, sperm are described as penetrating the egg, and specific substances on a sperm's head are described as binding to the egg. Recently, this description of events was rewritten in a biophysics lab at Johns Hopkins University—transforming the egg from the passive to the active party.[39]

Prior to this research, it was thought that the zona, the inner vestments of the egg, formed an impenetrable barrier. Sperm overcame the barrier by mechanically burrowing through, thrashing their tails and slowly working their way along. Later research showed that the sperm released digestive enzymes that chemically broke down the zona; thus, scientists presumed that the sperm used mechanical *and* chemical means to get through to the egg.

In this recent investigation, the researchers began to ask questions about the mechanical force of the sperm's tail. (The lab's goal was to develop a contraceptive that worked topically on sperm.) They discovered, to their great surprise, that the forward thrust of sperm is extremely weak, which contradicts the assumption that sperm are forceful penetrators.[40] Rather than thrusting forward, the sperm's head was now seen to move mostly back and forth. The sideways motion of the sperm's tail makes the head move sideways with a force that is ten times stronger than its forward movement. So even if the overall force of the sperm were strong enough to mechanically break the zona, most of its force would be directed sideways rather than forward. In fact, its strongest tendency, by tenfold, is to escape by attempting to pry itself off the egg. Sperm, then, must be exceptionally efficient at *escaping* from any cell surface they contact. And the surface of the egg must be designed to trap the sperm and prevent their escape. Otherwise, few if any sperm would reach the egg.

The researchers at Johns Hopkins concluded that the sperm and egg stick together because of adhesive molecules on the surfaces of each. The egg traps the sperm and adheres to it so tightly that the sperm's head is forced to lie flat against the surface of the zona, a little bit, they told me, "like Br'er Rabbit getting more and more stuck to tar baby the more he wriggles." The trapped sperm continues to wiggle ineffectually side to side. The mechanical force of its tail is so weak that a sperm cannot break even one chemical bond. This is where the digestive enzymes released by the sperm come in. If they start to soften the zona just at the tip of the sperm and the sides remain stuck, then the weak, flailing sperm can get oriented in the right direction and make it through the zona— provided that its bonds to the zona dissolve as it moves in.

Although this new version of the saga of the egg and the sperm broke through cultural expectations, the researchers who made the discovery continued to write papers and abstracts as if the sperm were the active party who attacks, binds, penetrates, and enters the egg. The only difference was that sperm were now seen as performing these actions weakly.[41] Not until August 1987, more than three years after the findings described above, did these researchers reconceptualize the process to give the egg a more active role. They began to describe the zona as an aggressive sperm catcher, covered with adhesive molecules that can capture a sperm with a single bond and clasp it to the zona's surface.[42] In the words of their published account: "The innermost vestment, the *zona pellucida*, is a glycoprotein shell, which captures and tethers the sperm before they penetrate it. . . . The sperm is captured at the initial contact between the sperm tip and the *zona*. . . . Since the thrust [of the sperm] is much smaller than the force needed to break a single affinity bond, the first bond made upon the tip-first meeting of the sperm and *zona* can result in the capture of the sperm."[43]

Experiments in another lab reveal similar patterns of data interpretation. Gerald Schatten and Helen Schatten set out to show that, contrary to conventional wisdom, the "egg is not merely a large, yolk-filled sphere into which the sperm burrows to endow new life. Rather, recent research suggests the almost heretical view that sperm and egg are mutually active partners."[44] This sounds like a departure from the stereotypical textbook view, but further reading reveals Schatten and Schatten's conformity to the aggressive-sperm metaphor. They describe how "the sperm and egg first touch when, from the tip of the sperm's triangular head, a long, thin filament shoots out and harpoons the egg." Then we learn that "remarkably, the harpoon is not so much fired as assembled at great speed, molecule by molecule, from a pool of protein stored in a specialized region called the acrosome. The filament may grow as much as twenty times longer than the sperm head itself before its tip reaches the egg and sticks."[45] Why not call this "making a bridge" or "throwing out a line" rather than firing a harpoon? Harpoons pierce prey and injure or kill them, while this filament only sticks. And why not focus, as the Hopkins lab did, on the stickiness of the egg, rather than the stickiness of the sperm?[46] Later in the article, the Schattens replicate the common view of the sperm's perilous journey into the warm darkness of the vagina, this time for the purpose of explaining its journey into the egg itself: "[The sperm] still has an arduous journey ahead. It must penetrate farther into the egg's huge sphere of cytoplasm and somehow locate the nucleus, so that the two cells' chromosomes can fuse. The sperm dives down into the cytoplasm, its tail beating. But it is soon interrupted by the sudden and swift migration of the egg nucleus, which rushes toward the sperm with a velocity triple that of the movement of chromosomes during cell division, crossing the entire egg in about a minute."[47]

Like Schatten and Schatten and the biophysicists at Johns Hopkins, another researcher has recently made discoveries that seem to point to a more interactive view of the relationship of egg and sperm. This work, which Paul Wassarman conducted on the sperm and eggs of mice, focuses on identifying the specific molecules in the egg coat (the zona pellucida) that are involved in egg-sperm interaction. At first glance, his descriptions seem to fit the model of an egalitarian relationship. Male and female gametes "recognize one another," and "interactions . . . take place between sperm and egg."[48] But the article in *Scientific American* in which those descriptions appear begins with a vignette that presages the dominant motif of their presentation: "It has been more than a century since Hermann Fol, a Swiss zoologist, peered into his microscope and became the first person to see a sperm penetrate an egg, fertilize it and form the first cell of a new embryo."[49] This portrayal of the sperm as the active party—the one that *penetrates* and *fertilizes* the egg and *produces* the embryo—is not cited as an example of an earlier, now outmoded view. In fact, the author reiterates the point later in the article: "Many sperm can bind to and penetrate the zona pellucida, or outer coat, of an unfertilized mouse egg, but only one sperm will eventually fuse with the thin plasma membrane surrounding the egg proper (*inner sphere*), fertilizing the egg and giving rise to a new embryo."[50]

The imagery of sperm as aggressor is particularly startling in this case: the main discovery being reported is isolation of a particular molecule *on the egg coat* that plays an important role in fertilization! Wassarman's choice of language sustains the picture. He calls the molecule that has been isolated, ZP3, a "sperm receptor." By allocating the passive, waiting role to the egg, Wassarman can continue to describe the sperm as the actor, the one that makes it all happen: "The basic process begins when many sperm first attach loosely and then bind tenaciously to receptors on the surface of the egg's thick outer coat, the zona pellucida. Each sperm, which has a large number of egg-binding proteins on its surface, binds to many sperm receptors on the egg. More specifically, a site on each of the egg-binding proteins fits a complementary site on a sperm receptor, much as a key fits a lock."[51] With the sperm designated as the "key" and the egg the "lock," it is obvious which one acts and which one is acted upon. Could this imagery not be reversed, letting the sperm (the lock) wait until the egg produces the key? Or could we speak of two halves of a locket matching, and regard the matching itself as the action that initiates the fertilization?

It is as if Wassarman were determined to make the egg the receiving partner. Usually in biological research, the *protein* member of the pair of binding molecules is called the receptor, and physically it has a pocket in it rather like a lock. As the diagrams that illustrate Wassarman's article show, the molecules on the sperm are proteins and have "pockets." The small, mobile molecules that fit into these pockets are called ligands. As shown in the diagrams, ZP3 on the egg is a polymer of "keys"; many small knobs stick out. Typically, molecules on the sperm would be called receptors and molecules on the egg would be called ligands. But Wassarman chose to name ZP3 on the egg the receptor and to create a new term, "the egg-binding protein," for the molecule on the sperm that otherwise would have been called the receptor.[52]

Wassarman does credit the egg coat with having more functions than those of a sperm receptor. While he notes that "the zona pellucida has at times been viewed by investigators as a nuisance, a barrier to sperm and hence an impediment to fertilization," his new research reveals that the egg coat "serves as a sophisticated biological security system that screens incoming sperm, selects only those compatible with fertilization and development, prepares sperm for fusion with the egg and later protects the resulting embryo from polyspermy [a lethal condition caused by fusion of more than one sperm with a single egg]."[53] Although this description gives the egg an active role, that role is drawn in stereotypically for fusion, and then *protects* the resulting offspring from harm. This is courtship and mating behavior as seen thorugh the eyes of a sociobiologist: woman as the hard-to-get prize, who, following union with the chosen one, becomes woman as servant and mother.

And Wassarman does not quit there. In a review article for *Science*, he outlines the "chronology of fertilization."[54] Near the end of the article are two subject headings. One is "Sperm Penetration," in which Wassarman describes how the chemical dissolving of the zona pellucida combines with the "substantial propulsive force generated by sperm." The next heading is "Sperm-Egg Fusion." This section details what happens inside the zona after a sperm "penetrates" it. Sperm "can make contact with, adhere to, and fuse with (that is, fertilize) an egg."[55] Wassarman's word choice, again, is astonishingly skewed in favor of the sperm's activity, for in the next breath he says that sperm *lose* all motility upon fusion with the egg's surface. In mouse and sea urchin eggs, the sperm enters at the *egg's* volition, according to Wassarman's description: "Once fused with egg plasma membrane [the surface of the egg], how does a sperm enter the egg? The surface of both mouse and sea urchin eggs is covered with thousands of plasma membrane-bound projections, called microvilli [tiny "hairs"]. Evidence in sea urchins suggests that, after membrane fusion, a group of elongated microvilli cluster tightly around and interdigitate over the sperm head. As these microvilli are resorbed, the sperm is drawn into the egg. Therefore, sperm motility, which ceases at the time of fusion in both sea urchins and mice, is not required for sperm entry."[56] The section called "Sperm Penetration" more logically would be followed by a section called "The Egg Envelops," rather than "Sperm-Egg Fusion." This would give a parallel—and more accurate—sense that both the egg and the sperm initiate action.

Another way that Wassarman makes less of the egg's activity is by describing components of the egg but referring to the sperm as a whole entity. Deborah Gordon has described such an approach as "atomism" ("the part is independent of and primordial to the whole") and identified it as one of the "tenacious assumptions" of Western science and medicine.[57] Wassarman employs atomism to his advantage. When he refers to processes going on within sperm, he consistently returns to descriptions that remind us from whence these activities came: they are part of sperm that penetrate an egg or generate propulsive force. When he refers to processes going on within eggs, he stops there. As a result, any active role he grants them appears to be assigned to the parts of the egg, and not to the egg itself. In the quote above, it is the microvilli that actively cluster around the sperm. In another example, "the driving force for engulfment of a fused sperm comes from a region of cytoplasm just beneath an egg's plasma membrane."[58]

SOCIAL IMPLICATIONS: THINKING BEYOND

All three of these revisionist accounts of egg and sperm cannot seem to escape the hierarchical imagery of older accounts. Even though each new account gives the egg a larger and more active role, taken together they bring into play another cultural stereotype: woman as a dangerous and aggressive threat. In the Johns Hopkins lab's revised model, the egg ends up as the female aggressor who "captures and tethers" the sperm with her sticky zona, rather like a spider lying in wait in her web.[59] The Schatten lab has the egg's nucleus "interrupt" the sperm's dive with a "sudden and swift" rush by which she "clasps the sperm and guides its nucleus to the center."[60] Wassarman's description of the surface of the egg "covered with thousands of plasma membrane-bound projections, called microvilli" that reach out and clasp the sperm adds to the spiderlike imagery.[61]

These images grant the egg an active role but at the cost of appearing disturbingly aggressive. Images of woman as dangerous and aggressive, the femme fatale who victimizes men, are widespread in Western literature and culture.[62] More specific is the connection of spider imagery with the idea of an engulfing, devouring mother.[63] New data did not lead scientists to eliminate gender stereotypes in their decriptions of egg and sperm. Instead, scientists simply began to describe egg and sperm in different, but no less damaging, terms.

Can we envision a less stereotypical view? Biology itself provides another model that could be applied to the egg and the sperm. The cybernetic model—with its feedback loops, flexible adaptation to change, coordination of the pats within a whole, evolution over time, and changing response to the environment—is common in genetics, endocrinology, and ecology and has a growing influence in medicine in general.[64] This model has the potential to shift our imagery from the negative, in which the female reproductive system is castigated both for not producing eggs after birth and for producing (and thus wasting) too many eggs overall, to something more positive. The female reproductive system could be seen as responding to the environment (pregnancy or menopause), adjusting to monthly changes (menstruation), and flexibly changing from reproductivity after puberty to nonreproductivity later in life. The sperm and egg's interaction could also be described in cybernetic terms. J. F. Hartman's research in reproductive biology demonstrated fifteen years ago that if an egg is killed by being pricked with a needle, live sperm cannot get through the zona.[65] Clearly, this evidence shows that the egg and sperm *do* interact on more mutual terms, making biology's refusal to portray them that way all the more disturbing.

We would do well to be aware, however, that cybernetic imagery is hardly neutral. In the past, cybernetic models have played an important part in the imposition of social control. These models inherently provide a way of thinking about a "field" of interacting components. Once the field can be seen, it can become the object of new forms of knowledge, which in turn can allow new forms of social control to be exerted over the components of the field. During the 1950s, for example, medicine began to recognize the psychosocial *environment* of the patient: the patient's family and its psychodynamics. Professions such as social work began to focus on this new environment, and the resulting knowledge became one way to further control the patient. Patients began to be seen not as isolated, individual bodies, but as psychosocial entities located in an "ecological" system: management of "the patient's psychology was a new entrée to patient control."[66]

The models that biologists use to describe their data can have important social effects. During the nineteenth century, the social and natural sciences strongly influenced each other: the social ideas of Malthus about how to avoid the natural increase of the poor inspired Darwin's *Origin of Species.*[67] Once the *Origin* stood as a description of the natural world, complete with competition and market struggles, it could be reimported into social science as social Darwinism, in order to justify the social order of the time. What we are seeing now is similar: the importation of cultural ideas about passive females and heroic males into the "personalities" of gametes. This amounts to the "implanting of social imagery on representations of nature so as to lay a firm basis for reimporting exactly that same imagery as natural explanations of social phenomena."[68]

Further research would show us exactly what social effects are being wrought from the biological imagery of egg and sperm. At the very least, the imagery keeps alive some of the hoariest old stereotypes about weak damsels in distress and their strong male rescuers. That these stereotypes are now being written in at the level of the *cell* constitutes a powerful move to make them seem so natural as to be beyond alteration.

The stereotypical imagery might also encourage people to imagine that what results from the interaction of egg and sperm—a fertilized egg—is the result of deliberate "human" action at the cellular level. Whatever the intentions of the human couple, in this microscopic "culture" a cellular "bride" (or femme fatale) and a cellular "groom" (her victim) make a cellular baby. Rosalind Petchesky points out that through visual representations such as sonograms, we are given "*images* of younger and younger, and tinier and tinier, fetuses being 'saved.'" This leads to "the point of visibility being 'pushed back' *indefinitely*."[69] Endowing egg and sperm with intentional action, a key aspect of personhood in our culture, lays the foundation for the point of viability being pushed back to the moment of fertilization. This will likely lead to greater acceptance of technological developments and new forms of scrutiny and manipulation, for the benefit of these inner "persons": court-ordered restrictions on a pregnant woman's activities in order to protect her fetus, fetal surgery, amniocentesis, and rescinding of abortion rights, to name but a few examples.[70]

Even if we succeed in substituting more egalitarian, interactive metaphors to describe the activities of egg and sperm, and manage to avoid the pitfalls of cybernetic models, we would still be guilty of endowing cellular entities with personhood. More crucial, then, than what *kinds* of personalities we bestow on cells is the very fact that we are doing it all. This process could ultimately have the most disturbing social consequences.

One clear feminist challenge is to wake up sleeping metaphors in science, particularly those involved in descriptions of the egg and the sperm. Although the literary convention is to call such metaphors "dead," they are not so much dead as sleeping, hidden within the scientific content of texts—and all the more powerful for it.[71] Waking up such metaphors, by becoming aware of when we are projecting cultural imagery onto what we study, will improve our ability to investigate and understand nature. Waking up such metaphors, by becoming aware of their implications, will rob them of their power to naturalize our social conventions about gender.

NOTES

1. James Hillman, *The Myth of Analysis* (Evanston, IL: Northwestern University Press, 1972), 220.

2. The textbooks I consulted are the main ones used in classes for undergraduate premedical students or medical students (or those held on reserve in the library for these classes) during the past few years at Johns Hopkins University. These texts are widely used at other universities in the country as well.

3. Arthur C. Guyton, *Physiology of the Human Body*, 6th ed. (Philadelphia: Saunders College Publishing, 1984), 624.

4. Arthur J. Vander, James H. Sherman, and Dorothy S. Luciano, *Human Physiology: The Mechanisms of Body Function*, 3d ed. (New York: McGraw Hill, 1980), 483–84.

5. Vernon B. Mountcastle, *Medical Physiology*, 14th ed. (London: Mosby, 1980), 2:1624.

6. Eldra Pearl Solomon, *Human Anatomy and Physiology* (New York: CBS College Publishing, 1983), 678.

7. For elaboration, see Emily Martin, *The Woman in the Body: A Cultural Analysis of Reproduction* (Boston: Beacon, 1987), 27–53.

8. Vander, Sherman, and Luciano, 568.

9. Melvin Konner, "Childbearing and Age," *New York Times Magazine* (December 27, 1987), 22–23, esp. 22.

10. I have found but one exception to the opinion that the female is wasteful: "Smallpox being the nasty disease it is, one might expect nature to have designed antibody molecules with combining sites that specifically recognize the epitopes on smallpox virus. Nature differs from technology, however: it thinks nothing of wastefulness. (For example, rather than improving the chance that a spermatozoon will meet an egg cell, nature finds it easier to produce millions of spermatozoa.)" (Niels Kaj Jerne, "The Immune System," *Scientific American* 229, no. 1 [July 1973]: 53). Thanks to a *Signs* reviewer for bringing this reference to my attention.

11. Bruce Alberts et al., *Molecular Biology of the Cell* (New York: Garland, 1983), 795.

12. In her essay "Have Only Men Evolved?" (in *Discovering Reality: Feminist Perspectives on Epistemology, Metaphysics, Methodology, and Philosophy of Science*, ed. Sandra Harding and Merrill B. Hintikka [Dordrecht: Reidel, 1983], 45–69, esp. 60–61), Ruth Hubbard points out that sociobiologists have said the female invests more energy than the male in the production of her large gametes, claiming that this explains why the female provides parental care. Hubbard questions

whether it "really takes more 'energy' to generate the one or relatively few eggs than the large excess of sperms required to achieve fertilization." For further critique of how the greater size of eggs is interpreted in sociobiology, see Donna Haraway, "Investment Strategies for the Evolving Portfolio of Primate Females," in *Body/Politics*, ed. Mary Jacobus, Evelyn Fox Keller, and Sally Shuttleworth (New York: Routledge, 1990), 155–56.

13. The sources I used for this article provide compelling information on interactions among sperm. Lack of space prevents me from taking up this theme here, but the elements include competition, hierarchy, and sacrifice. For a newspaper report, see Malcolm W. Browne, "Some Thoughts on Self Sacrifice," *New York Times* (July 5, 1988), C6. For a literary rendition, see John Barth, "Night-Sea Journey," in his *Lost in the Funhouse* (Garden City, N.Y.: Doubleday, 1968), 3–13.

14. See Carol Delaney, "The Meaning of Paternity and the Virgin Birth Debate," *Man* 21, no. 3 (September 1986): 494–513. She discusses the difference between this scientific view that women contribute genetic material to the fetus and the claim of long-standing Western folk theories that the origin and identity of the fetus comes from the male, as in the metaphor of planting a seed in soil.

15. For a suggested direct link between human behavior and purportedly passive eggs and active sperm, see Erik H. Erikson, "Inner and Outer Space: Reflections on Womanhood," *Daedalus* 93, no. 2 (Spring 1964): 582–606, esp. 591.

16. Guyton (n. 3 above), 619; and Mountcastle (n. 5 above), 1609.

17. Jonathan Miller and David Pelham, *The Facts of Life* (New York: Viking Penguin, 1984), 5.

18. Alberts et al., 796.

19. Ibid., 796.

20. See, e.g., William F. Ganong, *Review of Medical Physiology*, 7th ed. (Los Altos, Calif.: Lange Medical Publications, 1975), 322.

21. Alberts et al. (n. 11 above), 796.

22. Guyton, 615.

23. Solomon (n. 6 above), 683.

24. Vander, Sherman, and Luciano (n. 4 above), 4th ed. (1985), 580.

25. Alberts et al., 796.

26. All biology texts quoted above use the word "penetrate."

27. Solomon, 700.

28. A. Beldecos et al., "The Importance of Feminist Critique for Contemporary Cell Biology," *Hypatia* 3, no. 1 (Spring 1988): 61–76.

29. Gerald Schatten and Helen Schatten, "The Energetic Egg," *Medical World News* 23 (January 23, 1984): 51–53, esp. 51.

30. Alberts et al., 796.

31. Guyton (n. 3 above), 613.

32. Miller and Pelham (n. 17 above), 7.

33. Alberts et al. (n. 11 above), 804.

34. Ibid., 801.

35. Ruth Herschberger, *Adam's Rib* (New York: Pelligrini & Cudaby, 1948), esp. 84. I am indebted to Ruth Hubbard for telling me about Herschberger's work, although at a point when this paper was already in draft form.

36. Bennett M. Shapiro. "The Existential Decision of a Sperm," *Cell* 49, no. 3 (May 1987): 293–94, esp. 293.

37. Lennart Nilsson, "A Portrait of the Sperm," in *The Functional Anatomy of the Spermatozoan*, ed. Bjorn A. Afzelius (New York: Pergamon, 1975), 79–82.

38. Ludwik Fleck, *Genesis and Development of a Scientific Fact*, ed. Thaddeus J. Trenn and Robert K. Merton (Chicago: University of Chicago Press, 1979), 38.

39. Jay M. Baltz carried out the research I describe when he was a graduate student in the Thomas C. Jenkins Department of Biophysics at Johns Hopkins University.

40. Far less is known about the physiology of sperm than comparable female substances, which some feminists claim is no accident. Greater scientific scrutiny of female reproduction has long enabled the burden of birth control to be placed on women. In this case, the researchers' discovery did not depend on development of any new technology. The experiments made use of glass pipettes, a manometer, and a simple microscope, all of which have been available for more than one hundred years.

41. Jay Baltz and Richard A. Cone, "What Force Is Needed to Tether a Sperm?" (abstract for Society for the Study of Reproduction, 1985), and "Flagellar Torque on the Head Determines the Force Needed to Tether a Sperm" (abstract for Biophysical Society, 1986).

42. Jay M. Baltz, David F. Katz, and Richard A. Cone, "The Mechanics of the Sperm-Egg Interaction at the Zona Pellucida," *Biophysical Journal* 54, no. 4 (October 1988): 643–54. Lab members were somewhat familiar with work on metaphors in the biology of female reproduction. Richard Cone, who runs the lab, is my husband, and he talked with them about my earlier research on the subject from time to time. Even though my current research focuses on biological imagery and I heard about the lab's work from my husband every day, I myself did not recognize the role of imagery in the sperm research until many weeks after the period of research and writing I describe. There-

fore, I assume that any awareness the lab members may have had about how underlying metaphor might be guiding this particular research was fairly inchoate.

43. Ibid., 643, 650.
44. Schatten and Schatten (n. 29 above), 51.
45. Ibid., 52.
46. Surprisingly, in an article intended for a general audience, the authors do not point out that these are sea urchin sperm and note that human sperm do not shoot out filaments at all.
47. Schatten and Schatten, 53.
48. Paul M. Wassarman, "Fertilization in Mammals," *Scientific American* 259, no. 6 (December 1988): 78–84, esp. 78, 84.
49. Ibid., 78.
50. Ibid., 79.
51. Ibid., 78.
52. Since receptor molecules are relatively *immotile* and the ligands that bind to them relatively *motile*, one might imagine the egg being called the receptor and the sperm the ligand. But the molecules in question on egg and sperm are immotile molecules. It is the sperm as a *cell* that has motility, and the egg as a cell that has relative immotility.
53. Wassarman, 78–79.
54. Paul M. Wassarman, "The Biology and Chemistry of Fertilization," *Science* 235, no. 4788 (January 30, 1987): 553–60, esp. 554.
55. Ibid., 557.
56. Ibid., 557–58. This finding throws into question Schatten and Schatten's description (n. 29 above) of the sperm, its tail beating, diving down into the egg.
57. Deborah R. Gordon, "Tenacious Assumptions in Western Medicine," in *Biomedicine Examined*, ed. Margaret Lock and Deborah Gordon (Dordrecht: Kluwer, 1988), 19–56, esp. 26.
58. Wassarman, "The Biology and Chemistry of Fertilization," 558.

59. Baltz, Katz, and Cone (n. 42 above), 643, 650.
60. Schatten and Schatten, 53.
61. Wassarman, "The Biology and Chemistry of Fertilization," 557.
62. Mary Ellman, *Thinking about Women* (New York: Harcourt Brace Jovanovich, 1968), 140; Nina Auerbach, *Woman and the Demon* (Cambridge, Mass.: Harvard University Press, 1982), esp. 186.
63. Kenneth Alan Adams, "Arachnophobia: Love American Style," *Journal of Psychoanalytic Anthropology* 4, no. 2 (1981): 157–97.
64. William Ray Arney and Bernard Bergen, *Medicine and the Management of Living* (Chicago: University of Chicago Press, 1984).
65. J. F. Hartman, R. B. Gwatkin, and C. F. Hutchison, "Early Contact Interactions between Mammalian Gametes *In Vitro*," *Proceedings of the National Academy of Sciences* (U.S.) 69, no. 10 (1972): 2767–69.
66. Arney and Bergen, 68.
67. Ruth Hubbard, "Have Only Men Evolved?" (n. 12 above), 51–52.
68. David Harvey, personal communication, November 1989.
69. Rosalind Petchesky, "Fetal Images: The Power of Visual Culture in the Politics of Reproduction," *Feminist Studies* 13, no. 2 (Summer 1987): 263–92, esp. 272.
70. Rita Arditti, Renate Klein, and Shelley Minden, *Test-Tube Women* (London: Pandora, 1984); Ellen Goodman, "Whose Right to Life?" *Baltimore Sun* (November 17, 1987); Tamar Lewin, "Courts Acting to Force Care of the Unborn," *New York Times* (November 23, 1987), A1 and B10; Susan Irwin and Brigitte Jordan, "Knowledge, Practice, and Power: Court Ordered Cesarean Sections," *Medical Anthropology Quarterly* 1, no. 3 (September 1987): 319–34.
71. Thanks to Elizabeth Fee and David Spain, who in February 1989 and April 1989, respectively, made points related to this.

4
Sex in Primitive Society

Ruth Benedict

Columbia University

Sexual offenses rooted in deprivation

Dr. Wortis has discussed our American attitude toward "crimes against nature" as being not a simple instinctive horror, but as a product of social influence, i.e., as our cultural sanctions against infringements of *our* code, and from this fact that they are manmade, he draws the obvious conclusion that "both sexual life pattern and its regulatory tabus are proper subjects for critical evaluation." I wish to speak of a closely related point which can be carefully documented from comparative material: since sex offenses, both what they are and how frequently they occur are, according to Dr. Wortis' discussion, a cultural trait, the whole subject can be properly considered only in relation to many other aspects of the culture under discussion, for there is no axiom of cultural study which is more clearly established than the fact that a whole array of familial, political, economic and religious institutions mutually condition one another and conversely are unintelligible when considered in isolation. In the field of sex offenses this means that, from the comparative point of view, it is clear that many crucial factors do not have to do with sex specifically but with more general social adjustments. To put it another way, prevention is not solely a medical problem.

From comparative material I can best illustrate this from societies in which the most careful search does not uncover a sex crime, either in terms of their own code or in terms of a white court, more than once in several generations. What is so striking in such societies is that they have certain political arrangements, rules of distribution of property, certain familial institutions. There is, for example, no impairing of the morals of a minor since every adult has opportunity for sex expression among his own age-group, girl children are married at puberty and there are freely accessible means for changing sex partners. Sex relations, therefore, with an undeveloped child are no temptation and can be rated as thoroughly unsatisfactory. This same free access to an honorable and satisfac-

Source: Sex in primitive society, by Ruth Benedict. In *Journal of Orthopsychiatry*, 1937, pp. 570–573. © 1937 American Journal of Orthopsychiatry. Reprinted by permission of the publisher. Presented in discussion of Dr. Wortis' paper.

tory sex life also makes bestiality ridiculous in their eyes and, in the eyes of the men, rape is similarly ridiculous; women regard rape in much the same way, with the addition that in some tribes women would laugh a woman to scorn who could not prevent rape if it were necessary. The incest rules are supernaturally sanctioned and it is the joint responsibility of the whole group to uphold them, for not only the offender but the whole tribe are cursed if they are broken; besides, there is well marked etiquette which lessens temptations. Adultery is meaningless since it is easily permissible to set up a family with one's lover.

I have itemized these arrangements because it is clear that the crucial factors are not strictly in the sexual field. That is, the problem is not one of dealing with a specific perverted impulse to rape, incest or indulgence in bestiality. These may of course occur in individuals, but on a large community-wide scale it comes down rather to cultural arrangements which incidentally as it were, permit sex adjustments in adult life. On a community-wide basis these satisfactory sex adjustments will of course differ in different culture. What is true of all culture where sex offense is rare is that the adult is provided with a respected role in his society; he can count on getting a proper start in life, i.e., he can afford to marry and beget and bring up a family without being socially penalized.

I like Dr. Wortis' use of the phrase *faute de mieux*. He said perversions were preferences at least *faute de mieux*. The environment may deny an individual "the better way," as in the case where a man finds there is no woman left unmarried when he wants a wife, or where there is no way in which a household can be supported even by their joint efforts. The trouble may instead be in *himself;* though he would like to marry like his friends, he does not trust himself sufficiently or he cannot get away from an old attachment to his mother. Like neuroses, criminality provides "for want of a better" way of life which he can handle. It is rooted in deprivations.

Many of these deprivations are the correlates of poverty, insecurity, bad housing, isolated family life and the humiliations of minority groups, that is, they are a social problem over and above any intelligent medical or legal handling that society can provide. This is of course a point which does not depend alone upon comparative material; it is well recognized on the basis of studies restricted to our own culture. But the point is often not given due theoretical weight, i.e., crimes against nature, as observed in our own culture are too often taken as standard measure of their human inevitability, regarded too strictly as consequences of individual physiology or as essential consequences of the socialization of the organism. The fallacy of all these theoretical positions can be shown from comparative material.

I would not like, however, to leave the impression that the frustrations and humiliations which are so constantly associated with sex offenses in cultures where they are found, are specifically in the field of sex. They are, rather, those which interfere with self-respect in any field. It has been said by some sexologists that sex difficulties in our culture can be met only by relaxing sexual tabus. At least from the cross-cultural data this cannot be maintained. It is very common to find in a tribe sex tabus that from our standpoint seems a high point of frustration. There are often years-long pregnancy and lactation tabus between husband and wife in tribes which have, nevertheless, no polygamy, and participation as a religious officiant may impose drastic tabus. If such tabus are genuinely in the service of accepted social goals and hence minister to self-respect and the individual's conviction that he is serving the general good, such sexual restrictions, however likely it seems to us that they would pile up aggressions, do not show such a picture. For instance, if the whole value of life in the tribe is children and the lactation tabu is to make the child grow, the pregnancy and lactation tabu, though it may last two or three years, does not leave the consequences associated with frustration. Sociologically speaking, therefore, one could say it was not frustration. Rather, one can speak of under-evaluation of sex in such tribes; they do not manifest sex offenses and perversions.

There is another specific field in which anthropological materials can be used to cast light on the problems raised by Dr. Wortis. This has to do with the aetiology of sex perversions and offenses. In the case of sex *offenses* any discussion is handicapped by the fact that, in spite of the popular opinion of what savages are like, such offenses are rare in primitive societies. One cannot, therefore, give social correlations from any considerable number. It may be that in certain cases they are not rare but private, but privacy is extremely difficult in primitive life. Anyway, sex acts for which an individual is shunned and condemned and which make him a public mark at which to point or to punish or kill, are rare. Therefore I shall speak only of sex perversions. On the Plains of North America, the transvestite, a male who assumed women's clothes, occupation, and lived as wife with a husband, is an accepted institution. Among the Dakota he was exclusively a passive homosexual, active homosexuality being on the other hand a sexual offense; as was also the woman who lived as a man. The regular transvestite, the so-called berdache, was allowed but was regarded with a certain ambivalence. Behind his back he was called "he" and jokes were made. Fathers whipped little boys for dressing up in girls' costume—the only occasion on which informants remember ever having been whipped—because the danger of transvestitism was so real to them. Nevertheless once the role was chosen, the berdache was honored for his industry and strength; he was the "best wife" for he outshone women at their own occupations and also could provide game for the larder, which women did not do. The point of interest in connection with this discussion is that the berdaches were seldom to be distinguished physiologically from other men. Nor were their characteristics evident from early childhood. The choice was made at the time when they were trained for the war-path which was here exclusively a male occupation and required deeds of daring. A boy who balked at this masculine role—which alone proved manhood among the Dakota— took the role of woman. In other words this perversion ultimately goes back to the tribal distinctions between the role of men and that of women. The point becomes even clearer when one compares the next-door tribe, the Ojibwa; the latter do not culturally differentiate the roles of men and women, i.e., a woman can go on the war-path or be a shaman and divorce her spouse as can a man; *and* the Ojibwa have no berdaches. The aetiology of homosexuality, therefore, in this case and in many other instances, though it may be physiological in certain persons, is overwhelmingly social; Dakota homosexuality correlates with the allotment of contrasted role to men and women. Dr. Mead, in *Sex and Temperament*, has discussed how strikingly such a blanket conception of what is masculine and what is feminine is involved in a child's identification with its father or mother and how often it is basic in problems having to do with a male's or female's proper adjustment to masculinity or femininity.

The etiology of sex perversions, in instance after instance, can be shown to be unintelligible from the strictly physiological side—nor are the perverts insane—but intelligible from the social side, i.e., from a consideration of the whole culture. This is true also in the few cases one can give of sex *offenses* from primitive society and this agrees with observations made by Dr. Shaskan in cases in New York. The corollary would be that control on a community-wide basis can be not merely medical but also social. Deprivations, humiliations, discrimination against minority groups, all take their toll in that a certain proportion of people will take up asocial or unorthodox ways of life *faute de mieux*.

Whatever produces satisfaction is denominated virtue . . . Everything which gives uneasiness in human action is called vice. [If] the injustice is so distant from us as no way to affect our interest, it still displeases because we consider it as prejudicial to human society. Conscience is the judgment of society expressed as self-judgment (Hume, italics in the original).

◇ PART TWO ◇

THE NATURAL HISTORY OF GENDER AND REPRODUCTION

READINGS IN THIS PART

INTRODUCTION TO SUBJECT AND READINGS

Praying mantis females practice sexual cannibalism, eating their partners during the sex act. Kangaroo intromission reputedly lasts several hours. Elephants have gigantic penises that can move independently from the rest of the male elephant's body. Lorises will only copulate hanging upside down. Such sexual observations are fun, yet these examples of sexual behavior in the animal kingdom also offer us a glimpse of the wide world of sexual variation.

Many researchers have turned to evolution and applied Darwin's theory of "survival of the fittest" to explain such diversity. The same principles that revealed how the leopard got its spots and why giraffes have long necks are applied to understanding sexual behavior. We observe a trait or behavior and then try to figure out the advantage a physical or behavioral characteristic bestows on a species. For example, the elephant's penis can move independently because when a male elephant mounts a female, he lacks the agility necessary to insert the penis in the female's vagina. Rather than having to see what he is doing or move his entire body to reach his goal, his penis "has a mind of its own" and finds the vagina. Successfully finding the vagina and depositing his sperm inside would confer a reproductive advantage.

Human sexual behavior, however, is not nearly so easy to figure out. We have well-accepted theories about the evolution of our sexual apparatus; penis size, our permanently enlarged breast, and other physical features, but the role of evolution in human behavior is a highly contested subject. Reconstructing the evolution of human behavior in general, and sexuality in particular is problematic because sexualities and gender behavior, attitudes, and beliefs do not leave much data behind. To complement the paleoanthropological record, we turn to primate modeling. Accepting primates as our nearest relatives, we can study their sexual behavior to try to learn about our own past. Studying primate sexual behavior to try to understand human sexualities has benefits and drawbacks. On one hand, primates are not inhibited and researchers do not have to worry about the issues of privacy or dishonesty that are encountered in the study of human sexualities. On the other hand, there has been disagreement among the scientists concerning which primate best approximates our prehominid development and what conclusions can be drawn from these studies.

Jared Diamond, a physiologist, introduces us to peculiarities of human sexual behavior as seen through the eyes of a dog. In his article, *The Animal with the Weirdest Sex Life,* he contends that we need to get rid of specie-ism in order to put our own sexualities in perspective. We learn that our sexual behavior is "abnormal" by the standard in the animal kingdom. He details some of the major differences between nonhuman and human sexual behavior. Diamond introduces us to evolutionary biology and contends that it holds the key to understanding human sexualities.

Frans de Waal's article, *Bonobo Sex and Society*, provides a lively discussion about primate modeling. Baboons and chimps have been widely used to gain insights into prehominid behavior. Choosing these primates, rather than the bonobo, has had significant scientific and theoretical consequences. Frans de Waal introduces us to bonobos, the last great ape to be discovered and the least studied. He argues that bonobos have been undervalued as prehominid prototypes.

Bonobo sexuality breaks all the molds for sexual behavior, yet they also engage in some sexual behavioral traits that are uncannily human, such as face to face intercourse. Very importantly, studies of bonobo sexual behavior proves that sexual behavior is not all about reproduction. Bonobos engage in a tremendous amount of sex that has nothing to do with reproduction. And all Bonobos engage in same-sex sexual activity (homosexuality). In fact, in the "natural" setting of animals in the wild, numerous species, including giraffes, goats, penguins, and bears, engage in same-sex sexual behavior (Bagemihl 2000).

Alison Jolly, a primatologist, in her article *Human Apes,* tackles sexual dimorphism, pair bonding, concealed ovulation, male dominance, and child care. These features are the core of every discussion of the evolution of human sexuality. Jolly addresses the similarities between humans and primates in regard to these behaviors and reveals the function and consequence of these behaviors as they relate to gender and reproduction. She also discusses the uniqueness of human menopause and explains its benefits in terms of human survival. Jolly answers some of our most basic questions concerning gender and sexuality. Her article, along with each of the others, challenges some commonly held notions and encourages us to rethink our ideas about what is natural when it comes to sexual behavior.

TERMS AND CONCEPTS

concealed ovulation	phallocentrism
concealed sex	pheromones
conjugal	polyandry
estrus	polygyny
eurocentrism	precultural
evolutionary biology	primate modeling
intromission	protohuman
menarche	sexual dimorphism
natural selection	sexual selection

QUESTIONS TO CONSIDER

1. Jared Diamond notes that human sexuality is "abnormal by the standards of the world's thirty million other animal species." In what way is human sexual conduct different from other animals?
2. Describe sexual cannibalism and explain how such behavior is adaptive to reproductive success.
3. In what ways does the behavior of bonobos challenge current models of prehuman gender and sexual behavior?
4. Compare chimpanzee and bonobos sexual behavior. What does their behavior tell us about our evolutionary roots?
5. How would ideas about human sexualities and gender have been affected if Bonobo sexuality had been accepted as the prototype of prehuman sexuality?
6. Alison Jolly provides a hypothetical scenario regarding the evolutionary split in the great apes and early hominid. What assumptions were made to create this scenario?
7. Alison Jolly discusses pair-bonding among early humans. What is the suggested role of concealed ovulation and concealed sex in relation to pair-bonding? What are the different theories related to the evolution of these features?
8. How do our ideas and theories about the evolution of sexuality influence our ideas about male/female relationships?

FURTHER READINGS

Abramson, Paul R., and Steven D. Pinkerton (eds.). 1995. *Sexual Nature, Sexual Culture.* Chicago: University of Chicago Press.

Alison Jolly. 1999. *Lucy's Legacy: Sex and Intelligence in Human Evolution.* Cambridge: Harvard University Press.

Bagemihl, Bruce. 2000. *Biological Exuberance: Animal Sexuality and Natural Diversity.* New York: St. Martin's Press.

Buss, David M., and Neil M. Malamuth (eds.). 1996. *Sex, Power, Conflict: Evolutionary and Feminist Perspectives.* New York: Oxford University Press.

De Waal, Frans, and Frans Lanting. 1997. *Bonobo: The Forgotten Ape.* Berkeley: University of California Press.

Diamond, Jared. 1997. *Why is Sex Fun: The Evolution of Human Sexuality.* New York: Basic Books.

Hrdy, Sarah Blaffer. 1999. *Mother Nature: Maternal Instincts and How They Shape the Human Species.* New York: Ballantine Books.

Low, Bobbi S. 2000. *Why Sex Matters: A Darwinian Look at Human Behavior.* Princeton: Princeton University Press.

Ridley, Matt. 1993. *The Red Queen: Sex and the Evolution of Human Nature.* New York: Penguin Books.

Small, Meredith F. 1996. *What's Love Got to Do with It?: The Evolution of Human Mating.* New York: Bantam Doubleday Dell Publishing Group.

Taylor, Timothy. 1996. *The Prehistory of Sex: Four Million Years of Human Sexual Culture.* New York: Bantam Books.

RELATED WEBSITES

Darwin and Darwinism - Gender and the Brain
www.human-nature.com/darwin/links/evolution.html

Human Behavior and Evolution Society
www.hbes.com/

Human Nature: An Interdisciplinary Biosocial Perspective (Journal)
www.archaeoworld.com/journals/humannature

Journal of Evolutionary Biology, 1999, Volume 12, Issue 6 (Issue focusing on sex)
www.blackwell-science.com/

Nature vs. Nurture: How much free will do we really have?
www.trinity.edu/~mkearl/socpsy-2.html

Primate Lectures - Questions about sexual dimorphism and mating
www.indiana.edu/~origins/teach/A105/lectures/FAQ.html

Public Broadcast System's website about evolution and sex
www.pbs.org/wgbh/evolution/sex/index.html

Sex and Social Evolution
http://biology.uindy.edu/Biol504/HUMANSTRATEGY/35sexuality.htm

◈ 5
The Animal with the Weirdest Sex Life

Jared Diamond

UCLA Medical School

If your dog had your brain and could speak, and if you asked it what it thought of your sex life, you might be surprised by its response. It would be something like this:

> Those disgusting humans have sex any day of the month! Barbara proposes sex even when she knows perfectly well that she isn't fertile—like just after her period. John is eager for sex all the time, without caring whether his efforts could result in a baby or not. But if you want to hear something really gross—Barbara and John kept on having sex while she was pregnant! That's as bad as all the times when John's parents come for a visit, and I can hear them too having sex, although John's mother went through this thing they call menopause years ago. Now she can't have babies anymore, but she still wants sex, and John's father obliges her. What a waste of effort! Here's the weirdest thing of all: Barbara and John, and John's parents,

close the bedroom door and have sex in private, instead of doing it in front of their friends like any self-respecting dog!

To understand where your dog is coming from, you need to free yourself from your human-based perspective on what constitutes normal sexual behavior. Increasingly today, we consider it narrow-minded and despicably prejudiced to denigrate those who do not conform to our own standards. Each such form of narrow-mindedness is associated with a despicable "ism"—for instance, racism, sexism, Eurocentrism, and phallocentrism. To that list of modern "ism" sins, defenders of animal rights are now adding the sin of species-ism. Our standards of sexual conduct are especially warped, species-ist, and human-centric because human sexuality is so abnormal by the standards of the world's thirty million other animal species. It's also abnormal by the standards of the world's millions of species of plants, fungi, and microbes, but I'll ignore that broader perspective because I haven't yet worked through my own zoocentrism. This book confines itself to the

Source: The animals with the weirdest sex life. *From Why is Sex Fun?*, by Jared Diamond. New York: Basic Books, 1997, pp. 1–13. Copyright © 1997 by Jared Diamond. Reprinted by permission of Basic Books: a member of Perseus Books, L.L.C.

insights that we can gain into our sexuality merely by broadening our perspective to encompass other animal species.

As a beginning, let's consider normal sexuality by the standards of the world's approximately 4,300 species of mammals, of which we humans are just one. Most mammals do not live as a nuclear family of a mated adult male and adult female, caring jointly for their offspring. Instead, in many mammal species both adult males and adult females are solitary, at least during the breeding season, and meet only to copulate. Hence, males do not provide paternal care; their sperm is their sole contribution to their offspring and to their temporary mate.

Even most social mammal species, such as lions, wolves, chimpanzees, and many hoofed mammals, are not paired off within the herd/pride/pack/band into male/female couples. Within such a herd/pride/et cetera, each adult male shows no signs of recognizing specific infants as his offspring by devoting himself to them at the expense of other infants in the herd. Indeed, it is only within the last few years that scientists studying lions, wolves, and chimpanzees have begun to figure out, with the help of DNA testing, which male sired which infant. However, like all generalizations, these admit exceptions. Among the minority of adult male mammals that do offer their offspring paternal care are polygynous male zebras and gorillas with harems of females, male gibbons paired off with females as solitary couples, and saddleback tamarin monkeys, of which two adult males are kept as a harem by one polyandrous adult female.

Sex in social mammals is generally carried out in public, before the gazes of other membes of the troop. For instance, a female Barbary macaque in estrus copulates with every adult male in her troop and makes no effort to conceal each copulation from other males. The best-documented exception to this pattern of public sex is in chimpanzee troops, where an adult male and estrous female may go off by themselves for a few days on what human observers term a "consortship." However, the same female chimpanzee that has private sex with a consort may also have public sex with other adult male chimpanzees within the same estrus cycle.

Adult females of most mammal species use various means of conspicuously advertising the brief phase of their reproductive cycle when they are ovulating and can be fertilized. The advertisement may be visual (for instance, the area around the vagina turning bright red), olfactory (releasing a distinctive smell), auditory (making noises), or behavioral (crouching in front of an adult male and displaying the vagina). Females solicit sex only during those fertile days, are sexually unattractive or less attractive to males on other days because they lack the arousing signals, and rebuff the advances of any male that is nevertheless interested on other days. Thus, sex is emphatically not just for fun and is rarely divorced from its function of fertilization. This generalization too admits exceptions: sex is flagrantly separated from reproduction in a few species, including bonobos (pygmy chimpanzees) and dolphins.

Finally, the existence of menopause as a regular phenomenon is not well established for most wild mammal populations. By menopause is meant a complete cessation of fertility within a time span that is much briefer than the previous fertile career, and that is followed by an infertile life span of significant length. Instead, wild mammals either are still fertile at the time of death or else exhibit gradually diminishing fertility with advancing age.

*****

Now contrast what I have just said about normal mammalian sexuality with human sexuality. The following human attributes are among those that we take for granted as normal:

1. Most men and women in most human societies end up in a long-term pair relationship ("marriage") that other members of the society recognize as a contract involving mutual obligations. The couple has sex repeatedly, and mainly or exclusively with each other.

2. In addition to being a sexual union, marriage is a partnership for joint rearing of the resulting babies. In particular, human males as well as females commonly provide parental care.

3. Despite forming a couple (or occasionally a harem), a husband and wife (or wives) do not live (like gibbons) as a solitary couple in an exclusive territory that they defend against other couples, but instead they live embedded in a society of other couples with whom they cooperate economically and share access to communal territory.

4. Marriage partners usually have sex in private, rather than being indifferent to the presence of other humans.

5. Human ovulation is concealed rather than advertised. That is, women's brief period of fertility around the time of ovulation is difficult to detect for their potential sex partners as well as for most women themselves. A woman's sexual receptivity extends beyond the time of fertility to encompass most or all of the menstrual cycle. Hence, most human copulations occur at a time unsuitable for conception. That is, human sex is mostly for fun, not for insemination.

6. All women who live past the age of forty or fifty undergo menopause, a complete shutdown of fertility. Men in general do not undergo menopause: while individual men may develop fertility problems at any age, there is no age-clumping of infertility or universal shutdown.

Norms imply violation of norms: we call something a "norm" merely because it is more frequent than its opposite (the "violation of the norm"). That's as true for human sexual norms as for other norms. Readers of the last two pages will surely have been thinking of exceptions to the supposed generalizations that I have been describing, but they still stand as generalizations. For example, even in societies that recognize monogamy by law or custom there is much extramarital and premarital sex, and much sex that is not part of a long-term relationship. Humans do engage in one-night stands. On the other hand, most humans also engage in many-year or many-decade stands, whereas tigers and orangutans engage in nothing except one-night stands. The genetically based paternity tests developed over the last half-century have shown that the majority of American, British, and Italian babies are indeed sired by the husband (or steady boyfriend) of the baby's mother.

Readers may also bristle at hearing human societies described as monogamous; the term "harem," which zoologists apply to zebras and gorillas, is taken from the Arabic word for a human institution. Yes, many humans practice sequential monogamy. Yes, polygyny (long-term simultaneous unions between one man and multiple wives) is legal in some countries today, and polyandry (long-term simultaneous unions between one woman and multiple husbands) is legal in a few societies. In fact, polygyny was accepted in the great majority of traditional human societies before the rise of state institutions. However, even in officially polygynous societies most men have only one wife at a time, and only especially wealthy men can acquire and maintain a few wives simultaneously. The large harems that spring to mind at the mention of the word *polygamy*, such as those of recent Arabian and Indian royalty, are possible only in the state-level societies that arose very late in human evolution and that permitted a few men to concentrate great wealth. Hence the generalization stands: most adults in most human societies are at any given moment involved in a long-term pair bond that is often monogamous in practice as well as legally.

Still another cause for bristling may have been my description of human marriage as a partnership for the joint rearing of the resulting babies. Most children receive more parental care from their mothers than from their fathers. Unwed mothers form a significant proportion of the adult population in some modern societies, though it has been much harder for unwed mothers to rear children successfully in traditional societies. But the generalization again holds: most human children receive some parental care from their father, in the form of child care, teaching, protection, and provision of food, housing, and money.

All these features of human sexuality—long-term sexual partnerships, coparenting, proximity to the sexual partnerships of others, private sex, concealed ovulation, extended female receptivity, sex for fun, and female menopause—constitute what we humans assume is normal sexuality. It titillates, amuses, or disgusts us to read of the sexual habits of elephant seals, marsupial mice, or orangutans, whose lives are so different from ours. Their lives seem to us bizarre. But that proves to be a species-ist interpretation. By the standards of the world's 4,300 other species of mammals, and even by the standards of our own closest relatives, the great apes (the chimpanzee, bonobo, gorilla, and orangutan), we are the ones who are bizarre.

However, I am still being worse than zoocentric. I am falling into the even narrower trap of mammalo-centrism. Do we become more normal when judged by the standards of nonmammalian animals? Other animals do exhibit a wider range of sexual and social systems than do mammals alone. Whereas the young of most mammal species receive maternal care but no paternal care, the reverse is true for some species of birds, frogs, and fish in which the father is the sole caretaker for his offspring. The male is a parasitic appendage fused to the female's body in some species of deep-sea fish; he is eaten by the female immediately after copulation in some species of spiders and insects. While humans and most other mammal species breed repeatedly, salmon, octopus, and many other animal species practice what is termed big-bang reproduction, or semelparity: a single reproductive effort, followed by preprogrammed death. The mating system of some species of birds, frogs, fish, and insects (as well as some bats and antelope) resembles a singles bar—at a traditional site, termed a "lek," many males maintain stations and compete for the attention of visiting females, each of which chooses a male (often the same preferred male chosen by many other females), copulates with him, and then goes off to rear the resulting offspring without his assistance.

Among other animal species, it is possible to point out some whose sexuality resembles ours in particular respects. Most European and North American bird species form pair bonds that last for at least one breeding season (in some cases for life), and the father as well as the mother cares for the young. While most such bird species differ from us in that pairs occupy mutually exclusive territories, most species of sea birds resemble us further in that mated pairs breed colonially in close proximity to each other. However, all these bird species differ from us in that ovulation is advertised, female receptivity and the sex act are mostly confined to the fertile period around ovulation, sex is not recreational, and economic cooperation between pairs is slight or nonexistent. Bonobos (pygmy chimpanzees) resemble or approach us in many of these latter respects: female receptivity is extended through several weeks of the estrus cycle, sex is mainly recreational, and there is some economic cooperation between many members of the band. However, bonobos still lack our pair-bonded couples, our well-concealed ovulation, and our paternal recognition of and care for offspring. Most or all of these species differ from us in lacking a well-defined female menopause.

*****

Thus, even a non-mammalo-centric view reinforces our dog's interpretation: we are the ones who are bizarre. We marvel at what seems to us the weird behavior of peacocks and big-bang marsupial mice, but those species actually fall securely within the range of animal variation, and in fact we are the weirdest of them all. Species-ist zoologists theorize about why hammer-headed fruit bats evolved their lek mating system, yet the mating system that cries out for explanation is our own. Why did we evolve to be so different?

This question becomes even more acute when we compare ourselves with our closest relatives among the world's mammal species, the great apes (as distinguished from the gibbons or little apes). Closest of all are Africa's chimpanzee and bonobo, from which we differ in only about 1.6 percent of our nuclear genetic material (DNA). Nearly as close are the gorilla (2.3 percent genetic difference from us) and the orangutan of Southeast Asia (3.6 percent different). Our ancestors diverged "only" about seven million years ago from the ancestors of chimpanzees and bonobos, nine million years ago from the ancestors of gorillas, and fourteen million years ago from the ancestors of orangutans.

That sounds like an enormous amount of time in comparison to an individual human lifetime, but it's a mere eye-blink on the evolutionary time scale. Life has existed on Earth for more than three billion years, and hard-shelled, complex large animals exploded in diversity more than half a billion years ago. Within that relatively short period during which our ancestors and the ancestors of our great ape relatives have been evolving separately, we have diverged in only a few significant respects and to a modest degree, even though some of those modest differences—especially our upright posture and larger brains—have had enormous consequences for our behavioral differences.

Along with posture and brain size, sexuality completes the trinity of the decisive respects in which the ancestors of humans and great apes diverged. Orangutans are often solitary, males and females associate just to copulate, and males provide no paternal care; a gorilla male gathers a harem of a few females, with each of which he has sex at intervals of several years (after the female weans her most recent offspring and resumes menstrual cycling and before she becomes pregnant again); and chimpanzees and bonobos live in troops with no lasting male-female pair bonds or specific father-offspring bonds. It is clear how our large brain and upright posture played a decisive role in what is termed our humanity—in the fact that we now use language, read books, watch TV, buy or grow most of our food, occupy all continents and oceans, keep members of our own and other species in cages, and are exterminating most other animal and plant species, while the great apes still speechlessly gather wild fruit in the jungle, occupy small ranges in the Old World tropics, cage no animal, and threaten the existence of no other species. What role did our weird sexuality play in our achieving these hallmarks of humanity?

Could our sexual distinctiveness be related to our other distinctions from the great apes? In addition to (and probably ultimately as a product of) our upright posture and large brains, those distinctions include our relative hairlessness, dependence on tools, command of fire, and development of language, art, and writing. If any of these distinctions predisposed us toward evolving our sexual distinctions, the links are certainly unclear. For example, it is not obvious why our loss of body hair should have made recreational sex more appealing, nor why our command of fire should have favored menopause. Instead, I shall argue the reverse: recreational sex and menopause were as important for our development of fire, language, art, and writing as were our upright posture and large brains.

*****

The key to understanding human sexuality is to recognize that it is a problem in evolutionary biology. When Darwin recognized the phenomenon of biological evolution in his great book *On the Origin of Species*, most of his evidence was drawn from anatomy. He inferred that most plant and animal structures evolve—that is, they tend to change from generation to generation. He also inferred that the major force behind evolutionary change is natural selection. By that term, Darwin meant that plants and animals vary in their anatomical adaptations, that certain adaptations enable individuals bearing them to survive and reproduce more successfully than other individuals, and that those particular adaptations therefore increase in frequency in a population from generation to generation. Later biologists showed that Darwin's reasoning about anatomy also applies to physiology and biochemistry: an animal's or plant's physiological and biochemical characteristics also adapt it to certain lifestyles and evolve in response to environmental conditions.

More recently, evolutionary biologists have shown that animal social systems also evolve and adapt. Even among closely related animal species, some are solitary, others live in small groups, and still others live in large groups. But social behavior has consequences for survival and reproduction. Depending, for example, on whether a species' food supply is clumped or spread out, and on whether a species faces high risk of attack by predators, either solitary living or group living may be better for promoting survival and reproduction.

Similar considerations apply to sexuality. Some sexual characteristics may be more advantageous for survival and reproduction than others, depending on each species' food supply, exposure to predators, and other biological characteristics. At this point I shall mention just one example, a behavior that at first seems diametrically opposed to evolutionary logic: sexual cannibalism. The male of some species of spiders and mantises is routinely eaten by his mate just after or even while he is copulating with her. This cannibalism clearly involves the male's consent, because the male of these species approaches the female, makes no attempt to escape, and may even bend his head and thorax toward the female's mouth so that she may munch her way through most of his body while his abdomen remains to complete the job of injecting sperm into her.

If one thinks of natural selection as the maximization of survival, such cannibalistic suicide makes no sense. Actually, natural selection maximizes the transmission of genes, and survival is in most cases just one strategy that provides repeated opportunities to transmit genes. Suppose that opportunities to transmit genes arise unpredictably and infrequently, and that the number of offspring produced by such opportunities increases with the female's nutritional condition. That's the case for some species of spiders and mantises living at low population densities. A male is lucky to encounter a female at all, and such luck is unlikely to strike twice. The male's best strategy is to produce as many offspring bearing his genes as possible out of his lucky find. The larger a female's nutritional reserves, the more calories and protein she has available to transform into eggs. If the male departed after

mating, he would probably not find another female and his continued survival would thus be useless. Instead, by encouraging the female to eat him, he enables her to produce more eggs bearing his genes. In addition, a female spider whose mouth is distracted by munching a male's body allows copulation with the male's genitalia to proceed for a longer time, resulting in more sperm transferred and more eggs fertilized. The male spider's evolutionary logic is impeccable and seems bizarre to us only because other aspects of human biology make sexual cannibalism disadvantageous. Most men have more than one lifetime opportunity to copulate; even well-nourished women usually give birth to only a single baby at a time, or at most twins; and a woman could not consume enough of a man's body at one sitting to improve significantly the nutritional basis for her pregnancy.

This example illustrates the dependence of evolved sexual strategies on both ecological parameters nad the parameters of a species' biology, both of which vary among species. Sexual cannibalism in spiders and mantises is favored by the ecological variables of low population densities and low encounter rates, and by the biological variables of a female's capacity to digest relatively large meals and to increase her egg output considerably when well nourished. Ecological parameters can change overnight if an individual colonizes a new type of habitat, but the colonizing individual carries with it a baggage of inherited biological attributes that can change only slowly, through natural selection. Hence it is not enough to consider a species' habitat and lifestyle, design on paper a set of sexual characteristics that would be well matched to that habitat and lifestyle, and then be surprised that those supposedly optimal sexual characteristics do not evolve. Instead, sexual evolution is severely constrained by inherited commitments and prior evolutionary history.

For example, in most fish species a female lays eggs and a male fertilizes those eggs outside the female's body, but in all placental mammal species and marsupials a female gives birth to live young rather than to eggs, and all mammal species practice internal fertilization (male sperm injected into the female's body). Live birth and internal fertilization involve so many biological adaptations and so many genes that all placental mammals and marsupials have been firmly committed to those attributes for tens of millions of years. As we shall see, these inherited commitments help explain why there is no mammal species in which parental care is provided solely by the male, even in habitats where mammals live alongside fish and frog species whose males are the sole providers of parental care.

We can thus redefine the problem posed by our strange sexuality. Within the last seven million years, our sexual anatomy diverged somewhat, our sexual physiology further, and our sexual behavior even more, from those of our closest relatives, the chimpanzees. Those divergences must reflect a divergence between humans and chimpanzees in environment and lifestyle. But those divergences were also limited by inherited constraints. What were the lifestyle changes and inherited constraints that molded the evolution of our weird sexuality?

6

Bonobo Sex and Society
The Behavior of a Close Relative Challenges Assumptions about Male Supremacy in Human Evolution

Frans B. M. de Waal
Emory University

At a juncture in history during which women are seeking equality with men, science arrives with a belated gift to the feminist movement. Male-biased evolutionary scenarios—Man the Hunter, Man the Toolmaker and so on—are being challenged by the discovery that females play a central, perhaps even dominant, role in the social life of one of our nearest relatives. In the past few years many strands of knowledge have come together concerning a relatively unknown ape with an unorthodox repertoire of behavior: the bonobo.

The bonobo is one of the last large mammals to be found by science. The creature was discovered in 1929 in a Belgian colonial museum, far from its lush African habitat. A German anatomist, Ernst Schwarz, was scrutinizing a skull that had been ascribed to a juvenile chimpanzee because of its small size,

when he realized that it belonged to an adult. Schwarz declared that he had stumbled on a new subspecies of chimpanzee. But soon the animal was assigned the status of an entirely distinct species within the same genus as the chimpanzee, Pan.

The bonobo was officially classified as *Pan paniscus*, or the diminutive Pan. But I believe a different label might have been selected had the discoverers known then what we know now. The old taxonomic name of the chimpanzee, *P. satyrus*—which refers to the myth of apes as lustful satyrs—would have been perfect for the bonobo.

The species is best characterized as female-centered and egalitarian and as one that substitutes sex for aggression. Whereas in most other species sexual behavior is a fairly distinct category, in the bonobo it is part and parcel of social relations—and not just between males and females. Bonobos engage in sex in virtually every partner combination (although such contact among close family members may be suppressed). And sexual interactions occur more often among bonobos than among other primates. Despite the frequency of sex, the bonobo's rate of reproduction in the wild is about the same as that of the chimpanzee. A female gives birth to a single infant at intervals of between five and six years. So bonobos share at least one very important characteristic with our own species, namely, a partial separation between sex and reproduction.

A NEAR RELATIVE

This finding commands attention because the bonobo shares more than 98 percent of our genetic profile, making it as close to a human as, say, a fox is to a dog. The split between the human line of ancestry and the line of the chimpanzee and the bonobo is believed to have occurred a mere eight million years ago. The subsequent divergence of the chimpanzee and the bonobo lines came much later, perhaps prompted by the chimpanzee's need to adapt to relatively open, dry habitats [see "East Side Story: The Origin of Humankind," by Yves Coppens; *Scientific American*, May 1994].

In contrast, bonobos probably never left the protection of the trees. Their present range lies in humid forests south of the Zaire River, where perhaps fewer than 10,000 bonobos survive. (Given the species' slow rate of reproduction, the rapid destruction of its tropical habitat and the political instability of central Africa, there is reason for much concern about its future.)

If this evolutionary scenario of ecological continuity is true, the bonobo may have undergone less transformation than either humans or chimpanzees. It could most closely resemble the common ancestor of all three modern species. Indeed, in the 1930s Harold J. Coolidge—the American anatomist who gave the bonobo its eventual taxonomic status—suggested that the animal might be most similar to the primogenitor, since its anatomy is less specialized than is the chimpanzee's. Bonobo body proportions have been compared with those of the australopithecines, a form of prehuman. When the apes stand or walk upright, they look as if they stepped straight out of an artist's impression of early hominids.

Not too long ago the savanna baboon was regarded as the best living model of the human ancestor. That primate is adapted to the kinds of ecological conditions that prehumans may have faced after descending from the trees. But in the late 1970s, chimpanzees, which are much more closely related to humans, became the model of choice. Traits that are observed in chimpanzees—including cooperative hunting, food sharing, tool use, power politics and primitive warfare—were absent or not as developed in baboons. In the laboratory the apes have been able to learn sign language and to recognize themselves in a mirror, a sign of self-awareness not yet demonstrated in monkeys.

Although selecting the chimpanzee as the touchstone of hominid evolution represented a great improvement, at least one aspect of the former model did not need to be revised: male superiority remained the natural state of affairs. In both baboons and chimpanzees, males are conspicuously dominant over females; they reign supremely and often brutally. It is highly unusual for a fully grown male chimpanzee to be dominated by any female.

Enter the bonobo. Despite their common name—the pygmy chimpanzee—bonobos cannot be distinguished from the chimpanzee by size. Adult males of the smallest subspecies of chimpanzee weigh some 43 kilograms (95 pounds) and females 33 kilograms (73 pounds), about the same as bonobos. Although female bonobos are much smaller than the males, they seem to rule.

GRACEFUL APES

In physique, a bonobo is as different from a chimpanzee as a Concorde is from a Boeing 747. I do not wish to offend any chimpanzees, but bonobos have more style. The bonobo, with its long legs and small head atop narrow shoulders, has a more gracile build than does a chimpanzee. Bonobo lips are reddish in a black face, the ears small and the nostrils almost as wide as a gorilla's. These primates also have a flatter, more open face with a higher forehead than the chimpanzee's and—to top it all off—an attractive coiffure with long, fine, black hair neatly parted in the middle.

Like chimpanzees, female bonobos nurse and carry around their young for up to five years. By the age of seven the offspring reach adolescence. Wild females give birth for the first time at 13 or 14 years of age, becoming full grown by about 15. A bonobo's longevity is unknown, but judging by the chimpanzee it may be older than 40 in the wild and close to 60 in captivity.

Fruit is central to the diets of both wild bonobos and chimpanzees. The former supplement with more pith from herbaceous plants, and the latter add meat. Although bonobos do eat invertebrates and occasionally capture and eat small vertebrates, including mammals, their diet seems to contain relatively little animal protein. Unlike chimpanzees, they have not been observed to hunt monkeys.

Whereas chimpanzees use a rich array of strategies to obtain foods—from cracking nuts with stone tools to fishing for ants and termites with sticks—tool use in wild bonobos seems undeveloped. (Captive bonobos use tools skillfully.) Apparently as intelligent as chimpanzees, bonobos have, however, a far more sensitive temperament. During World War II bombing of Hellabrun, Germany, the bonobos in a nearby zoo all died of fright from the noise; the chimpanzees were unaffected.

Bonobos are also imaginative in play. I have watched captive bonobos engage in "blindman's bluff." A bonobo covers her eyes with a banana leaf or an arm or by sticking two fingers in her eyes. Thus handicapped, she stumbles around on a climbing frame, bumping into others or almost falling. She seems to be imposing a rule on herself: "I cannot look until I lose my balance." Other apes and monkeys also indulge in this game, but I have never seen it performed with such dedication and concentration as by bonobos.

Juvenile bonobos are incurably playful and like to make funny faces, sometimes in long solitary pantomimes and at other times while tickling one another. Bonobos are, however, more controlled in expressing their emotions—whether it be joy, sorrow, excitement or anger

—than are the extroverted chimpanzees. Male chimpanzees often engage in spectacular charging displays in which they show off their strength: throwing rocks, breaking branches and uprooting small trees in the process. They keep up these noisy performances for many minutes, during which most other members of the group wisely stay out of their way. Male bonobos, on the other hand, usually limit displays to a brief run while dragging a few branches behind them.

Both primates signal emotions and intentions through facial expressions and hand gestures, many of which are also present in the nonverbal communication of humans. For example, bonobos will beg by stretching out an open hand (or, sometimes, a foot) to a possessor of food and will pout their lips and make whimpering sounds if the effort is unsuccessful. But bonobos make different sounds than chimpanzees do. The renowned low-pitched, extended "huuu-huuu" pant-hooting of the latter contrasts with the rather sharp, high-pitched barking sounds of the bonobo.

LOVE, NOT WAR

My own interest in bonobos came not from an inherent fascination with their charms but from research on aggressive behavior in primates. I was particularly intrigued with the aftermath of conflict. After two chimpanzees have fought, for instance, they may come together for a hug and mouth-to-mouth kiss. Assuming that such reunions serve to restore peace and harmony, I labeled them reconciliations.

Any species that combines close bonds with a potential for conflict needs such conciliatory mechanisms. Thinking how much faster marriages would break up if people had no way of compensating for hurting each other, I set out to investigate such mechanisms in several primates, including bonobos. Although I expected to see peacemaking in these apes, too, I was little prepared for the form it would take.

For my study, which began in 1983, I chose the San Diego Zoo. At the time, it housed the world's largest captive bonobo colony—10 members divided into three groups. I spent entire days in front of the enclosure with a video camera, which was switched on at feeding time. As soon as a caretaker approached the enclosure with food, the males would develop erections. Even before the food was thrown into the area, the bonobos would be inviting each other for sex: males would invite females, and females would invite males and other females.

Sex, it turned out, is the key to the social life of the bonobo. The first suggestion that the sexual behavior of bonobos is different had come from observations at European zoos. Wrapping their findings in Latin, primatologists Eduard Tratz and Heinz Heck reported in 1954 that the chimpanzees at Hellabrun mated more canum (like dogs) and bonobos more hominum (like people). In those days, face-to-face copulation was considered uniquely human, a cultural innovation that needed to be taught to preliterate people (hence the term "missionary position"). These early studies, written in German, were ignored by the international scientific establishment. The bonobo's humanlike sexuality needed to be rediscovered in the 1970s before it became accepted as characteristic of the species.

Bonobos become sexually aroused remarkably easily, and they express this excitement in a variety of mounting positions and genital contacts. Although chimpanzees virtually never adopt face-to-face positions, bonobos do so in one out of three copulations in the wild. Furthermore, the frontal orientation of the bonobo vulva and clitoris strongly suggest that the female genitalia are adapted for this position.

Another similarity with humans is increased female sexual receptivity. The tumescent phase of the female's genitals, resulting in a pink swelling that signals willingness to mate, covers a much longer part of estrus in bonobos than in chimpanzees. Instead of a few days out of her cycle, the female bonobo is almost continuously sexually attractive and active.

Perhaps the bonobo's most typical sexual pattern, undocumented in any other primate, is genito-genital rubbing (or GG rubbing) between adult females. One female facing another clings with arms and legs to a partner that, standing on both hands and feet, lifts her off the ground. The two females then rub their genital swellings laterally together, emitting grins and squeals that probably reflect orgasmic experiences. (Laboratory experiments on stump-tailed macaques have demonstrated that women are not the only female primates capable of physiological orgasm.)

Male bonobos, too, may engage in pseudocopulation but generally perform a variation. Standing back to back, one male briefly rubs his scrotum against the buttocks of another. They also practice so-called penis-fencing, in which two males hang face to face from a branch while rubbing their erect penises together.

The diversity of erotic contacts in bonobos includes sporadic oral sex, massage of another individual's genitals and intense tongue-kissing. Lest this leave the impression of a pathologically oversexed species, I must add, based on hundreds of hours of watching bonobos, that their sexual activity is rather casual and relaxed. It appears to be a completely natural part of their group life. Like people, bonobos engage in sex only occasionally, not continuously. Furthermore, with the average copulation lasting 13 seconds, sexual contact in bonobos is rather quick by human standards.

That sex is connected to feeding, and even appears to make food sharing possible, has been observed not only in zoos but also in the wild. Nancy Thompson-Handler, then at the State University of New York at Stony Brook, saw bonobos in Zaire's Lomako Forest engage in sex after they had entered trees loaded with ripe figs or when one among them had captured a prey animal, such as a small forest duiker. The flurry of sexual contacts would last for five to 10 minutes, after which the apes would settle down to consume the food.

One explanation for the sexual activity at feeding time could be that excitement over food translates into sexual arousal. This idea may be partly true. Yet another motivation is probably the real cause: competition. There are two reasons to believe sexual activity is the bonobo's answer to avoiding conflict.

First, anything, not just food, that arouses the interest of more than one bonobo at a time tends to result in sexual contact. If two bonobos approach a cardboard box thrown into their enclosure, they will briefly mount each other before playing with the box. Such situations lead to squabbles in most other species. But bonobos are quite tolerant, perhaps because they use sex to divert attention and to diffuse tension.

Second, bonobo sex often occurs in aggressive contexts totally unrelated to food. A jealous male might chase another away from a female, after which the two males reunite and engage in scrotal rubbing. Or after a female hits a juvenile, the latter's mother may lunge at the aggressor, an action that is immediately followed by genital rubbing between the two adults.

I once observed a young male, Kako, inadvertently blocking an older, female juvenile, Leslie, from moving along a branch. First, Leslie pushed him; Kako, who was not very confident in trees, tightened his grip, grinning nervously. Next Leslie gnawed on one of his hands, presumably to loosen his grasp. Kako uttered a sharp peep and stayed put. Then Leslie rubbed her vulva against his shoulder. This gesture calmed Kako, and he moved along the branch. It seemed that Leslie had been very close to using force but instead had reassured both herself and Kako with sexual contact.

During reconciliations, bonobos use the same sexual repertoire as they do during feeding time. Based on an analysis of many such incidents, my study yielded the first solid evidence for sexual behavior as a mechanism to overcome aggression. Not that this function is absent in other animals—or in humans, for that matter—but the art of sexual reconciliation may well have reached its evolutionary peak in the bonobo. For these animals, sexual behavior is indistinguishable from social behavior. Given its peacemaking and appeasement functions, it is not surprising that sex among bonobos occurs in so many different partner combinations, including between juveniles and adults. The need for peaceful coexistence is obviously not restricted to adult heterosexual pairs.

FEMALE ALLIANCE

Apart from maintaining harmony, sex is also involved in creating the singular social structure of the bonobo. This use of sex becomes clear when studying bonobos in the wild. Field research on bonobos started only in the mid-1970s, more than a decade after the most important studies on wild chimpanzees had been initiated. In terms of continuity and invested (wo)manpower, the chimpanzee projects of Jane Goodall and Toshisada Nishida, both in Tanzania, are unparalleled. But bonobo research by Takayoshi Kano and others of Kyoto University is now two decades under way at Wamba in Zaire and is beginning to show the same payoffs.

Both bonobos and chimpanzees live in so-called fission-fusion societies. The apes move alone or in small parties of a few individuals at a time, the composition of which changes constantly. Several bonobos traveling together in the morning might meet another group in the forest, whereupon one individual from the first group wanders off with others from the second group, while those left behind forage together. All associations, except the one between mother and dependent offspring, are of a temporary character.

Initially this flexibility baffled investigators, making them wonder if these apes formed any social groups with stable membership. After years of documenting the travels of chimpanzees in the Mahale Mountains, Nishida first reported that they form large communities: all members of one community mix freely in ever changing parties, but members of different communities never gather. Later, Goodall added territoriality to this picture. That is, not only do communities not mix, but males of different chimpanzee communities engage in lethal battles.

In both bonobos and chimpanzees, males stay in their natal group, whereas females tend to migrate during adolescence. As a result, the senior males of a chimpanzee or bonobo group have known all junior males since birth, and all junior males have grown up together. Females, on the other hand, transfer to an unfamiliar and often hostile group where they may know no one. A chief difference between chimpanzee and bonobo societies is the way in which young females integrate into their new community.

On arrival in another community, young bonobo females at Wamba single out one or two senior resident females for special attention, using frequent GG rubbing and grooming to establish a relation. If the residents reciprocate, close associations are set up, and the younger female gradually becomes accepted into the group. After producing her first offspring, the young female's position becomes more stable and central. Eventually the cycle repeats with younger immigrants, in turn, seeking a good relation with the now established female. Sex thus smooths the migrant's entrance into the community of females, which is much more close-knit in the bonobo than in the chimpanzee.

Bonobo males remain attached to their mothers all their lives, following them through the forest and being dependent on them for protection in aggressive encounters with other males. As a result, the highest-ranking males of a bonobo community tend to be sons of important females.

What a contrast with chimpanzees! Male chimpanzees fight their own battles, often relying on the support of other males. Furthermore, adult male chimpanzees travel together in same-sex parties, grooming each other frequently. Males form a distinct social hierarchy with high levels of both competition and association. Given the need to stick together against males of neighboring communities, their bonding is not surprising: failure to form a united front might result in the loss of lives and territory. The danger of being male is reflected in the adult sex ratio of chimpanzee populations, with considerably fewer males than females.

Serious conflict between bonobo groups has been witnessed in the field, but it seems quite rare. On the contrary, reports exist of peaceable mingling, including mutual sex and grooming, between what appear to be different communities. If intergroup combat is indeed unusual, it may explain the lower rate of all-male associations. Rather than being male-bonded, bonobo society gives the impression of being female-bonded, with even adult males relying on their mothers instead of on other males. No wonder Kano calls mothers the "core" of bonobo society.

The bonding among female bonobos violates a fairly general rule, outlined by Harvard University anthropologist Richard W. Wrangham, that the sex that stays in the natal group develops the strongest mutual bonds. Bonding among male chimpanzees follows naturally because they remain in the community of their birth. The same is true for female kinship bonding in Old World monkeys, such as macaques and baboons, where males are the migratory sex.

Bonobos are unique in that the migratory sex, females, strongly bond with same-sex strangers later in life. In setting up an artificial sisterhood, bonobos can be said to be secondarily bonded. (Kinship bonds are said to be primary.) Although we now know HOW this happens—through the use of sexual contact and grooming—we do not yet know WHY bonobos and chimpanzees differ in this respect. The answer may lie in the different ecological environments of bonobos and chimpanzees—such as the abundance and quality of food in the forest. But it is uncertain if such explanations will suffice.

Bonobo society is, however, not only female-centered but also appears to be female-dominated. Bonobo specialists, while long suspecting such a reality, have been reluctant to make the controversial claim. But in 1922, at the 14th Congress of the International Primatological Society in Strasbourg, investigators of both captive and wild bonobos presented data that left little doubt about the issue.

Amy R. Parish of the University of California at Davis reported on food competition in identical groups (one adult male and two adult females) of chimpanzees and bonobos at the Stuttgart Zoo. Honey was provided in a "termite hill" from which it could be extracted by dipping sticks into a small hole. As soon as honey was made available, the male chimpanzee would make a charging display through the enclosure and claim everything for himself. Only when his appetite was satisfied would he let the females fish for honey.

In the bonobo group, it was the females that approached the honey first. After having engaged in some GG rubbing, they would feed together, taking turns with virtually no competition between them. The male might make as many charging displays as he wanted; the females were not intimidated and ignored the commotion.

Observers at the Belgian animal park of Planckendael, which currently has the most naturalistic bonobo colony, reported similar findings. If a male bonobo tried to harass a female, all females would band together to chase him off. Because females appeared more successful in dominating males when they were together than on their own, their close association and frequent genital rubbing may represent an alliance. Females may bond so as to outcompete members of the individually stronger sex.

The fact that they manage to do so not only in captivity is evident from zoologist Takeshi Furuichi's summary of the relation between the sexes at Wamba, where bonobos are enticed out of the forest with sugarcane. "Males usually appeared at the feeding site first, but they surrendered preferred positions when the females appeared. It seemed that males appeared first not because they were dominant, but because they had to feed before the arrival of females," Furuichi reported at Strasbourg.

Occasionally, the role of sex in relation to food is taken one step further, bringing bonobos very close to humans in their behavior. It has been speculated by anthropologists—including C. Owen Lovejoy of Kent State University and Helen Fisher of Rutgers University—that sex is partially separated from reproduction in our species because it serves to cement mutually profitable relationships between men and women. The human female's capacity to mate throughout her cycle and her strong sex drive allow her to exchange sex for male commitment and paternal care, thus giving rise to the nuclear family.

This arrangement is thought to be favored by natural selection because it allows women to raise more offspring than they could if they were on their own. Although bonobos clearly do not establish the exclusive heterosexual bonds characteristic of our species, their behavior does fit important elements of this model. A female bonobo shows extended receptivity and uses sex to obtain a male's favors when—usually because of youth—she is too low in social status to dominate him.

At the San Diego Zoo, I observed that if Loretta was in a sexually attractive state, she would not hesitate to approach the adult male, Vernon, if he had food. Presenting herself to Vernon, she would mate with him and make high-pitched food calls while taking over his entire bundle of branches and leaves. When Loretta had no genital swelling, she would wait until Vernon was ready to share. Primatologist Suehisa Kuroda reports similar exchanges at Wamba: "A young female approached a male, who was eating sugarcane. They copulated in short order, whereupon she took one of the two canes held by him and left."

Despite such quid pro quo between the sexes, there are no indications that bonobos form humanlike nuclear families. The burden of raising offspring appears to rest entirely on the female's shoulders. In fact, nuclear families are probably incompatible with the diverse use of sex found in bonobos. If our ancestors started out with a sex life similar to that of bonobos, the evolution of the family would have required dramatic change.

Human family life implies paternal investment, which is unlikely to develop unless males can be reasonably certain that they are caring for their own, not someone else's, offspring. Bonobo society lacks any such guarantee, but humans protect the integrity of their family units through all kinds of moral restrictions and taboos. Thus, although our species is characterized by an extraordinary interest in sex, there are no societies in which people engage in it at the drop of a hat (or a cardboard box, as the case may be). A sense of shame and a desire for domestic privacy are typical human concepts related to the evolution and cultural bolstering of the family.

Yet no degree of moralizing can make sex disappear from every realm of human life that does not relate to the nuclear family. The bonobo's behavioral peculiarities may help us understand the role of sex and may have serious implications for models of human society.

Just imagine that we had never heard of chimpanzees or baboons and had known bonobos first. We would at present most likely believe that early hominids lived in female-centered societies, in which sex served important social functions and in which warfare was rare or absent. In the end, perhaps the most successful reconstruction of our past will be based not on chimpanzees or even on bonobos but on a three-way comparison of chimpanzees, bonobos and humans.

SOCIAL ORGANIZATION AMONG VARIOUS PRIMATES

Bonobo

Bonobo communities are peace-loving and generally egalitarian. The strongest social bonds are those among females, although females also bond with males. The status of a male depends on the position of his mother, to whom he remains closely bonded for her entire life.

Chimpanzee

In chimpanzee groups the strongest bonds are established between the males in order to hunt and to protect their shared territory. The females live in overlapping home ranges within this territory but are not strongly bonded to other females or to any one male.

Gibbon

Gibbons establish monogamous, egalitarian relations, and one couple will maintain a territory to the exclusion of other pairs.

Human

Human society is the most diverse among the primates. Males unite for cooperative ventures, whereas females also bond with those of their own sex. Monogamy, polygamy and polyandry are all in evidence.

Gorilla

The social organization of gorillas provides a clear example of polygamy. Usually a single male maintains a range for his family unit, which contains several females. The strongest bonds are those between the male and his females.

Orangutan

Orangutans live solitary lives with little bonding in evidence. Male orangutans are intolerant of one another. In his prime, a single male establishes a large territory, within which live several females. Each female has her own, separate home range.

FURTHER READING

The Pygmy Chimpanzee: Evolutionary Biology and Behavior. Edited by Randall L. Susman. Plenum Press, 1984.

The Communicative Repertoire of Captive Bonobos (Pan Paniscus) Compared to that of Chimpanzees. F.B.M. de Waal in *Behaviour*, Vol. 106, Nos. 3–4, pages 183–251; September 1988.

Peacemaking among Primates. F.B.M. de Waal. Harvard University Press, 1989.

Understanding Chimpanzees. Edited by Paul Heltne and Linda A. Marquardt. Harvard University Press, 1989.

The Last Ape: Pygmy Chimpanzee Behavior and Ecology. Takayoshi Kano. Stanford University Press, 1992.

Chimpanzee Cultures. R. Wrangham, W. C. McGrew, F.B.M. de Waal and P. Heltne. Harvard University Press, 1994.

7

Human Apes

Alison Jolly

Lemur, monkey, and ape societies reflect many bits and pieces of our own behavior; humans can live in almost any grouping. Conjugal families are always framed by a larger group, with strong elements of male bonding. This gives us the social subtlety to play off allies and rivals, the way chimpanzees do. The really rare mating structures are a strict solitary life, polyandry, and group marriage—all usually thought rather odd by surrounding society.

Women in any given human population are only 85–90 percent as large as the men. A baboon male is twice the female's size, and so are gorillas and orangutans. The baboon lives in a multisexed social group; the gorilla has a true harem; the orang is alone except when his bellowing attracts amorous mates.

Body size ratio clearly does not reflect any particular group structure, only that males are proportionately larger in species where a few honchos impregnate many females, leaving other males with none. The female's size relates to efficient foraging and reproduction, in other words, to her ecology. She has not grown smaller; it is rather that competing males have evolved to be big and dangerous.

Conversely, in monogamous animals, males and females are essentially the same size, with the same size antlers and tusks. They may be different colors or have small fluffy headdresses, but they are physically a match for each other. The variance in reproduction between sexes is relatively slight. Adultery happens, but most reproductive effort is bound up with the partner's success. Gibbons are the closest of our cousins who are monogamous. Gibbon partners have equally large canines, as each fends off rivals of her or his own sex. In mammalian societies generally, male-to-female size ratio correlates closely to male-to-female ratio of mates: the bigger the size difference, the more mates the males "expect" to have.

Source: Reprinted by permission of the publisher from "Human Apes" in *Lucy's Legacy; Sex and Intelligence in Human Evolution* by Alison Jolly, Cambridge, Mass.: Harvard University Press, Copyright © 1999 by the President and Fellows of Harvard College.

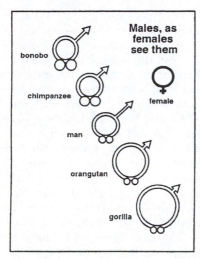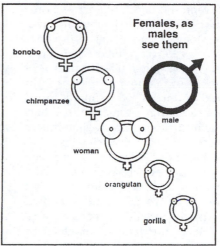

FIGURE 1 The bigger a male body is compared to females of his species, the more mates he is evolved to have. The bigger the sexual attribute of either sex, the more mates a female is evolved to have, although humans also choose monogamy and other lifestyles. (After Short, 1994; bonobos added)

If we turn to men and women and apply this formula, we conclude that human males "expect" perhaps two or three mates. In other words, the difference in size between men and women probably evolved through mild polygamy, on average, in spite of our behavioral scope for men to take either one wife or several hundred.

What do we conclude about the number of mates if we look at another revealing trait—the ratio of testis weight to body weight? Again, humans are intermediate, at least when compared with our primate cousins. Human testes weigh about the same as those of a 450-pound gorilla, which suggests that men compete with other men at the sperm level more than gorillas compete with other gorillas. Because gorilla groups are widely separated, a gorilla female is not likely to go off among the giant nettles to mate with a neighboring male unless she opts to change groups completely. It would be taking a huge physical risk to sneak off for an adulterous liaison and sneak back, hoping to escape detection. Occasionally there may be two adult males in a single harem, and both may even be allowed to mate; but then the younger one is generally the favored son of the harem leader. Gorillas compete by muscle power to establish a harem; they do not need to compete by quantities of sperm.[1]

Common chimpanzees and bonobos, by contrast, who live in multimale groups, are well equipped for sperm competition. Humans are partially so, both in testis size and even by quantity of ejaculate, depending on the length of time the pair have been apart. This implies that men hedge their bets against likely infidelity. They are evolved to defend at the sperm level against their mates having another lover in the same fertile period—not many others, but one or two.[2]

In other words, body size suggests, on average, that early human males might have had two or three mates at a given time, while testis size suggests that women also found more than one simultaneous mate over the eons that our bodies were evolving.

EXTENDED SEX AND PAIR BONDING

In prehuman societies, during most of their reproductive life females were not cycling, being almost permanently pregnant or lactating.

When our foremothers evolved, we spent only two or three years of the life span having menstrual cycles. Modern women, in contrast, may spend as many as 35 "reproductive" years neither gestating nor lactating. Birth control technology is the major reason for the change. In industrialized countries today, family size is commonly two children, or in Spain and Italy one or none. In Africa, completed family size was six children 25 years ago, whereas it has now dropped to three. A second factor is age of menarche: in the West it has dropped from about eighteen to about twelve during the last century, due to improved health and diet. Finally, when modern women do become pregnant and give birth, they tend to breastfeed for just a few months or none at all, as compared with several years that our foremothers spent nursing each child. The physiologist Roger Short has pointed out that the upshot—year after year of monthly bleeding—is a highly unnatural life course for modern women.[3] In earlier times, when human females were evolving, menstrual cycles were a rarity.

Among gibbons, the absence of cycling leads to a nearly sexless monogamy that lasts for much of the three or four years between infants. Among baboons, male "friends" shadow and guard females, and often carry their infants, again over years before the female returns to estrus. Pregnant or lactating protowomen, too, might well have figured out a way to attract the help and interest of males without having sex with them, but we found another route. Our solution was to extend sex to become a social, not just a reproductive, function.

Sex for passion, for intimacy, for relief of tension, even for material reward, for all the reasons people now make love—sex in early humans became a social lubricant. It seems to serve this function predominantly between sexes. Although people have much capacity for homosexuality and bisexuality, we are a long way from the equal-time arrangement of bonobos. Given their reproductive interests, it seems reasonable that protowomen's extended sexiness evolved in such a way as to attract primarily—but not only—males.

Sexual eagerness evolved in women along with their other social needs. This is extended, not constant, interest. As Frank Beach, who has devoted his professional life to studying sex in animals, remarked: "No human female is 'constantly sexually receptive' (Any male who entertains this illusion must be a very old man with a short memory or a very young man due for bitter disappointment)."[4]

Sex outside estrus is rare among mammals. It does happen. Even in chimpanzees, half of the mating goes on when the female is already pregnant. The chimp's labia continue monthly swelling while the fetus is already growing. Hanuman langur females give sexual invitations to a new and potentially infanticidal male whatever their reproductive state. They judder their heads from side to side and present their hindquarters, which is their species' sexual invitation. Some are definitely pregnant already, but perhaps the new male, having mated, might accept the infant and let it live. It is only humans and bonobos, however, who have managed to prolong female sexual appetite over months on end, not just a few days of real or apparent estrus.[5]

Concealed ovulation. In multimale primate species, sexual swellings signaling estrus have evolved at least seven separate times. The bright red advertising balloons flaunted by chimps and bonobos appear in species that attract many males at a distance. Human chimpwatchers can spot the pink flash of a swollen bottom on an opposite hillside—much more so an eager chimp male. Male chimpanzees and baboons are exquisitely sensitive to the flamboyant sexual swellings of females. Dominants allow subordinates or even subadults to mate in the days before and after the peak of a female's ovulation but claim their rights at the peak itself.

Orangutans and gorillas have almost no visual sign of ovulation, but pheromones and behavior cue in the males to the relevant days. Visually concealed estrus is widespread in multimale species, and it is common in single-male and monogamous species as well. It does not tell you much about the mating system—only that the female lives in a group where scent and behavioral cues serve to notify all the males she needs.

Human females, by contrast, conceal the moment of ovulation. Throughout human evolution, the moment when conception was likely was unknown even to women, let alone to their mates. In recent times, some women have learned to take their temperature daily and monitor their cervical mucus for clues to ovulation. However, we are apparently alone among mammals in needing technology to ascertain our own state of fertility.[6]

Instead of hormonally varying swellings, human females have evolved breasts and buttocks—permanent advertisements for receptivity, even if cycling is absent. Along with "faking" fertility, women can also fake desire and orgasm. Men can't. A female chimp can't either. She is not above trying it on a bit: estrous chimps are more likely to mate with males who give them meat, and much of the male's hunting seems to be centered around having tidbits to give to estrous females. All the same, a chimp prostitute could earn a living only a few days in the month.[7]

There are two main theories why concealed ovulation and extended sex evolved in humans, and at first they seem diametrically opposed. Jared Diamond has called them the "daddy-at-home" theory versus the "many-fathers" theory.[8]

"Daddy-at-home" has a long paternity, including the gleefully mischievous ethologist Desmond Morris, who in 1967 wrote a paean of tribute to explicit but monogamous sex in *The Naked Ape*.[9] A woman who wants to keep a husband interested in her and their children (and away from other females) can jump him any time she likes. All the better if neither she nor he knows just when they may actually produce a child. This can exploit a man's justified paranoia about fatherhood. If nobody knows just when the right time is, he had best keep at it, not leave his wife to find other men in the intervals.

This is certainly not the function of bonobo free-for-all sex. Sarah Hrdy opts instead for the "many-fathers" hypothesis. Perhaps extended sex is a way for a female to interest many men, not just to nail down one. If females live among males so jealous they actually kill rivals' children, then there are two ways out. The gorilla route is to get

a powerful male committed to defending you and his own offspring. The bonobo route is to mate so widely that rival males must all treat your children as possibly their own. What better way than being ready to mate whenever a good opportunity comes? Bonobos clearly mate to defuse tension, especially over feeding. Males often swap food for sex, though both parties act as if they appreciate both the food and the sex.[10]

Setting up "many-fathers" and "daddy-at-home" as a contradiction ducks the fact that both apply. David Pilbeam of Harvard has been pointing out to students for years that evolution does not have to have an either-or explanation for every trait. Two good reasons are better than one. If human women can have sex just about whenever we want, and can fake an interest even when we do not want, we can have our cake and eat it too. Men are quite right to feel threatened on occasion and deeply and warmly and wholeheartedly loved on other occasions. We play it both ways.

Concealed sex. Seeking privacy to mate is just as extraordinary a development as ovulating in private. There is almost no primate parallel. The nearest one is the "safari" of chimpanzees, when a male chimp inveigles a female to follow him in silence for days away from the group until her estrus has finished. Of course, many primates, like other mammals and furtively mating birds, are onto the principle of hiding momentarily from interference. Dominants and legitimate nesting mates, however, do not need to seek privacy.[11]

The trait seems to have developed along with the evolution of publicly recognized mating partners. As our ancestors' groups coalesced into recognized liaisons, each couple tried to keep away from interference by the others. This implies as its obverse that each couple also needed the others. After all, if they could afford to break up into separate territories like birds or gibbons, they would not just seek privacy for sex but for a lifetime.[12]

Our peculiar system comes from strong personal bonding within a larger group. It is the safari of the chimpanzees extended to a two-week honeymoon and then into spending nights in the couple's own nest or hut, yet in the daytime foraging and hunting in cooperation with the rest of the group. This strategy strengthens paternal certainty and support while allowing participation in a larger, more integrated social group, including friends who help with child care.

Is concealed estrus critical to making the system work? Privacy might be harder to maintain if females advertised with overwhelming smell, or brilliant bottoms, to all the men of the tribe just when the moment comes. However, you could argue that it is just as hard to restrain indiscriminate coupling with permanently sexy females like ourselves and the bonobos. Bonobos don't have restraints; we do. Sex in private is human.

Male control of females.   How did humans turn toward fidelity? It is often the hope of both parties, but sometimes it is forced on the female by male coercion. Why the asymmetry, where women take far more pains to conceal their secondary lovers, if any, than men do? Recall the crack of billionaire James Goldsmith: "A man who marries his mistress creates a vacancy."

It isn't enough to go back to the male-female difference in overall mating strategy, even as ratcheted up by mammalian pregnancy and lactation. We take on *obligations* to our principal mates. The verbal contract is one that only *Homo sapiens sapiens* could make, but the limiting of obligations to so few partners, and the asymmetry between partners in their degree of commitment, is perhaps much older.

One primate illuminates our own situation: the hamadryas baboon, the silver-maned Ethiopian species with its true harems. One afternoon I watched a film of an experiment conducted by Hans Kummer, in which a brown savanna female was introduced to a male hamadryas. I happened onto a particularly antagonistic version of *The Taming of the Shrew* that same evening, which played up Kate the shrew's feminist independence rather than her sexual chemistry. The brown savanna baboon kept wandering off to feed; in her own species' troop she would go where she pleased. A hamadryas female, in contrast, would have known her place, following her

harem overlord but also expecting his support and protection. The silver, scarlet-bottomed hamadryas male seemed furious at the brown female's behavior; he herded and bit her ever more viciously, while she seemed to become more and more disoriented by his behavior. At last, on a narrow cliff path, she stopped fleeing and began to follow him. She learned her new role through straight aversive conditioning. It spoiled any possible pleasure I might have taken in *The Taming of the Shrew*.

I am pleased to report that after two or three days the brown female evaded her hamadryas lord and ran away. I should also add that Kummer, one of the most sensitive as well as clearest-minded of primatologists, used as few animals in these experiments as possible to understand the situation and now says he might not even have embarked on such experiments if he had foreseen how devastating it is to wild primates to be taken from their social context.[13]

The hamadryas provides all-too-familiar a model of those human couples where males enforce the pair bond and females submit. The crucial factor is not just the difference in muscle power between the sexes but the pact of mutual respect between males. This makes it difficult for hamadryas or, as Barbara Smuts points out, human females to escape to another protector or to live in personal independence.[14]

The converse of the male pact is male jealousy. Some have suggested that jealousy in a man, especially "irrational" jealousy, is a mark of low self-esteem. It may, of course, reflect an accurate assessment by the man of his own undesirable status. And if his wife shares this view, he may soon have grounds for jealousy—which at that point may not be "irrational" at all. Throughout the world, male jealousy is invoked as a legal defense for so-called crimes of passion, even murdering a wife. The phrase "rule of thumb" derives from the eighteenth-century English judgment that beating one's wife with a stick is a crime only if the stick is thicker than the husband's thumb.[15]

The evolution of two-parent families and marriage. If the down side of pair bonding is coercion, the up side is that, in humans, men want to care for the kids. All single parents know how badly they need help with finances, housing, personal safety, just somebody to take a shift when the baby is howling with earache or has vomited over the last pair of sheets. Sometimes being on your own is just too much to cope with. Of course we want long-term partners. Both sexes do. Our love for each other has risen out of an evolutionary need for co-parenting. This does not mean that the pair must be biological parents of the children: present and future bonding matters more than the past—and an extended family of grandparents, aunts, and uncles also helps mightily. Male-female asymmetry remains, but a woman who is the only wife, or the official wife, or the favored wife, can enjoy her husband's support. Marriage—the formal recognition of partners with rites and rights—is a human universal, and so is love.

Raising up
from my weeding
of ripening cane

my eyes
make four
with this man

there ain't
no reason
to laugh

but
I laughing
in confusion

his hands
soft his words
quick his lips
curling as in
prayer

I nod

I like this man

Tonight
I go to meet him
like a flame[16]

BIRTH SPACING AND CHILD CARE

Human infants and children are more dependent for longer than any other primate. At birth, they don't even have prehensile toes to support themselves on our fur, if we had enough fur for them to hold. They may be thirty and just emerging from graduate or professional school before they are financially self-supporting.

However, an ape-child's physical demands on its own mother are even greater. Orang birth spacing in Tanjung Puting in Borneo (before the fires of 1997–98) has been about eight years. The mother carries her baby for much of the first two years. She suckles it for five or six years and only resumes cycling after seven. She is also the sole tutor for the child in the complexities of rainforest food supply and travel routes and its sole defense against clouded leopards.[17]

Chimpanzee females, who often range alone, have a similar challenge. The birth interval is slightly shorter, five or six years. They meet more often, and siblings stay till about age eight, so the children do play with aunts and uncles and older sibs. Six-year-old males can tag along after adult male "heroes." But by far the major energy demand for care, carrying, and lactation falls on the mother. Among the great apes, only gorilla females, in their tight harem groups, have constant companions to watch for predators, and playmates always at hand. Gorilla birth spacing in the giant nettle meadows of the Virungas also adds up to five or six years.[18]

One measure of the mother's role in infant survival is what happens to orphans. Among chimpanzees, four-year-old orphans die; five-year-olds go into depression, fail to develop and learn, and also die except in the rare cases when a competent older sibling or adult essentially adopts them. Among bonobos, the limitation may not be so strict. After Shijimi of Wamba lost his mother to hunters as a tiny three-year-old, he was raised by the group at large, especially grooming and cuddling with the three big group males. However, even Shijimi has suffered. An extraordinary BBC film followed his growing up and recorded a jealous adult female biting off one of his fingers. His own mother might have defended him from such an attack, as well as providing milk and comfort.[19]

Birth spacing is a sum of the physical and energetic needs of the mother and child. In zoos with plenty of food and no work, great ape mothers give birth every two to three years. Human Hutterites and other well-fed women who do not use any birth control except breastfeeding have the same interval. Our physiological potential for reproduction is thus much like that of other apes, but no known population of humans takes as long as wild apes to conceive again.[20]

Consider the archetypal society of the !Kung San, studied by Marjorie Shostak. It is archetypal not because it is the only way hunter-gatherers have lived but because the San until recently kept their traditional lifestyle, roaming the Kalahari Desert. Among these groups, the birth interval amounted to four years, during which a mother nursed her toddler and carried it on the long daily trek for food. But even among the !Kung San almost any adult would look after an infant for a while. Older children—the four-year-olds who, like Nisa, were displaced by new baby siblings—ran round the camp watching adult behavior and began their own apprenticeship in adult skills. Meanwhile a four- or five-year-old chimpanzee or orangutan would be still almost wholly fixated on its mother. The contrast becomes even sharper if you look at the Hadza, hunter-gatherers of Tanzania. During the 1980s when they were studied, they lived in richer gathering grounds, with fewer predators than the San. Even babies and toddlers could be put in the care of older children, so mothers nursed less often, carried their offspring less far, and conceived after a mere 2.5 years.[21]

It is perfectly true that human young need care from birth to puberty and beyond. However, there is no human society where all the care comes from the mother. That is what I mean by the relative independence of human children. Mothers could not bring them up without help. Even if our kids left home at eight, they would need help from someone.

Throughout the species, help is given. In modern human groups, much of the care comes from other women and older children, particularly girl children. Some comes from husbands; almost no physical or material help is offered by men who are not the mother's father, brother, or mate. It seems that human childhood, and all the dependence it entails, evolved within the mother's support group. The support group may have been kin, especially female kin, and friends, especially female friends but also male "friends" in the sense of potential or long-term mates.

One primate social system that we do not adopt, except for madmen and anchorites, is solitary life. This is odd since our female chimp relatives may range alone for weeks, and orangs for many months. Our need for support is such that "the heart of a person is only a jelly-fish in the human ocean, and when the ocean is removed from the jelly-fish, the latter dries up."[22]

A SCENARIO

Here is one possible scenario. The ancestors of all the African apes lived as a group of related males, like chimpanzees, bonobos, and the minority of gorilla groups where young males stay at home to inherit the territory and females. Young females came to join the males, crossing the forest on their own to find attractive mates. They also made friends with older females already in the group, though possibly with some continued tension toward these mothers-in-law.

First the gorillas split off. Their groups grew smaller, more focused on the dominant male, until most were true harems. The chimp-human line instead foraged on resources that led groups sometimes to fission but often to feed in large assemblages. Possibly females even then were beginning to extend the period of sexual interest, mating with many of the males.

Again two lineages split. One, the chimp-bonobos, grew large sexual swellings that advertised receptivity over a limited time to any male in eyeshot. The protohuman line continued extending the timing of sexual receptivity. They grew enlarged breasts and buttocks, permanent advertisements to any male around. Females of this second lot were not only attracting several males for their own choice but, with their sexually selected displays, were themselves subjects of choice.

The chimp line split a final time. Chimp sex swellings were originally temporary, but bonobos converted theirs into the equivalent of buttocks. By keeping them for a large part of each cycle, they showed their own prolonged sexual receptivity, although they were still aware of changes in the intensity of the signal. Meanwhile, the protohuman line went still further in blurring their signal. More and more, the time of ovulation was concealed until nobody—not even the woman herself—could be sure of it. And any occurrence of ovulation was rare, perhaps only once or twice over the course of two or three years.

The protohuman females, in their multimale, multifemale groups, mated with many males and befriended many females, including, at times, female kin who remained home. The males protected them all. They lived in the kind of forest-edge or savanna habitat that encouraged a fission-fusion society and mutual attacks between groups. Within the group, however, personal links coalesced. Males made compacts with one another, unconsciously at first and later consciously, to respect mating rights. Females also encouraged particular males to think themselves the father of particular infants, and they grew jealous of their own mates' attention to other females. They enticed the males to bond, heading off harm to the infants.

On the whole, peace within the group would help them raise the needy infants. This was, of course, a conditional strategy: you could change partners, or just plain stir up trouble, then as now. Sex in private was doubly helpful. Females hid like any other primate if mating with a non-legit male. But hiding with the main or recognized mate also helped deflect jealousy. For the taboo against public sex to have become so strong and universal, it must have been a very important factor in keeping the peace, for all parties.

One crucial part of the story is almost pure speculation. This is what happened between neighboring troops. Among most primates there is an uneasy truce, punctuated by stand-offs between females over food and territory. Males do fight, sometimes lethally, to take over females, as witness the "demonic males" among Wrangham's chimps. It matters if they have kin in other groups; immigrant vervet monkey males fight less hard against their own kin.[23]

Chimplike warfare intensified among the evolving human apes. Still, the females had kin in other groups—the mothers and brothers they, as adventurous adolescents, had left behind. In spite of the tribalism of modern chimps and humans, for most of the time human neighbors live in peace. When, and how, did humans start keeping in touch with both mother's and father's kin? My scenario would be that it was long, long before conscious "traffic in women" by males swapping sisters between groups. Perhaps, just perhaps, it was the mediation of the sisters, who maintained links between their husbands and brothers. With, of course, the agreement of the men, who found ways to extend the male pact of mutual respect to their in-laws.

MENOPAUSE AND THE VALUE OF AGE

One final group to consider: the old. Life does not stop with fertility. It is extraordinary that among women, fertility stops long before life or even sex does. This is not true in many primates. I remember meeting the oldest female of the Arashiyama Japanese macaque troop. She was 33—silver-haired, rheumy-eyed, arthritic. It hurt just to watch her hips move. Her infant clung to her back, bright-eyed, wrinkle-snouted, with the newborn's part in its topknot. It was just the age of her great-grandchild born the same spring.

In fact, most female mammals decline in fertility as they age. Women, pilot whales, and some elephants and chimpanzees stop cycling completely, as do individuals of many other species. Why do we give up reproduction so long before out time? Or, conversely, why do we live so long afterward?

It could just be a by-product. If genetically influenced breakdown of reproduction—and other bodily functions—are delayed long enough, animals will die anyhow of disease and starvation. In other words, natural selection acts to favor living vigorously and reproducing robustly up until the point when the animal is likely to be knocked off anyway. There is little selective pressure on genes to keep you healthy after that point, say until age 200, if the lion or the TB germ would have got to you first. Craig Packer and his colleagues examined the extensive records for wild lions and baboons and concluded that they live just long enough past their last child's birth to "fledge" that child. Both lions and baboons do offer child care for their grandchildren. However, having a grandmother alive, or a grandmother alive but not herself reproducing, does not seem to influence the grandchildren's survival.[24]

Lion mothers need only live on for a year, baboons only two, to launch their own offspring with as good a chance of survival as they are likely to get. Human mothers need more. Further, human mothers overlap their broods: we do not wait until one is "fledged" before starting on the next. This means that a risky final childbirth, in an older mother, may also put her existing children at risk. The "by-product" of putting off the effects of genes that lower reproduction until late in life may turn into a "spandrel" for us, which lets women stop having children in order to take better care of the ones we have. (Men seem to be in no particular danger from late reproduction, except the real possibility of a heart attack during intercourse—apparently worth it.)[25]

A second tier of benefits accrues to grandchildren, though the statistics do not show that it aids survival. Lions and baboons and even little vervet monkeys lick, cuddle, and protect their grandchildren. Human grandmothers do all that and share food as well—surely a part of the aid that allows our longer childhood and relatively shorter birth spacing than other apes, and a contribution to survival and success of the family.

The other aspect of postmenopausal life is not the stopping of fertility but life span itself. We are all too well aware in our aging society that old women are likely to live longer than old men. John M. Allman and his students have compiled life tables for a wide variety of primate species, in the cossetted conditions of zoos: not survival at the margins but, for a primate, life in the middle class. Strikingly, in species where the females do the bulk of child care, females live to be older. In the firmly monogamous species—gibbons and siamang, little New World owl monkeys and titis—males also live to be old. In other words, males who carry, play with, feed and defend their babies are chosen by natural selection for ripe old age. There is a politically correct moral here, though unfortunately helpful men can only expect to reap the benefits over evolutionary time. There is a politically uncomfortable conclusion, too: that females in our prehuman past did most of the work to care for their young.[26]

For humans, of course, the benefits given by aged parents and grandparents are not mere food and care. Sometimes they share wisdom. When Jared Diamond was inquiring about edible wild plants on the island of Rennell in the Solomon Archipelago of the Pacific, the tribesmen led him to their ultimate authority. "There, in the back of the hut, once my eyes had become accustomed to the dim light, was the inevitable, frail, very old woman, unable to walk without support. She was the last living person with direct experience of the plants found safe and nutritious to eat after the hungi kengi [the catastrophic cyclone of 1910] until people's gardens began producing again . . . Her survival after the 1910 cyclone had depended on information remembered by aged survivors of the last big cyclone before the hungi kengi. Now, the ability of her people to survive another cyclone would depend on her own memories."[27]

Again, this is foreshadowed faintly among other mammals. There was an aged mangabey female who led the group to a distant swamp at the height of a drought when all other water sources were dry, as, on a grander scale, do aged elephant matriarchs. Having at least a few elders to be the troop's memory could mean survival for children and grandchildren, and the tribe of all one's kin.[28] It is better for everyone that women should live to be old.

The two of us sit in the doorway
chatting about our children and grandchildren.
We sink happily
Into our oldwomanhood

like two spoons
sinking
into a bowl of hot porridge.[29]

NOTES

1. Harcourt, A. H., P. H., Larson, S. G., and Short, R. (1981); Fossey, D. (1983); Watts, D. P. (1990); Harcourt, A. H., Purvis, A., and Liles, L. (1995).

2. Baker, R. R., and Bellis, M. A. (1993).

3. Short, R. V. (1976).

4. Frank Beach, in Wolfe, L. D., Gray, J. P., Robinson, J. G., Lieberman, L. S., and Peters, E. H. (1982), p. 302.

5. Hrdy, S. B. (1977); Hrdy, S. B. (1993); Wallis, J. (1995).

6. Sillén-Tullberg, B., and Møller, A. P. (1993).

7. Stanford, C. B. (1995b); Stanford, C. B. (in press).

8. Diamond, J. (1997).

9. Morris, D. (1967).

10. Hrdy, S. B. (1981); Furuichi, T. (1987); Hrdy, S. B. (1993); Takahata, Y., Ihobe, H., and Idani, G. (1996).

11. Tutin, C. E. G. (1979).

12. Diamond, J. (1992); Diamond, J. (1997).

13. Kummer, H. (1995).

14. Smuts, B. (1992); Smuts, B. (1995).

15. Daly, M., and Wilson, M. (1983).

16. Nichols, Grace, "Like a Flame," in Nichols, G. (1984). Reprinted by permission of Little, Brown for Virago Press.

17. Galdikas, B. M. F. (1981); Galdikas, B. (1995a).

18. Goodall, J. (1986); Watts, D. P. (1990).

19. Goodall, J. (1986); Bass, K. (1997).

20. Short, R. V. (1976).

21. Short, R. V. (1976); Blurton-Jones, N. G., Hawkes, K., and O'Connell, J. (1989).

22. White, T. H., in Warner, S. T. (1967/1989), p. 169.

23. Cheney, D. L. (1981); Wrangham, R., and Peterson, D. (1996).

24. Packer, C., Tatar, M., and Collins, A. (1998).

25. Diamond, J. (1992); Caro, T. M., Sellen, D. W., Parish, A., Frank, R., Brown, D. M., Voland, E., and Borgerhoff Mulder, M. (1995); Diamond, J. (1997).

26. Allman, J. M. (1999).

27. Diamond, J. (1997), pp. 131–132.

28. Waser, P. M. (1978); Foley, Charles (personal communication).

29. Swirszczynska, Anna, "Two Old Women," trans. Marshment, M., and Baran, G., in Rumens, C., ed. (1985), p. 52.

◇ PART THREE ◇

SEXUAL POTENTIALITIES
LESSONS FROM EARLY ETHNOGRAPHIES

READINGS IN THIS PART

INTRODUCTION TO THE SUBJECT AND READINGS

A few years ago while rummaging through used books at a library sale, I happened upon a book with the title, *The Strangest Human Sex, Ceremonies and Customs* (Talalaj 1994). I imagined it would be a kind of cross-cultural *Ripley's Believe it or Not* of sexual behavior, and the book did not disappoint. Like *Ripley's*, the descriptions of the "strangest human sex" were sensationalized in ways that increased their exoticism. The author prepared us for "truly revolting sexual customs" warning that "the reader will find many descriptions almost impossible to grasp as true. . . . " (Talalaj 1994:3, vii).

Below, I provide a sampling of the strangest customs. I have omitted the names and locations of the cultures because some of these behaviors are misrepresented.

"It was custom in some societies that a girl had to lose her virginity before she attained puberty. Among the . . . a young girl had to be deflowered by a stranger." p. 21
". . . in some cultures, for the pleasure of women, men mutilated their penises and inserted a wide range of devices into the glans." p. vii.[1]

"The . . . wanted females to have pendulous breasts. Local girls tied special bands tightly across their bosom to force the breasts to hang down." p. 10

". . . a tribe in . . . use to spit on each other's faces while engaging in sexual intercourse." p. 4

"Among . . . the husband felt most honoured when his wife engaged in a sexual union with a stranger." p. 19

While these sexual tidbits successfully grab our attention and interest as eccentric behavior, the question of how to seriously address the sexualities of "others" has long been an issue in the social sciences. Studying or simply reporting sexual behavior in any culture is problematic. Although some research issues are consistent across cultures and through time, studying sexualities among small groups of people or encountering behaviors that differ dramatically from that of the researcher presents a special set of problems.

Working with small populations in ethnographic settings, means that the researcher cannot find safety in numbers, e.g., if you ask 1000 people about masturbation and 100 are dishonest, the resulting statistics will not be 100 percent accurate, but will only be off by 10 percent—in other words, conclusions will be in the ballpark (and you could try to calculate and correct for dishonesty). However, if your study population consists of only 50 people, each dishonest answer will carry considerably more weight, making conclusions about averages and norms less accurate.

Another major issue when studying sexualities in a "foreign" culture is definitions. For example, in some cultures mothers will sooth their infants by stroking their genitals. Within these cultures, such behavior is parenting, not sexual. Some researchers would, however, define anything that involves genital stimulation as a sex act. Whose definition should be used? Sexuality also has different meanings for different members of the same culture. What does sexuality mean to a 50-year-old man with three wives? And what does sexuality mean to the 16-year-old who just became his third wife?

Another major pitfall when studying sexualities in an ethnographic setting has been the tendency to take sexual behavior out of its cultural context. Learning, as we did earlier in this introduction, that culture X has a preference for pendulous breasts teaches us virtually nothing about sexualities in that culture. It did not provide the information needed to understand the value of this aspect of their sexuality? Why did it develop? What does it mean to the people of culture X? How does it fit into the bigger picture of their culture? Engaging in ethnographic research involves analyzing a cultural practice or behavior holistically and situating it within the culture. Cultural relativity is crucial to understanding behavior and helps prevent the ultimate ethnographic sin—ethnocentrism. Many ethnographic accounts have suffered because the researchers judged a cultural practice by the standards of their own culture. Consider the quote from the beginning of this section: "The inhabitants of . . . had truly revolting sexual customs." Revolting to whom? By whose standards? In this case, the practices were revolting to the author of the book.

Rather than step into the sexual quagmire, many of the early ethnographers simply ignored sexual behavior and avoided the topic. They provided thorough descriptions about land use, social etiquette, and local cuisine. In addition, kinship and marriage were usually explained in great detail. Yet ethnographies too often stopped at the "bedroom" door. Like television shows from the 1950s that portrayed married couples, in full pajamas, happily reading in their twin beds. Ethnographers brave enough to write about sexual behavior were often guilty of the sex-research sins listed above. By being judgmental or taking sexual behavior out of its cultural context, they often failed to realize that sexualities are enmeshed in a web of cultural meanings. For these reasons, the ethnographic record of sexualities is incomplete and some of it should not be taken at face value.

Later, progressive researchers, such as the authors featured in this part, understood that psychosexual socialization creates norms very different from our own. Their mini-ethnographies are offered not only because they demonstrate the wide range of sexual behavior recorded among the world's people, but also because each one of these articles has become a classic. Keep in mind that the cultures featured in these articles have changed since these studies were done, maybe dramatically. The data that form the basis for this writing were collected years ago. Since then, TV, birth control, AIDS, and even the Internet may have had profound effects on these cultures. These writings also predated social constructionism; therefore, these scholars employ the cultural influence model that dominated anthropology for several years. The cultural influence model proposed that biological theories provided neutral truths about human needs and that human variation occurred because socialization influenced the ways in which these biological needs were met. Simply put, the libido was shaped by the culture a person grew up in.

The first article in this section was written by Bronislaw Malinowski (1884–1942), one of the "fathers" of anthropological research. His interest in sexuality is reflected in his ethnographic work such as *Sex and Repression in Savage Society* and *Sex, Culture, and Myth*. The article presented here, *Prenuptial Intercourse Between the Sexes* explores the psychosexual development of Trobriand children. Through Malinowski's work we learn that sexual education begins at infancy with the socialization process. Children learn what is right and wrong by interacting with and observing adults and other children. Malinowski provides a picture of a youthful sexuality free from many of the constraints imposed in our own culture. At the same time, despite a seemingly unfettered sexual atmosphere, there are norms and mores. Some of their rules are almost the opposite to our own. We learn that, "To take a girl out to dinner without having previously married her . . . would be to disgrace her in the eyes of a Trobriander" p. 81. Thus, Malinowski's account demonstrates that morality is culturally specific. Ideas about virginity, childhood sexuality, marriage, and jealousy vary from culture to culture, as is demonstrated in other articles throughout this reader.

Many people mistakenly believe that sex in "simple" societies is free and easy. The sexual behavior of the Dani, as detailed in Karl Heider's article, *Dani Sexuality: A Low Energy System* dispels such misconceptions. Dani sexual behavior offers a sharp contrast to the sexual freedoms of the Trobriand Islands. The Dani have been become rather infamous in anthropological circles because of their lack of interest in sex. The idea of the libido was so strongly held that when Heider's article was first published it was met with disbelief by many in the academic community. Descriptions of Dani sexuality challenged many dearly held beliefs about human sexualities.

Sexual Inversion among the Azande by E.E. Evans-Pritchard is another article that expanded our knowledge of the potential for human sexual behavior. He described how some Azande boys would act as wives for young men. As these boy-brides aged and moved up the economic ladder, they would take on their own boy-brides. However, as soon as it became economically possible (due to bride-price) these men would marry women. Evans-Pritchard also recounts reports of lesbianism taking place between married women and also among co-wives in polygamous unions.

Evans-Pritchard calls male/male and female/female sexual interaction "sexual inversion," a term commonly used among sexologists in the 1900s to identify same-sex sexual relations. Inversion means to turn inside out or upside down, implying that same-sex sexual relations are the opposite of heterosexual relations. Once we get past the terminology, Evans-Pritchard's account of Azande sexual behavior challenges our ideas about sexual orientation. How could boy brides grow up to be heterosexual husbands? Azande women also displayed a fluid sexuality, engaging in sex with women in addition to their married heterosexual relations.

The first three mini-ethnographies in this section are from non-Western cultures. Most anthropological research was conducted in non-Western cultures. The last reading, *Sex and Repression in an Irish Folk Community* by John Messenger, details sexualities in a European community. Messenger agrees with Freud that our largest sex organ is the brain, and his analysis of the psychosexual development on Inis Beag supports this idea. We learn how several cultural factors conjoin to create a sexually repressive environment on this Irish island. Given the Inis Beag's lack of sex, it is tempting to draw similarities between the Dani and the population of Inis Beag. This, however would be a mistake. Whereas the Dani do not seem interested in sex, the people on Inis Beag have a dramatically different relationship with sexuality. In their culture discussions of all things sexual are taboo, and this extends beyond the obvious. No one learns to swim because it requires "bared" bodies and dogs are not allowed to lick their own genitals. On Inis Beag, sexuality is everywhere and has an important role within the culture—denying or pretending it does not exist.

The readings in this section demonstrate that using the cross-cultural ethnographic record to understand sexual potentialities is not simply about finding "the strangest human sex ceremonies and customs." Understanding what people do not do, and why, is just as important as understanding what they do, and why. The study of sexualities is not just about behavior—who does what to whom. It is also about beliefs, attitudes, and aspirations. Sexualities are embedded in political, ideological, social, and economic systems. Reading ethnographies about sexualities increases our knowledge about what it means to be human and what role sexualities plays in humanness and humanity.

TERMS AND CONCEPTS

bridewealth	pan-cultural
concubinage	pederasty
copulation	postpartum sexual abstinence
cultural relativity	psychosexual development
ethnography	puberty
fornication	sexual inversion
holism/holistic	tribadism
libidinous plasticity	taboo

QUESTIONS TO CONSIDER

1. How does Heider's characterization of the Dani sexualities challenge Freudian ideas about the human libido?
2. How does Heider's description of the Dani sexualities challenge our views about human sexualities? What was your reaction to this article?
3. How does adolescent sexuality in the Trobriand Islands, as described by Malinowski, compare with ideas about adolescent sexuality in the United States?
4. How do Trobriand children learn about sexual conduct? Give examples from the readings that demonstrate socialization.
5. What are the rules regarding sexual conduct among young people in the Trobriand Islands?
6. E.E. Evans-Pritchard used the phrase "libidinous plasticity" to describe sexual conduct among the Azande. What does he mean by this phrase and why does he apply it to Azande?
7. Does the Azande sexual behavior described by E.E. Evans-Pritchard challenge or support our ideas about sexual orientation? Why?
8. Messenger describes Inis Beag as "one of the most sexually naive of the world's societies." What behaviors and beliefs lead him to this conclusion?
9. What similarities do you find in the sexual behavior/conduct of these four cultures? What are the differences?

NOTES

1. See also Brown, 1990, for an ethnographic account of these practices.

FURTHER READINGS

Brown, Donald E. 1990. The penis pen: An unsolved problem in the relations between the sexes in Borneo. In *Female and Male in Borneo*, edited by V. Sutlive, The Borneo Research Council, pp. 435–454.

Crocker, William, and Jean Crocker. 1994. *The Canela: Bonding through Kinship, Ritual, and Sex.* New York: Harcourt Brace College Publishers.

Davis, D.L. and R.G. Whitten. 1987. The cross-cultural study of human sexuality. *Annual Review of Anthropology*, 16:69–98.

Ford, Clellan S. and Frank A. Beach. 1951. *Patterns of Sexual Behavior.* New York: Harper & Brothers.

Francouer, Robert T. (ed.). 1997. *The International Encyclopedia of Sexuality*, Vol. 1–3. New York: Continuum Publishing.

Frayser, Suzanne G. 1985. *Varieties of Sexual Experience.* New Haven: Human Relations Area Files.

Gregersen, Edgar. 1996. *The World of Human Sexuality: Behaviors, Customs, and Beliefs.* New York: Irvington Press.

Heider, Karl G. 1997. *Grand Valley Dani: Peaceful Warriors.* New York: Harcourt Brace Publishers.

Malinowski, Bronislaw. 1927. *Sex and Repression in Savage Society.* New York: Meridian Books.

Marshall, Donald S. and Robert C. Suggs (eds.). 1971. *Human Sexual Behavior: Variations in the Ethnographic Spectrum.* New York: Basic Books.

Mead, Margaret. 1929. *Coming of Age in Samoa: A Psychological Study of Primitive Youth for Western Civilization.* New York: Harperperennial Library.

Ortner, Sherry B., and Harriet Whitehead (eds.). 1981. *Sexual Meanings: The Cultural Construction of Gender and Sexuality.* New York: Cambridge University Press.

Shostak, Marjorie. 1981. *Nisa: The Life and Words of a !Kung Woman.* New York: Vintage Books.

Talalaj, J., and S. Talalaj. 1994. *The Strangest Human, Sex, Ceremonies and Customs.* Melbourne: Hill of Content.

RELATED WEBSITES

AnthroGlobe - Bibliography of sex, gender, and fieldwork
www.coombs.anu.edu.au/Biblio_fieldwork4.html

The Electronic Journal of Human Sexuality
www.ejhs.org

Human Relations Area Files (HRAF) - Outline of World Cultures
www.yale.edu/hraf/fiche_collection.html

The International Lesbian and Gay Association
www.ilga.org

The International Encyclopedia of Sexuality, Vol 1-3.
www.rki.de/gesund/archiv/ies

Oceania Newsletter: Dani Bibliography
www.kun.nl/cps/12/nb12i/html

SIECUS (Sexuality, Information, and Education Council of the United States)
www.siecus.org

8

Prenuptial Intercourse Between the Sexes

Bronislaw Malinowski

University of London

The Trobrianders are very free and easy in their sexual relations. To a superficial observer it might indeed appear that they are entirely untrammeled in these. This, however, is not the case; for their liberty has certain very well-defined limits. The best way of showing this will be to give a consecutive account of the various stages through which a man and a woman pass from childhood to maturity—a sort of sexual life-history of a representative couple.

We shall have first to consider their earliest years, for these natives begin their acquaintance with sex at a very tender age. The unregulated and, as it were, capricious intercourse of these early years becomes systematized in adolescence into more or less stable intrigues, which later on develop into permanent liaisons. Connected with these latter stages of sexual life, there exists in the Trobriand Islands an extremely interesting

institution, the bachelors' and unmarried girls' house, called by the natives *bukumatula*; it is of considerable importance, as it is one of those arrangements sanctioned by custom which might appear on the surface to be a form of "group-marriage."

THE SEXUAL LIFE OF CHILDREN

Children in the Trobriand Islands enjoy considerable freedom and independence. They soon become emancipated from a parental tutelage which has never been very strict. Some of them obey their parents willingly, but this is entirely a matter of the personal character of both parties: there is no idea of a regular discipline, no system of domestic coercion. Often as I sat among them, observing some family incident or listening to a quarrel between parent and child, I would hear a youngster told to do this or that, and generally the thing, whatever it was, would be asked as a favour, though sometimes the request might be backed up by a threat of violence. The parents would either coax or scold or ask as from one equal to

Source: Prenuptial intercourse between the sexes. In *The Sexual Life of Savages in North-Western Melanesia*, by Bronislaw Malinowski, 1929, pp. 44–64, new edition 1987. Boston: Beacon Press.

another. A simple command, implying the expectation of natural obedience, is never heard from parent to child in the Trobriands.

People will sometimes grow angry with their children and beat them in an outburst of rage; but I have quite as often seen a child rush furiously at his parent and strike him. This attack might be received with a good-natured smile, or the blow might be angrily returned; but the idea of definite retribution, or of coercive punishment, is not only foreign, but distinctly repugnant to the native. Several times, when I suggested, after some flagrant infantile misdeed, that it would mend matters for the future if the child were beaten or otherwise punished in cold blood, the idea appeared unnatural and immoral to my friends, and was rejected with some resentment.

Such freedom gives scope for the formation of the children's own little community, an independent group, into which they drop naturally from the age of four or five and continue till puberty. As the mood prompts them, they remain with their parents during the day, or else join their playmates for a time in their small republic. And this community within a community acts very much as its own members determine, standing often in a sort of collective opposition to its elders. If the children make up their minds to do a certain thing, to go for a day's expedition, for instance, the grown-ups and even the chief himself, as I often observed, will not be able to stop them. In my ethnographic work I was able and was indeed forced to collect my information about children and their concerns directly from them. Their spiritual ownership in games and childish activities was acknowledged, and they were also quite capable of instructing me and explaining the intricacies of their play or enterprise.

Small children begin also to understand and to defer to tribal tradition and custom; to those restrictions which have the character of a taboo or of a definite command of tribal law, or usage or propriety.[1]

The child's freedom and independence extend also to sexual matters. To begin with, children hear of and witness much in the sexual life of their elders. Within the house, where the parents have no possibility of finding privacy, a child has opportunities of acquiring practical information concerning the sexual act. I was told that no special precautions are taken to prevent children from witnessing their parents' sexual enjoyment. The child would merely be scolded and told to cover its head with a mat. I sometimes heard a little boy or girl praised in these terms: "Good child, he never tells what happens between his parents." Young children are allowed to listen to baldly sexual talk, and they understand perfectly well what is being discussed. They are also themselves tolerably expert in swearing and the use of obscene language. Because of their early mental development some quite tiny children are able to make smutty jokes, and these their elders will greet with laughter.

Small girls follow their fathers on fishing expeditions, during which the men remove their pubic leaf. Nakedness under these conditions is regarded as natural, since it is necessary. There is no lubricity or ribaldry associated with it. Once, when I was engaged in the discussion of an obscene subject, a little girl, the daughter of one of my informants, joined our group. I asked the father to tell her to go away. "Oh no," he answered, "she is a good girl, she never repeats to her mother anything that is said among men. When we take her fishing with us we need not be ashamed. Another girl would describe the details of our nakedness to her companions or her mothers.[2] Then these will chaff us and repeat what they have heard about us. This little girl never says a word." The other men present enthusiastically assented, and developed the theme of the girl's discretion. But a boy is much less in contact with his mother in such matters, for here, between maternal relations, that is, for the natives, between real kindred, the taboo of incest begins to act at an early age, and the boy is removed from any intimate contact of this sort with his mother and above all with his sisters.

There are plenty of opportunities for both boys and girls to receive instruction in erotic matters from their companions. The children initiate each other into the mysteries of sexual life in a directly practical manner at a very early age. A premature amorous existence begins among them long before they are able really to carry out the act of sex. They indulge in plays and pastimes in which they satisfy their curiosity concerning the appearance and function of the organs of generation, and incidentally receive, it would seem, a certain amount of positive pleasure. Genital manipulation and such minor perversions as oral stimulation of the organs are typical forms of this amusement. Small boys and girls are said to be frequently initiated by their somewhat older companions, who allow them to witness their own amorous dalliance. As they are untrammelled by the authority of their elders and unrestrained by any moral code, except that of specific tribal taboo, there is nothing but their degree of curiosity, of ripeness, and of "temperament" or sensuality, to determine how much or how little they shall indulge in sexual pastimes.

The attitude of the grown-ups and even of the parents towards such infantile indulgence is either that of complete indifference or of complacency—they find it natural, and do not see why they should scold or interfere. Usually they show a kind of tolerant and amused interest, and discuss the love affairs of their children with easy jocularity. I often heard some such benevolent gossip as this: "So-and-so (a little girl) has already had intercourse with So-and-so (a little boy)." And if such were the case, it would be added that it was her first experience. An exchange of lovers, or some small love drama in the little world would be half-seriously, half-jokingly discussed. The infantile sexual act, or its substitute, is regarded as an innocent amusement. "It is their play to *kayta* (to have intercourse). They give each other a coconut, a small piece of betel-nut, a few beads or some fruits from the bush, and then they go and hide, and *kayta*." But it is not considered proper for the children to carry on their affairs in the house. It has always to be done in the bush.

The age at which a girl begins to amuse herself in this manner is said to coincide with her putting on the small fibre skirt, between, that is, the ages of four and five. But this obviously can refer only to incomplete practices and not to the real act. Some of my informants insisted that such small female children actually have intercourse with penetration. Remembering, however, the Trobriander's very strong tendency to exaggerate in the direction of the grotesque, a tendency not altogether devoid of a certain malicious Rabelaisian humour, I am inclined to discount these statements of my authorities. If we place the beginning of real sexual life at the age of six to eight in the case of girls, and ten to twelve in the case of boys, we shall probably not be erring very greatly in either direction. And from these times sexuality will gradually assume a greater and greater importance as life goes on, until it abates in the course of nature.

Sexual, or at least sensuous pleasure constitutes if not the basis of, at least an element in, many of the children's pastimes. Some of them do not, of course, provide any sexual excitement at all, as for instance those in imitation of the grown-up economic and ceremonial activities, or games of skill or childish athletics; but all sorts of round games, which are played by the children of both sexes on the central place of the village, have a more or less strongly marked flavour of sex, though the outlets they furnish are indirect and only accessible to the elder youths and maidens who also join in them. Indeed, we shall have to return later (chs. ix and xi) to a consideration of sex in certain games, songs, and stories, for as the sexual association becomes more subtle and indirect it appeals more and more to older people alone and has, therefore, to be examined in the contexts of later life.

There are, however, some specific games in which the older children never participate, and into which sex directly enters. The little ones sometimes play, for instance, at house-building, and at family life. A small hut of sticks and boughs is constructed in a secluded part of the jungle, and a couple or more repair thither and play at husband and wife, prepare food and carry out or imitate as best they can the act of sex. Or else a band of them, in imitation of the amorous expeditions of their elders, carry food to some favourite spot on the sea-shore or in the coral ridge, cook and eat vegetables there, and "when they are full of food, the boys sometimes fight with each other, or sometimes *kayta* (copulate) with the girls." When the fruit ripens on certain wild trees in the jungle they go in parties to pick it, to exchange presents, make *kula* (ceremonial exchange) of the fruit, and engage in erotic pastimes.[3]

Thus it will be seen that they have a tendency to palliate the crudity of their sexual interest and indulge by associating it with something more poetic. Indeed, the Trobriand children show a great sense of the singular and romantic in their games. For instance, if a part of the jungle or village has been flooded by rain, they go and sail their small canoes on this new water; or if a very strong sea has thrown up some interesting flotsam, they proceed to the beach and inaugurate some imaginative game around it. The little boys, too, search for unusual animals, insects, or flowers, and give them to the little girls, thus lending a redeeming aesthetic touch to their premature eroticisms.

In spite of the importance of the sexual motive in the life of the youngest generation, it must be kept in mind that the separation of the sexes, in many matters, obtains also among children. Small girls can very often be seen playing or wandering in independent parties by themselves. Little boys in certain moods—and these seem their more usual ones—scorn the society of the female and amuse themselves alone. Thus the small republic falls into two distinct groups which are perhaps to be seen more often apart than together; and, though they frequently unite in play, this need by no means be necessarily sensuous.

It is important to note that there is no interference by older persons in the sexual life of children. On rare occasions some old man or woman is suspected of taking a strong sexual interest in the children, and even of having intercourse with some of them. But I never found such suspicions supported even by a general consensus of opinion, and it was always considered both improper and silly for an older man or woman to have sexual dealings with a child. There is certainly no trace of any custom of ceremonial defloration by old men, or even by men belonging to an older age class.

AGE DIVISIONS

I have just used the expression "age class," but I did so in a broad sense only: for there are no sharply distinguished age grades or classes among the Trobriand natives. The following table of age designations only roughly indicates the stages of their life; for these stages in practice merge into one another.

The terms used in this table will be found to overlap in some instances. Thus a very small infant may be referred to as *waywaya* or

TABLE 8–1 Designations of Age

1. *Waywaya* (fœtus; infant till the age of crawling, both male and female).		I. Stage: *Gwadi*—Word used as a generic designation for all these stages 1–4, meaning *child*, male or female, at any time between birth and maturity
2. *Pwapwawa* (infant, till the stage of walking, male or female).		
3. *Gwadi* (child, till puberty, male or female).		
4. *Monagwadi* (male child)	4. *Inagwadi* (female child)	
5. *To'ulatile* (youth from puberty till marriage)	5. *Nakapugula* or *Nakubukwabuya* (girl from puberty till marriage)	II. Stage: Generic designations— *Ta'u* (man), *Vivila* (woman).
6. *Tobubowa'u* (mature man)	6. *Nabubowa'u* (ripe woman)	
6a. *Tovavaygile* (married man)	6a. *Navavaygile* (married woman)	
7. *Tomwaya* (old man)	7. *Numwaya* (old woman)	III. Stage: Old age.
7a. *Toboma* (old honoured man)		

pwapwawa indiscrimately, but only the former term as a rule would be used in speaking of a fœtus or referring to the pre-incarnated children from Tuma.[4] Again, you might call a few months' old child either *gwadi* or *pwapwawa*, but the latter term would be but seldom used except for a very small baby. The term *gwadi* moreover can be used generically, as "child" in English, to denote anything from a fœtus to a young boy or girl. Thus, it will be seen that two terms may encroach on each other's field of meaning, but only if they be consecutive. The terms with sex prefixes (4) are normally used only of elder children who may be distinguished by their dress.

There are, besides these more specific subdivisions, the three main distinctions of age, between the ripe man and woman in the full vigour of life and the two stages—those of childhood and of old age—which limit manhood and womanhood on either side. The second main stage is divided into two parts, mainly by the fact of marriage. Thus, the words under (5) primarily designate unmarried people and to that extent are opposed to (6a), but they also imply youthfulness or unripeness, and in that respect are opposed to (6).

The male term for old age, *tomwaya* (7) can also denote rank of importance. I myself was often so addressed, but I was not flattered, and much preferred to be called *toboma* (literally "the tabooed man"), a name given to old men of rank, but stressing the latter attribute rather than the former. Curiously enough, the compliment or distinction implied in the word *tomwaya* becomes much weaker, and almost disappears in its feminine equivalent. *Numwaya* conveys that tinge of scorn or ridicule inseparable from "old woman" in so many languages.

THE AMOROUS LIFE OF ADOLESCENCE

When a boy reaches the age of from twelve to fourteen years, and attains that physical vigour which comes with sexual maturity, and when, above all, his increased strength and mental ripeness allow him to take part, though still in a somewhat limited and fitful manner, in some of the economic activities of his elders, he ceases to be regarded as a child (*gwadi*), and assumes the position of adolescent (*ulatile* or *to'ulatile*). At the same time he receives a different status, involving some duties and many privileges, a stricter observance of taboos, and a greater participation in tribal affairs. He has already donned the pubic leaf for some time; now he becomes more careful in his wearing of it, and more interested in its appearance. The girl emerges from childhood into adolescence through the obvious bodily changes "her breasts are round and full; her bodily hair begins to grow; her menses flow and ebb with every moon," as the natives put it. She also has no new change in her attire to make, for she has much earlier assumed her fibre skirt, but now her interest in it from the two points of view of elegance and decorum is greatly increased.

At this stage a partial break-up of the family takes place. Brothers and sisters must be segregated in obedience to that stringent taboo which plays such an important part in tribal life.[5] The elder children, especially the males, have to leave the house, so as not to hamper by their embarrassing presence the sexual life of their parents. This partial disintegration of the family group is effected by the boy moving to a house tenanted by bachelors or by elderly widowed male relatives or friends. Such a house is called *bukumatula*, and in the next section we shall become acquainted with the details of its arrangement. The girl sometimes goes to the house of an elderly widowed maternal aunt or other relative.

As the boy or girl enters upon adolescence the nature of his or her sexual activity becomes more serious. It ceases to be mere child's play and assumes a prominent place among life's interests. What was before an unstable relation culminating in an exchange of erotic manipulation or an immature sexual act becomes now an absorbing passion, and a matter for serious endeavour. An adolescent gets definitely attached to a given person, wishes to possess her, works purposefully towards this goal, plans to reach the fulfilment of his desires by magical and other means, and finally rejoices in achievement. I have seen young people of this age grow positively miserable through ill-success in love. This stage, in fact, differs from the one before in that personal preference has now come into play and with it a tendency towards a greater permanence in intrigue. The boy develops a desire to retain the fidelity and exclusive affection of the loved one, at least for a time. But this tendency is not associated so far with any idea of settling down to one exclusive relationship, nor do adolescents yet begin to think of marriage. A boy or girl wishes to pass through many more experiences; he or she still enjoys the prospect of complete freedom and has no desire to accept obligations. Though pleased to imagine that his partner is faithful, the youthful lover does not feel obliged to reciprocate this fidelity.

We have seen in the previous section that a group of children forming a sort of small republic within the community is conspicuous in every village. Adolescence furnishes the community with another small group, of youths and girls. At this stage, however, though the boys and girls are much more bound up in each other as regards amorous interests, they but rarely mix in public or in the daytime. The group is really broken up into two, according to sex. To this division there correspond two words, *to'ulatile* and *makubukwabuya*, there being no one expression—such as there is to describe the younger age group, *gugwadi*, children—to define the adolescent youth of both sexes.

The natives take an evident pride in this, "the flower of the village," as it might be called. They frequently mention that "all the *to'ulatile* and *nakubukwabuya* (youths and girls) of the village were there." In speaking of some competitive game, or dance or sport, they compare the looks or performance of their own youths with those of some other village, and always to the advantage of their own. This group leads a happy, free, arcadian existence, devoted to amusement and the pursuit of pleasure.

Its members are so far not claimed by any serious duties, yet their greater physical strength and ripeness give them more independence and a wider scope of action than they had as children. The adolescent boys participate, but mainly as freelancers, in garden work, in the fishing and hunting and in oversea expeditions; they get all the excitement and pleasure, as well as some of the prestige, yet remain free from a great deal of the drudgery and many of the restrictions which trammel and weigh on their elders. Many of the taboos are not yet quite binding on them, the burden of magic has not yet fallen on their shoulders. If they grow tired of work, they simply stop and rest. The self-discipline of ambition and subservience to traditional ideals, which moves all the elder individuals and leaves them relatively little personal freedom, has not yet quite drawn these boys into the wheels of the social machine. Girls, too, obtain a certain amount of the enjoyment and excitement denied to children by joining in some of the activities of their elders, while still escaping the worst of the drudgery.

Young people of this age, besides conducting their love affairs more seriously and intensely, widen and give a greater variety to the setting of their amours. Both sexes arrange picnics and excursions and thus their indulgence in intercourse becomes associated with an enjoyment of novel experiences and fine scenery. They also form sexual connections outside the village community to which they belong. Whenever there occurs in some other locality one of the ceremonial occasions on which custom permits of licence, thither they repair, usually in bands either of boys or of girls, since on such occasions opportunity of indulgence offers for one sex alone (see ch. ix, esp. secs. 6 and 7).

It is necessary to add that the places used for lovemaking differ at this stage from those of the previous one. The small children carry on their sexual practices surreptitiously in bush or grove as a part of their games, using all sorts of make-shift arrangements to attain privacy, but the *ulatile* (adolescent) has either a couch of his own in a bachelors' house, or the use of a hut belonging to one of his unmarried relatives. In a certain type of yam-house, too, there is an empty closed-in space in which boys sometimes arrange little "cozy-corners," affording room for two.

In these, they make a bed of dry leaves and mats, and thus obtain a comfortable *garçonnière*, where they can meet and spend a happy hour or two with their loves. Such arrangements are, of course, necessary now that amorous intercourse has become a passion instead of a game.

But a couple will not yet regularly cohabit in a bachelors' house *(bukumatula)*, living together and sharing the same bed night after night. Both girl and boy prefer to adopt more furtive and less conventionally binding methods, to avoid lapsing into a permanent relationship which might put unnecessary restraint upon their liberty by becoming generally known. That is why they usually prefer a small nest in the *sokwaypa* (covered yam-house), or the temporary hospitality of a bachelors' house.

We have seen that the youthful attachments between boys and girls at this stage have ripened out of childish games and intimacies. All these young people have grown up in close propinquity and with full knowledge of each other. Such early acquaintances take fire, as it were, under the influence of certain entertainments, where the intoxicating influence of music and moonlight, and the changed mood and attire of all the participants, transfigure the boy and girl in each other's eyes. Intimate observation of the natives and their personal confidences have convinced me that extraneous stimuli of this kind play a great part in the love affairs of the Trobrianders. Such opportunities of mutual transformation and escape from the monotony of everyday life are afforded not only by the many fixed seasons of festivity and permitted licence, but also by that monthly increase in the people's pleasure-seeking mood which leads to many special pastimes at the full of the moon.[6]

Thus adolescence marks the transition between infantile and playful sexualities and those serious permanent relations which precede marriage. During this intermediate period love becomes passionate and yet remains free.

As time goes on, and the boys and girls grow older, their intrigues last longer, and their mutual ties tend to become stronger and more permanent. A personal preference as a rule develops and begins definitely to overshadow all other love affairs. It may be based on true sexual passion or else on an affinity of characters. Practical considerations become involved in it, and, sooner or later, the man thinks of stabilizing one of his liaisons by marriage. In the ordinary course of events, every marriage is preceded by a more or less protracted period of sexual life in common. This is generally known and spoken of, and is regarded as a public intimation of the matrimonial projects of the pair. It serves also as a test of the strength of their attachment and extent of their mutual compatibility. This trial period also gives time for the prospective bridegroom and for the woman's family to prepare economically for the event.

Two people living together as permanent lovers are described respectively as "his woman" *(la vivila)* and "her man" *(la ta'u)*. Or else a term, also used to describe the friendship between two men, is applied to this relationship *(lubay-*, with pronominal suffixes). In order to distinguish between a passing liaison and one which is considered preliminary to marriage, they would say of the female concerned in the latter: *"la vivila mokita; imisiya yambwata yambwata"*—"his woman truly; he sleeps with her always always." In this locution the sexual relationship between the two is denoted by the verb "to sleep with" *(imisiya)*, the durative and iterative form of *masisi*, to sleep. The use of this verb also emphasizes the lawfulness of the relation, for it is used in talking of sexual intercourse between husband and wife, or of such relations as the speaker wishes to discuss seriously and respectfully. An approximate equivalent in English would be the verb "cohabit." The natives have two other words in distinction to this. The verb *kaylasi*, which implies an illicit element in the act, is used when speaking of adultery or other forms of non-lawful intercourse. Here the English word "fornicate" would come nearest to rendering the native meaning. When the natives wish to indicate the crude, physiological fact, they use the word *kayta*, translatable, though pedantically, by the verb "copulate with."

The pre-matrimonial, lasting intrigue is based upon and maintained by personal elements only. There is no legal obligation on either party. They may enter into and dissolve it as they like. In fact, this relationship differs from other liaisons only in its duration and stability. Towards the end, when marriage actually approaches, the element of personal responsibility and obligation becomes stronger. The two now regularly cohabit in the same house, and a considerable degree of exclusiveness in sexual matters is observed by them. But they have not yet given up their personal freedom; on the several occasions of wider licence affianced couples are invariably separated and each partner is "unfaithful" with his or her temporary choice. Even within the village, in the normal course, the girl who is definitely going to marry a particular boy will bestow favours on other men, though a certain measure of decorum must be observed in this; if she sleeps out too often, there will be possibly a dissolution of the tie and certainly friction and disagreement. Neither boy nor girl may go openly and flagrantly with other partners on an amorous expedition. Quite apart from nocturnal cohabitation, the two are supposed to be seen in each other's company and to make a display of their relationship in public. Any deviation from the exclusive liaison must be decent, that is to say, clandestine. The relation of free engagement is the natural outcome of a series of trial liaisons, and the appropriate preliminary test of marriage.

THE BACHELORS' HOUSE

The most important feature of this mode of steering towards marriage, through gradually lengthening and strengthening intimacies, is an institution which might be called "the limited bachelors' house," and which, indeed, suggests at first sight the presence of a "group concubinage." It is clear that in order to enable pairs of lovers permanently to cohabit, some building is needed which will afford them seclusion. We have seen the makeshift arrangements of children and the more comfortable, but not yet permanent love-nests of adolescent boys and girls, and it is obvious that the lasting liaisons of youth and adult girls require some special institution, more definitely established, more physically comfortable, and at the same time having the approval of custom.

To meet this need, tribal custom and etiquette offer accommodation and privacy in the form of the *bukumatula*, the bachelors' and unmarried girls' house of which mention has already been made. In this a limited number of couples, some two, three, or four, live for longer or shorter periods together in a temporary community. It also and incidentally offers shelter for younger couples if they want amorous privacy for an hour or two.

We must now give some more detailed attention to this institution, for it is extremely important and highly significant from many points of view. We must consider the position of the houses in the village, their internal arrangements and the manner in which life within the *bukumatula* shapes itself.

In the description of the typical village in the Trobriands (ch. i, sec. 2), attention was drawn to its schematic division into several parts. This division expresses certain sociological rules and regularities. As we have seen, there is a vague association between the central place and the male life of the community; between the street and feminine activities. Again, all the houses of the inner row, which consists principally of storehouses, are subject to certain taboos, especially to the taboo of cooking, which is believed to be inimical to the stored yam. The outer ring, on the other hand, consists of household dwellings, and there cooking is allowed. With this distinction is associated the fact that all the establishments of married people have to stand in the outer ring, whereas a bachelor's house may be allowed among the storehouses in the middle. The inner row thus consists of yam-houses (*bwayma*), personal huts of a chief and his kinsmen (*lisiga*), and bachelors' houses (*bukumatula*). The outer ring is made up of matrimonial homes (*bulaviyaka*), closed yam-houses (*sokwaypa*), and widows' or widowers' houses (*bwala nakaka'u*). The main distinction between the two rings is the taboo on cooking. A young chief's *lisiga* (personal hut) is as a rule used also to accommodate other youths and thus becomes a *bukumatula* with all that this implies.

At present there are five bachelors' establishments in Omarakana, and four in the adjoining village of Kasana'i. Their number has greatly diminished owing to missionary influence. Indeed, for fear of being singled out, admonished and preached at, the owners of some *bukumatula* now erect them in the outer ring, where they are less conspicuous. Some ten years ago my informants could count as many as fifteen bachelors' homes in both villages, and my oldest acquaintances remember the time when there were some thirty. This dwindling in number is due, of course, partly to the enormous decrease of population, and only partly to the fact that nowadays some bachelors live with their parents, some in widowers' houses, and some in the missionary compounds. But whatever the reason, it is needless to say that this state of affairs does not enhance true sex morality.

The internal arrangements of a *bukumatula* are simple. The furniture consists almost exclusively of bunks with mat coverings. Since the inmates lead their life in association with other households in the day-time, and keep all their working implements in other houses, the inside of a typical *bukumatula* is strikingly bare. It lacks the feminine touch, the impression of being really inhabited.

In such an interior the older boys and their temporary mistresses live together. Each male owns his own bunk and regularly uses it. When a couple dissolve their liaison, it is the girl who moves, as a rule, to find another sleeping-place with another sweetheart. The *bukumatula* is, usually, owned by the group of boys who inhabit it, one of them, the eldest, being its titular owner. I was told that sometimes a man would build a house as a *bukumatula* for his daughter, and that in olden days there used to be unmarried people's houses owned and tenanted by girls. I never met, however, any actual instance of such an arrangement.

At first sight, as I have said, the institution of the *bukumatula* might appear as a sort of "Group Marriage" or at least "Group Concubinage," but analysis shows it to be nothing of the kind. Such wholesale terms are always misleading, if we allow them to carry an extraneous implication. To call this institution "Group Concubinage" would lead to misunderstanding; for it must be remembered that we have to deal with a number of couples who sleep in a common house, each in an exclusive liaison, and not with a group of people all living promiscuously together; there is never an exchange of partners, nor any poaching nor "complaisance." In fact, a special code of honour is observed within the *bukumatula*, which makes an inmate much more careful to respect sexual rights within the house than outside it. The word *kaylasi*, indicating sexual trespass, would be used of one who offended against this code; and I was told that "a man should not do it, because it is very bad, like adultery with a friend's wife."

Within the *bukumatula* a strict decorum obtains. The inmates never indulge in orgiastic pastimes, and it is considered bad form to watch another couple during their love-making. I was told by my young friends that the rule is either to wait till all the others are asleep, or else for all the pairs of a house to undertake to pay no attention to the rest. I could find no trace of any "voyeur" interest taken by the average boy, nor any tendency to exhibitionism. Indeed, when I was discussing the positions and technique of the sexual act, the statement was volunteered that there are specially unobtrusive ways of doing it "so as not to wake up the other people in the *bukumatula*."

Of course, two lovers living together in a *bukumatula* are not bound to each other by any ties valid in tribal law or imposed by custom. They foregather under the spell of personal attraction, are kept together by sexual passion or personal attachment, and part at will. The fact that in due course a permanent liaison often develops out of a temporary one and ends in marriage is due to a complexity of causes, which we shall consider later; but even such a gradually strengthening liaison is not binding until marriage is contracted. *Bukumatula* relationships, as such, impose no legal tie.

Another important point is that the pair's community of interest is limited to the sexual relation only. The couple share a bed and nothing else. In the case of a permanent liaison about to lead to marriage, they share it regularly; but they never have meals together; there are no services to be mutually rendered, they have no obligation to help each other in any way, there is, in short, nothing which would constitute a common ménage. Only seldom can a girl be seen in front of a bachelors' house, and this as a rule means that she is very much at home there, that there has been a liaison of long standing and that the two are going to be married soon. This must be clearly realized, since such words as "liaison" and "concubinage," in the European use, usually imply a community of household goods and interests. In the French language, the expression *vivre en ménage*, describing typical concubinage, implies a shared domestic economy, and other phases of life in common, besides sex. In Kiriwina this phrase could not be correctly applied to a couple living together in the *bukumatula*.

In the Trobriands two people about to be married must never have a meal in common. Such an act would greatly shock the moral susceptibility of a native, as well as his sense of propriety. To take a girl out to dinner without having previously married her—a thing permitted in Europe—would be to disgrace her in the eyes of a Trobriander. We object to an unmarried girl sharing a man's bed—the Trobriander would object just as strongly to her sharing his meal. The boys never eat within, or in front of, the *bukumatula*, but always join their parents or other relatives at every meal.

The institution of the *bukumatula* is, therefore, characterized by: (1) individual appropriation, the partners of each couple belonging exclusively to one another; (2) strict decorum and absence of any orgiastic or lascivious display; (3) the lack of any legally binding element; (4) the exclusion of any other community of interest between a pair, save that of sexual cohabitation.

Having described the liaisons which lead directly to marriage, we end our survey of the various stages of sexual life previous to wedlock. But we have not exhausted the subject—we have simply traced the normal course of sexuality and that in its main outlines only. We have yet to consider those licensed orgies to which reference has already been made, to go more deeply into the technique and psychology of love-making, to examine certain sexual taboos, and to glance at erotic myth and folklore. But before we deal with these subjects, it will be best to carry our descriptive narrative to its logical conclusion—marriage.

NOTES

1. The processes by which respect for tribal taboo and tradition is instilled in the child are described throughout this book, especially in ch. xiii. Custom must not be personified nor is its authority absolute or autonomous, but it is derived from specific social and psychological mechanisms. Cf. my *Crime and Custom*, 1926.

2. That is, "classificatory mothers" mother, maternal aunts, etc. Cf. ch. xiii, secs. 5 and 6, *Crime and Custom*.

3. For a description of the real *kula*, cf. *Argonauts of the Western Pacific*.

4. Cf. ch. vii, sec. 2, *Crime and Custom*.

5. Cf. ch. xiii, 6, and ch. xiv, *Crime and Custom*.

6. Cf. ch. ix, *Crime and Custom*.

REFERENCES

Malinowski, Bronislaw. 1922. *Argonauts of the Western Pacific*. London: George Routledge and Sons.

———. 1926. *Crime and Custom in Savage Society*. New York: Harcourt, Brace & Co.

9
Dani Sexuality
A Low Energy System

Karl G. Heider
University of South Carolina

ABSTRACT

The Grand Valley Dani of Irian Jaya, Indonesia (West New Guinea) have an extremely low level of sexual interst and activity. Especially striking is their five year post-partum sexual abstinence, which is uniformly observed and is not a subject of great concern or stress. This low level of sexuality appears to be a purely cultural phenomenon, not caused by any biological factors. It is consistent with other Dani features such as scanty intellectual elaboration and general absence of peak activity in rituals and interpersonal interactions. This leads to a characterisation of Dani behaviour as a low-energy system. Some causal factors are suggested.

Source: Dani: A low energy system by Karl Heider, *Man* 11(2), 1976, pp. 188–201. © 1976 Royal Anthropological Association.

I

The Grand Valley Dani have a four-to-six year postpartum sexual abstinence.

The period of abstinence is invariably observed.

The norm of a long postpartum sexual abstinence is neither supported by powerful explanations nor enforced by strong sanctions.

Most people have no alternative sexual outlets.

No one shows signs of unhappiness or stress during their abstinence (cf. Heider 1970: 74).

Most people find these five statements difficult to accept. Even an anthropological audience, which is accustomed to hearing the most exotic facts about different cultures, feels somehow that these statements stretch their credulity. Anthropologists, together with most other social scientists, hold Freudian assumptions about a high pan-cultural level of sexuality. These assumptions make the description of the Dani behaviour extremely improbable. A fair example of conventional thinking is found in a recent (1972) cross-cultural study of the postpartum sexual abstinence by Saucier, who was trained in both psychoanalysis and anthropology. Saucier considers that a long postpartum sexual abstinence is one of more than one year, and says that such a long abstinence places a great burden on the women and those men who are monogamous. Therefore, he concludes,

> to explain such a taboo we must postulate serious reasons for its introduction and a strong social organization for its maintenance (1972:238).

This is a strong position, one which Saucier feels is self-evident, based on indisputable assumptions, and so not necessary to elaborate on. His paper was published as part of a symposium on population in *Current Anthropology*. The symposium papers were sent to fifty scholars for comment, and eight comments were published, but no one challenged Saucier. So it is fair to say that Saucier has accurately represented anthropological thinking on sexuality and the postpartum sexual abstinence. In fact, the Freudian ideas about sexuality have permeated our intellectual atmosphere. They are often passed off as an unchallenged part of general knowledge. Anthropologists, who are culturally relativistic in many matters, are quite comfortable with assumptions of an innate sexual drive, or quotient of sexual energy which must be expressed somehow, directly or indirectly. Certainly anthropologists have long been interested in the performance ethnography of sex, but even this is based on covert Freudian assumptions of pan-cultural or biologically-innate levels of sexuality.

But my problem, as the anthropologist reporting these statements about the Dani postpartum sexual abstinence, is compound. In the first place, since the statements are unlikely, or go against expectation, a special degree of proof is required: a proof far more rigorous than that demanded of claims which, however strange they may be, fall within an expectable range of variation. What compounds the problem is that these statements refer to sexual behaviour and to internal psychic states, both of which are extremely diffi-

cult to document. And, further, they are negative statements. They claim an absence of expected occurrences, and nothing is more difficult to demonstrate than that people *never* do or feel a certain thing.

Yet, if this is a true description of the Dani, as I think it is, the subject is worth pursuing. It has important implications for the understanding of a few thousand people in the mountains of Irian Jaya, Indonesia. And it has more general implications for our understanding of the range of human sexual behaviour. Particularly it speaks to the issue of whether the level of sexuality is culturally learned, or is more innate. As we shall see, the Dani data provide a strong argument for the importance of cultural conditioning.

It seems best to broaden the scope of the discussion from a consideration of just the Dani postpartum abstinence to a consideration of Dani sexuality in general. There are two reasons for this, one theoretical, and the other more practical. In theoretical terms, the Dani postpartum sexual abstinence is mainly significant as an indication, or manifestation, of a remarkably low level of sexuality. So, rather than just examine a single trait, we can look at a number of traits which contribute to a complex pattern or tendency, which runs throughout Dani life.

The more practical reason is simply one of strategy. It would be virtually impossible to prove the postpartum sexual abstinence case. It is hard to imagine any anthropologist being able to obtain the sort of data which could conclusively prove that a couple does not have sexual intercourse for a five year period. Certainly I do not have such data. But if the very suggestive data on the postpartum sexual abstinence are put together with other, related data on sexuality, a strong circumstantial case can be made.

The proposition to be shown in this article, then, is: The Grand Valley Dani have an extraordinarily low level of sexuality.

For convenience, I will use the term 'Dani'. In fact, I am discussing only Grand Valley Dani men. (For a general ethnographic description of the Dani, see Heider 1970.) There is reason to believe that other Dani—

especially the Western Dani—are quite different in this respect from the Grand Valley Dani. And my data come mainly from men. I observed Grand Valley Dani women, but rarely discussed anything with them.

By 'sexuality' I mean both sexual behaviour and sexual attitudes. I mean to say that Dani do not often behave sexually nor does sex have much interest for them.

Although the proposition will demonstrate 'an extraordinarily low level' of sexuality, it does not support a general proposition that the sexuality of cultures can be calibrated on a scale. Rather, I would suggest that most cultures have fairly similar levels of sexuality (expressed, of course, in a myriad of ways) and that it would serve no purpose to try to rank them in terms of precise levels of sexuality. But the Dani level of sexuality is so clearly beyond the general range that we will have no trouble in saying that it is 'extraordinarily low'.

This is an unorthodox essay, more than description and less than explanation. By drawing together the various behaviours which are relevant to sexuality, I shall present an interrelated contextualised behavioural and cognitive pattern, one which forms a major theme in Dani life: namely, the low level of psychical or emotional energy which the Dani invest in sexuality and, indeed, in many other sorts of behaviour. My own understanding of the Dani pattern began with noticing negatives, or absences: the lack of theatrical climax in ceremonies, the casual attitudes toward death, the unconcern about sex. But this article is not merely a list of what the Dani lack. It tries to build an understanding of what a low energy cultural system implies.

II

The place to begin a description of Dani sexuality is with the postpartum sexual abstinence. Let us take up, one by one, the statements at the beginning of the article.

1. The Grand Valley Dani have a four- to six-year postpartum sexual abstinence.

There is no question that the Dani claim this. In many circumstances many different

Dani men have told me that the parents of a child refrain from sexual intercourse with each other from the time when the child is born until the child is about five years old.

The time period is only approximate. The Dani do not reckon time units like months or years. They have little interest in quantification (in contrast to the neighbouring Kapauku, who are similar in many respects to the Dani, but are avid quantifiers—cf. Pospisil 1958). Indeed, the Dani have no words for four, five, or six, although they can be pushed into expressing these as a combination of 'one' or 'two'. When I asked the length of the postpartum sexual abstinence, my informant would express it in relation to the age of some child we both knew, or he would simply indicate it by holding his hand at the height of a child of the appropriate age. Since the Dani do not reckon people's ages in years even these data are only approximate. But it seems very safe to say that when the Dani describe the length of the postpartum sexual abstinence, they are referring to a period of between four and six years.

It is worth noting that a similarly long period of postpartum sexual abstinence was reported, independently, from the Jalé, who are a neighbouring Dani-speaking group (Koch 1968: 90). There seem to be no reports of any society which has a longer postpartum sexual abstinence as a general norm. The Cheyenne are often cited as having a ten-year postpartum sexual abstinence, but this was apparently a very unusual and virtuous undertaking, and not a general Cheyenne practice (cf. Grinnell 1924: 149).

2. The period of the postpartum sexual abstinence is invariably observed.

This is a broad claim, but I have no reason to doubt it. There are two sets of evidence in favour of it. First, there is the fact that the Dani say that the postpartum sexual abstinence is invariably observed. Although I was often told quite scurrilous things about people, no one ever told me that someone else had prematurely broken their abstinence. I assume that if such an explicit norm were casually violated, I would have learned about it casually. And I did not. On the other hand, if the violation of the norm were of great consequence, I would have heard about it as a serious accusation. And I did not. It is worth adding that Dani life is generally quite public. Neither the landscape nor the architecture provides much privacy, so it would be extremely difficult to do anything in secret.

The second kind of evidence is biological. No full siblings are closer in age than about five years. This conclusion is based on those siblings whom I knew or saw, and, since the Dani do not reckon ages in years, on my estimate of their age differences. But the genealogical data were quite good, and the estimates of age were fairly good, at least for those under age 25 or so.

Since the norm only prohibits sexual intercourse between the parents of a child, and is not a general prohibition on intercourse for them as individuals, there were several men and one woman who were parents of half-siblings only a couple of years apart in age.

Of course, the pattern of siblings five or more years apart in age is one which could be produced by other means than a long postpartum sexual abstinence. Contraception, coitus interruptus, abortion, or infanticide could be used singly or in combination to produce such a pattern. But all my data suggest that none of these is actually practised and that the pattern of widely-spaced siblings is indeed due to the observance of the postpartum sexual abstinence.

3. The norm of a long postpartum sexual abstinence is neither supported by powerful explanation nor enforced by strong sanctions.

I was never able to learn a reason for the long postpartum sexual abstinence. When I pushed the line of questioning, people would say that violations of the abstinence would cause trouble with the ghosts, who might hurt or even kill the adults involved, and might cripple a child conceived during a violation of the abstinence. But it is important to realise that this ghostly sanction is neither very salient nor very powerful. Elsewhere I have described at some length the casual attitude which the Dani have toward their ghosts (1970: 37 sqq). Briefly, the Dani explain much of their ritual, including warfare, in terms of the need to pla-

cate the ghosts of their own dead. But in fact they were extremely casual in discussing the ghosts, and in performing the supposedly-necessary placatory behaviour. So while it is literally correct to say that this postpartum sexual abstinence has a supernatural sanction, it must be understood as a fairly casual, pro forma sanction.

Of course, it would be possible to enforce a five-year postpartum sexual abstinence in any society, given a powerful enough external control system. I found no evidence of such a system in Dani society. I think that it is fair to say that in most societies the control system would have to be very powerful and obvious. So obvious, in fact, that no anthropologist could miss it—certainly not after staying for some 30 months, as I did amongst the Dani.

4. Most people have no alternative sexual outlets.

An obvious 'solution' to the deprivation of a long postpartum sexual abstinence would be polygyny. But although the Dani practise polygyny, it is not very effective in this way. None of the women and a minority of the men have more than one spouse. The figures for the 148 males in the neighbourhood which I studied are:

Dugum neighbourhood males: marital status.

Status		N
Not yet married		53
Never married (permanent bachelors)		3
One wife		49
More than one wife		43
2 wives	23	
3 wives	14	
4 wives	5	
9 wives	1	
Total		148

(from Heider 1970: 72, table 2.2)

But even these figures are misleading, since not all the 47 per cent of married men (29 per cent. of all males) with multiple wives would actually have free access to another wife throughout the five years of their postpartum sexual abstinence with one wife. Two wives may have borne children within a few years of each other; and often co-wives do not get along well together, and live in different compounds. During the first year or so of a child's life, a man is likely to stay in the compound with the infant, and not with the wife to whom he has sexual access.

Other possible sexual outlets for a couple would be coitus interruptus with each other, extramarital sexual intercourse, masturbation, homosexuality, or bestiality. To the best of my knowledge, none of these is practised by any Dani, whether or not subject to a postpartum sexual abstinence.

5. No one shows any signs of unhappiness or stress during the period of abstinence.

The strongest evidence for a lack of concern, or anxiety, during the long post-partum sexual abstinence is my own ethnographic authority, based on more than two years' work with the Dani, in the course of which I explicitly probed into these matters. The information about the postpartum sexual abstinence was always given me in a quite matter-of-fact manner, and no man even hinted that he or anyone else might be in the least unhappy or stressed by such a long deprivation.

In order to investigate this point more systematically, I designed an elicitation experiment, utilising a Facial Expression Reaction Test. The experiment attempted to find some difference in sexual anxiety between men who were deep into their postpartum sexual abstinence and men who had sexual access to one or more wives. I have described the experiment in some detail elsewhere (Heider ms.). Although it has some general methodological interest, the results were not very conclusive. Certainly it did not turn up any overwhelming evidence for anxiety caused by celibacy.

III

Other data

The birth rate.   There are no hard data for frequency of sexual intercourse among the Dani other than that absolute minimal figure represented by the birth rate. Even though the Dani have low interest in sex, they do perform it frequently enough to maintain the population. However, the apparent birth rate is rather low. The following table shows the number of children per married woman.

Number of children per woman in the Dugum neighbourhood.

Married women having borne:	N
No children	13 (all young married women who have not yet begun to have children)
1 child	86
2 children	57
3 children	13 (includes two women with twins)
4 children	1 (woman with two children by each of two husbands)

(Heider 1970: 73, table 2.4)

These data come from genealogical data supplied in most cases by someone other than the woman involved, and so they represent remembered children—not total births, and certainly not total conceptions. Nevertheless, they do indicate the relatively low birth rate of the Dani. And, in turn, they indicate the low frequency of sexual intercourse for the Dani, since there is no good evidence of anything other than abstinence to account for the low birth rate. Dani men do talk about abortion. They are certainly aware of the possibility and they say that it is common, but I was never able to get convincing evidence that it is actually practised. Some Dani women have told me of a plant which they claim is a contraceptive, but I have no convincing data on that either. I cannot completely rule out the possibility that the Dani use abortion or contraception rather than abstinence to keep down the birth rate, but it seems reasonable that if they were major factors I would have been able to learn more about them. Infanticide seems completely out of the question; no Dani ever hinted that it was ever practised, and I have no data to suggest that inadvertent infanticide occurred.

Extramarital sexual intercourse

There seems to be remarkably little extra-marital or premarital sexual activity. This con-clusion is based on lack of evidence but it is a significant lack. If such affairs occurred, I should have learned about them through either casual gossip or serious accusation, and I did not. In the two years when I lived in the Dugum neighbourhood, I came to know of only one adulterous affair, and it precipitated a serious fight within the neighbourhood.

Even courting does not involve sexual inter-course. In fact, the Dani say that a couple do not begin to have sexual intercourse until a specific ceremony is held, two years after the major wedding exchange ceremony and thus two years after the couple has established a common residence (cf. Heider 1972: 182).

The wedding ceremonies themselves are very much group affairs. Weddings take place only at the major Pig Feast, held every four to six years, and never during the intervals. Although the marriage matches themselves are generally arranged by the two principals, marital sex is very much subject to the slow pace of the ceremonial cycle. This is further strong evidence for the unimportance of sex in Dani life.

Homosexuality

Another obvious possible locus for expression of sexuality would be homosexuality. But apparently the Dani do not practise it. Al-though most married men in a compound sleep most nights in the sleeping loft of the one men's house, this seems to invovle no erotic homosexual behaviour.

Child-rearing. Infant eroticism is another obvi-ous locus for sexuality, but the Dani infants receive remarkably little erotic input. This had been my general impression during my earlier research in 1961–1963. In 1970, Eleanor Rosch and I carried out systematic one-day (6 to 10 hours) observations on ten mother-preverbal infant pairs in the Grand Valley, and for com-parative purposes we replicated those obser-vations with another ten closely matched mother-infant pairs in the Western Dani region around Karubaga (the site of Denise O'Brien's research in 1961–1963). The obser-vations were recorded on audio- and video-tape. Although we have not yet analysed the data, it became obvious to us during the obser-vations that although we were seeing among the Western Dani an expectable amount of mothers erotically manipulating their infants, there was virtually none of this among the Grand Valley Dani.

Initiation. Boys' initiation ceremonies often emphasise the sexual aspect of manhood, but the comparable Dani ceremony (which may not even be properly called 'initiation') emphasises moiety membership and not any masculine coming of age. In fact, only half the boys ever go through the ceremony, and in the one which I observed in 1970, the ages of the initiates ranged from about four to eighteen (cf. Heider 1970). There is one event with erotic symbolism, where the initi-ates throw reed spears into a tree as an explicit metaphor of the sexual intercourse they will later engage in. This is a rare and fleeting evidence of sexuality in Dani life.

The penis gourd. The penis gourd would seem to be as obvious a focus for sexuality as the postpartum sexual abstinence. Dani males from about the age of six wear a long upright penis gourd at virtually all times except when they are urinating or having sex-ual intercourse. Penis gourds, or other simi-lar phallocrypts which exaggerate the size and erection of the penis, have been used in many regions of the world, including late medieval and early Renaissance Europe. But the Dani penis gourd does not have any explicit sex-ual connotations for the Dani (this is not so true for non-Dani) nor do the different sizes and shapes of the penis gourd have apparent sexual connotations (cf. Heider 1969: 386–8; 1970: 244–7).

Teenagers' play. One of the very few areas of Dani life where there is any significant level of sexuality is in the songs, drawings, and string figures done by teenage boys and girls.

The songs, called *silon*, have a standard tune with regular form. Some are merely about natural phenomena, but others are quite explicitly sexual. They are sung by one or more boys, accompanied by laughter and nudging, in full recognition of their improper humour (cf. Heider 1970: 305–9).

The same teenage boys are responsible for crude charcoal drawings on rock overhangs throughout the neighbourhood. One common design, a short-stemmed down-pointing arrow, is called 'vulva'. The same symbol is scratched in sand or, after the introduction of machetes, chopped in tree bark (cf. Heider 1970: 181–4).

Also, one of the standard string figures performed by either a boy or a girl is called 'copulation' and involves moving loops together to represent a man and a woman copulating (Heider 1970: 205).

These three areas of sexual reference are extremely mild, and are remarkable only because they represent the most explicit sexuality—indeed, practically the only explicit sexuality—in Dani culture.

IV

Associated cultural phenomena

There are a number of other factors which seem relevant to this discussion of Dani sexuality, and which support the general picture of the Dani drawn so far.

On the whole, Dani interpersonal interaction is marked by low affect. The Dani are congenial and even-tempered, with few emotional peaks. Anger is rarely expressed, and confrontations are simply avoided through early withdrawal. There are rarely brawls, fights, or even shouting matches in a compound. An experiment designed to elicit facial expressions of affects confirmed this, showing that the Dani tended to express disgust expressions when given situations that might have been expected to arouse anger (cf. Heider ms.).

Low intellectuality. One of the essential features of Freudian thought is that each person has a certain innate fixed amount of sexual energy which must be expressed in some fashion (cf. the excellent discussion in Gagnon and Simon 1973: 11 sqq). Freud himself, in *Civilization and its discontents*, wrote

> Since a man does not have unlimited quantities of psychical energy at his disposal, he has to accomplish his tasks by making an expedient distribution of his libido. What he employs for cultural aims he to a great extent withdraws from women and sexual life (Freud 1930; English translation 1961: 103–4).

If this is true, then one might expect that the Dani, who do not use their energy in sexual directions, would have made notable achievements in intellectual or aesthetic directions. In fact, there is no sign of such achievements.

In most areas the Dani show very little intellectual elaboration (cf. Heider 1970). The Dani counting system, already described above, is a good example of this. The Dani have numbers 'one', 'two', (a rarely used) 'three', if necessary a 'two-two', and 'many'. Certainly Dani men are not stupid (whatever that might mean). But they do not live in an intellectualised, abstract world.

Likewise, the Dani have very little that one could call art (I have discussed Dani art and the difficult problem of defining art in the Dani case in 1970: 180–93). This is especially true if one excludes ornamenting the body with feathers and grease, and the fine craftsmanship of a five-metre spear. The Dani are a direct, practical, pragmatic people.

Conservatism. It seems logical to mention here the extraordinary resistance of the Grand Valley Dani to change. Elsewhere I have attempted to explain this conservatism as the result of deep satisfaction with their traditional culture (Heider 1975). Whatever the causes, there is no question that the Dani show little adventurous innovation, despite a good deal of microflexibility. That is, the norms of behaviour allow considerable variation of behaviour, but the norms themselves do not change.

Finally I must emphasise that the Dani are a healthy, vigorous, strong people. Certainly through the early 1960's there was no malaria or other apparent debilitating endemic disease. As well as I could judge by the people's appearance and activity level, their diet was quite adequate. The various Dutch and Indonesian doctors who worked in the Grand Valley had found no serious diseases. It seems very unlikely that some undiscovered physical factor could be responsible for the Dani pattern which I have described.

V

Sexuality and relativism

The Dani data speak directly to a fundamental controversy about the nature of human sexuality, a controversy which is succinctly described in Gagnon and Simon (1973): namely, do all humans have an innate high level of sexual energy which must be expressed directly or indirectly (the Freudian view); or is the level of sexual energy determined by the cultural and social circumstances (the relativistic position)? The low level of Dani sexuality gives clear support to the relativistic position. Even the loophole of rechannelled, indirect expression of sexual energy, postulated by Freudian theorists, is of no avail. The Dani are a clear case of a culture with low sexuality. It is not necessary to explain why this occurs, although causal explanations are desirable in the long run. For now it is sufficient to have established the ethnographic facts.

The apparent uniqueness of the Dani case makes it especially important. Although Gagnon and Simon have argued strongly for the relativistic position, their data are primarily from groups within U.S. society—e.g., prison populations—which demonstrate (to use the subtitle of their book) 'the social sources of human sexuality' (1973). But even they, in what is admittedly only a very cursory glance at cross-cultural data, do not even postulate an entire society with low sexuality (cf. 1973: 306–7). They use the term 'sexuality' in much the same way as I do, to refer to both activity and affect. They refer to cultures with high affect, or concern about sex, but little

activity (e.g. the Irish community studied by Messenger [1971]); and, at the opposite extreme, cultures with high sexual activity levels but low affect, or concern about sex (e.g., the Polynesian community studies by Marshall [1971]). This is an ironic situation indeed. These sociological champions of the relativistic position have challenged the Freudian assumptions when applied to individuals and groups. Yet, when they think of entire societies they implicitly (and intuitively?) utilise Freudian assumptions about pan-cultural levels of activity. It would be hard to find better testimony to the powers of these assumptions. This is also a strong testimony to the importance of the Dani data which so directly contradict the pan-cultural validity of these assumptions.

VI

Dani sexuality as a low-energy system

The goal of this article has been to bring together many diverse features of Dani culture and present them as manifestations of a single basic pattern. The features on which we have been focusing are the postpartum sexual abstinence and other aspects of sexual expression. At the beginning it seemed reasonable to speak of the Dani's low level of sexuality. As a first-level descriptive label for the Dani sexuality pattern, this is acceptable, but we can now move a step further.

The low level of sexuality seems to be consistent with the low level of intellectual elaboration, and the low level of affect. All these are part of a larger pattern of Dani behaviour which can be thought of as a set of low energy systems.

To term Dani sexuality a low energy system is merely to say that the Dani put little energy into sexual activities and into thinking about sexual activities. Much of Dani behaviour and thought is characterised by low energy expenditure. This concept of a low energy culture is a very imprecise one, difficult to define, and impossible to calibrate. But it is one way of looking at a great deal of Dani behaviour, and making sense of it.

The Dani do not invest much energy in their activities. They have little sustained, systematic, elaborated achievement. Certainly they live comfortably, and even well. No Dani ever goes hungry. They procreate, feed and shelter themselves, have ceremonies—and they do all these things quite adequately. They are not a deprived, broken down, or unhealthy society. But in none of these realms do the Dani act intensively, elaborately, or with great dramatic peaks of intellectual or emotional achievement.

This is not simply physical energy. If so, it would be fairly easy to describe and measure. And, to anticipate a bit, it would probably be fairly easy to explain low physical activity in purely physical terms. This energy is as much psychic or emotional as it is purely physical. There are situations in which Dani act strenuously and energetically. A good example of this is Dani behaviour in battle, which has been well-documented in Robert Gardner's film, *Dead birds* (1963). A battle lasts for part of a day, and exertion is very sporadic. Men spend most of the time relaxing behind the lines, talking, watching, and only occasionally moving forward to engage the enemy for an hour or so, before falling back to the rear again. But most significant in this context is the marked absence of aggression, hatred for the enemy, or even much at all in the way of sustained excitement (cf. Heider 1970: 127–8). Dani men reach an even more intense peak in the secular phase of war, a concentrated two or three days of ambushes and battles. However, this occurs only every decade or so. In fact, the overwhelming majority of the time which Dani spend in warfare and warfare associated activity is devoted to casual, low-energy activity.

VII

Energy and steady states

In a famous exploratory essay (1949), Gregory Bateson had grappled with a somewhat analogous problem in tring to understand the Balinese value system. In particular, he wrote about a set of attitudes and activities which were characterised by non-climaxing, balanced, plateaux of behaviour. Bateson used the term 'steady state' to describe the Balinese system. Bateson had been concerned with what he called 'schismogenic sequences'—competitive opposition which culminates in climax, followed by a lowered state. This had been one subject of *Naven*, his book on the New Guinea Iatmül. But he did not find the same pattern among the Balinese. This was surprising, and contrary to the expectations which he held, based on 'so many theories of social opposition and Marxian determinism' (1949: 39) and, in particular, the earlier formulations of game theory.

In the Dani case, it is a high level of sexuality, which was predicted by Freudian and Freudian-derived theories, which was found to be lacking.

The analogy goes a step further, for in some respects the Balinese culture resembles Dani culture. Particularly, Bateson's metaphor of plateau, or steady state lacking cumulative climaxing, seems very appropriate for the Dani. However, the differences are even more striking than the similarity. In Bateson's work there is the sense that this Balinese plateau is one of high intensity. I understand the Dani plateau to be one of very low intensity. The Balinese maintain a steady state at a high energy level, the Dani a steady state at a low energy level. To use a culturally-apt metaphor, the difference is between a person balancing on a high wire and a person sitting on the ground. Both may appear nearly motionless, but the difference in energy level is considerable.

VIII

Causality

This all raises the question of causality. Of course, I am assuming that there is something to be explained: that we have established that Dani sexuality is a low-energy system—and indeed, that much of Dani life can be called a low-energy system; and I am assuming that the Dani are quite exceptional in this respect, and are not merely towards the low end of some normal curve of cultural energy.

The question can be phrased, then, either as 'Why are the Dani the way they are?' or 'Why are the Dani so different from other cultures?' The answers might be biological, or they might be cultural. However, it seems to me thoroughly unlikely that the Dani situation can be accounted for by some unique genetic, nutritional, or medical circumstances. My own predilection as an anthropologist is to look for a cultural factor as cause. I would think somewhat along the lines which Bateson took when he suggested that an explanation for the Balinese 'steady state' could be seen as the outcome of Balinese childhood experiences which resulted in 'some sort of modification, deconditioning, or inhibition' of a basic tendency of human beings to 'involve themselves in sequences of cumulative interactions' (1949: 42). In the Dani case, we can assume that something has happened to impede 'a basic tendency' of human beings to develop a high level of sexual energy which may be expressed in a variety of ways.

But what factors could account for the Dani situation? Better yet: what sorts of factors should we look for? It would be easy to fit some biological factors into our explanatory scheme: a unique gene pool, a debilitating disease, or a major nutritional deficiency could easily account for low energy level. But, alas for easy explanation, there are no apparent biological candidates. (We must be somewhat tentative here, for a thoroughgoing physiological investigation of the Dani could possibly turn up something which has so far escaped notice.)

But there are two factors, one environmental and the other more cultural, which might have some relevant causal status on the grounds that they involve a low input of stress into Dani life.

The first factor is the environment of the Grand Valley itself. It is remarkably benign. Flora, fauna, climate, and topography combine to create optimal comfort and minimal stimulation for human life (cf. Heider 1970: 212 sqq). All is mild, and there are no excesses: no dangerous plants or animals, moderate rainfall (around 78.5 inches per year) with no excessive floods or drought;

mild temperature, with extremes of 29.5°C (85°F) and 6°C (42°F). Perhaps even more important, the Dani recognise no regular yearly rhythm of hot and cold or wet and dry. Indeed, even non-Dani who live in Grand Valley but come from Europe and North America, and are looking for seasonal cycles, have the greatest difficulty in satisfying their need for climatic order. Now, if it is true that the Dani experience no seasons, this may have powerful cognitive implications. For most cultures, the seasonal cycle forces a long-term organisation of subsistence activities and thereby promotes the development of an associated ceremonial cycle and a set of time units with which to handle it all. One can imagine that out of the cognitive demands of this periodicity grow intellectual opportunities for an even wider range of cognitive and intellectual elaborations. But the Dani lack the demands and therefore, perhaps, the opportunities. Instead, they plant and harvest the year round, and their ceremonies are either triggered by the accidents of birth or death, or, like the great Pig Feast, are held irregularly every few years. And the Dani do not use temporal units like day, month, or year to order their life. Obviously, the Dani do act with reference to the future, as when they plant sweet potato cuttings, or taboo the killing of pigs in order to build up the herds in anticipation of a ceremony a few months in the future. But they do not act in terms of a timetable of future demands as people must do to a certain extent if their environment has seasons.

Elsewhere I have suggested that the Dani lack 'the cognitive pacing that a strong yearly seasonal round might provide' (1970: 296). I had also argued that the absence of seasons is a contributory factor to the low level of sexuality. But now I think that both propositions, however ingenious they might seem, are vastly overstated. They are based on the assumption that regular seasonal changes of climate (like those found in the temperate zone) make certain cognitive demands on a people, and are themselves a sort of energising force. For the purposes of this present discussion of Dani sexuality, there are two important considerations: first, although the

Dani themselves do not recognise seasons, and have no activities geared to a regular seasonal cycle, a Western scientist looking at the rainfall charts for the Grand Valley can talk of 'a short season of heavy rain and cloud' (Brookfield 1964: 36). Both Peter (1965: 15) and I (1970: 212) have emphasised the great variability in the occurrence of the rainy period, and the rainfall itself does vary in the Grand Valley from about 60 mm to about 350 mm a month (cf. Heider 1970: 213 Diagram 7.1). So there is variation in rainfall, even though its regularity is minimal and goes unnoticed by the Dani. (This is not the place to go into the question of how much variation it takes to invalidate a concept of regularity like 'seasons' [but cf. Brookfield & Brown 1963: 20–4].)

And second, although the Dani pattern of sexuality is unique, their climate is not. It is still fair to say that the climate of the Grand Valley is remarkably equable. But the attempt to link this causally with Dani sexuality is seriously compromised as soon as one looks at data from elsewhere in the New Guinea Highlands. Pospisil described an almost identical climate for the temperamentally very different Kapauku to the West (1963: 81), as did Glasse for the Huli to the East (1968: 19). At best we are left with a weak causal statement: the relatively benign natural environment of the Grand Valley is consistent with (and perhaps even contributory to) the low level of Dani sexuality.

The social environment of the Grand Valley Dani, like their natural environment, is fairly blank and uniform. Although the peoples of the New Guinea Highlands are known for their cultural (or at least linguistic) diversity, in fact the Grand Valley Dani are quite effectively isolated from other peoples by high uninhabited mountain ranges. Until regular European contact began in 1954, few Grand Valley Dani had experienced—or even seen—people with cultures and languages different from their own. Anthropologists and historians have long thought that the interaction between different cultures was an important stimulation for the evolution of culture. It is also reasonable to assume the converse: that extreme cultural isolation would have some effects. And certainly the Grand Valley Dani receive comparatively little stress or stimulation from either natural or cultural environment.

The second factor which seems suggestive here is the extremely low stress which Dani infants receive. For the first year or so, a Grand Valley Dani infant spends much of its time in the warm, shaded, softly-padded carrying net against its mother's back. This became especially apparent only when Eleanor Rosch and I carried out systematic observations of mother-infant pairs among both Grand Valley Dani and the Western Dani. The Western Dani infant was often taken out of the carrying net and held or carried in the open, exposed to massive stimulation even when this hampered the mother's work. Thus, during the several hours a day which the mothers spend working in their gardens, the Western Dani infants are squirming, clinging, seeing, and hearing, while the Grand Valley Dani are snugly snoozing.

Toilet training—and, indeed all training—is remarkably gentle and non-coercive for the Grand Valley Dani child. In short, Dani childhood is a period of little stress or stimulation.

Certainly I can make no conclusive causal claim for either environmental factors or child-rearing practices. Both are further evidence of low level stress, and so they are at least significant as further aspects of the entire complex of low energy, whatever their causal status. In any case, for the moment at least it is not possible to demonstrate that the level of sexuality varies significantly with climate and child care, even within the New Guinea Highlands.

Conclusions

I began this essay by advancing a problematic ethnographic fact about a small group of Dani in the central highlands of Irian Jaya. In attempting to account for this fact, I used the strategy of holistic accumulation. More and more ethnographic facts were brought together, and were shown to constitute ever more inclusive patterns of behaviour. The extremely long postpartum sexual abstinence was shown to be part of a generally low level of sexuality; the low level of sexuality is consistent with generally low energy levels in much of Dani life; and the low energy levels are found in demands or inputs, as well as performance, or output for Dani individually and as a group, from infancy onwards. There are suggestive causal threads, but no single satisfactory conclusive causal chain emerges. The concept of energy levels is an effective one for understanding Dani behaviour. It remains to be seen whether it will have a comparative, cross-cultural use. Certainly the most important finding of general interest is that the Dani do have a low level of sexuality. This constitutes solid support for a relativistic view of sexuality.

NOTE

This article is based on research carried out among the Grand Valley Dani of Irian Jaya, Indonesia (West New Guinea), during two and a half years between 1961 and 1970. The research was supported by grants from the Foundations' Fund for Research in Psychiatry, the Cross-Cultural Study of Ethnocentrism Project, and others. So many people have helped me to think about these problems during the last fifteen years that it would be hopeless to try to name them all, but at least I would like to acknowledge Eleanor Rosch, my collaborator in research among the Dani in 1968 and 1970. While preparing the final version of this article I was a Fellow at the Center for Advanced Study in the Behavioral Sciences.

REFERENCES

Bateson, Gregory. 1936. *Naven.* Cambridge: Univ. Press.

————. 1949. Bali: the value system of a steady state. In *Social structure: studies presented to A. R. Radcliffe-Brown* (ed.) Meyer Fortes. Oxford: Clarendon Press.

Brookfield, H. C. 1964. The ecology of highland settlement: some suggestions. *Am. Anthrop.* **66**, 20–38.

————. & P. Brown. 1963. *Struggle for land: agricultural and group territories among the Chimbu of the New Guinea Highlands.* Mclbourne: Oxford Univ. Press.

Freud, Sigmund. 1961. Civilization and its discontents. In *The Standard Edition of the complete psychological works of Sigmund Freud* (ed.) J. Strachey, vol. **21**. London: Hogarth.

Gagnon, John H., and William Simon. 1973. *Sexual conduct: the social sources of human sexuality.* Chicago: Aldine.

Gardner, Robert. 1963. *Dead birds* [film]. Film Study Center, Harvard University. New York: McGraw-Hill/Contemporary Films (distributors).

Glasse, Robert M. 1968. *Huli of Papua: a cognatic descent system* (Cah. Homme N.S. **8**). Paris: Mouton.

Grinnell, George Bird. 1924. *The Cheyenne Indians: their history and ways of life,* vol. **I**. New Haven: Yale Univ. Press.

Heider, Karl G. 1969. Attributes and categories in the study of material culture: New Guinea Dani attire. *Man* (N.S.) **4**, 379–91.

————. 1970. *The Dugum Dani: a Papuan culture in the highlands of west New Guinea.* Chicago: Aldine.

————. 1972. The Grand Valley Dani pig feast: a ritual of passage and intensification. *Oceania* **42**, 169–87.

————. 1975. Societal intensification and cultural stress as determining factors in the innovation and conservatism of two Dani groups. *Oceania* **46**, 53–67.

————. ms. Nonverbal studies of Dani anger and sexual expression: experimental method in videotape ethnography. Paper presented to the American Anthropological Association meetings, Nov. 1973, New Orleans.

Koch, Klaus-Friedrich. 1968. Marriage in Jalémo. *Oceania* **39**, 85–109.

Marshall, Donald S. 1971. Sexual behavior on Magaia. In *Human sexual behavior* (eds.) Donald S. Marshall & Robert C. Suggs. New York: Basic Books.

Messenger, John C. 1971. Sex and repression in an Irish folk community. In *Human sexual behavior* (eds) Donald S. Marshall & Robert C. Suggs. New York: Basic Books.

Peter, H. L. 1965. *Enkele hoofdstuukken uit het sociaal-religieuze leven van een Dani-groep.* Venlo: Dagblad voor Noord-Limburg.

Pospisil, Leopold 1958. *Kapauku Papuans and their law* (Yale Univ. Publ. Anthrop. **54**). New Haven: Yale Univ. Press.

————. 1963. *Kapauku Papuan economy* (Yale Univ. Publ. Anthrop. **67**). New Haven: Yale Univ. Press.

Saucier, Jean-François. 1972. Correlates of the long postpartum taboo: a cross-cultural study. *Curr. Anthrop.* **13**, 238–49.

Postscript
Revisiting *Dani Sexuality* (December 2001)

Karl G. Heider
University of South Carolina

When I first went to the Dani, in what was then called Netherlands New Guinea, in 1961, I had not intended to study sexuality. I had been trained mainly as an archaeologist, with just enough cultural anthropology to do a holistic ethnography of Dani material culture. When, after more than two years of fieldwork with the Dani, I began to write my dissertation, I had enough information to make a broad description of Dani culture, contextualizing the material objects. I sometimes think of this work as one of the last old fashioned pre-modern ethnographies. I did discuss the Dani postpartum sexual abstinence very briefly in my (1965) dissertation, but did not make much of it. However, as I mentioned aspects of Dani life to my family and friends in the mid-1960s, they expressed mild interest in the warfare, the penis gourds, and the complex nouns, but were amazed at my claims for the five year postpartum sexual abstinence. So, having to think about it, and explain it, I focused my next research on it.

Together with Eleanor Rosch, an experimental cognitive psychologist, I returned to the Dani for a few weeks in 1968 and for seven months in 1970. Meanwhile, as I rewrote my dissertation for publication I expanded the section on the postpartum sexual abstinence to nearly two pages (1970:74–75) and then, in 1976, published this paper.

The reception of the paper was mixed. To my surprise, American anthropologists have on the whole ignored it (I know of only one anthropology textbook [other than my own] that takes it seriously) (Schultz and Lavenda 2001:494). A more interesting reaction is that of Thomas Gregor, who writes, in a footnote, that "the jury is still out on a final verdict of sex neutrality for the Dani" and seems to endorse a suggestion by Pontius (1977) "that their low levels of sexuality may have a simple biological cause" (1985:5). In my own response to Pontius (1977), I had reaffirmed my position that we have to seek a cultural basis for such a complex pattern.

Psychologists and psychiatrists, on the other hand, have been more receptive to it. Our research proposal for the 1970 research was rejected by the anthropology panel of the National Science Foundation but was funded by the Foundations' Fund for Research in Psychiatry. The popular reaction, however, was overwhelming. After the article appeared in *Man*, the Journal of the Royal Anthropological Society, in the Summer of 1976, the wire services picked it up and friends sent me clippings from many newspapers around the world. News magazines like *Time* ran stories on it, and I was flown to New York for an interview on the television news program, Good Morning America (giving me $7\frac{1}{2}$ of my 15 minutes of fame). To my real surprise, though, the most accurate account appeared in *Playboy* (which I read in those days for its scientific reporting).

But the long Dani postpartum sexual abstinence remains a significant instance of the bio-cultural model, the cultural shaping of a biological feature basic to *Homo sapiens*. Sexual intercourse between male and female is common to all human groups, but there is a wide latitude in how different cultures perform it and construe it.

So why the reluctance of anthropologists to consider this claim? No one has put forth any contrary evidence or justification. I suspect that these attitudes are due to an unexamined and naïve Freudianism held by most Westerners, particularly those who would not call themselves Freudians.

Today I have no new data to add beyond what I describe in the article. I no longer describe the Dani pattern as "a low energy system," but use the phrase "low intensity" (e.g., Heider 2001:308). "Low energy" has too many possibly misleading meanings. But the pattern itself is still valid, at least for those Dani I studied as they were in the 1960s. But now it seems useful to ask what would be the next steps in this research (assuming that one could obtain a research visa from the Indonesian government). Certainly, we would need Dani women's understandings. More in depth interviewing of both men and women, especially those old enough to have been married and subject to the postpartum sexual abstinence in the 1960s would be important. Meanwhile, we are left with a problematic pattern of culture, perhaps limited to one area of the Grand Valley Dani (and Koch's Jale, the Eastern Dani), which has triggered an even more problematical response from the anthropological community.

BIBLIOGRAPHY

Gregor, Thomas. 1985. *Anxious Pleasures: The Sexual Lives of an Amazon People.* Chicago: The University of Chicago Press.

Heider, Karl G. 1976. Dani sexuality: A low energy system. *Man* 11:188–201.

———. 1977. Dani sexuality: A reply to Pontius. *Man* 12.1:167–8.

———. 2001. *Seeing Anthropology: Cultural Anthropology Through Film.* 2nd ed. Boston: Allyn & Bacon.

Pontius, A. 1977. Dani sexuality. *Man* 12.1: 166–167.

Schultz, Emily A. and Robert H. Lavenda. 2001. *Anthropology: A Perspective on the Human Condition.* 3rd ed. Mountain View, California: Mayfield Press.

◈ 10
Sexual Inversion among the Azande

E. E. Evans-Pritchard
Oxford University

Male and female homosexual relationship seems to have been common among the Azande in past times. Between males it was approved of in the bachelor military companies. Between females it is said to have been a frequent, though highly disapproved of, practice in polygamous homes. [Sudan (southern); Azande; sexual inversion] Accepted for publication 16 January 1970.

It is beyond question that male homosexuality, or rather a sexual relationship between young warriors and boys, was common in pre-European days among the Azande, and as Czekanowski (1924:56), citing Junker (1892: 3–4), has pointed out, there is no reason to suppose that it was introduced by Arabs as some have thought. All Azande I have known well enough to discuss this matter have asserted also that female homosexuality (lesbianism) was practiced in polygamous homes in the past and still (1930) is sometimes. This

paper brings together information about both practices and presents translations of a few texts on the subject taken down from Azande of the Sudan forty years ago.

Before European rule was imposed on the Azande there was a good deal of fighting between kingdoms (Evans-Pritchard 1957b, 1957c). Part of the adult male population of each kingdom was organized in military companies of *abakumba* 'married men' and *aparanga* 'bachelors'; the same companies, besides their military functions, served at courts in various capacities and were called on for labor in the royal and princely cultivations (Evans-Pritchard 1957a). In this account we do not have to refer again to the companies of married men. It was the custom for members of bachelor companies, some of whom would always be living in barracks at court, to take boy-wives. This was undoubtedly brought about by the scarcity of marriageable women in the days when the nobility and also the richer commoners kept large harems and were able to do so because bridewealth was hard to come by and they were able to acquire it more easily than poorer men. Most young

Source: Sexual inversion among the Azande, by E. E. Evans-Pritchard. In *American Anthropologist*, 1970, 72: 1428–1434. © 1970 American Anthropological Association.

men consequently married late—well into their twenties and thirties—and, because girls were engaged (in a legal sense married) very young, often at birth, the only way youths could obtain satisfaction from a woman was in adultery. But that was a very dangerous solution to a young man's problem, for the fine his father would have to pay was heavy—twenty spears and a woman, which meant in effect the payment of two women to the husband; it sometimes happened that the husband was so enraged that he refused compensation and chose instead to mutilate the offender, cutting off his ears, upper lip, genitals, and hands. So, the risk being too great, it was the custom for cautious bachelors in the military companies who were living at court, if they were not content to masturbate—a practice to which no shame is attached, though a young man would not do it in public—to marry boys and satisfy their sexual needs with them. A youth of position in his company might have more than one boy (*kumba gude*). To these boys their warrior mates were *badiya ngbanga* 'court lovers.'

That it was on account of the difficulties of getting satisfaction in heterosexual relationships that boy marriage was a recognized temporary union is, I believe, shown by the fact that boy marriage has in post-European times entirely disappeared. It is true that the military companies disappeared also; but Azande, I think rightly, attribute the giving up of the custom to its having become easier for youths to marry and, in the general breakdown of morals and of the suppression of customary punishments, to indulge in adultery and fornication. Boy marriage was owing, Azande say, to *zanga ade* 'lack of women.' As one man put it, "What man would prefer a boy to a woman? A man would be a fool to do so. The love of boys arose from lack of women." So the Azande in my day spoke of it as *kuru pai* 'old custom,' though I have never heard anyone speak of sleeping with a boy with distaste—at worst it is regarded as something of a joke; even in my time one heard it said of a man that he used to be some well-known older man's boy much as we in England might say that someone at school was fag to some celebrity. It should also be made clear that, as in ancient Greece, so far as one can judge, when the boy-wives grew up and when they and their husbands married females they had a normal married life like everyone else. There were no urnings in the modern European sense.

The custom of boy marriage had died out before I first visited Zandeland, and as direct observation no longer was possible, I had to rely on statements about the past, but such statements by senior men were unanimous. I have pointedly used the terms "wife," "husband," and "marriage," for, as the texts will make clear, the relationship was, for so long as it lasted, a legal union on the model of a normal marriage. The warrior paid bridewealth (some five spears or more) to the parents of his boy and performed services for them as he would have done had he married their daughter; if he proved to be a good son-in-law they might later replace the son by a daughter. Also, if another man had relations with his boy he could, I was told, sue him at court for adultery.

The boys were "women": "*Ade nga ami,*" they would say, "we are women." A boy was addressed by his lover as *diare* 'my wife,' and the boy addressed him as *kumbami* 'my husband.' The boys used to eat out of sight of the warriors in the same way as women do not eat in the presence of their husbands. The boys performed many of the smaller services a woman performs daily for her husband, such as gathering leaves for his ablutions, gathering leaves for his bed, drawing water and breaking off firewood for him, helping him in hoeing his father's cultivations, bearing messages for him, and bringing him cooked provisions from his home to court to supplement those provided by the prince; but he did not cook porridge for him. With regard to these services it should be borne in mind that a young man at court had no mother or sisters to look after him there. Also, the boy-wife carried his husband's shield when on a journey. It should be understood that he performed these services lest it might be thought that the relationship was entirely of a sexual nature; it will be appreciated that it had an educational side to it. With regard to the sexual side, at night the boy slept with his lover, who had intercourse with him between his thighs (Azande expressed disgust at the suggestion of anal penetration). The boys got what pleasure they could by friction of their organs on the husband's belly or groin. However, even though there was this side to the relationship, it was clear from Zande accounts that there was also the comfort of a nightly sharing of the bed with a companion.

The word "boy" (*kumba gude*) must, it would appear, be interpreted liberally, for as far as I could judge from what I was told the lads might have been anywhere between about twelve and twenty years of age. When they ceased to be boys they joined the companies of warriors to which their at-one-time husbands belonged and took boys to wife on their own account; so the period of marriage was also one of apprenticeship. I cannot present figures for boy marriages, but the practice was certainly both accepted and common. I obtained lists of a succession of such marriages from several senior men but there would be little profit after this lapse of time (sixty-five years after King Gbudwe's death) in recording just strings of names.

Before giving the texts it should be further stated that some members of the noble ruling class indulged in homosexual intercourse. In the main these were those young sons of princes who hung about court till their fathers saw fit to give them wives and districts to administer. They kept well away from their fathers' harems and took commoner boys as servants and for sexual pleasure. It appears also that a prince, however many wives he might have, might sleep with a boy rather than by himself during the night before consulting the poison oracle, for intercourse with a woman was taboo on these occasions. It was said that *kumba gude na gberesa nga benge te* 'a boy does not spoil the poison oracle.' Otherwise I have heard of only one senior prince—deposed by the administration—who, although he had several wives, still habitually slept with boys. For this and other reasons he was regarded by Azande as slightly crazy. One must not jump to conclusions, as Czekanowski did on what Junker had recorded about boys accompanying a Zande prince wherever he went; all kings and princes are accompanied by pages who are treated by their masters with notable indulgence in contrast with the severe aloofness with which their seniors are usually treated.

Text (Evans-Pritchard 1963a:277–280) was taken down from Kuagbiaru, a man well acquainted with the court life of the past who had himself been a boy-wife and, as head of a company of warriors at the court of Prince Gangura, several times a husband to boys.

In the past men used to have sexual relations with boys as they did with wives. A man paid compensation to another if he had relations with his boy. People asked for the hand of a boy with a spear, just as they asked for the hand of a maiden of her parents.[1] All those young warriors who were at court, all had their boys. Those huts of the young men which were around the court, all their boy-loves were in those huts. They built their huts large and long, and there were many youths to each hut, each in his own place, together with their captain. Their boy-loves also slept in the huts. When night fell they all kindled fires in front of their husbands' beds, each kindled a fire in front of his lover's bed. When the young warriors began to be very hungry at court they sent their boy-loves to their [the boys'] parents to fetch food for them. Their boy-loves went and returned with fine lots of porridge and cooked fowls and beer. The relatives of a boy escorted him [when he was married] in the same way as they escorted a bride [on her marriage] to her husband with much good food. However, the boys did not cook porridge for their lovers themselves; they cooked manioc and sweet potatoes for their lovers. It was their mothers [the boys'] who cooked porridge in their homes, and nice meats; and some of them cooked fowls. They collected all these lots of food together where their husbands were. All these youths and their loves, there was no forgetfulness of the boys' part about giving food to the lovers. But that porridge which they gave them, they broke off part of it together with part of the meats to hide it for their husbands, for they were like wives.[2] Their lovers did not approve of their laughing loud like men, they desired them to speak softly, as women speak.

When all the young warriors went to hoe the prince's cultivations each took his love with him. When they reached the cultivations they built a big hut for their captain and they set up a palsade around it. In this enclosure, filled with boys, otherwise was the captain alone. Then the youths began to build their little shelters adjacent to the hut of the captain, and they stretched far, crossing streams. But all their boys were in the enclosure they had erected for the captain. When it was dusk the boys scattered, each to the hut of his lover to kindle a fire there for his lover. Each went to kindle a fire in the hut of his own lover. Next morning they gathered together in the enclosure of the captain. No youth could enter there without permission. The captain gave them their meals behind the enclosure. Only if the captain felt well-disposed towards him might he summon one of the senior youths into the enclosure to share his meal with him. All the rest of them never entered the enclosure; they saw their loves at night. The youths hoed the cultivations till evening and then they returned to their sleeping places. Their loves had already made their husbands' beds and kindled fires for them in their huts.

Text (Evans-Pritchard 1962:16–17) was taken down from Ganga, one of King Gbudwe's captains of companies of warriors.

This is about how men married boys when Gbudwe was lord of his domains. In those days, if a man had relations with the wife of another the husband killed him or he cut off his hands and his genitals. So for that reason a man used to marry a boy to have orgasm between his thighs, which quieted his desire for a woman. If this boy was a good wife to his husband five spears might be paid for him, and for another as many as ten might be paid. A husband who was liberal to his in-laws, they would later give him a woman, saying that good for a boy, how much better for a woman; so if he married a girl his in-laws would greatly profit, and so they gave him a wife [girl]. This his boy, he did not abide seeing another near him; they would quarrel, and if they took the matter before [King] Gbudwe, Gbudwe told the one who went after the other's boy to pay him spears [in compensation] since he had gone after the other's boy. Also there were some men who, although they had [female] wives, still married boys. When war broke out they took their boys with them,[3] but they did not take them to the place of fighting; the boys remained behind in the camp, for they were like women; and they collected firewood for their husbands and plucked *nzawa* leaves [for the toilet] and they

cooked meals for when their husbands returned from the fighting. They did for their husbands everything a wife does for her husband. They drew water and presented it before their husbands on their knees and they took food and brought it to them, and the husbands washed their hands and ate this meal and then recounted what had happened in the fighting to their boy-wives.

So far something has been said about male homosexuality. What about lesbianism? That also must be regarded as a product, like male homosexuality, of polygamy on a large scale; for if this precluded young men from normal sex, so in large polygamous homes it prevented the wives, or some of them, from receiving the amount of sexual attention they wished for from their common husband, who, moreover, might well have been elderly and not at the height of his sexual vigor. Though men have slightly different habits, it can be said generally that a woman who is one of three wives would not sleep with her husband more than some ten nights a month, one of six wives more than five nights, and so on. One of the many wives of a prince or of an important commoner in the past might not have shared her husband's bed for a month or two, whereas some of the dozens, even hundreds, of wives of a king must have been almost totally deprived of the sex life normal in smaller homes. Adulterous intercourse was very difficult for a wife in such large polygamous families, for the wives were kept in seclusion and carefully watched; death on discovery, or even on suspicion, would have been the penalty for both the wife and her lover.

It was in such polygamous families, Azande say, that lesbianism was practiced. Obviously I had no opportunity of knowing anything about it by observation, so that I can only tell what I was told (by males only, though women admitted that some women practiced it). Wives would cut a sweet potato or manioc root in the shape of the male organ, or use a banana for the purpose. Two of them would shut themselves in a hut and one would lie on the bed and play the female role while the other, with the artificial organ tied round her stomach, played the male role. They then reversed roles.

Women were certainly underprivileged in old Zande society, and it is a further indication of male dominance that what was encouraged among males was condemned among females. Zande men, princes especially, have a horror of lesbianism, and they regard it as highly dangerous, being more or less equivalent to *adandara*, a kind of cat born, it is believed, of women (Evans-Pritchard 1937:51–56). It would be fatal were a man to see one of these women suckling her kittens. I have heard it said that some of the great kings of the past—Bazingbi, Gbudwe, Wando, and others—died on account of lesbian practices between their wives, and it is alleged that in Gbudwe's home one of his senior wives, Nanduru, a wizened old lady in my day, executed several of his cowives for this offense. Some Azande have told me that lesbianism was much practiced by daughters and sisters of ruling nobles in whose homes they lived in an incestuous relationship. A ruler might give a girl slave to one of his daughters, who would anoint and paint the girl to make her attractive and then lie with her. Azande further say that once a woman has started homosexual intercourse she is likely to continue it because she is then her own master and may have gratification when she pleases and not just when a man cares to give it to her, and the gratification may also last as long as she pleases.

It would seem, if Zande statements are correct, that a lesbian relationship is often brought about in the first instance by a simple rite. When two women are very friendly they may seek to give formality to their friendship through a ceremony called *bagburu*, having obtained permission from their husbands to do so. A husband finds it difficult to refuse his consent for it would not normally mean that any sexual element was involved. One of the women makes a small gift to the other and the other makes a return gift. They then take a maize cob and divide it, and each plants the seeds of her half in her garden.[4] Later the women perform various mutual services and will from time to time exchange gifts. However, though a husband may give his consent he may do so with reluctance because Zande men think that this bond of friendship between women may be a respectable cover for homosexual intimacies.

Text (Evans-Pritchard 1963b:13–14) was taken down from Kuagbiaru.

Among the Azande many women do the same as men. There are many of them who have intercourse among themselves as a husband with his wife. Lesbianism began with a maize the name of which is *kaima*, a maize with a cob red like blood. They take this cob and utter a spell over it in the same way as men utter a spell over the blood in making blood-brotherhood; and when that is done one of them [the two women] takes hold of the top of it on her side and the other takes hold of the bottom of it for her part and they break it between them. After this they should not call each other by their proper names, but they call each other *bagburu*. The one who is the wife cooks porridge and a fowl and brings them to the one who is the husband. They do this between them many times. They have sexual intercourse between them with sweet potatoes carved into the shape of a circumcised penis, with carved manioc also, and also with bananas. At the top it is just like the male organ. The husband dislikes her wife conversing with other women. She beats her wife just as a husband beats his wife for bad behaviour, such as going with a man. However, when Gbudwe was alive he was very much opposed to anything to do with lesbianism.

Text (Evans-Pritchard) was taken down from Kisanga, a man with a very wide knowledge of Zande customs.

Women get together and one says to another "Oh my friend, you, why don't you like me mistress!" The other replies "O lady, my mistress, why should I bear you ill-will?" The first says "Lady, come the day after tomorrow as I have a little something to tell you." She replies "Eh lady, what is it that you do not now tell me? For unless you tell it to me now I cannot survive the night waiting to hear it!" So the one tells the other "Lady, I am greatly in love with you. O lady how shall we manage this horrible husband?"

"Hm! Eh lady, do they keep all that watch on a woman lady!"

"Ahe lady, let us play a trick. You come after my husband and we will make a pact of love-friendship (*bagburu*) between us and he will think it is just a friendship between women, and you lady can pleasure me." She adds "Early tomorrow you come with a little gift for him." Early in the morning she takes a gift, such as a spear, and she comes to visit the husband in his home. She says to the husband:

"So, will you listen well to what I am going to say to you?"

"Lady, say what the lady has come to my home here for."

"Eh sir, sir it is about my friend, master. I said to myself sir that I would come to ask the prince about her; no man am I who could deceive you with a woman."

He says "O lady may be I shall consent."

"O sir by your head! O sir by your head! Let me have the woman sir. Sir I will grind her flour for her, and if she is sick I will gather her firewood."

"I must consult the oracles first lady, I must consult the oracles first. I think I must first consult the oracles."

"Eh sir, does one refuse with a woman? Is she a man?"

"All right my friend, you leave the spear and go home and I will think the matter over."

She wipes the ground before him [thanks him], saying "O my master I go about by myself among people sir!" Then she goes home. She sleeps two nights and then grinds flour and she comes with flour and porridge. When she appears on the path her lover runs to meet her on the path:

"O my love, O my friend, O lady have you not come today?" She puts down the flour and porridge at the side of the homestead. Her lover takes a stool and puts it for her to be seated. The husband sulks:

"You have come my friend?"

"Yes sir."

"Lady let me be, I am feeling chilly today."

They take his food and bring it. He is embarrassed: "Child pour water over my hands." His wife goes and takes water and pours it over his hands. He says "Lady that is good, lady, it is good." He breaks off one lump of porridge. He sulks and goes on sulking, telling his daughters "Now then come on and take it away and give it to the children."

"Ahe sir! A person brings her food and a man is not well—it should not be given away, it should be kept for him to eat at another time?"

"Hm! Eh woman, does one argue with a father in this manner!" They deceive him. "Oh no sir, I am not disputing anything sir."

"Mistress I do not feel well today, today is not a good day for me. I shall retire."

"He! Look at that spying husband of mine lady, what an unpleasant character!"

The wife puts water before her lover as though she were her [male] husband. She has her penis in her bag—she takes it around with her. They carve a sweet potato into the shape of a circumcised penis. The woman-husband makes a hole through the sweet potato and then ties it with cord through it to her loins so that she is like a male. She washes herself with water and anoints herself with oil.

Meanwhile the husband is eating his meal in the hut of his senior wife. He says to her: "O mistress since you have been a long time with me you have never done me ill. My wife, that which I have seen, do you see it too?"

"No sir, but I have an idea about it. I am not sure of things sir! Eh sir! As you are a man, in a matter of this kind why do you not hear what she has to say to satisfy yourself in your mind?"

He coughs: "All right, this death of mine they speak of, I will get to the bottom of it."

The two women get up to lie on the ground because their movements on the bed make a noise. The wife of the man says: "That spying husband of mine, he is nasty enough to try and trap people in a hut!"

"If he does he will die if he sees it. Madam do not weary yourself with thinking about women's affairs, you will see what happens."

"Let us do what we are going to do. Just stop talking about my husband." She makes her keep quiet by shaking her head at her while she takes her pleasure of her love. The husband comes and crouches in the porch and he hears the sounds of them in the hut; he hear the movement in the hut, as they say to each other "O my brother, O my darling, O my husband, O lady." He enters the hut and when they see him they rise from the ground. He seizes his wife and says (to the other woman):

"O my friend you kill me. I thought you had come to my home in goodwill, but it seems that it is my death you bring." Then he calls his senior wife:

"Mistress come here and see what evil has befallen me—this woman I have taken hold of together with her companion. . . ."

"Heyo! My husband, do you summon me to a woman's affair—your wives can be very malicious sir."

"Eh woman, we share a home with you in double-talk (*sanza*). So you are all moved by wish for my death!"

"Hi! Leave off that talk with me—is it my fault that you went and entered the hut?"

Perhaps I should add in conclusion to this note that it is not of course being suggested that pederasty and tribadism are explained by social conditions such as those obtaining among the Azande. Obviously they are not. What is perhaps accounted for, given libidinous plasticity, are the institutional forms prevalent in Zande society and the (male) attitudes toward them.

NOTES

1. A man asking a girl's parents for her hand in marriage gave them a spear or two as a first installment of bridewealth. In the case of boys, the acceptance of a spear likewise constituted a legal marriage.

2. In preparing a meal for guests a Zande wife often kept part of it back before serving it so that her husband could have a second meal secretly when the guests had departed.

3. Intercourse with women was taboo for warriors during periods of fighting.

4. The rite corresponds to exchange of blood among men. That it is copied from the latter is suggested by the blood-red maize cob (Evans-Pritchard 1933).

REFERENCES CITED

Czekanowski, Jan. 1924. *Forschungen im Nil-Kongo Zwischengebiet*. Vol. 2. Leipzig: Klinkhardt & Biermann.

Evans-Pritchard, E. E. 1933. Zande blood-brotherhood. *Africa* 6:369–401.

———. 1937. *Witchcraft, oracles and magic among the Azande*. Oxford: Clarendon Press.

———. 1957a. The Zande royal court. *Zaï're* 5:495–511.

———. 1957b. Zande border raids. *Africa* 28:217–232.

———. 1957c. Zande warfare. *Anthropos* 52:239–262.

———. 1962. Zande texts: part 1. Oxford: Oxonian Press.

———. 1963a. Some Zande texts. Kush 11.

———. 1963b. Zande texts: part 3:1–43.

———. n.d. Vernacular text. Manuscript. Zande text collection. Oxford: Institute of Social Anthropology.

Junker, Wilhelm. 1892. *Travels in Africa*. London: Chapman and Hall.

11

Sex and Repression in an Irish Folk Community

John C. Messenger
Ohio State University

In this chapter I will discuss sexual repression—its manifestations in behavior and beliefs, its causes, its inculcation, and its broader historical and cultural implications—in a small island community of the Gaeltacht that I will call Inis Beag.[1] My wife and I conducted ethnographic research there for nineteen months, between 1958 and 1966, which included a one-year stay and eight other visits of from one to seven weeks—at Christmas or during the summer. Ours is the only holistic ethnographic study of this community, although archeologists, linguists, philologists, folklorists, geographers, anthropometricians, and other scientists have undertaken research there for over a century. We collected a large body of culture and personality data on three

other Irish islands for the purposes of making comparisons and testing hypotheses concerning culture and personality concomitants of island living. Inis Beag is ideally suited to ethnographic and folklore research in that its population possesses a tradition which is less acculturated than that of any other local Irish group.

According to anthropological definition (Lewis 1960: 1–2), the islanders qualify as folk people in almost every respect. The community has maintained its stability for at least 200 years; there is a strong bond between the peasants and their land, and agriculture provides them with the major source of their livelihood; production is mainly for subsistence and is carried on with a simple technology, using the digging stick, spade, and scythe as primary implements; the island folk participate in a money economy, but barter still persists; a low standard of living prevails, and the birth rate is high; the family is of central importance, and marriage figures prominently as a provision of economic welfare; the island is integrated into the county and national governments and is subject to their

Source: Sex and repression in an Irish folk community, by John C. Messenger. From *Human Sexual Behavior*, by Donald S. Marshall and Robert C. Suggs. New York: Basic Books. Copyright © 1971 by The Institute for Sex Research, Inc. Reprinted by permission of Basic Books, a member of Perseus Books, L.L.C.

laws; the people have long been exposed to urban influences and have borrowed cultural forms from other rural areas on the mainland, integrating them into a relatively stable system; and, finally, the experience of living under English rule for centuries has created in the islanders an attitude of dependence on—yet hostility toward—government which continues to this day. The only conditions in Inis Beag which run counter to those found in most other peasant communities are low death and illiteracy rates and bilateral, rather than unilineal, descent (although inheritance is patrilineal).

Inis Beag culture also characterizes people of nearby islands, and the traditions of the several together might be regarded as forming a subculture of the total Irish system. Many island customs are shared with rural peasants on the mainland (where numerous regional subcultures exist), and some are part of a broader European matrix. The island has experienced considerable cultural change since the establishment of the Congested Districts Board (forerunner of the Gaeltacht) in 1891 and the growth of tourism in this century. But conditions there still approximate those which must have prevailed two generations ago, and earlier, throughout this region of peasant Ireland.

Inis Beag has a population of approximately 350 persons living in seventy-one "cottages" distributed among four settlements, called "villages." Bordering a "strand" and a large tract of common land on the northeastern side of the island are a series of limestone terraces, separated by water-bearing shales and faced by small cliffs, on which the villages are situated. Most of the arable land is found on this side, where the shales have been broken down by weathering and alien soils deposited by wind and by ice of the Weichsel glacier. Over many generations, the islanders have deepened these soils and created new soils on rock surfaces by adding seaweed, sand, and human manure. On the southwestern side of Inis Beag, known as the "back of the island," limestone pavements slope rather evenly, almost as the gentle dip of the strata, from the crest of the highest terrace to the sea a mile away. The bared surfaces are intersected in all directions by crevices, which contain a large portion of the natural flora—herbs and shrubs—of the island. Stone fences delimit many hundreds of plots which compose most of the two-square-mile land surface of Inis Beag.

The island boasts a post office with radio-telephone facilities, a "national school" in which three teachers instruct ninety pupils in the seven "standards," two provision shops with attached "pubs," a former coast guard station now housing the nurse and a knitting industry which employs local girls, a lighthouse, and a chapel served by a curate who resides nearby. Inis Beag lacks electricity and running water, and the only vehicles are several ass-drawn carts which are able to travel the narrow, fence-bordered trails. A small "steamer" carrying supplies, passengers, and mail to and from a mainland port visits the island at least once each week. That Inis Beag has experienced far less cultural change than other island communities of Ireland is largely due to the fact that, in absence of a deep water quay, the steamer has had to stand off the strand and be met by "canoes." Most of the tourists who come to the island stay only for the hours that the steamer is anchored and go ashore mainly for the thrill of riding in the canoes, which the island men row with consummate skill. Insofar as I can discover, the inhabitants of Inis Beag are less prone to visit the mainland than are the peoples of other Irish islands.

INIS BEAG HISTORY AND CULTURE[2]

The prehistory and history of Inis Beag are recorded dramatically in a multitude of monuments and artifacts of stone and metal, including Neolithic axe-heads and kitchen middens, Copper-Bronze Age gallery grave tombs and burial mounds of earth and stone, an Iron Age promontory fort, and medieval Christian monasteries, churches, cemeteries, stone houses, and a sacred well, as well as a three-story tower house built by the political overlords of the island. Irish nativists claim that the contemporary folk are lineal descendants of ancient, once civilized Celts.

But local legend, historical evidence, and genealogical data collected by my wife and me indicate that the present population is descended from immigrants who came to the island from many parts of Ireland following the Cromwellian incursion of the seventeenth century. The islanders still express bitterness over conditions of poverty and servitude experienced by their ancestors during the 300 years that they lived under absentee Anglo-Irish landlords. All of the excesses of foreign domination suffered by mainland peasants were suffered by the inhabitants of Inis Beag, but were aggravated by the ordinary hardships of island living. Little was known about events in Inis Beag during the eighteenth and early nineteenth centuries until the island was visited by archeologists and publicized in their scientific writings. The surrounding area of the mainland was very much isolated and seldom visited at that time, although trading between Inis Beag and nearby communities was carried on, and passing ships sometimes called at the island.

Agricultural pursuits have always dominated the subsistence economy of Inis Beag. Most householders own land on which they grow potatoes and other vegetables, grass, and sometimes rye and sally rods and where they pasture cattle, sheep, goats, asses, and horses. The back of the island, behind the communities, is divided into four strips, and each landowner possesses numerous plots located along the "quarter" on which his village fronts. The average combined holding is sixteen acres, and almost 50 percent of the land is composed of arable indigenous and manufactured soils. Potatoes are the staple crop, and they are supplemented by various other vegetables, milk from cattle and goats, meat from island sheep, fish, eggs, and other foods, many of which are imported and sold in the shops. Rye is grown for thatching, and sally rods are used to weave several types of containers. Other subsistence activities (which also provide income for some folk) are knitting, weaving, crocheting, tailoring, and sandal making.

A slowly expanding cash economy features the export of cattle and sheep fattened on the island and of surplus potatoes and fish, the collection of seaweed for extraction of iodine at a mainland factory, the keeping of tourists in private homes, and the manufacturing of craft objects for sale to visitors and for export. At the turn of the century, fishing from canoes—with nets and lines often many miles out in the ocean— was an important subsistence and income activity. A few islanders who owned little or no land lived primarily by fishing and kelp-making. But over the past few decades, fish have become less plentiful and the weather more inclement, especially during winter months; less than a dozen crews now fish regularly, and most fish are consumed locally rather than exported. Government subsidies of many sorts and remittances from relatives who have emigrated supplement the cash economy. The government further aids the islanders by not collecting "rates" and by setting low rents on land. Income information is as difficult to come by as data on sex, disputes, and pagan religious retentions; since the people do not wish to jeopardize their unemployment benefits (most of them receive the "dole") and old age pensions and fear taxation in the future, they are secretive about sources and amounts of income.

More important than the formal political structure of Inis Beag are the local informal system and social control techniques of gossip, ridicule, satire, and the like. Crime is rare in Inis Beag, and there are no "guards" stationed there. The island is seldom visited by politicians, and many inhabitants are either apathetic or antagonistic toward the county and national governments. Those asked to account for their antigovernment attitude cite widespread nepotism and corruption among officials, the slight differences between the platforms of the two major parties, and "foolish" government schemes in Inis Beag—usually instituted without consulting the islanders. Government aid is sought and even expected as a "right," but it is seldom considered adequate. Taxation in any form, especially of tobacco and stout, is bitterly opposed.

The informal political system is dominated by the curate, the "headmaster" of the national school, and a self-appointed local "king." In the past, the amount of influence exerted by curates has varied; some have been concerned mostly with fulfilling spiritual responsibilities, while others have attacked by sermon, threat, and even physical action such activities as courting, dancing, visiting, gossiping, and drinking spirits. Anticlerical sentiment (seldom manifested in overt acts) is as strong as, or stronger than, its antigovernment counterpart. The clergy are said to interfere too much in secular affairs, to live too "comfortably," to be absent from the island too often, and to act overly aloof and supercilious. The most outspoken anticlerics assert that curates have employed informers, allocated indulgences, withheld the sacraments, and placed curses ("reading the Bible at") in their efforts to regulate the secular life of Inis Beag. The headmaster, appointed and rigidly supervised by the parish priest and curate, presides over social events and serves as an adviser to the islanders in many matters, in addition to carrying out his official duties.

Inis Beag lacks a class system, and the status symbols which affect human relationships are few. There is, in fact, little difference in the style of life between the most and the least prosperous of the islanders. The web of kinship rather than the possession of status attributes, for the most part, determines who will interact with whom and in what manner. Land and money are the principal symbols, with formal education and influential relatives (particularly priests, nuns, and teachers), on the mainland and abroad, becoming more important. Two generations ago, strength, courage, economic skills, and musical and storytelling abilities were highly regarded as well, but acculturation has lessened their significance.

Although there are fifty-nine nuclear families, only thirteen surnames exist today. There is much inbreeding, as might be expected, and the church carefully checks the genealogies of prospective spouses to ascertain their degree of consanguinity. Courtship is almost nonexistent, and most marriages are arranged with little concern for the desires of the young people involved. Late marriage and celibacy are as prevalent in Inis Beag as elsewhere in Ireland. The average marriage age for men is thirty-six and for women twenty-five, and 29 percent of those persons eligible for marriage are single.[3] The functions of the family are mainly economic and reproductive, and conjugal love is extremely rare. A sharp dichotomy exists between the sexes; both before and after marriage men interact mostly with men and women with women. The average family has seven offspring, and many women are unhappy about being forced by the unauthorized decree of local priests to produce as many children as possible. They feel that the constant bearing and rearing of offspring increase their work, restrict their freedom, and perpetuate the poverty of their families. Jealousy of the greater freedom of men is commonly expressed by women who have many young children. Mothers bestow a considerable amount of attention and affection on their offspring, especially on their sons. However, tensions between fathers and sons which develop in childhood often flare into scarcely repressed hostility later on, particularly in those families where competition for the inheritance of property is engendered among siblings by the fathers' attempts to ensure favored treatment in old age.

Men are far more active socially than are women. The latter are restricted by custom mostly to visiting, attending parties during the winter, and participating in church-associated activities. Many women leave their cottages only to attend mass, wakes, and funerals or to make infrequent calls on relatives; my wife and I talked with some elderly women who had not visited other villages or walked to the back of the island for thirty or more years. Men not only attend parties with their womenfolk but go to dances during the summer, frequent the pubs, play cards almost nightly during November and December (the period when once people congregated to hear storytellers), visit the homes of kin and friends or meet along the trails at night, and range the entire island and the sea about it in their economic pursuits. Before the age of benevolent government, women shared many economic tasks with men, such as collecting seaweed, baiting lines, and gutting fish. But now they tend to household chores and only milk cows and perform some of the lighter farming jobs with their fathers and husbands.

The island folk are devout Catholics, despite the fact that they are critical of their priests and hold pagan religious beliefs. Youth of Inis Beag overtly disallow the existence of other than church-approved supernatural entities. However, their elders cling to traditional pagan beliefs and practices (many of which are Druidic in origin) about which they are extremely secretive for fear of being ridiculed by outsiders and their more skeptical neighbors. The non-Christian array of spiritual beings includes various spirits and demons, ghosts, witches, phantom ships, and animals and material objects possessing human attributes and volitions. Prominent among the spirits thought to inhabit Inis Beag are the trooping and solitary fairies, sea creatures, mermaids, and the banshee. The most formidable of the demons is a pooka which lives in a Bronze Age burial mound and roams the strand and common land at night altering its shape and size at will; during the day it will twist the limbs of unwary persons who choose the hill for a resting place. Ghosts, called "shades," are frequently seen after dark performing economic tasks. They are thought to be doing penance in purgatory, which embraces the earth as well as a spiritual locus; this is one example of the many reinterpretations of Christian and pagan belief effected by the islanders. The only form of witchcraft practiced today is the casting of the evil eye. At least three persons, suitably ostracized, are believed to be able to perpetrate evil by the act of complimenting their victims. Other religious retentions found in Inis Beag are a multitude of taboos, divination through the seeking of omens, magical charms and incantations of a protective nature, and an emphasis on "natural" foods, folk medicines, and other products impinging on the human body.

It is believed by many people in Ireland that the Catholicism of the islanders embodies an ideal unattained on the mainland, where the faith is thought to set an example for the world. In fact, the worship of the folk is obsessively oriented toward salvation in the next world, with a corresponding preoccupation with sin in this world; there is a resemblance to polytheism in the manner in which they relate to the Blessed Virgin and Irish saints; Christian as well as pagan rituals and religious artifacts are often employed to serve magical ends; and many beliefs that they hold to be orthodox Catholic are in reality idiosyncratic to Inis Beag or Ireland. Christian morality in its "outward" manifestations is realized to a remarkable degree. This can be attributed, in part, to the emphasis placed on good works as a means of gaining salvation; but, more importantly, it results from the already-mentioned techniques of social control exercised by the clergy, based on an overwhelming fear of damnation. . . .

SEXUAL REPRESSION: ITS MANIFESTATIONS

Both lack of sexual knowledge and misconceptions about sex among adults combine to brand Inis Beag as one of the most sexually naive of the world's societies. Sex never is discussed in the home when children are about; only three mothers admitted giving advice, briefly and incompletely, to their daughters. We were told that boys are better advised than girls, but that the former learn about sex informally from older boys and men and from observing animals. Most respondents who were questioned about sexual instructions given to youths expressed the belief that "after marriage nature takes its course," thus negating the need for anxiety-creating and embarrassing personal confrontation of parents and offspring. We were unable to discover any cases of childlessness based on sexual ignorance of spouses, as reported from other regions of peasant Ireland. Also, we were unable to discover knowledge of the sexual categories utilized by researchers in sex: insertion of tongue while kissing, male mouth on female breast, female hand on penis, cunnilingus, fellatio, femoral coitus, anal coitus, extramarital coitus, manifest homosexuality, sexual contact with animals, fetishism, and sado-masochistic behavior. Some of these activities may be practiced by particular individuals and couples; however, without a doubt they are deviant forms in Inis Beag, about which information is difficult to come by.

Menstruation and menopause arouse profound misgivings among women of the island, because few of them comprehend their physiological significance. My wife was called on to explain these processes more than any other phenomena related to sex. When they reach puberty, most girls are unprepared for the first menstrual flow and find the experience a traumatic one—especially when their mothers are unable to provide a satisfactory explanation for it. And it is commonly believed that the menopause can induce "madness"; in order to ward off this condition, some women have retired from life in their mid-forties and, in a few cases, have confined themselves to bed until death, years later. Others have so retired as a result of depressive and masochistic states. Yet the harbingers of "insanity" are simply the physical symptoms announcing the onset of menopause. In Inis Beag, these include severe headaches, hot flashes, faintness in crowds and enclosed places, and severe anxiety. Mental illness is also held to be inherited or caused by inbreeding (or by the Devil, by God punishing a sinner, or by malignant pagan beings) and stigmatizes the family of the afflicted. One old man came close to revealing what is probably the major cause of neuroses and psychoses in Ireland, when he explained the incarceration of an Inis Beag curate in a mental institution for clerics as caused by his constant association with a pretty housekeeper, who "drove him mad from frustration." This elder advocated that only plain-appearing older women (who would not "gab" to "our man") be chosen for the task. Earlier, according to island opinion, the same priest had caused to be committed to the "madhouse" a local man who publicly challenged certain of his actions. The unfortunate man was released six months later, as per law, since he was not mentally ill.

Sexual misconceptions are myriad in Inis Beag. The islanders share with most Western peoples the belief that men by nature are far more libidinous than women. The latter have been taught by some curates and in the home that sexual relations with their husbands are a "duty" which must be "endured," for to refuse coitus is a mortal sin. A frequently encountered assertion affixes the guilt for male sexual strivings on the enormous intake of potatoes of the Inis Beag male. (In Nigeria, among the people whom my wife and I studied, women are thought to be more sexually disposed than men and are the repositories of sexual knowledge; it is they who initiate coitus and so pose a threat to their spouses. Nigerian men place the blame on clitoridectomy performed just prior to marriage.) Asked to compare the sexual proclivities of Inis Beag men and women, one mother of nine said, "Men can wait a long time before wanting 'it,' but we can wait a lot longer." There is much evidence to indicate that the female orgasm is unknown—or at least doubted, or considered a deviant response. One middle-aged bachelor, who considers himself wise in the ways of the outside world and has a reputation for making love to willing tourists, described one girl's violent bodily reactions to his fondling and asked for an explanation; when told the "facts of life" of what obviously was an orgasm, he admitted not realizing that women also could achieve a climax, although he was aware that some of them apparently enjoyed kissing and being handled.

Inis Beag men feel that sexual intercourse is debilitating, a common belief in primitive and folk societies. They will desist from sex the night before they are to perform a job which will require the expenditure of great energy. Women are not approached sexually during menstruation or for months after childbirth, since they are considered "dangerous" to the male at these times. Returned "Yanks" have been denounced from the pulpit for describing American sexual practices to island youths, and such "pornographic" magazines as *Time* and *Life,* mailed by kin from abroad, have aroused curates to spirited sermon and instruction.

The separation of the sexes, started within the family, is augmented by separation in almost all segments of adolescent and adult activity. Boys and girls are separated to some extent in classrooms, and completely in recess play and movement to and from school. During church services, there is a further separation of adult men and women, as well as boys and girls, and each of the four groups leaves the chapel in its turn. The pubs are frequented only by men or by women tourists and female teachers who have spent several years on the mainland while training and thus are "set apart" (and, of course, by inquisitive female ethnographers). Women occasionally visit the shops to procure groceries, but it is more common for them to send their children to do so, since supplies and drinks are proffered across the same counter, and men are usually to be found on the premises. Even on the strand during summer months, male tourists tend to bathe at one end and women at the other. Some swimmers "daringly" change into bathing suits there, under towels and dresses—a custom practiced elsewhere in Ireland which has overtones of sexual catharsis.

It is often asserted that the major "escape valve" of sexual frustration among single persons in Ireland is masturbation; frustration-aggression theorists, however, would stress the ubiquity of drinking, alcoholism, disputes, and pugnacity as alternative outlets. Pugnacity can also be linked to the widespread problem of male identity. Our study revealed that male masturbation in Inis Beag seems to be common, premarital coitus unknown, and marital copulation limited as to foreplay and the manner of consummation. My wife and I never witnessed courting—"walking out"—in the island. Elders proudly insist that it does not occur, but male youths admit to it in rumor. The claims of young men focus on "petting" with tourists and a few local girls, whom the "bolder" of them kiss and fondle outside of their clothing. Island girls, it is held by their "lovers," do not confess these sins because they fail to experience pleasure from the contact. The male perpetrators also shun the confessional because of their fear of the priest.

We were unable to determine the frequency of marital coitus. A considerable amount of evidence indicates that privacy in the act is stressed and that foreplay is limited to kissing and rough fondling of the lower body, especially the buttocks. Sexual activity invariably is initiated by the husband. Only the male superior position is employed; intercourse takes place with underclothes not removed; and orgasm, for the man, is achieved quickly, almost immediately after which he falls asleep. (I must stress the provisional nature of these data, for they are based on a limited sample of respondents and relate to that area of sexual behavior least freely discussed.)

Many kinds of behavior disassociated from sex in other societies, such as nudity and physiological evacuation, are considered sexual in Inis Beag. Nudity is abhorred by the islanders, and the consequences of this attitude are numerous and significant for health and survival. Only infants have their entire bodies sponged once a week, on Saturday night; children, adolescents, and adults, on the same night, wash only their faces, necks, lower arms, hands, lower legs, and feet. Several times my wife and I created intense embarrassment by entering a room in which a man had just finished his weekly ablutions and was barefooted; once when this occurred, the man hurriedly pulled on his stockings and said with obvious relief, "Sure, it's good to get your clothes on again." Clothing always is changed in private, sometimes within the secrecy of the bedcovers, and it is usual for the islanders to sleep in their underclothes.

Despite the fact that Inis Beag men spend much of their time at sea in their canoes, as far as we could determine none of them can swim. Four rationales are given for this deficiency: the men are confident that nothing will happen to them, because they are excellent seamen and weather forecasters; a man who cannot swim will be more careful; it is best to drown immediately when a canoe capsizes far out in the ocean rather than swim futilely for minutes or even hours, thus prolonging the agony; and, finally, "When death is on a man, he can't be saved." The truth of the matter is that they have never dared to bare their bodies in order to learn the skill. Some women claim to have "bathed" at the back of the island during the heat of summer, but this means wading in small pools with skirts held knee-high, in complete privacy. Even the nudity of household pets can arouse anxiety, particularly when they are sexually aroused during time of heat. In some homes, dogs are whipped for licking their genitals and soon learn to indulge this practice outdoors. My wife, who can perform Irish stepdances and sing many of the popular folk songs, was once requested to sing a seldomheard American Western ballad; she chose "The Lavendar Cowboy," who "had only two hairs on his chest." The audience response was perfunctory and, needless to say, she never again was "called out" to sing that particular song.

The drowning of seamen, who might have saved themselves had they been able to swim is not the only result of the sexual symbolism of nudity; men who were unwilling to face the nurse when ill, because it might have meant baring their bodies to her, were beyond help when finally treated. While my wife and I were on the island, a nurse was assaulted by the mother of a young man for diagnosing his illness and bathing his chest in the mother's absence. (In this case, Oedipal and sexual attitudes probably were at work in tandem.)

It must be pointed out that nudity is also shunned for "health" reasons, for another obtrusive Inis Beag character trait is hypochondria. In some cases, however, it is hard to determine whether concern with modesty or health is dominant in a particular behavioral response. Fear of colds and influenza is foremost among health concerns; rheumatism and related muscular joint ailments, migraine headaches and other psychosomatic disorders, tooth decay, indigestion ("nervous stomach"), and hypermetropia are other widespread pathologies which cause worry among the folk—not to mention those of supernatural origin.

Secrecy surrounds the acts of urination and defecation. The evacuation of infants before siblings and strangers is discouraged, and animals that discharge in the house are driven out. Chickens that habitually "dirty" their nests while setting are soon killed and eaten. Although some women drink spirits privately, they seldom do so at parties. In part this is because of the embarrassment involved in visiting the outside toilet with men in the "street" looking on. One of the most carefully guarded secrets of Inis Beag, unreported in the many works describing island culture, is the use of human manure mixed with sand as a fertilizer. We were on the island eight months before we discovered that compost is not "street drippings" and "scraw," but decomposed feces. With "turf" becoming more difficult to procure from the mainland, some islanders have taken to importing coal and processed peat and burning cattle dung. The dung is prepared for use in difficult-to-reach plots at the back of the island when tourists are few in number; it is burned covertly because of the overtones of sex and poverty. Another custom that my wife and I learned of late in our research, due to the secrecy surrounding it, concerns the thickening of wool; men are required to urinate in a container and tread the wool therein with their bare feet.

Other major manifestations of sexual repression in Inis Beag are the lack of a "dirty joke" tradition (at least as the term is understood by ethnologists and folklorists) and the style of dancing, which allows little bodily contact among participants. I have heard men use various verbal devices—innuendoes, puns, and asides—that they believed bore sexual connotations; relatively speaking, they were pallid. In the song that I composed, one line of a verse refers to an island bachelor arising late in the day after "dreaming perhaps of a beautiful mate"; this is regarded as a highly suggestive phrase, and I have seen it redden cheeks and lower glances in a pub. Both step- and set-dancing are practiced in Inis Beag, although the former type is dying out. This rigid-body dancing, from which sex is removed by shifting attention below the hips, appears to have originated in Ireland during the early nineteenth century. The set patterns keep partners separated most of the time; but, even so, some girls refuse to dance, because it involves touching a boy. Inis Beag men, while watching a woman step-dance, stare fixedly at her feet, and they take pains to appear indifferent when crowding at a party necessitates holding women on their laps and rubbing against them when moving from room to room. But they are extremely sensitive, nevertheless, to the entire body of the dancer and to these casual contacts, as are the women. Their covert emotional reactions (which become overt as much drink is taken) are a form of catharsis. . . .

SEXUAL REPRESSION: ITS INCULCATION

. . . The seeds of repression are planted early in childhood by parents and kin through instruction supplemented by rewards and punishments, conscious imitation, and unconscious internalization. Although mothers bestow considerable affection and attention on their offspring, especially on their sons, physical love as manifested in intimate handling and kissing is rare in Inis Beag. Even breast feeding is uncommon because of its sexual connotation, and verbal affection comes to replace contact affection by late infancy. Any form of direct or indirect sexual expression—such as masturbation, mutual exploration of bodies, use of either standard or slang words relating to sex, and open urination and defecation—is severely punished by word or deed. Care is taken to cover the bodies of infants in the presence of siblings and outsiders, and sex is never discussed before children. Several times my wife inadvertently inquired as to whether particular women were pregnant, using that word before youths, only to be "hushed" or to have the conversation postponed until the young people could be herded outside. The adults were so embarrassed by the term that they found it difficult to communicate with her after the children had departed. She once aroused stupefaction among men on the strand when she attempted unsuccessfully to identify the gender of a bullock about to be shipped off.

It is in the home that the separation of sexes, so characteristic of Inis Beag life, is inaugurated among siblings in early childhood. Boys and girls in the family remain apart not only when interacting with the parent of the same sex at work, but when playing in and near the cottage and traveling to and from school. Parents and their older offspring read popular religious journals, found in most homes, many of the articles in which deal with sexual morality of the Irish Catholic variety.

One sociologist (Berger 1963: 66–92) classifies social control methods as those which involve physical violence or its threat (e.g., political and legal sanctions), those which result in economic pressures (e.g., occupation and market place relations), and, finally, those which govern our "morality, custom, and manners" (e.g., persuasion, ridicule, and gossip). I will not consider political and economic manipulation; more significant are other techniques that I have labelled secular social control. Inis Beag, as much as any human community, is characterized by gossip, ridicule, and opprobrium. Influenced by nativism, primitivism, and structural-functional theory, writers and social scientists have painted a distorted picture of culture and personality equilibrium among Irish peasants. Actually, the folk are neither glorified Celts nor "noble savages," and dysfunctional sociocultural forms, mental aberrations (neuroses, psychoses, and psychosomatic disorders), and exaggerated defense postures abound.

Inis Beag people are ambivalent about gossip; they welcome every opportunity to engage in it, yet detest the practice when they are its victims. When asked to cite the major deficiencies of their way of life, islanders usually place the prevalence of malicious gossiping near the top of their list. Boys and men hide themselves in the darkness or behind fences to overhear the conversations of passersby; they maintain close scrutiny of visitors during the summer, both day and night, in order to discover them in "compromising" situations. Parties are organized at the last moment and persons will leave the island without any previous announcement—often to emigrate or enter the hospital or join a religious order—in order to circumvent gossip. Rumors run rife in Inis Beag, especially when they concern, for example, the "nude" sun bathing of a visiting actress (bared shoulders and lower thighs) or the "attack" on a Dublin girl late at night by an island youth (an effort to hold her hand while under the influence of stout). Over a dozen efforts on our part to determine the truth behind the most pernicious rumors of this genre revealed sexual fantasy at their core in every case.

The force most responsible for limiting the potential social activities of women—which would make their lot much easier and possibly stem the tide of emigration—is the fear of gossip: "If I went for a walk, they'd wonder why I wasn't home tending my chores." Even couples who might otherwise disregard religious teachings and the wrath of the priest do not court, because it might be observed and reported through gossip to the entire population.[4] An islander must carefully regulate his own words and actions in the presence of others so that the fires of factionalism are not ignited. Equally feared are informers of the curate and relatives or close friends of persons in an audience who might be offended by a heedless remark brought to their attention by the listeners.

It is sometimes heard in Ireland, from those aware of, and willing to admit, the fact, that the inability of most Irish to "share themselves" with one another, even husbands and wives, is a heritage of the fear of gossip—a fear that one's intimate revelations will become common knowledge and lead to censure and "loss of face." A more likely explanation, according to those of Freudian bent, is the Oedipus configuration, which numbers among its many effects the following: the prevalence of romantic attachments and the rarity of conjugal love; the lack of sexual foreplay, marked by little or no concern with the female breast; the brevity of the coital act and the frequent spurning of the woman following it; the need to degrade the woman in the sexual encounter and the belief that the "good" woman does not like sex, and, conversely, that the sexually disposed woman is by virtue of the fact "bad." All of these widely reported phenomena bespeak the overwhelming influence of the mother image.

Ridicule and opprobrium, as well as satire in song and tale, are effective control mechanisms in light of the emphasis placed by Inis Beag folk on saving face. Most islanders could not believe that I was author of the ballad referred to in footnote 5 because several stanzas attack my character; they find it difficult to conceive of anyone publicly proclaiming their own faults, under any circumstances. Opinions, once formed, are clung to tenaciously, even in light of obviating circumstances, since to alter them would be an admittance that they were ill advised in the first instance. The folk pride themselves on being able to judge a stranger's character immediately on meeting him, and this initial impression is rarely modified no matter how long their interaction continues. A seldom revealed tradition of satirical balladry exists in Inis Beag, but its employment is infrequent and then calculated according to singer and audience so as not to offend directly. Apprehensiveness and anxiety about real and imagined ego assaults by others are dominant personality traits of the islanders. . . .

Paramount among external factors stimulating emigration are prosperity on the mainland and abroad, the impact of the mass media of communication, the increasing number of tourists visiting Inis Beag, the return of former emigrants, and the fact that, with an increase in incomes and scholarship funds, more island children are going to the mainland for their schooling each year. America has been a land of freedom and prosperity to the Irish since before the famine, and, until the Second World War, most islanders migrated there never to return. But the growth of prosperity in England following 1946 shifted the stream of emigration in that direction, for not only were jobs plentiful across the Irish Sea, but large, viable ethnic communities served by Irish clergy had sprung up in big cities. And it was possible to visit Ireland frequently, as the distance and cost are slight compared to a journey across the Atlantic. It is common for youths vacationing in Inis Beag from England to talk others into returning with them. The latter declare that they will soon come back to the island to settle permanently, hopefully with "great riches," but they seldom return. Since the war, a number of "Yanks" have also returned home, and their stories of life in America make the youthful islanders restive. Tourists who remain for weeks and months in Inis Beag and come to know many folk also sow the seeds of discontent.

Television was introduced into Inis Beag during 1963, and the two sets now installed always have ready and willing audiences. Almost every cottage has a radio, and, although the islanders seldom read books, a wide assortment of domestic and foreign magazines and newspapers find their way into most homes. These mass media also are an emancipating force making for restiveness and discontent, as they allow the islanders to glimpse behind the "lace curtain" at what appears to be a happier and freer world. Television and radio programs are censored, but, even so, the morality expressed in them—especially the sex and violence drenched American ones—presents a striking contrast to locally conceived moral precepts. A censor from Inis Beag would most certainly create more discontinuities in films with his shears than do his much maligned "secularized" colleagues in Dublin.

Most of what I have written in this essay is to be found expressed in the works of such older Irish writers as James Joyce, Sean O'Casey, Austin Clarke, and Patrick Kavanaugh, and such younger ones as William Murray, John McGahern, Edna O'Brien, John Broderick, Brian Moore, and Benedict Kiely. Irish reviewers of the writings of the younger authors often criticize them for portraying an Ireland of the distant past. But, although conditions there are changing quite rapidly, sexual repression is still a force active enough to command the attention of creative artists and social scientists.[5] The subtle influences of nationalism, religion, and sexual puritanism were very apparent in the revisions suggested by most of the twenty-six "unbiased" scholars of Irish descent—in Ireland, England, and America—to whom I submitted the first version of this article for comment.

NOTES

1. For other reports on Inis Beag, consult Messenger 1962, 1968, and 1969.
2. The culture described herein is that of 1959–1960 and excludes important changes which

have occurred since then, such as those resulting from the introduction of television, a summer language school for pupils from the mainland, and free secondary education.

3. Twenty-nine percent of those islanders of marriageable age are single. This rises to a high of 37 percent among first and second generation Inis Beag emigrants, indicating the actions of more than just economic causes. Irish scholars, for obvious reasons, tend to stress economic and other (climate, race, English oppression, the famine, loss of the Irish tongue, etc.) monistic causes in their analyses of culture and personality phenomena. Inadequate statistics for second and third generation migrants from Inis Beag suggest that the celibacy rate lowers markedly only when descendants of immigrants dissociate themselves from Irish ethnic communities and Irish-American priests. Ethnographic research is sorely needed among Irish of several generations in the countries to which they have migrated to probe this and other phenomena.

4. The fear of being observed, as well as repression, may account for the apparent lack of sexual contact with animals. This practice may be common among mainland peasants, if one is willing to accept as evidence the existence of a genre of dirty jokes popular there, and hearsay among certain scholars concerning confessional materials.

5. I am confident that one of the major "lines of attack" on my ethnography by Irish nativist reviewers will be that the community described is atypical and conditions in urbanized Ireland no longer bear any resemblance to those in Inis Beag. Since 1957, I have been much criticized by African elitists for describing in my writings a primitive culture which they claim is no longer characteristic of that developing continent.

REFERENCES

Arensberg, C. M., and Kimball, S. T. 1968. *Family Community in Ireland.* Cambridge: Harvard University Press.

Bales, R. F. 1962. "Attitudes Toward Drinking in the Irish Culture." In *Society, Culture, and Drinking Patterns,* eds. David J. Pittman and Charles R. Snyder, pp. 157–187. New York: John Wiley and Sons, Inc.

Berger, P. L. 1963. *Invitation to Sociology: A Humanistic Perspective.* Garden City: Anchor Books.

Blanshard, P. 1954. *The Irish and Catholic Power.* London: Derek Verschoyle.

Coxhead, E. 1961. *Lady Gregory.* London: MacMillan and Co., Ltd.

de Freine, S. 1965. *The Great Silence.* Dublin: Foilseachain Naisiunta Teoranta.

Delargy, J. H. 1957. "Folklore." In *A View of Ireland,* eds. James Meenan and David A. Webb, pp. 178–187. Dublin: Hely's Limited.

Humphreys, Fr. A. J. 1966. *New Dubliners.* New York: Fordham University Press.

Lewis, O. 1960. *Tepoztlan: Village in Mexico.* New York: Holt, Rinehart and Winston, Inc.

McCarthy, J. 1964. *Ireland.* New York: Time Incorporated.

McGahern, J. 1965. *The Dark.* London: Faber and Faber.

Messenger, J. C. 1962. "A Critical Reexamination of the Concept of Spirits." *American Anthropologist,* 64, No. 2: 267–272.

———. 1968. "Types and Causes of Disputes in an Irish Community." *Eire-Ireland,* 3, No. 3: 27–37.

———. 1969. *Inis Beag: Isle of Ireland.* New York: Holt, Rinehart and Winston, Inc.

Murray, W. C. 1965. *Michael Joe.* New York: Appleton-Century.

O'Brien, Fr. J. A., ed. 1953. *The Vanishing Irish.* New York: McGraw-Hill Book Company.

Opler, M. K. and Singer, J. L. 1956. "Ethnic Differences in Behavior and Psychopathology: Italian and Irish." *The International Journal of Social Psychiatry,* 2, No. 1: 11–23.

O'Suilleabhain, S. 1963. *A Handbook of Irish Folklore.* Hatboro: Folklore Associates, Inc.

Tracy, H. 1953. *Mind You I've Said Nothing.* London: Methuen and Co., Ltd.

◇ PART FOUR ◇

RITES OF PASSAGE AND GENITAL MUTILATION

INTRODUCTION TO THE SUBJECT AND READINGS

In the most "simple" and most "complex" cultures throughout the world peoples have been piercing their bodies, inserting lip plates, elongating their necks and labia, filing their teeth, shaping their skulls, and tattooing their skin. A trip to almost any high school in the United States will convince skeptics that body modification is alive and well in the postindustrial world. While superficial alterations such as pierced nipples and neck tattoos are upsetting parents across our country, the severest forms of body modification, genital mutilations, have generated serious debates in academic, political, and human rights arenas.

Most of us are familiar with the practice of male circumcision, and many people are also aware of the African custom of female genital mutilation (FGM).[1] Very few people, however, know about subincision, superincision, penis palangs, and introcision. Genital mutilation occurs in Africa, North America, Central America, South America, the Middle East, Oceania, and Australia. The widespread existence of genital cutting is one of the bigger mysteries in human behavior. Records of genital mutilation, found in Egypt, date back to about 2000 B.C.E, but this evidence does not explain its origin or original meanings. What prompts people from all around the world to cut the genitalia of their young? Why do we find variations in different cultures? How did it come to be viewed as a functional, positive cultural tradition? Why didn't the pain and health consequences deter or halt the practices? What are the origins and why have they persisted for so long?

Although there is no unifying theory or consensus regarding genital mutilation, various theories for the motivation behind genital mutilation have been put forth and can be summarized to provide three separate but related explanations. It has been argued that the different forms of genital cutting fulfills one of the following three cultural necessities:

1. Some forms of genital mutilation, mainly subincision and superincision, make male and female genitalia less distinct. Cutting the penis so that it looks more like a vagina and causing men to bleed (like women), has the affect of diminishing genital/sexual differences, thus equalizing and bringing the community together;

2. Other forms of genital cutting, like some types of FGM, remove the clitoris, the part of female genitalia that most resembles the penis, thus making the male and female genitalia more distinct from each other. In other words, it maximizes genital/sexual differences and creates a greater separation between women and men;

3. Genital cutting as a rite of passage promotes social conformity and group membership.

The debates about the practice of male subincision in Oceania demonstrate the problem of looking for simple answers to complex behaviors. Psychologists argued that this invasive form of mutilation, slitting the underside of the penis straight through to the urethra, was a form of vagina envy (the flip side of Freud's famous idea about penis envy). The people who practiced subincision claimed it was an attempt to imitate the kangaroo's bifid (two-headed) penis and its intromission performance (several hours) (Singer 1967). Scholarly consensus was never reached—a fact that had no effect on the people engaged in the practice.

One important aspect of genital mutilation is undeniable; it is deeply imbedded in gender. With the exception of introcision, a procedure to enlarge the vagina that is practiced by a few groups of Australian aborigines, FGM is about controlling women's sexualities. On the other hand, male genital mutilation has been about increasing the health or sexual enjoyment of men.

The gender related differences of male and female genital mutilation has resulted in a division of discussion, research, theories, and activism. The articles in this section reflect this division. *The Geography of Genital Mutilation* by James DeMeo primarily addresses male circumcision. It is estimated that about 500 million men in the world have been circumcised; male infants in the United States are circumcised at birth for health reasons, Jewish males are circumcised eight days after birth in a religious ceremony called Bris, and several different cultures in Africa circumcise boys during adolescence as a rite of passage to manhood (NOHARM 2000). DeMeo presents a cross-cultural survey of male genital mutilations, including the geographic distribution of the practice. He identifies similarities in cultures that practice male circumcision and argues that deep psychological processes are responsible for the practice.

Despite its illegality and efforts to stop the practice, FGM has been performed on approximately 100–130 million girls in Africa. The article *Unmasking Tradition: A Sudanese anthropologist confronts female "circumcision" and its terrible tenacity* by Rogaia Mustafa Abusharaf begins with a disturbing description of one girl's ordeal. Although this woman's story incites our outrage, Abusharaf reminds us: "Barbaric though the ritual may seem to Westerners, female circumcision is deeply enmeshed in local tradition and beliefs . . . Mothers who bring their daughters for the operations believe they are doing the right things—and indeed, their children would likely become social outcasts if left uncut." (p. 128) Abusharaf argues that we need to understand the ideology underlying FGM and how it relates to the status of women in general. Simply put, women have low status, cannot be independent, and must marry, but no one wants to marry uncut girls. Parents who refuse to have their daughters undergo genital cutting have to worry that their unmarried daughters could become sexually active and destroy the family's honor. They would have to police her and support her for life. All these factors bring a great deal of pressure on parents and help perpetuate the practice. Abusharaf offers hope for the eventual eradication of FGM, but she also reminds us that FGM is only one of many problems in Africa that need to be addressed.

TERMS AND CONCEPTS

clitoridectomy	minimizing genital difference
female genital mutilation (FGM)	patristic
excision	penis envy
incision	rites of passage
infibulation	shamanistic
introcision	subincision
maximizing genital difference	superincision

QUESTIONS TO CONSIDER

1. DeMeo argues that genital mutilation is correlated to other cultural practices. What are those practices and how do they relate to genital mutilation?
2. What are the various reasons given for male circumcision?
3. DeMeo states that "unconscious motivations" are responsible for the tradition of genital mutilation. Why is this explanation problematic?
4. Abusharaf notes that some American women undergo unnecessarily painful and potentially dangerous body modifications to conform to United States standards of beauty. What are the differences and the similarities between a sixteen-year-old American girl getting breast implants and a twelve-year-old Sudanese girl being circumcised?
5. Do you believe that genital cutting of girls in Africa is best labeled FGM and is a violation of human rights, or should it be considered female circumcision and be protected as the preservation of cultural traditions?

NOTE

1. This practice is sometimes called female circumcision, but the invasiveness and severity of FGM are so much greater than male circumcision that many researchers and activists believe that the label circumcision has falsely minimized the consequences.

FURTHER READINGS

Dirie, Waris and Cathleen Miller. 1998. *Desert Flower: The Extraordinary Journey of a Desert Nomad.* New York: William Morrow & Company.

Dorkenoo, Efua. 1996. *Cutting the Rose: Female Genital Mutilation: The Practice and Its Prevention.* Auckland: Paul & Co Publishers Consortium.

Gollaher, David L. 2000. *Circumcision: A History of the World's Most Controversial Surgery.* New York: Basic Books.

Graber, Robert Bates. 1981. A psychocultural theory of male genital mutilation. *Journal of Psychoanalytic Anthropology,* 4(4):413–434.

Gruenbaum, Ellen. 2000. *The Female Circumcision Controversy: An Anthropological Perspective.* Philadelphia: University of Pennsylvania Press.

Harrington, Charles. 1968. Sexual differentiation in socialization and some male genital mutilations. *American Anthropologist,* 70:951–956.

Kenyetta, Jomo. 1962. *Facing Mt. Kenya.* New York: Random House.

Lighthouse-Klein, Hanny. 1989. *Prisoners of Ritual: An Odyssey into Female Genital Circumcision in Africa.* New York: Harrington Park Press.

Marshall, Donald S. 1971. Sexual Aspects of the Life-Cycle. In *Human Sexual Behavior,* Donald S. Marshall and Robert C. Suggs, eds. New York: Basic Books.

NOHARM. 2000.

Rahman, Anika and Nahid Toubia (eds.). 2000. *Female Genital Mutilation: A Guide to Laws and Policies Worldwide.* London: Zed Books.

Saitoti, Tepilit Ole. 1986. *The Worlds of a Maasai Warrior: An Autobiography.* Berkeley: University of California Press.

Shell-Duncan, Bettina and Ylva Hernlund (eds.). 2001. *Female Circumcision in Africa: Culture, Controversy, and Change.* Boulder, CO: Lynne Rienner Publishers.

Singer, Philip and Daniel E. Desole. 1967. The Australian subincision ceremony reconsidered: Vaginal envy or kangaroo bifid penis envy. *American Anthropologist,* 69: 355–358

RELATED WEBSITES

Circumcision, A Virtual Journal
http://faculty.washington.edu/gcd/circumcision/

Circumcision Information and Resources Pages
www.cirp.org

Circumcision Issues
www.eskimo.com/~gburlin/cir.html

Circumcision Resource Center
www.circumcision.org

The Female Genital Mutilation Education and Networking Project
www.fgmnetwork.org

Info-Circumcision
  www.infocirc.org/index-e.htm

National Organization to Halt the Abuse and Routine Mutilation of Males (NOHARM)
  www.noharm.org

National Organization of Circumcision Information Resource Center
  www.nocirc.org/introduction.htm

Research Action and Information Network for the Bodily Integrity of Women
  www.rainbow.org

12

The Geography of Genital Mutilations

James DeMeo

Director, Orgone Biophysical Research Laboratory

This paper summarizes portions of a prior study of the geographical aspects of human behavior among subsistence-level aboriginal peoples (DeMeo, 1986, 1988). The focus here will specifically be on the phenomenon of male genital mutilations. Genital mutilations are often classified as a "cultural practice," but there is growing evidence that this benign-sounding label merely serves to dismiss or evade the painful and contractive effects the mutilations have upon the psyche and soma of the child. Genital mutilations elicit severe pain and terror in infants and children and are often very dangerous to health, which raises important questions how

they could have gotten started in the first instance. People who do not engage in such practices view them almost always with horror and disbelief, while people who do them often have difficulty imagining life without the practice. Oftentimes, the presence or the absence of the rites are seen as important requirements for the selection of a marriageable partner, and very powerful emotions focus upon them. Genital mutilations are among the most strongly defended, or defended against, of all cultural practices. Among the various theories developed to account for the mutilations, their geographical distribution has only rarely been discussed (DeMeo 1986).

The global distributions of the male and female genital mutilations among native, non-Western peoples, along with history and archaeology, suggest their genesis in the deserts of Northeast Africa and the Near East, with a subsequent diffusion outward into sub-Saharan Africa, Oceania and possibly even into parts of the New World. They have generally been transmitted from one region to another by virtue of relocation diffusion, accompanied by phases of military conquest of cultures which do not mutilate by invading cultures which do, or by voluntary adoption in association with other cultural changes of an antisexual and antichild nature. One must keep in mind the **premarital**, **pubertal** character of the mutilations as originally practiced by most cultures, performed at a time of otherwise great sexual interests and passion. *I have demonstrated elsewhere that the global distributions of genital mutilations are similar to that of other patrist antichild, antifemale, and antisexual cultural factors, such as infant cranial deformation, swaddling, the virginity taboo, vaginal blood taboo, male domination of kinship and inheritance, and so on (DeMeo 1986).*

Figures 1 and 2 show the overlapping distributions of various types of male and female genital mutilations, respectively, as they existed among aboriginal, subsistence-level peoples within the last several hundred years. As such, the maps greatly minimize or eliminate the influences of the diffusion of European peoples within the last several hundred years. For example, the maps do not reflect the existence of male circumcision as adopted in the USA over the last 100 years;

North and South American data are composed from aboriginal peoples only. The various forms of the mutilations, and the source for the mapped data, are discussed below. A detailed discussion of female genital mutilation will be given later by Fran Hosken, whose work (1979) provided the basis for the map of female mutilations.

MALE GENITAL MUTILATIONS

Incision, the least harsh of the male genital mutilations, consists of either a simple cut on the foreskin to draw blood, or a complete cutting through of the foreskin in a single place so as to partly expose the glans. Incision existed primarily among peoples of the East African coast, in Island Asia and Oceania, and among a few peoples of the New World. **Circumcision**, a harsher mutilation where the foreskin of the penis is cut or torn away, was and is practiced across much of the Old World desert belt, and in a number of Sub-Saharan, Central Asian, and Pacific Ocean groups. When performed during puberty, circumcision was largely a premarital rite of pain endurance.

FIGURE 1   Male Genital Mutilations

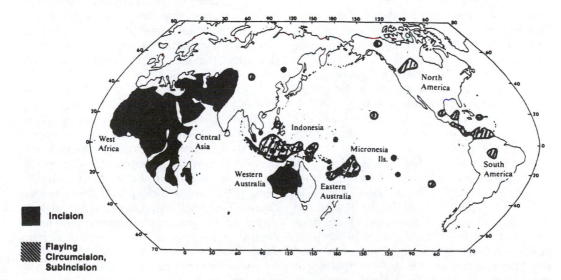

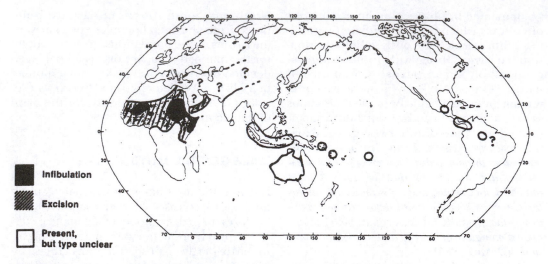

FIGURE 2   Female Genital Mutilations (After Hosken 1979 and Montagu 1945)

Circumcision only gained the status of being a "hygienic operation" in relatively recent times, although the most recent and best medical evidence has in fact shown that routine circumcision has neither short nor long-term hygienic benefits; indeed, it has mild to severe negative psychological and physiological effects. Particularly in the bush, under less than sanitary conditions, the circumcised boy infant or child would have been at greater risk than the uncircumcised boy. The most severe male genital mutilation, a form of **skinstripping**, was practiced along the Red Sea coast in Arabia and Yemen, at least into the 1800s. Here, in an endurance ritual performed on a potential marriage candidate, skin was flayed from the entire penile shaft as well as from a region of the pubis. The community blessing would only be bestowed upon the young man who could refrain from expressing emotion during the event (DeMeo 1986).

Another harsh ritual, **subincision**, was practiced primarily among Australian aborigines and on a few Pacific Islands. It consisted of a cutting open of the urethra on the underside of the penis down to as far as near the scrotum; the subincision ritual was generally preceded by a circumcision ritual. The practice did not confer any contraceptive advantage, and no claims as such were made

for it by the Australian aborigines. The geographical aspects of the Australian genital mutilations has been studied previously, and two competing theories were developed: Northwest Australia, specifically the Kimberly region, was identified as a location where genital skin stripping was performed, and some believed that circumcision and subincision spread into Australia from that region, diffusing to the east and south. On the other hand, independent development of the traits within Australia has been argued, based upon the observation that the most intense forms of subincision occurred in the desert center of the continent, being absent in a few border regions where only circumcision was practiced (DeMeo 1986).

The *Ethnographic Atlas* of G. P. Murdock (1967) provided most of the data for Figure 1. Murdock's *Atlas* also contains raw data on the age at which the mutilations were customarily done among a globally-balanced sample of 350 cultures. A map of that data which I constructed indicated that genital mutilations possessed a widespread distribution, centered on Northeast Africa and Arabia. Furthermore, the greater the distance from those central regions, the older was the male at the time of the mutilation (DeMeo 1986, p. 159). As one moves farther and farther from Africa and the Near East, the males are progressively older at the time of the mutilation. Furthermore, the practices occur less frequently and undergo a gradual dilution of harshness as distance from those central regions increases. Genital skin stripping, the harshest mutilation, was centered on the Red Sea region, and was surrounded by a region practicing only male circumcision. Circumcision, in turn, gives way to the less harsh practice of incision as one moves eastward across the Pacific. Genital mutilations were not practiced at all among most of the aboriginal peoples of the Americas or Eastern Oceania. It was precisely in these regions of mutilation absence where the decorative "penis tops" were most frequently found among native peoples, indicating a similar interest in the genitalia, but only in a decorative and pleasurable sense.

From the standpoint of the pain involved in circumcision as a puberty or premarital rite, the easterly decline in mutilation frequency and dilution of the rite towards less painful methods, and to older ages, makes perfect sense if we **also** assume that the emotional attitudes, beliefs, and cultural institutions which originally mandated the painful ritual were likewise diluted as they were carried eastward from a Northeast African or Arabian point of origin (DeMeo 1986). With the social and emotional root reasons for the rituals becoming diluted with time and distance, less painful methods such as incision were substituted, or it was put off as long as possible, certainly well past the period just before marriage, preferably into the period of old age. Or it was relinquished altogether. In the Near Eastern desert regions where the social institutions and emotional roots for the ritual remained, but where the pain of the mutilation was feared as a puberty/premarital rite, it was occasionally shifted into infancy, or adopted as such from the start.

There have been several phases of diffusion of the mutilations. Egyptian bas-reliefs give the earliest known unambiguous evidence of male genital mutilations, performed as a puberty rite during the early Dynastic era, about 2300 BC (Paige 1978, Montagu 1946). However, it seems probable that genital mutilations, were introduced before 2300 BC, when the Nile Valley was invaded by militant

pastoral nomads, and culturally transformed around 3100 BC. These invaders, who possessed Asian and Semitic characteristics, ushered in an era of divine kings, ritual widow murder, a military and priestly caste, massive graves and fabulous grave wealth, temple architecture, and other trappings of extreme patriarchal authoritarian culture (DeMeo 1986, p. 218–294). As discussed below, cultural tendencies of a similar direction, but of lesser intensity, are positively correlated with genital mutilating cultures of more recent times.

According to biblical scripture, the Hebrews institutionalized the mutilations after the Exodus from Egypt, and it thereafter became a special mark of the tribe. The mutilations appeared widely across the Near East prior to the eruptions of Moslem armies in the 600s AD, but were subsequently spread wherever Moslem armies ventured. While neither male nor female genital mutilations have any specific Koranic mandate, Mohammed thought them to be "desirable," and they predominate in Moslem areas. Still, there are regions of non-Moslem Africa and Oceania which possess the mutilations as a probable diffusion from ancient, pre-Moslem times. Diffusion from these earliest periods may also yet account for isolated, rare examples of the traits in the New World (DeMeo 1986, p. 358–426). [See Figure 3.]

Male genital mutilations were never adopted widely in Europe, European Australia, Canada, Latin America, in the Orient, or by Hindus, Southeast Asians, or Native Americans. The spread of the rite of infant circumcision to the United States during the late 1800s and early 1900s is a most recent phenomenon not reflected on the maps. *Circumcision gained in importance in the USA only after allopathic medical doctors, playing upon prevailing sexual anxieties, urged it as a "cure" for a long list of childhood diseases and "disorders," to include polio, tuberculosis, bedwetting, and a new syndrome which appeared widely in the medical literature known as "masturbatory insanity."* Circumcision was then advocated along with a host of exceedingly harsh, pain-inducing devices and practices designed to thwart any vestige of genital pleasure in children (Paige 1978).

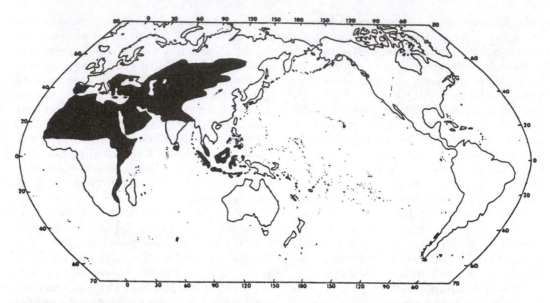

FIGURE 3 Areas Influenced or Occupied by Arab Armies Since 632 AD (after Pitcher 1972). The Islamic empire spread genital mutilations into many new areas of the globe, and reinforced it in others. However, genital mutilations had spread into sub-Saharan Africa, Oceania, and the New World, prior to the Islamic period, notably among caste, high god, and warrior-emphasizing peoples.

Freud and other psychoanalysts have discussed male genital mutilations as inducing a form of "castration anxiety" in the child by which the taboo against incest and parricide is pathologically strengthened (DeMeo 1986). Montagu (1946) and Bettleheim (1962) have discussed their connections to the male fear of vaginal blood, where menstruation is imitated (subincision), or where the male must be ritually absolved of contact with poisonous childbirth blood (infant circumcision), or hymenal blood (pubertal circumcision). Reich identified genital mutilations as but one, albeit a major one, of a series of brutal and cruel acts directed toward infants and children which possess hidden motives **designed** to cause a painful, permanent contraction of the child's physical and emotional self. Reich saw the real purpose of circumcision, and other assaults upon the child's sexuality, to be the reduction of the child's emotional fluidity and energy level, and their ability to experience maximal pleasurable genital excitation later in life, a major step in, as he put it, transmuting **Homo sapiens** into armored **Homo normalis**. Reich

argued *that parents and doctors blindly advocated or performed the genital mutilations, and other painful shamanistic medical procedures, in proportion to their own emotional armoring and pleasure-anxiety, in order to make children more like themselves: obedient, docile, and reduced in sexual vigor and emotional vitality (Reich 1967, 1973).*

These ideas, as disturbing as they may be, find support in cross-cultural comparisons of cultures which mutilate the genitals of their males. Textor's Cross-Cultural Summary (1967) demonstrates positive correlations between male genital mutilations and the following other cultural characteristics (also see Prescott 1975, DeMeo 1986):

High narcissism index
Slavery and Castes are present
Class stratification is high
Land inheritance favors male line
Cognatic kin groups are absent
Patrilineal descent is present
Female barrenness penalty is high
Bride price is present
Father has family authority

Polygamy is present
Marital residence near male kin
Painful female initiation rites are present
Segregation of adolescent boys is high
Oral anxiety potential is high
Average satisfaction potential is low
Speed of attention to infant needs is low
High God present, active, supportive of
   human morality

One cannot extract a list of correlated prochild, profemale, or sex-positive traits from Textor's work as cultures which mutilate the male genitalia do not generally possess such characteristics. Male genital mutilations are found prespent in a cultural complex where children, females, and weaker social ethnic groups are subordinated to elder, dominant males in rigid social hierarchies of one form or another. While the cross-cultural analysis contrasted only aboriginal, subsistence-level cultures, many of the factors identified in the above list are or once were applicable to the USA, where male circumcision predominates. It must be noted, however, that many or most of those patristic characteristics may be present in cultures where genital mutilations are absent, but which can be accounted for by deprivation of physical affection in the maternal infant and adolescent sexual relationships (Prescott, 1975, 1979, 1989).

SUMMARY

The underlying psychology of genital mutilations is anxiety regarding sexual pleasure, mainly heterosexul genital intercourse, as indicated by the associated virginity taboos and ritual absolutions against vaginal blood. In the final analysis, these mutilations say more about predominant attitudes regarding sexual pleasure than anything else.

Given their similar distributions, similar cross-cultural aspects, and similar psychological motifs, the time and location of origins of male and female genital mutilations are probably identical, the use of each being mandated and widely expanded by groups where dominance of the sexual lives of children by adults, and of females by males, was most extreme. The use of eunuchs has died out over the last 100 years with the decline of the harem system, but female infibulations and other forms of female genital mutilation persist in accordance with the arranged marriage system, and other vestiges of a powerful and hysterical virginity taboo.

The genital mutilations of young males and females are major examples of cultural "traits" or "practices" which, on deeper analysis, reveal roots in severe pleasure-anxiety, with sadistic overtones. The parent or tribal elder who cuts the genitals of young children, was subject to the rite himself as a child, and is made very anxious or angry when confronted with a child whose genitals are not mutilated. This incapacity to tolerate pleasurable movement or feeling in others (pleasure anxiety) was first identified for **Homo sapiens** by Reich, who also identified the role that social institutions play in demanding a systematic recreation of trauma and damage in each new generation; primatologists have identified similar processes of abuse transmission at work in monkeys deprived of maternal love in infancy (DeMeo 1986). Prescott (1975) previously confirmed many of these relationships in a cross-cultural manner. The materials summarized here in geographical form further confirm these processes which possess historically identifiable roots in specific regions. The urge to mutilate the genitals of children stems from deeply ingrained cultural anxieties regarding sexual pleasure and happiness. *Genital mutilations always exist within a complex of other social institutions that provide for the socially sanctioned expression of adult sadism and destructive aggression towards the infant and child, with unconscious motivations aimed at destroying or damaging the capacity for pleasurable emotional/ sexual bonding between mothers and babies, and between young males and females.* In the absence of such deeper motivations, genital mutilations would not be welcomed or championed by parents or birth attendants.

REFERENCES

Bettleheim, B. (1962). *Symbolic Wounds*, Collier Books, NY.

DeMeo, J. (1986). On the origins and diffusion of patrism: The saharasian connection, Dissertation, U. of Kansas, Geography Department. University Microfilms, Ann Arbor: see section on "Male and Female Genital Mutilations," p. 153–178.

DeMeo, J. (1987, 1988). Desertification and the origins of armoring: The saharasian connection, *J. Orgonomy*, 21(2):185–213, 22(1):101–122, 22(2):268–289.

Hosken, F. (1979). *The Hosken Report on Genital and Sexual Mutilation of Females*, 2nd Ed., Women's International Network News, Lexington, Mass.

Montagu, A. (1945). Infibulation and defibulation in the Old and New Worlds, *Am. Anthropologist*, 47:464–7.

Montagu, A. (1946). Ritual Mutilation Among Primitive Peoples, *Ciba Symposium*, October, p. 424.

Murdock, G. P. (1967). *Ethnographic Atlas*, Pittsburgh, HRAF Press.

Paige, K. (1978). The ritual of circumcision, *Human Nature*, May.

Pitcher, D. (1972). *An Historical Geography of the Ottoman Empire*, E. J. Brill, Leiden, Map V.

Prescott, J. W. (1975). Body pleasure and the origins of violence, *The Futurist*, April, p. 64–74.

Prescott, J. W. (1979). Deprivation of physical affection as a primary process in the development of physical violence. In *Child Abuse and Violence*, (David G. Gil, Ed.). AMS Press, New York, pp. 66–137.

Prescott, J. W. (1989). Affectional bonding for the prevention of violent behaviors: Neurobiological, psychological and religious spiritual determinants. In *Violent Behavior* Vol. 1: Assessment and intervention. (Hertzberg, L. J., et al., eds) PMA Publishing Corp. New York 1989, p. 109–142.

Reich, W. (1967). *Reich Speaks of Freud*, Farrar, Straus & Giroux New York, p. 27–31.

Reich, W. (1973). *Ether, God & Devil*, Farrar, Straus & Giroux New York, p. 67–70.

Textor, R. (1967). *A Cross-Cultural Summary*, HRAF Press, New Haven.

13

Unmasking Tradition
A Sudanese Anthropologist Confronts Female "Circumcision" and Its Terrible Tenacity

Rogaia Mustafa Abusharaf

Abstract: Female circumcision, or genital mutilation, is a common practice in Africa, where it is performed on young girls, often by those with no medical training and with implements that may not be clean. For Westerners to condemn the practice unilaterally does little good because mothers who bring daughters for the operation believe they are doing the right thing. Long-established social mores are involved. Estimates are that 100 million–130 million women now living have undergone the surgery, which takes several forms, and that each year 2 million girls aged 4–12 do so. Some groups in Asia perform the procedure.

I will never forget the day of my circumcision, which took place forty years ago. I was six years

Source: Unmasking tradition: A Sudanese anthropologist confronts female "circumcision" and its terrible tenacity, by Rogaia Mustafa Abusharaf. In *The Sciences*, March-April 1988 v. 38 n2 p. 22(6). © 1998 The Sciences/New York Academy of Sciences. This article is reprinted by permission of *The Sciences* and is from the March/April 1998 issue.

old. One morning during my school summer vacation, my mother told me that I had to go with her to her sisters' house and then to visit a sick relative in Halfayat El Mulook [in the northern part of Sudan]. We did go to my aunts' house, and from there all of us went straight to [a] red brick house [I had never seen].

While my mother was knocking, I tried to pronounce the name on the door. Soon enough I realized that it was Hajja Alamin's house. She was the midwife who performed circumcisions on girls in my neighborhood. I was petrified and tried to break loose. But I was captured and subdued by my mother and two aunts. They began to tell me that the midwife was going to purify me.

The midwife was the cruelest person I had seen. . . . [She] ordered her young maid to go buy razors from the Yemeni grocer next door. I still remember her when she came back with the razors, which were enveloped in purple wrapping with a crocodile drawing on it.

The women ordered me to lie down on a bed [made of ropes] that had a hole in the middle. They held me tight while the midwife started to cut my flesh without anesthetics. I screamed till I lost my voice. The midwife was saying to me, "Do you want me to be taken into police custody?" After the job was done I could not eat, drink or even pass urine for three days. I remember one of my uncles who discovered what they did to me threatened to press charges against his sisters. They were afraid of him and they decided to bring me back to the midwife. In her sternest voice she ordered me to squat on the floor and urinate. It seemed like the most difficult thing to do at that point, but I did it. I urinated for a long time and was shivering with pain.

It took a very long time [before] I was back to normal. I understand the motives of my mother, that she wanted me to be clean, but I suffered a lot.

—from a 1989 interview with Aisha Abdel Majid, a Sudanese woman working as a teacher in the Middle East.

Aisha Abdel Majid's story echoes the experience of millions of African women who have undergone ritualized genital surgeries, often as young girls, without anesthesia, in unsanitary conditions, the surgical implement a knife, a razor blade or a broken bottle wielded by a person with no medical training. The pain and bleeding are intense; the girls sometimes die. Survivors are prone to a host of medical complications that can plague them throughout their lives, including recurrent infections, pain during intercourse, infertility and obstructed labor that can cause babies to be born dead or brain-damaged.

Female circumcision, also known as genital mutilation, is a common practice in at least twenty-eight African countries, cutting a brutal swath through the center of the continent—from Mauritania and the Ivory Coast in the west to Egypt, Somalia and Tanzania in the east. The ritual also takes place among a few ethnic groups in Asia. Where it is practiced, female circumcision is passionately perpetuated and closely safeguarded; it is regarded as an essential coming-of-age ritual that ensures chastity, promotes cleanliness and fertility, and enhances the beauty of a woman's body. In Arabic the colloquial word for circumcision, tahara, means "to purify." It is estimated that between 100 million and 130 million women living today have undergone genital surgeries, and each year two million more—mostly girls from four to twelve years old—will be cut.

Last December genital mutilation became illegal in Egypt, thanks to a closely watched court and women's groups in Africa and that the landmark ruling will bolster eradication efforts worldwide. But most people working for change recognize that government action, though an important and useful symbol, is ultimately not the answer. Barbaric though the ritual may seem to Westerners, female circumcision is deeply enmeshed in local traditions and beliefs. Treating it as a crime and punishing offenders with jail time would in many cases be unfair. Mothers who bring their daughters for the operation believe they are doing the right thing—and indeed, their children would likely become social outcasts if left uncut. You cannot arrest an entire village.

Make no mistake: I believe that genital mutilation must end if women are to enjoy the most basic human rights. But it does little good for a Westerner, or even an African-born woman such as myself, to condemn the practice unilaterally. We must learn from history: when colonial European powers tried to abolish the surgery in the first half of this century, local people rejected the interference and clung even more fiercely to their traditions. Without an understanding of indigenous cultures, and without a deep commitment from within those cultures to end the cutting, eradication efforts imposed from the outside are bound to fail. Nothing highlights the problem more clearly than the two terms used to describe the procedure: is it circumcision, an "act of love," as some women call it, or mutilation? Contradictory though the answer might seem, it is both.

Because genital cutting is considered an essential aspect of a woman's identity, abolishing it has profound social implications. Think of the politics and emotions in Western countries that have swirled around issues such as abortion, the right of homosexuals to be parents and the ethics of human cloning. Any change that requires a readjustment of long-established social mores makes people highly uncomfortable.

The justifications for female circumcision vary. Some ethnic groups in Nigeria believe that if a woman's clitoris is not removed, contact with it will kill a baby during childbirth.

Other people believe that, unchecked, the female genitalia will continue to grow, becoming a grotesque penislike organ dangling between a woman's legs. Vaginal secretions, produced by glands that are often removed as part of the surgery, are thought to be unclean and lethal to sperm.

Circumcision is also intended to dull women's sexual enjoyment, and to that end it is chillingly effective. In a survey conducted in Sierra Leone, circumcised women reported feeling little or no sexual responsiveness. The clitoris is always at least partially removed during the operation, and without it orgasm becomes practically impossible. Killing women's desire is thought to keep them chaste, in fact, genital cutting is so closely associated with virginity that a girl who is spared the ordeal by enlightened parents is generally assumed to be promiscuous, a man-chaser.

Such beliefs may seem absurd to outsiders. But in the nineteenth century respected doctors in England and the United States performed clitoridectomies on women as a supposed "cure" for masturbation, nymphomania and psychological problems. Today some girls and women in the West starve themselves obsessively. Others undergo painful and potentially dangerous medical procedures—face lifts, liposuction, breast implants and the like—to conform to cultural standards of beauty and femininity. I am not trying to equate genital cutting with eating disorders or cosmetic surgery; nevertheless, people in the industrialized world must recognize that they too are influenced, often destructively, by traditional gender roles and demands.

Local custom determines which kind of genital surgery, part or all of [which] is called clitoridectomy. A second kind of operation [occurs when] the clitoris and part or all minora, the inner lips of the vagina, are cut away. Clitoridectomy and excision are practiced on the west coast of Africa, in Chad and the Central African Republic, and in Kenya and Tanzania.

The most drastic form of genital surgery is infibulation, in which the clitoris and labia minora are removed, and then the labia majora, the outer lips of the vagina, are stitched together to cover the urethral and vaginal entrances. The goal is to make the genital area a blank patch of skin. A Sudanese woman in her sixties I interviewed told me that the midwife performing the surgery is often reminded by a girl's kinswomen to "make it smooth and beautiful like the back of a pigeon." A new opening is created for the passage of urine and menstrual blood and for sex—but the opening is made small, to increase the man's enjoyment. After the operation a girl's legs may be tied together for weeks so that skin grows over the wound. Women who have undergone infibulation must be cut open before childbirth and restitched afterward. Infibulation is practiced in Mali, Sudan, Somalia and parts of Ethiopia and northern Nigeria.

Genital surgery is usually performed by a midwife, either at her home, in the girl's home or in some cases in a special hut where a group of girls is sequestered during the initiation period. Midwives often have no medical training and little anatomical knowledge; if a girl struggles or flinches from the pain, the surgical instrument may slip, causing additional damage. There is also concern that unsterilized circumcision instruments may be spreading the AIDS virus. Among affluent Africans there is a growing trend to have the operation performed by physicians in private clinics—sometimes as far away as Europe—where general anesthesia is administered and conditions are hygienic.

The word circumcision (literally, "cutting around"), which was borrowed from the male operation, is a striking misnomer when applied to the procedures performed on women. Male circumcision, in which the foreskin of the penis is removed, is not associated with health problems, nor does it interfere with sexual functioning or enjoyment. By contrast, the immediate complications of female genital surgery include tetanus and other infections, severe pain, and hemorrhaging, which can in turn lead to shock and death. In July 1996 the Western press reported that an eleven-year-old Egyptian girl had died following a circumcision performed by a barber. The following month a fourteen-year-old girl died, also in Egypt. Countless other deaths go unreported.

Long-term complications of genital surgery are also common, particularly for women who have been infibulated. Scar tissue blocking the urethral or vaginal opening can lead to a buildup or urine and menstrual blood, which, in turn, can cause chronic pelvic and urinary-tract infections. The infections can lead to back pain, kidney damage, severe uterine cramping and infertility. If sebaceous glands in the skin become embedded in the stitched area during the surgery, cysts the size of grapefruits may form along the scar. Nerve endings can also become entrapped in the scar, causing extreme pain during sex.

Childbirth poses many special dangers for the infibulated woman. The baby's head may push through the perineum, the muscular area between the vagina and the anus. Sometimes a fistula, or abnormal passage, between the bladder and the vagina develops because of damage caused by obstructed labor. Women who develop fistulas may suffer frequent miscarriages because of urine seeping into the uterus. In addition, they smell of urine and often become outcasts.

Not surprisingly, depression and anxiety are also frequent consequences of genital surgery—whether spurred by health problems, fears of infertility, or the loss of a husband's attention because of penetration difficulties.

In spite of its grim nature, female circumcision is cloaked in festivity. Girls are feted and regaled with gifts after the operation. In some societies the experience includes secret ceremonies and instruction in cooking, crafts, child care and the use of herbs. After circumcision adolescent girls suddenly become marriageable, and they are allowed to wear jewelry and womanly garments that advertise their charms. Among the Masai of Kenya and Tanzania, girls undergo the operation publicly; then the cutting becomes a test of bravery and a proof that they will be able to endure the pain of childbirth. Circumcision gives girls status in their communities. By complying, they also please their parents, who can arrange a marriage and gain a high bridal price for a circumcised daughter.

The consequences of not undergoing the ritual are equally powerful: teasing, disrespect and ostracism. Among the Sabiny people of Uganda, an uncircumcised woman who marries into the community is always lowest in the pecking order of village women, and she is not allowed to perform the public duties of a wife, such as serving elders. Uncut women are called girls, whatever their age, and they are forbidden to speak at community gatherings. The social pressures are so intense that uncircumcised wives often opt for the operation as adults.

Girls, too, can be driven to desperation. A Somali woman identified as Anab was quoted in a report by a local women's group:

> When girls of my age were looking after the lambs, they would talk among themselves about their circumcision experiences and look at each other's genitals to see who had the smallest opening. Every time the other girls showed their infibulated genitals, I would feel ashamed I was not yet circumcised. Whenever I touched the hair of infibulated girls, they would tell me not to touch them since I was [still] "unclean." . . . One day I could not stand it anymore. I took a razor blade and went to an isolated place. I tied my clitoris with a thread, and while pulling at the thread with one hand I tried to cut part of my clitoris. When I felt the pain and saw the blood coming from the cut I stopped. . . . I was seven years old.

Yet despite the peer pressure and the benefits to be gained from being circumcised, the prospect of the operation can loom threateningly over a girl's childhood, poisoning everyday activities and filling her with fear and suspicion. Memuna M. Sillah, a New York City college student who grew up in Sierra Leone, described in a recent story in *Natural History* how as a child, whenever her mother sent her on an unusual errand, she feared that it might be a trick, that this might be the moment when strange women would grab her and cut her flesh. And Taha Baashar, a Sudanese psychologist, has reported the case of a seven-year-old girl who suffered from insomnia and hallucinations caused by fear of the operation. The problems reportedly improved when the girl was promised she would not be circumcised.

The origins of female circumcision are uncertain. Folk wisdom associates it with ancient Egypt, though the examination of mummies has so far provided no corroboration. Ancient Egyptian myths stressed the bisexuality of the gods, and so circumcision may have been introduced to clarify the femininity of girls. (In some African countries the clitoris is considered a masculine organ, and in the fetus, of course, both clitoris and penis develop from the same precursor tissue.) At any rate, the ritual certainly dates back more than 1,000 years: the eighth-century poet El Farazdaq denounced the tribe of Azd in the Arabian peninsula in one of his lampoons, writing that their women had never experienced the pain of circumcision and were therefore "of inferior stock."

Although female circumcision is practiced by Africans of all religions—Muslims, Christians and Ethiopian Jews, as well as followers of animist religions, such as the Masai—it is particularly associated with Islam. Many Muslims believe the ritual is a religious obligation. In fact, however, **female** circumcision is not mentioned in the Koran, and it is unknown in predominantly Muslim countries outside of Africa, such as Saudi Arabia and Iraq. What seems likely is that when Islam came to Africa, its emphasis on purity became associated with the existing practice of genital cutting—much the way early Christianity assimilated existing pagan rituals such as decorating evergreen trees.

Female circumcision came to European attention long ago. An early historical record can be found in the writings of Pietro Bembo, the sixteenth-century Italian cardinal:

They now . . , sailed into the Red Sea and visited several areas inhabited by blacks, excellent men, brave in war. Among these people the private parts of the girls are sewn together immediately after birth, but in a way not to hinder the urinary ways. When the girls have become adults, they are given away in marriage in this condition and the husbands' first measure is to cut open with a knife the solidly consolidated private parts of the virgin. Among the barbarous people virginity is held in high esteem.

Other Europeans also wrote about genital cutting in accounts that were read by generations of foreign travelers to Africa. But despite some attempts by Christian missionaries and colonial powers to intervene, genital mutilation remained largely unknown abroad until the 1950s, when nationalist struggles gave rise to the women's movement in Africa. It was then that local activists and medical professionals began publicly condemning the practice.

After college I lived in Khartoum and worked for two years at a development corporation. A secretary I became friendly with there, whom I will call Shadia, confided in me that she found intercourse painful because of the effects of her circumcision. She and her husband had agreed, she told me, that any daughters of theirs would not be cut.

Two years ago I returned to Sudan to visit friends, and I looked up Shadia. We had not seen each other for a decade. We embraced; I asked about her children and she pulled out a photograph. I gasped. The three girls, the youngest of whom was about six, were dressed in jewelry and fancy clothes, their hands and feet patterned with henna, and around their shoulders they wore traditional maroon-and-gold satin shawls called firkas. It was unmistakably a picture from a circumcision celebration. How could my friend have had such a change of heart? I was shocked.

Shadia explained. One day while she was at work her mother-in-law, who lived with the family, had secretly taken the girls to be circumcised, in defiance of their parents' wishes. When Shadia's husband, a truck driver, returned home, he was so distraught that he left the house and did not return for a week. Shadia was also heartbroken but she consoled herself that the girls had "only" been given clitoridectomies; at least they had not been infibulated, as she had. "It could have been worse," she told me resignedly.

Entrenched customs die hard, and the task facing anti-circumcisionists is daunting. They can take heart, however, from the precedents: foot binding and widow burning, once widespread in China and India, respectively, have been abolished.

International efforts to end genital mutilation began in 1979, when the World Health Organization published statements against it.

Then, after a gathering of African women's organizations in Dakar, Senegal, in 1984, the Inter-African Committee Against Traditional Practices Affecting the Health of Women and Children was formed; since then, affiliates in twenty-three African countries have been working to end the practice. In 1994 the International Conference on Population and Development in Cairo adopted the first international document to specifically address female genital mutilation, calling it a "basic rights violation" that should be prohibited.

A variety of projects have aimed to end genital cutting:

- Alternative initiation rituals: In 1996 in the Meru district of Kenya, twenty-five mother-daughter pairs took part in a six-day training session, during which they were told about the health effects of circumcision and coached on how to defend the decision not to be cut. The session culminated in a celebration in which the girls received gifts and "books of wisdom" prepared by their parents.
- Employment for midwives: In several African countries, programs have aimed at finding other ways for midwives and traditional healers to make a living. A soap factory set up near Umbada, Sudan, with help from Oxfam and UNICEF is one example.
- Health education: Many African governments have launched public-information campaigns. In Burkina Faso, for instance, a national committee has held awareness meetings and distributed teaching materials. A documentary film, *Ma fille ne sera pas excisee* ("My daughter will not be excised"), has been shown on national television. And in Sierra Leone, health workers found that when it was explained to women that genital surgery had caused their physical ailments, they were more willing to leave their daughters uncut.

So far the success of such pilot projects remains uncertain. The available statistics are disheartening: in Egypt, Eritrea and Mall the percentages of women circumcised remain the same among young and old. Attitudes, however, do seem to be shifting. In Eritrea men and women under twenty-five are much more likely than people in their forties to think the tradition should be abandoned. And in recent years in Burkina Faso, parents who are opposed to circumcision but who fear the wrath of aunts or grandmothers have been known to stage fake operations.

Refugees and immigrants from Africa who arrive in Australia, Canada, Europe or the United States have brought genital mutilation more immediately to Western attention. On the basis of the 1990 U.S. Census, the Centers for Disease Control and Prevention in Atlanta, Georgia, has estimated that at least 168,000 girls and women in the United States have either been circumcised or are at risk. In the past four years the U.S. Congress and nine state governments have criminalized the practice, and similar laws have been passed in several European countries. So far in the United States, no one has been prosecuted under the new laws.

Meanwhile, Fauziya Kassindja, a twenty-year-old woman from Togo, spent more than a year behind bars, in detention centers and prisons in New Jersey and Pennsylvania, after fleeing to the United States in 1994 to avoid circumcision. Her mother, who remained in Togo, had sacrificed her inheritance and defied the family patriarch to help her escape. A U.S. immigration judge initially denied Kassindja's claim of persecution, saying her story lacked "rationality." Later, his ruling was overturned, and Kassindja was granted political asylum.

Western ignorance and incredulity regarding female circumcision have made life difficult and even dangerous for immigrant Africans. I recently met an infibulated Sudanese woman living in New England who was having trouble finding a gynecologist trained to treat her. "I am six months pregnant and I don't know what to expect," she told me fearfully. While pressing for an end to the practice, advocates must not ignore its victims. Perhaps exchange programs should be arranged for American gynecologists and obstetricians, to enable them to learn appropriate prenatal care from their African counterparts.

Every society has rules to which its members are expected to conform. But for African women, belonging exacts too high a price. Whereas African men often have more than one wife and freely engage in extramarital sex, "the acceptable image of a woman with a place in society [is] that of one who is circumcised, docile, fertile, marriageable, hardworking, asexual and obedient," writes Olayinka Koso-Thomas, a Nigerian physician.

The irony is that, in a society that forces women to reconstruct their bodies in order to be socially and sexually acceptable, most men prefer sex with uncircumcised women. In a study of 300 Sudanese men, each of whom had one wife who had been infibulated and one or more who had not, 266 expressed a strong sexual preference for the uninfibulated wife. A second irony is that circumcision does not guarantee a woman a secure marriage; in fact, the opposite may be true. Infibulated women are more prone to fertility problems, which in Africa is grounds for being cast off by a husband. One study has shown that infibulated women in Sudan are more than twice as likely as other women to be divorced.

It might seem odd that women, not men, are the custodians of the ritual—in fact, a Sudanese man recently made headlines by filing a criminal lawsuit against his wife for having their two daughters circumcised while he was out of the country. Why do women subject their daughters to what they know firsthand to be a wrenchingly painful ordeal? Many are simply being practical. "I think that it is very important for the virginity of women to be protected if they want to get husbands who respect them," a fifty-five-year-old Sudanese mother of five girls told me. To get married and have children is a survival strategy in a society plagued by poverty, disease and illiteracy. The socioeconomic dependence of women on men colors their attitude toward circumcision.

But male oppression is not the biggest problem women face in Africa. Africans—men and women alike—must still cope with the ugly remnants of colonialism, the fact that they and their land have been exploited by Western nations and then abandoned. They are struggling to build democratic systems and economic stability from scratch. For African feminists, Western outrage about genital mutilation often seems misplaced. On a continent where millions of women do not have access to the basics of life—clean water, food, sanitation, education and health care—genital mutilation is not necessarily the top priority.

Studies have shown that the more educated women are, the less willing they are to have their daughters circumcised. I have no doubt that when African women have taken their rightful places in the various spheres of life, when they have gained social equality, political power, economic opportunities, and access to education and health care, genital mutilation will end. Women will make sure of that.

◻ PART FIVE ◻

MARRIAGE AND LOVE

READINGS IN THIS PART

INTRODUCTION TO SUBJECT AND READINGS

You may be surprised to learn that in many cultures in the world, your preferred marriage partner would be your cousin. All cultures have regulations about who can marry whom and under what circumstances. In some cultures, partners should come from outside of the group (exogamy), in other cultures the partner should come from within the group (endogamy). In many cultures men are allowed to have more than one wife at the same time (polygyny). In a few cultures, women are allowed to be married to more than one man at the same time (polyandry). There are rules about where the couple goes to live after the wedding; with or near the groom's family (patrilocality), with or near the bride's family (matrilocality), off on their own (neolocality). Rules regarding the economics of marriage also exist. In some cultures a transfer of goods or services moves from the groom or his family to the bride or her family (bride service, bride wealth, or bride price). In other cultures the wealth moves in the opposite direction, from the bride's family to the groom or his family (dowry). There are also rules about divorces, who keeps the children, and property.

The reason for all these regulations relates to the fact that marriage has several important functions in society. It has an economic component, providing for a gendered division of labor, for example, women gather roots and nuts while men hunt large game. Marriage has a political component—it helps to create alliances, a man from one family forms a bond with a woman from another family, and their bonds extend beyond their immediate relationships out to the other family members. Marriage has a social function—it gives people a place in society. Finally, marriage has a physical component—it grants sexual rights and channels sexual activity into culturally appropriate behavior.

The one feature of marriage that I have yet to mention is love. In Western cultures any discussion of marriage would not get very far without raising the subject of love—something that many people believe is a human universal. To test this idea, anthropologists surveyed 168 cultures detailed in the Human Relation Areas Files. They found the concept of romantic love in 87 percent of the cultures. In the article *Mehinaku Men and Women: A Sociology of Marriage, Sex, and Affection* by Thomas Gregor, we are introduced to a culture that would not have been included in the 87 percent. Gregor reports that the Mehinaku consider romantic love to be "absurd." In this mini-ethnography about gender relations in an Amazonian culture, Gregor demonstrates that marriage is about the gendered division of labor. Although the Mehinaku reject notions of romantic love, "A Mehinaku child grows up in an erotically charged social environment." (p. 142) Sex dominates the culture in many ways through sexual jokes, gossip, extramarital affairs, and myths. Yet Mehinaku sexuality is gendered, men and women are supposed to have different sexual natures, and this shapes the relationships between men and women. Thus, although the Mehinaku culture may be new to us, some of the themes running through this mini-ethnography will sound familiar.

Arranging a Marriage in India by Serena Nanda, offers insights into the practice of arranged marriages. In the West we compete for mates, engaging in a courtship system that involves considerable time, energy, money, and anxiety. Marriages are supposed to be about love, attraction, and compatibility. Letting someone else choose our marriage partners for us is unthinkable. To explore this idea, I often begin my marriage lecture by asking my students if they would agree to an arranged marriage. Almost no one ever raises their hand. Next, I ask them to think of themselves as parents. Would they allow their fourteen-year-old daughter to choose her own spouse? Or would they prefer to choose one for her? Almost every hand in the room shoots up. We would not want our children to have the responsibility of making such an important decision. In most countries marriage occurs at an early age, making the arranged marriage an attractive solution for finding marriage partners. Nanda's discussion of the advantages of arranged marriages and the downside to our system raises some interesting issues about how we choose our mates.

What should the role of love be in our lives? In the article *Against Love*, Laura Kipnis critiques love in modern society. The concept of romantic love is old—Eros, the Greek god of love, dates back to 750 B.C.E., the Kama Sutra, penned around 300 C.E., explored love and sexuality unabashedly, and Chinese literature from 600 C.E. details the agony of women and men torn between complying with their arranged marriages and their romantic love for each other. Kipnis discusses how the concept of love has changed through the centuries and about how our expectations of love have also changed. In our postmodern era, we are independent people, making independent decisions and living independently with independently chosen partners. Why then do we have so much trouble with love? Kipnis offers the idea of mutuality, "recognizing that your partner has needs and being prepared to meet them." But are we able to meet all the needs of our partners? Our postmodern independence has led many of us to put all of our eggs into one basket. Our partners are supposed to be our lovers, our best friends, our parents, and siblings. Instead of surrounding ourselves with several people to fill many roles, we choose one person and invest all our emotional/social eggs in the partnered basket. That is why we have to work so hard at our relationships. Love requires work and work is not a very romantic notion.

One of the enduring and oft quoted lines is: "It is better to have loved and lost than never to have loved at all" (Tennyson). By holding this notion dear to our hearts we have perpetuated the mystical and mysterious nature of love. Poets and social scientists have loved love, analyzed love, and now deconstructed love. Now the discourse on love is being taken to a different level. Researchers claim to have found that love affects the brain, and the "chemistry" that is so often sought after is, in fact, a reality (Viegas 2000). Like mutuality, this is not a very romantic notion, but then again, progress has no obligation to be sexy.

TERMS AND CONCEPTS

bride service/wealth/price	incest taboo
caste	matrilocal
courtesans	men's house
division of labor	mutuality
dowry	neolocality
endogamy	Oedipal complex
exogamy	patrilocal
gender antagonism	serial monogamy

CRITICAL THINKING AND QUESTIONS TO CONSIDER

1. In Mehinaku society bachelorhood is an undesirable state. How are bachelors disadvantaged? What gender role "rules" make bachelors' lives uncomfortable?
2. Gregor notes that among the Mehinaku "romance between spouses borders on bad taste." Why is this true? And what is Mehinaku marriage about, if not romance?
3. Gregor argues that extramarital attachments among the Mehinaku contribute to village cohesion. Explain how this works.
4. Nanda notes that Indian brides are highly motivated to make their marriages work. In what ways are marriages in India more difficult for women than they are for men?
5. Make a list of all the advantages to arranged marriages. Make a list of all the disadvantages. Which list is longer? Why?
6. Kipnis states that modern love has developed to "maximize submission" and "minimize freedom." Using her article, support her assertion.

7. In the United States we have bonded love with sex and with marriage. Kipnis discusses the difficulty we have created for ourselves by trying to hold these three things together with one person. According to Kipnis, what is the key to successful long-term intimacy?

FURTHER READINGS

Bledsoe, Carolilne H., and Gilles Pison (eds.). 1994. *Nuptiality in Sub-Saharan Africa: Contemporary Anthropological and Demographic Perspectives.* New York: Oxford University Press.

Bretschneider, Peter. 1995. *Polygyny: A cross-cultural study.* Philadelphia, PA: Coronet Books.

Croutier, Alev Lythe. 1998. *Harem: The world beyond the veil.* New York: Abbeville Press.

Fisher, Helen. 1992. *Anatomy of Love: A natural history of adultery, monogamy and divorce.* New York: Simon & Schuster.

Giddens, Anthony. 1992. *The Transformation of Intimacy: Sexuality, love, & erotism in modern societies.* Stanford: Stanford University Press.

Gough, E. Kathleen. 1959. The Nayars and the definitions of marriage. *Journal of the Royal Anthropological Institute,* 89, pp. 23–34.

Gregor, Thomas. 1985. *Anxious Pleasures: The sexual lives of an Amazonian people.* Chicago: The University of Chicago Press.

Levi-Strauss, Claude. 1971. *The Elementary Structures of Kinship.* New York: Beacon Press.

Schuler, Sidney R. 1987. *Other Side of Polyandry: Property, stratification, and non-marriage in the Nepal Himalayas.* New York: Westville Press.

Stern, Pamela R., and Richard G. Condon. 1995. A good spouse is hard to find: Marriage, spouse exchange and infatuation among the Copper Inuit. In *Romantic Passion,* edited by William Jankowiak, pp. 196–218. New York: Columbia University Press.

Trawick, Margaret. 1992. *Notes on Love in a Tamil Family.* Berkeley: University of California Press.

Van Wagner, Richard S. 1989. *Mormon Polygamy: A history.* Salt Lake City: Signature Books.

Viegas, Jennifer. 2000. Love on the Brain: True love affects brain activity. *Discovery.com News,* 7-12-00.

RELATED WEBSITES

Gender and Sexuality—links to numerous websites dealing with issues
   http://eserver.org/gender/

Marriage Customs, Family, and Rituals—University of Alberta
   www.ualberta.ca/~slis/guides/canthro/marriage.htm

Marriage Systems, Brian Schwimmer, University of Manitoba
   www.umanitoba.ca/anthropology/tutor/marriage/

On the Economics of Polygyny, Ted Berstrom, University of California, Santa Barbara
   http://netec.mcc.ac.uk/BibEc/data/papers/elsercls042.html

Polygyny in Sub-Saharan African by Ian Timaeus, Centre for Population Studies
   www.Ishtm.ac.uk/eps/cps/dfid/37.htm

Population Research Institute Working Papers—Offers dozens of papers on marriage
   www.pop.psu.edu/info-core/library/wp_lists/psu.htm

Sinclair Intimacy Institute
   www.intimacyinstitute.com

◈ 14

Mehinaku Men and Women
A Sociology of Marriage, Sex, and Affection

Thomas Gregor
Vanderbilt University

Kikyala! your "little hammock" just went down to the water.

> —Kama, referring to his
> friend's wife

Among the Mehinaku, the "battle of the sexes" is more than a metaphor. Men and women make insulting sexual jokes in each others' presence and engage in knock-down, drag-out brawls in the course of certain rituals. Much of this book describes the antagonistic character of men's and women's relationships and the price the men pay in fear of women and insecurity about their masculine selves. This focus is of theoretical interest, and it reflects the concerns of Mehinaku masculine culture. It is the oppositional nature of male and female interaction that draws the attention of the villagers. But it is well to remember that

Source: Mehinaku men and women: A sociology of marriage, sex, and affection. In *Anxious Pleasures*, by Thomas Gregor. Chicago, IL: The University of Chicago Press, 1985, pp. 22–38. © 1985 The University of Chicago Press. Reprinted by permission of the publisher.

Mehinaku men and women are also united in enduring relationships of work, residence, kinship, and affection. Before describing the tensions between the sexes, we must document the institutions that link village men and women and provide a basic background in the sociology of Mehinaku male-female relations.

WORK, MARRIAGE, AND AFFECTION

Men, Women, and the Division of Labor

A division of labor is a separation of tasks, yet a basis for interdependence. Among the Mehinaku, the assignment of separate jobs to men and women is the fundamental economic contract. Even a casual observer of village life will notice that men and women are usually found in different places, following different schedules, and engaged in different tasks.

The six haystack-shaped houses that surround the central plaza are the focus of female activities. . . . A glance into one of these buildings during the late morning hours

The village is conceived by the Mehinaku as a great circle formed by the perimeter of houses and the brush and scrub forest beyond. Within the circle is the public plaza and the men's house. These are primarily masculine areas of the community, and they are used for public oratory, rituals associated with the men's house, and wrestling. The houses and the "trashyards" immediately behind them are feminine regions where the women process manioc and take care of young children. Bisecting the community are broad paths that the men clear in order to see visitors well in advance of their arrival in the village. Also visible are two houses under construction and several manioc drying racks, which are built during the rainless months of the dry season.

catches the women of the house at work: making hammocks, processing manioc flour, spinning cotton, or making twine cord. All of these tasks, like women's work in most cultures, are compatible with child care. The job can be quickly put aside to keep a child away from the open hearth or the hot tub of manioc porridge and then resumed with little difficulty. The association of women with the houses and domestic activities is built into the way the villagers conceive of their community. The village is perceived as two concentric rings. In the innermost are the plaza (*wenekutaku,* "frequented place") and the men's house. These are public regions for casual male interaction and organization of community activities. In the outermost ring are the houses and their backyards. This region is feminine in its connotations. A man who hangs around the backyards is derisively called a "trash-yard man," and he is said to be "like' a woman. Boys who spend too much time in these areas are scolded by their parents and ordered away. Only women properly belong in these regions. When they leave, it is for specific tasks, such as getting water, visiting their gardens, and participating in public rituals.

But the women are never quite comfortable beyond the house and yard and move about in circumspect groups of two or three close relatives. On the paths and in the gardens, they are uneasy about the hazards of jaguars, snakes, and "wild" Indians. And on the plaza, the younger women are concerned that the men are staring at them from the men's house and perhaps making sexual comments. The men are more wide ranging in their movements. At a random moment, we find them dispersed about the village. Some are hunting or fishing many miles from home. Others are clearing distant gardens or working on arrows and baskets in the men's house. And a few are to be found aimlessly wandering through the forest in search of whatever adventure may befall them. The men feel at home where the women are out of place.

A Mehinaku feminist who added up the many tasks allotted to the sexes would sense that, as in our own society, the equation does not balance. Steel tools and fish hooks have greatly eased men's work as farmers and fishermen but made no dent in the women's drudgery of producing manioc flour. Following Robert Carneiro's comparable data gathered among the neighboring Kuikuru Indians (1957, 223), I estimate that the Mehinaku men spend only three-and-one-half hours a day in subsistence tasks. Admittedly the work is hard and occasionally dangerous, but it is far less time-consuming than the women's seven to nine hours of processing manioc, fetching firewood, and carrying tubs of water from the stream. When at last these tasks are done, the women are still the main caretakers of small children. Meanwhile, rich in free time, their husbands are off on trading trips to the Indian post, meanders through the forest, and long periods of socializing in the men's house. Only for a few weeks during the dry season when the men clear new fields do they face work that is as demanding of time as that of their wives.

The Mehinaku have made rough but similar calculations, and most will agree that women work longer hours than men. But they do not draw the conclusion that the women are therefore exploited. Rather, they maintain, men and women have different jobs for which they are suited by temperament and biology. Thus Kalu, one of the more assertive women, remarks, "I could not go fishing. The line would cut my hands. I am afraid of big animals. We women have no strength . . . the men are worthy of respect." For Kalu and the other women, the significance of the division of labor between men and women lies in exchange and interdependence. The principal institution that mediates this economic relationship is marriage.

Marriage as the Basic Economic Partnership

On the first morning of his marriage, a young man awakens long before any of the other residents of his house. Slipping out as quietly as possible, he goes to fish in a distant but well-stocked lake. The trip is long, but he would be ashamed if he were to return empty-handed on such an important day. His bride is busy at home, making the sweetest and most delicate manioc bread of the finest flour. On her husband's return, she greets him at the door, takes his catch, and cooks the fish stew. Called the "mistress of the fish stew" (*wakula weketu*), she sends gifts of fish and bread to her relatives and in-laws. Neither manioc or fish alone would make a meal, but when they are distributed together, they are a powerful symbol of the new economic partnership of husband and wife.

Men's and women's craft work is also connected to the symbolism of marriage. Women are known for their ability as hammock makers, and everyone speaks admiringly of the best craftswomen in the village. An essential reason for making a hammock is to fulfill an obligation owed to a man, especially a husband. Properly, a man's hammock is woven from cotton thread, while a woman's hammock is a loosely tied net of palm fiber. As Palui put it as she wove a cotton hammock, "A man's hammock is hard to make, a woman's is easy. A woman's hammock breaks easily. It has so many holes that the mosquitoes eat you when you sleep. This good woven hammock that I am making I will give to my husband." Unlike

Palui, some village women weave poorly made hammocks and make them so infrequently that their families are said to sleep "practically on the ground." The contemptuous and derisive descriptions of these women underscore the more than utilitarian significance of the hammock within marriage. The gift of food and well-crafted material goods celebrates the relationship of husband and wife.

The Plight of the Bachelor

There is no better way to appreciate the value of Mehinaku marriage than to look at the pitiable bachelor. Consider, for example, the case of Tala, a man in his fifties, who has been without a wife for nearly fifteen years. His tattered hammock barely keeps him off the ground, and he has been unable to obtain a manufactured one at the trading post despite his constant importuning. Thinner than many of the other villagers, Tala complains that he never gets enough manioc bread. His sister-in-law usually keeps him supplied, but he cannot ask her to start the fire and bake a new batch as her husband can. Tala is also dependent on other men's women for manioc porridge and water. None of the women, however, get him firewood. On the coldest of nights, he reluctantly hauls his own. When the evening chill has less bite, he wraps himself in a ragged blanket cadged from the post and shivers through the night. But at least he has avoided women's work.

When Tala leaves his house, his frayed arm bands and bead belt show that he has no wife to supply him with cotton thread essential for masculine adornment. Moreover, his unmarried status prevents him from participating in the public ritual and political life of the village as an equal of other men. Only married adults may become "owners" of significant spirits, sponsors of important rituals, and respected chiefs. Bachelors cannot provide the bread and porridge that is the spirit's food and a chief's hospitality. The Mehinaku marital partnership is therefore a unit of participation in vital social events.

Tala is fully aware of the advantages of marriage, and only a shortage of eligible women among the Mehinaku and neighboring tribes has kept him from finding a wife. Once he brought home a woman from the despised Carib-speaking Txicão tribe, but she was never accepted by the village women and soon left. At all times, Tala tries to compensate for his low status by being a particularly energetic fisherman and farmer. Each year when the rains come, he keeps his household well supplied with fish caught in his extensive network of traps along the Tuatuari River. And yet he is never on the same footing as the other men. Lacking basic possessions and living on the margins of the village system of ritual and politics, he is not respected. To his friends, he is an object of pity.

Affection between Husbands and Wives

For the Mehinaku, the idea of romantic love is absurd. Nothing is more ridiculous to the young men who understand some Portuguese than the love songs they hear on their transistor radios: "What is this 'I love you, I love you'?" Amairi asked me. "I don't understand it. I don't like it. Why does the white man make himself a fool?"

Although all romantic love is suspect, romance between spouses borders on bad taste. Husband and wife should respect one another and, to a degree, stand apart. Each represents a set of in-laws to whom the other owes work, gifts, and deference. Whatever potential remains for romantic attachment is further diluted by coresidence with many kinsmen and an elaborate network of extramarital affairs. In this setting, only a new couple (*autsapalui*) is permitted anything more than a low-keyed expression of affection. Typically, a newly married husband and wife sleep together in the same large hammock and spend much of the day in each other's company. As their marriage matures, however, this degree of affection seems foolish. Those who persist risk the laughter of their comrades and supernatural dangers. Excessive thoughts about one's spouse, the villagers say, attract snakes, jaguars, and deadly spirits.

Despite the absence of romance, some husbands and wives take an enduring pleasure in one another's company. Ketepe tells me that his wife is "good" and that she is "dear" (*kakai-apai*; literally, precious or expensive) to him. He likes to take her and his children on long fishing trips so that they can be alone together. Far away from in-laws, village gossips, and the tension of sexual intrigues, they spend the days fishing, collecting wild fruits, and paddling together in their canoe to explore distant streams and lakes. On my most recent visit to the Mehinaku, Ketepe asked that I buy him a large tarpaulin as a roof for his family when they pitched their hammocks together under the trees.

Even couples who are less affectionate than Ketepe and his wife spend a fair amount of time together. It is true that their daily work separates them, but each day, a husband and wife go bathing together and speak to the other couples whom they meet on the trail. In the late afternoon, they may pair off to visit their garden. On the way, they talk about the day's events, their children, and the social life of the community. Unlike the communal houses, the gardens are intimate places where husband and wife have sexual relations and speak in privacy. Returning home, couples eat together around a common hearth, share a common water bowl, and rest in hammocks that are slung closely together. Each of these activities is regarded as an expression of the solidarity of the marital relationship. When husband and wife no longer eat together, when they drink from different bowls and separate their hammocks, they are not far from divorce. Hammock position is an especially good barometer of the pressures and pleasures of marriage. When spouses get along well, they hang their hammocks so that the woman is suspended just a few inches below her husband. Whispering to each other after the children are asleep, they discuss the day's events.

More often, husbands and wives prefer to separate their hammocks, suggesting a degree of distance (though not hostility) in their relationship. In this position, the hammocks are tied to separate poles so that the intimacy of the first arrangement is broken. To place even greater distance between themselves and their mates, spouses attach their hammocks to separate house poles and build the family hearth between them. During severe quarrels, a wife may sleep so that no matter how her husband turns, her feet lie alongside his head. Hammock positions are part of the Mehinaku language of marital intimacy and estrangement, just as double beds, twin beds, and separate bedrooms can make the same point in middle-class American homes. But the Mehinaku use the system to convey one message that is beyond the scope of American sleeping arrangements. When enraged at her husband, a wife may take a machete and cut down her husband's hammock. More than ropes are severed, for this symbolic act may initiate divorce.

The most dramatic evidence of the concern that most spouses feel for one another occurs during prolonged absences. The men's two-week fishing expeditions take them through forest that is believed to be the haunt of dangerous spirits and "wild" Indians who prowl the borders of Mehinaku territory. Wives worry about their absent husbands. The men are concerned about the well-being of their women and families. When the men are away, the village is a quiet, empty place, but in each house there is a symbol of connectedness and concern. On his departure, a husband gives his wife a knotted cord and retains an identical one for himself. Each knot stands for "one sleep," and in the evening, husband and wife loosen a tie, so that they can keep track of the days. When at last the string is untied, a wife knows that her husband will return no later than the next evening.

On one occasion, I recall that Kikayala did not return after the final knot had been loosened and night had fallen. Even though his wife, Pialu, had never seemed to display any special affection for her husband, she became increasingly concerned. Anxiously peering down the trail, she wondered if her husband had been carried off by a forest spirit or attacked by a jaguar. She finally borrowed my flashlight and walked with her son to the edge of the woods to wait. When at last Kikayala arrived, she greeted him calmly, but he must have sensed Pialu's concern and her pleasure in his safe return.

The most extreme form of separation is that occasioned by death. Among the Mehinaku, the death of a spouse initiates a period of seclusion and mourning that is more prolonged and intense than for any other class of relative. The villagers say that the purpose of mourning seclusion is to cry for one's lost spouse. The period of isolation, closely supervised by the deceased's kin, can last as long as a year. The mourner (*katumbachu*) must stay behind a palm-wood partition and speak in a hushed voice. Although initially the bereaved cry copiously, the meaning of mourning seclusion varies. For some it is an expression of propriety and an obligation to in-laws rather than an outpouring of grief. It is a mistake to interpret the institution too romantically, as we might be inclined to do from the perspective of our own society, which lacks long periods of formal mourning. Nonetheless, Mehinaku mourning is a ceremonialization of marriage and an expression of one facet of the idealized relationship of spouses.

SEXUAL RELATIONSHIPS

Within the roles of marriage and kinship, Mehinaku men and women express mutual affection and respect and advance their economic well-being. The bond of sexual attraction is basic to understanding their complex relationships.

Early Sexual Experiences

A Mehinaku child grows up in an erotically charged social environment. Living on close terms with his sexually active older kin and occasionally following them out to the gardens to watch their assignations, a ten-year-old child is already a sophisticate by American standards. His parents openly joke about sex in his presence, and he is likely to be well informed about the village's latest extramarital intrigues. In the open setting of the Mehinaku community, parents cannot wall off sex in a secret adult world. Many of them do just the opposite, openly attributing sexual motivation to their children. As toddlers play and tussle in a promiscuous huddle on the floor, parents make broad jokes about their having sexual relations: "Look! Glipe is having sex with Pairuma's daughter." As a result, there are few mysteries about the facts of life, and some children grow up with a relatively matter-of-fact attitude toward sexuality. "I haven't had sex yet," one eight-year-old remarked to me, "but in a few years I will."

Sex and marriage, like virtually every adult activity, have their counterpart in children's games. In a game called "marrying" (*kanupai*; literally, "taking a wife") little boys and girls sling their hammocks in the trees around the village. The boys bring home "fish" (actually big leaves) to be cooked by their "wives." After the "food" is cooked and consumed, the game has a number of variants. In one, "being jealous" (*ukitsapai*), the children sneak off on extramarital assignations, only to be surprised by furious spouses. In all versions of the game, however, a few of the children may drift off in pairs to experiment in sexual play. Parents do not seem overly concerned about this kind of activity while their children are young and so long as they are discreet. If exposed, mothers and fathers are merciless in their teasing. Children rapidly learn that sexual activity and public exposure do not mix.

By early adolescence, parents are far more concerned about their children's, and especially their sons' sexuality. Maturation, say the villagers, is not an inevitable process. Sexual and physical development must be induced by medicines and sexual abstinence. When a boy is eleven or twelve years of age, his father erects a seclusion barrier of palm-wood staves across one end of the house. The son ties his hammock behind the partition and begins a term of seclusion that, with interruptions, will last for approximately three years. Watching over him during this lengthy period is a spirit, "the master of the medicines," who makes sure that his charge confines himself to quarters, takes medicines to augment his growth, speaks softly, and follows all the dietary rules. Above all, the boy in seclusion must avoid sexual relations. Unlike the little girls he played with when he was young, sexually mature women are dangerous. Their menstrual blood and vaginal secretions can poison the medicines and even induce the medicine spirit to pass a fatal sentence: *makatsiki*, a paralytic disease striking young men in seclusion. . . .

The Network of Sexual Affairs

A boy in seclusion is almost invariably celibate, especially while taking medicines. Toward the end of his stay, however, it is common for him to succumb to temptation and sneak out at night for an affair. Upon hearing of such adventures his father rips down the seclusion barrier and expels his son into public village life. Now the boy is nearly a man, ready to cut his own garden, go on long trips away from the village by himself, and get married. At this point, too, he gingerly enters the elaborate village network of sexual relationships. Arranging sexual encounters with most village women can be a risky and humiliating business. Unmarried girls present no problem since they have no jealous husbands. Their fathers are pleased by a potential son-in-law who sends occasional gifts of fish over to the house as an acknowledgment of his indebtedness. So casual is the attitude toward premarital courtship that girls are said to unabashedly return from an assignation smeared with their boyfriends' body paint.

Unfortunately, from a young man's point of view, there are never many unmarried women. Despite the villagers' toleration of premarital sex, pregnancy out of wedlock is wrong. The *pukapi'inu*, "mother of the illegitimate child," is an object of scorn. The "fatherless" child is himself subject to abuse. As a result, most girls are married as soon as they emerge from the period of adolescent seclusion that follows their first menses. Virtually all sexual affairs, therefore, are extramarital affairs. These are fraught with danger because husbands and wives are sexually jealous. To use the Mehinaku idiom, they "prize each other's genitals" and do not like to see them appropriated by an interloper. Numerous cautionary tales warn the would-be adulterer against the fury of the jealous spouse. In these myths, adulterous couples are beaten, dismembered, put to death, and in one story, glued together in a permanent copulatory embrace. The tale of Patijai and his girlfriend is very much in this genre of cautionary myths (see Gregor 1977, 139, 145–46 for other examples). Our narrator is Ketepe, who has both more girl friends and more cautionary tales than anyone else in the village.

PATIJAI

Patijai went to the garden to have sex with another man's wife. He did not know it, but the husband was following close behind. Patijai and his girlfriend had sex together, and then they worked a little in the garden, weeding. Just then, they heard the husband coming, whistling as he walked on the path. Quickly, Patijai hid in a pile of sticks and leaves. But his foot was not covered up, and the husband said, "Oh, I think I'll clean the garden a little and burn off these sticks and leaves."

"No, don't do that. My mother hid her knife there," said the wife.

"Well, then, look for it."

"No, only mother knows where it is."

"I'll burn it all the same," said the husband, and he did. A huge fire sprang up, and out of the blaze ran Patijai, his hair ablaze.

"There goes your mother's knife, there goes your mother's knife, there goes your mother's knife!" shouted the husband. "You had sex with your lover. I'll club you."

And he struck her, and that was the end of her and the end of her former lover's semen, still in her vagina.

Meanwhile Patijai, his hair burned off completely, went to hide. "What has become of my son," his mother asked the villagers.

"We don't know. Maybe he went off fishing," everyone replied. But one woman had seen what had happened, and she said, "It's good that your son caught on fire after having sex with another man's wife. Sex fiends like Patijai are no good."

In real life, extramarital affairs seldom provoke serious confrontations. Only in the early years of marriage are spouses so jealous that they openly quarrel. As they mature, jealousy is tempered by social pressure that enjoins discretion in managing affairs and avoiding confrontations. A Mehinaku like the jealous husband in the myth is called an *itsula*, "kingfisher," a bird noted for its raucous scolding and aimless flapping about. Only a few of the younger villagers seem to deserve the title.

Even though sexual jealousy is muted, entering the network of sexual affairs is still a delicate matter. One low risk strategy is "buying" (*aiyatapai*) the girl's services with the help of one of her established lovers. In exchange for a small gift to both the lover and the girl, she will agree to meet him for sexual relations and perhaps become a regular girlfriend. A second, bolder alternative is to approach the girl when she is alone in a public place. The path to the river and the bushes behind the houses are favored areas. Here the young man takes the girl firmly by the wrist and says, "Come, let us have sexual relations together." On occasion, the suitor may sweeten his offer with a gift, such as a bar of soap, a comb, or a small handful of beads. If the girl accepts, they will have sexual relations immediately in the bushes; or, fearing her husband, she may suggest that her lover come "alligatoring" (*aiyakatapai*) later in the day. "To alligator," in the vernacular of the Mehinaku men, means to summon women to assignations from small areas behind the houses known as "alligator places" (*yaka epuga*). The use of the alligator (actually the cayman, *Caiman crocodilus*) as a sexual metaphor derives from Mehinaku mythology, which describes the alligator as a libidinous animal who in ancient times had repeated assignations with two village women.

Like the real-life alligator who lies submerged for hours until his prey comes into range, the would-be lover remains concealed in his "alligator place" until his girlfriend comes into view. Even though she may not appear for an hour or more, he has to be patient, knowing how risky a direct approach may be. At last she steps outside of her house, perhaps to prepare some manioc flour. Smacking his lips, he signals her to come to him. The sexual behavior that ensues varies according to the participants' preferences. The most common position is "having intercourse while seated" (*putakene aintyawakapai*), in which the couple sit flat on the ground facing each other, the women's legs over and around the man's thighs. In a frequent variation of the position, the man kneels, resting on his legs, knees spread apart. As in the first case, his partner places her legs over his thighs while he clutches her about the back so that they are both supported. The prone position favored in our society is less frequently used by the Mehinaku, since lying on the ground leaves one vulnerable to insects and is considered unattractive. Most commonly, this position is reserved for "having sex on top of a log" (*ata penwitsa aintyawakapai*), with both partners lying down, the man on top.

These positions are employed when couples have sufficient time and privacy. There are a number of other methods, however, adapted to particular situations and considerably less privacy. The most demanding of these is "having intercourse in the hammock" (*amakwaitsa aintyawakapai*), a feat that requires considerable gymnastics on the part of both partners. Although the basic side-to-side position has been described to me, I cannot understand how a couple can arrange themselves in a small swinging hammock so that they can have intercourse. The task is made doubly difficult by the minimal privacy in which such encounters occur. Occasionally, I am told, a woman will have sexual relations with a lover in her hammock even though her husband sleeps only a few inches away. "Danger," say some of the villagers, "is pepper for sex."

"Standing intercourse" (*enwitsa aintywakapai*) is a fourth position, best adapted to the fleeting moments of chance encounters along the side of a path or in back of a house. Holding his partner about the buttocks and lower back, the man lifts her slightly off the ground while she raises one knee. "In-the-water intercourse" (*unya aintyawakapai*) is the final commonly used position, occurring in the bathing area when a man is briefly alone with his girlfriend. Easiest to perform when the water is about chest level, the physical arrangements resemble those in standing intercourse.

This list of five coital positions does not exhaust the Mehinaku repertory and indicates somewhat more inventiveness than is typical of many societies, including America.[1] Not limiting themselves to one stereotyped act, the Mehinaku vary their techniques to match their mood and situation. Ketepe, for example, prefers the prone position because the penetration is deepest; but, he says "the women usually makes the choice."

Repression and Desire

"All men," Ketepe informs me, "like sex. But women are different." My data support Ketepe's belief to the extent that sexuality has a somewhat different meaning for the women than it does for the men. Men are more overtly sexual, and hence it is possible for women to use their sexuality to secure food and support in exchange for intercourse. Moreover, women are subject to repressive beliefs and practices that confine and even suffocate their sexual natures. From an early age, a girl knows that she is "just a girl" and in many respects inferior to boys. As she matures, she learns that her vagina is "smelly" and "disgusting." She must take care that others do not see it when she sits or walks. With her first menses, she discovers that she is a danger to others. She can be held responsible for contaminating food, defiling sacred rituals, and making men sick. When she enters the network of sexual affairs, she finds that she must comport herself carefully. A casual boyfriend may seize on any unusual or uninhibited conduct in sexual relations and joke about it among his friends. One of the reasons that a woman expects gifts of her lovers is that a token of commitment is insurance that she will not be denigrated in village gossip. Even discreet sexual relationships are risky, however, since pregnancy is known to be painful and dangerous.

A Mehinaku woman's sexuality is thus linked to a sense of inferiority to men, to feelings of disgust about the genitalia, to concern about menstrual contamination, and to fear of unwanted pregnancy. No wonder that some of the women are *kanatalalu*, literally "rejecting women," and in this context "women who do not like sex." At the moment there is only one Mehinaku woman who is widely stigmatized as a kanatalalu, but the men complain that the others are less than enthusiastic. They are, in the male vernacular, "stingy with their genitals." This lack of interest is disturbing to the men. It puts into question both their own attractiveness and the legitimacy of their sexual demands. Women who consistently reject their suitors are the subject of gossip and are referred to as "worthless women" (*teneju malu*).

The men's complaints about the low level of female sexuality may also be related to their own lack of sophistication in sexual technique. With a few notable exceptions, the men do not engage in foreplay or touch the genitals of their partners. Significantly, there is no word in the Mehinaku language for a woman's sexual climax. From my questioning of male and female informants, I am uncertain if any of the women are orgasmic. Certainly it is not an expectation that they have in participating in sexual relations.[2]

Most women, however, take some pleasure in sexual relations even though their level of interest is lower than that of the men. As Kama puts it, "Women act as if they do not want to have sex. You take them by the wrist and say, 'let's go over there.' And they say, 'Not me. I don't want to have sex.' I don't know why they say that. Perhaps they are afraid of the semen. Perhaps it is revolting to them. But when you sit on the ground and the penis goes in, then they like it. They thrust their hips. It is sensual for them."

Once a couple begin to have sexual relations regularly, they regard themselves as "boyfriend" and "girlfriend," a relationship that is in some respects like marriage. Boyfriends and girlfriends exchange food, spindles of cotton, baskets, and even shell jewelry, just as do spouses. As we shall see, men may even assume a quasi-parental role in relation to the children they have fathered.

As of my last visit to the Mehinaku, the thirty-seven adults were conducting approximately 88 extramarital affairs. This figure is only an estimate because the relationship is noncontractual, and opinions vary within the village as to who is having a genuine affair, and who is engaging in an occasional liaison. To put this number in perspective, it would be possible for the villagers to pair off in 340 extramarital (heterosexual) partnerships if they were unrestrainedly promiscuous. If affairs that are in violation of in-law avoidances, the incest taboo, and the respect owed older persons are eliminated, 150 theoretically possible pairings remain. Given that the actual number of partners is 88, I conclude that the villagers' taste for extramarital liaisons is limited primarily by social barriers, such as the incest taboo, and only secondarily by personal preference. In short, village men and women tend to have relations with each other unless they are specifically prohibited from doing so by the rules of their culture.

The sheer number of affairs is evidence of the villagers' intensely sexual orientation. The network of liaisons, however, is more impressive than the modest frequency of actual sexual encounters. These are limited by long taboos associated with rituals and the life cycle, by the absence of privacy within the community, by competition from jealous husbands and more attractive rivals, and especially by the difficulty of finding a willing female partner. These constraints on sex create shortages in the midst of apparent abundance. Nonetheless, several of the young men have told me that when they make the effort (importuning, gifts, verbal coercion), they are able to have sex on a once-a-day basis. The frequency of sex for the average Mehinaku, however, is far less.

Motives for Becoming Lovers and Some Standards of Attractiveness

Table 1 below shows that the number of affairs per person varies widely from zero to fourteen, with age and physical appearance as the main source of variation. Young, physically attractive men and women have more lovers. A youthful woman with long sleek hair, heavy yet firm calves and thighs, large breasts and nipples, small close-set eyes, little body hair and "attractive genitals" (those that do not show the inner labia) is an avidly sought after sex partner.

TABLE 14–1   Mehinaku Sexual Affairs (1972)

Number of Affairs per Person	Number of Persons Having the Affairs	
	Men	Women
0	0	3
1	2	0
2	3	0
3	4	3
4	3	1
5	0	4
6	4	1
7	2	1
8	1	1
9	0	1
10	1	0
11	0	1
14	0	1
	20	17

Appearance in men is also important. A heavily muscled, imposingly built man is likely to accumulate many girlfriends, while a small man, deprecatingly referred to as a *peritsi*, fares badly. The mere fact of height creates a measurable advantage. Men over 5′4″ (N = 7) had an average of six girlfriends at the time of my study, while those under 5′4″ (N = 8) had only 3.4 girlfriends. To a degree, these data reflect the advantage height gives men in their political relations with other men rather than simply their sexual attractiveness. As in our own society, men who are socially successful are more attractive to women as sexual partners.

An additional factor that correlates with numbers of affairs is gender. The average man engages in 4.4 affairs, and most of the men are fairly close to that average. In the case of the women, however, the range or variation is greater. The three most sexually active women in the village account for almost forty percent of the total number of liaisons, while the three least active women account for none of the community's extramarital relationships. In contrast, all of the men have at least one sexual partner, and the three most active men engage in only twenty-eight percent of the total number of extramarital affairs.

The data reflect the different meaning of extramarital relationships for men and women. The men's principal motivation for initiating affairs is sexual desire. The women, on the other hand, seem to value the social contact and the gifts they receive in the course of the affair as well as the physical side of the relationship. The result is that women who do not excite sexual interest (the old, the sick, the extremely unattractive) have little opportunity to engage in affairs. All the men, however, no matter what their age or appearance, can have an affair, or at least a sexual encounter, by offering a gift. All village men, therefore, have some sexual contacts, while some women have none.

The case of Tamalu, the most sexually active woman in the village, illustrates the different meaning of affairs for men and women. At the time of my study, Tamalu had fourteen lovers whom she had rapidly accumulated upon her arrival among the Mehinaku. Her initial reception in the village had been less than enthusiastic, since she sought refuge there after abandoning a husband in another Xingu tribe. Though she was welcomed by her cousins and aunts, the men grumbled about her voracious and bothersome children. Each day, her two daughters were mercilessly teased by the village boys and girls. After Tamalu had been in the village for a while, however, these problems largely abated. Gifts of fish from her lovers began to arrive with clockwork regularity, making it apparent she was an economic asset to her household. In addition, some of her paramours took it upon themselves to protect her daughters from the other village children. Tamalu's case suggests that the pressures and incentives for a woman to engage in extramarital affairs sometimes leave her very vulnerable to the men's advances.

Extramarital Affairs and Mehinaku Society

Despite husbands' and wives' occasional jealous quarrels, I believe extramarital attachments among the Mehinaku contribute to village cohesion. Within the community, affairs may consolidate relationships between persons in different kindreds. Not only must a man find most of his mistresses among distantly related kinswomen, but he may be obliged to recognize children born of the relationship as his own. The network of blood kinship is thereby greatly expanded. There are few Mehinaku, no matter how marginal they may be to the village kindreds, who are wholly outside the orbit of these extensions of normal paternity (see Gregor 1977, 292–94).

Liaisons also enhance community stability by promoting enduring relationships based on mutual affection. Many lovers are very fond of one another and regard separation as a privation to avoid. In a community whose boundaries and unity are not structured by fear of war or by regular patterns of marriage with other groups, the relationship of lovers is centripetal. The traveler to other villages or the man who takes his family to a distant dry-season garden is never far from home in his thoughts. Eventually, he will return to his community and the pleasures of his extramarital affairs. Finally, even invidious gossip and jealous intrigues are a part of the beat of Mehinaku community life. The culture of sexual liaisons makes the village an exciting and interesting place. As Ketepe often explained to me, "Good fish get dull, but sex is always fun."

Mehinaku men and women enjoy an organic and complex relationship. Attracted to each other by an enthusiastic heterosexuality, benefiting from the affection they owe each other as spouses and kinsmen, and profiting from their exchanges of material goods, they appear to stand united and indivisible. Yet within this pattern of attraction, they are in many respects opposed. Mehinaku society is separated into a male and a female world by fears of sexual pollution, antagonism, and anxiety. . . .

NOTES

1. The relatively stereotyped pattern of sexual relations is noted in Kinsey's classic study of American male sexuality: "Universally, at all social levels in our Anglo-American culture, the opinion is held that there is one coital position which is biologically natural, and that all others are man-devised variants which become perversions when regularly engaged in" (Kinsey, Pomeroy, and Martin 1948, 373).

2. The preceding discussion was suggested to me by Emilienne Ireland, whose research among the Waura (neighbors of the Mehinaku) has increased my awareness of the difficulties faced by the Mehinaku women.

15
Arranging a Marriage in India

Serena Nanda

John Jay College of Criminal Justice

Sister and doctor brother-in-law invite correspondence from North Indian professionals only, for a beautiful, talented, sophisticated, intelligent sister, 5′3″, slim, M.A. in textile design, father a senior civil officer. Would prefer immigrant doctors, between 26–29 years. Reply with full details and returnable photo.

A well-settled uncle invites matrimonial correspondence from slim, fair, educated South Indian girl, for his nephew, 25 years, smart, M.B.A., green card holder, 5′6″. Full particulars with returnable photo appreciated.

Matrimonial Advertisements,
India Abroad

In India, almost all marriages are arranged. Even among the educated middle classes in modern, urban India, marriage is as much a concern of the families as it is of the individuals. So customary is the practice of arranged marriage that there is a special

name for a marriage which is not arranged: It is called a "love match."

On my first field trip to India, I met many young men and women whose parents were in the process of "getting them married." In many cases, the bride and groom would not meet each other before the marriage. At most they might meet for a brief conversation, and this meeting would take place only after their parents had decided that the match was suitable. Parents do not compel their children to marry a person who either marriage partner finds objectionable. But only after one match is refused will another be sought.

As a young American woman in India for the first time, I found this custom of arranged marriage oppressive. How could any intelligent young person agree to such a marriage without great reluctance? It was contrary to everything I believed about the importance of romantic love as the only basis of a happy marriage. It also clashed with my strongly held notions that the choice of such an intimate and permanent relationship could be made only by the individuals involved. Had

Source: Arranging a marriage in India, by Serena Nanda (1992) in *The Naked Anthropologist*, edited by Phillip R. Devita. New York: Wadsworth Publishing Company, pp. 34–45. © 1992 Serena Nanda.

anyone tried to arrange my marriage, I would have been defiant and rebellious!

At the first opportunity, I began, with more curiosity than tact, to question the young people I met on how they felt about this practice. Sita, one of my young informants, was a college graduate with a degree in political science. She had been waiting for over a year while her parents were arranging a match for her. I found it difficult to accept the docile manner in which this well-educated young woman awaited the outcome of a process that would result in her spending the rest of her life with a man she hardly knew, a virtual stranger, picked out by her parents.

"How can you go along with this?" I asked her, in frustration and distress. "Don't you care who you marry?"

"Of course I care," she answered. "This is why I must let my parents choose a boy for me. My marriage is too important to be arranged by such an inexperienced person as myself. In such matters, it is better to have my parents' guidance."

I had learned that young men and women in India do not date and have very little social life involving members of the opposite sex. Although I could not disagree with Sita's reasoning, I continued to pursue the subject.

"But how can you marry the first man you have ever met? Not only have you missed the fun of meeting a lot of different people, but you have not given yourself the chance to know who is the right man for you."

"Meeting with a lot of different people doesn't sound like any fun at all," Sita answered. "One hears that in America the girls are spending all their time worrying about whether they will meet a man and get married. Here we have the chance to enjoy our life and let our parents do this work and worrying for us."

She had me there. The high anxiety of the competition to "be popular" with the opposite sex certainly was the most prominent feature of life as an American teenager in the late fifties. The endless worrying about the rules that governed our behavior and about our popularity ratings sapped both our self-esteem and our enjoyment of adolescence. I reflected that absence of this competition in India most certainly may have contributed to the self-confidence and natural charm of so many of the young women I met.

And yet, the idea of marrying a perfect stranger, whom one did not know and did not "love," so offended my American ideas of individualism and romanticism, that I persisted with my objections.

"I still can't imagine it," I said. "How can you agree to marry a man you hardly know?"

"But of course he will be known. My parents would never arrange a marriage for me without knowing all about the boy's family background. Naturally we will not rely only on what the family tells us. We will check the particulars out ourselves. No one will want their daughter to marry into a family that is not good. All these things we will know beforehand."

Impatiently, I responded, "Sita, I don't mean know the family, I mean, know the man. How can you marry someone you don't know personally and don't love? How can you think of spending your life with someone you may not even like?"

"If he is a good man, why should I not like him?" she said. "With you people, you know the boy so well before you marry, where will be the fun to get married? There will be no mystery and no romance. Here we have the whole of our married life to get to know and love our husband. This way is better, is it not?"

Her response made further sense, and I began to have second thoughts on the matter. Indeed, during months of meeting many intelligent young Indian people, both male and female, who had the same ideas as Sita, I saw arranged marriages in a different light. I also saw the importance of the family in Indian life and realized that a couple who took their marriage into their own hands was taking a big risk, particularly if their families were irreconcilably opposed to the match. In a country where every important resource in life—a job, a house, a social circle—is gained through family connections, it seemed foolhardy to cut oneself off from a supportive social network and depend solely on one person for happiness and success.

Six years later I returned to India to again do fieldwork, this time among the middle class in Bombay, a modern, sophisticated city. From the experience of my earlier visit, I decided to include a study of arranged marriages in my project. By this time I had met many Indian couples whose marriages had been arranged and who seemed very happy. Particularly in contrast to the fate of many of my married friends in the United States who were already in the process of divorce, the positive aspects of arranged marriages appeared to me to outweigh the negatives. In fact, I thought I might even participate in arranging a marriage myself. I had been fairly successful in the United States in "fixing up" many of my friends, and I was confident that my matchmaking skills could be easily applied to this new situation, once I learned the basic rules. "After all," I thought, "how complicated can it be? People want pretty much the same things in a marriage whether it is in India or America."

An opportunity presented itself almost immediately. A friend from my previous Indian trip was in the process of arranging for the marriage of her eldest son. In India there is a perceived shortage of "good boys," and since my friend's family was eminently respectable and the boy himself personable, well educated, and nice looking, I was sure that by the end of my year's fieldwork, we would have found a match.

The basic rule seems to be that a family's reputation is most important. It is understood that matches would be arranged only within the same caste and general social class, although some crossing of subcastes is permissible if the class positions of the bride's and groom's families are similar. Although dowry is now prohibited by law in India, extensive gift exchanges took place with every marriage. Even when the boy's family do not "make demands," every girl's family nevertheless feels the obligation to give the traditional gifts, to the girl, to the boy, and to the boy's family. Particularly when the couple would be living in the joint family—that is, with the boy's parents and his married brothers and their families, as well as with unmarried siblings—which is still very common even among the urban, upper-middle class in India, the girl's parents are anxious to establish smooth relations between their family and that of the boy. Offering the proper gifts, even when not called "dowry," is often an important factor in influencing the relationship between the bride's and groom's families and perhaps, also, the treatment of the bride in her new home.

In a society where divorce is still a scandal and where, in fact, the divorce rate is exceedingly low, an arranged marriage is the beginning of a lifetime relationship not just between the bride and groom but between their families as well. Thus, while a girl's looks are important, her character is even more so, for she is being judged as a prospective daughter-in-law as much as a prospective bride. Where she would be living in a joint family, as was the case with my friend, the girl's ability to get along harmoniously in a family is perhaps the single most important quality in assessing her suitability.

My friend is a highly esteemed wife, mother, and daughter-in-law. She is religious, soft-spoken, modest, and deferential. She rarely gossips and never quarrels, two qualities highly desirable in a woman. A family that has the reputation for gossip and conflict among its womenfolk will not find it easy to get good wives for their sons. Parents will not want to send their daughter to a house in which there is conflict.

My friend's family were originally from North India. They had lived in Bombay, where her husband owned a business, for forty years. The family had delayed in seeking a match for their eldest son because he had been an Air Force pilot for several years, stationed in such remote places that it had seemed fruitless to try to find a girl who would be willing to accompany him. In their social class, a military career, despite its economic security, has little prestige and is considered a drawback in finding a suitable bride. Many families would not allow their daughters to marry a man in an occupation so potentially dangerous and which requires so much moving around.

The son had recently left the military and joined his father's business. Since he was a college graduate, modern, and well traveled, from such a good family, and, I thought, quite handsome, it seemed to me that he, or rather his family, was in a position to pick and choose. I said as much to my friend.

While she agreed that there were many advantages on their side, she also said, "We must keep in mind that my son is both short and dark; these are drawbacks in finding the right match." While the boy's height had not escaped my notice, "dark" seemed to me inaccurate; I would have called him "wheat" colored perhaps, and in any case, I did not realize that color would be a consideration. I discovered, however, that while a boy's skin color is a less important consideration than a girl's, it is still a factor.

An important source of contacts in trying to arrange her son's marriage was my friend's social club in Bombay. Many of the women had daughters of the right age, and some had already expressed an interest in my friend's son. I was most enthusiastic about the possibilities of one particular family who had five daughters, all of whom were pretty, demure, and well educated. Their mother had told my friend, "You can have your pick for your son, whichever one of my daughters appeals to you most."

I saw a match in sight. "Surely," I said to my friend, "we will find one there. Let's go visit and make our choice." But my friend held back; she did not seem to share my enthusiasm, for reasons I could not then fathom.

When I kept pressing for an explanation of her reluctance, she admitted, "See, Serena, here is the problem. The family has so many daughters, how will they be able to provide nicely for any of them? We are not making any demands, but still, with so many daughters to marry off, one wonders whether she will even be able to make a proper wedding. Since this is our eldest son, it's best if we marry him to a girl who is the only daughter, then the wedding will truly be a gala affair." I argued that surely the quality of the girls themselves made up for any deficiency in the elaborateness of the wedding. My friend admitted this point but still seemed reluctant to proceed.

"Is there something else?" I asked her, "some factor I have missed?" "Well," she finally said, "there is one other thing. They have one daughter already married and living in Bombay. The mother is always complaining to me that the girl's in-laws don't let her visit her own family often enough. So it makes me wonder, will she be that kind of mother who always wants her daughter at her own home? This will prevent the girl from adjusting to our house. It is not a good thing." And so, this family of five daughters was dropped as a possibility.

Somewhat disappointed, I nevertheless respected my friend's reasoning and geared up for the next prospect. This was also the daughter of a woman in my friend's social club. There was clear interest in this family and I could see why. The family's reputation was excellent; in fact, they came from a sub-caste slightly higher than my friend's own. The girl, who was an only daughter, was pretty and well educated and had a brother studying in the United States. Yet, after expressing an interest to me in this family, all talk of them suddenly died down and the search began elsewhere.

"What happened to that girl as a prospect?" I asked one day. "You never mention her any more. She is so pretty and so educated, what did you find wrong?"

"She is too educated. We've decided against it. My husband's father saw the girl on the bus the other day and thought her forward. A girl who 'roams about' the city by herself is not the girl for our family." My disappointment this time was even greater, as I thought the son would have liked the girl very much. But then I thought, my friend is right, a girl who is going to live in a joint family cannot be too independent or she will make life miserable for everyone. I also learned that if the family of the girl has even a slightly higher social status than the family of the boy, the bride may think herself too good for them, and this too will cause problems. Later my friend admitted to me that this had been an important factor in her decision not to pursue the match.

The next candidate was the daughter of a client of my friend's husband. When the client learned that the family was looking for a match for their son, he said, "Look no further, we have a daughter." This man then invited my friends to dinner to see the girl. He had already seen their son at the office and decided that "he liked the boy." We all went together for tea, rather than dinner— it was less of a commitment—and while we were there, the girl's mother showed us around the house. The girl was studying for her exams and was briefly introduced to us.

After we left, I was anxious to hear my friend's opinion. While her husband liked the family very much and was impressed with his client's business accomplishments and reputation, the wife didn't like the girl's looks. "She is short, no doubt, which is an important plus point, but she is also fat and wears glasses." My friend obviously thought she could do better for her son and asked her husband to make his excuses to his client by saying that they had decided to postpone the boy's marriage indefinitely.

By this time almost six months had passed and I was becoming impatient. What I had thought would be an easy matter to arrange was turning out to be quite complicated. I began to believe that between my friend's desire for a girl who was modest enough to fit into her joint family, yet attractive and educated enough to be an acceptable partner for her son, she would not find anyone suitable. My friend laughed at my impatience: "Don't be so much in a hurry," she said. "You Americans want everything done so quickly. You get married quickly and then just as quickly get divorced. Here we take marriage more seriously. We must take all the factors into account. It is not enough for us to learn by our mistakes. This is too serious a business. If a mistake is made we have not only ruined the life of our son or daughter, but we have spoiled the reputation of our family as well. And that will make it much harder for their brothers and sisters to get married. So we must be very careful."

What she said was true and I promised myself to be more patient, though it was not easy. I had really hoped and expected that the match would be made before my year in India was up. But it was not to be. When I left India my friend seemed no further along in finding a suitable match for her son than when I had arrived.

Two years later, I returned to India and still my friend had not found a girl for her son. By this time, he was close to thirty, and I think she was a little worried. Since she knew I had friends all over India, and I was going to be there for a year, she asked me to "help her in this work" and keep an eye out for someone suitable. I was flattered that my judgment was respected, but knowing now how complicated the process was, I had lost my earlier confidence as a matchmaker. Nevertheless, I promised that I would try.

It was almost at the end of my year's stay in India that I met a family with a marriageable daughter whom I felt might be a good possibility for my friend's son. The girl's father was related to a good friend of mine and by coincidence came from the same village as my friend's husband. This new family had a successful business in a medium-sized city in central India and were from the same subcaste as my friend. The daughter was pretty and chic; in fact, she had studied fashion design in college. Her parents would not allow her to go off by herself to any of the major cities in India where she could make a career, but they had compromised with her wish to work by allowing her to run a small dressmaking boutique from their home. In spite of her desire to have a career, the daughter was both modest and home-loving and had had a traditional, sheltered upbringing. She had only one other sister, already married, and a brother who was in his father's business.

I mentioned the possibility of a match with my friend's son. The girl's parents were most interested. Although their daughter was not eager to marry just yet, the idea of living in Bombay—a sophisticated, extremely fashion-conscious city where she could continue her education in clothing design—was a great inducement. I gave the girl's father my friend's address and suggested that when they went to Bombay on some business or whatever, they look up the boy's family.

Returning to Bombay on my way to New York, I told my friend of this newly discovered possibility. She seemed to feel there was potential but, in spite of my urging, would not make any moves herself. She rather preferred to wait for the girl's family to call upon them. I hoped something would come of this introduction, though by now I had learned to rein in my optimism.

A year later I received a letter from my friend. The family had indeed come to visit Bombay, and their daughter and my friend's daughter, who were near in age, had become very good friends. During that year, the two girls had frequently visited each other. I thought things looked promising.

Last week I received an invitation to a wedding: My friend's son and the girl were getting married. Since I had found the match, my presence was particularly requested at the wedding. I was thrilled. Success at last! As I prepared to leave for India, I began thinking, "Now, my friend's younger son, who do I know who has a nice girl for him . . . ?"

Further Reflections on Arranged Marriage

Serena Nanda

John Jay College of Criminal Justice

The previous essay was written from the point of view of a family seeking a daughter-in-law. Arranged marriage looks somewhat different from the point of view of the bride and her family. Arranged marriage continues to be preferred, even among the more educated, Westernized sections of the Indian population. Many young women from these families still go along, more or less willingly, with the practice, and also with the specific choices of their families. Young women do get excited about the prospects of their marriage, but there is also ambivalence and increasing uncertainty, as the bride contemplates leaving the comfort and familiarity of her own home, where as a "temporary guest" she has often been indulged, to live among strangers. Even in the best situation, she will now come under the close scrutiny of her husband's family. How she dresses, how she behaves, how she gets along with others, where she goes, how she spends her time, her domestic abilities—all of this and much more—will be observed and commented on by a whole new set of relations. Her interaction with her family of birth will be monitored and curtailed considerably. Not only

will she leave their home, but with increasing geographic mobility, she may also live very far from them, perhaps even on another continent. Too much expression of her fondness for her own family, or her desire to visit them, may be interpreted as an inability to adjust to her new family, and may become a source of conflict. In an arranged marriage, the burden of adjustment is clearly heavier for a woman than for a man. And that is in the best of situations.

In less happy circumstances, the bride may be a target of resentment and hostility from her husband's family, particularly her mother-in-law or her husband's unmarried sisters, for whom she is now a source of competition for the affection, loyalty, and economic resources of their son or brother. If she is psychologically, or even physically abused, her options are limited, as returning to her parent's home, or divorce, are still very stigmatized. For most Indians, marriage and motherhood are still considered the only suitable roles for a woman, even for those who have careers, and few women can comfortably contemplate remaining unmarried. Most families still consider "marrying off" their daughters as a compelling religious duty and social necessity. This increases a bride's sense of obligation to make the marriage a success, at whatever cost to her own personal happiness.

The vulnerability of a new bride may also be intensified by the issue of dowry, that although illegal, has become a more pressing issue in the consumer conscious society of contemporary urban India. In many cases, where a groom's family is not satisfied with the amount of dowry a bride brings to her marriage, the young bride will be constantly harassed to get her parents to give more. In extreme cases, the bride may even be murdered, and the murder disguised as an accident or suicide. This also offers the husband's family an opportunity to arrange another match for him, thus bringing in another dowry. This phenomenon, called dowry death, calls attention not just to the "evils of dowry" but to larger issues of the powerlessness of women as well.

16

Against Love
A Treatise on the Tyranny of Two

Laura Kipnis
Northwestern University

nontraditional empirical research piece

Love is, as we know, a mysterious and controlling force. It has vast power over our thoughts and life decisions. It demands our loyalty, and we, in turn, freely comply. Saying no to love isn't simply heresy; it is tragedy—the failure to achieve what is most essentially human. So deeply internalized is our obedience to this most capricious despot that artists create passionate odes to its cruelty, and audiences seem never to tire of the most deeply unoriginal mass spectacles devoted to rehearsing the litany of its torments, fixating their very beings on the narrowest glimmer of its fleeting satisfactions.

Yet despite near total compliance, a buzz of social nervousness attends the subject. If a society's lexicon of romantic pathologies reveals its particular anxieties, high on our own list would be diagnoses like "inability to settle down" or "immaturity," leveled at those who stray from the norms of domestic coupledom either by refusing entry in the first place or, once installed, pursuing various escape routes: excess independence, ambivalence, "straying," divorce. For the modern lover, "maturity" isn't a depressing signal of impending decrepitude but a sterling achievement, the sine qua non of a lover's qualifications to love and be loved.

This injunction to achieve maturity—synonymous in contemporary usage with 30-year mortgages, spreading waistlines and monogamy— obviously finds its raison d'être in modern love's central anxiety, that structuring social contradiction the size of the San Andreas Fault: namely, the expectation that romance and sexual attraction can last a lifetime of coupled togetherness despite much hard evidence to the contrary.

Ever optimistic, heady with love's utopianism, most of us eventually pledge ourselves to unions that will, if successful, far outlast the desire that impelled them into being. The prevailing cultural wisdom is that even if sexual desire tends to be a short-lived phenomenon, "mature love" will kick in to save the

Source: Against love by Laura Kipnis. In *The New York Times Magazine*, 10–14–2001, pp. 98–102. Copyright © 2001 by the New York Times Co. Reprinted by permission.

day when desire flags. The issue that remains unaddressed is whether cutting off other possibilities of romance and sexual attraction for the more muted pleasures of mature love isn't similar to voluntarily amputating a healthy limb: a lot of anesthesia is required and the phantom pain never entirely abates. But if it behooves a society to convince its citizenry that wanting change means personal failure or wanting to start over is shameful or simply wanting more satisfaction than what you have is an illicit thing, clearly grisly acts of self-mutilation will be required.

There hasn't always been quite such optimism about love's longevity. For the Greeks, inventors of democracy and a people not amenable to being pushed around by despots, love was a disordering and thus preferably brief experience. During the reign of courtly love, love was illicit and usually fatal. Passion meant suffering: the happy ending didn't yet exist in the cultural imagination. As far as togetherness as an eternal ideal, the 12th-century advice manual "De Amore et Amor is Remedio" ("On Love and the Remedies of Love") warned that too many opportunities to see or chat with the beloved would certainly decrease love.

The innovation of happy love didn't even enter the vocabulary of romance until the 17th century. Before the 18th century—when the family was primarily an economic unit of production rather than a hothouse of Oedipal tensions—marriages were business arrangements between families; participants had little to say on the matter. Some historians consider romantic love a learned behavior that really only took off in the late 18th century along with the new fashion for reading novels, though even then affection between a husband and wife was considered to be in questionable taste.

Historians disagree, of course. Some tell the story of love as an eternal and unchanging essence; others, as a progress narrative over stifling social conventions. (Sometimes both stories are told at once; consistency isn't required.) But has modern love really set us free? Fond as we are of projecting our own emotional quandaries back through history, construing vivid costume dramas featuring medieval peasants or biblical courtesans sharing their feelings with the post-Freudian savvy of lifelong analysands, our amatory predecessors clearly didn't share all our particular aspirations about their romantic lives.

We, by contrast, feel like failures when love dies. We believe it could be otherwise. Since the cultural expectation is that a state of coupled permanence is achievable, uncoupling is experienced as crisis and inadequacy—even though such failures are more the norm than the exception.

As love has increasingly become the center of all emotional expression in the popular imagination, anxiety about obtaining it in sufficient quantities—and for sufficient duration—suffuses the population. Everyone knows that as the demands and expectations on couples escalated, so did divorce rates. And given the current divorce statistics (roughly 50 percent of all marriages end in divorce), all indications are that whomever you love today—your beacon of hope, the center of all your optimism—has a good chance of becoming your worst nightmare tomorrow. (Of course, that 50 percent are those who actually leave their unhappy marriages and not a particularly good indication of the happiness level or nightmare potential of those who remain.) Lawrence Stone, a historian of marriage, suggests—rather jocularly, you can't help thinking—that today's rising divorce rates are just a modern technique for achieving what was once taken care of far more efficiently by early mortality.

Love may or may not be a universal emotion, but clearly the social forms it takes are infinitely malleable. It is our culture alone that has dedicated itself to allying the turbulence of romance and the rationality of the long-term couple, convinced that both love and sex are obtainable from one person over the course of decades, that desire will manage to sustain itself for 30 or 40 or 50 years and that the supposed fate of social stability is tied to sustaining a fleeting experience beyond its given life span.

Of course, the parties involved must "work" at keeping passion alive (and we all know how much fun that is), the presumption being that even after living in close proximity to someone for a historically unprecedented length of time, you will still muster the requisite desire to achieve sexual congress on a regular basis. (Should passion fizzle out, just give up sex. Lack of desire for a mate is never an adequate rationale for "looking elsewhere.") And it is true, many couples do manage to perform enough psychic retooling to reshape the anarchy of desire to the confines of the marriage bed, plugging away at the task year after year (once a week, same time, same position) like diligent assembly-line workers, aided by the occasional fantasy or two to help get the old motor to turn over, or keep running, or complete the trip. And so we have the erotic life of a nation of workaholics: if sex seems like work, clearly you're not working hard enough at it.

But passion must not be allowed to die! The fear—or knowledge—that it does shapes us into particularly conflicted psychological beings, perpetually in search of prescriptions and professional interventions, regardless of cost or consequence. Which does have its economic upside, at least. Whole new sectors of the economy have been spawned, with massive social investment in new technologies from Viagra to couples' porn: capitalism's Lourdes for dying marriages.

There are assorted low-tech solutions to desire's dilemmas too. Take advice. In fact, take more and more advice. Between print, airwaves and the therapy industry, if there were any way to quantify the G.N.P. in romantic counsel, it would be a staggering number. Desperate to be cured of love's temporality, a love-struck populace has molded itself into an advanced race of advice receptacles, like some new form of miracle sponge that can instantly absorb many times its own body weight in wetness.

Inexplicably, however, a rebellious breakaway faction keeps trying to leap over the wall and emancipate themselves, not from love itself—unthinkable!—but from love's domestic confinements. The escape routes are well trodden—love affairs, midlife crises—though strewn with the left-behind luggage of those who encountered unforeseen obstacles along the way (panic, guilt, self-engineered exposures) and beat self-abashed retreats to their domestic gulags, even after pledging body and soul to new-found loves in the balmy utopias of nondomesticated romances. Will all the adulterers in the audience please stand up? You know who you are. Don't be embarrassed! Adulterers aren't just "playing around." These are our home-grown closet social theorists, because adultery is not just a referendum on the sustainability of monogamy; it is a veiled philosophical discussion about the social contract itself. The question on the table is this: "How much renunciation of desire does society demand of us, versus the degree of gratification it provides?" Clearly, the adulterer's answer, following a long line of venerable social critics, would be, "Too much."

But what exactly is it about the actual lived experience of modern domestic love that would make flight such a compelling option for so many? Let us briefly examine those material daily life conditions.

Fundamentally, to achieve love and qualify for entry into that realm of salvation and transcendence known as the couple (the secular equivalent of entering a state of divine grace), you must *be* a lovable person. And what precisely does being lovable entail? According to the tenets of modern love, it requires an advanced working knowledge of the intricacies of *mutuality*.

Mutuality means recognizing that your partner has needs and being prepared to meet them. This presumes, of course, that the majority of those needs can and should be met by one person. (Question this, and you question the very foundations of the institution. So don't.) These needs of ours run deep, a tangled underground morass of ancient, gnarled roots, looking to ensnarl any hapless soul who might accidentally trod upon their outer radices.

Still, meeting those needs is the most effective way to become the object of another's desire, thus attaining intimacy, which is required to achieve the state known as psychological maturity. (Despite how closely it reproduces the affective conditions of our childhoods, since trading compliance for love is the earliest social lesson learned; we learn it in our cribs.)

You, in return, will have your own needs met by your partner in matters large and small. In practice, many of these matters turn out to be quite small. Frequently, it is the tensions and disagreements over the minutiae of daily living that stand between couples and their requisite intimacy. Taking out the garbage, tone of voice, a forgotten errand—these are the rocky shoals upon which intimacy so often founders.

Mutuality requires *communication*, since in order to be met, these needs must be expressed. (No one's a mind reader, which is not to say that many of us don't expect this quality in a mate. Who wants to keep having to tell someone what you need?) What you need is for your mate to understand you—your desires, your contradictions, your unique sensitivities, what irks you. (In practice, that means what about your mate irks you.) You, in turn, must learn to understand the mate's needs. This means being willing to hear what about yourself irks your mate. Hearing is not a simple physiological act performed with the ears, as you will learn. You may think you know how to *hear*, but that doesn't mean that you know how to *listen*.

With two individuals required to coexist in enclosed spaces for extended periods of time, domesticity requires substantial quantities of compromise and adaptation simply to avoid mayhem. Yet with the post-Romantic ideal of unconstrained individuality informing our most fundamental ideas of the self, this can prove a perilous process. Both parties must be willing to jettison whatever aspects of individuality might prove irritating while being simultaneously allowed to retain enough individuality to feel their autonomy is not being sacrificed, even as it is being surgically excised.

Having mastered mutuality, you may now proceed to *advanced intimacy*. Advanced intimacy involves inviting your partner "in" to your most interior self. Whatever and wherever our "inside" is, the widespread—if somewhat metaphysical—belief in its existence (and the related belief that whatever is in there is dying to get out) has assumed a quasi-medical status. Leeches once served a similar purpose. Now we "express our feelings" in lieu of our fluids because everyone knows that those who don't are far more prone to cancer, ulcers or various dire ailments.

With love as our culture's patent medicine, prescribed for every ill (now even touted as a necessary precondition for that other great American obsession, longevity), we willingly subject ourselves to any number of arcane procedures in its quest. "Opening up" is required for relationship health, so lovers fashion themselves after doctors wielding long probes to penetrate the tender regions. Try to think of yourself as one big orifice: now stop clenching and relax. If the procedure proves uncomfortable, it just shows you're not open enough. Psychotherapy may be required before sufficient dilation can be achieved: the world's most expensive lubricant.

Needless to say, this opening-up can leave you feeling quite vulnerable, lying there psychically spread-eagled and shivering on the examining table of your relationship. (A favored suspicion is that your partner, knowing exactly where your vulnerabilities are, deliberately kicks you there—one reason this opening-up business may not always feel as pleasant as advertised.) And as anyone who has spent much time in—or just in earshot of—a typical couple knows, the "expression of needs" is often the Trojan horse of intimate warfare, since expressing needs means, by definition, that one's partner has thus far failed to meet them.

In any long-term couple, this lexicon of needs becomes codified over time into a highly evolved private language with its own rules. Let's call this couple grammar. Close observation reveals this as a language composed of one recurring unit of speech: the interdiction—highly nuanced, mutually imposed commands and strictures extending into the most minute areas of household affairs, social life, finances, speech, hygiene, allowable idiosyncrasies and so on. From bathroom to bedroom, car to kitchen, no aspect of coupled life is not subject to scrutiny, negotiation and codes of conduct.

A sample from an inexhaustible list, culled from interviews with numerous members of couples of various ages, races and sexual orientations:

You can't leave the house without saying where you're going. You can't not say what time you'll return. You can't go out when the other person feels like staying at home. You can't be a slob. You can't do less than 50 percent of the work around the house, even if the other person wants to do 100 percent more cleaning than you find necessary or even reasonable. You can't leave the dishes for later, load them the way that seems best to you, drink straight from the carton or make crumbs. You can't leave the bathroom door open—it's offensive. You can't leave the bathroom door closed—your partner needs to get in. You can't not shave your underarms or legs. You can't gain weight. You can't watch soap operas. You can't watch infomercials or the pregame show or Martha Stewart. You can't eat what you want—goodbye Marshmallow Fluff; hello tofu meatballs. You can't spend too much time on the computer. And stay out of those chat rooms. You can't take risks, unless they are agreed-upon risks, which somewhat limits the concept of "risk." You can't make major purchases alone, or spend money on things the other person considers excesses. You can't blow money just because you're in a bad mood, and you can't be in a bad mood without being required to explain it. You can't begin a sentence with "You always. . . . " You can't begin a sentence with "I never . . . " You can't be simplistic, even when things are simple. You can't say what you really think of that outfit or color combination or cowboy hat. You can't be cynical about things the other person is sincere about. You can't drink without the other person counting your drinks. You can't have the wrong laugh. You can't bum cigarettes when you're out because it embarrasses your mate, even though you've explained the unspoken fraternity between smokers. You can't tailgate, honk or listen to talk radio in the car. And so on. The specifics don't matter. What matters is that the operative word is "can't."

Thus is love obtained.

Certainly, domesticity offers innumerable rewards: companionship, child-rearing convenience, reassuring predictability and many other benefits too varied to list. But if love has power over us, domesticity is its enforcement wing: the iron dust mop in the velvet glove.

The historian Michel Foucault has argued that modern power made its mark on the world by inventing new types of enclosures and institutions, places like factories, schools, barracks, prisons and asylums, where individuals could be located, supervised, processed and subjected to inspection, order and the clock. What current social institution is more enclosed than modern intimacy? What offers greater regulation of movement and time, or more precise surveillance of body and thought, to a greater number of individuals?

Of course, it is your choice—as if any of us could really choose not to desire love or not to feel like hopeless losers should we fail at it. We moderns are beings yearning to be filled, yearning to be overtaken by love's mysterious power. We prostrate ourselves at love's portals, like social strivers waiting at the rope line outside some exclusive club hoping to gain admission and thereby confirm our essential worth. A life without love lacks an organizing narrative. A life without love seems so barren, and it might almost make you consider how empty the rest of the world is, as if love were vital plasma and everything else just tap water.

Exchanging obedience for love comes naturally—after all, we all were once children whose survival depended on the caprices of love. And there you have the template for future intimacies. If you love me, you'll do what I want—or need, or demand—and I'll love you in return. We all become household dictators, petty tyrants of the private sphere, who are, in our turn, dictated to.

And why has modern love developed in such a way as to maximize submission and minimize freedom, with so little argument about it? No doubt a citizenry schooled in renouncing desire instead of imagining there could be something more would be, in many respects, advantageous. After all, wanting more is the basis for utopian thinking, a path toward dangerous social demands, even toward imagining the possibilities for altogether different social arrangements. But if the most elegant forms of social control are those that came packaged in the guise of individual needs and satisfactions, so wedded to the individual psyche that any opposing impulse registers as the anxiety of unlovability, who needs a soldier on every corner? We are more than happy to police ourselves and those we love and call it living happily ever after. Perhaps a secular society needed another metaphysical entity to subjugate itself to after the death of God, and love was available for the job. But isn't it a little depressing to think we are somehow incapable of inventing forms of emotional life based on anything other than subjugation?

lose part of yourself but find part of yourself
theories of control →accountability

◈ PART SIX ◈

CONSTRUCTING AND DECONSTRUCTING BODIES

READINGS IN THIS PART

INTRODUCTION TO SUBJECT AND READINGS

Image that you are at the hospital giving birth or helping your partner give birth. As a healthy infant emerges from the womb, you ask the two most basic questions: (1) Is it a boy or a girl? and (2) Does it have ten fingers and ten toes? The sex and the health of newborns are usually the first concerns of new parents. The doctor reassures you that your baby has ten fingers and toes, and then breaks the news that you are one of the one out of 1,000/2000 parents who have given birth to an infant with ambiguous genitalia (Fausto-Sterling 2000). In other words, your baby is not clearly a boy or a girl. Your world starts to spin. Think of all the things that could start running through your head. What to name it? How to introduce it? How to dress it? What to say when people ask, "Is it a boy or is it a girl? Your mind moves forward to potential problems in the future. Which bathroom in school? Which locker room? What to say? Who to tell?

If you try to walk through the world as a not-woman/not-man you will begin to see how gendered our world really is. Many girls are still engulfed in pink and told stories of princesses and heroic knights as they are carted off to ballet class. Just as many boys are expected to skin their knees, are told to be brave as they are read stories about trucks and astronauts. It is simply not possible to raise a child in the United States without gendered bias and learned stereotypes. As soon as you turn on the television, gender jumps out at you. Miss Piggy with her dyed blonde hair is batting false eyelashes at Kermit. Commercials feature little girls playing with the latest Barbie fashion accessories, while boys have action figures armed with weapons.

Even if you could somehow avoid all the stereotyping on television, you must venture out to the world where store windows, magazine covers, toy displays, and other children and adults all have the potential to relate gender messages. Eventually your child will attend school and mainstream gendering begins whether you like it or not. Sometimes it is obvious—a story with a woman as a nurse and a male doctor, but lots of gendering happens unconsciously. For example, studies have shown that some teachers unintentionally reward little girls for certain behaviors while rewarding little boys for other actions. All this gendering, and your child has not yet graduated from kindergarten!

Now image that shortly after the birth, a doctor approaches and tells you that they can surgically "fix" your infant. A few procedures now and a few more procedures may be needed as the child grows up. Hormones therapy may also be necessary, but with these efforts you will be able to have an almost normal boy or girl.

Most of us have never had to make such decisions or even think through this scenario. How would you respond? What would you do? What considerations would help you make your decision?

The readings in this section explain and detail the issues of what used to be called hermaphroditism. This term, Greek in origin refers to the son of Hermes and Aphrodite, who became physically united in one body with a nymph—one person combined as male and female. Today we use the term intersexuality, which means biologically having sexual characteristics intermediate of those of typically male or typically female. In the article, *The Five Sexes: Why Male and Female Are Not Enough*, Anne Fausto-Sterling, a developmental geneticist, argues that "biologically speaking, there are many gradations running from female to male. . . . " She identifies five sexes and suggests that sex is better thought of as a continuum. Fausto-Sterling describes the biological variations that can occur and provides us with a short history of intersexuality. She then introduces and employs Foucault's concept of biopower and explains how biopower changed how we think and treat the intersexed.

Whereas, Fausto-Sterling focused on the biological aspects and the history of intersexuality, Cheryl Chase, the author of *Hermaphrodites with Attitude* examines how the medical world intervenes in the lives of the intersexed. She shares her own personal history as an intersexed person and details the operations and lies that shaped her life. Chase founded the Intersexed Society of North America (ISNA), an organization dedicated to challenging the medicalization of intersexuality. She argues that intersexuality is not a disability or something that needs to be fixed and is outraged that infants are subjected to unnecessary surgery to "normalize" them. Chase asks the questions: Do we surgically alter infants because we are made uncomfortable by their ambiguous genitalia? How can we justify such procedures? And who is there to protect those who are too young to speak for themselves?

TERMS AND CONCEPTS

androgens   hermaphroditism (herms)
Aphrodite   heteronormal
biopower   hormones
chromosomes   intersexuality
endocrinologists   male pseudohermaphroditism (merms)
estrogens   psychosocial
female pseudohermaphroditism (ferms)

QUESTIONS TO CONSIDER

1. According to Fausto-Sterling, in what ways does the medical "intervention" of intersexed individuals illustrate Foucault's concept of biopower?
2. Are doctors shaping the intersexed because it is easier to make them fit our notions of sex/gender identity than to change our society's ideas sex/gender identity? Support your answer.
3. What does Chase mean when she states that "the birth of an intersex infant today is deemed a "psychosocial emergency"?
4. The belief that an infant can be assigned a sex and socialized into an assigned gender suggests a complete malleability of sex/gender identity. How does Chase's article challenge this assumption?
5. Critique the management of Cheryl Chase's own intersexuality. Write a new version based on what you have learned from these articles.
6. Chase compares genital surgery performed on intersex infants with the practices of FGM in Africa (the United States has outlawed the latter but not the former). What are the similarities and differences?

FURTHER READINGS

Atkins, Dawn (ed.). 1998. *Looking Queer*. Binghamton, NY: Haworth Press.
Colapinto, John. 2001. *As Nature Made Him: The Boy Who was Raised as a Girl*. New York: Harper Trade.
Dreger, Alice (ed.). 1999. *Intersex in the Age of Ethics*. Hagerstown, MD: University Publishing Group.
———. 2000. *Hermaphrodites and the Medical Invention of Sex*. Boston: Harvard University Press.
Fausto-Sterling, Anne. 1985. *Myth of Gender: Biological Theories about Women and Men*. New York: Basic Books.
———. 1999. *Sexing the Body: How Biologists Construct Human Sexuality*. New York: Basic Books.
———. 2000. The five sexes, revisited. *The Sciences*, July/August, pp.19–23.
Hegarty, Peter. and Cheryl Chase. 2000. Intersex activism, feminism, and psychology: Opening a dialogue on theory, research, and clinical practice. *Feminism & Psychology* 10: 117–132.
Kessler, Susan J. 1990. The medical construction of gender: Case management of intersexed infants. *Signs: Journal of Women in Culture and Society*, vol.16, no.1, pp. 3–26.
———. 1998. *Lessons from the Intersexed*. Piscataway, NJ: Rutgers University Press.

Miller, Suzanne. 2000. When sex 'needs' to be fixed. *World and I*, September 2000 v15:9, pp.148–155.

Nussbaum, Emily. 2000. A question of gender. *Discover*, January 2000 v2:1, pp.92–98.

RELATED WEBSITES

The Intersex Society of North America (ISNA)
www.isna.org/

Intersex Support Group International
www.isgi.org

The True Story of John/Joan in *Press for Change*
www.pfc.orguk/news/1998/johnjoan.htm

Whatever I feel . . . in *Press for Change*
www.pfc.org.uk/news/1998/whatever.htm

The UK Intersex Association
www.ukia.co.uk

◈ 17

The Five Sexes
Why Male and Female Are Not Enough

Anne Fausto-Sterling

Brown University

In 1843 Levi Suydam, a twenty-three-year-old resident of Salisbury, Connecticut, asked the town board of selectmen to validate his right to vote as a Whig in a hotly contested local election. The request raised a flurry of objections from the opposition party, for reasons that must be rare in the annals of American democracy: it was said that Suydam was more female than male and thus (some eighty years before suffrage was extended to women) could not be allowed to cast a ballot. To settle the dispute a physician, one William James Barry, was brought in to examine Suydam. And, presumably upon encountering a phallus, the good doctor declared the prospective voter male. With Suydam safely in their column the Whigs won the election by a majority of one.

Source: The five sexes: Why male and female are not enough, by Anne Fausto-Sterling. In *The Sciences* 1993 (33)2, pp. 20–24. © 1993 The Sciences/New York Academy of Sciences. This article is reprinted by permission of *The Sciences* and is from the March/April 1993 issue.

Barry's diagnosis, however, turned out to be somewhat premature. Within a few days he discovered that, phallus notwithstanding, Suydam menstruated regularly and had a vaginal opening. Both his/her physique and his/her mental predispositions were more complex than was first suspected. S/he had narrow shoulders and broad hips and felt occasional sexual yearnings for women. Suydam's "feminine propensities, such as a fondness for gay colors, for pieces of calico, comparing and placing them together, and an aversion for bodily labor, and an inability to perform the same, were remarked by many," Barry later wrote. It is not clear whether Suydam lost or retained the vote, or whether the election results were reversed.

Western culture is deeply committed to the idea that there are only two sexes. Even language refuses other possibilities; thus to write about Levi Suydam I have had to invent conventions—*s/he* and *his/her*—to denote someone who is clearly neither male nor female or who is perhaps both sexes at once. Legally, too, every adult is either man or woman, and the difference, of course, is not trivial. For Suydam it meant the franchise; today it means being available for, or exempt from, draft registration, as well as being subject, in various ways, to a number of laws governing marriage, the family and human intimacy. In many parts of the United States, for instance, two people legally registered as men cannot have sexual relations without violating anti-sodomy statutes.

But if the state and the legal system have an interest in maintaining a two-party sexual system, they are in defiance of nature. For biologically speaking, there are many gradations running from female to male; and depending on how one calls the shots, one can argue that along that spectrum lie at least five sexes—and perhaps even more.

For some time medical investigators have recognized the concept of the intersexual body. But the standard medical literature uses the term *intersex* as a catch-all for three major subgroups with some mixture of male and female characteristics: the so-called true hermaphrodites, whom I call herms, who possess one testis and one ovary (the sperm- and egg-producing vessels, or gonads); the male pseudohermaphrodites (the "merms"), who have testes and some aspects of the female genitalia but no ovaries; and the female pseudohermaphrodites (the "ferms"), who have ovaries and some aspects of the male genitalia but lack testes. Each of those categories is in itself complex; the percentage of male and female characteristics, for instance, can vary enormously among members of the same subgroup. Moreover, the inner lives of the people in each subgroup—their special needs and their problems, attractions and repulsions—have gone unexplored by science. But on the basis of what is known about them I suggest that the three intersexes, herm, merm, and ferm, deserve to be considered additional sexes each in its own right. Indeed, I would argue further that sex is a vast, infinitely malleable continuum that defies the constraints of even five categories.

Not surprisingly, it is extremely difficult to estimate the frequency of intersexuality, much less the frequency of each of the three additional sexes: it is not the sort of information one volunteers on a job application. The psychologist John Money of Johns Hopkins University, a specialist in the study of congenital sexual-organ defects, suggests intersexuals may constitute as many as 4 percent of births. As I point out to my students at Brown University, in a student body of about 6,000 that fraction, if correct, implies there may be as many as 240 intersexuals on campus—surely enough to form a minority caucus of some kind.

In reality though, few such students would make it as far as Brown in sexually diverse form. Recent advances in physiology and surgical technology now enable physicians to catch most intersexuals at the moment of birth. Almost at once such infants are entered into a program of hormonal and surgical management so that they can slip quietly into society as "normal" heterosexual males or females. I emphasize that the motive is in no way conspiratorial. The aims of the policy are genuinely humanitarian, reflecting the wish that people be able to "fit in" both physically and psychologically. In the medical community, however, the assumptions behind that wish—that there be only two sexes, that heterosexuality alone is normal, that there is one true model of psychological health—have gone virtually unexamined.

The word *hermaphrodite* comes from the Greek names Hermes, variously known as the messenger of the gods, the patron of music, the controller of dreams or the protector of livestock, and Aphrodite, the goddess of sexual love and beauty. According to Greek mythology, those two gods parented Hermaphroditus, who at age fifteen became half male and half female when his body fused with the body of a nymph he fell in love with. In some true hermaphrodites the testis and the ovary grow separately but bilaterally; in others they grow together within the same organ, forming an ovo-testis. Not infrequently, at least one of the gonads functions quite well, producing either sperm cells or eggs, as well as functional levels of the sex hormones—androgens or estrogens. Although in theory it might be possible for a true hermaphrodite to become both father and mother to a child, in practice the appropriate ducts and tubes are not configured so that egg and sperm can meet.

In contrast with the true hermaphrodites, the pseudohermaphrodites possess two gonads of the same kind along with the usual male (XY) or female (XX) chromosomal makeup. But their external genitalia and secondary sex characteristics do not match their chromosomes. Thus merms have testes and XY chromosomes, yet they also have a vagina and a clitoris, and at puberty they often develop breasts. They do not menstruate, however. Ferms have ovaries, two X chromosomes and sometimes a uterus, but they also have at least partly masculine external genitalia. Without medical intervention they can develop beards, deep voices and adult-size penises.

No classification scheme could more than suggest the variety of sexual anatomy encountered in clinical practice. In 1969, for example, two French investigators, Paul Guinet of the Endocrine Clinic in Lyons and Jacques Decourt of the Endocrine Clinic in Paris, described ninety-eight cases of true hermaphroditism—again, signifying people with both ovarian and testicular tissue—solely according to the appearance of the external genitalia and the accompanying ducts. In some cases the people exhibited strongly feminine development. They had separate openings for the vagina and the urethra, a cleft vulva defined by both the large and the small labia, or vaginal lips, and at puberty they developed breasts and usually began to menstruate. It was the oversize and sexually alert clitoris, which threatened sometimes at puberty to grow into a penis, that usually impelled them to seek medical attention. Members of another group also had breasts and a feminine body type, and they menstruated. But their labia were at least partly fused, forming an incomplete scrotum. The phallus (here an embryological term for a structure that during usual development goes on to form either a clitoris or a penis) was between 1.5 and 2.8 inches long; nevertheless, they urinated through a urethra that opened into or near the vagina.

By far the most frequent form of true hermaphrodite encountered by Guinet and Decourt—55 percent—appeared to have a more masculine physique. In such people the urethra runs either through or near the phallus, which looks more like a penis than a clitoris. Any menstrual blood exits periodically during urination. But in spite of the relatively male appearance of the genitalia, breasts appear at puberty. It is possible that a sample larger than ninety-eight so-called true hermaphrodites would yield even more contrasts and subtleties. Suffice it to say that the varieties are so diverse that it is possible to know which parts are present and what is attached to what only after exploratory surgery.

The embryological origins of human hermaphrodites clearly fit what is known about male and female sexual development. The embryonic gonad generally chooses early in development to follow either a male or a female sexual pathway; for the ovo-testis, however, that choice is fudged. Similarly, the embryonic phallus most often ends up as a clitoris or a penis, but the existence of intermediate states comes as no surprise to the embryologist. There are also uro-genital swellings in the embryo that usually either stay open and become the vaginal labia or fuse and become a scrotum. In some hermaphrodites, though, the choice of opening or closing is ambivalent. Finally, all mammalian embryos have structures that can become the female uterus and the fallopian tubes, as well as structures that can become part of the male sperm-transport system. Typically either the male or the female set of those primordial genital organs degenerates, and the remaining structures achieve their sex-appropriate future. In hermaphrodites both sets of organs develop to varying degrees.

Intersexuality itself is old news. Hermaphrodites, for instance, are often featured in stories about human origins. Early biblical scholars believed Adam began life as a hermaphrodite and later divided into two people—a male and a female—after falling from grace. According to Plato there once were three sexes—male, female and hermaphrodite—but the third sex was lost with time.

Both the Talmud and the Tosefta, the Jewish books of law, list extensive regulations for people of mixed sex. The Tosefta expressly forbids hermaphrodites to inherit their fathers' estates (like daughters), to seclude themselves with women (like sons) or to shave (like men). When hermaphrodites menstruate they must be isolated from men (like women); they are disqualified from serving as witnesses or as priests (like women), but the laws of pederasty apply to them.

In Europe a pattern emerged by the end of the Middle Ages that, in a sense, has lasted to the present day: hermaphrodites were compelled to choose an established gender role and stick with it. The penalty for transgression was often death. Thus in the 1600s a Scottish hermaphrodite living as a woman was buried alive after impregnating his/her master's daughter.

For questions of inheritance, legitimacy, paternity, succession to title and eligibility for certain professions to be determined, modern Anglo-Saxon legal systems require that newborns be registered as either male or female. In the U.S. today sex determination is governed by state laws. Illinois permits adults to change the sex recorded on their birth certificates should a physician attest to having performed the appropriate surgery. The New York Academy of Medicine, on the other hand, has taken an opposite view. In spite of surgical alterations of the external genitalia, the academy argued in 1966, the chromosomal sex remains the same. By that measure, a person's wish to conceal his or her original sex cannot outweigh the public interest in protection against fraud.

During this century the medical community has completed what the legal world began—the complete erasure of any form of embodied sex that does not conform to a male–female, heterosexual pattern. Ironically, a more sophisticated knowledge of the complexity of sexual systems has led to the repression of such intricacy.

In 1937 the urologist Hugh H. Young of Johns Hopkins University published a volume titled *Genital Abnormalities, Hermaphroditism and Related Adrenal Diseases.* The book is remarkable for its erudition, scientific insight and open-mindedness. In it Young drew together a wealth of carefully documented case histories to demonstrate and study the medical treatment of such "accidents of birth." Young did not pass judgment on the people he studied, nor did he attempt to coerce into treatment those intersexuals who rejected that option. And he showed unusual even-handedness in referring to those people who had had sexual experiences as both men and women as "practicing hermaphrodites."

One of Young's more interesting cases was a hermaphrodite named Emma who had grown up as a female. Emma had both a penis-size clitoris and a vagina, which made it possible for him/her to have "normal" heterosexual sex with both men and women. As a teenager Emma had had sex with a number of girls to whom s/he was deeply attracted; but at the age of nineteen s/he had married a man. Unfortunately, he had given Emma little sexual pleasure (though *he* had had no complaints), and so throughout that marriage and subsequent ones Emma had kept girlfriends on the side. With some frequency s/he had pleasurable sex with them. Young describes his subject as appearing "to be quite content and even happy." In conversation Emma occasionally told him of his/her wish to be a man, a circumstance Young said would be relatively easy to bring about. But Emma's reply strikes a heroic blow for self-interest:

> Would you have to remove that vagina? I don't know about that because that's my meal ticket. If you did that, I would have to quit my husband and go to work, so I think I'll keep it and stay as I am. My husband supports me well, and even though I don't have any sexual pleasure with him, I do have lots with my girlfriends.

Yet even as Young was illuminating intersexuality with the light of scientific reason, he was beginning its suppression. For his book is also an extended treatise on the most modern surgical and hormonal methods of changing intersexuals into either males or females. Young may have differed from his successors in being less judgmental and controlling of the patients and their families, but he nonetheless supplied the foundation on which current intervention practices were built.

By 1969, when the English physicians Christopher J. Dewhurst and Ronald R. Gordon wrote *The Intersexual Disorders*, medical and surgical approaches to intersexuality had neared a state of rigid uniformity. It is hardly surprising that such a hardening of opinion took place in the era of the feminine mystique—of the post–Second World War flight to the suburbs and the strict division of family roles according to sex. That the medical consensus was not quite universal (or perhaps that it seemed poised to break apart again) can be gleaned from the near-hysterical tone of Dewhurst and Gordon's book, which contrasts markedly with the calm reason of Young's founding work. Consider their opening description of an intersexual newborn:

> One can only attempt to imagine the anguish of the parents. That a newborn should have a deformity . . . [affecting] so fundamental an issue as the very sex of the child . . . is a tragic event which immediately conjures up visions of a hopeless psychological misfit doomed to live always as a sexual freak in loneliness and frustration.

Dewhurst and Gordon warned that such a miserable fate would, indeed, be a baby's lot should the case be improperly managed; "but fortunately," they wrote, "with correct management the outlook is infinitely better than the poor parents—emotionally stunned by the event—or indeed anyone without special knowledge could ever imagine."

Scientific dogma has held fast to the assumption that without medical care hermaphrodites are doomed to a life of misery. Yet there are few empirical studies to back up that assumption, and some of the same research gathered to build a case for medical treatment contradicts it. Francies Benton, another of Young's practicing hermaphrodites, "had not worried over his condition, did not wish to be changed, and was enjoying life." The same could be said of Emma, the opportunistic hausfrau. Even Dewhurst and Gordon, adamant about the psychological importance of treating intersexuals at the infant stage, acknowledged great success in "changing the sex" of older patients. They reported on twenty cases of children reclassified into a different sex after the supposedly critical age of eighteen months. They asserted that all the reclassifications were "successful," and they wondered then whether reregistration could be "recommended more readily than [had] been suggested so far."

The treatment of intersexuality in this century provides a clear example of what the French historian Michel Foucault has called biopower. The knowledge developed in biochemistry, embryology, endocrinology, psychology and surgery has enabled physicians to control the very sex of the human body. The multiple contradictions in that kind of power call for some scrutiny. On the one hand, the medical "management" of intersexuality certainly developed as part of an attempt to free people from perceived psychological pain (though whether the pain was the patient's, the parents' or the physician's is unclear). And if one accepts the assumption that in a sex-divided culture people can realize their greatest potential for happiness and productivity only if they are sure they belong to one of only two acknowledged sexes, modern medicine has been extremely successful.

On the other hand, the same medical accomplishments can be read not as progress but as a mode of discipline. Hermaphrodites have unruly bodies. They do not fall naturally into a binary classification; only a surgical shoehorn can put them there. But why should we care if a "woman," defined as one who has breasts, a vagina, a uterus and ovaries and who menstruates, also has a clitoris large enough to penetrate the vagina of another woman? Why should we care if there are people whose biological equipment enables them to have sex "naturally" with both men and women? The answers seem to lie in a cultural need to maintain clear distinctions between the sexes. Society mandates the control of intersexual bodies because they blur and bridge the great divide. Inasmuch as hermaphrodites literally embody both sexes, they challenge traditional beliefs about sexual difference: they possess the irritating ability to live sometimes as one sex and sometimes the other, and they raise the specter of homosexuality.

But what if things were altogether different? Imagine a world in which the same knowledge that has enabled medicine to intervene in the management of intersexual patients has been placed at the service of multiple sexualities. Imagine that the sexes have multiplied beyond currently imaginable limits. It would have to be a world of shared powers. Patient and physician, parent and child, male and female, heterosexual and homosexual—all those oppositions and others would have to be dissolved as sources of division. A new ethic of medical treatment would arise, one that would permit ambiguity in a culture that had overcome sexual division. The central mission of medical treatment would be to preserve life. Thus hermaphrodites would be concerned primarily not about whether they can conform to society but about whether they might develop potentially life-threatening conditions—hernias, gonadal tumors, salt imbalance caused by adrenal malfunction—that sometimes accompany hermaphroditic development. In my ideal world medical intervention for intersexuals would take place only rarely before the age of reason; subsequent treatment would be a cooperative venture between physician, patient and other advisers trained in issues of gender multiplicity.

I do not pretend that the transition to my utopia would be smooth. Sex, even the supposedly "normal," heterosexual kind, continues to cause untold anxieties in Western society. And certainly a culture that has yet to come to grips—religiously and, in some states, legally—with the ancient and relatively uncomplicated reality of homosexual love will not readily embrace intersexuality. No doubt the most troublesome arena by far would be the rearing of children. Parents, at least since the Victorian era, have fretted, sometimes to the point of outright denial, over the fact that their children are sexual beings.

All that and more amply explains why intersexual children are generally squeezed into one of the two prevailing sexual categories. But what would be the psychological consequences of taking the alternative road—raising children as unabashed intersexuals? On the surface that tack seems fraught with peril. What, for example, would happen to the intersexual child amid the unrelenting cruelty of the school yard? When the time came to shower in gym class, what horrors and humiliations would await the intersexual as his/her anatomy was displayed in all its nontraditional glory? In whose gym class would s/he register to begin with? What bathroom would s/he use? And how on earth would Mom and Dad help shepherd him/her through the mine field of puberty?

In the past thirty years those questions have been ignored, as the scientific community has, with remarkable unanimity, avoided contemplating the alternative route of unimpeded intersexuality. But modern investigators tend to overlook a substantial body of case histories, most of them compiled between 1930 and 1960, before surgical intervention became rampant. Almost without exception, those reports describe children who grew up knowing they were intersexual (though they did not advertise it) and adjusted to their unusual status. Some of the studies are richly detailed—described at the level of gym-class showering (which most intersexuals avoided without incident); in any event, there is not a psychotic or a suicide in the lot.

Still, the nuances of socialization among intersexuals cry out for more sophisticated analysis. Clearly, before my vision of sexual multiplicity can be realized, the first openly intersexual children and their parents will have to be brave pioneers who will bear the brunt of society's growing pains. But in the long view—though it could take generations to achieve—the prize might be a society in which sexuality is something to be celebrated for its subtleties and not something to be feared or ridiculed.

18

Hermaphrodites with Attitude
Mapping the Emergence of Intersex Political Activism

Cheryl Chase

Executive Director, Intersex Society of North America

The insistence on two clearly distinguished sexes has calamitous personal consequences for the many individuals who arrive in the world with sexual anatomy that fails to be easily distinguished as male or female. Such individuals are labeled "intersexuals" or "hermaphrodites" by modern medical discourse.[1] About one in a hundred births exhibits some anomaly in sex differentiation,[2] and about one in two thousand is different enough to render problematic the question "Is it a boy or a girl?"[3] Since the early 1960s, nearly every major city in the United States has had a hospital with a standing team of medical experts who intervene in these cases to assign— through drastic surgical means—a male or female status to intersex infants. The fact that this system for preserving the boundaries of the categories male and female has existed for so long without drawing criticism or

scrutiny from any quarter indicates the extreme discomfort that sexual ambiguity excites in our culture. Pediatric genital surgeries literalize what might otherwise be considered a theoretical operation: the attempted production of normatively sexed bodies and gendered subjects through constitutive acts of violence. Over the last few years, however, intersex people have begun to politicize intersex identities, thus transforming intensely personal experiences of violation into collective opposition to the medical regulation of bodies that queer the foundations of heteronormative identifications and desires.

HERMAPHRODITES: MEDICAL AUTHORITY AND CULTURAL INVISIBILITY

Many people familiar with the ideas that gender is a phenomenon not adequately described by male/female dimorphism and that the interpretation of physical sex differences is culturally constructed remain surprised to learn just how variable sexual anatomy is.[4] Though the male/female binary is constructed as natural presumed to be immutable, the phenomenon of intersexuality offers clear evidence to the contrary and furnishes an opportunity to deploy "nature" strategically disrupt heteronormative systems of sex, gender, and sexuality. The concept of bodily sex, in popular usage, refers to multiple components including karyoty (organization of sex chromosomes), gonadal differentation (e.g., ovarian or testicular), genital morphology, configuration of internal reproductive organs, and pubertal sex characteristics such as breasts and facial hair. Because these characteristics are expected to be concordant in each individual—either all male or all female—an observer, once having attributed male or female sex to a particular individual, assumes the values of other unobserved characteristics.[5]

Because medicine intervenes quickly in intersex births to change the infant's body, the phenomenon of intersexuality is today largely unknown outside specialized medical practices. General public awareness of intersex bodies slowly vanished in modern Western European societies as medicine gradually appropriated to itself the authority to interpret—and eventually manage—the category which had previously been widely known as "hermaphroditism." Victorian medical taxonomy began to efface hermaphroditism as a legitimated status by establishing mixed gonadal histology as a necessary criterion for "true" hermaphroditism. By this criterion, both ovarian and testicular tissue types had to be present. Given the limitations of Victorian surgery and anesthesia, such confirmation was impossible in a living patient. All other anomalies were reclassified as "pseudo-hermaphroditisms" masking a "true sex" determined by the gonads.[6]

With advances in anesthesia, surgery, embryology, and endocrinology, however, twentieth-century medicine moved from merely labeling intersexed bodies to the far more invasive practice of "fixing" them to conform with a diagnosed true sex. The techniques and protocols for physically trans-

forming intersexed bodies were developed primarily at Johns Hopkins University in Baltimore during the 1920s and 1930s under the guidance of urologist Hugh Hampton Young. "Only during the last few years," Young enthused in the preface to his pioneering textbook, *Genital Abnormalities*, "have we begun to get somewhere near the explanation of the marvels of anatomic abnormality that may be portrayed by these amazing individuals. But the surgery of the hermaphrodite has remained a terra incognita." The "sad state of these unfortunates" prompted Young to devise "a great variety of surgical procedures" by which he attempted to normalize their bodily appearances to the greatest extents possible.[7]

Quite a few of Young's patients resisted his efforts. One, a "'snappy' young negro woman with a good figure" and a large clitoris, had married a man but found her passion only with women. She refused "to be made into a man" because removal of her vagina would mean the loss of her "meal ticket," namely, her husband.[8] By the 1950s, the principle of rapid postnatal detection and intervention for intersex infants had been developed at John Hopkins with the stated goal of completing surgery early enough so that the child would have no memory of it.[9] One wonders whether the insistence on early intervention was not at least partly motivated by the resistance offered by adult intersexuals to normalization through surgery. Frightened parents of ambiguously sexed infants were much more open to suggestions of normalizing surgery, while the infants themselves could of course offer no resistance whatever. Most of the theoretical foundations justifying these interventions are attributable to psychologist John Money, a sex researcher invited to Johns Hopkins by Lawson Wilkins, the founder of pediatric endocrinology.[10] Wilkins's numerous students subsequently carried these protocols to hospitals throughout the United States and abroad.[11] Suzanne Kessler notes that today Wilkins and Money's protocols enjoy a "consensus of approval rarely encountered in science."[12]

In keeping with the Johns Hopkins model, the birth of an intersex infant today is deemed a "psychosocial emergency" that propels a multidisciplinary team of intersex specialists into action. Significantly, they are surgeons and endocrinologists rather than psychologists, bioethicists, representatives from intersex peer support organizations, or parents of intersex children. The team examines the infant and chooses either male or female as a "sex of assignment," then informs the parents that this is the child's "true sex." Medical technology, including surgery and hormones, is then used to make the child's body conform as closely as possible to that sex.

The sort of deviation from sex norms exhibited by intersexuals is so highly stigmatized that the likely prospect of emotional harm due to social rejection of the intersexual provides physicians with their most compelling argument to justify medically unnecessary surgical interventions. Intersex status is considered to be so incompatible with emotional health that misrepresentation, concealment of facts, and outright lying (both to parents and later to the intersex person) are unabashedly advocated in professional medical literature.[13] Rather, the systematic hushing up of the fact of intersex births and the use of violent techniques to normalize intersex bodies have caused profound emotional and physical harm to intersexuals and their families. The harm begins when the birth is treated as a medical crisis, and the consequences of that initial treatment ripple out ever afterward. The impact of this treatment is so devastating that until just a few years ago, people whose lives have been touched by intersexuality maintained silence about their ordeal. As recently as 1993, no one publicly disputed surgeon Milton Edgerton when he wrote that in forty years of clitoral surgery on intersexuals, "not one has complained of loss of sensation, *even when the entire clitoris was removed.*"[14]

The tragic irony is that, while intersexual anatomy occasionally indicates an underlying medical problem such as adrenal malfunction, ambiguous genitals are in and of themselves neither painful nor harmful to health. Surgery is essentially a destructive process.

It can remove and to a limited extent relocate tissue, but it cannot create new structures. This technical limitation, taken together with the framing of the feminine as a condition of lack, leads physicians to assign 90 percent of anatomically ambiguous infants as female by excising genital tissue. Members of the Johns Hopkins intersex team have justified female assignment by saying, "You can make a hole, but you can't build a pole."[15] Positively heroic efforts shore up a tenuous masculine status for the remaining 10 percent assigned male, who are subjected to multiple operations—twenty-two in one case[16]—with the goal of straightening the penis and constructing a urethra to enable standing urinary posture. For some, the surgeries end only when the child grows old enough to resist.[17]

Children assigned to the female sex are subjected to surgery that removes the troubling hypertrophic clitoris (the same tissue that would have been a troubling micropenis if the child had been assigned male). Through the 1960s, feminizing pediatric genital surgery was openly labeled "clitorectomy" and was compared favorably to the African practices that have been the recent focus of such intense scrutiny. As three Harvard surgeons noted, "Evidence that the clitoris is not essential for normal coitus may be gained from certain sociological data. For instance, it is the custom of a number of African tribes to excise the clitoris and other parts of the external genitals. Yet normal sexual function is observed in these females."[18] A modified operation that removes most of the clitoris and relocates a bit of the tip is variously (and euphemistically) called clitoroplasty, clitoral reduction, or clitoral recession and is described as a "simple cosmetic procedure" to differentiate it from the now infamous clitorectomy. However, the operation is far from benign. Here is a slightly simplified summary (in my own words) of the surgical technique—recommended by Johns Hopkins Surgeons Oesterling, Gearhart, and Jeffs—that is representative of the operation:

> They make an incision around the phallus, at the corona, then dissect the skin away from its underside. Next they dissect the skin away from

the dorsal side and remove as much of the corpora, or erectile bodies, as necessary to create an "appropriate size clitoris." Next, stitches are placed from the pubic area along both sides of the entire length of what remains of the phallus; when these stitches are tightened, it folds up like pleats in a skirt, and recesses into a concealed position behind the mons pubis. If the result is still "too large," the glans is further reduced by cutting away a pieshaped wedge.[19]

For most intersexuals, this sort of arcane, dehumanized medical description, illustrated with close-ups of genital surgery and naked children with blacked-out eyes, is the only available version of *Our Bodies, Ourselves*. We as a culture have relinquished to medicine the authority to police the boundaries of male and female, leaving intersexuals to recover as best they can, alone and silent, from violent normalization.

MY CAREER AS A HERMAPHRODITE: RENEGOTIATING CULTURAL MEANINGS

I was born with ambiguous genitals. A doctor specializing in intersexuality deliberated for three days—sedating my mother each time she asked what was wrong with her baby—before concluding that I was male, with a micropenis, complete hypospadias, undescended testes, and a strange extra opening behind the urethra. A male birth certificate was completed for me, and my parents began raising me as a boy. When I was a year and a half old my parents consulted a different set of experts, who admitted me to a hospital for "sex determination." "Determine" is a remarkably apt word in this context, meaning both "to ascertain by investigation" and "to cause to come to a resolution." It perfectly describes the two-stage process whereby science produces through a series of masked operations what it claims merely to observe. Doctors told my parents that a thorough medical investigation would be necessary to determine (in the first sense of that word) what my "true sex" was. They judged my genital appendage to be inadequate as a penis, too short to mark masculine status effectively or

to penetrate females. As a female, however, I would be penetrable and potentially fertile. My anatomy having been relabeled as vagina, urethra, labia, and outsized clitoris, my sex was determined (in the second sense) by amputating my genital appendage. Following doctors' orders, my parents then changed my name, combed their house to eliminate all traces of my existence as a boy (photographs, birthday cards, etc.), changed my birth certificate, moved to a different town, instructed extended family members no longer to refer to me as a boy, and never told anyone else—including me—just what had happened. My intersexuality and change of sex were the family's dirty little secrets.

At age eight, I was returned to the hospital for abdominal surgery that trimmed away the testicular portion of my gonads, each of which was partly ovarian and partly testicular in character. No explanation was given to me then for the long hospital stay or the abdominal surgery, nor for the regular hospital visits afterward, in which doctors photographed my genitals and inserted fingers and instruments into my vagina and anus. These visits ceased as soon as I began to menstruate. At the time of the sex change, doctors had assured my parents that their once son/now daughter would grow into a woman who could have a normal sex life and babies. With the confirmation of menstruation, my parents apparently concluded that that prediction had been borne out and their ordeal was behind them. For me, the worst part of the nightmare was just beginning.

As an adolescent, I became aware that I had no clitoris or inner labia and was unable to orgasm. By the end of my teens, I began to do research in medical libraries, trying to discover what might have happened to me. When I finally determined to obtain my medical records, it took me three years to overcome the obstruction of the doctors whom I asked for help. When I did obtain them, a scant three pages, I first learned that I was a "true hermaphrodite" who had been my parents' son for a year and a half and who bore a name unfamiliar to me. The records also documented my clitorectomy. This was the middle 1970s, when I was in my early twenties.

I had come to identify myself as lesbian, at a time when lesbianism and a biologically based gender essentialism were virtually synonymous: men were rapists who caused war and environmental destruction; women were good and would heal the earth; lesbians were a superior form of being uncontaminated by "men's energy." In such a world, how could I tell anyone that I had actually possessed the dreaded "phallus"? I was no longer a woman in my own eyes but rather a monstrous and mythical creature. Because my hermaphroditism and long-buried boyhood were the history behind the clitorectomy, I could never speak openly about that or my consequent inability to orgasm. I was so traumatized by discovering the circumstances that produced my embodiment that I could not speak of these matters with anyone.

Nearly fifteen years later, I suffered an emotional meltdown. In the eyes of the world, I was a highly successful businesswoman, a principal in an international high tech company. To myself, I was a freak, incapable of loving or being loved, filled with shame about my status as a hermaphrodite and about my sexual dysfunction. Unable to make peace with myself, I finally sought help from a psychotherapist, who reacted to each revelation about my history and predicament with some version of "no, it's not" or "so what?" I would say, "I'm not really a woman," and she would say, "Of course you are. You look female." I would say, "My complete withdrawal from sexuality has destroyed every relationship I've ever entered." She would say "Everybody has their ups and downs." I tried another therapist and met with a similar response. Increasingly desperate, I confided my story to several friends, who shrank away in embarrassed silence. I was in emotional agony, feeling utterly alone, seeing no possible way out. I decided to kill myself.

Confronting suicide as a real possibility proved to be my personal epiphany. I fantasized killing myself quite messily and dramatically in the office of the surgeon who had cut off my clitoris, forcibly confronting him with the horror he had imposed on my life. But in acknowledging the desire to put my pain to some use, not to utterly waste my life, I turned a crucial corner, finding a way to direct my rage productively out into the world rather than destructively at myself. I had no conceptual framework for developing a more positive self-consciousness. I knew only that I felt mutilated, not fully human, but that I was determined to heal. I struggled for weeks in emotional chaos, unable to eat or sleep or work. I could not accept my image of a hermaphroditic body any more than I could accept the butchered one the surgeons left me with. Thoughts of myself as a Frankenstein's monster patchwork alternated with longings for escape by death, only to be followed by outrage, anger, and a determination to survive. I could not accept that it was just or right or good to treat any person as I had been treated—my sex changed, my genitals cut up, my experience silenced and rendered invisible. I bore a private hell within me, wretchedly alone in my condition without even my tormentors for company. Finally, I began to envision myself standing in a driving storm but with clear skies and a rainbow visible in the distance. I was still in agony, but I was beginning to see the painful process in which I was caught up in terms of revitalization and rebirth, a means of investing my life with a new sense of authenticity that possessed vast potentials for further transformation. Since then, I have seen this experience of movement through pain to personal empowerment described by other intersex and transsexual activists.[20]

I slowly developed a newly politicized and critically aware form of self-understanding. I had been the kind of lesbian who at times had a girlfriend but who had never really participated in the life of a lesbian community. I felt almost completely isolated from gay politics, feminism, and queer and gender theory. I did possess the rudimentary knowledge that the gay rights movement had gathered momentum only when it could effectively deny that homosexuality was sick or inferior and assert to the contrary that "gay is good." As impossible as it then seemed, I pledged similarly to affirm that "intersex is good," that the body I was born with was not diseased, only different. I vowed to embrace the sense of being "not a woman" that I initially had been so terrified to discover.

I began searching for community and consequently moved to San Francisco in the fall of 1992, based entirely on my vague notion that people living in the "queer mecca" would have the most conceptually sophisticated, socially tolerant, and politically astute analysis of sexed and gendered embodiment. I found what I was looking for in part because my arrival in the Bay Area corresponded with the rather sudden emergence of an energetic transgender political movement. Transgender Nation (TN) had developed out of Queer Nation, a post-gay/lesbian group that sought to transcend identity politics. TN's actions garnered media attention—especially when members were arrested during a "zap" of the American Psychiatric Association's annual convention when they protested the psychiatric labeling of transsexuality as mental illness. Transsexual performance artist Kate Bornstein was introducing transgender issues in an entertaining way to the San Francisco gay/lesbian community and beyond. Female-to-male issues had achieved a new level of visibility due in large part to efforts made by Lou Sullivan, a gay FTM activist who had died an untimely death from HIV-related illnesses in 1991. And in the wake of her underground best-selling novel, *Stone Butch Blues*, Leslie Feinberg's manifesto *Transgender Liberation: A Movement Whose Time Has Come* was finding a substantial audience, linking transgender social justice to a broader progressive political agenda for the first time.[21] At the same time, a vigorous new wave of gender scholarship had emerged in the academy.[22] In this context, intersex activist and theoretician Morgan Holmes could analyze her own clitorectomy for her master's thesis and have it taken seriously as academic work.[23] Openly transsexual scholars, including Susan Stryker and Sandy Stone, were visible in responsible academic positions at major universities. Stone's "*Empire* Strikes Back: A Posttranssexual Manifesto" refigured open, visible transsexuals not as gender conformists propping up a system of rigid, binary sex but as "a set of embodied texts whose potential for productive disruption of structured sexualities and spectra of desire has yet to be explored."[24]

Into this heady atmosphere, I brought my own experience. Introduced by Bornstein to other gender activists, I explored with them the cultural politics of intersexuality, which to me represented yet another new configuration of bodies, identities, desires, and sexualities from which to confront the violently normativizing aspects of the dominant sex/gender system. In the fall of 1993, TN pioneer Anne Ogborn invited me to participate in a weekend retreat called the New Woman Conference, where postoperative transsexual women shared their stories, their griefs and joys, and enjoyed the freedom to swim or sunbathe in the nude with others who had surgically changed genitals. I saw that participants returned home in a state of euphoria, and I determined to bring that same sort of healing experience to intersex people.

BIRTH OF AN INTERSEX MOVEMENT: OPPOSITION AND ALLIES

Upon moving to San Francisco, I started telling my story indiscriminately to everyone I met. Over the course of a year, simply by speaking openly within my own social circles, I learned of six other intersexuals—including two who had been fortunate enough to escape medical attention. I realized that intersexuality, rather than being extremely rare, must be relatively common. I decided to create a support network. In the summer of 1993, I produced some pamphlets, obtained a post office box, and began to publicize the Intersex Society of North America (ISNA) through small notices in the media. Before long, I was receiving several letters per week from intersexuals throughout the United States and Canada and occasionally some from Europe. While the details varied, the letters gave a remarkably coherent picture of the emotional consequences of medical intervention. Morgan Holmes: "All the things my body might have grown to do, all the possibilities, went down the hall with my amputated clitoris to the pathology department. The rest of me went to the recovery room— I'm still recovering." Angela Moreno: "I am horrified by what has been done to me and by the conspiracy of silence and lies. I am filled with grief and rage, but also relief finally to believe that maybe I am not the only one." Thomas: "I pray that I will have the means to repay, in some measure, the American Urological Association for all that it has done for my benefit. I am having some trouble, though, in connecting the timing mechanism to the fuse."

ISNA's most immediate goal has been to create a community of intersex people who could provide peer support to deal with shame, stigma, grief, and rage as well as with practical issues such as how to obtain old medical records or locate a sympathetic psychotherapist or endocrinologist. To that end, I cooperated with journalists whom I judged capable of reporting widely and responsibly on our efforts, listed ISNA with self-help and referral clearinghouses, and established a presence on the Internet (http://www.isna.org). ISNA now connects hundreds of intersexuals across North America, Europe, Australia, and New Zealand. It has also begun sponsoring an annual intersex retreat, the first of which took place in 1996 and which moved participants every bit as profoundly as the New Woman Conference had moved me in 1993.

ISNA's longer-term and more fundamental goal, however, is to change the way intersex infants are treated. We advocate that surgery not be performed on ambiguous genitals unless there is a medical reason (such as blocked or painful urination), and that parents be given the conceptual tools and emotional support to accept their children's physical differences. While it is fascinating to think about the potential development of new genders or subject positions grounded in forms of embodiment that fall outside the familiar male/female dichotomy, we recognize that the two-sex/gender model is currently hegemonic and therefore advocate that children be raised either as boys or girls, according to which designation seems most likely to offer the child the greatest future sense of comfort. Advocating gender assignment without resorting to normalizing surgery is a radical position given that it requires the willful disruption of the assumed concordance between body shape and gender category. However, this is the only position that prevents irreversible physical damage to the intersex person's body, that respects the intersex person's agency regarding his/her own flesh, and that recognizes genital sensation and erotic functioning to be at least as important as reproductive capacity. If an intersex child or adult decides to change gender or to undergo surgical or hormonal alteration of his/her body, that decision should also be fully respected and facilitated. The key point is that intersex subjects should not be violated for the comfort and convenience of others.

One part of reaching ISNA's long-term goal has been to document the emotional and physical carnage resulting from medical interventions. As a rapidly growing literature makes abundantly clear (see the bibliography on our website, http://www.isna.org/bigbib.html), the medical management of intersexuality has changed little in the forty years since my first surgery. Kessler expresses surprise that "in spite of the thousands of genital operations performed every year, there are no meta-analyses from within the medical community on levels of success."[25] They do not know whether postsurgical intersexuals are "silent and happy or silent and unhappy."[26] There is no research effort to improve erotic functioning for adult intersexuals whose genitals have been altered, nor are there psychotherapists specializing in working with adult intersex clients trying to heal from the trauma of medical intervention. To provide a counterpoint to the mountains of medical literature that neglect intersex experience and to begin compiling an ethnographic account of that experience, ISNA's *Hermaphrodites with Attitude* newsletter has developed into a forum for intersexuals to tell their own stories. We have sent complimentary copies of the newsletter filled with searing personal narratives to academics, writers, journalists, minority rights organizations, and medical practitioners—to anybody we thought might make a difference in our campaign to change the way intersex bodies are managed.

ISNA's presence has begun to generate effects. It has helped politicize the growing number of intersex organizations, as well as intersex identities themselves. When I first began organizing ISNA, I met leaders of the Turner's Syndrome Society, the oldest known support group focusing on atypical sexual differentiation, founded in 1987. Turner's Syndrome is defined by an XO genetic karyotype that results in a female body morphology with nonfunctioning ovaries, extremely short stature, and a variety of other physical differences described in the medical literature with such stigmatizing labels as "web-necked" and "fish-mouthed." Each of these women told me what a profound, life-changing experience it had been simply to meet another person like herself. I was inspired by their accomplishments (they are a national organization serving thousands of members), but I wanted ISNA to have a different focus. I was less willing to think of intersexuality as a pathology or disability, more interested in challenging its medicalization entirely, and more interested still in politicizing a pan-intersexual identity across the divisions of particular etiologies in order to destabilize more effectively the heteronormative assumptions underlying the violence directed at our bodies.

When I established ISNA in 1993, no such politicized groups existed. In the United Kingdom in 1988, the mother of a girl with androgen-insensitivity syndrome (AIS, which produces genetic males with female genital morphologies) formed the AIS Support Group. The group, which initially lobbied for increased medical attention (better surgical techniques for producing greater vaginal depth, more research into the osteoporosis that often attends AIS), now has chapters in five countries. Another group, K. S. and Associates, was formed in 1989 by the mother of a boy with Klinefelter's Syndrome and today serves over one thousand families. Klinefelter's is characterized by the presence of one or more additional X chromosomes, which produce bodies with fairly masculine external genitals, above-average height, and somewhat gangly limbs. At puberty, people with K. S. often experience pelvic broadening and the development of breasts. K. S. and Associates continues to be dominated by parents, is highly medical in orientation, and has resisted attempts by adult Klinefelter's Syn-drome men to discuss gender identity or sexual orientation issues related to their intersex condition.

Since ISNA has been on the scene, other groups with a more resistant stance vis-à-vis the medical establishment have begun to appear. In 1995, a mother who refused medical pressure for female assignment for her intersex child formed the Ambiguous Genitalia Support Network, which introduces parents of intersexuals to each other and encourages the development of pen-pal support relationships. In 1996, another mother who had rejected medical pressure to assign her intersex infant as a female by removing his penis formed the Hermaphrodite Education and Listening Post (HELP) to provide peer support and medical information. Neither of these parent-oriented groups, however, frames its work in overtly political terms. Still, political analysis and action of the sort advocated by ISNA has not been without effect on the more narrowly defined service-oriented or parent-dominated groups. The AIS Support Group, now more representative of both adults and parents, noted in a recent newsletter,

> Our first impression of ISNA was that they were perhaps a bit too angry and militant to gain the support of the medical profession. However, we have to say that, having read [political analyses of intersexuality by ISNA, Kessler, Fausto-Sterling, and Holmes], we feel that the feminist concepts relating to the patriarchal treatment of intersexuality are extremely interesting and do make a lot of sense. After all, the lives of intersexed people are stigmatized by the cultural disapproval of their genital appearance, [which need not] affect their experience as sexual human beings.[27]

Other more militant groups have now begun to pop up. In 1994, German intersexuals formed both the Workgroup on Violence in Pediatrics and Gynecology and the Genital Mutilation Survivors' Support Network, and Hijra Nippon now represents activist intersexuals in Japan.

Outside the rather small community of intersex organizations, ISNA's work has generated a complex patchwork of alliances and oppositions. Queer activists, especially transgender activists, have provided encouragement, advice, and logistical support to the intersex movement. The direct action group Transsexual Menace helped an ad hoc group of militant intersexuals calling themselves Hermaphrodites with Attitude plan and carry out a picket of the 1996 annual meeting of the American Academy of Pediatrics in Boston—the first recorded instance of intersex public protest in modern history.[28] ISNA was also invited to join GenderPAC, a recently formed national consortium of transgender organizations that lobbies against discrimination based on atypical expressions of gender or embodiment. More mainstream gay and lesbian political organizations such as the National Gay and Lesbian Task Force have also been willing to include intersex concerns as part of their political agendas. Transgender and lesbian/gay groups have been supportive of intersex political activism largely because they see similarities in the medicalization of these various identities as a form of social control and (especially for transsexuals) empathize with our struggle to assert agency within a medical discourse that works to efface the ability to exercise informed consent about what happens to one's own body.

Gay/lesbian caucuses and special interest groups within professional medical associations have been especially receptive to ISNA's agenda. One physician on the Internet discussion group glb-medical wrote:

> The effect of Cheryl Chase's postings—admittedly, after the shock wore off—was to make me realize that THOSE WHO HAVE BEEN TREATED might very well think [they had not been well served by medical intervention]. This matters a lot. As a gay man, and simply as a person, I have struggled for much of my adult life to find my own natural self, to disentangle the confusions caused by others' presumptions about how I am/should be. But, thankfully, their decisions were not surgically imposed on me!

Queer psychiatrists, starting with Bill Byne at New York's Mount Sinai Hospital, have been quick to support ISNA, in part because the psychological principles underlying the current intersex treatment protocols are manifestly unsound. They seem almost will-

fully designed to exacerbate rather than ameliorate already difficult emotional issues arising from sexual difference. Some of these psychiatrists see the surgical and endocrinological domination of a problem that even surgeons and endocrinologists acknowledge to be psychosocial rather than biomedical as an unjustified invasion of their area of professional competence.

ISNA has deliberately cultivated a network of nonintersexed advocates who command a measure of social legitimacy and can speak in contexts where uninterpreted intersex voices will not be heard. Because there is a strong impulse to discount what intersexuals have to say about intersexuality, sympathetic representation has been welcome—especially in helping intersexuals reframe intersexuality in nonmedical terms. Some gender theory scholars, feminist critics of science, medical historians, and anthropologists have been quick to understand and support intersex activism. Years before ISNA came into existence, feminist biologist and science studies scholar Anne Fausto-Sterling had written about intersexuality in relation to intellectually suspect scientific practices that perpetuate masculinist constructs of gender, and she became an early ISNA ally.[29] Likewise, social psychologist Suzanne Kessler had written a brilliant ethnography of surgeons who specialize in treating intersexuals. After speaking with several "products" of their practice, she, too, became a strong supporter of intersex activism.[30] Historian of science Alice Dreger, whose work focuses not only on hermaphroditism but on other forms of potentially benign atypical embodiment that become subject to destructively normalizing medical interventions (conjoined twins, for example), has been especially supportive. Fausto-Sterling, Kessler, and Dreger will each shortly publish works that analyze the medical treatment of intersexuality as being culturally motivated and criticize it as harmful to its ostensible patients.[31]

Allies who help contest the medicalization of intersexuality are especially important because ISNA has found it almost entirely fruitless to attempt direct, nonconfrontational interactions with the medical specialists who themselves determine policy on the treatment of intersex infants and who actually carry out the surgeries. Joycelyn Elders, the Clinton administration's first surgeon general, is a pediatric endocrinologist with many years of experience managing intersex infants but, in spite of a generally feminist approach to health care and frequent overtures from ISNA, she has been dismissive of the concerns of intersexuals themselves.[32] Another pediatrician remarked in an Internet discussion on intersexuality: "I think this whole issue is preposterous. . . . To suggest that [medical decisions about the treatment of intersex conditions] are somehow cruel or arbitrary is insulting, ignorant and misguided. . . . To spread the claims that [ISNA] is making is just plain wrong, and I hope that this [on-line group of doctors and scientists] will not blindly accept them." Yet another participant in that same chat asked what was for him obviously a rhetorical question: "Who is the enemy? I really don't think it's the medical establishment. Since when did we establish the male/female hegemony?" While a surgeon quoted in a *New York Times* article on ISNA summarily dismissed us as "zealots,"[33] there is considerable anecdotal information supplied by ISNA sympathizers that professional meetings in the fields of pediatrics, urology, genital plastic surgery, and endocrinology are buzzing with anxious and defensive discussions of intersex activism. In response to the Hermaphrodites with Attitude protests at the American Academy of Pediatrics meeting, that organization felt compelled to issue the following statement to the press: "The Academy is deeply concerned about the emotional, cognitive, and body image development of intersexuals, and believes that successful early genital surgery minimizes these issues." Further protests were planned for 1997.

The roots of resistance to the truth claims of intersexuals run deep in the medical establishment. Not only does ISNA critique the normativist biases couched within most scientific practice, it advocates a treatment protocol for intersex infants that disrupts conventional understandings of the relationship between bodies and genders. But on a level more personally threatening to medical practitioners, ISNA's position implies that they have—unwittingly at best, through willful denial at worst—spent their careers inflicting a profound harm from which their patients will never fully recover. ISNA's position threatens to destroy the assumptions motivating an entire medical subspecialty, thus jeopardizing the ability to perform what many surgeons find to be technically difficult and fascinating work. Melissa Hendricks notes that Dr. Gearhart is known to colleagues as a surgical "artist" who can "carve a large phallus down into a clitoris" with consummate skill.[34] More than one ISNA member has discovered that surgeons actually operated on their genitals at no charge. The medical establishment's fascination with its own power to change sex and its drive to rescue parents from their intersex children are so strong that heroic interventions are delivered without regard to the capitalist model that ordinarily governs medical services.

Given such deep and mutually reinforcing reasons for opposing ISNA's position, it is hardly surprising that medical intersex specialists have, for the most part, turned a deaf ear toward us. The lone exception as of April 1997 is urologist Justine Schober. After watching a videotape of the 1996 ISNA retreat and receiving other input from HELP and the AIS Support Group, she suggests in a new textbook on pediatric surgery that while technology has advanced to the point that "our needs [as surgeons] and the needs of parents to have a presentable child can be satisfied," it is time to acknowledge that problems exist that "we as surgeons . . . cannot address. Success in psychosocial adjustment is the true goal of sexual assignment and genitoplasty. . . . Surgery makes parents and doctors comfortable, but counseling makes people comfortable too, and is not irreversible."[35]

While ISNA will continue to approach the medical establishment for dialogue (and continue supporting protests outside the closed doors when doctors refuse to talk), perhaps the most important aspect of our current activities is the struggle to change public perceptions. By using the mass media, the Internet, and our growing network of allies and sympathizers to make the general public aware of the frequency of intersexuality and of the intense suffering that medical treatment has caused, we seek to create an environment in which many parents of intersex children will have already heard about the intersex movement when their child is born. Such informed parents we hope will be better able to resist medical pressure for unnecessary genital surgery and secrecy and to find their way to a peer-support group and counseling rather than to a surgical theater.

FIRST-WORLD FEMINISM, AFRICAN CLITORECTOMY, AND INTERSEX GENITAL MUTILATION

> We must first locate and challenge our own position as rigorously as we challenge that of others. (Salem Mekuria, "Female Genital Mutilation in Africa")

Traditional African practices that remove the clitoris and other parts of female genitals have lately been a target of intense media coverage and feminist activism in the United States and other industrialized Western societies. The euphemism *female circumcision* largely has been supplanted by the politicized term *female genital mutilation* (FGM). Analogous operations performed on intersexuals in the United States have not been the focus of similar attention—indeed, attempts to link the two forms of genital cutting have met with multiform resistance. Examining how first-world feminists and mainstream media treat traditional African practices and comparing that treatment with their responses to intersex genital mutilation (IGM) in North America exposes some of the complex interactions between ideologies of race, gender, colonialism, and science that effectively silence and render invisible intersex experience in first-world contexts. Cutting intersex genitals becomes yet another hidden mechanism for imposing normalcy upon unruly flesh, a means of containing the potential anarchy of desires and identifications within oppressive heteronormative structures.

In 1994, the *New England Journal of Medicine* paired an article on the physical harm resulting from African genital surgery with an editorial denouncing clitorectomy as a violation of human rights but declined to run a reply drafted by University of California at Berkeley medical anthropologist Lawrence Cohen and two ISNA members detailing the harm caused by medicalized American clitorectomies.[36] In response to growing media attention, Congress passed the Federal Prohibition of Female Genital Mutilation Act in October 1996, but the act specifically exempted from prohibition medicalized clitorectomies of the sort performed to "correct" intersex bodies. The bill's principal author, former Congresswoman Patricia Schroeder, received and ignored many letters from ISNA members and Brown University professor of medical science Anne Fausto-Sterling asking her to recast the bill's language. The *Boston Globe*'s syndicated columnist Ellen Goodman is one of the few journalists covering African FGM to respond to ISNA. "I must admit I was not aware of this situation," she wrote to me in 1994. "I admire your courage." She continued, however, regularly to discuss African FGM in her column without mentioning similar American practices. One of her October 1995 columns on FGM was promisingly titled, "We Don't Want to Believe It Happens Here," but it discussed only immigrants to the United States from third-world countries who performed clitorectomies on their daughters in keeping with the practices of their native cultures.

While clitorectomized African immigrant women doing anti-FGM activism in the United States have been receptive to the claims made by intersex opponents to medicalized clitorectomies and are in dialogue with us, first-world feminists and organizations working on African FGM have totally ignored us. To my knowledge, only two of the many anti-FGM groups contacted have responded to repeated overtures from intersex activists. Fran Hosken, who since 1982 has regularly published a catalogue of statistics on female genital mutilation worldwide, wrote me a terse note saying that "we are not concerned with biological exceptions."[37] Forward International, another anti-FGM organization, replied to an inquiry from German intersexual Heike Spreitzer that her letter was "most interesting" but that they could not help because their work focuses only on "female genital mutilation that is performed as a harmful cultural or traditional practice on young girls." As Forward International's reply to Spreitzer demonstrates, many first-world anti-FGM activists seemingly consider Africans to have "harmful cultural or traditional practices," while we in the modern industrialized West presumably have something better. We have science, which is linked to the metanarratives of enlightenment, progress, and truth. Genital cutting is condoned to the extent that it supports these cultural self-conceptions.

Robin Morgan and Gloria Steinem set the tone for subsequent first-world feminist analyses of FGM with their pathbreaking article in the March 1980 issue of *Ms.* magazine, "The International Crime of Genital Mutilation."[38] A disclaimer warns, "These words are painful to read. They describe facts of life as far away as our most fearful imagination—and as close as any denial of women's sexual freedom." For *Ms.* readers, whom the editors imagine are more likely to experience the pain of genital mutilation between the covers of their magazine than between their thighs, clitorectomy is presented as a fact of foreign life whose principal relevance to their readership is that it exemplifies a loss of "freedom," that most cherished possession of the liberal Western subject. The article features a photograph of an African girl with her legs held open by the arm of an unseen woman to her right. To her left is the disembodied hand of the midwife, holding the razor blade with which she has just performed a ritual clitorectomy. The girl's face—mouth open, eyes bulging—is a mask of pain. In more than fifteen years of coverage, Western images of African practices have changed little. "Americans made a horrifying discovery this year," *Life* soberly informed its readers in January 1997 while showing a two-page photo spread of a Kenyan girl held from behind as unseen hands cut her genitals.[39] The 1996 Pulitzer Prize for feature photography went to yet another portrayal of a Kenyan clitorectomy.[40] And in the wake of Fauziya Kassindja's successful bid for asylum in the United States after fleeing clitorectomy in Togo, the number of FGM images available from her country has skyrocketed.[41]

These representations all manifest a profound othering of African clitorectomy that contributes to the silence surrounding similar medicalized practices in the industrialized West. "Their" genital cutting is barbaric ritual; "ours" is scientific. Theirs disfigures; ours normalizes the deviant. The colonialist implications of these representations of genital cutting are even more glaringly obvious when images of intersex surgeries are juxtaposed with images of African FGM. Medical books describing how to perform clitoral surgery on white North American intersex children are almost always illustrated with extreme genital close-ups, disconnecting the genitals not only from the individual intersexed person but from the body itself. Full-body shots always have the eyes blacked out. Why is it considered necessary to black out the eyes of clitorectomized American girls—thus preserving a shred of their privacy and helping ward off the viewer's identification with the abject image—but not the eyes of the clitorectomized African girls in the pages of American magazines?[42]

First-world feminist discourse locates clitorectomy not only "elsewhere," in Africa, but also "elsewhen" in time. A recent *Atlantic Monthly* article on African clitorectomy asserted that the "American medical profession stopped performing clitoridectomies decades ago," and the magazine has since declined to publish a contradictory letter to the editor from ISNA.[43] Academic publications are as prone to this attitude as the popular press. In the recent *Deviant Bodies* anthology, visual artist Susan Jahoda's "Theatres of Madness" juxtaposes nineteenth- and twentieth-century material depicting "the conceptual interdependence of sexuality, reproduction, family life, and 'female disorders.'"[44] To represent twentieth-century medical clitorectomy practices, Jahoda quotes a July 1980 letter written to *Ms.* magazine in response to Morgan and Steinem. The letter writer, a nurse's aide in a geriatric home, said she had been puzzled by the strange scars she saw on the genitals of five of the forty women in her care: "Then I read your article. . . . My God! Why?

Who decided to deny them orgasm? Who made them go through such a procedure? I want to know. Was it fashionable? Or was it to correct 'a condition'? I'd like to know what this so-called civilized country used as its criteria for such a procedure. And how widespread is it here in the United States?"[45] While Jahoda's selection of this letter does raise the issue of medicalized American clitorectomies, it safely locates the genital cutting in the past, as something experienced a long time ago by women now in their later stages of life.

Significantly, Jahoda literally passed over an excellent opportunity to comment on the continuing practice of clitorectomy in the contemporary United States. Two months earlier, in the April 1980 issue of *Ms.*, feminist biologists Ruth Hubbard and Patricia Farnes also replied to Morgan and Steinem:

> We want to draw the attention of your readers to the practice of clitoridectomy not only in the Third World . . . but right here in the United States, where it is used as part of a procedure to "repair" by "plastic surgery" so-called genital ambiguities. Few peole realize that this procedure has routinely involved removal of the entire clitoris and its nerve supply—in other words, total clitoridectomy. . . . In a lengthy article, [Johns Hopkins intersex expert John] Money and two colleagues write . . . that "a three-year old girl about to be clitoridectomized . . . should be well informed that *the doctors will make her look like all other girls and women*" (our emphasis), which is not unlike what North African girls are often told about their clitoridectomies. . . . But to date, neither Money nor his critics have investigated the effect of clitoridectomies on the girls' development. Yet one would surely expect this to affect their psychosexual development and their feelings of identity as young women.[46]

While Farnes and Hubbard's prescient feminist exposé of medicalized clitorectomies in the contemporary United States sank without a trace, there has been an explosion of work that keeps "domestic" clitorectomy at a safe distance. Such conceptualizations of clitorectomy's geographical and temporal cultural remoteness allow first-world feminist outrage to be diverted into potentially colonialist meddling in the social affairs of others while hampering work for social justice at home.[47]

Feminism represents itself as being interested in unmasking the silence that surrounds violence against women. Most medical intersex management is another form of violence based on a sexist devaluing of female pain and female sexuality. Doctors consider the prospect of growing up as a boy with a small penis to be a worse alternative than growing up as a girl sans clitoris and ovaries; they gender intersex bodies accordingly and cut them up to make the assigned genders support cultural norms of embodiment. These medical interventions transform many transgressive bodies into ones that can be labeled safely as women and subjected to the many forms of social control with which women must contend. Why then have most first-world feminists met intersexuals with a blank stare?

Intersexuals have had such difficulty generating mainstream feminist support not only because of the racist and colonialist frameworks that situate clitorectomy as a practice foreign to proper subjects within the first world but also because intersexuality undermines the stability of the category "woman" that undergirds much of first-world feminist discourse. We call into question the assumed relation between genders and bodies and demonstrate how some bodies do not fit easily into male/female dichotomies. We embody viscerally the truth of Judith Butler's dictum that "sex," the concept that accomplishes the materialization and naturalization of power-laden, culturally constructed differences, has really been "gender all along."[48] By refusing to remain silenced, we queer the foundations upon which depend not only the medical management of bodies but also widely shared feminist assumptions of properly embodied feminine subjectivity. To the extent that we are not normatively female or normatively women, we are not considered the proper subjects of feminist concern.

As unwilling subjects of science and improper subjects of feminism, politicized intersex activists have deep stakes in allying with and participating in the sorts of poststructuralist cultural work that exposes the foundational assumptions about personhood shared by the dominant society, conventional feminism, and many other identity-based oppositional social movements. We have a stake, too, in the efforts of gender queers to carve out livable social spaces for reconfigured forms of embodiment, identity, and desire. In 1990, Suzanne Kessler noted that "the possibilities for real societal transformations would be unlimited" if physicians and scientists specializing in the management of gender could recognize that "finally, and always, people construct gender as well as the social systems that are grounded in gender-based concepts. . . . Accepting genital ambiguity as a natural option would require that physicians also acknowledge that genital ambiguity is 'corrected' not because it is threatening to the infant's life but because it is threatening to the infant's culture."[49] At that time, intersexuals had not yet been heard from, and there was little reason to think that physicians or other members of their culture would ever reflect on the meaning or effect of what they were doing. The advent of an activist intersex opposition changes everything.

NOTES

My appreciation goes to Susan Stryker for her extensive contributions to the structure and substance of this essay.

1. Claude J. Migeon, Gary D. Berkovitz, and Terry R. Brown, "Sexual Differentiation and Ambiguity," in *Wilkins: The Diagnosis and Treatment of Endocrine Disorders in Childhood and Adolescence*, ed. Michael S. Kappy, Robert M. Blizzard, and Claude J. Migeon (Springfield, Ill.: Charles C. Thomas, 1994), 573–715.

2. Lalitha Raman-Wilms et al., "Fetal Genital Effects of First-Trimester Sex Hormone Exposure: A Meta-Analysis," *Obstetrics and Gynecology* 85 (1995): 141–48.

3. Anne Fausto-Sterling, *Body Building: How Biologists Construct Sexuality* (New York: Basic Books, forthcoming).

4. Judith Butler, *Gender Trouble: Feminism and the Subversion of Identity* (New York: Routledge, 1990); Thomas Laqueur, *Making Sex: Body and Gender from the Greeks to Freud* (Cambridge, Mass.: Harvard University Press, 1990).

5. Suzanne Kessler and Wendy McKenna, *Gender: An Ethnomethodological Approach* (New York: John Wiley and Sons, 1978).

6. Alice Domurat Dreger, "Doubtful Sex: Cases and Concepts of Hermaphroditism in France and Britain, 1868–1915," (Ph.D. diss., Indiana University, 1995); Alice Domurat Dreger, "Doubtful Sex: The Fate of the Hermaphrodite in Victorian Medicine," *Victorian Studies* (spring 1995): 336–70; Alice Domurat Dreger, "Hermaphrodites in Love: The Truth of the Gonads," *Science and Homosexualities*, ed. Vernon Rosario (New York: Routledge, 1997), 46–66; Alice Domurat Dreger, "Doctors Containing Hermaphrodites: The Victorian Legacy," *Chrysalis: The Journal of Transgressive Gender Identities* (fall 1997): 15–22.

7. Hugh Hampton Young, *Genital Abnormalities, Hermaphroditism, and Related Adrenal Diseases* (Baltimore: Williams and Wilkins, 1937), xxxix–xl.

8. Ibid., 139–42.

9. Howard W. Jones Jr. and William Wallace Scott, *Hermaphroditism, Genital Anomalies, and Related Endocrine Disorders* (Baltimore: Williams and Wilkins, 1958), 269.

10. John Money, Joan G. Hampson, and John L. Hampson, "An Examination of Some Basic Sexual Concepts: The Evidence of Human Hermaphroditism," *Bulletin of the Johns Hopkins Hospital* 97 (1955): 301–19; John Money, Joan G. Hampson, and John L. Hampson, "Hermaphroditism: Recommendations Concerning Assignment of Sex, Change of Sex, and Psychologic Management," *Bulletin of Johns Hopkins Hospital* 97 (1955): 284–300; John Money, *Venuses Penuses* (Buffalo: Prometheus, 1986).

11. Robert M. Blizzard, "Lawson Wilkins," in Kappy et al., *Wilkins*, xi–xiv.

12. Suzanne Kessler, "The Medical Construction of Gender: Case Management of Intersexual Infants," *Signs: Journal of Women in Culture and Society* 16 (1990): 3–26.

13. J. Dewhurst and D. B. Grant, "Intersex Problems," *Archives of Disease in Childhood* 59 (1984): 1191–94; Anita Natarajan, "Medical Ethics and Truth-Telling in the Case of Androgen Insensitivity Syndrome," *Canadian Medical Association Journal* 154 (1996): 568–70; Tom Mazur, "Ambiguous Genitalia: Detection and Counseling," *Pediatric Nursing* (1983): 417–22; F. M. E. Slijper et al., "Neonates with Abnormal Genital Development Assigned the Female Sex: Parent Counseling," *Journal of Sex Education and Therapy* 20 (1994): 9–17.

14. Milton T. Edgerton, "Discussion: Clitoroplasty for Clitoromegaly due to Adrenogenital Syndrome without Loss of Sensitivity (by Nobuyuki Sagehashi)," *Plastic and Reconstructive Surgery* 91 (1993): 956.

15. Melissa Hendricks, "Is It a Boy or a Girl?" *Johns Hopkins Magazine*, November 1993, 10–16.

16. John F. Stecker et al., "Hypospadias Cripples," *Urologic Clinics of North America: Symposium on Hypospadias* 8 (1981): 539–44.

17. Jeff McClintock, "Growing Up in the Surgical Maelstrom," *Chrysalis: The Journal of Transgressive Gender Identities* (fall 1997): 53–54.

18. Robert E. Gross, Judson Randolph, and John F. Crigler, "Clitorectomy for Sexual Abnormalities: Indications and Technique," *Surgery* 59 (1966): 300–308.

19. Joseph E. Oesterling, John P. Gearhart, and Robert D. Jeffs, "A Unified Approach to Early Reconstructive Surgery of the Child with Ambiguous Genitalia," *Journal of Urology* 138 (1987): 1079–84.

20. Kira Triea, "The Awakening," *Hermaphrodites with Attitude* (winter 1994): 1; Susan Stryker, "My Words to Victor Frankenstein above the Village of Chamounix: Performing Transgender Rage," *GLQ* 1 (1994): 237–54.

21. Leslie Feinberg, *Stone Butch Blues* (Ithaca, N.Y.: Firebrand, 1993); Leslie Feinberg, *Transgender Liberation: A Movement Whose Time Has Come* (New York: World View Forum, 1992).

22. See, for example, Judith Butler, *Bodies That Matter: On the Discursive Limits of "Sex"* (New York: Routledge, 1993); Butler, *Gender Trouble*; Laqueur, *Making Sex*; and Julia Epstein and Kristina Straub, eds., *Body Guards: The Cultural Politics of Gender Ambiguity* (New York: Routledge, 1991).

23. Morgan Holmes, "Medical Politics and Cultural Imperatives: Intersexuality Beyond Pathology and Erasure" (master's thesis, York University, Toronto, 1994).

24. Sandy Stone, "The *Empire* Strikes Back: A Posttranssexual Manifesto," in Epstein and Straub, *Body Guards*, 280–304, quotation on 296.

25. Suzanne Kessler, *Lessons from the Intersexed* (New Brunswick, N.J.: Rutgers University Press, forthcoming).

26. Robert Jeffs, quoted in Ellen Barry, "United States of Ambiguity," Boston *Phoenix*, 22 November 1996, 6–8, quotation on 6.

27. AIS Support Group, "Letter to America," *ALIAS* (spring 1996): 3–4.

28. Barry, "United States of Ambiguity," 7.

29. Anne Fausto-Sterling, "The Five Sexes: Why Male and Female Are Not Enough," *The Sciences* 33, no. 2 (March/April 1993): 20–25; Anne Fausto-Sterling, *Myths of Gender: Biological Theories about Women and Men*, 2d ed. (New York: Basic Books, 1985), 134–41.

30. Kessler, "The Medical Construction of Gender"; Suzanne Kessler, "Meanings of Genital Variability," *Chrysalis: The Journal of Transgressive Gender Identities* (fall 1997): 33–38.

31. Anne Fausto-Sterling, *Building Bodies: Biology and the Social Construction of Sexuality* (New York: Basic Books, forthcoming); Kessler, "Meanings of Genital Variability"; Alice Domurat Dreger, *Hermaphrodites and the Medical Invention of Sex* (Cambridge, Mass.: Harvard University Press, forthcoming).

32. "Dr. Elders' Medical History," *New Yorker*, 26 September 1994: 45–46; Joycelin Elders and David Chanoff, *From Sharecropper's Daughter to Surgeon General of the United States of America* (New York: William Morrow, 1996).

33. Natalie Angier, "Intersexual Healing: An Anomaly Finds a Group," *New York Times*, 4 February 1996, E14.

34. Hendricks, "Is It a Boy or a Girl?" 10.

35. Justine M. Schober, "Long Term Outcomes of Feminizing Genitoplasty for Intersex," in *Pediatric Surgery and Urology: Long Term Outcomes*, ed. Pierre Mouriquant (Philadelphia: W. B. Saunders, forthcoming).

36. Patricia Schroeder, "Female Genital Mutilation," *New England Journal of Medicine* 331 (1994): 739–40; Nahid Toubia, "Female Circumcision as a Public Health Issue," *New England Journal of Medicine* 331 (1994): 712–16.

37. Fran P. Hosken, *The Hosken Report: Genital/Sexual Mutilation of Females*, 4th ed. (Lexington, Mass.: WIN News, 1994).

38. Robin Morgan and Gloria Steinem, "The International Crime of Genital Mutilation," *Ms.*, March 1980, 65–67ff.

39. Mariella Furrer, "Ritual Agony," *Life*, January 1997, 38–39.

40. Pulitzer Prize Board, "Feature Photography: Stephanie Welsh," 1996. Available online at http://www.pulitzer.org/winners/1996/winners/works/feature-photography/.

41. Celia Dugger, "U.S. Grants Asylum to Woman Fleeing Genital Mutilation Rite," *New York Times*, 14 June 1996, A1; Celia Dugger, "New Law Bans Genital Cutting in the United States," *New York Times*, 12 October 1996, 1; Furrer, "Ritual Agony."

42. Dugger, "U.S. Grants Asylum"; Salem Mekuria, "Female Genital Mutilation in Africa: Some African Views," *Association of Concerned African Scholars Bulletin* (winter/spring 1995): 2–6.

43. Linda Burstyn, "Female Circumcision Comes to America," *Atlantic Monthly*, October 1995, 28–35.

44. Susan Jahoda, "Theatres of Madness," *Deviant Bodies*, ed. Jennifer Terry and Jacqueline Urla (Bloomington: Indiana University Press, 1995), 251–76.

45. Letter to the editor, *Ms.*, July 1980, 12.

46. Ruth Hubbard and Patrica Farnes, letter to the editor, *Ms.*, April 1980, 9–10.

47. Seble Dawit and Salem Mekuria, "The West Just Doesn't Get It," *New York Times*, 7 December 1993, A27.

48. Butler, *Gender Trouble*, 8.

49. Kessler, "Medical Construction of Gender," 25.

◈ PART SEVEN ◈

BEYOND THE BINARY

INTRODUCTION TO SUBJECT AND READINGS

In the early days of gender studies, it was commonly held that sex was biological and gender was social. Sex was precultural—you were born with it. Gender, on the other hand, was learned. Infants were considered to be blank slates waiting to be gendered by society, as if gender was plastic and could be molded into any shape. These beliefs led surgeons to think that they could assign a gender, enabling parents to raise intersexed children as either gender. Today we know that gender is more complex than this. In the last section, Anne Fausto-Sterling argued that two sexes are not enough and that in fact, five sexes would be more appropriate. Given this premise, the idea of a world that allows for more than two genders would also make good sense.

Westerners tend to think in twos—pairs and opposites—and we classify or categorize the things in our lives as consisting of two complementary or contrary components. For example, if I say *tall*, you say *short*, not taller. If I say *woman*, you say *man*—because in our society you need to be one or the other. There is no room for anything in-between. In fact, we consider women to be the "opposite" sex *of* men and vice-versa. The idea of the opposite sex is deeply ingrained in our culture. This is an old model; for two thousand years women were considered, genitally, to be men turned inside-out (Angier 1999). We often hear partners referred to as "my better half." Love songs, popular movies, and religious ideology all reinforce these beliefs. The binary system of gender may seem so "natural" that it may be difficult for us to image a nonbinary gender system.

Nevertheless, third genders exist/have existed in several cultures around the world. Some of the well-researched third genders include the mahu of Polynesia, katheoys of South East Asia, xaniths of Oman, sworn virgins of Albania, hijras of India, and berdaches of North America.[1] Depending on the culture, third genders can be biologically male or female (although usually male) and are allowed to occupy a social/gender space that is neither male or female. The readings in this section detail two of the most researched third genders: hijras of India and berdaches (two-spirits) of North America.

The article *Hijra and Sādhin: Neither Man nor Woman in India,* by Serena Nanda, explains that Hinduism has gods that change from male to female and who are not perfect but succumb to desires and temptation. The gender flexibility of Hindu gods allows for Indian gender diversity. Nanda describes two forms of gender variance in India, hijras and sādhin. Hijras are defined as men who adopt the clothing and behavior of women. Culturally, they are neither male nor female. The hijra identity is available to the intersexed or men who are willing to undergo surgical removal of their genitals. Infertility and identification with the Hindu Mother Goddess empower hijras and allows them to exist in Indian society with some dignity. Hijras are more visible and widespread than sādhin, a gender variant role available to Indian women. Sādhin are women ascetics who adopt male clothing and forgo marriage and sex.

The article *Lesbians, Men-Women and Two-Spirits: Homosexuality and Gender in Native American Cultures,* by Sabine Lang, introduces the third gender found in North America commonly referred to as berdache. The earliest accounts of berdaches date back to the 1600s and were written by traders, explorers, and missionaries who offered contradictory descriptions of the roles and status of berdaches. They were depicted as homosexuals, transvestites, intersexed, shamans, and cowards who were revered or reviled. Many Westerners condemned berdaches because of their transgender behavior and/or homosexuality. This homophobia not only affected the ethnographic record; it was instrumental in destroying the institution of berdaches.

Although berdaches were reported in 113 Native American cultures, from all across North America, there were significant variations. In some cultures, the berdache role was available only to men, in others it was available to both men and women. Lang discusses the role of berdaches in traditional Native American culture and connects the traditional role with gay and lesbian Native Americans today. The identity of two-spirit, a pan-Native American lesbian/gay identity that embraces traditional ideas of spirituality, has emerged as a source of empowerment. Like the hijras, there is a lot of variation within the two-spirits' identity and behavior. Both identities suffered but survived Western homophobia, and today they celebrate their gender variance even amid continued discrimination.

TERMS AND CONCEPTS

androgynous	mahu
asceticism	ritual castration
berdaches	sādhin
binary sex/gender system	third genders
dharma	transgender
gender variance	transvestite
hijras	two-spirit
katheoys	xaniths

QUESTIONS TO CONSIDER

1. Explain the religious affiliation and Hindu ideology that help to legitimize the status of the hijras?
2. Compare the status, the sexuality, prevalence and freedoms of the hijras and sādhins?
3. Are hijras and berdaches really third genders? Why? Or why not?
4. Why are some cultures more comfortable with gender flexibility, while others, like our own, are not?
5. According to Lang, what are the differences between a two-spirit identity and a lesbian identity?
6. What does Lang mean when she observes that in "Native American cultures where multiple genders were still intact, a same-sex relationship was by no means identical with a same-gender relationship"?

NOTE

1. Berdaches is now considered a derogatory term. I use it because most of the ethnographic accounts of North American third genders use this term and no one has suggested an appropriate replacement. Lang (1997) also uses the term "berdache," asserting that it cannot be replaced by the term "two-spirit."

FURTHER READINGS

Blackwood, Evelyn. 1984. Sexuality and gender in certain Native American tribes: The case of cross-gender females. *Signs: Journal of Women in Culture and Society*, Vol 10, no 11, pp. 27–42.

Greenberg, David F. 1985. Why was the Berdache ridiculed. *Journal of Homosexuality*, vol 11, pp. 179–189.

Herdt, Gilbert H. 1996. *Third Sex, Third Gender: Beyond Sexual Dimorphism in Culture and History*. New York: Zone Books.

Jacobs, Sue-Ellen, Wesley Thomas, and Sabine Lang (eds.). 1997. *Two-Spirited People*. Chicago: The University of Chicago Press.

Matzer, Andrew. 2001. '*O Au No Keia: Voices from Hawaii's Mahu and Transgender Communities*. Philadelphia, PA: Xlibris Corporation.

Nanda, Serena. 1999. *Neither Man nor Woman: The Hijras of India.* New York: Wadsworth Publishing.

———. 2000. *Gender Diversity: Crosscultural Variations.* Prospect Heights, IL: Waveland Press, Inc.

Roscoe, Will. 1992. *The Zuni Man-Woman.* Albuquerque: University of New Mexico Press.

Roscoe, Will (ed.). 2000. *The Changing Ones: Third and Fourth Genders in Native North American.* New York: St. Martins Press.

Williams, Walter L. 1986. *The Spirit and the Flesh.* Boston: Beacon Press.

Young, Antonia. 1999. *Women Who Become Men: Albanian Swore Virgins.* New York: Berg Publishers.

RELATED WEBSITES

There is a dearth of websites relating strictly to third genders. There are, however, numerous websites related to transgenderism that include discussions and information on third genders.

Baylan, Asog, Transvestism, and Sodomy: Gender, Sexuality and the Sacred in Early Colonial Philippines by Carolyn Brewer
　　www.sshe.murdoch.edu.au/intersections/issues2/carolyn2.html

Welcome to Transgender in Thailand—information about katheoys
　　http://home.att.net/~leela2/home.htm

◆ 19
Hijra and Sādhin
Neither Man nor Woman in India

Serena Nanda
John Jay College of Criminal Justice

As in native North America, gender diversity in Hindu India is mainly set within a religious context. Unlike North America, however, gender diversity in India is set within a basically binary sex/gender system that is hierarchical and patriarchal rather than one that is egalitarian.

In Hindu India, male and female/man and woman are viewed as natural categories in complementary opposition. This binary construction incorporates—and conflates—biological qualities (sex) and cultural qualities (gender). Males and females are born with different sexual characteristics and reproductive organs, have different sexual natures, and take different and complementary roles in marriage, sexual behavior, and reproduction. The biological or "essential" nature of the differences between male and female, man and woman, is amply demonstrated in the medical and ritual texts of classical Hinduism, in which body fluids and sexual organs are presented as both the major sources of the sex/gender dichotomy and its major symbols (O'Flaherty 1980).

In Hinduism, in contrast to Western culture, the female principle is the more active, animating the male principle, which is more inert and latent. This active female principle has an erotic, creative, life-giving aspect and a destructive, life-destroying aspect. The erotic aspect of female power is dangerous unless it is controlled by the male principle. Powerful women, whether deities or humans, must be restrained by male authority. Thus, the Hindu Mother Goddess is kind and helpful when subordinated to her male consort, but when dominant, the goddess is aggressive, devouring, and destructive. The view that unrestrained female sexuality is dangerous characterizes a more down-to-earth sexual ideology as well. In India, both in Hinduism and in Islam, women are believed to be more sexually voracious than men; in order to prevent their sexual appetites from causing social chaos and distracting men from their higher spiritual duties, women must be controlled.

THE RELIGIOUS CONTEXT OF GENDER DIVERSITY

The most important context for understanding sex/gender diversity in Indian society is Hindu religious concepts (Nanda 1999). In Hinduism, in spite of the importance of the basic complementary opposition of male and female, many sex/gender variants and transformations are also acknowledged. Unlike Western cultures and religions, which try to resolve, repress, or dismiss sexual contradictions and ambiguities as jokes or trivia, Hinduism has a great capacity to allow opposites to confront each other without necessarily resolving the opposition, "celebrating the idea that the universe is boundlessly various, and . . . that all possibilities may exist without excluding each other" (O'Flaherty 1973:318). The presence of alternative genders and gender transformations in Hinduism gives positive meaning to the lives of many individuals with a variety of alternative gender identifications, physical conditions, and erotic preferences. Despite the criminalization of many kinds of transgender behavior under British rule and even by the Indian government after independence, Indian society has not yet permitted cultural anxiety about transgenderism to express itself in culturally institutionalized phobias and repressions.

Ancient Hindu origin myths often feature androgynous or hermaphroditic ancestors. The Rg Veda (a classical Hindu religious text), for example, says that before creation the world lacked all distinctions, including those of sex and gender. Ancient poets often expressed this concept with androgynous or hermaphroditic images, such as a male with a womb, a male deity with breasts, or a pregnant male (Zwilling and Sweet n.d.:3). In Hinduism, then, multiple sexes and genders are acknowledged as possibilities, albeit ambivalently regarded possibilities, both among humans and deities. Individuals who do not fit into society's major sex/gender categories may be stigmatized but may also find, within Hinduism, meaningful and valued gender identifications.

Hinduism has been characterized as having a "propensity towards androgynous thinking" (Zwilling and Sweet n.d.:2). Within the Hindu sex/gender system, the interchange of male and female qualities, transformations of sex and gender, the incorporation of male and female within one person, and alternative sex and gender roles among deities and humans are meaningful and positive themes in mythology, ritual and art. Among the many kinds of male and female sex/gender variants, the most visible and culturally institutionalized are the *hijras*.

Hijras are culturally defined as "neither man nor woman." They are born as males and through a ritual surgical transformation become an alternative, third sex/gender category (Nanda 1999). Hijras worship Bahuchara Mata, a form of the Hindu Mother Goddess particularly associated with transgenderism. Their traditional employment is to perform at marriages and after a child (especially a son) has been born. They sing and dance and bless the child and the family for increased fertility and prosperity in the name of the goddess. They then receive traditional payments of money, sweets, and cloth in return.

HIJRAS AS NOT-MEN . . .

The recognition of more than two sex/genders is recorded in India as early as the eighth century BCE; like the hijras, alternative or third sex/gendered persons were primarily considered to be defective males. The core of their deficiency centered on their sexual impotence, or inability to procreate (Zwilling and Sweet 1996:361). In India today, the term hijra is most commonly translated as "eunuch" or intersexed, and emphasizes sexual impotence. Hijras are culturally defined as persons who are born as males but who adopt the clothing, behavior and occupations of women, and who are neither male nor female, neither man nor woman.

Hijra sexual impotence is popularly understood as a *physical* defect impairing the male sexual function in intercourse (in the inserter role) and in reproduction. This is the major way in which hijras are "not-men." Hijras attribute their impotence to a defective male sexual organ. A child who at birth is classified as male but whose genitals are subsequently noticed to be ambiguous, culturally would be defined as a hijra, or as potentially a hijra (though in fact not all such individuals become hijras).

Like their counterparts in native North America, hijras (as receptors) frequently have sexual relationships with men. While hijras are not defined by their sexual practices, they often define themselves as "men who have no desire for women." Linguistically and culturally, hijras are distinguished from other men who take the receptor role in sex and are identified by their same-sex sexual orientation (Cohen 1995). It is the hijras' sexual impotence and in-between sex/gender status that is at the core of their cultural definition. A male who is not biologically intersexed who wishes to become a hijra must transform his sex/gender through the emasculation operation (discussed later in this chapter).

Although all hijras explain their deficient masculinity by saying, "I was born this way," this statement is not factually true. Rather, it expresses the Hindu view that qualities of both sex and gender are inborn, and is also consistent with the Hindu view that fate is important in shaping one's life chances and experiences.

HIJRAS AS WOMEN AND NOT-WOMEN

While hijras are "man minus man," they are also "man plus woman." Hijras adopt many aspects of the feminine gender role. They wear women's dress, hairstyle, and accessories; they imitate women's walk, gestures, voice, facial expressions and language; they have only male sexual partners and they experience themselves positively as sexual objects of men's desires. Hijras take feminine names as part of their gender transformation and use female kinship terms for many of their

relationships with each other, such as sister, aunty, and grandmother (Hall 1995). They request "ladies only" seating in public transportation and they periodically demand to be counted as women (rather than men) in the census. Being a hijra means not only divesting oneself of one's masculine identity, but also taking on a feminine one.

Although hijras are "like" women, they are also "not-women." Their feminine dress and manners are often exaggerations and their aggressive female sexuality contrasts strongly with the normatively submissive demeanor of ordinary women. Hijra performances do not attempt a realistic imitation of women but rather a burlesque, and the very act of dancing in public violates norms of feminine behavior. Hijras also use coarse and abusive speech, both among themselves and to their audiences, which is also deviant for Indian women. Hijras' use of verbal insult is an important component in the construction of their gender variance, as noted by early European observers and the contemporary Indian media (Hall 1997).

Because hijras are defined as neither men nor women they were sometimes prohibited from wearing women's clothing exclusively: some Indian rulers in the eighteenth century required that hijras distinguish themselves by wearing a man's turban with their female clothing. A century later, hijras were reported as wearing "a medley of male and female clothing," with a female sari under a male coat-like, outer garment (Preston 1987:373). This seems similar to North American gender variant transvestism, though hijras today for the most part do not wear gender-mixed clothing.

The major reason why hijras are considered—by themselves and others—as not-woman is that they do not have female reproductive organs and therefore cannot have children. The hijras tell a story about a hijra who prayed to god to bear a child. God granted her wish, but since she had not specifically prayed for the child to be born, she could not give birth. She remained pregnant until she could not stand the weight any more and slit her stomach open to deliver the baby. Both the hijra and the baby died. This story illustrates that it is against the nature of hijras to reproduce like women do, thereby denying them full identification as women.

RELIGIOUS IDENTIFICATIONS

An important sex/gender identification of hijras is with Arjun, hero of the great Hindu epic, the Mahabharata. In one episode Arjun is exiled and lives for a year in the disguise of a eunuch-transvestite, wearing women's dress and bracelets, braiding his hair like a woman, and teaching singing and dancing to the women of the king's court. In this role he also participates in weddings and childbirths, a clear point of identification with the hijras (Hiltelbeitel 1980).

The hijras' identification with Arjun is visually reinforced by Arjun's representation in popular drama as a vertically divided half-man/half-woman. In this form Arjun is identified with the sexually ambivalent deity, Shiva, who is also frequently represented as a vertically divided half-man/half-woman, symbolizing his union with his female energy.

Shiva is particularly associated with the concept of creative asceticism, which is the core of hijra identity and power. In Hinduism, sexual impotence can be transformed into procreative power through the practice of asceticism, or the renunciation of sex. The power that results from sexual abstinence (called *tapas*) paradoxically becomes an essential feature in the process of creation.

In one Hindu creation myth, Shiva was asked to create the world, but took so long to do so that the power of creation was given to another deity, Brahma (The Creator). When Shiva was finally ready to begin creation he saw that the universe was already created and got so angry, he broke off his phallus saying "there is no use for this," and threw it into the earth. Paradoxically, as soon as Shiva's phallus ceased to be a source of individual fertility, it became a source of universal fertility (O'Flaherty 1973). This paradox expresses the power of the hijras who as emasculated men are individually impotent but nevertheless are able to confer blessings for fertility on others. As creative ascetics

hijras are considered auspicious and powerful, and this underlies their ritual performances at marriages and childbirth.

While at one level the hijras' claim to power is through Shiva's ritual sacrifice of the phallus, at a more conscious and culturally elaborated level, the power of the hijras is based on their identification with the Mother Goddess. In Hindu India, salvation and success are equated with submission, particularly in regard to the Mother Goddess. The Mother Goddess must offer help when confronted with complete surrender of the devotee, but those who deny her wishes put themselves in danger. Thus, underlying the surrender is fear. The protective and destructive aspects of the Mother Goddess, expressed in myth and ritual, represent the ambivalence toward the real mother that is perhaps universal. But the Hindu Mother Goddess is singularly intense in her destructive aspects, which, nevertheless, contain the seeds of salvation (for a comparison of female goddesses with eunuch priests, see Roller 1999). Popular Hindu mythology (and its hijra versions) abounds in images of the aggressive Mother Goddess as she devours, beheads, and castrates—destructive acts that nevertheless contain the possibility of rebirth, as in the hijra emasculation ritual. This dual nature of the goddess provides the powerful symbolic and psychological context in which the hijras become culturally meaningful as an alternative sex/gender.

Deficient masculinity by itself does not make a hijra. Hijras are deficient men who receive a call from their goddess—which they ignore at the peril of being born impotent for seven future rebirths—to undergo a sex and gender change, wear their hair long, and dress in women's clothes. The sex change, which involves surgical removal of the genitals, is called "the operation" (even by hijras who do not otherwise speak English). For hijras, the operation is a form of rebirth and it contains many of the symbolic elements of childbirth. Only after the operation do hijras become vehicles of the power of the Mother Goddess whose blessings they bestow at weddings and childbirth. For hijras not born intersexed, the operation transforms an impotent, "useless" male into a hijra, and a vehicle of the procreative power of the Mother Goddess.

The operation is explicitly identified with the hijras' devotion to Bahuchara Mata, who is particularly associated with male transvestism and transgenderism. Several hijras are always present at Bahuchara's temple, near Ahmedabad, in Gujerat, to bless visitors and tell them about the power of the goddess.

The surgery is (ideally) performed by a hijra, called a "midwife." The client is seated in front of a picture of the goddess and repeats Bahuchara's name over and over, which induces a trancelike state. The midwife then severs all or part of the genitals (penis and testicles) from the body with two diagonal cuts with a sharp knife. The blood from the operation, which is considered part of the male identity, is allowed to flow freely; this rids the person of their maleness. The resulting wound is healed by traditional medical practices and a small hole is left open for urination. After the operation the new hijra is subject to many of the same restrictions as a woman after childbirth and is supervised and taken care of by hijra elders. In the final stage of the ritual, the hijra is dressed as a bride, signifying the active sexuality potential in marriage, and is taken through the streets in procession. This completes the ritual and the sex/gender transformation. Although emasculation is prohibited by Indian law, hijras continue to practice it secretly (Ranade 1983).

HIJRAS AS ASCETICS

In India, gender is an important part of being a full social person. Through marriage, men and women are expected to produce children, especially sons, in order to continue the family line. An individual who dies without being married, an impotent man, or a woman who does not menstruate is considered an incomplete person. However, the individual who is not capable of reproduction, as either a man or a woman, or who does not wish to marry, is not necessarily excluded from society (see female gender variants later in this chapter). In India, a meaningful role that transcends the categories of (married) man and (married) woman is that of the ascetic, or renouncer, a person both outside society yet also part of it. In identifying with the ascetic role, individuals who are sexually "betwixt and between" for any number of biological reasons or personal choices are able to transform an incomplete personhood into a transcendent one. Within the Hindu religion, the life path of an ascetic is one of the many diverse paths that an individual may take to achieve salvation.

Hijras identify themselves as ascetics in their renunciation of sexual desire, in abandoning their family and kinship ties, and in their dependence on alms (religiously inspired charity) for their livelihood. As ascetics, hijras transcend the stigma of their sex/gender deficiencies.

An important Hindu belief, called *dharma*, is that every individual has a life path of his/her own that he/she must follow, because every individual has different innate essences, moral qualities, and special abilities. This leads to an acceptance of many different occupations, behaviors, and personal styles as legitimate life paths. This is particularly so when the behavior is sanctified by tradition, formalized in ritual, and practiced within a group (Kakar 1982:163). Hinduism thus affords the individual personality wide latitude in behavior, including that which Euro-American cultures might label criminal or pathological and attempt to punish or cure. This Hindu concept of the legitimacy of many different life paths applies to hijras and to other sex/gender variants as well.

RITUAL ROLES AND SOCIAL ACCEPTANCE

In India, the birth of a son is viewed as a major purpose of marriage. As auspicious and powerful ritual figures, on this occasion hijras bless the child and the family and provide entertainment for friends, relatives, and neighbors. These hijra performances, which include folk and current film songs and dances, also have comic aspects. These mainly derive from the hijras' burlesque of women's behavior, especially aggressive sexuality, and mimicking the pains of pregnancy at each month.

At some point in the performance, one hijra inspects the genitals of the newborn to ascertain its sex. Hijras claim that any baby born intersexed belongs to their community and it is widely believed in India that this claim cannot be resisted. The hijras then confer the power of the Mother Goddess to bless the child for what they themselves do not possess—the power of creating new life, of having many sons, and of carrying on the continuity of a family line. When the performance is completed, the hijras claim their traditional payment.

Hijras also perform after a marriage, when the new bride has come to her husband's home (traditionally, and even today ideally, the couple lives with the groom's parents). The hijras bless the couple so that they will have many sons, which is not only the desire of the family, but also means more work for the hijras. These performances contain flamboyant sexual displays and references to sexuality, which break all the rules of normal social intercourse in gender-mixed company and on this occasion are a source of humor. The hijras' skits and songs refer to potentially conflicting relationships in Indian marriages, for example between mother-in-law and daughter-in-law, or between sisters-in-law. As outsiders to the social structure because of their ambiguous sex/gender status, the hijras are uniquely able to expose the points of tension in a culture where sex, gender, and reproduction are involved. In humorously expressing this tension, the hijras defuse it, yet at the same time, their very ambiguity of sex and gender keep the tension surrounding sex, gender, and fertility alive.

Hijras are generally regarded with ambivalence; social attitudes include a combination of mockery, fear, respect, contempt, and even compassion. Fear of the hijras is related to the "virility complex" in India, which has an ancient history and which is also part of contemporary culture. This complex identifies manhood with semen and sexual potency,

both of central concern in India's patriarchal culture (Zwilling and Sweet n.d.:6). Hijras have the power to curse as well as to bless, and if they are not paid their due, they will insult a family publicly and curse it with a loss of virility. The ultimate weapon of a hijra is to raise her skirt and display her mutilated genitals; this is both a source of shame and a contamination of the family's reproductive potential.

Hijras are also feared for another reason. Having renounced normal family life, hijras are outside the social roles and relationships of caste and kinship, which define the social person in Hindu culture and which are the main sources of social control of an individual (Ostor, Fruzzetti, and Barnett 1982). Hijras (and other ascetics) are thus an implicit threat to the social order (Lannoy 1975; O'Flaherty 1973). The hijras use their sexual and social marginality to manipulate and exploit the public to their own advantage. Hijras themselves say that because they are marginal to the social rules that govern the behavior of men and women, they are a people without "shame" (Hall 1995; 1997:445). Hijra audiences know this and feel vulnerable to economic extortion, as they weigh the financial cost of giving in to the hijras' coercive demands for payment against the likelihood that if they do not pay, they will be publicly abused, humiliated, and cursed.

Nevertheless, if hijras challenge their audiences, their audiences also challenge the hijras. Sometimes a member of the hijras' audience will challenge the performers' authenticity by lifting their skirts to see whether they are emasculated and thus "real" hijras or "fake" hijras, men who have male genitals and are thus only impersonating hijras. If hijra performers are found to be "fakes" they are insulted and chased away without payment.

HIJRA SEXUALITY

Part of the ambivalence surrounding hijras focuses on their sexuality. Sexuality is also a source of conflict within the hijra community. As noted above, the term hijra translates as eunuch not homosexual; the power of the hijra role resides in their renunciation of sexuality and the transformation of sexual desire into sacred power. In reality, however, many hijras do engage in sexual activities, exclusively in the receptor role with men and frequently as prostitutes. This is an "open secret" in Indian cities, although known to a different degree among different sections of the population. Sometimes, as in Bombay, hijra prostitutes work out of houses of prostitution located in "red light" districts; in smaller cities and towns they may simply use their own homes to carry on prostitution discretely.

In addition to the exchange of money for sex with a variety of male clients, hijras also have long-term sexual relationships with men they call their "husbands." These relationships may be one-sided and exploitative, as when the "husband" lives off his hijra "wife," but they may also be affectionate and involve some economic reciprocity. Most hijras prefer having a husband to prostitution and many speak of their husbands in very loving terms, as indeed husbands sometimes do of their hijra wives. For many hijras, joining the hijra community provides an opportunity to engage in sexual relations with men in a safer, more organized and orderly environment than is afforded by street prostitution.

Hijra sexual relationships cause conflict within the hijra community, however. Because active sexuality runs counter to the cultural definition of hijras as ascetics, knowledge of hijra prostitution and sexuality undermines their respect in society. In cities where the hijra population is large, hijra prostitutes are not permitted to live with hijra ritual performers. Hijra elders are often jealous of the attachment of individual hijras to their husbands, as this undercuts the economic contribution of a hijra to her household. Some hijras complain that prostitution has increased because the opportunities for ritual performances have declined. In fact, prostitution has been associated with the hijras for hundreds of years, an association that hijras vehemently deny and attribute to those who imitate their effeminacy but who are not "real" hijras.

SOCIAL STRUCTURE OF THE HIJRA COMMUNITY

Indian social structure is built on castes, which are ethnically distinct corporate social units associated with occupational exclusivity, control over their members, and a hierarchically based group allocation of rights and privileges. The Indian caste system includes many different kinds of groups, such as Muslims and tribal peoples, who, though originally outside the Hindu system, were incorporated into it as caste-like groups.

Hijra communities have many caste-like features, which, along with their kinship networks, contribute to their social reproduction (Nanda 1999). Like a caste, the hijra community claims a monopoly over their occupation as ritual performers; exercises control over its members, with outcasting as the ultimate sanction; and rests its legitimacy on origin myths associated with high-status legendary figures like Arjun or deities like Ram or Shiva.

The census of India does not count hijras separately, so estimates of their numbers are unreliable; a common "guesstimate" is 50,000 nationwide. Hijras predominantly live in the cities of northern India, where they find the greatest opportunity to perform their traditional ritual roles, but small groups of hijras are found all over India, in the south as well as the north, and in rural areas and small towns as well as in big cities.

Hijras are highly organized and participate in a special subculture that extends throughout the nation, with some regional variations. Hijras normally live in households containing between five and twenty members with one elder as a "manager." Each hijra contributes to the running of the household, either with money or by performing domestic tasks. Household composition is flexible, and individuals commonly move from one household to another in a different part of a city or in a different city or region, out of boredom, dissatisfaction, or as the result of a dispute.

The nationwide hijra community is composed of "houses," or named subgroups; houses are not domestic units, but are similar to lineages or clans. Each house recognizes a common "ancestor" and has its own history and special rules. Any particular household contains members of several houses. Each house (not household) has a leader, called a *naik* (chief), and within the major cities, the naiks of the different houses form a kind of executive council, making policy and resolving disputes.

Below the level of the naiks are the gurus. The most significant relationship among hijras is that of *guru* (master, teacher) and *chela* (disciple). An individual is formally initiated into the hijra community under the sponsorship of a guru, who bestows a new female name and pays the initiation fee. The new chela vows to obey her guru and the rules of the house and the community. The guru presents the new chela with some gifts and records her name in the guru's record book. This guru-chela relationship, which replicates the ideals of an extended family, is ideally a lifelong bond of reciprocity in which the guru is obligated to "take care of" and help the chela, while the chela is obligated to be loyal and obedient to the guru. The chela must also give her guru a portion of whatever she earns.

Through the extension of guru-chela relationships, hijras all over India are related by (fictive) kinship (Hall 1995). "Daughters" of one "mother" consider themselves "sisters," and elders are regarded as "grandmothers" or as "mother's sister" (aunt). These relationships involve warm and reciprocal regard and are sometimes formalized by the exchange of small amounts of money, clothing, jewelry, and sweets. In addition to the constant movement of hijras who visit their gurus and fictive kin in different cities, religious and secular annual gatherings also bring together thousands of hijras from all over India.

Hijras come from all castes and from Hindu, Muslim and Christian families. Most hijras seem to be from the lower, though not unclean (formerly, untouchable), castes. Within the hijra community, however, all caste affiliations are disregarded and there are no distinctions of purity and pollution. Like other ascetics, hijra identity transcends caste and kinship affiliation.

In pre-independent India, the caste-like status of the hijras was recognized in the princely states, where one hijra in each district was granted hereditary rights to a parcel of land and the right to collect food and small sums of money from each agricultural household in a stipulated area. These rights were protected against other hijras and legitimately inherited within the community. This granting of rights was consistent with the Indian concept of the king's duty to ensure the ancient rights of his subjects (Preston 1987:380). Even today, although in a vague and somewhat confused way, hijras refer back to these rights as part of their claims to legitimacy.

Under British rule in India the hijras lost some of their traditional legitimacy when the British government refused to lend its legal support to the hijras' "right of begging or extorting money, whether authorized by former governments or not." The British thereby hoped to discourage what they found to be "the abominable practices of the wretches." Through a law disallowing any land grant or entitlement from the state to any group that "breach[ed] the laws of public decency," the British finally removed state protection from the hijras (Preston 1987:382). In some British-controlled areas, laws criminalizing emasculation, aimed specifically at the hijras, were enacted. These laws were later incorporated into the criminal code of independent India.

Though emasculation continues, criminalization undercuts social respect for the hijras, particularly when criminal cases are sensationalized in the media. This is also true about the association of hijras with AIDS, though in fact, the spread of AIDS in India is primarily through heterosexual prostitution. In addition, as a result of increasing Westernization of Indian values and culture, at least at a surface level, the role of many traditional ritual performers like the hijras is becoming less compelling. Traditional life-cycle ceremonies are shorter, and expensive and nonessential ritual features are dropping off. In an attempt to compensate for lost earnings, hijras have tried to broaden the definition of occasions on which they claim their performances are necessary, for example, at the birth of a girl as well as a boy or at the opening of a public building or business.

The hijra role incorporates many kinds of contradictions. Hijras are both men and women, yet neither men nor women; their ideal identity is that of chaste ascetics, yet they widely engage in sexual relationships; they are granted the power of the goddess and perform rituals in her name, but they are held in low esteem and are socially marginal. Yet, with all its contradictions and ambiguities, the hijra role continues to be sustained by a culture in which religion still gives positive meaning to gender variance and even accords it a measure of power.

THE SĀDHIN: A FEMALE GENDER VARIANT

Although female gender variants are mentioned in ancient Hindu texts, none are as widespread, visible, or prominent as the hijras. One female gender variant role is the *sādhin* or female ascetic. This role becomes meaningful within the context of Hindu values and culture, particularly regarding the position of women in India (see Humes 1996) and the concept of the ascetic.

As noted above, marriage and reproduction are essential to recognition as a social person in Hindu India, and "spinsters" rarely exist in rural areas. Among the Gaddis, a numerically small pastoral people of the Himalayan foothills, a female gender variant role called sādhin emerged in the late-nineteenth century. Sādhins renounce marriage (and thus, sexuality), though they otherwise live in the material world. They are committed to celibacy for life. Sādhins do not wear women's clothing, but rather the everyday clothing of men, and they wear their hair close cropped (Phillimore 1991).

A girl voluntarily decides to become a sādhin. She usually makes this decision around puberty, before her menarche, though in one reported case, the parents of a six-year-old girl interpreted her preference to dress in boy's clothing and cut her hair like a boy, as an indication of her choice to be a sādhin. For most sādhins, this role choice, which is considered irreversible, is related to their determined rejection of marriage. A sādhin must be a virgin; she is viewed, however, not just as a celibate woman but as a female asexual. Although the transition from presexual child to an asex-

ual sādhin denies a girl's sexual identity, the girl is not considered to have changed her gender, so much as transcended it.

Entering the sādhin role is not marked by ritual, but it is publicly acknowledged when the sādhin adopts men's clothing and has her hair cut in a tonsure, like a boy for his initiation rite into adulthood. Despite her male appearance, however, a sādhin remains socially a woman in many ways, and she retains the female name given to her when she was a child. Sādhins may (but are not obliged to) engage in masculine productive tasks from which women are normally excluded, for example, ploughing, sowing crops, sheep herding, and processing wool. They also, however, do women's work. On gender-segregated ceremonial occasions, adult sādhins may sit with the men as well as smoke the water pipe and cigarettes, definitely masculine behaviors. Yet sādhins do not generally attend funerals, a specifically male prerogative.

Ethnographer Peter Phillimore characterizes the role of the sādhin as an "as if" male (1991:337). A sādhin's gender is not in question, but she can nevertheless operate in many social contexts "like a man." A sādhin can, for example, make the necessary offerings for her father's spirit and the ancestors, a ceremony otherwise performed only by a son. Unlike hijras, though, sādhins have no special ritual or performance roles in society, nor are they considered to have any special sacred powers. Sādhins, like hijras, are ascetics in their renunciation of sexuality, although sādhins are only ambiguous ascetics because they do not renounce other aspects of the material world.

Hindu asceticism is primarily identified with males so that female ascetics behave in significant respects like men; this maleness makes visible and legitimates female asceticism, though it is different from male asceticism in important ways (Humes 1996; Phillimore 1991:341). Unlike male ascetics, who transcend sex/gender classification and who can renounce the world at any age or stage of life, the sādhin's asceticism must begin before puberty and her lifelong chastity, or purity, is essential to the public acceptance of her status. These differences suggest that within orthodox Hinduism, the sādhin role is a way of controlling female sexuality and providing a social niche for the woman who rejects the only legitimate female roles in traditional Hindu India, those of wife and mother.

Because of the importance of women in the subsistence economy, Gaddi society was substantially more gender egalitarian than orthodox Hindus. When Gaddi migration in the late-nineteenth century brought them into contact with more orthodox Hindus, Gaddis came under increasing cultural pressure to curtail the relative equality and freedom of their women. However, because a woman's decision to reject marriage is an unacceptable challenge to gender conventions among the orthodox Hindus, the sādhin role, defined as an asexual female gender variant, acts as a constraint on the potential, unacceptable, sexuality of unmarried women. The definition of the sādhin as asexual transforms "the negative associations of spinsterhood" into the "positive associations of sādhin-hood" (Phillimore 1991:347).

The sādhin role provides one kind of response to the cultural challenge of adult female virginity in a society where marriage and motherhood are the dominant feminine ideals, while the hijra role, despite its many contradictions, gives meaning and even power to male sex/gender ambiguity in a highly patriarchal culture. While all cultures must deal with those whose anatomy or behavior leaves them outside the classification of male and female, man and woman, it is the genius of Hinduism that allows for so many different ways of being human.

REFERENCES

Cohen, Lawrence. 1995. "The Pleasures of Castration: The Postoperative Status of Hijras, Jankhas and Academics." In *Sexual Nature, Sexual Culture*, edited by Paul R. Abramson and Steven D. Pinkerton, pp. 276–304. Chicago: University of Chicago Press.

Hall, Kira. 1995. "Hijra/Hijrin: Language and Gender Identity." Unpublished doctoral dissertation in Linguistics, University of California, Berkeley. Ann Arbor, MI: UMI Dissertation Services.

———. 1997. "'Go Suck Your Husband's Sugarcane!': Hijras and the Use of Sexual Insult." In *Queerly Phrased: Language, Gender, and Sexuality*, edited by Anna Livia and Kira Hall, pp. 430–60. New York: Oxford.

Hiltelbeitel, Alf. 1980. "Siva, the Goddess, and the Disguises of the Pandavas and Draupadi." *History of Religions* 20 (1–2): 147–74.

Humes, Cynthia Ann. 1996. "Becoming Male: Salvation through Gender Modification in Hinduism and Buddhism." In *Gender Reversals and Gender Cultures: Anthropological and Historical Perspectives*, edited by Sabrina Petra Ramet, pp. 123–37. London: Routledge.

Kakar, Sudhir. 1982. *Shamans, Mystics and Doctors: A Psychological Inquiry into India and Its Healing Traditions*. New York: Knopf.

Lannoy, Richard. 1975. *The Speaking Tree*. New York: Oxford University Press.

Nanda, Serena. 1996. "Hijras: An Alternative Sex and Gender Role in India." In *Third Sex, Third Gender: Beyond Sexual Dimorphism in Culture and History*, edited by Gilbert Herdt, pp. 373–418. New York: Zone (MIT).

———. 1999. *The Hijras of India: Neither Man nor Woman*, 2nd ed. Belmont, CA: Wadsworth.

O'Flaherty, Wendy Doniger. 1973. *Siva: The Erotic Ascetic*. New York: Oxford.

———. 1980. *Women, Androgynes, and Other Mythical Beasts*. Chicago: University of Chicago Press.

Ostor, Akos, Lina Fruzetti, and Steve Barnett, eds. 1982. *Concepts of Person: Kinship, Caste, and Marriage in India*. Cambridge, MA: Harvard University Press.

Phillimore, Peter. 1991. "Unmarried Women of the Dhaula Dhar: Celibacy and Social Control in Northwest India." *Journal of Anthropological Research* 47 (3): 331–50.

Preston, Laurence W. 1987. "A Right to Exist: Eunuchs and the State in Nineteenth-Century India." *Modern Asian Studies* 21 (2): 371–87.

Ranade, S. N. 1983. *A Study of Eunuchs in Delhi*. Unpublished manuscript. Government of India, Delhi.

Roller, Lynn E. 1999. *In Search of God the Mother: The Cult of Aatolian Cybele*. Berkeley: University of California Press.

Zwilling, L., and M. Sweet. 1996. "Like a City Ablaze: The Third Sex and the Creation of Sexuality in Jain Religious Literature." *Journal of the History of Sexuality* 6 (3): 359–84.

———. n.d. "The Evolution of Third Sex Constructs in Ancient India: A Study in Ambiguity." In *Constructing Ideologies: Religion, Gender, and Social Definition in India*, edited by Julia Leslie. Delhi: Oxford University Press (forthcoming).

20

Lesbians, Men-Women and Two-Spirits
Homosexuality and Gender in Native American Cultures

Sabine Lang

In the following, I first set the stage for an understanding of how homosexual behavior is viewed and constructed in North American cultures past and present by providing a general introduction to systems of multiple genders that traditionally existed and that, to some extent, still exist in those cultures. "Traditionally" here refers to the tribal cultures of prereservation time. Then I discuss the identities and life situations of contemporary Native American lesbians and gays with a special focus on lesbian women.[1]

People who belonged to special, "alternative" genders within the traditional systems of multiple genders often entered into sexual relationships with people of the same sex. Thus, quite a number of (especially) urban contemporary Native American lesbians and gays have come to view the "women-men" and "men-women" of the prereservation days as their immediate predecessors in the tribal cultures, and to refer to themselves as *two-spirit people* in order to express that continuum. For that reason, I explore both the traditional and contemporary identities and roles of people who had, and have, same-sex relationships. I suggest that the self-identity of present-day two-spirit people is shaped by a variety of factors, including the tribal traditions of gender variance, influences from the Western urban lesbian/gay communities, the experience of being Native American and homosexual as opposed to gay and lesbian from other ethnic groups, and homophobia within the Indian communities.[2]

GENDER VARIANCE AND HOMOSEXUAL BEHAVIOR IN NATIVE AMERICAN CULTURES: WOMEN-MEN AND MEN-WOMEN

The so-called "berdache,"[3] a Native American male who partially or completely adopts the

Source: Lesbians, men-women and two-spirits: Homosexuality and gender in Native American cultures, by Sabine Lang. In *Same-Sex Relations and Female Desires*, edited by Evelyn Blackwood and Saskia E. Wieringa. New York: Columbia University Press, 1999, pp. 91–116. © 1999 Columbia University Press. Used with permission of the publisher.

culturally defined role of a woman, often also donning women's garb, has been widely discussed in anthropological literature (e.g., Callender and Kochems 1983; Jacobs 1968; Jacobs and Cromwell 1992; Lang 1990, 1998; Roscoe 1987, 1991; Williams 1986a,b). Sources referring to females in Native American cultures who take up the ways of men, however, are comparatively rare, and they have mostly been touched on only peripherally in studies on the "berdache" traditions, with some exceptions (Blackwood 1984; Callender and Kochems 1983; Lang 1990, 1998; Roscoe 1988; Whitehead 1981; Williams 1986b).

Since women-men (males in Native American cultures who had partially or completely adopted the socially defined women's role) often entered into sexual relationships or even marriages with men, their roles, as well as the roles of men-women (females in a man's role), have long been viewed as examples of culturally institutionalized homosexuality, a homosexuality that was often considered innate or was categorized under Western culture's psychiatric concepts of deviance and perversion (e.g., Benedict 1934; Ford and Beach 1965; Katz 1985; Kiev 1964; Minturn et al. 1969; Stewart 1960; Werner 1979).[4] Within the past twenty years, however, the essentialist view that interpreted the "berdache" roles as a way to culturally integrate innately abnormal individuals has been replaced in anthropological literature by a view that takes into consideration the cultural and historical context (cf. Blackwood 1986:4f). Moreover, feminist approaches opened the path to a new understanding of the ways sex and gender are viewed and constructed differently in different societies. This view also made possible a reinterpretation of women-men's and men-women's roles and statuses in terms of gender rather than sexuality (cf. Callender and Kochems 1983; Jacobs and Cromwell 1992; Jacobs, Thomas, and Lang 1997; Kessler and McKenna 1977; Lang 1990, 1998; Martin and Voorhies 1975; Whitehead 1981; Williams 1986a,b). Martin and Voorhies to my knowledge were the first to refer to the North American male-bodied "berdaches" as a third gender and to their

female-bodied counterparts as a fourth gender, implying that they constitute part of cultural constructions of gender that recognize additional genders apart from man and woman (Martin and Voorhies 1975:92ff.). Such "cultural expressions of multiple genders (i.e., more than two) and the opportunity for individuals to change gender roles and identities over the course of their lifetimes" (Jacobs and Cromwell 1992:63) are termed *gender variance* in recent anthropological literature.

Within their respective cultures women-men and men-women are classified as neither men nor women, but as genders of their own. This is also reflected in words used in Native American languages to refer to them. These words are different from the words for woman and man, and often indicate that women-men and men-women are seen, one way or another, as combining the masculine and the feminine (cf. Roscoe 1988; Lang 1990:299–302, 312–313; also Callender and Kochems 1983). The Cheyenne, for example, called women-men *heemaneh,* "half men, half women" (Grinnell 1962 2:39). Women-men in the Pueblo of Isleta were called *lhunide,* "man-woman" (Parsons 1932:246), the Subarctic Ingalik called them "woman pretenders" (Osgood 1958:261). A certain female at the Pueblo of Zuni who manifested masculine manners was called *katsotse,* "boy-girl" (Parsons 1939:38), and among the Shoshoni both males in a woman's role and females in a man's role were called *tainna wa'ippe,* "man-woman" (Clyde Hall, taped conversation; see also Steward 1941:353, where the spelling is *tavgowaip,* the phonetic letter *ϑ* resembling the Greek *eta*). In Shoshoni, *tainkwa* or *tainna* means "man," *wa'ippe* "woman" (Miller 1972:136, 172).

Apart from gender constructions, the roles and statuses of individuals who are neither men nor women in Native American cultures are embedded within worldviews that emphasize and appreciate transformation and change. Due to the scope and subject of this contribution, such religious aspects cannot be discussed in detail here but have been elaborated upon elsewhere (Lang 1994, 1997b, forthcoming). Within such worldviews, an individual who changes her or his gender once or more often in the course of her or his life is not viewed as an abnormality but rather as part of the natural order of things. As Tafoya has observed, the emphasis on transformation and change in Native American cultures also includes the idea that an individual is expected to go through many changes in a lifetime (1992:257).

People who are familiar with their culture's traditions of gender variance emphasize elements of spirituality that were crucial to the roles of women-men and men-women and still are important where such roles continue to exist. This even holds true for contemporary "two-spirited" Native Americans who for that reason may feel restricted by categories like "gay" or "lesbian." These categories are defined in terms of sexual behavior instead of personhood, spirituality, and specific, complex identities deriving from the experience of being Native American (cf. Tafoya 1992:257), as opposed to being white or of any other ethnic heritage.

Gender variance at least traditionally was a widespread trait of Native American cultures in North America (see map 1). Its individual expressions, however, were very diverse, more diverse than can be elaborated upon here. Parents in quite a number of tribes would recognize a child that was to become a woman-man or man-woman by the way he or she acted while very young (cf. Lang 1990:256ff, 351f). In the Native American cultures of the Plains and the Prairies, and also in parts of California and the Northeast, women-men and men-women were/are seen as acting upon a vision or dream, which both explained and legitimized their choice to become a gender other than woman or man. Among the Canadian Dene-Tha, a phenomenon akin to gender variance occurs within a complex system of reincarnation beliefs, including the possibility of cross-sex reincarnation (Goulet 1982:9f).

The statuses and roles of women-men and men-women also varied from tribe to tribe, even though some writers evoke the image of some timeless, universally present, and universally revered "berdache" role in Native American cultures, sometimes elevating especially women-men above everyone else.[5]

In a small number of cultures special supernatural powers were attributed to women-men, and therefore special ceremonial roles, because of their gender status and their vision, just as special religious roles were attributed to other people because of other kinds of supernatural powers and instructions they received in visions. In yet other cultures, women-men were healers or "shamans" apparently not because of their special gender status, but because of the gender role they had chosen. Thus, in tribes where predominantly the women were healers, women-men would choose that profession also; likewise, men-women might pick up the profession of a healer as part of their masculine gender role in cultures where healers were predominantly men. In still other Native American cultures, there is no predominance of either men or women in the healing profession, and women-men or men-women apparently picked up that profession if they were gifted for it, but did not—and did not have to—become healers if they did not possess that gift (cf. Lang 1990:173ff., 337).

In quite a number of Native American cultures, no supernatural impetus seems to have been needed for the members of a community to accept a child's choice to partially or completely adopt the role and manners of the opposite sex. Women-men and men-women were mixing, blending, and splitting gender roles to varying degrees, some of them taking up the role of the opposite sex completely, others only part of it. This mixing did not affect their classification as genders other than women and men. In some Native American cultures cross-dressing was an integral part of their role, in others it was not. In most cases people would take up the role and status of a gender that was neither man nor woman permanently; sometimes, however, they eventually might become a man or a woman again. Gender variance is as diverse as Native American cultures themselves. About the only common denominator is that in many Native American tribal cultures systems of multiple genders existed, classifying people of either sex according to their occupational preferences and expression of gender-specific personality traits and mannerisms as either men, women, women-men, or men-women.

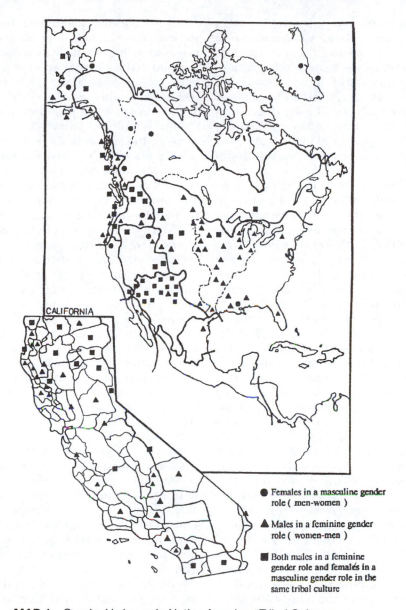

Females in a masculine gender role (men-women)

Males in a feminine gender role (women-men)

Both males in a feminine gender role and females in a masculine gender role in the same tribal culture

MAP 1   Gender Variance in Native American Tribal Cultures

DEFINITIONS OF "HOMOSEXUALITY" AND "HETEROSEXUALITY" IN TRIBAL CULTURES

Often—but, as has been pointed out above, by no means always—women-men and men-women entered into sexual relationships with partners of the same sex. Since multiple genders were recognized in many Native American cultures, however, sexual relations between a woman-man or a man-woman and her/his same-sexed partner may be homosexual on the level of (physical) sex, but they are not so on the level of gender. If a man, for example, is having sex with a woman-man, he is not seen as having sex with another man, he is having sex with someone who belongs to a gender different from his own.

The same holds true, of course, for a woman who has sex with either a woman-man or a man-woman. The partners in such relationships are never of the same gender, regardless whether they are of the same sex or not (cf. Tafoya in Levy et al. 1991). Thus, at least in the prereservation and early reservation Native American cultures where systems of multiple genders were still intact, a same-sex relationship was by no means identical with a same-gender relationship.

Little is known about homosexual relationships as defined by Western culture in Native American tribal societies, even though there are some scant references in the literature (Lang 1990:375ff). Regarding the Yuma, for example, Forde notes that "casual secret homosexuality among both women and men is well known. The latter is probably more common. This is not considered objectionable but such persons would resent being called *elxa'* or *kwe'rhame*" (Forde 1931:157). *Elxa'* and *kwe'rhame* are the Yuma terms for women-men and men-women, respectively. Thus, among the Yuma there existed sexual relationships between women-men and men-women and partners of the same sex and also sexual contacts between two men and two women, and these two kinds of same-sex behavior were clearly distinguished from each other by the Yuma themselves. Among the Flathead there apparently existed words that referred to sexual relations between two women and two men (Turney-High 1937:85, 156f). The word for lesbianism, which according to Turney-High contains the root "kiss," was *ntalá* (Turney-High 1937:156).

Within systems of multiple genders native definitions on homosexuality were based on the gender rather than the physical sex of the people involved, and also took into account such factors as visionary experiences. Among the Navajo, for example, there traditionally existed four genders—women, men, women-men and men-women, the two latter categories being called *nádleehé*, "someone who is in a constant process of change." An individual who is classified as nádleehé is usually already recognized in childhood because she/he shows a marked preference for occupations culturally assigned to the opposite sex. A homosexual relationship as defined by the Navajo is a sexual relationship between two individuals of the same gender (two men, two women, two female-bodied nádleehé, two male-bodied nádleehé), or of closely related genders (a woman and a male-bodied nádleehé, a man and a female-bodied nádleehé). While a homosexual relationship in Western culture is basically defined as a relationship between individuals of the same sex and the same gender, the Navajo definition of homosexuality is more subtle and based on gender rather than on characteristics of biological sex and anatomy. Thus it might more appropriately be termed a *homogender relationship* (cf. Tietz 1996). Quasi-heterosexual (or *heterogender*) relationships among the Navajo include relationships between a man and a woman, a man and a male-bodied nádleehé, and a woman and a female-bodied nádleehé. Such relationships are met with approval, whereas relationships between members of the same gender or closely related genders are considered to be culturally inappropriate, at least traditionally (Thomas 1993). The idea, for example, of two nádleehé of either sex having a sexual relationship with each other is unthinkable to traditionally raised Navajo (cf. Thomas 1993).

Among the Shoshoni, on the other hand, the difference between a "gay," or homosexual, individual and a woman-man and a man-woman is traditionally defined in terms of both occupational preferences and spirituality. *Tainna wa'ippe* (women-men and men-women who, as among the Navajo, are both subsumed under one term) act on a powerful vision that causes them to adopt and manifest the ways, occupations, and clothing of the other sex, but their tainna wa'ippe status does not limit their choices as far as sexual partners are concerned. Unlike nádleehé, male- and female-bodied tainna wa'ippe can have relationships with both men and women, the only kind of relationship considered inappropriate being a relationship between two tainna wa'ippe of either sex, which apparently is viewed as incestuous since, according to Clyde Hall (personal communication 1992), at least male-bodied tainna wa'ippe refer to each other as "sisters." A "gay" person as opposed to a tainna wa'ippe is largely defined as lacking the spiritual element, acting on personal preference instead of manifesting spiritual power. Homosexuality in this case is defined on the basis of the presence or absence of the spiritual element. A "gay" relationship, therefore, in Shoshoni culture is a relationship between two persons of the same sex and the same gender that does not involve a tainna wa'ippe. To my knowledge, such relationships were, and are, not considered inappropriate.

While constructions of homosexuality and heterosexuality, or rather of homogender and heterogender relationships, differed among the tribal and early reservation cultures, the general way of classifying relationships and the attitude toward these various kinds of relationships are summarized in the figure below (see Figure 1).

NATIVE AMERICAN LESBIANS AND GAYS TODAY

The attitude toward sexuality in general and same-sex relationships in particular has changed dramatically on many reservations over the past century due to colonization and acculturation.[6] In many cases the traditions of gender variance have been forgotten or repressed; in other cases they have gone underground and become invisible to white government officials, researchers, and others, sometimes even to other Native Americans. Today only very few individuals living on reservations adopt the role and manners of the "other" sex, or more importantly, are classified as women-men or men-women by the other members of their communities within a still functioning system of multiple genders (cf. Lang 1997a). There are exceptions, of course. On some reservations people were still familiar with the traditions of gender variance in the 1950s and 1960s. Even today in some cases an elder or relative, usually a grandmother, who recognizes that a child is manifesting personality and behavioral traits of a woman-man or man-woman, will see to it that that child is allowed to grow up to fulfill a gender role according to this special gender status.

Gender Status	Woman	Man	(female-bodied) Man-Woman	(male-bodied) Woman-Man
Woman	homo-gender	hetero-gender	hetero-gender	hetero-gender
Man	hetero-gender	homo-gender	hetero-gender	hetero-gender
(female-bodied) Man-Woman	hetero-gender	hetero-gender	homo-gender (?)	hetero-gender
(male-bodied) Woman-Man	hetero-gender	hetero-gender	hetero-gender	homo-gender*

FIGURE 1 Classifications of Sexual Relationships in Native American Tribal Cultures (following Thomas, in print, and Tietz 1996, and based on the data compiled in Lang 1990)

☐ Relationships that are culturally acknowledged, accepted, and sanctioned

☐ Relationships that may be tolerated, but not formally acknowledged

* Relationships that are culturally tabooed universally in North America (Relationships between two women-men are the only kind of relationships that traditionally are considered inappropriate almost universally.)

(?) No information obtainable about cultural acceptance or nonacceptance

Recognition of a potential woman-man or man-woman on the grounds of occupational preferences requires a sexual/gendered division of labor. But the sexual division of labor that existed in tribal cultures has disappeared just as the life of the prereservation days has disappeared. Life—especially economy—on Indian reservations has become integrated into twentieth-century capitalist society. In many areas, the differences between "man's work" and "woman's work" have become blurred. Still, there are areas of work that are cross-culturally considered more masculine or more feminine. People pick non-Native or at least not culturally specific occupations that best fit their gender identity. Contemporary men-women (as well as "butch" lesbians) become, for example, firefighters, road construction workers, crane operators, and the like; that is, they choose physically strenuous occupations dominated by men. In the rural areas, they may also choose to compete with men by participating in rodeos, riding bulls, and roping cows. Erna Pahe (Navajo) told me about such a woman whom she had witnessed in the late 1950s and 1960s. Among the Shoshoni on the reservation I visited, I was told that contemporary mannish females hunt deer and elk, as do the men, while most women do not. Present-day Native American women-men (as well as gays), on the other hand, have a tendency to choose occupations defined as feminine and "nurturing" in the Western sense, such as nurses and social workers.

The issue of identity has become complex over the past decades. Some people, usually raised in families that are oriented toward the traditions of their cultures, still identify themselves as women-men or men-women, and are viewed and labeled that way by the other members of their respective communities. Such individuals are to be found almost exclusively on the reservations. Often they do not have any role models, that is, women-men or men-women of the generations before them. In order to recreate a role for themselves, they turn to the elders (and sometimes to anthropological and other writings about Native American gender variance) and refashion their role to fit into the late twentieth century. Their identity and status is still,

as in the old days, based on occupational preferences and/or spiritual experiences rather than on sexual preference. As a rule they do not identify themselves as gay or lesbian due to the cultural constructions of sexuality noted above.

Other people on and off the reservations set themselves apart from others of their community not by cross-gender occupational interests and personality traits, but by a sexual preference for partners of the same sex. They identify with Western concepts of lesbian and gay; they do not view themselves as women-men or men-women but as gay *men* or lesbian *women*. In defining their identity, they emphasize sexuality and deemphasize occupational aspects and spirituality.

Still other, usually urban, Native Americans manifest an identity that is a combination of the traditions of gender variance and of Western concepts of homosexuality. Their identity is, on the one hand, gay and lesbian, so they exclusively or predominantly enter into relationships with same-sex partners. On the other hand, they perceive themselves, as Native American homosexual individuals, as inherently combining elements of both the masculine and the feminine within themselves on a spiritual rather than an occupational level. For them a combination of the masculine and the feminine is tied to sexual orientation rather than to gender status. While two-spirit people may be "butches" or "queens," most of them unambiguously identify themselves as women or men, not as an intermediate gender that combines both.

There are also Native Americans who on some reservations basically live a contemporary version of the ways of women-men and men-women but do not necessarily label themselves as such. Many people in the respective communities remember that cross-gender behavior once was culturally acceptable, but they do not necessarily remember the details of women-men's and men-women's roles and statuses or the terminology used to refer to them. Masculine females in such cases may or may not identify themselves as belonging to a gender different from both man and woman, but they are perceived by others in their community as being masculine in their personal expressions and occupational choices, and thus as being different from other females.

COLONIZATION AND HOMOPHOBIA

Due to the influences of white concepts and Christianity, gender variance and homosexual behavior have come to be met with strong disapproval on and off the reservations. People either adopted white attitudes and values or did not wish to see their cultures criticized by Whites for permitting expressions of "perversion."[7] On the other hand I have also heard stories about—and have witnessed this myself—contemporary women-men and men-women as well as lesbian or gay couples living on the reservation unharmed and quite comfortable. It is my impression that on a number of reservations it is possible for same-sex couples to live undisturbed unless they make their sex life a public issue the way urban lesbians and gays in the cities do. A common remark people made to me was that same-sex relationships "are not talked about" on the reservations, neither by those involved in them nor by other members of their communities. At first I took this as an indication of discrimination. At least in some cases it seems to be a matter of decorum, however.

People of whatever sexual inclination are expected to fit into the everyday life of their rural reservation community. It is considered inappropriate to set oneself apart on the grounds of sexuality. The inappropriateness here does not necessarily lie in the fact that sexuality is concerned, but that certain people try to set themselves apart on whatever grounds from the community at large. Erna Pahe (Navajo) for example, said that for one thing it is considered bad taste to hurl one's sex life or sexual preference into everyone's face. She also pointed out to me:

> [On the reservation] you wouldn't go out and advertise a gay barbecue, gay picnic, or something like that, because in their [the other Navajos'] eyes it would show that there is this group of people that are trying to be separate from the People, you know, all of our people on the reservation.

Thus lesbians and gays on the reservations will get together for informal private gatherings, barbecues, or parties, but it seems uncommon—or sometimes maybe even unnecessary—for them to formally organize themselves. Male-bodied nádleehé know each other but apparently do not feel any need to formally organize themselves on the grounds of their gender or sexuality because they are integrated within their families and local communities. A Nez Percé woman I talked to said that it is her impression that back on the reservation "everybody knows, but they just don't pay attention, they don't really care, you know, it's not a big deal. They tease you about it, [but] the only ones that really gave me any trouble were the ones that were Christian Indians."

But it is impossible to generalize about the presence or absence of homophobia in Indian communities. As Paula Gunn Allen (Laguna/Sioux) remarked, "there are people being raised even today in a number of tribal universes . . . in the rural areas, not the big cities, and they're raised with complete acceptance. . . . But it's a pretty mixed bag. There are a number of reservations that are throwing queers off and won't let them come back. . . . It's pretty horrifying in a lot of respects because we're still going through the agonies of colonization and the remnants of the colonial mind that has been imposed upon us" (quoted in Levy et al. 1991).

TWO-SPIRITED PEOPLE: IDENTITY ISSUES

Many Native Americans who at some point in their lives have had a same-sex relationship have also had heterosexual relationships, a fact that confuses the more narrowly defined Western categories of "gay," "lesbian," "bisexual," and "straight." To identify themselves as lesbian to many Native American women means that for the time being they prefer women as partners, and maybe they will continue to do so, but it does not necessarily mean that they exclusively live or intend to live in relationships with women. Moreover, mannish women on and off the reservation will not seldom prefer the company of (heterosexual) men over that of women, because it is the men and not the women who share their way of life and personal manners. Still other Native American self-identified lesbians greatly enjoy the company of Native American gays.

The idea of being restricted to one kind of sexual choice for all of their lives or of even banning men from their lives altogether seems to be far-fetched to many Native American lesbians I talked to, even though some prefer a way of life centered entirely around women. Many of the lesbians I talked to had a history of relationships with men, which they did not seem to remember with repugnance. Amelia (pseudonym), an urban woman in her late thirties who is of mixed heritage and identifies herself as bisexual, recalled how she felt alienated by the codes of the white lesbian community in the 1970s:

> I think my first big romance was [with] a girl, another girl, when I was in junior high. I was thirteen, she was fifteen. She was an older woman. [Chuckles.] I think I fell in love with girls first, but I was also attracted to boys. I think that sometimes in trying to fit in with some of the lesbian stuff in the seventies—I wasn't really experimenting with men that much, but it's like a lot of the lesbians just wouldn't talk about any attraction to men, although I think that there is probably lesbians who occasionally sleep with men, more than people want to talk about, but there's so much denial around it. So I mean to some extent I'm perfectly happy to sleep with women for the rest of my life, but if it turns into a real iron-clad thing like that, it kind of loses its appeal.

My data indicate that a high proportion of self-identified lesbian/two-spirited Native American women have given birth to children (who were not conceived by artificial insemination but by intercourse with men). The importance of children for Native American women was repeatedly emphasized to me by lesbian women. Erna Pahe said that in Navajo culture

> there is a special role that women play, too, I mean, as the bearers of the next generation. There's a distinct position that women play within the tribe, and so even though nádleehé women [in the sense of lesbian/two-spirited,

S. L.] exist, it's of a different level. They're mothers. I mean, like myself, I'm a mother. The first thing is you're a child. And you become a young woman. And then you become a mother, so whether you're a nádleehé or not, the first, before anything else, is, you are a mother. . . . So when you speak about nádleehé women, the thing is that they're mothers first.

Another example of the connection of motherhood with sexual preferences that are not exclusively homosexual is a Shoshoni woman, Shirley (pseudonym), and her first partner. They decided they wanted to raise a child, so Shirley, who was many years younger than her partner, got pregnant by a relative of her partner's and gave birth to a daughter. The partner had guardianship of the girl from the time she was born, so they decided that the partner should adopt the child, which was finally arranged by a (two-spirited) tribal judge. When the two women separated, the girl stayed with the partner, but Shirley regularly spent time with the child.

While Shirley apparently has spent most of her adult life in relationships with older women, she did not exclude the possibility of entering into a long-term relationship with a man. She dreamt of having her own cattle and cultivating alfalfa, and an older, male, cowboy-type partner would have been just as welcome to her in that imaginary future as the kind of female partners she had. The possibility for a mannish female to choose either a woman or a man for her partner is consistent with the traditional pattern among the Shoshoni.

Within their Native American cultural frames of reference, conceiving and giving birth to children is an essential part of womanhood regardless of a woman's sexual preference. Thus, some of them label themselves bisexual rather than lesbian, which some women perceive to be a rigid Western category created by self-identified lesbian white women that runs contrary to lived life where sexual preferences may change.[8]

URBAN LESBIANS AND GAY MEN

Because of problems many encounter within their families and communities, but also to find better opportunities for work and education, a considerable number of lesbian and gay Native Americans leave their reservations to join Native American lesbian and gay communities in the cities. They may return to their reservations periodically to see their relatives, which often also means going back into the closet (Randy Burns, personal communication 1992). Even though the lesbian and gay subcultures in the cities might still not provide specific role models for Native American lesbians and gays, the latter at least find themselves in a position to express same-sex relationships in a noncloseted way. Erna Pahe recalls:

> On the [Navajo] reservation, you never see a lot of touching of lovers. Even in straight relationships, they don't do much touching, you know, holding hands is about the extent of any public showing that you're in a relationship, right? So it was nice, going down the Castro [Castro Street, the heart of the gay/lesbian neighborhood of San Francisco, S. L.], and you're actually able to put your arms around your lover, and, you know, *touching* women has always been exciting for me. I mean, it was just so different.

This example also illustrates the influence of the urban gay/lesbian context on urban Native American lesbians' and gays' lives. While the experience of being Native American is a strong part of their identity, they do incorporate behaviors that are available to them in the lesbian/gay subcultures in the cities but not on the reservations.

Many lesbian and gay Native Americans basically identify themselves as members of the lesbian/gay/bisexual communities (Tafoya 1992:257). Yet others do not quite feel at home there because of the racist discrimination they face. These individuals are searching for identities and lifestyles that are, in the broadest sense, specifically "Indian," as opposed to white gay and lesbian, and different from other gays and lesbians of color. Many turn to their native cultures in search of identities and role models and rediscover the tribal traditions of multiple genders, of women-men and men-women whose same-sex relationships were accepted and who, moreover, sometimes were very respected members of their communities.

Many Native American gays and lesbians in the cities see their contemporary roles as a continuation of the roles of women-men and men-women in tribal cultures. They view the women-men and men-women of the tribal cultures as their "gay" and "lesbian" predecessors. Consequently, they also see the "traditional" role as a "gay" role. "Gay" in this context assumes a meaning that in some respects differs from Western definitions, referring not only to sexual preferences but also to special roles and responsibilities (artists, providers, healers) that are linked to homosexual individuals in tribal cultures (cf. Burns 1988:1f).

This perception is reflected in the term "two-spirit" that urban lesbian and gay Native Americans have coined for themselves. The term two-spirit/two-spirited refers to tribal traditions of gender variance, to the roles and statuses in Indian cultures of women-men and men-women who combined both masculine and feminine traits. Such a concept of two-spirit/two-spirited both helps Native American lesbians and gays to gain acceptance within the Indian communities and provides them with positive role models. While women-men and men-women in the tribal societies often were such in very tangible ways (e.g., by combining masculine and feminine work activities), contemporary urban two-spirited people view such a combination in a more abstract way. A combination of the masculine and the feminine is more often seen as a spiritual quality innately inherent in homosexual women and men. The choice of the term "two-*spirit*" (and not, for example, "two-gendered") also reflects an emphasis on spiritual gifts Native American gays and lesbians perceive to be innately bestowed on them.

Even though Native American lesbians, for example, who label themselves two-spirited draw on the tribal traditions of men-women, they do not usually view themselves as being of a gender different from "woman" and "man." The combination of abstract, spiritual masculine and feminine energies that they perceive to dwell within themselves does not affect their classification in terms of gender. As a rule, they view themselves as women-loving *women*, not as men-women.

The postulated historical continuum from the women-men and men-women of the tribal cultures to the urban Native American lesbians and gays of today is not entirely unproblematic, however. According to both the written sources and various people who are intimately familiar with the traditions of gender variance in their respective cultures, the last "old-time" women-men and men-women on many reservations were alive in the 1920s and 1930s, in a few cases up to the 1940s. Even by then, the institution had already dramatically declined due to acculturation, as has been outlined above. The contemporary two-spirit identity is strongly based on research done by urban lesbian and gay Native Americans since the mid-1970s into the written anthropological and historical sources. In many ways, this identity reflects the way white researchers up to the 1980s have interpreted women-men's and men-women's roles and statuses—as ways to culturally integrate innately homosexual individuals, who at the same time often held special, highly respected statuses.

In the old-time roles and statuses of women-men and men-women there is an emphasis on gender while in those of contemporary two-spirit people the emphasis is on sexuality, ethnicity, and a spirituality that is viewed as innate in Native American homosexual women and men. Thus, in many ways the concept of two-spirit reinterprets the old-time traditions of gender variance in a way to fit the needs of Native American lesbians and gays in the late twentieth century. As gender variance has ceased to exist on the reservations, urban Native American lesbians and gays have been reinventing a new tradition of two-spiritness that draws on tribal cultures, on the experience of being Native American in an urban multiethnic environment, and on urban gay and lesbian lifestyles.

Two-spirit can probably best be characterized as a largely pan-Indian gay/lesbian identity that emphasizes ethnicity and spirituality. During the past years, the term has sometimes come to encompass also the traditions of gender variance past and present, Native American bisexuals, transgendered people, butches and queens as well as gender variance in indigenous cultures outside North America (cf. Tietz 1996:205). The urban two-spirit communities are comprised of people of various tribal backgrounds and of a number of people who are of mixed heritage. Their knowledge of tribal culture varies widely, depending on how and where they were brought up. Interaction during intertribal two-spirit gatherings is facilitated by the use of pan-Indian symbols and actions, mostly of Plains origin, such as the use of sage (or other plants that are connected with special cleansing power) for smudging, sweat lodges, talking circles, pow-wows, and giveaways.

Not all Native American lesbians and gays consider themselves two-spirited in the sense outlined above. Two-spirited is a concept prevalent in the cities and at intertribal gatherings that are mostly attended by urban Indian gays and lesbians, and it has not yet spread to the reservations on a large scale. Moreover, a considerable number of lesbian and gay native Americans still choose an identity and lifestyle closer to white homosexual identities, trying to merge into the gay and lesbian urban subculture with their bars and other gathering places.

NATIVE AMERICAN LESBIANS: A SKETCH

As I talked to more and more people, very diverse life histories began to unfold. It is impossible to go into many details here because of this diversity (the results of the project will be presented in detail in Lang forthcoming).[9] It may suffice, however, to offer a few glimpses of the lives of a few contemporary Native American lesbians.

One theme usually runs through each of these life histories like a red thread. With Amelia (pseudonym), the main theme was her mixed heritage and attempts to find an identity that harmoniously combines both sides of her heritage instead of denying one of them. With Joan (pseudonym), a Nez Percé woman, the main theme was the experience of having grown up as a tomboy, always different from other children. Joan was born around 1953 and lived in urban surroundings since her family relocated in the 1950s, but she still has ties to her reservation.

I was really a tomboy. By the time I came out it was more or less suspected already, you know? I just always was very different! So when I finally really came out and started bringing lovers home and stuff, then they started treating me more like I was just like a guy. As I was growing up some of these Indian males on the reservation that are straight and that I visited growing up, they just treat me like a guy. I've always been the kind of person who hung out with the guys.

Another experience she elaborated on was being nonmonogamous. At the time we talked she had one main relationship and a number of more loose ones.

Michael Owlfeather told me about an earlier generation of women on the Shoshoni reservation, his grandmother and several of her women friends, who had husbands and children and who were nevertheless considered specially gendered:

My grandmother was a two-spirited person herself, and it's known among the lesbian people there. . . . There's another woman that always hung around her . . . , and people like that, that took pride in doing anything that a man could do, and doing it better. But these women also had children, got married, you know? But they had their women friends and were always respected for that and everything else. But it was nothing overt, they didn't hold it out to the community. But everybody knew what was going on.

Some Shoshoni women (about ten to twelve according to Michael Owlfeather) on the reservation today are contemporary examples of gender variance. They are quite "butch" in appearance and manners and seem to identify as mannish women rather than as a gender of their own. While they enter into relationships with each other (and, interestingly, *not* with feminine women), it nevertheless appears to be not unusual for them to also have sex with men and give birth to and raise children.

While one woman I talked to referred to herself and others like her on the reservation as lesbian, it eventually became apparent that this was not identical with the Western concept of lesbian. She used the term to refer to the masculine females on the reservation and their way of life, including sexual relationships that are by no means exclusively homosexual. "Lesbian" to her meant a contemporary "man-woman," although I am not sure how familiar she was with her culture's traditions of gender variance. She told me about a woman who lives a quite masculine life and, according to my consultant, competed with men in boxing matches. She characterized her friend with the words: "She's a lesbian, too."

I do not know what generic term is used among the other Shoshoni to refer to those women or if any term is used. It is my impression that it is sufficient to drop one or two names of the women concerned, and everyone knows what particular group of women is being talked about—the reservation is small (the Indian population there numbers a little over 3,000), and everyone knows everyone else. Among the general population on the reservation, the way of life and relationships of these mannish women is apparently not disapproved of. Michael Owlfeather half jokingly described them to me as a female version of "good old boys." Moreover, they seem to be ready to pick a fight if someone insults them, so people who do not condone their way of life usually leave them alone. They have a reputation of roughness and toughness.

The lives of the Shoshoni mannish women on the reservation I visited (as well as the life of the modern Shosoni woman-man at whose home I stayed for various periods of time) did not seem closeted. They are rural people with interests centering around rural occupations and recreational activities. Shoshoni mannish women take up male-dominated pursuits. At least two women I met used to work as firefighters; they also hunt elk.

The mannish females on the reservation are integrated into the life of their community and socialize with both straights and other two-spirits. Of course there are people who try to discriminate against them, an action sometimes prompted by the women's overall way of life rather than by their sexual behavior. My consultant Shirley told me about an incident where one of her brothers showed up drunk and started to insult her and her partner, asking whether they thought they were men. "I'm more of a man than you are," Shirley replied, adding that she had regular work and led an orderly life, whereas he had lived on welfare all his life. One word led to another, until a fight ensued. Finally the brother was lying on the floor, Shirley and her partner pinning him down. They called the police and had him thrown into jail. While there may be discrimination on the reservations, Native American lesbians and gays are by no means always helpless victims but may very well take a stand against it.

There was another side to Shirley, her proneness to physical violence. People told me that the lesbians on the reservation resort to physical fights among each other when quarrels arise, especially when they have been drinking in bars in the nearby towns. People did not necessarily find this objectionable since physical fights under the influence of alcohol occur among straight women as well. Shirley was no exception. When drunk, she had a tendency toward violence, which she was herself very aware of. She told me that she once broke the jaw of a woman barkeeper who had somehow offended her and went to jail for it.[10]

In spite of the fact that many Native American lesbians cooperate and organize with gay men, they recognize that their own specific experiences and needs sometimes require women-only gatherings. Thus even though Native American lesbians often work closely with men in organizations like Gay American Indians, and attend the annual two-spirit gatherings with gay Native men, there are a few events that are restricted to Native American lesbians or to Native Americans and other lesbians of color and designed specifically to empower them. One example is the Women's Sun Dance, which is held annually. Only women of color may pledge to dance and be the actual performers of the Sun Dance, even though white women are welcome to attend, provided they show respect for the ceremony and its participants and help with the many things that have to be done (cooking, keeping the fire near the sweat lodge going, cutting firewood, hauling water).

Native American lesbians are acutely aware of the impacts of triple discrimination directed at them as women, lesbians, and Native Americans/women of color. An Ojibwa (Aniishnabe) woman summarized her experiences and those of other Native American lesbians as follows:

> As a two-spirited woman of the First Nations, you become aware of "triple oppression." You are lesbian, female and Native in a society dominated by a world that does not honor women or indigenous peoples and by a world that says your sexuality is non-existent, a phase, a threat or a sin against God. . . . [You] find yourself in a city built on racism and fed on the oppression of everyone who is not heterosexual, white, and male (quoted in Tietz 1994:1).

There are some Native American lesbians who have become so disenchanted with white people, including white lesbian women, or who have come to reject white/Western society that they have established small communities restricted to Native American women or people of color. Two women I know live on women's land in the Midwest. Other women, mostly of mixed heritage, have recently purchased land in northern California where they plan to live self-sufficiently in the traditions of their tribal ancestors, turning their backs to the white culture, which they perceive as disrespectful toward nature and humans and as destructive.

The identities of contemporary Native American lesbians emerge at the intersection of traditional tribal models of multiple genders, ways of life that have emerged in the lesbian/gay subcultures in the cities, and an awareness of being Native American as opposed to being white or of any other ethnic heritage. In the tribal societies, there were no roles and identities that are strictly comparable to those of late twentieth-century lesbian women. In those societies systems of more than two genders led to the cultural acknowledgment and valuation of other genders in addition to the genders "woman" and "man." These additional genders accommodated males and females who markedly manifested personality traits and occupational preferences culturally attributed to the other sex. The roles of such women-men and men-women often included socially condoned sexual or marital relationships with partners of the same physical sex, but not of the same gender.

The women-men and men-women of tribal cultures have been presented as the predecessors of contemporary Native American lesbians and gays in numerous publications by white and Native writers alike. Urban lesbian and gay Native Americans view the traditions of gender variance as examples of how people who had same-sex relationships were traditionally accepted and valued in Native American cultures. As a result of this, during the last decade the term and concept of "two-spirit" has emerged at intertribal gatherings of mostly urban Native American lesbians and gays. Two-spirit, an identity that is largely pan-Indian, combines the experience of being Native American with that of being lesbian/gay.

On some reservations the once favorable attitude toward same-sex relationships and manifestations of cross-gender behavior gave way to a homophobia that condemns both gender variance and homosexuality. On other reservations, while the traditions of gender variance may be forgotten or repressed, masculine females and feminine males may still be treated with acceptance. The roles of lesbians on some reservations seem to reflect the tribal roles of men-women rather than urban lesbian identities, which are influenced by the white lesbian/gay subcultures. At the same time, their sexual relationships are usually not exclusively homosexual, which is a trait they share with many urban Native American lesbians. Motherhood is perceived as an essential component of Native American womanhood regardless of sexual preference. Thus, "lesbian" to many self-identified lesbian women on and off the reservation does not imply an exclusive preference for sexual relationships with women.

The lives of Native American lesbians are just as diverse as were the lives of men-women and women-men in the tribal societies. It is problematic to make any generalizations that may not do justice to individual life experiences. An oversimplified and misleading picture results if one reduces women-men's and men-women's lives to their sexuality. The same holds true for contemporary Native American lesbians and gays.

NOTES

1. This work is based on literature research and fifteen months of fieldwork conducted in 1992–1993.

2. Lesbian and gay Native Americans emphasize common ground and their common struggle as Native Americans for a specifically "Indian" lesbian/gay identity rather than differences in their experiences. In the mid-1980s when some lesbian members of Gay American Indians, an organization based in San Francisco, suggested a renaming of the organization to include the word "lesbian," the suggestion was rejected by women and men alike on the grounds that "gay" encompasses both men and women and it would be disruptive to the common cause if the women set themselves apart (Randy Burns and Erna Pahe, personal communication). Much of what is said here holds true for lesbians as well as gays, yet an effort has been made to highlight lesbian women's experiences.

3. The term "berdache" originally derived from an Arab term for male prostitutes or "kept boys" (Angelino and Shedd 1955). Even though in anthropological literature that term has never been used to imply that the individuals concerned were male prostitutes but only to refer to males in a woman's role in Native American cultures, the term has come to be rejected as inappropriate or even discriminating by quite a number of Native Americans and native and nonnative anthropologists alike. Thus, wherever it seemed necessary to use the word "berdache" in the present contribution, it is in quotation marks. I do not, however, follow the suggestion to replace "berdache" with "two-spirit." As becomes apparent from the present contribution, the term "two-spirit" originally came into being under specific historical circumstances and with specific political intentions (the postulation of a historical continuum between the old-time women-men and men-women and present-day Native American gays and lesbians, in order to counteract homophobia in modern Native American communities). Instead of replacing one "loaded" term with another, I have decided to use the descriptive terms *women-men* (for males in a woman's role) and *men-women* (for females in a man's role).

4. It will be noted that the use of "man-woman" in this essay differs from the way the word is used both in Native American languages and in anthropological writings (e.g., Roscoe 1991; Fulton and Anderson 1992). There, "man-woman" usually refers to males in a woman's role. Yet, as will be pointed out in the section on the classification of

sexual relationships, in Native American cultures a person's gender status in a sense overrides her or his (physical) sex. It therefore makes sense to refer to males in a woman's role by a term that puts the gender to which the chosen gender role belongs first and the physical sex second. This usage has already been recognized by Bleibtreu-Ehrenberg (1984), who titled her book on male gender variance in various cultures *Der Weibmann* (The woman-man). For the same reason, it seems appropriate to refer to females in a man's role as "men-women."

5. For a critique of such writings that do not take into account cultural variations and changes of Native American gender variance traditions and related phenomena within the historical context, therefore blurring diversities, see Blackwood's (1987) review of Williams (1986b).

6. Williams (1986a,b) provides a very optimistic view of the status especially male-bodied "berdaches" held in Native American tribal cultures. Trexler's book (1995) is the other extreme, stressing persecution faced by women-men in aboriginal North America. The historical truth lies probably somewhere in the middle (cf. Lang forthcoming).

7. The latter has already been pointed out by Lurie in the early 1950s where she observed that the Winnebago had become ashamed of the custom of *shiaᵭge* (woman-man) "because the white people thought it amusing or evil" (Lurie 1953:708). Even back then—Lurie did her fieldwork in 1945–47—the last woman-man among the Winnebago had died fifty years earlier.

8. The limitations of using Western categories such as gay, lesbian, or bisexual in trying to understand the lives of Native American two-spirited people are aptly pointed out by Tafoya (1992:257).

9. As a matter of fact, while there are quite a number of references to Native American female gender variance in the sources (see, for example, Blackwood 1984), hardly anything has ever been written about lesbians, with the exception of some contributions by Native Americans themselves to women-of-color anthologies (e.g., Brant 1984; Moraga and Anzaldúa 1981; Silvera 1991), the anthology *Living the Spirit* (Gay American Indians and Roscoe 1988), and other pieces of prose and poetry contained in collections of writings of explicitly lesbian Native American writers (e.g., Chrystos 1988, 1991).

10. Some time after I last visited the reservation, friends from the reservation wrote me that Shirley started to "act crazier and crazier as time passed." She acted aggressively toward various people. One day early in 1994, she got drunk, got her rifle, and shot her partner to death.

REFERENCES

Allen, Paula Gunn. 1981. "Lesbians in American Indian Culture." *Conditions* 7:67–87.

Angelino, Henry and Charles L. Shedd. 1955. "A Note on Berdache." *American Anthropologist* 57 (1): 121–126.

Benedict, Ruth. "Anthropology and the Abnormal." *Journal of General Psychiatry* 10 (1934): 59–82.

Blackwood, Evelyn. 1984. "Sexuality and Gender in Certain Native American Tribes. The Case of Cross-Gender Females." *Signs: Journal of Women in Culture and Society* 10: 1–42.

———. 1986. "Breaking the Mirror: The Construction of Lesbianism and the Anthropological Discourse on Homosexuality." In Evelyn Blackwood, ed., *The Many Faces of Homosexuality: Anthropological Approaches to Homosexual Behavior*, pp. 1–18. New York: Harrington Park Press.

———. 1987. "Review of *The Spirit and the Flesh* by Walter L. Williams." *Journal of Homosexuality* 15 (3/4): 165–176.

Bleibtreu-Ehrenberg, Gisela. 1984. *Der Weibmann: Kultischer Geschlechtswechsel im Schamanismus.* Frankfurt: Fischer.

Brant, Beth, ed. 1984. *A Gathering of Spirit: A Collection by North American Indian Women.* Ithaca and New York: Firebrand Books.

Burns, Randy. 1988. "Preface." In Gay American Indians and Will Roscoe, eds., *Living the Spirit: A Gay American Indian Anthology*, pp. 1–5. New York: St. Martin's Press.

Callender, Charles and Lee Kochems. 1983. "The North American Berdache." *Current Anthropology* 24: 443–470.

Chrystos. 1988. *Not Vanishing.* Vancouver: Press Gang Publishers.

———. 1991. *Dream On.* Vancouver: Press Gang Publishers.

Ford, Clellan S. and Frank Beach. 1965. *Formen der Sexualität.* Hamburg: Rowohlt.

Forde, C. Daryll. 1931. "Ethnography of the Yuma Indians." *University of California Publications in American Archaeology and Ethnology* 28 (4): 83–278.

Fulton, Robert and Steven W. Anderson. 1992. "The Amerindian 'Man-Woman': Gender, Liminality, and Cultural Continuity." *Current Anthropology* 33: 603–610.

Gay American Indians and Will Roscoe, eds. 1988. *Living the Spirit: A Gay American Indian Anthology.* New York: St. Martin's Press.

Goulet, Jean-Guy. 1982. "Religious Dualism among Athapaskan Catholics." *Canadian Journal of Anthropology* 3 (1): 1–18.

Grinnell, George B. 1962. *The Cheyenne Indians*. 2 Vols. New York: Cooper Square.

Jacobs, Sue-Ellen. 1968. "Berdache: A Brief Review of the Literature." *Colorado Anthropologist* 1: 25–40.

———— and Jason Cromwell. 1992. "Visions and Revisions of Reality: Reflections on Sex, Sexuality, Gender, and Gender Variance." *Journal of Homosexuality* 23 (4): 43–69.

————, Wesley Thomas, and Sabine Lang, eds. 1997. *Two-Spirit People: Native American Gender Identity, Sexuality, and Spirituality*. Urbana: University of Illinois Press.

Katz, Jonathan N. 1985. *Gay American History: Lesbians and Gay Men in the USA*. New York: Harper & Row.

Kessler, Suzanne and Wendy McKenna. 1977. *Gender: An Ethnomethodological Approach*. New York: Wiley.

Kiev, Ari. 1964. "The Study of Folk Psychiatry." In Ari Kiev, ed., *Magic, Faith, and Healing: Studies in Primitive Psychiatry*, pp. 3–35. New York: The Free Press of Glencoe.

Lang, Sabine. 1990. *Männer als Frauen—Frauen als Männer: Geschlechtsrollen-wechsel bei den Indianern Nordamerikas*. Hamburg: Wayasbah.

————. 1994. "Hermaphrodite Twins, Androgynous Gods: Reflections of Gender Variance in Native American Religions." Paper presented at the 93d Annual Meeting of the American Anthropological Association, Atlanta, Ga.

————. 1997a. "Various Kinds of Two-Spirit People: Gender Variance and Homosexuality in Native American Communities." In Sue-Ellen Jacobs, Wesley Thomas, and Sabine Lang, eds., *Two-Spirit People: Native American Gender Identity, Sexuality, and Spirituality*, pp. 100–118. Urbana: University of Illinois Press.

————. 1997b. "Zwillingshermaphroditen und androgyne Götter: Geschlechtliche Ambivalenz in oralen Traditionen indianischer Kulturen." *kuckuck* 1 (1997): 29–34.

————. 1998. *Men as Women, Women as Men: Changing Gender in Native American Cultures*. Austin: University of Texas Press.

————. Forthcoming. *Visions and Choices: Glimpses of Native American Two-Spirited People's Lives*. Austin: University of Texas Press.

Levy, Lori, Michel Beauchemin, and Gretchen Vogel. 1991. *Two-Spirited People: The Berdache Tradition in Native American Cultures*. Videotape, Dept. of Anthropology, University of California, Berkeley.

Lurie, Nancy O. 1953. "Winnebago Berdache." *American Anthropologist* 55 (5): 708–712.

Martin, M. Kay and Barbara Voorhies. 1975. *Female of the Species*. New York: Columbia University Press.

Miller, Wick. 1972. "Newe Natekwinappeh: Shoshoni Stories and Dictionary." *University of Utah Anthropological Papers* 94: 1–172.

Minnesota Indian AIDS Task Force. 1989. *Honored by the Moon*. Videotape, Minneapolis, Minn.

Minturn, Leigh, Martin Grosse, and Santoah Haider. 1969. "Cultural patterning of Sexual Beliefs and Behavior." *Ethnology* 8: 303–318.

Moraga, Cherríe and Gloria Anzaldúa, eds. 1981. *This Bridge Called my Back: Writings by Radical Women of Color*. New York: Kitchen Table Women of Color Press.

Osgood, Cornelius. 1958. "Ingalik Social Culture." *Yale University Publications in Anthropology* 53: 1–289.

Owlfeather, Michael. 1988. "Children of Grandmother Moon." In Gay American Indians and Will Roscoe, eds., *Living the Spirit: A Gay American Indian Anthology*, pp. 97–105. New York: St. Martin's Press.

Parsons, Elsie C. 1932. "Isleta, New Mexico." *Annual Report, Bureau of American Ethnology* 47: 193–466.

————. 1939. "The Last Zuni Transvestite." *American Anthropologist* 41 (2): 338–340.

Roscoe, Will. 1987. "Bibliography of Berdache and Alternative Gender Roles among North American Indians." *Journal of Homosexuality* 14 (3/4): 81–171.

————. 1988. "North American Tribes with Berdache and Alternative Gender Roles." In Gay American Indians and Will Roscoe, eds., *Living the Spirit: A Gay American Indian Anthology*, pp. 217–222. New York: St. Martin's Press.

————. 1991. *The Zuni Man-Woman*. Albuquerque: University of New Mexico Press.

Silvera, Makeda, ed. 1991. *Piece of my Heart: A Lesbian of Color Anthology*. Toronto: Sister Vision Press.

Steward, Julian H. 1941. "Culture Element Distributions 13: Nevada Shoshoni." *Anthropological Records* 4 (2): 209–359.

Stewart, Omer C. 1960. "Homosexuality among the American Indians and other Peoples of the World." *Mattachine Review* 6 (1): 9–15, (2): 13–19.

Tafoya, Terry. 1992. "Native Gay and Lesbian Issues: The Two-Spirited." In Betty Berzon, ed., *Positively Gay: New Approaches to Gay and Lesbian Life*, pp. 253–259. Berkeley: Celestial Arts Publishing.

Thomas, Wesley. 1993. "A Traditional Navajo's Perspectives on the Cultural Construction of Gender in the Navajo World." Paper presented at the University of Frankfurt, Germany.

————. 1997. "Navajo Cultural Constructions of Gender and Sexuality." In Sue-Ellen Jacobs, Wesley Thomas, and Sabine Lang, eds., *Two-Spirit*

People: Native American Gender Identity, Sexuality, and Spirituality, pp. 156–173. Urbana: University of Illinois Press.

Tietz, Lüder. 1994. "Two-Spirited People in Canada: Between Triple Discrimination and Empowerment." Paper presented at the 93d Annual Meeting of the American Anthropological Association, Atlanta, Ga.

———. 1996. "Moderne Rückbezüge auf Geschlechtsrollen indianischer Kulturen." Master's thesis, University of Hamburg, Institut für Ethnologie.

Trexler, Richard T. 1995. *Sex and Conquest: Gendered Violence, Political Order, and the European Conquest of the Americas.* Ithaca: Cornell University Press.

Turney-High, Harry H. 1937. "The Flathead Indians of Montana." *Memoirs of the American Anthropological Association* 48: 1–161.

Voegelin, Erminie W. 1942. "Culture Element Distributions 20: Northwest California." *Anthropological Records* 7 (2): 47–251.

Werner, Dennis. 1979. "A Cross-Cultural Perspective on Theory and Research on Male Homosexuality." *Journal of Homosexuality* 4: 345–362.

Whitehead, Harriet. 1981. "The Bow and the Burden-Strap: A New Look at Institutionalized Homosexuality in Native North America." In Sherry Ortner and Harriet Whitehead, eds., *Sexual Meanings: The Cultural Construction of Gender and Sexuality,* pp. 80–115. London: Cambridge University Press.

Williams, Walter L. 1986a. "Persistence and Change in the Berdache Tradition among Contemporary Lakota Indians." In Evelyn Blackwood, ed., *The Many Faces of Homosexuality: Anthropological Approaches to Homosexual Behavior,* pp. 191–200. New York: Harrington Park Press.

———. 1986b. *The Spirit and the Flesh: Sexual Diversity in American Indian Culture.* Boston: Beacon Press.

◨ PART EIGHT ◨

TRANS-ISMS/ GENDER/SEXUAL/CULTURAL

READINGS IN THIS PART

INTRODUCTION TO THE SUBJECT AND READINGS

One of the opening scenes from the movie, *Mi Vie en Rose* (My Life in Pink), is the moment a six-year-old boy adorns his mother's fancy clothes and jewelry and makes a dramatic entrance at the barbeque his newly relocated family is hosting. His belief in his beauty is confirmed when the guests stop, take note, and applaud his efforts. However, when the parents reveal that this beauty queen is their son, the guests freeze. The moment is heavy with uncertainty—no one seems to know what to do. Here is a child committing, in reality, a harmless social transgression, yet the cultural baggage that accompanies the event is oppressive. The boy, unaware of the implication of his actions, is innocently proud of himself. When the applause is replaced with looks of disbelief, his moment is shattered and he runs to hide.

It is hard not to empathize with this little boy and be angered by the superficiality of a gender system that demands behavioral conformity based on anatomy. In another film, *Boys Don't Cry,* based on the true story of Teena Brandon, we see the tragic results of the same binary gender system. Whereas, *Mi Vie en Rose* ends on an optimistic note concerning acceptance and appreciation of gender diversity, in the real life story, Teena Brandon paid for his transgender behavior with his life.

Definitions vary, but simply put, transgender refers to people whose expression of gender is outside the current cultural expectations or norms—their behavior crosses gender lines. Many students are confused about the difference between transgenderism and transsexuality. Their confusion reflects the fact that various definitions exist. Many people make the distinction based on anatomy, considering transsexuals to be persons who have surgically transformed themselves into members of the opposite sex. These persons, however, also fit the definition of transgender. Therefore, using this distinction, transsexuals are transgendered, but not all transgendered people are transsexuals—many are not interested in surgical "solutions."

The medical profession has labeled the transgendered and transsexuals as having a disorder termed gender dysphoria, a condition that occurs when a person's anatomical sex does not match their gender identity. Labeling transgenderism as a disorder has created controversy and raises important questions. Are these "conditions" that need "fixing"? If we feel uncomfortable by another person's identity, do we have the right to argue that they should change? Does the problem lie within a society that embraces a binary gender/sex system that only offers its members one option—identifiable anatomy with the "proper" accompanying gender behavior?

Transgenderism has been on the forefront of politicizing sexual and gender stereotypes and pushing to expand our gender boundaries. Transgendered activists are the gender outlaws and rebels, often in the front lines fighting for gender change, educating and raising awareness of the danger associated with our society's inflexible gender identities. Make no mistake about it, each one of us benefits by the struggles of the transgender movement. We benefit in ways that may not be obvious at first, but freedom of personal expression is increased through the work of transgendered advocates.

The article, *Who Put the "Trans" in Transgender? Gender Theory and Everyday Life*, by Suzanne Kessler and Wendy McKenna, raises a radical possibility by taking transgenderness to its ultimate conclusion—the end of gender. This idea has been widely debated. Interestingly, one of the issues is that if we eliminate gender what will happen to women's studies and the women's movement? You need solidarity of an oppressed group to fight for rights and the end of discrimination. The end of gender would eliminate an identifiable oppressed group and replace it with a gender continuum. Imagine the end of racial categories with peoples identifying with a rainbow of color and multiculturalism. What would happen to the African American/Black rights movement?

Kessler and McKenna began questioning our assumptions about gender twenty years ago. They were pioneers in the field of social construction and addressed the problems of a binary system of sex and gender. In their article, they first offer a history of theoretical arguments and perspectives on transsexuality. Then, moving forward, they summarize the findings of research they conducted. Their results may or may not shock or disturb you, but it is unlikely that anyone could read this article without confronting their own ideas about gender, transsexuality, and transgenderism.

The sexualities of the transgendered have raised some important questions in relation to concept of sexual orientation. If a transgender male—a man who behaves and dresses like a woman—has sexual relations with a male, should their interactions be considered homosexuality? After all, the word *homo* is taken from the Greek word meaning alike or the same (not to be confused with *homo* taken from Latin, meaning man, as in *homo sapiens*). Thus, homosexuality is engaging in or having sexual relations or being attracted to people like yourself. A person dressed and behaving as a woman who has sex with a man does not fit this description very well.

Don Kulick's *The Gender of Brazilian Transgendered Prostitutes* is a dramatically different discussion about transgenderism. He presents a mini-ethnography about gender/sexual systems in Latin America and how they differ from those in the United States. He introduces the idea that in Latin America not all men who engage in sexual relations with other men are considered gay. Men who penetrate other men are not gay, it is the role in the sex act that determines gayness. In other words, this system defines people by what they *do* in bed rather than whom they go to bed with.

Being in the receptor role during sex places Brazilian transgendered prostitutes, *travesti* as they are called in Brazil, in the category of not-men. Kulick explains that travesti are not women, nor do they want to be women. He introduces us to a world where gender, genitalia, ideals of beauty, sexualities, and manhood are different than in the United States. His analysis of the interrelationship between all these factors illustrates, once again, the futility of trying to apply our definitions and values to sex/gender systems in other cultures.

TERMS AND CONCEPTS

deconstructing gender	mollies
gender dysphoria	queer theory
heterosexuality	sexual reassignment
homophobia	transsexuality
homosexuality	transvestism
the medicalization of sex	travesti

CRITICAL THINKING AND QUESTIONS TO CONSIDER

1. Drawing on the research findings of Kessler and McKenna, answer the following questions. Has the notion of transgenderism led to an expansion of gender categories in the United States? Why? Or why not?

2. In what ways does Kulick's description of travesti sexuality differ from U.S. definitions of transsexuality?

3. Kulick notes that there are only two genders in Brazil, but adds that gender is not divided into people being men and women. What is the basis for gender differentiation in Brazil?

4. Discuss the similarities and differences between "third genders" (as discussed in the previous section) and transgender?

FURTHER READINGS

Blackwood, Evelyn, and Saskia E. Wieringa (eds.). 1998. *Female Desires: Same-Sex Relations and Transgendered Practices Across Cultures.* New York: Columbia University Press.

Bolin, Anne. 1987. *In Search of Eve: Transsexual Rites of Passage.* Greenwood Publishing Group.

Bornstein, Kate. 1994. *Gender Outlaw: On Men, Women and the Rest of Us.* New York: Routledge.

Bullough, Bonnie, Vern L. Bullough, and James Elias (eds.). 1997. *Gender Blending.* Amherst, New York: Prometheus Books.

Bulter, Judith. 1990. *Gender Trouble: Feminism and the Subversion of Identity.* New York: Routledge.

Denny, Dallas (ed.). 1997. *Current Concepts in Transgender Identity.* New York: Garland Publishing.

Devor, Holly. 1999. FTM: Female to male transsexuals in society. Bloomington: Indiana University Press.

Kulick, Don. 1998. *Travesti: Sex, Gender, and Culture among Brazilian Transgendered Prostitutes.* Chicago: University of Chicago Press.

Namaste, Viviane K. 2000. *Invisible Lives: The Erasure of Transsexual and Transgendered People.* Chicago: University of Chicago Press.

Newton, Esther. 1972. *Mother Camp: Female Impersonators in America.* Chicago: University of Chicago.

Wilchins, Riki Anne. 1997. *Read My Lips.* Firebrand Books: Ithaca, New York.

RELATED WEBSITES

Altsex Organization/Transgender Issues
  www.altsex.org/transgender

The International Foundation for Gender Education
  www.ifge.org

The International Journal of Transgenderism
  www.symposion.com/ijt/default.htm

The National Transgender Advocacy Coalition
  www.ntac.org

Transgender Book Reviews
  www.alchemist-light.com

Transgender Forum Community Center
  www.transgender.org

Transgender Law and Policy Institute
  www.transgenderlaw.org

Transgender Renaissance Organization
  www.ren.org

Transgender Support Site
  www.heartcorps.com/journeys

21
Who Put the "Trans" in Transgender?
Gender Theory and Everyday Life

Suzanne Kessler
Purchase College, State University of New York

Wendy McKenna
Barnard College

Abstract

In theory, transgender is a challenge to the social construction of gender. In practice, it usually is not. Transgendered people—in one way or another—place themselves outside the conventional female/male dichotomy, yet live in a social world that recognizes only females and males. How could a self-identified transgendered person earn and maintain a transgender attribution, when others are constrained to attribute an unproblematic "male" or "female" gender to him/her? Is it possible to alter, in practice, what seems to be the incorrigibility of the gender attribution process? Is this, in fact, what transgendered people want to do? In the light of three possible meanings of trans, we consider whether there is any point to deconstructing gender.

Source: Who put the "trans" in transgender? Gender theory and everyday life, by Suzanne Kessler and Wendy McKenna. In *The International Journal of Transgenderism*, V4, no3, July-September 2000. © 2000 Suzanne Kessler and Wendy McKenna. Used with permission of the authors.

The prefix "trans" has 3 different meanings. Trans means change, as in the word "transform." In this first sense transgendered people change their bodies to fit the gender they feel they always were. They change from male to female or vice versa. Transgender in this sense is synonymous with what is typically meant by the term "transsexual." Trans means across as in the word "transcontinental." In this second sense a transgendered person is one who moves across genders (or maybe aspects of the person cross genders). This meaning does not imply being essentially or permanently committed to one or the other gender and therefore has a more social-constructionist connotation. Nevertheless, the transgendered person in this meaning does not leave the realm of two genders. Persons who assert that although they are "really" the other gender they do not need to change their genitals, are transgendered in this sense of "trans." The emphasis is on the crossing and not on any surgical transformation accompanying it. Such a person might say, "I want people to attribute the gender 'female' to me, but I'm not going to get my genitals changed. I don't mind having my penis." This type of identity is relatively recent as an open, public identity, but it does not seem to be an identity separate from male and female. It is more like a previously unthinkable combination of male and female. But even a combination of male and female reflexively gives credence to these categories. There are still two genders. The third meaning of "trans" is beyond or through as in the word "transcutaneous." In this third sense a transgendered person is one who has gotten through gender, beyond gender. No clear gender attribution can be made, or is allowed to be made. Gender ceases to exist, both for this person and those with whom they interact. This third meaning is the most radical and the one of greatest importance to gender theorists like us who are interested in the possibility, both theoretical and real, of eliminating gender.

THE SOCIAL CONSTRUCTION OF GENDER" TRANSSEXUALS

Over 20 years ago we wrote a book asserting that all aspects of gender, including the physical/biological aspects, which people refer to as "sex," are socially constructed. Our point was that the male/female dichotomy is not essentially given in nature. In developing our argument, we analyzed the natural attitude toward gender. These taken-for-granted beliefs of the culture include:

- There are two and only two genders. Apparent violations are not really violations. If you look long enough, ask enough questions, or do enough medical tests, the "real" gender will be revealed.
- Gender exists as a biological "fact" independently of anyone's ideas about gender.
- A person's gender never changes.
- Genitals are the essential defining feature of gender. That is, if you do not have the right organ between your legs, you cannot be what you say you are. You are not the "genuine article," even if you have everything else. (That is why transsexuals, at least

historically, were not really the gender they claimed until they had surgery, and that is why intersexed infants are required to have genital "reconstructive" surgery.)

By the mid-1970s most people, in and out of academia, were beginning to accept that roles, appearances, and characteristics (what they called "gender") were socially defined and culturally varied. However, biological features (what they called "sex") were considered to be given in nature. We argued that the biological is as much a construction as the social is. Although hormones, chromosomes, gonads, and genitals, are real parts of the body, seeing them as dichotomous and essential to being a female or male is a social construction. That is why we believed (and continue to believe) that in discussions of this topic it is critical to only use "gender" and never use "sex" (in the conventional meanings). If anything is primary, it is not some biological sign, but what we called "gender attribution"—the decision one makes in every concrete case that someone is either a male or a female. Virtually all of the time, gender attribution is made with no direct knowledge of the genitals or any other biological "sex marker."

It seemed to us in the mid-1970's that transsexuals exemplified the social construction of gender. We talked to as many as we could about what their experience was with gender attributions made to them and how they insured that "mistakes" were not made. As we pondered our conversations with them, we were struck by how the immediate and interactive presentation of gender is impossible to ignore. In a social setting we do not see one another's chromosomes, genitals, or gender history. In fact, once we make a gender attribution, we are able to discount or reinterpret chromosomes, genitals, or gender history that does not "match" the gender attribution. If you are "obviously" a man and then you tell new acquaintances that you were given a female gender assignment at birth and do not have a penis, they have an adjustment to make, but that will probably not mean that they will change their minds about whether you are a man. We asserted that the primacy of gender attribution benefits transsexuals—if they make an initial credible gender presentation—because other people will interpret contradictory information (like the gender on a driver's license) as a clerical error rather than as evidence of the person's intent to deceive. What we did not consider 25 years ago was the possibility that someone might not want to make a credible gender presentation—might not want to be seen as clearly either male or female. In addition, although we advocated that because of the primacy of gender attribution, persons could be whatever gender they wanted without costly and dangerous surgery, it did not seem to us that this would happen for a very long time, if ever. It did not even occur to us that within 20 years there would be some people who would want to confront others with the contradiction between their gender presentation and other "facts" such as their genitals or gender history. In other words, we did not address what has come to be called "transgender." Transgender was neither a concept nor a term 25 years ago. Transsexual was radical enough.

TRANSGENDER: TRANSFORMATION, TRANSFER, OR TRANSCENDENCE?

Recently, we did a Web search for "transgender," using the Google search engine and found over 3300 matches for that term. Clearly "it" exists, but what is "it"? And what is the meaning of "gender" now? Realizing that we needed more information about this, especially from younger people, in the Fall of 1999 we gave a questionnaire to 83 students in a human sexuality class at a college with a reputation for attracting and reasonably tolerating all types of genders and sexualities. The students' answers to our questions are some indication of what is different now and what is the same, at least among young, liberal and presumably gender-progressive people. Our first two questions, "What is the meaning of the category 'gender'?" and "How do you know someone's gender?" were treated as reasonable questions—not nonsensical ones. In 1975 we suspect most people would have been mystified as to why we were asking

questions like that. It would have been like asking "How can you tell if someone is dead or alive?" a question about a simple, objective fact. The students still believe there are two genders, but they seem to have more of a sense that gender is a complex, not a simple, dichotomy; yet it is still a dichotomy. There is the acknowledgment by some that gender characteristics can be mixed. (Perhaps we have Jerry Springer and other purveyors of the atypical to thank for this.) The answers to "how do you know" in any given case were those things that we had described as important in gender attribution like breasts, Adam's apples, body shape, and voice.

Although students rarely wrote that they use genitals to decide a person's gender, they did write that genitals are the essential defining feature of what it means to be a gender. Men have penises and women have vaginas, even if later on in the questionnaire they said that other combinations are possible like men with vaginas and women with penises. The equation gender = genitals is no different from what we found 25 years ago. However, there has been a significant change regarding genitals. In our original work we provided evidence that the penis was the only socially real genital. People held the often unstated belief that males had penises and females had no penises. In this recent questionnaire though, the vagina was mentioned almost as often as the penis. It appears that the vagina and vulva have become more socially real. How and why has this happened, and what that implies are intriguing areas for further inquiry.

Although these students may consider gender extremely complex and allow for the possibility that it is not that important to categorize people by gender, in everyday life not knowing a person's gender still makes them very uncomfortable. They try to find out what the person "really" is. Gender continues to be real and dichotomous, even if an ambiguous presentation is tolerated.

The students said that what has changed in the way their generation thinks about gender compared to their parents is awareness and acceptance of alternatives (mainly homosexuality) and more flexibility/inclusion in expectations for women. Whatever changes in expectations there have been for men, this was not acknowledged by the students. Why has the "trans"formation only gone in one direction?

In light of the question "Who put the 'trans' in transgender?" of particular interest is the students' answers to the question, "What does transgendered mean?" Almost none of the students indicated that they knew what it meant. A few who did, said that it referred to someone who changes gender, and then they described what most people mean by "transsexual." One person said the term referred to someone being "torn between a physical existence and a mental existence," but only one or two referred to a person who feels comfortable with physical aspects of both genders, e.g. having breasts and a penis. Only four of the students said they knew a transgendered person. However, there were others who understood that their belief that they did not know transgendered people only meant that "as far as they knew" they did not, but they might. We think that in 1975 basically everyone would have believed that they would know if a person was not "all man or all woman." Judging from this one sample, as well as observations and discussions with others, we could conclude that in the last 25 years the absolute either/or aspect of biological gender has been reduced, at least for some people. But just because more people acknowledge that gender features can be mixed together or that a person can move more easily between categories, this has not led to an expansion of or transcendence of the gender categories. There are still two and only two genders, even if some of the women have penises and some of the men have vaginas. Twenty-five years ago we thought that because transsexualism seemed to violate the rule that you can not change gender, it had revolutionary potential. Now what seems radical are those who identify as "transgender" and reject "transsexual" as too restrictive and too diagnostic. But even if there are transgendered people for whom the gender dichotomy ceases to exist, of what import is that if transgendered people live in a world of two conventional genders? Could a person with a transgendered identity translate it into a public transgendered attribution, where the attributor would say "That's neither a woman nor a man," rather than "I can't tell if that's a woman or a man"?

To cultivate such an attribution in this third sense of transgender (beyond or through) is extraordinarily difficult and might be impossible.

Transgendered people (even those who are publicly "out" on stage, in print, or among trustworthy others) know that unless they do what it takes to get a male or female gender attribution, their physical safety may be in jeopardy. How do we reconcile the desire to radically transform gender (which some transgenderists and theorists share) with the practical need to transform the publicly visible body in gender dichotomous ways? People with a public transgender identity still have one of the standard gender attributions made about them by the casual passerby, even if the passerby has questions. This is because the gender attribution process is an interactive one, grounded in the attributors' unshakable belief that everyone can and must be classified as female or male. In everyday life even gender theorists do not treat the gender dichotomy as problematic. Twenty-five years of our and others' theorizing about gender has in many ways unsettled the meaning of gender, but it has done no damage to the gender dichotomy. The next challenge is understanding why.

REFERENCES

Garfinkel, Harold. 1967. *Studies in Ethnomethodology.* Upper Saddle River, NJ: Prentice Hall. This analysis was based on Harold Garfinkel's description of the natural attitude toward gender.

Kessler, Suzanne, and Wendy McKenna. 1978. *Gender: An Ethnomethodological Approach.* New York: Wiley.

Prince, Virginia C.F. 1979. "Charles to Virginia: Sex Research as a Personal Experience." In *The Frontiers of Sex Research*, ed. Vern Bullough, 167–175. Buffalo, NY: Prometheus Books. Virginia Prince should probably be credited as having introduced the term "transgender." Because she needed a term to describe her decision to become a woman without changing her genitals (what she would call her "sex,") the term "transsexual" would not do.

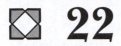

22

The Gender of Brazilian Transgendered Prostitutes

Don Kulick
Stockholm University

Males who enjoy being anally penetrated by other males are, in many places in the world, an object of special cultural elaboration. Anywhere they occur as a culturally recognized type, it is usually they who are classified and named, not the males who penetrate them (who are often simply called "men"). Furthermore, to the extent that male same-sex sexual relations are stigmatized, the object of social vituperation is, again, usually those males who allow themselves to be penetrated, not the males who penetrate them. Anywhere they constitute a salient cultural category, men who enjoy being penetrated are believed to think, talk, and act in particular, identifiable, and often cross-gendered manners. What is more, a large number of such men do in fact behave in these culturally intelligible ways. So whether they are the *mahus*,

The gender of Brazilian transgendered prostitutes, by Don Kulick. In *American Anthropologist* 99 (3): 574–585. © 1999 American Anthropological Association. Reproduced by permission of the American Anthropological Association from *American Anthropologist* 99 (3). Not for sale or further reproduction.

hijras, kathoeys, xaniths, or *berdaches* of non-Western societies, or the mollies and fairies of our own history, links between habitual receptivity in anal sex and particular effeminate behavioral patterns structure the ways in which males who are regularly anally penetrated are perceived, and they structure the ways in which many of those males think about and live their lives.[1]

One area of the world in which males who enjoy being anally penetrated receive a very high degree of cultural attention is Latin America. Any student of Latin America will be familiar with the effervescent figure of the effeminate male homosexual. Called *maricón, cochón, joto, marica, pajara, loca, frango, bicha,* or any number of other names depending on where one finds him (see Murray and Dynes 1987 and Dynes 1987 for a sampling), these males all appear to share certain behavioral characteristics and seem to be thought of, throughout Latin America, in quite similar ways.[2]

One of the basic things one quickly learns from any analysis of Latin American sexual categories is that sex between males in this part of the world does not necessarily result in both partners being perceived as homosexual. The crucial determinant of a homosexual classification is not so much the fact of sex as it is the role performed during the sexual act. A male who anally penetrates another male is generally not considered to be homosexual. He is considered, in all the various local idioms, to be a "man"; indeed, in some communities, penetrating another male and then bragging about it is one way in which men demonstrate their masculinity to others (Lancaster 1992:241; cf. Brandes 1981:234). Quite different associations attach themselves to a male who allows himself to be penetrated. That male has placed himself in what is understood to be an unmasculine, passive position. By doing so, he has forfeited manhood and becomes seen as something other than a man. This cultural classification as feminine is often reflected in the general comportment, speech practices, and dress patterns of such males, all of which tend to be recognizable to others as effeminate.

A conceptual system in which only males who are penetrated are homosexual is clearly very different from the modern heterosexual-homosexual dichotomy currently in place in countries such as the United States, where popular understanding generally maintains that a male who has sex with another male is gay, no matter how carefully he may restrict his behavior to the role of penetrator.[3] This difference between Latin American and northern Euro-American understandings of sexuality is analyzed with great insight in the literature on male same-sex relations in Latin America, and one of the chief merits of that literature is its sensitive documentation of the ways in which erotic practices and sexual identities are culturally organized.

Somewhat surprisingly, the same sensitivity that informs the literature when it comes to sexuality does not extend to the realm of gender. A question not broached in this literature is whether the fundamental differences that exist between northern Euro-American and Latin American regimes of sexuality might also result in, or be reflective of, different regimes of gender. This oversight is odd in light of the obvious and important links between sexuality and gender in a system

where a simple act of penetration has the power to profoundly alter a male's cultural definition and social status. Instead of exploring what the differences in the construction of sexuality might mean for differences in the construction of gender, however, analysis in this literature falls back on familiar concepts. So just as gender in northern Europe and North America consists of men and women, so does it consist of men and women in Latin America, we are told. The characteristics ascribed to and the behavior expected of those two different types of people are not exactly the same in these two different parts of the world, to be sure, but the basic gender categories are the same.

This article contests that view. I will argue that the *sexual division* that researchers have noted between those who penetrate and those who are penetrated extends far beyond sexual interactions between males to constitute the basis of the *gender division* in Latin America. Gender, in this particular elaboration, is grounded not so much in sex (like it is, for example, in modern northern European and North American cultures) as it is grounded in sexuality. This difference in grounding generates a gender configuration different from the one that researchers working in Latin America have postulated, and it allows and even encourages the elaboration of cultural spaces such as those inhabited by effeminate male homosexuals. Gender in Latin America should be seen not as consisting of men and women, but rather of men and not-men, the latter being a category into which both biological females and males who enjoy anal penetration are culturally situated. This specific situatedness provides individuals—not just men who enjoy anal penetration, but everyone—with a conceptual framework that they can draw on in order to understand and organize their own and others' desires, bodies, affective and physical relations, and social roles.

THE BODY IN QUESTION

The evidence for the arguments developed here will be drawn from my fieldwork in the

Brazilian city of Salvador, among a group of males who enjoy anal penetration. These males are effeminized prostitutes known throughout Brazil as *travestis* (a word derived from *transvestir*, to cross-dress).[4]

Trasvestis occupy a strikingly visible place in both Brazilian social space and in the Brazilian cultural imaginary.[5] All Brazilian cities of any size contain travestis, and in the large cities of Rio de Janeiro and São Paulo, travestis number in the thousands. (In Salvador, travestis numbered between about 80 and 250, depending on the time of year.)[6] Travestis are most exuberantly visible during Brazil's famous annual Carnival, and any depiction or analysis of the festival will inevitably include at least a passing reference to them, because their gender inversions are often invoked as embodiments of the Carnival spirit. But even in more mundane contexts and discourses, travestis figure prominently. A popular Saturday afternoon television show, for example, includes a spot in which female impersonators, some of whom are clearly travestis, get judged on how beautiful they are and on how well they mime the lyrics to songs sung by female vocalists. Another weekly television show regularly features Valéria, a well-known travesti. *Tieta*, one of the most popular television *novelas* in recent years, featured a special guest appearance by Rogéria, another famous travesti. And most telling of the special place reserved for travestis in the Brazilian popular imagination is the fact that the individual widely acclaimed to be most beautiful woman in Brazil in the mid-1980s was . . . a travesti. That travesti, Roberta Close, became a household name throughout the country. She regularly appeared on national television, starred in a play in Rio, posed nude (with demurely crossed legs) in *Playboy* magazine, was continually interviewed and portrayed in virtually every magazine in the country, and had at least three songs written about her by well-known composers. Although her popularity declined when, at the end of the 1980s, she left Brazil to have a sex-change operation and live in Europe, Roberta Close remains extremely well-known. As recently as 1995, she appeared in a nationwide advertisement for Duloren lingerie, in which a photograph of

her passport, bearing her male name, was transposed with a photograph of her looking sexy and chic in a black lace undergarment. The caption read, "Você não imagina do que uma Duloren é capaz" (You can't imagine what a Duloren can do).

Regrettably, the fact that a handful of travestis manage to achieve wealth, admiration, and, in the case of Roberta Close, an almost iconic cultural status says very little about the lives of the vast majority of travestis. Those travestis, the ones that most Brazilians only glimpse occasionally standing along highways or on dimly lit street corners at night or read about in the crime pages of their local newspapers, comprise one of the most marginalized, feared, and despised groups in Brazilian society. In most Brazilian cities, travestis are so discriminated against that many of them avoid venturing out onto the street during the day. They are regularly the victims of violent police brutality and murder.[7] The vast majority of them come from very poor backgrounds and remain poor throughout their lives, living a hand-to-mouth existence and dying before the age of 50 from violence, drug abuse, health problems caused or exacerbated by the silicone they inject into their bodies, or, increasingly, AIDS.

The single most characteristic thing about travestis is their bodies. Unlike the drag performers examined by Esther Newton (1972) and recently elevated to the status of theoretical paragons in the work of postmodernist queer scholars such as Judith Butler (1990), travestis do not merely don female attributes. They incorporate them. Sometimes at ages as young as 10 or 12, boys who self-identify as travestis begin ingesting or injecting themselves with massive doses of female hormones in order to give their bodies rounded features, broad hips, prominent buttocks, and breasts. The hormones these boys take either are medications designed to combat estrogen deficiency or are contraceptive preparations designed, like "the pill," to prevent pregnancy. In Brazil such hormones are cheap (a month's supply, which would be consumed by a travesti in a week or less, costs the equivalent of only a few dollars) and are sold over the counter in any pharmacy.

Boys discover hormones from a variety of sources. Most of my travesti friends told me that they learned about hormones by approaching adult travestis and asking them how they had achieved the bodies they had. Others were advised by admirers, boyfriends, or clients, who told them that they would look more attractive and make more money if they looked more like girls.

Hormones are valued by travestis because they are inexpensive, easy to obtain, and fast working. Most hormones produce visible results after only about two months of daily ingestion. A problem with them, however, is that they can, especially after prolonged consumption, result in chronic nausea, headaches, heart palpitations, burning sensations in the legs and chest, extreme weight gain, and allergic reactions. In addition, the doses of female hormones required to produce breasts and wide hips make it difficult for travestis to achieve erections. This can be quite a serious problem, since a great percentage of travestis' clients want to be penetrated by the travesti (a point to which I shall return below). What usually happens after several years of taking hormones is that most individuals stop, at least for a while, and begin injecting silicone into their bodies.

Just as hormones are procured by the individual travestis themselves, without any medical intervention or interference, so is silicone purchased from and administered by acquaintances or friends. The silicone available to the travestis in Salvador is industrial silicone, which is a kind of plastic normally used to manufacture automobile parts such as dashboards. Although it is widely thought to be illegal for industrial outlets to sell this silicone to private individuals, at least one or two travestis in any city containing a silicone manufacturing plant will be well connected enough to be able to buy it. Whenever they sense a demand, these travestis contact their supplier at the plant and travel there in great secrecy to buy several liters. They then resell this silicone (at a hefty profit) to other travestis, who in turn pay travestis who work as *bombadeiras* (pumpers) to inject it directly into their bodies.

Most travestis in Salvador over the age of 17 have some silicone in their bodies. The amount of silicone that individual travestis choose to inject ranges from a few glasses to up to 18 liters. (Travestis measure silicone in liters and water glasses (*copos*), six of which make up a liter.) Most have between two and five liters. The majority have it in their buttocks, hips, knees, and inner thighs. This strategic placement of silicone is in direct deference to Brazilian aesthetic ideals that consider fleshy thighs, expansive hips, and a prominent, teardrop-shaped *bunda* (buttocks) to be the hallmark of feminine beauty. The majority of travestis do *not* have silicone in their breasts, because they believe that silicone in breasts (but not elsewhere in the body) causes cancer, because they are satisfied with the size of the breasts they have achieved through hormone consumption, because they are convinced that silicone injections into the chest are risky and extremely painful, or because they are waiting for the day when they will have enough money to pay for silicone implants (*prótese*) surgically inserted by doctors. A final reason for a general disinclination to inject silicone into one's breasts is that everyone knows that this silicone shifts its position very easily. Every travesti is acquainted with several unfortunate others whose breasts have either merged in the middle, creating a pronounced undifferentiated swelling known as a "pigeon breast" (*peito de pomba*), or whose silicone has descended into lumpy protrusions just above the stomach.

THE BODY IN PROCESS

Why do they do it? One of the reasons habitually cited by travestis seems self-evident. Elizabeth, a 29-year-old travesti with 1 1/2 liters of silicone in her hips and one water-glass of silicone in each breast, explained it to me this way: "To mold my body, you know, be more feminine, with the body of a woman." But why do travestis want the body of a woman?

When I first began asking travestis that question, I expected them to tell me that they wanted the body of a woman because they felt themselves to be women. That was not the answer I received. No one ever offered the explanation that they might be women trapped in male bodies, even when I suggested it. In fact, there is a strong consensus among travestis in Salvador that any travesti who claims to be a woman is mentally disturbed. A travesti is not a woman and can never be a woman, they tell one another, because God created them male. As individuals, they are free to embellish and augment what God has given them, but their sex cannot be changed. Any attempt to do so would be disastrous. Not only do sex-change operations not produce women (they produce, travestis say, only *bichas castradas*, castrated homosexuals), they also inevitably result in madness. I was told on numerous occasions that, without a penis, semen cannot leave the body. When trapped, it travels to the brain, where it collects and forms a "stone" that will continue to increase in size until it eventually causes insanity.

So Roberta Close notwithstanding, travestis modify their bodies not because they feel themselves to be women but because they feel themselves to be "feminine" (*feminino*) or "like a woman" (*se sentir mulher*), qualities most often talked about not in terms of inherent predispositions or essences but rather in terms of behaviors, appearances, and relationships to men.[8] When I asked Elizabeth what it meant when she told me she felt feminine, for example, she answered, "I like to dress like a woman. I like when someone— when men—admire me, you know? . . . I like to be admired, when I go with a man who, like, says: 'Sheez, you're really pretty, you're really feminine.' That . . . makes me want to be more feminine and more beautiful every day, you see?" Similar themes emerged when travestis talked about when they first began to understand that they were travestis. A common response I received from many different people when I asked that question was that they made this discovery in connection with attraction and sexuality. Eighteen-year-old Cintia told me that she understood she was a travesti from the age of seven:

> I already liked girls' things, I played with dolls, played with . . . girls' things; I only played with girls. I didn't play with boys. I just played with these two boys; during the afternoon I always played with them . . . well, you know, rubbing

penises together, rubbing them, kissing on the mouth. *[Laughs.]*

Forty-one-year-old Gabriela says that she knew that she was a travesti early on largely because "since childhood I always liked men, hairy legs, things like that, you know?" Banana, a 34-year-old travesti, told me "the [understanding that I was a] travesti came after, you know, I, um, eight, nine years, ten years old, I felt attracted, really attracted to men."

The attraction that these individuals felt for males is thus perceived by them to be a major motivating force behind their self-production as travestis, both privately and professionally. Travestis are quick to point out that, in addition to making them feel more feminine, female forms also help them earn more money as prostitutes. At night when they work on the street, those travestis who have acquired pronounced feminine features use them to attract the attention of passing motorists, and they dress (or rather, undress) to display those features prominently.

But if the goal of a travesti's bodily modifications is to feel feminine and be attractive to men, what does she think about her male genitals?

The most important point to be clear about is that virtually every travesti values her penis: "There's not a better thing in the whole world," 19-year-old Adriana once told me with a big smile. Any thought of having it amputated repels them. "Deus é mais" (God forbid), many of them interject whenever talk of sex-change operations arises. "What, and never cum (i.e., ejaculate, *gozar*) again?!" they gasp, horrified.

Despite the positive feelings that they express about their genitals, however, a travesti keeps her penis, for the most part hidden, "imprisoned" (*presa*) between her legs. That is, travestis habitually pull their penises down between their legs and press them against their perineums with their underpants. This is known as "making a cunt" (*fazer uma buceta*). This cunt is an important bodily practice in a travesti's day-to-day public appearance. It is also crucial in another extremely important context of a travesti's life, namely in her relationship to her *marido* (live-in boyfriend). The maridos of travestis are typically attractive, muscular, tattooed young men with little or no education and no jobs. Although they are not pimps (travestis move them into their rooms because they are impassioned *[apaixonada]* with them, and they eject them when the passion wears thin), maridos are supported economically by their travesti girlfriends. All these boyfriends regard themselves, and are regarded by their travesti girlfriends, as *homens* (men) and, therefore, as nonhomosexual.

One of the defining attributes of being a *homen* (man) in the gender system that the travestis draw on and invoke is that a man will not be interested in another male's penis. A man, in this interpretative framework, will happily penetrate another male's anus. But he will not touch or express any desire for another male's penis. For him to do so would be tantamount to relinquishing his status as a man. He would stop being a man and be reclassified as a *viado* (homosexual, faggot), which is how the travestis are classified by others and how they see themselves.

Travestis want their boyfriends to be men, not viados. They require, in other words, their boyfriends to be symbolically and socially different from, not similar to, themselves. Therefore, a travesti does not want her boyfriend to notice, comment on, or in any way concern himself with her penis, even during sex. Sex with a boyfriend, consists, for the most part, of the travesti sucking the boyfriend's penis and of her boyfriend penetrating her, most often from behind, with the travesti on all fours or lying on her stomach on the bed. If the boyfriend touches the travesti at all, he will caress her breasts and perhaps kiss her. But no contact with the travesti's penis will occur, which means, according to most travestis I have spoken to, that travestis do not usually have orgasms during sex with their boyfriends.

What surprised me most about this arrangement was that the ones who are the most adamant that it be maintained are the travestis themselves. They respect their boyfriends and maintain their relationships with them only as long as the boyfriends remain "men." If a boyfriend expresses interest in a travesti's penis, becomes concerned that the travesti ejaculate during sex, or worst of all, if the boyfriend expresses a desire to be anally penetrated by the travesti, the relationship, all travestis told me firmly, would be over. They would comply with the boyfriend's request, they all told me, "because if someone offers me their ass, you think I'm not gonna take it?" Afterward, however, they were agreed, they would lose respect for the boyfriend. "You'll feel disgust (*nojo*) toward him," one travesti put it pithily. The boyfriend would no longer be a man in their eyes. He would, instead, be reduced to a viado. And as such, he could no longer be a boyfriend. Travestis unfailingly terminate relationships with any boyfriend who deviates from what they consider to be proper manly sexuality.

This absolute unwillingness to engage their own penises in sexual activity with their boyfriends stands in stark contrast to what travestis do with their penises when they are with their clients. On the street, travestis know they are valued for their possession of a penis. Clients will often request to see or feel a travesti's penis before agreeing to pay for sex with her, and travestis are agreed that those travestis who have large penises are more sought after than those with small ones. Similarly, several travestis told me that one of the reasons they stopped taking hormones was because they were losing clients. They realized that clients had begun avoiding them because they knew that the travesti could not achieve an erection. Travestis maintain that one of the most common sexual services they are paid to perform is to anally penetrate their clients.

Most travestis enjoy this. In fact, one of the more surprising findings of my study is that travestis, in significant and highly marked contrast to what is generally reported for other prostitutes, enjoy sex with clients.[9] That is not to say they enjoy sex every time or with every client. But whenever they talk about thrilling, fulfilling, or incredibly fun sex, their partner is always either a client or what they call a *vício*, a word that literally means "vice" or "addiction" and that refers to a male, often encountered on the street while they are working, with whom they have sex for free. Sometimes, if the vício is especially attractive, is known to have an especially large penis, or is known to be especially versatile in bed, the travesti will even pay *him*.

THE BODY IN CONTEXT

At this point, having illustrated the way in which the body of a travesti is constructed, thought about, and used in a variety of contexts, I am ready to address the question of cultural intelligibility and personal desirability. Why do travestis want the kind of body they create for themselves? What is it about Brazilian culture that incites and sustains desire for a male body made feminine through hormones and silicone?

By phrasing that question primarily in terms of culture, I do not mean to deny that there are also social and economic considerations behind the production of travesti bodies and subjectivities. As I noted above, a body full of silicone translates into cash in the Brazilian sexual marketplace. It is important to understand, however—particularly because popular and academic discourses about prostitution tend to frame it so narrowly in terms of victimization, poverty, and exploitation— that males do not become travestis because they were sexually abused as children or just for economic gain. Only one of the approximately 40 travestis in my close circle of acquaintances was clearly the victim of childhood sexual abuse. And while the vast majority of travestis (like, one must realize, the vast majority of people in Brazil) come from working-class or poor backgrounds, it is far from impossible for poor, openly effeminate homosexual males to find employment, especially in the professions of hairdressers, cooks, and housecleaners, where they are quite heavily represented.

Another factor that makes it problematic to view travestis primarily in social or economic terms is the fact that the sexual marketplace does not require males who prostitute themselves to be travestis. Male prostitution (where the prostitutes, who are called *michês*, look and act like men) is widespread in Brazil and has been the topic of one published ethnographic study (Perlongher 1987). Also, even transgendered prostitution does not require the radical body modifications that travestis undertake. Before hormones and silicone became widely available (in the mid-1970s and mid-1980s, respectively) males dressed up as females, using wigs and foam-rubber padding (*pirelli*), and worked successfully as prostitutes. Some males still do this today.

Finally, it should be appreciated that travestis do not need to actually have sex with their clients to earn money as prostitutes. A large percentage (in some cases, the bulk) of a travesti's income from clients is derived from robbing them. In order to rob a client, all that is required is that a travesti come into close physical proximity with him. Once a travesti is in a client's car or once she has begun caressing a passerby's penis, asking him seductively if he "quer gozar" (wants to cum), the rest, for most travestis, is easy. Either by pickpocketing the client, assaulting him, or if she does have sex with him, by threatening afterward to create a public scandal, the travesti will often walk away with all the client's money (Kulick 1996a). Thus it is entirely possible to derive a respectable income from prostitution and still not consume hormones and inject silicone into one's body.

In addition to all those considerations, I also phrase the question of travestis in terms of culture because, even if it were possible to claim that males who become travestis do so because of poverty, early sexual exploitation, or some enigmatic inner psychic orientation, the mystery of travestis as a sociocultural phenomenon would remain unsolved. What is it about the understandings, representations, and definitions of sexuality, gender, and sex in Brazilian society that makes travesti subjectivity imaginable and intelligible?

Let me begin answering that question by noting an aspect of travesti language that initially puzzled me. In their talk to one another, travestis frequently refer to biological males by using feminine pronouns and feminine adjectival endings. Thus the common utterance "ela ficou doida" (she was furious) can refer to a travesti, a woman, a gay male, or a heterosexual male who has allowed himself to be penetrated by another male. All of these different people are classified by travestis in the same manner. This classificatory system is quite subtle, complex, and context sensitive; travestis narrating their life stories frequently use masculine pronouns and adjectival endings when talking about themselves as children but switch to feminine forms when discussing their present-day lives. In a similar way, clients are often referred to as "she," but the same client will be referred to with different gendered pronouns depending on the actions he performs. When a travesti recounts that she struggled with a client over money or when she describes him paying, for example, his gender will often change from feminine to masculine. The important point here is that the gender of males is subject to fluctuation and change in travesti talk. Males are sometimes referred to as "she" and sometimes as "he." Males, in other words, can shift gender depending on the context and the actions they perform. The same is not true for females. Females, even the several extremely brawny and conspicuously unfeminine lesbians who associate with the travestis I know, are never referred to as "he" (Kulick 1996b). So whereas the gender of females remains fixed, the gender of males fluctuates and shifts continually.

Why can males be either male or female, but females can only be female? The answer, I believe, lies in the way that the gender system that the travestis draw on is constituted. Debates about transgendered individuals such as 18th-century mollies, Byzantine eunuchs, Indian hijras, Native American berdaches, U.S. transsexuals, and others often suggest that those individuals constitute a third, or intermediate, gender, one that is neither male or female or one that combines both male and female.[10] Journalists and social commentators in Brazil sometimes take a similar line when they write about travestis, arguing that travestis transcend maleness and femaleness and constitute a kind of postmodern androgeny.

My contention is the opposite. Despite outward physical appearances and despite local claims to the contrary, there is no third or intermediate sex here; travestis only arise and are only culturally intelligible within a gender system based on a strict dichotomy. That gender system, however, is structured according to a dichotomy different from the one with which many of us are familiar, anchored in and arising from principles different from those that structure and give meaning to gender in northern Europe and North America.

The fundamental difference is that, whereas the northern Euro-American gender system is based on sex, the gender system that structures travestis' perceptions and actions is based on sexuality. The dominant idea in northern Euro-American societies is that one is a man or a woman because of the genitals one possesses. That biological difference is understood to accrete differences in behavior, language, sexuality, perception, emotion, and so on. As scholars such as Harold Garfinkel (1967), Suzanne Kessler and Wendy McKenna (1985[1978]), and Janice Raymond (1979) have pointed out, it is within such a cultural system that a transsexual body can arise, because here biological males, for example, who do not feel or behave as men should, can make sense of that difference by reference to their genitals. They are not men; therefore they must be women, and to be a woman means to have the genitals of a female.

While the biological differences between men and women are certainly not ignored in Brazil, the possession of genitals is fundamentally conflated with what they can be used for, and in the particular configuration of sexuality, gender, and sex that has developed there, the determinative criterion in the identification of males and females is not so much the genitals as it is the role those genitals perform in sexual encounters. Here the locus of gender difference is the act of penetration. If one *only* penetrates, one is a man, but if one gets penetrated, one is not a man, which, in this case, means that one is either a viado (a faggot) or a mulher (a woman). Tina, a 27-year-old travesti, makes the parallels clear in a story about why she eventually left one of her ex-boyfriends:

1. TINA: For three years [my marido] was a man for me. A total man (*foi homíssimo*). Then I was the man, and he was the faggot (viado).
2. DON: What?
3. TINA: Do you see?
4. DON: Yes. . . . But no, how?
5. TINA: For three years he was a man for me, and after those three years he became a woman (*ele foi mulher*). I was the man, and

he was the woman. The first three years I was together with him, do you see, he penetrated me (*ele me comia*) and I sucked [his penis]. I was his woman.

6. DON: Yeah . . .

7. TINA: And after those three years, I was his man. Do you understand now? Now you get it.

8. DON: But what happened? What, what made him . . .

9. TINA: Change?

10. DON: Change, yeah.

11. TINA: It changed with him touching my penis. . . . He began doing other kinds of sex things. "You don't have to cum [i.e., have orgasms] on the street [with clients]" [he told me], "I can jerk you off (*eu bato uma punhetinhe pra você*). And later on we can do other new things." He gives me his ass, he gave me his ass, started to suck [my penis], and well, there you are.

Note how Tina explains that she was her boyfriend's woman, in that "he penetrated me and I sucked [his penis]" (line 5). Note also how Tina uses the words *viado* (faggot) and *mulher* (woman) interchangeably (lines 1 and 5) to express what her boyfriend became after he started expressing an interest in her penis and after he started "giving his ass" to her. This discursive conflation is similar to that used when travestis talk about their clients, the vast majority of whom are believed by travestis to desire to be anally penetrated by the travesti—a desire that, as I just explained, disqualifies them from being men and makes them into viados, like the travestis themselves. Hence they are commonly referred to in travestis' talk by the feminine pronoun *ela* (she).

Anal penetration figures prominently as an engendering device in another important dimension of travestis' lives, namely, their self-discovery as travestis. When I asked travestis to tell me when they first began to understand that they were travestis, the most common response, as I noted earlier, was that they discovered this in connection with attraction to males. Sooner or later, this attraction always led to sexuality, which in practice means that the travesti began allow-

ing herself to be penetrated anally. This act is always cited by travestis as crucial in their self-understanding as travestis.

A final example of the role that anal penetration plays as a determining factor in gender assignment is the particular way in which travestis talk about gay men. Travestis frequently dismiss and disparage gay men for "pretending to be men" (*[andar/passar] como se fosse homem*), a phrase that initially confounded me, especially when it was used by travestis in reference to me. One Sunday afternoon, for example, I was standing with two travesti friends eating candy in one of Salvador's main plazas. As two policemen walked by, one travesti began to giggle. "They see you standing here with us," she said to me, "and they probably think you're a man." Both travestis then collapsed in laughter at the sheer outrageousness of such a profound misunderstanding. It took me, however, a long time to figure out what was so funny.

I finally came to realize that as a gay man, a viado, I am assumed by travestis to *dar* (be penetrated by men). I am, therefore, the same as them. But I and all other gay men who do not dress as women and modify their bodies to be more feminine disguise this sameness. We hide, we deceive, we pretend to be men, when we really are not men at all. It is in this sense that travestis can perceive themselves to be more honest, and much more radical, than "butch" (*machuda*) homosexuals like myself. It is also in this sense that travestis simply do not understand the discrimination that they face throughout Brazil at the hands of gay men, many of whom feel that travestis compromise the public image of homosexuals and give gay men a bad name.

What all these examples point to is that for travestis, as reflected in their actions and in all their talk about themselves, clients, boyfriends, vícios, gay men, women, and sexuality, there are two genders; there is a binary system of opposites very firmly in place and in operation. But the salient difference in this system is not between men and women. It is, instead, between those who penetrate (*comer*, literally "to eat" in Brazilian Portuguese) and those who get penetrated (*dar*, literally "to give"), *in a system where the act of being penetrated has transformative force.* Thus those who *only* "eat" (and *never* "give") in this system are culturally designated as "men"; those who give (even if they *also* eat) are classified as being something else, a something that I will call, partly for want of a culturally elaborated label and partly to foreground my conviction that the gender system that makes it possible for travestis to emerge and make sense is one massively oriented towards, if not determined by, male subjectivity, male desire, and male pleasure, as those are culturally elaborated in Brazil: "not men." What this particular binarity implies is that females and males who enjoy being penetrated belong to the same classificatory category, they are on the same side of the gendered binary. They share, in other words, a gender.

This sharing is the reason why the overwhelming majority of travestis do not self-identify as women and have no desire to have an operation to become a woman even though they spend their lives dramatically modifying their bodies to make them look more feminine. Culturally speaking, travestis, because they enjoy being penetrated, are structurally equivalent to, even if they are not biologically identical to, women. Because they already share a gender with women, a sex-change operation would (again, culturally speaking) give a travesti nothing that she does not already have. All a sex-change operation would do is rob her of a significant source of pleasure and income.

It is important to stress that the claim I am making here is that travestis share a gender with women, not that they *are* women (or that women are travestis). Individual travestis will not always or necessarily share individual women's roles, goals, or social status. Just as the worldviews, self-images, social statuses, and possibilities of, say, a poor black mother, a single mulatto prostitute, and a rich white businesswoman in Brazil differ dramatically, even though all those individuals share a gender, so will the goals perspectives, and possibilities of individual travestis differ from those of individual women, even though all those individuals share a gender. But inasmuch as travestis share the same gender as women,

they are understood to share (and feel themselves to share) a whole spectrum of tastes, perceptions, behaviors, styles, feelings, and desires. And one of the most important of those desires is understood and felt to be the desire to attract and be attractive for persons of the opposite gender.[11] The desire to be attractive for persons of the opposite gender puts pressure on individuals to attempt to approximate cultural ideals of beauty, thereby drawing them into patriarchal and heterosexual imperatives that guide aesthetic values and that frame the direction and the content of the erotic gaze.[12] And although attractive male bodies get quite a lot of attention and exposure in Brazil, the pressure to conform to cultural ideals of beauty, in Brazil as in northern Euro-American societies, is much stronger on females than on males. In all these societies, the ones who are culturally incited to look (with all the subtexts of power and control that that action can imply) are males, and the ones who are exhorted to desire to be looked *at* are females.

In Brazil, the paragon of beauty, the body that is held forth, disseminated, and extolled as desirable—in the media, on television, in popular music, during Carnival, and in the day-to-day public practices of both individual men and women (comments and catcalls from groups of males at women passing by, microscopic string bikinis, known throughout the country as *fio dental* [dental floss], worn by women at the beach)—is a feminine body with smallish breasts, ample buttocks, and high, wide hips. Anyone wishing to be considered desirable to a man should do what she can to approximate that ideal. And this, of course, is precisely what travestis do. They appropriate and incorporate the ideals of beauty that their culture offers them in order to be attractive to men: both real men (i.e., boyfriends, some clients, and *vícios*), and males who publicly "pretend to be men" (clients and *vícios* who enjoy being penetrated).

CONCLUSION: PENETRATING GENDER

What exactly is gender and what is the relationship between sex and gender? Despite several decades of research, discussion, and intense debate, there is still no agreed-upon, widely accepted answer to those basic questions. Researchers who discuss gender tend to either not define it or, if they do define it, do so by placing it in a seemingly necessary relationship to sex. But one of the main reasons for the great success of Judith Butler's *Gender Trouble* (and in anthropology, Marilyn Strathern's *The Gender of the Gift*) is surely because those books called sharp critical attention to understandings of gender that see it as the cultural reading of a precultural, or prediscursive, sex. "And what is 'sex' anyway?" asks Butler in a key passage:

> Is it natural, anatomical, chromosomal, or hormonal, and how is a feminist critic to assess the scientific discourses which purport to establish such "facts" for us? Does sex have a history? Does each sex have a different history, or histories? Is there a history of how the duality of sex was established, a genealogy that might expose the binary options as variable construction? Are the ostensibly natural facts of sex discursively produced by various scientific discourses in the service of other political and social interests? If the immutable character of sex is contested, perhaps this construct called "sex" is as culturally constructed as gender; indeed, perhaps it was always already gender, with the consequence that the distinction between sex and gender turns out to be no distinction at all. [1990:6–7]

It is only when one fully appreciates Butler's point and realizes that sex stands in no particularly privileged, or even necessary, relation to gender that one can begin to understand the various ways in which social groups can organize gender in different ways. My work among travestis has led me to define gender, more or less following Eve Sedgwick (1990: 27–28), as a social and symbolic arena of ongoing contestation over specific identities, behaviors, rights, obligations, and sexualities. These identities and so forth are bound up with and productive of male and female persons, in a hierarchically ordered cultural system in which the male/female dichotomy functions as a primary and perhaps a model binarism for a wide range of values, processes, relationships, and behav-

iors. Gender, in this rendering, does not have to be about "men" and "women." It can just as probably be about "men" and "not-men," a slight but extremely significant difference in social classification that opens up different social configurations and facilitates the production of different identities, understandings, relationships, and imaginings.

One of the main puzzles I have found myself having to solve about Brazilian travestis is why they exist at all. Turning to the rich and growing literature on homosexuality in Latin America was less helpful than I had hoped, because the arguments developed there cannot account for (1) the cultural forces at work that make it seem logical and reasonable for some males to permanently alter their bodies to make them look more like women, even though they do not consider themselves to be women and (2) the fact that travestis regularly (not to say daily) perform both the role of penetrator and penetrated in their various sexual interactions with clients, vícios, and boyfriends. In the first case the literature on homosexuality in Latin America indicates that it should not be necessary to go to the extremes that Brazilian travestis go to (they could simply live as effeminate, yet still clearly male, homosexuals), and in the second case, the literature leads one to expect that travestis would restrict their sexual roles, by and large, to that of being penetrated.[13] Wrong on both counts.

What is lacking in this literature, and what I hope this essay will help to provide, is a sharper understanding of the ways in which sexuality and gender configure with one another throughout Latin America. My main point is that for the travestis with whom I work in Salvador, gender identity is thought to be determined by one's sexual behavior.[14] My contention is that travestis did not just pull this understanding out of thin air; on the contrary, I believe that they have distilled and clarified a relationship between sexuality and gender that seems to be widespread throughout Latin America. Past research on homosexual roles in Latin America (and by extension, since that literature builds on it, past research on male and female roles in Latin America) has perceived the links to sexuality and gender to which I have drawn attention (see, for example, Parker 1986: 157; 1991: 43–53, 167), but it has been prevented from theorizing those links in the way I have done in this article because it has conflated sex and gender. Researchers have assumed that gender is a cultural reading of biological males and females and that there are, therefore, two genders: man and woman. Effeminate male homosexuals do not fit into this particular binary; they are clearly not women, but culturally speaking they are not men either. So what are they? Calling them "not quite men, not quite women," as Roger Lancaster (1992: 274) does in his analysis of Nicaraguan cochones, is hedging: a slippage into "third gender" language to describe a society in which gender, as Lancaster so carefully documents, is structured according to a powerful and coercive binary. It is also not hearing what cochones, travestis, and other effeminate Latin American homosexuals are saying. When travestis, maricas, or cochones call each other "she" or when they call men who have been anally penetrated "she," they are not just being campy and subcultural, as analyses of the language of homosexual males usually conclude; I suggest that they are perceptively and incisively reading off and enunciating core messages generated by their cultures' arrangements of sexuality, gender, and sex.

I realize that this interpretation of travestis and other effeminate male homosexuals as belonging to the same gender as women will seem counterintuitive for many Latin Americans and students of Latin America. Certainly in Brazil, people generally do not refer to travestis as "she," and many people, travestis will be the first to tell you, seem to enjoy going out of their way to offend travestis by addressing them loudly and mockingly as "o senhor" (sir or mister).[15] The very word *travesti* is grammatically masculine in Brazilian Portuguese (*o travesti*), which makes it not only easy but logical to address the word's referent using masculine forms.[16]

There are certainly many reasons why Brazilians generally contest and mock individual travestis' claims to femininity, not least among them being travestis' strong associations with homosexuality, prostitution, and AIDS—all highly stigmatized issues that tend to elicit harsh condemnation and censure from many people. Refusal to acknowledge travestis' gender is one readily available way of refusing to acknowledge travestis' right to exist at all. It is a way of putting travestis back in their (decently gendered) place, a way of denying and defending against the possibilities that exist within the gender system itself for males to shift from one category to the other.[17]

During the time I have spent in Brazil, I have also noted that the harshest scorn is reserved for unattractive travestis. Travestis such as Roberta Close and some of my own acquaintances in Salvador who closely approximate cultural ideals of feminine beauty are generally not publicly insulted and mocked and addressed as men. On the contrary, such travestis are often admired and regarded with a kind of awe. One conclusion I draw from this is that the commonplace denial of travestis' gender as not-men may not be so much a reaction against them as gender crossers as it is a reaction against unattractiveness in people (women and other not-men), whose job it is to make themselves attractive for men. Seen in this light, some of the hostility against (unattractive) travestis becomes intelligible as a reaction against them as failed women, not failed men, as more orthodox interpretations have usually argued.

Whether or not I am correct in claiming that the patterns I have discussed here have a more widespread existence throughout Latin America remains to be seen. Some of what I argue here may be specific to Brazil, and some of it will inevitably be class specific. In a large, extraordinarily divided, and complex area like Latin America, many different and competing discourses and understandings about sexuality and gender will be available in different ways to different individuals. Those differences need to be investigated and documented in detail. My purpose here is not to suggest a monolithic and immutable model of gender and sexuality for everyone in Latin America. I readily admit to having close firsthand understanding only of the travestis with whom I worked in Salvador, and the arguments presented in this essay have been developed in an ongoing attempt to make sense of their words, choices, actions, and relationships.

At the same time, though, I am struck by the close similarities in gender and sexual roles that I read in other anthropologists' reports about homosexuality and male-female relations in countries and places far away from Salvador, and I think that the points discussed here can be helpful in understanding a number of issues not explicitly analyzed, such as why males throughout Latin America so violently fear being anally penetrated, why men who have sex with or even live with effeminate homosexuals often consider themselves to be heterosexual, why societies like Brazil can grant star status to particularly fetching travestis (they are just like women in that they are not-men, and sometimes they are more beautiful than women), why women in a place like Brazil are generally not offended or outraged by the prominence in the popular imagination of travestis like Roberta Close (like women, travestis like Close are also not-men, and hence they share women's tastes, perceptions, feelings, and desires), why many males in Latin American countries appear to be able to relatively unproblematically enjoy sexual encounters with effeminate homosexuals and travestis (they are definitionally not-men, and hence sexual relations with them do not readily call into question one's self-identity as a man), and why such men even pay to be penetrated by these not-men (for some men being penetrated by a not-man is perhaps not as status- and identity-threatening as being penetrated by a man; for other men it is perhaps more threatening, and maybe, therefore, more exciting). If this essay makes any contribution to our understanding of gender and sexuality in Latin America, it will be in revitalizing exploration of the relationship between sexuality and gender and in providing a clearer framework within which we might be able to see connections that have not been visible before.

NOTES

Acknowledgments. Research support for fieldwork in Brazil was generously provided by the Swedish Council for Research in the Humanities and Social Sciences (HSFR) and the Wenner-Gren Foundation for Anthropological Research. The essay has benefited immensely from the critical comments of Inês Alfano, Lars Fant, Mark Graham, Barbara Hobson, Kenneth Hyltenstam, Heather Levi, Jerry Lombardi, Thaïs Machado-Borges, Cecilia McCallum, Stephen Murray, Bambi Schieffelin, Michael Silverstein, Britt-Marie Thurén, David Valentine, Unni Wikan, and Margaret Willson. My biggest debt is to the travestis in Salvador with whom I work and, especially, to my teacher and coworker, Keila Simpsom, to whom I owe everything.

1. Chauncey 1994; Crisp 1968; Jackson 1989; Nanda 1990; Trumbach 1989; Whitehead 1981; Wikan 1977.

2. See, for example, Almaguer 1991, Carrier 1995, Fry 1986, Guttman 1996, Lancaster 1992, Leiner 1994, Murray 1987, 1995, Parker 1991, Prieur 1994, and Trevisan 1986.

3. One of the few contexts in which ideas similar to Latin American ones are preserved in North American and northern European understandings of male sexuality is prisons. See, for example, Wooden and Parker 1982.

4. This article is based on 11 months of anthropological fieldwork and archival research and more than 50 hours of recorded speech and interviews with travestis between the ages of 11 and 60 in Salvador, Brazil's third-largest city, with a population of over 2 million people. Details about the fieldwork and the transcriptions are in Kulick n.d.

5. Travestis are also the subject of two short anthropological monographs in Portuguese: de Oliveira 1994 and Silva 1993. There is also an article in English on travestis in Salvador: Cornwall 1994. As far as I can see, however, all the ethnographic data on travestis in that article are drawn from de Oliveira's unpublished master's thesis, which later became her monograph, and from other published sources. Some of the information in the article, such as the author's claim that 90 percent of the travestis in Salvador are devotees of the Afro-Brazilian religion *candomblé*, is also hugely inaccurate.

6. In the summer months leading up to Carnival, travestis from other Brazilian cities flock to Salvador to cash in on the fact that the many popular festivals preceding Carnival put men in festive moods and predispose them to spend their money on prostitutes.

7. de Oliveira 1994; Kulick 1996a; Mott and Assunção 1987; Silva 1993.

8. The literal translation of *se sentir mulher* is "to feel woman," and taken out of context, it could be read as meaning that travestis feel themselves to be women. In all instances in which it is used by

travestis, however, the phrase means "to feel like a woman," "to feel as if one were a woman (even though one is not)." Its contrastive opposite is *ser mulher* (to be woman).

9. In her study of female prostitutes in London, for example, Day explains that "a prostitute creates distinctions with her body so that work involves very little physical contact in contrast to private sexual contacts. Thus . . . at work . . . only certain types of sex are acceptable while sex outside work involves neither physical barriers nor forbidden zones" (1990: 98). The distinctions to which Day refers here are inverted in travesti sexual relationships.

10. Bornstein 1994; Elkins and King 1996; Herdt 1994.

11. One gendered, absolutely central, and culturally incited desire that is almost entirely absent from this picture is the desire for motherhood. Although some readers of this article have suggested to me that the absence of maternal desires negates my thesis that travestis share a gender with women, I am more inclined to see the absence of such desire as yet another reflex of the famous Madonna-Whore complex: travestis align themselves, exuberantly and literally, with the Whore avatar of Latin womanhood, not the Mother incarnation. Also, note again that my claim here is not that travestis *are* women. The claim is that the particular configurations of sex, gender, and sexuality in Brazil and other Latin American societies differ from the dominant configurations in northern Europe and North America, and generate different arrangements of gender, those that I am calling men and not-men. Motherhood is indisputably a crucial component of female roles and desires, in that a female may not be considered to have achieved full womanhood without it (and in this sense, travestis [like female prostitutes?] can only ever remain incomplete, or failed, women). I contend, however, that motherhood is not *determinative* of gender in the way that I am claiming sexuality is.

12. I use the word *heterosexuality* purposely because travesti-boyfriend relationships are generally considered, by travestis and their boyfriends, to be *hetero*sexual. I once asked Edilson, a 35-year-old *marido* who has had two long-term relationships in his life, both of them with travestis, whether he considered himself to be heterosexual, bisexual, or homosexual. "I'm heterosexual; I'm a man," was his immediate reply. "I won't feel love for another heterosexual," he continued, significantly, demonstrating how very lightly the northern Euro-American classificatory system has been grafted onto more meaningful Brazilian ways of organizing erotic relationships: "[For two males to be able to feel love], one of the two has to be gay."

13. One important exception to this is the Norwegian sociologist Annick Prieur's (1994) sensitive work on Mexican *jotas*.

14. Note that this relationship between sexuality and gender is the *opposite* of what George Chauncey reports for early-20th-century New York. Whereas Chauncey argues that sexuality and gender in that place and time were organized so that "one's sexual behavior was necessarily thought to be determined by one's gender identity" (1994: 48), my argument is that for travestis in Salvador, and possibly for many people throughout Latin America, one's gender identity is necessarily thought to be determined by one's sexual behavior.

One more point here. I wish to note that Unni Wikan, upon reading this paper as a reviewer for the *American Anthropologist*, pointed out that she made a similar claim to the one I argue for here in her 1977 article on the Omani xanith. Rereading that article, I discovered this to be true (see Wikan 1977: 309), and I acknowledge that here. A major difference between Wikan's argument and my own, however, is that it is never entirely clear whether Omanis (or Wikan) conceptualize(s) xaniths as men, women, or as a third gender. (For a summary of the xanith debate, see Murray 1997.)

15. The exceptions to this are boyfriends, who often—but, interestingly, not always—use feminine grammatical forms when speaking to and about their travesti girlfriends, and clients, who invariably use feminine forms when negotiating sex with travestis.

16. In their day-to-day language practices, travestis subvert these grammatical strictures by most often using the grammatically feminine words *mona* and *bicha* instead of *travesti*.

17. The possibility for males to shift gender—at least temporarily, in (hopefully) hidden, private encounters—seems to be one of the major attractions that travestis have for clients. From what many different travestis told me, it seems clear that the erotic pleasure that clients derive from being anally penetrated is frequently expressed in very specific, heavily gender-saturated, ways. I heard numerous stories of clients who not only wanted to be penetrated but also, as they were being penetrated, wanted the travesti to call them *gostosa* (delicious/sexy, using the feminine grammatical ending) and address them by female names. Stories of this kind are so common that I find it hard to escape the conclusion that a significant measure of the erotic delight that many clients derive from anal penetration is traceable to the fact that the sexual act is an engendering act that shifts their gender and transforms them from men into not-men.

REFERENCES CITED

Almaguer, Tomás. 1991. Chicano Men: A Cartography of Homosexual Identity and Behavior. *Differences* 3: 75–100.

Bornstein, Kate. 1994. Gender Outlaw: On Men, Women and the Rest of Us. London: Routledge.

Brandes, Stanley. 1981. Like Wounded Stags: Male Sexual Ideology in an Andulusian Town. In *Sexual Meanings: The Cultural Construction of Gender and Sexuality.* S. B. Ortner and H. Whitehead, eds. Pp. 216–239. Cambridge: Cambridge University Press.

Butler, Judith. 1990. *Gender Trouble: Feminism and the Subversion of Identity.* London: Routledge.

Carrier, Joseph. 1995. *De los Otros: Intimacy and Homosexuality among Mexican Men.* New York: Columbia University Press.

Chauncey, George. 1994. *Gay New York: Gender, Urban Culture and the Making of the Gay Male World, 1890–1940.* New York: Basic Books.

Cornwall, Andrea. 1994. Gendered Identities and Gender Ambiguity among Travestis in Salvador, Brazil. In *Dislocating Masculinity: Comparative Ethnographies.* A. Cornwall and N. Lindisfarne, eds. Pp. 111–132. London: Routledge.

Crisp, Quentin. 1968. *The Naked Civil Servant.* New York: New American Library.

Day, Sophie. 1990. Prostitute Women and the Ideology of Work in London. In *Culture and AIDS.* D. A. Feldman, ed. Pp. 93–109. New York: Praeger.

de Oliveira, Neuza Maria. 1994. *Damas de paus: O jogo aberto dos travestis no espelho da mulher.* Salvador, Brazil: Centro Editorial e Didático da UFBA.

Dynes, Wayne. 1987. Portugayese. In *Male Homosexuality in Central and South America.* S. O. Murray, ed. Pp. 183–191. San Francisco: Instituto Obregón.

Elkins, Richard, and Dave King. 1996. *Blending Genders: Social Aspects of Cross-dressing and Sex-changing.* London: Routledge.

Fry, Peter. 1986. Male Homosexuality and Spirit Possession in Brazil. In *The Many Faces of Homosexuality: Anthropological Approaches to Homosexual Behavior.* E. Blackwood, ed. Pp. 137–153. New York: Harrington Park Press.

Garfinkel, Harold. 1967. *Studies in Ethnomethodology.* Englewood Cliffs, NJ: Prentice-Hall.

Guttman, Matthew C. 1996. *The Meanings of Macho: Being a Man in Mexico City.* Berkeley: University of California Press.

Herdt, Gilbert, ed. 1994. *Third Sex, Third Gender: Beyond Sexual Dimorphism in Culture and History.* New York: Zone Books.

Jackson, Peter A. 1989. *Male Homosexuality in Thailand: An Interpretation of Contemporary Thai Sources.* New York: Global Academic Publishers.

Kessler, Suzanne J., and Wendy McKenna. 1985 [1978]. *Gender: An Ethnomethodological Approach.* Chicago: University of Chicago Press.

Kulick, Don. 1996a. Causing a Commotion: Public Scandals as Resistance among Brazilian Transgendered Prostitutes. *Anthropology Today* 12 (6): 3–7.

———. 1996b. Fe/male Trouble: The Unsettling Place of Lesbians in the Self-images of Male Transgendered Prostitutes in Salvador, Brazil. Paper presented at 95th annual meeting of the American Anthropological Association, San Francisco.

———. n.d. Practically Woman: The Lives, Loves and Work of Brazilian Travesti Prostitutes. Manuscript under review.

Lancaster, Roger N. 1992. *Life is Hard: Machismo, Danger, and the Intimacy of Power in Nicaragua.* Berkeley: University of California Press.

Leiner, Marvin. 1994. *Sexual Politics in Cuba: Machismo, Homosexuality and AIDS.* Boulder, CO: Westview Press.

Mott, Luis, and Aroldo Assunção. 1987. Gilete na carne: Etnografia das automutilações dos travestis da Bahia. Revista do Instituto de Medicina Social de São Paulo 4 (1): 41–56.

Murray, Stephen O. 1997. The Sohari Khanith. In *Islamic Homosexualities: Culture, History, and Literature.* S. O. Murray and W. Roscoe. Pp. 244–255. New York: New York University Press.

Murray, Stephen O., ed. 1995. *Latin American Male Homosexualities.* Albuquerque: University of New Mexico Press.

———. 1987. *Male Homosexuality in Central and South America.* San Francisco: Instituto Obregón.

Murray, Stephen O., and Wayne Dynes. 1987. Hispanic Homosexuals: Spanish Lexicon. In *Male Homosexuality in Central and South America.* S. O. Murray, ed. Pp. 170–182. San Francisco: Instituto Obregón.

Nanda, Serena. 1990. *Neither Man nor Woman: The Hijras of India.* Belmont, CA: Wadsworth Publishing.

Newton, Esther. 1972. *Mother Camp: Female Impersonators in America.* Englewood Cliffs, NJ: Prentice-Hall.

Parker, Richard G. 1986. Masculinity, Femininity, and Homosexuality: On the Anthropological Interpretation of Sexual Meanings in Brazil. In *The Many Faces of Homosexuality: Anthropological Approaches to Homosexual Behavior.* E. Blackwood, ed. Pp. 155–163. New York: Harrington Park Press.

————. 1991. *Bodies, Pleasures and Passions: Sexual Culture in Contemporary Brazil.* Boston: Beacon Press.

Perlongher, Nestor. 1987. *O negócio do michê: Prostituição viril em São Paulo.* São Paulo: Editora Brasiliense.

Prieur, Annick. 1994. *Iscensettelser av kjønn: Tranvestitter og machomenn i Mexico by.* Oslo: Pax Forlag.

Raymond, Janice. 1979. *The Transsexual Empire.* London: Women's Press.

Sedgwick, Eve Kosofsky. 1990. *Epistemology of the Closet.* Berkeley: University of California Press.

Silva, Hélio R. S. 1993. *Travesti: A invenção do feminino.* Rio de Janeiro: Relume-Dumará.

Strathern, Marilyn. 1988. *The Gender of the Gift: Problems with Women and Problems with Society in Melanesia.* Berkeley: University of California Press.

Trevisan, João Silvério. 1986. *Perverts in Paradise.* London: Gay Men's Press.

Trumbach, Randolph. 1989. The Birth of the Queen: Sodomy and the Emergence of Gender Equality in Modern Culture, 1660–1750. In *Hidden from History: Reclaiming the Gay and Lesbian Past.* M. B. Duberman, M. Vicinus, and G. Chauncey Jr., eds. Pp. 129–140. New York: New American Library.

Whitehead, Harriet. 1981. The Bow and the Burden Strap: A New Look at Institutionalized Homosexuality in Native North America. In *Sexual Meanings: The Cultural Construction of Gender and Sexuality.* S. B. Ortner and H. Whitehead, eds. Pp. 80–115. Cambridge: Cambridge University Press.

Wikan, Unni. 1977. Man Becomes Woman: Transsexualism in Oman as a Key to Gender Roles. *Man,* n.s., 12: 304–319.

Wooden, Wayne S., and Jay Parker. 1982. *Men Behind Bars: Sexual Exploitation in Prison.* New York: Da Capo Press.

PART NINE

SAME-SEX SEXUALITIES
CULTURE, DESIRE,
AND FREEDOM

READINGS IN THIS PART

INTRODUCTION TO SUBJECT AND READINGS[1]

In September 2001, as I was reading a journal while riding through Manhattan on a crowded D-train, a man with a Jamaican accent tapped my arm and said, "Excuse me, I'm sorry to be looking over your shoulder, but I have to tell you that the second line there is wrong." The sentence the man referred to read, "[It is also a] badly kept secret that Jamaica has a perceptibly vibrant gay population." As I turned to look at him, he added, "It is not true, we don't love gay people in Jamaica." The sentence was from a journal article titled "Homophobia and Gay Rights Activism in Jamaica," a subject so volatile that the author published it under a pseudonym.[2]

I was not surprised by this man's reaction. A number of recent incidents demonstrate the magnitude of homophobia in Jamaica:

• Sixteen men, presumed gays, were killed in a prison riot in 1997 after it was announced that condoms would be distributed to prisoners to curb HIV/AIDS. Apparently the "straight" inmates wanted to demonstrate their disapproval of homosexual acts in their prison.

- The lyrics of several popular dancehall songs openly advocate murdering gays.
- In 2000, P. J. Patterson, the Prime Minister, stated "Under my watch . . . , we have no intention whatsoever of changing those laws that make homosexuality illegal."[3]
- Although there is no law specifically prohibiting lesbianism, the law against male/male sex is broad and can carry a penalty of ten years in prison.[4]
- In June 2001, P. J. Patterson, long believed to be gay (a fact many Jamaicans believe is responsible for their failing economy), felt he needed to publicly affirm his sexual orientation with the statement: "My credentials as a lifelong heterosexual are impeccable."[5]
- The Village People, because of their "pro-gay" music were blocked from coming to the island.
- There has been a call to prohibit gay cruise ships from visiting the island.
- Finally, when the lone Jamaican gay rights organization, J-FLAG, declared that they were going to rally and march through a major commercial area in Kingston, hundreds of citizens, women and men, young and old, armed themselves and lined the streets daring any *battyman/ Chi Chi man* [homosexuals] to show themselves.[6] None did.

My interviewees confirm these attitudes by claiming that they would disown their children if they "came out" as gay. Homosexuality was described as a disease and sinful, and lesbians were just as "sick" as male homosexuals. In contrast to the blatant sexual intolerance of gays, a visit to the island reveals sexually explicit advertisements, announcements for Bare-as-You-Dare fetes that offer prizes for the most revealing outfit, and dancehall lyrics that boast of the singers' sexual (heterosexual) capabilities.

Back to the objections of man on the D train. Is the line "[It is also a] badly kept secret that Jamaica has a perceptibly vibrant gay population" wrong? I think that depends on your definition of "vibrant." There is a *brave* gay population fighting a difficult moral and political battle. Tolerance of homosexuality in Jamaica is seen not only as morally reprehensible but also as un-Jamaican. Homophobia is championed as evidence of Jamaica's moral superiority over Western liberal sexual mores. Although the country has received international criticism for its open homophobia, Jamaicans view such pressure as post-colonial imperialism. They believe that upholding their sexual mores is an integral part of their cultural rights.

Jamaicans are not particularly exceptional in their intolerance and discrimination against gays. Sex between members of the same sex is criminalized in over 100 countries in the world. In a few countries, it is a capital offense. In the United States, several states have sodomy laws that apply only to same-sex couples, and in some states the age of consent is older for gay people than it is for heterosexuals. Discrimination relating to partner benefits, taxes, and adoption are some of the more subtle forms of inequality. In general, Austria, Australia, Canada, Germany, the Netherlands are the most tolerant countries in the world, and South Africa is the only nation with "sexual orientation" protection in its constitution.

Research about same-sex sexualities has suffered due to researcher and research design bias, assumptions, and misinformation. The articles in this section tackle the question about what constitutes homosexuality? Same-sex sexual activity occurs under a variety of circumstances, each with different meanings. Four major categories can be identified: (1) situational same-sex sexual activity, such as occurs in prison;

(2) experimental same-sex sexual activity, such as sex play among children or the college students who are exploring and formulating their sexualities; (3) lifestyle same-sex sexualities, adults who identify and live as gays and lesbians; and (4) ritual same-sex sexual activity, such as insemination rituals found in New Guinea.

Sambia Sexual Culture, by Gilbert Herdt, addresses ritualized homoerotic practices among the Sambia, a culture living in the highlands of New Guinea. It is their cultural belief that boys will not become masculine or attain manhood without ingesting semen. All boys engage in a cycle of insemination rituals, first as fellators, then as the fellated. As boy grow to men, their involvement in the rituals ends, they marry women, and live the rest of their lives as heterosexuals.

The Sambia are not the only culture with insemination rites; the practice, however, seems to be concentrated in Melanesia. The idea of rituals that require young boys (aged seven to eleven) to fellate older boys may be disturbing to us. Such behavior violates our strongly held belief that children should not engage in sexual activity. But rather than dismiss it as perverted or deviant, Herdt unravels how these rituals are replete with many levels of meaning and symbolism. He explains how they relate to Sambian gender ideology, procreation, strength, and spiritual transmission. Thus, what looks like an exotic sexual ritual is revealed to be a social transaction. Sambia sexual culture, as described by Herdt, challenges more than our ideas about cultural relativity; it forces us to confront our ideas about childhood sexual behavior and sexual orientation.

Evelyn Blackwood's article, *Culture and Women's Sexualities,* also explores same-sex relationships in non-Western cultures. Rather than focusing on one culture, as Herdt did, Blackwood presents a cross-cultural comparison of women's same-sex sexual relations. She notes that although same-sex sexuality is varied throughout the world, it has often been taken out of its cultural context and treated as a "thing" rather than being a part of a gender/sexual system relating to power. By employing holism and exploring variability, Blackwood demonstrates that sexuality is not and does not have to be a fixed identity.

Blackwood also explores how gender ideologies and gender relations shape women's and men's sexualities differently. Women in all cultures are expected to marry and bear children. Enforced heterosexuality runs deep and is tied to women's lack of economic and political power. Despite this, women around the world have subverted male hegemony and engaged in sexual behaviors which exclude men. Yet, as Blackwood notes, same-sex sexualities between women is not the same as it is for men. The act of having sex with members of your own sex is not only culturally defined, but it is culturally defined in different ways for men and women.

The introduction to this section began with a description of a culture where many people believe that homosexuality is a disease and a sin. Not so long ago, many people in the United States held similar beliefs. Timothy F. Murphy, in the article *Redirecting Sexual Orientation: Techniques and Justifications,* discusses how many of our ideas about homosexuality were shaped by the medical profession. As the responsibility of sexualities moved from religion to medicine, the status of same-sex sexualities changed from sin to disease. Once homoerotism was deemed a disease, it was believed that it could and should be cured. Thus, began the relationship between the medical profession and people with same-sex sexual desires. Murphy provides us with the details of the disasters caused by behavioral therapy, drug and hormonal therapy, and surgery (including lobotomies).

Despite this sordid history, Murphy notes that the relationship between medical intervention and sexual orientation is not over. Today one of the issues concerning sexual orientations is whether to try to reorient people who want to be reoriented. However, because lesbianisms and male homosexualities are not diseases, they do not need to be treated. Image the flip side of current reorientation justification, a person wanting to be reorientated from heterosexuality to homosexuality. Murphy shows us that if one is not ethical, neither is the other.

TERMS AND CONCEPTS

boy-insemination rites	psychopathology
congenital condition	sadomasochism
control group	same-gender sexual relations
diagnostic nomenclature	same-sex sexual relations
exhibitionism	semen transaction
menstrual huts	sexual orientation
orgasmic reconditioning	sexual reorientation
psychodynamic	

QUESTIONS TO CONSIDER

1. What does Blackwood mean when she states "gender ideologies are critical to the production of men's and women's sexualities"? Support your answer with the ethnographic data.
2. Using Blackwood's data describe how kinship systems such as marriage can shape female and male sexuality.
3. In what ways does Herdt's description of age-graded homoerotic relations among the Sambia challenge the concept of a fixed sexual orientation?
4. Using Herdt's ethnographic data explain the value of semen in Sambia culture from the Sambian point of view.
5. Describe the use of drugs, surgery, and orgasmic reconditioning in attempts at sexual reorientation, and discuss the outcomes of these interventions.
6. One criticism for evaluating reorientation therapy was the researchers' lack of control groups. What types of research problems would such a control group present?
7. How does the Western concept of a fixed sexual orientation encourage attempts at sexual reorientation?

NOTES

1. This introduction is a brief version of my article, Very straight sex: The development of sexual mores in Jamaica, published in *Journal of Colonialism and Colonial History*, 2001 (2)3.

2. Williams, Lawson (pseudonym). Homophobia and gay rights activism in Jamaica. *Small Axe: A Journal of Criticism*, 4(2000): 106–111.

3. Gay cruises in question, *The Gleaner*, 9-26-2000.

4. Williams, 2000.

5. White, Nicole. Rhythm of hatred: Anti-gay lyrics reflect an island's intolerance. *Miami Herald* (8-5-2001). *www.geocities.com/privacylaws/World?Jamaica?JAnews05.htm*

6. J-FLAG stands for the Jamaican Forum of Lesbians, All-Sexuals and Gays. Launched in 1998, J-FLAG's mission is "working towards a Jamaican society in which the human rights and equality of lesbians, all-sexuals [all those included in the non-heterosexual continuum who defy labels] and gays are guaranteed." *http://village.fortunecity.com/garland/704/*

FURTHER READINGS

Barale, Michele Aina, Henry Abelove, and David M. Halperin (eds.). 1993. *The Lesbian and Gay Studies Reader*. New York: Routledge.

Faderman, Lillian. 1991. *Odd Girls and Twilight Lovers: A History of Lesbian Life in Twentieth-Century America*. New York: Penguin Books.

Fone, Byrne. 2000. *Homophobia: A History*. New York: Metropolitan Books.

Herdt, Gilbert H. 1997. *Same Sex, Different Cultures: Gays and Lesbians Across Cultures*. New York: Westview Press.

———. 1999. *Sambia Sexual Culture: Essays from the Field*. Chicago: University of Chicago Press.

Hogan, Steve, and Lee Hudson. 1998. *Completely Queer: The Gay and Lesbian Encyclopedia*. New York: Henry Holt and Company.

Katz, Jonathan Ned. 1995. *The Invention of Heterosexuality*. New York: Plume.

Murphy, Timothy F. 1999. *Gay Science: Between Men~Between Women: Lesbian and Gay Studies*. New York: Columbia University Press.

Murray, Stephan O. 2000. *Homosexualities*. Chicago: University of Chicago.

Murray, Stephen O., and Will Roscoe (eds.). 2001. *From Boy-Wives and Female Husbands: Studies in African Homosexualities*. New York: St. Martin's Press.

Rich, Adrienne. 1986. Compulsory heterosexuality and lesbian experience. In *Blood, Bread and Poetry: Selected Prose 1979–1985*. New York: W.W. Norton & Company. Pp. 23–75.

Spencer, Colin. 1995. *Homosexuality in History*. London: Harcourt Brace & Company.

Weston, Kath. 1993. Lesbian/gay studies in the house of anthropology. *Annual Review of Anthropology*, Vol 22. Pp. 339–67.

RELATED WEBSITES

The Bisexual Resource Center
www.biresource.org

The Center for Lesbian and Gay Civil Rights
www.center4civilrights.org/index.htm

Gay and Lesbian Alliance Against Defamation (GLAAD)
www.glaad.org

Gay and Lesbian Studies—Resources (University of Chicago)
www.lib.uchicago.edu/e/su/gaylesb/

A Gay, Lesbian, Bisexual, Transsexual Search Engine
www.rainbowquery.com

Human Rights Campaign—Working for Lesbian, Gay, Bisexual, and Transgender Equal Rights
www.hrc.org

The National Gay and Lesbian Task Force
www.ngltf.org

The National Institute for Gay, Lesbian, Bisexual and Transgender Education
www.thenationalinstitute.org/eyc.html

ONE Institute and Archives - International Gay and Lesbian Archives (University of Southern California)
www.usc.edu/isd/archives/oneigla

Solga@online—Society of Lesbian and Gay Anthropologist
www.usc.edu/isd/archives/one/ssolga/main.html

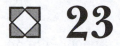

23
Sambia Sexual Culture

Gilbert Herdt
San Francisco State University

The sexual and the social ultimately belong within the same framework of personal and cultural reality, and the main effort of my work among the Sambia has been to restore this holistic sense of things. Thus in this chapter I focus on how Sambia traditions of social practices and meanings, values, and beliefs regulate sexual behavior and, in turn, how these sexual transactions create a unique sexual culture.

In each instance, the concept of a particular "sexual culture" is meant to inflect relations between sexuality and meaning at the most fundamental level of the local cultural history, knowledge, power, sociality, the reg-

Source: From Gilbert Herdt, *Ritualized Homosexuality in Melanesia.* Berkeley: University of California Press, 1984, pp. 167–210. Copyright © 1984 The Regents of the University of California. Reprinted from Sambia sexual culture. In *Sambia Sexual Culture: Essays from the Field*, by Gilbert H. Herdt. Chicago: University of Chicago Press, 1999, pp. 56–88. © 1999 University of Chicago Press. Reprinted with permission of the publisher, The University of Chicago Press.

ulation of markets, and the development of the person and selfhood. This does not mean that the content of sexual culture is everywhere particularistic and diverse, since, in general, full personhood, in the Maussian sense of rights and duties, involves being married and parenting children. Thus every sexual culture must grapple with the norms and exigencies of marriage, sexual partnerships, parenting, childhood socialization, and the exceptions that depart from these norms. In this sense, the sexual is but one of many overlapping domains of shared meanings, which would include kinship, politics, religion, and economy in virtually all human communities.

Sambia sexual culture creates these sexual meanings—both at a symbolic level of representations and institutional discourses and at the level of practices of embodiment and subjectivity of the individual, the values and understandings, rights and duties, of being a sexual actor in the flood of social relations that exist among the Sambia. Sexual culture has an extremely wide scope, in this view, and is actually a window that opens onto the widest topography of cultural and social life. This includes the classification of sexual relationships, definitions of sexuality which impose norms (and resistance to norms), the creation and maintenance of local theories of "human nature," as well as a kind of local ontology of psychological types of sexual actors, according to folk concepts registered by social status, gender, age, personality, sexual proclivities, marital status, and so on. Beliefs about the nature of the genders and their difference or similarity are of significance as well, and of greater import in New Guinea than in certain other culture areas of the world. Of special importance to the Sambia are the variety of institutional forms of sexual transactions, and the beliefs and values relevant to the larger society which Sambia bring to their erotic encounters with one another. These can be studied as a kind of lexicon of forms because the Sambia have heavily ritualized and tabooed these sexual transactions.

But precisely how is the student of human society and history to go about describing a phenomenon, such as sexual culture, which seems all-encompassing? We can employ a variety of strategies in answering the question, though the answer of anthropology is different. Every anthropologist has certain choices when he or she sets out to write a particular ethnographic piece. In another era the answer would always have been staid, formal, impersonal (see Herdt and Stoller 1990). Today, however, the relentless battering of postmodernism has made accounts which omit the personal seem old-fashioned, passé. We cannot do without an account of the cultural environment, nevertheless. And we must pay special attention to the fact that many people tend to project their own "natural" meanings and assumptions onto what they read about "sex." The following symbolic and structural account of Sambia culture elucidates these matters by providing the key domains of sexual beliefs, their constraints upon semen transactions in same and opposite sexual relation, as these regulate social and sexual life.

PRECOLONIAL SOCIETY AND CULTURE

The Sambia dwell on the fringe area of the Eastern Highlands of Papua New Guinea.

Traditional society and economy revolve around small hamlets built atop high mountain ridges for defense. Gardening and hunting are the main economic pursuits. Sweet potatoes and taro are the chief staples. Women do most of the garden work. Men do all the hunting, primarily for possum, cassowary, birds, and eels. Pigs are few and are of little ceremonial importance. Descent is ideally organized on the basis of patriliny. Postmarital residence is patrivirilocal, so males grow up in their father's hamlet, inherit his land, and reside there. Marriage is by infant betrothal or sister exchange; bride-wealth was introduced only in the mid-1970s. Some men, especially senior leaders, have several wives. All marriage is arranged by elders, women being traded between exogamous clans, which tend to be internally organized as an extended family. Inside hamlets, nuclear (or polygamous) families live together in small, separate huts, but there are also one or two men's houses wherein all initiated, unmarried males over age seven live. The hamlet tends to function as a corporate group in warfare, subsistence activities, marriage, ritual, and dispute settlements.

Sambia society is comprised of six different population clusters of hamlets in adjacent river valleys. These population clusters are divided, in turn, into subgroups (phratries) believed related by ancestry, ritual, and common geographic origin. Each phratry has between two and six hamlets, situated on ridges often within sight of one another. These local hamlet groups, known as confederacies, intermarry and engage in joint ritual initiations every three or four years.[1] But they sometimes fight among themselves. Warfare has indeed been rife throughout the entire area of the Sambia, taking two forms: intertribal war raids to kill and loot and intratribal bow fights designed to bluster and get revenge for perceived wrongs. In other words, within the Sambia Valley, hamlets have intermarried, initiated, and fought—sociopolitical dynamics that are crucial for understanding social and sexual life.

Relationships between the sexes are highly polarized. One sees this gender polarization in virtually every social domain. A strict division of labor and ritual taboos forbids men and women from doing each other's tasks in hunting and gardening. Women are responsible for food preparation and child care. Authority rests in the hands of elders and war leaders. Men are in charge of public affairs. The hamlet itself is divided into male and female spaces and paths tabooed to the opposite sex after initiation. Men's rhetoric disparages older married women as oversexed or lecherous and younger women as prudish or shy. Men fear being contaminated and sapped of their strength (*jerungdu*) by marriageable women.

Furthermore, male-female sexual relationships are generally antagonistic, and many marital histories reveal arguments, fights, jealousies, sorcery fears, some wife beating, and even suicides, especially by women. Wives (more than female kin) are stigmatized as inferior, as polluting and depleting to men, because of their menstrual and vaginal fluids. Sexual intercourse is supposed to be spaced to avoid depletion and premature aging or death. (Couples may have sex every three to five days, or as infrequently as once every two or three weeks, depending on their ages, length of marriage, personalities, etc.) Prolonged postpartum taboos prohibit couples from engaging in coitus for up to two-and-a-half years following the birth of a child. These generalizations indicate trends, but Sambia are generally highly sexually regulated compared with other Highlands groups (Langness 1967 [reviewed in Herdt and Poole 1982]; Strathern 1988).

How do Sambia understand the nature and functioning of the sexes? Male is the socially preferred and valued sex. Female is perceived by men as inferior, except reproductively. Infants are assigned to the male, female, or hermaphroditic sex, and sex typing of behaviors and gender traits is rigid. Females, however, are believed to mature quickly and without external aids, for their bodies contain a menstrual blood organ (*tingu*) that hastens physical and mental development, puberty, and eventually menarche—the key sign a woman is ready for marriage and procreation. (Menarche occurs late in New Guinea and in precolonial times was about age nineteen for Sambia.) At menarche a woman is initiated

through secret ceremonies in the menstrual hut forbidden to all males (see Godelier 1986:74ff.). Males, by contrast, do not naturally mature as fast or as competently. Womb blood and maternal care not only hold them back but endanger their health. Males cannot reach puberty or acquire secondary sex traits (e.g., facial hair, mature penis) without semen; their bodies, their semen organs (*keriku-keriku*), do not internally produce semen, Sambia believe. Therefore males require inseminations and magical ritual treatments over many years to "catch up" with females and become strong, manly men.

Male development and masculinization after childhood are the responsibility of the men's secret cult and its initiation system. This cult is organized and perpetuated by the confederacy of hamlets. Boys are initiated at seven to ten years of age, when they are separated from their mothers, natal households, older sisters, and younger siblings. Thereafter, they must avoid all females for many years while living in the men's house. Avoidance taboos are rigidly enforced with shaming, beatings, and ultimately death (the last used to keep boys from revealing ritual secrets).

Males undergo six initiations in all over the next ten or fifteen years. First initiation (*moku*) graduates are called *choowinoku;* second-stage initiation (*imbutu*) occurs between ages eleven and thirteen; and third-stage initiation (*ipmangwi*), bachelorhood puberty rites, is for youths fourteen to sixteen years of age. These initiations are all done in sequence on large groups of age-mate boys, who are from neighboring hamlets, thus making them members of a regional age grade. Initiates also become members of warriorhoods, which as local units are responsible for defending their own hamlets. Fourth-stage initiation (*nuposha*) may occur anytime afterward. It is a public marriage ceremony associated with secret male rites and sexual teachings for youths to whom girls have been individually assigned for their marriage. But genital intercourse does not yet occur between the couple. Fifth-stage initiation (*taiketnyi*) occurs when a man's wife has her menarche, typically in her late teens. The bride then has her secret initiation in the menstrual hut. Afterward, the couple can engage in coitus. The final, sixth-stage initiation *(moondangu)*, is held when a man's wife bears her first child. She then undergoes a final women's secret ceremony too. Two children bring full adult manhood *(aatmwunu)* for males and personhood for both sexes.

The men's secret cult is ideally organized in the men's house as a social hierarchical system according to ritual rank. Initiates are lumped into ritual categories: *kuwatni'u* is a category term for first- and second-stage prepubescent initiates (who may also be referred to as *choowinuku* or *imbutnuku*, ritual-grade titles); *ipmangwi* (or *moongenyu*, "new bamboo") bachelors are third-stage initiates of higher adolescent status. Pubescent bachelors dominate prepubescent initiates; older youths and young married men dominate bachelors; elders are seen as politically and spiritually superior to everyone (Herdt 1981). War leaders and shamans lead in fights and healing ceremonies, respectively. There is nothing unique about this ritual system, for many similar forms can be found in Eastern Highlands (e.g., Read 1952), Papuan Gulf (e.g., Williams 1936a), and Telefomin (e.g., Barth 1975) societies. What is special, and what links Sambia and their Anga neighbors with Papuan lowland systems (e.g., Keraki, Kiwai Island, Marind-anim), are the wide-scale institutionalization of age-graded homoerotic relations (see Herdt 1984a, for a review).

Sambia practice secret homoerotic fellatio, which is taught and instituted in first-stage initiation. Boys learn to ingest semen from older youths through oral sexual contacts. First- and second-stage initiates may only serve as fellators; they are forbidden to reverse erotic roles with older partners. Third-stage pubescent bachelors and older youths thus act as fellateds, inseminating prepubescent boys. All males pass through both erotic stages, being first fellators, then fellated; there are no exceptions, since all Sambia males are initiated into homoerotic insemination.

The symbolism of the first homoerotic teaching in initiation is elaborate and rich; the meaning of fellatio is related to secret bamboo flutes, and ritual equations are made between flutes, penis, and mother's breast, as between semen and breast milk. . . . Boys must drink semen to grow big and strong. At third-stage initiation, bachelors may experience personal difficulty in making the erotic switch in roles (see Herdt 1987a). Thereafter, they may continue having oral sex with boys until they father children. Essentially, youths pass from an exclusively homoerotic behavioral period to a briefer bisexual period, during which they may have both homoerotic and heteroerotic contacts in secret, and finally to exclusive heterosexual relationships. Social and sexual inadequacies in masculine personhood are regarded as individual failures to achieve these social transitions. . . .

SEXUAL SUBJECTS AND OBJECTS

For the Sambia, who ritualize male obligatory homoerotic practices on a broad scale, it may be said that two forms of sexual behavior characterize their culture and developmental experience. For males, first sexual contacts are secret, transitional, male-male oral sexual behaviors. For adult males and females, the parallel form is initial male-female oral (the woman is fellator) sex in marriage. Later, heterosexual genital contacts occur. To my knowledge, no other customary form of sexual behavior occurs, including masturbation to orgasm or anal intercourse. The rules and norms surrounding these two sexual modes are parallel. But in both cases, semen acquisition is an imperative organizing principle of people's social interaction and sexual behavior. Its magical power does things to people, changing and rearranging them, as if it were a generator. They, however, can do little to affect this semen principle: it does not reflect on but merely passes through them— as an electrical current through a wire—winding its way into bodies, like generator coils, for temporary storage. Because it is instrumental to growth, reproduction, and regeneration, semen (and its substitutes, detailed below) is needed to spark and mature human life. Humans are its objects.

This strange view may seem upside-down to us, since it animates a body fluid with agency and life force in a way that seems "magical." However, this belief system is fundamental to the Sambia worldview, and such a parallel view was once common in premodern Europe as influenced by alchemy. By thus beginning with the novelty of Sambia sexual culture, we may hope to achieve a better understanding of the relationship between heteroerotic and homoerotic life, a subject about which we Westerners assume so much. I shall first examine cultural ideas about semen and then study how these ideas influence sociologic types of semen transactions between males and males and males and females. Taken together, these ideas and social transactions form a system of objects of the semen. Though these two perspectives are conceptually distinct, their complementarity suggests how normative goals affect individual social action and the developmental cycle of the group. When viewed as a total system, all of these valuations structure the sexual interactions and subjectivities of Sambi participants.

Semen predicates two different sorts of relationships: direct sexual transactions between semen donors and recipients, on either the individual or group level (in the latter sense, I am speaking normatively); and indirect semen transactions that affect changes in a third party via the semen recipient, who is believed to serve as a transformer of semen (e.g., father to mother to baby). The concept "transformer" is analogous to Meig's (1976) use of "transmitter," in which she argues that a person's body may store or deliver fluids (e.g., blood or semen) or essences to someone else. "Transformer" differs because of another dimension needed, transformation: that is, changing semen into something else, as medieval alchemists were thought to change lead into gold. I shall later disentangle these levels of description and analysis.

CULTURAL IDEAS OF SEMEN VALUE

Sambia have five main cultural categories of semen valuation. These include erotic play, procreation, growth, strength, and spirituality, all of which are connected with sexual behavior. The metaphoric and analogic uses in rhetoric and imagination of these categories can be found in other domains too (see Herdt 1981). Here, though, I shall explore their social significance for insemination.[2] The study of these categories will involve us in understanding how people (and in some ways, nonhuman entities) are represented as potential semen donors or recipients, transformers, or transmitters of semen value in Sambia culture. This section is concerned with the cultural level of these concepts.[3]

There are two analytic senses in which I shall use the term "value." First, the anthropologic sense of conventional valuations in a culture: attributed or assumed meanings shared by and assigned to people, institutions, and substances. Thus we can speak of the cultural regard for semen and the social esteem with which it thus endows bodies and social relationships. (There is also a libidinal value, present in conscious and unconscious thought, which will not concern us.)[4] Second, there is the Marxist sense of the value of a commodity, such as gold, which "when impressed upon products, obtains fixity only by reason of their acting and reacting upon each other as quantities of value" (Marx 1977:248).[5] Hence, we can analyze semen as a scarce resource that can be consumed and produced, conserved, invested, or otherwise spent. Persons and relationships may be valuated (as a means to an end) in regard to their status as donors or recipients of the commodity semen.

There are several tacit assumptions underlying the relation between semen information and the categories examined below, and I begin with them. (1) Semen is the most precious human fluid. Because it is believed vital for procreation and growth and is in short supply, semen is more precious than even mother's milk, its closest cultural equivalent. But precious does not necessarily mean powerful. Menstrual blood is the logical antithesis of semen; it is dangerous and, in some rituals, is equally efficacious as semen (cf. Faithorn 1975). (2) Sambia are by character prudish people. (May I refer to them as "prudish lechers" [see Meggitt 1964]?) Semen, other body fluids, and sexuality are sensitive subjects: the data and viewpoints described below took years to accumulate, even though the presentation makes them seem obvious. (3) Sexual pleasure is seen by Sambia only in relation to another person; that is, there is no equivalent to the Western category "sex" (used in relation to masturbation, pornography, etc., as an indefinite noun; e.g., "Sex is . . . good, bad, fun, boring, etc."). Sex, in the Sambia sense, is only spoken of as *duvuno* (pushing or penetrating into) a boy's mouth or a woman's vagina, in the sense of a battle between one's erect penis (lit., *lakelu mulu*, "penis fight") and the sexual partner: "his bamboo orifice" (metaphor for boy's mouth) or "her thing down below" (euphemism for vagina). Again, the verb *duvuno* is not used for masturbation (which is not a cultural concept among the Sambia) and is only rarely applied to wet dreams, in which the dream images concern copulating with persons (e.g., always interpreted as spirits).[6] (4) When men refer to erotic desire (e.g., "I swallow my saliva [thinking about sex] with him/her"), they tend to refer to their sexual outlets as if their alter's orifice (mouth or vagina) were a fetishized object, like a commodity: "My penis is hungry" (i.e., they use "food" as a metaphor for their sexual needs). (5) All sexual intercourse may be defined as either work *(wumdu)* or play *(chemonyi)*, but usually not both. For example, it is *wumdu* to produce a baby by copulating with a woman many times, but it is *chemonyi* to inseminate a boy once or twice, knowing he will not procreate. Insemination is also an action (e.g., like ritual, *pweiyu*) that mediates between work and play, sacred and profane. Let us examine each category in turn.

EROTIC PLAY

When Sambia use *chemonyi* (play) as a noun in relation to sexual intercourse, they normatively refer to sexual interaction as "erotic pleasure."[7] Semen is expended and orgasm *(imbimboogu)* achieved. I begin with this category not because it is most crucial—Sambia themselves would rank procreation first (Herdt 1981)—but because semen valuations

are contingent upon orgasm, and anthropologists often ignore orgasm and its erotic manifestations, including erotic motivation, as native categories.

The most general cultural attributes of erotic play may be sketched as follows. First, the factor of the sex of one's partner: erotic play symbolically typifies male-male more than male-female erotic contacts. Male-male sexual transactions are culturally defined as behaviorally casual. Male-female contacts, normative only in marriage, are viewed (unless adulterous) as noncasual transactions aimed toward procreation. Erotic play is of course an aspect of all male-female sex, but it is not their most important one. Exclusive sexual access to a person seems in time to be inversely related to erotic play: a man's wife, as his sexual property, as Sambia see it, is less exciting than a boy or woman taken at first (i.e., as a virgin), or only once, on the sly. Age is a contributing factor here: sexual partners are perceived as having more "heat" and being more exciting the younger they are, especially females. A second factor is reciprocity: the more unequal the sexual partners (youth/boy), the more erotic play seems to define their contact culturally. (By contrast, the husband-wife dyad is the most symmetrical sexual relationship in Sambia culture [see chapter 4].) Third, sexual constancy, that is, greater frequency and permanence of sexual contacts, generally transforms sexual contacts from being erotic play into something else. Husband-wife contacts are the most constant, though not necessarily the most frequent, in Sambia sexual culture.

Erotic play may be defined also according to the social purpose of insemination. Erotic pleasure is attached to male-male and male-female sexual contacts and to both oral and vaginal intercourse.[8] But only heterosexual genital contacts result in procreation; all other sexual contacts fulfill other quasi-reproductive functions (e.g., growth of spouse) or are for erotic play. Since homoerotic fellatio cannot result in reproduction (marriage consummation), it becomes a demonstration of the older male's maturity, that is, of his power to masculinize a boy. But this valuation is significant only for donors; the boy-recipients value semen for their own growth. What donors value also is the fellator's mouth as a sexual outlet: the social purpose is sexual release in appropriate relationships that demonstrate status.

Erotic play may be defined, lastly, according to the flow of a scarce commodity. Semen is viewed as a very scarce resource by Sambia, for, in reproduction, it is believed instrumental from conception to adulthood. It takes many inseminations to procreate: large expenditures of time, energy, semen. From this viewpoint, all male-female contacts may be construed as benefiting procreation (as we shall see next). Homoerotic play unevenly fits this paradigm. It is, after all, play, not work: procreative work is defined as producing babies. So how do homoerotic transactions benefit the donor? Essentially, homoerotic play is culturally defined as an unequal exchange of commodities: recipients acquire semen; donors get sexual services. This exchange is unequal because (as Sambia see it) a man's semen is being depleted, but he gets only erotic pleasure in return ("which is insubstantial"). Homoerotic activity thus creates a dilemma for bachelors, which is perhaps why some engage in it less frequently as they approach marriage. Homoerotic play is, however, less depleting than heterosexual intercourse (work), which is, in part, why bachelors are less worried about replenishing the semen lost during their early homoerotic activities compared with later sex with their wives.

PROCREATION

Procreation is defined as genital-to-genital heterosexual contacts that lead to the birth of offspring. Sambia regard vaginal intercourse as primarily focused on the production of babies. Oral insemination prepares a wife's body for making babies by strengthening her as well as by precipitating her menarche (if she has not already attained it). Fellatio also prepares her for lactation by semen's being transformed into breast milk. Oral sexual contacts are not believed to make babies in anyone; only vaginal intercourse does that. All heterosexual genital intercourse contributes directly to procreation in one's marriage, and all sexual contacts may be viewed as contributing directly to the recipients' procreative competence (wife or boy-fellator) or reproduction (wife).[9]

Procreation is jurally defined as resulting from genital-to-genital sexual contacts between formally married husband and wife. Since heterosexual contact is not morally or jurally allowed outside marriage, privilege of sexual access to a woman's body is restricted by marriage; exclusive sexual rights belong to her husband. Likewise, exclusive access to a husband's body and semen, after the birth of their first child, is his wife's right (which view is a key argument women use to resist polygyny). Traditionally, only infant betrothal and bride-service marriage (which was rare) required the transfer of goods or services to the donors bestowing a wife. Infant betrothal, though, required meat and small food prestations only, whereas bride-service required more wealth, in addition to the bridegroom's years-long work for his prospective affines. Sister exchange requires no exchange other than that of the women. Since infant betrothal is preferred and sister exchange marriages far outnumber those of bride-service, marriage transactions are largely unrelated to bride-wealth.

Genital-to-genital intercourse creates a fetus by successively "injecting" semen into a woman's womb. After initial oral sexual contacts, a woman's body is viewed as ready to procreate. One instance of vaginal intercourse does not a fetus make: Sambia have no notion of conception in our Western scientific sense. The womb is the container and transformer of semen. It changes semen into fetal tissue: primarily bone and skin but also muscle and internal organs. The semen coagulates inside the birth sac; this "biological" process is central to fetal development, and its imagery is important in social thought (Herdt 1981:167–72ff.). Womb and umbilical blood also become circulatory blood in the fetus; they do not produce any hard body parts of the child, which result only from semen. Social ideology thus defines procreation as productive work (not erotic play) in two senses: it is hard work to feed enough semen into a woman's womb to create a fetus; and it is hard work for the woman's body to change this semen into a whole baby, sapping her own blood and carrying the child in her body for so long.

Blood and semen also differentially contribute to the sex of the offspring and his or her gender differentiation. First, both parents can magically influence the fetus's sex by ingesting various plants. They do this both because Sambia ideally prefer a boy as the first born and because they want to make the infant more attractive. Second, it takes more semen to create a girl than a boy. Two other beliefs explain why, and they pertain to the procreative/economic productive capacities of males versus females (i.e., in social reproduction). The most important is that females do more hard work (i.e., garden work) all the time; therefore, the female fetus "pulls" more semen from the mother to make itself. (A magical elaboration of this idea is that since females think about garden work constantly, their fetal thought anticipates and drains more semen strength in preparation.) The other belief is that a female fetus has a *tingu* (menstrual-blood organ), which makes the mother's vagina hot and therefore drains off more semen from the father during sexual contacts that create the fetus. During womb life, the sexes receive blood in differential amounts too. Essentially, girls have some of their mother's menstrual blood transmitted to their own menstrual-blood organs in utero. Later, during postnatal growth, this blood stimulates girls' psychobiological feminization (sexual and gender differentiation). Boys, by contrast, have no blood transmitted to their inactive *tingus*. Nor do they receive their father's semen for use in their own semen organs; father's semen in both male and female offspring merely creates fetal tissue.

Marriage is fully consummated after the birth of a child. Procreation results in final but distinct initiation ceremonies for the husband-father and wife-mother alike. The new father and his clan bestow a meat prestation on the wife's cognatic kin, especially patrilateral female kin, and her ritual sponsor, in public village ceremonies. Because pro-

creation defines full adulthood for men and women, childless adults are not perceived as full persons. Nonetheless, all childlessness in marriage is attributed to barrenness in the woman or contraceptive sorcery by other men (usually thought to be envious fellow villagers who wanted the woman for themselves). Sambia men dogmatically deny the possibility of sterility in a husband (see also Read 1955); indeed, such is never discussed in social discourse, and the only category for sterility is "barren woman" *(kwoliku)*. Childlessness is thus an acceptable reason for taking a second wife but not for divorce. Once a marriage is consummated, it is contracted for life; a woman is rarely taken back by the donor. When warfare occurs, a woman's ties with her natal group (i.e., enemies) are severed. Divorce is thus extremely rare and usually instigated by a husband over his wife's perceived adultery; their children become jural members of the father's clan. And so only death breaks the marital bond.

GROWTH

Sambia believe that biologic growth in humans results from ingesting semen and equivalent substances (mother's milk, pandanus nuts). Sexual intercourse for growth is described as *pinu pungooglumonjapi* ("pushing" to "grow" him or her, where *pinu* is an alternate verbal form of *duvuno*). This idiomatic form may be applied to both male-male and male-female sexual transactions.

The value of semen for human growth comes in successive stages, which differ according to the mode of semen transmission and one's sex. Initial growth for every fetus occurs through semen accumulations in the mother's womb. Postnatal growth in babies results mainly from breast-feeding. A woman's body is again treated as a biologic transformer of semen in this regard: a man's inseminations (especially oral) amass in and are transformed by his wife's breasts into mother's milk *(nu-tokeno,* breast food). After weaning, growth is aided by eating pandanus nuts, which are seasonal but are treated as nearly equal nourishment to that of mother's milk. (The productive source of this nut food is one's father's trees and his hard work in tending and scaling to procure the nuts.) Meat fed to children also contributes smaller increments to growth. Following weaning, though, girls continue to grow without further aids, whereas boys falter, staying weak and puny.

Male growth after weaning comes mostly from homoerotic inseminations following initiation. This semen-nourishment form is male *monjapi'u*, which men liken to breast-feeding (Herdt 1981:234–36).[10] Oral sexual contacts feed semen into a boy's body, distributing semen to his maturing skin, bones, and skull and producing changes toward masculinization (eventuating in puberty). The bulk of ingested semen goes to the boy's semen organ, where it accumulates as a pool. This pool is drawn on after puberty for two purposes: it produces pubescent secondary sex traits, especially muscle, body hair, and a mature penis; and it provides semen for later sexual contacts. (The first sign of surplus semen in the body comes from wet dreams.)

Girls require and are permitted no inseminations until marriage. Postmarital oral sexual contacts in cases of marriage before menarche provide a young wife's body with semen to stimulate the final changes necessary for childbearing. Men also argue, as noted above, that women need semen to create breast milk. (Some women dispute these views and say that a woman's body creates its milk; however, other women disagree.)

In sum, semen creates biologic growth directly in initiates and wives through sexual contact, primarily fellatio, whereas it creates growth indirectly in the fetus and newborn through being transformed by a woman's body into fetal tissue and milk. For spouses, then, growth and procreation are concepts that refer to different aspects of the same sexual contacts. For the offspring, as third-party semen recipient, growth is vital after birth, and long postpartum taboos prohibit marital sexual intercourse for fear the infant will be harmed (be stunted or ugly, an outcome that would shame the parents, especially the father, who would be viewed as lacking sexual restraint). In homoerotic activity, men offer boys the normative goal that semen "grows" them. But from the donor's standpoint, though initiates' growth does provide vicarious long-term confirmation of the fellated's manhood, a fellator's growth is not of direct importance to a bachelor's personhood. Rather, homoerotic play takes precedence as the fellated's motive; the boy's growth is a latent social function of the bachelor's behavior (and is, I think, often a rationalization on the men's part).

STRENGTH

Strength *(jerungdu)* is one of the key concepts of insemination in Sambia culture; we shall here examine only its implications for semen transmission and thereby human maturation.

"Strength" is absolutely derived from semen and its equivalents: mother's milk and pandanus nuts. But more than those substances, semen masculinizes a male's body; there is no substitute for it. Unlike procreation or growth valuations, strength can be obtained directly only through semen. In Sambia thought, there is a tendency to play down strength and stress growth as characteristic of the breast-feeding relationship. Suckling milk makes a baby grow, but it is much less associated with strengthening it. Semen in the womb forms the skeletal fetus; nursing helps create the baby's teeth, the hardening of its skin and skull. But milk is more for growth. The strong results of milk, Sambia believe, are transformations of semen: the mother ingests semen, which her breasts convert into milk. The strong part of milk is also more crucial for male infants, but it alone will not masculinize them. Thus, strength is not intrinsically produced but is rather derived from the mother-infant relationship, itself a product of marriage. In male subjectivity, however, strength is a transactional product that makes use of the father's secret sexual acquisition of semen from other men, which he feeds to his wife, whose body, in turn, has a natural capacity to store the fluid and turn it into breast food that strengthens and matures the infant.

As with growth, a father can indirectly add small amounts of strength over the years following weaning by providing meat and pandanus nuts to children. Cassowary meat, too, which may be eaten only by males, has fat *(moo-nugu)* that sometimes is treated as a second-rate semen equivalent (Herdt 1981:110). (Other kinds of fat, e.g., from pigs or eels, are never likened to semen.) But these are small increments.

If one follows the semen cycle, we see a chain of links in which men strengthen people: husband strengthens wife through initial fellatio; father strengthens baby through mother's milk; bachelor strengthens initiate through fellatio. Symbolically, homoerotic fellatio provides the key ritualized strengthening of boys' postpartum bodies. As I have emphasized elsewhere, male insemination is chiefly seen as making a boy grow, the perceived outcome of which is strength. Culturally, the act of feeding/inseminating is equivalent to the verbal category *monjapi'u*, male nursing, the social/perceptual outcome of which is the state of being *jerungdu*, as seen in both its physical and psychosocial manifestations: larger size, attractiveness, valor, forceful speech, sexual potency, and many social achievements, including progeny.

There is another secret source of strength that is important in male thought and that concerns the nonhuman sources for replenishing semen expended in sexual intercourse. Analytically, this semen valuation might be treated as separate from the "strength" concept because of its ontogenetic status in the male life cycle (adults give semen away and then must replace it to stay strong). But Sambia do not think of the matter in this way, for this replenishment is seen simply as a further extension of strength building. Yet, since this replenishment practice is learned later in ritual life and comes from trees, not men, we shall here examine it as an auxiliary strengthening process.

In semen transactions, one person's loss is another's gain: semen, which embodies strength, depletes the donor, whose strength therefore diminishes. Fear of semen depletion is an important theme in male ritual discourse and ideology. (It is registered, too, in individual sexual aberrations. . . . Concern with too-frequent semen loss inhibits initial homoerotic contacts, bachelors being cautioned to go easy. (Here, again, fellateds and fellators are at odds.) Yet bachelors' fears are

not great, and the early use of ritual mechanisms for semen replenishment in fellateds is played down. Among married men, the situation is different. A key pragmatic focus of fifth- and sixth-stage initiation ceremonies is teaching about secret ingestion of white milk sap from trees, which is believed to replace semen lost to women. (Pandanus nuts are another semen replacement, though of less importance because they are not always available.) This milk sap comes from several forest trees and vines, and the sap is referred to as *iaamoonaalyu*, "tree mother's milk."

Trees are, in general, regarded as if they and their products were female, for example, as with pandanus trees. Myth also "genderizes" them this way (Herdt 1981). There seems little doubt that the imagery and symbolization of the adult man's semen replenishment is not, then, symbolic insemination but rather that of symbolic breast-feeding. This interpretation is confirmed by men's drinking sap from long aerial roots of pandanus nut trees: the trees are ritually referred to as "females," and the roots are likened to women's breasts. We see, therefore, that semen comes at first from homoerotic fellatio, later to be replaced by milk sap (and, to a lesser extent, by pandanus nuts and cassowary fat), and semen, in turn, is transformed into milk and fetal tissue by women. At bottom, male ideology seems to postulate that these forest trees create new semen.

SPIRITUAL TRANSMISSION

The final category of semen valuations I shall refer to as spiritual transmission, or "spirituality" for short, though it is not a marked category in Sambia culture or language. Spirituality is, in our terms, an animistic composite of both "natural" and "supernatural" elements. These elements include, most noticeably, spirit familiars *(numelyu)* of various sorts, believed to be transmitted (not transformed) through semen for males (and through blood for females). The reproduction of spiritual elements in individuals and groups is a social outcome of sexual intercourse over which individuals have little control.

Before I describe spirit familiars, two other matters deserve mention. The first is the concept of soul *(koogu)*, a spiritual aspect of personhood that is related to sexuality and parenting. There is no clearly formulated theory of the soul's origin in individual development. Some men attribute it only to the father's semen. Others say it is a combination of semen and material in the mother's womb (they do not specify which parts of semen and/or blood). Though the womb is important, some people attribute the birth of a child's soul not to fetal life but to postnatal socialization. Men normatively relate the father's semen to the child's soul in both sexes, especially boys. This ambiguity is no doubt an expression of all persons' normative blood ties to mother and matrilateral kin. Yet, since the soul survives death and becomes a ghost, forest spirit (big man), or hamlet spirit (prominent woman) haunting its clan's territory, its patrilineal origin and afterlife influence seem clear in sociopolitical organization. The skull and bones of the deceased also become powerful weapons in sorcery and are most efficacious when used by biologic kinsmen, sons especially. In both cases—souls and bones—spiritual essences of semen are thought to survive death. The other concept is "thought," or *koontu*, which I gloss as personhood. "Thought" is the totality of one's experience, beliefs, and knowledge. Personhood is mainly a product of social training; its relation to body substance and biologic inheritance is less certain. Socialization is its chief source, however, and this means that both mother and father influence personhood.

Without question the most significant semen valuation for spirituality is the child's inheritance of spirit familiars. Transmission of familiars is ideologically clear and sex linked. Boys inherit only their father's familiars via his semen. Girls inherit their mother's familiars through her blood. (Mother's milk, a semen derivative, is ignored in this domain.) Genealogical inheritance of clan familiars (i.e., totems) among males seems to derive from the semen that creates a son's body tissue. Later, males acquire other familiars attracted to them through ritual ceremonies: the nature of this attraction again implies that father's semen is instrumental. Shamanic familiars, transmitted through semen from father to son in the mother's womb, are a clear case of necessary patrilineal inheritance required for legitimate performance of the shamanic role (Herdt 1977), though some women shamans claim inheritance of father's familiars. Other familiars, both personal and clan related, ensure longevity, spiritual protection, or strength. Male ideology generally denies women such blessings from their natal clan familiars. Men may have their familiars stolen unwittingly by male children, which leads to sickness or premature death. Homoerotic inseminations do not transmit familiars to semen recipients (cf. Schieffelin 1976). Finally, men's ingestion of milk sap from trees is consistent with the perpetuation of their clan familiars (though this is not fully conscious in Sambia thought).

SEMEN VALUE IN SOCIAL TRANSACTIONS

Who may and should have sexual intercourse with what categories of persons in Sambia society? What are the principles of these social transactions? In this section I examine social action in relation to the cultural ideas of semen valuation already described. The sociology of semen transactions involves two viewpoints. First, there are direct semen transactions between persons resulting from sexual intercourse. Second, there are indirect semen transactions with a third party, believed to occur by transforming semen into something else by a second party, whether the source of semen is human or nonhuman (i.e., trees), though the semen transformers are always humans. A subcategory of indirect inseminations may be seen as delayed exchanges between social groups, semen being returned to donor groups via former recipients in the subsequent generation. I shall study each of these types in turn.

DIRECT SEMEN TRANSACTIONS

All sexual contacts are restricted by exogamous taboos and social norms. Sexual contacts are permissible only between unrelated people; that is, those related through common cognatic links, especially agnates, are forbidden sexual partners. Marriage should be arranged between different clans, preferably of different villages. Statistically, though, up to 50 percent of all marriages are contracted within large, consolidated hamlets; father's sister's daughter marriage is normatively permitted in delayed-exchange marriage contracts, and mother's brother's daughter marriage, though frowned on, occurs rarely, when no alternate wife can be found (Herdt 1981). Homoerotic contacts are likewise prohibited between all clansmen, matrilateral kin, age mates, and with ritual sponsors. (Homoerotic infractions occur, however, as between matrilateral cross-cousins or distant kin not normally encountered, though these are unusual.) Male initiates' ritual sponsors are called "mother's brother," a social title, since only some sponsors are actual or classificatory mother's brother. Nonetheless a boy's sponsor becomes, in effect, a pseudo-kinsman who combines both maternal and paternal attributes, making it very wrong for any sexual contact to occur between them. In general, all sexual transactions are highly regulated and tend to occur with people of other hamlets (who are potential or real enemies), so sexual relations distinguish kin from non-kin and friendly from hostile persons.

In direct sexual transactions, all the above cultural ideas of semen value come into play, but the domain of erotic play is especially important. Erotic play is a social motive and goal that applies mainly to adult men. Their motive for erotic play is orgasm. Boy-fellators never have orgasms in homoerotic play. And men deny, in general, that women experience orgasm, though they believe women are lascivious and enjoy sexual play.

Men's enjoyment of erotic play changes through the life cycle. Some older boy-fellators do experience vicarious erotic pleasure from homoerotic fellatio, as indicated by their reports (near puberty) of their own erections while sucking a bachelor, or by certain feelings or body sensations during fellatio. Bachelors inseminate in homoerotic play to (in local idiom) "straighten their penises,"

that is, to reduce sexual tension/frustration, or to "feel *ilaiyu*" (here meaning pleasure) from orgasm. Men get erotic pleasure from copulating with their wives, first through fellatio, and then in genital-to-genital intercourse, which most men favor over fellatio. To repeat: male-female oral sexual contacts, like those with boys, are regarded more as erotic play.

Male social ideology defines both homoerotic and heteroerotic play as transactions in which the older male is always the inseminator. No role reversals are ever situationally permitted. The older male is viewed as the socially active party who should control the behavior interchanges that lead to the insemination. A man's control over sexual contacts is established by the social norms regulating the behavioral conditions of sexual intercourse. Men are physically bigger than boys and most women. During intercourse the man either stands over his fellator (who kneels) or lies on top of his wife (in the missionary position), methods that allow a man instant freedom to withdraw from body contact at will. Men are also usually years older than their insertees, either boys or women (even though, curiously, men regard younger wives as of like age and maturity [see Herdt 1981:177, 181]). Again, these interactions are defined as unequal: women and boys get semen; men get erotic pleasure. Most men are (consciously) uninterested in the erotic arousal of either boys or women, so direct sexual transactions emphasize the sexual excitement of the inserter.

In spite of the men's view, the concept "erotic play" admits of some social reciprocity between all sexual partners. Men recognize that women have erotic interests; for instance, sexually experienced women are rhetorically described as lascivious harlots consumed by insatiable erotic appetites (Herdt 1981:187). Perhaps this dogma is the men's response to knowing that women favor certain men over others as mates. Men also know that boys joke about fellatio among themselves and that initiates favor some bachelors over others in regard to the amount and taste of their semen.[11] Bachelors likewise favor certain boys over others: those who are more attractive to them are either more or less sexually aggressive and/or willing to perform fellatio. These reciprocal aspects thus underscore the frame of play, and they are not found in notions of sex for procreation, growth, strength, or spirituality, all of which stem from insemination.

Since semen is highly valued as a means to valuable social ends—personal strength, marriage, offspring, personhood—it should be conserved and wisely spent. Men assume that women and boys desire their semen for those social ends; no other motive is searched for in understanding why insertees engage in sexual intercourse. (We know the situation is more complex. For instance, boys must at first be coerced into fellatio, but men also know this.) The seeming personal conflict on men's part, at least in homoerotic contacts, is that they get only sexual release in return for their semen. They recognize this in idioms that depict the penis as having a mind of its own: for example, "that no-good man down there [penis] gets up and we follow its nose" (euphemism for glans penis), as if men inseminate from sexual impulse, almost against their will. Here, then, is a perceived conflict between private impulses and public norms.

This conflict is felt in two other ways. First, women are prized as sexual outlets more than boys. Women are owned: this ownership is a contributing dynamic to the sexual excitement of Sambia men. Power is a critical part of this excitement. Male-female relationships are, in general, filled with more power than are male-male contacts, for heterosexuality is more highly regulated. Sexually, women are also more powerful, for they can contaminate as well as deplete, and women deplete semen more than do boys. Moreover, sexual impulses leading to adultery are a tremendous social problem in Sambia society (see below). Second, when orgasm occurs, it is treated as being beyond conscious control. Wet dreams are the best example. For women, breast-feeding may also apply: some women report that they experience *imbimboogu*, which they liken to orgasm, when feeding, though it is not clear yet what this social labeling of their experience means (Herdt and

Stoller 1990: chapter 6).[12] All these points support the conclusion that individual sexual impulses are stronger than the need for semen constraint in hetero- versus homoerotic relations.

Underlying this conflict is the fact that sex for erotic play is the only sexual mode that produces no social advantage to the semen donor. Because all ejaculation is debilitating and semen is a male's most valuable resource, all sexual contacts are viewed as a "careful metering of semen" (Gell 1975:252). Seen this way, erotic play represents what Gell (1975) refers to as a "nemesis of reproductivity": it makes no sense in the scheme of things, even though it is personally pleasurable. All other categories of direct sexual transactions may be defined as work, not play, for this reason; like other forms of work (e.g., gardening), sex for procreation, growth, and so forth produces social products. One's semen is spent to reproduce heirs and perpetuate one's clan. With this view in mind I will now contrast other cultural ideas pertaining to hetero- and homoerotic transactions.

The idea of procreation applies only to male-female sexual contacts. In native theory all heterosexual contacts, oral or vaginal, contribute to a woman's reproductive competence. In practice, however, only early marital sex is treated this way: oral sex is infrequent after a woman bears children. My impression is that both men and women in later years prefer genital-to-genital contact (and I think most women always prefer vaginal sex). Though homoerotic transactions are not procreative (but cf. individual boys' fears of becoming pregnant [Herdt 1981] and similar beliefs about male pregnancy elsewhere [Meigs 1976: Williams 1936a]), semen in boys does assist in becoming reproductively competent adults.

The concepts of growth and strength are applied to both homo- and heteroerotic transactions. In theory, boy-fellators as semen recipients use sexual contact first to grow and then to get strong. Until third-stage initiation this norm holds; youths are thereafter accorded physical maturity and may no longer serve as insertees. Growth and strength apply differentially to women as semen recipients. Essentially, all heterosexual fellatio makes a woman grow and strengthens her until she is a mother. Later oral sex does not make a woman grow, for she is viewed as biologically mature. It does replenish her strength, however—a sort of perpetual fountain of youth men must give up after bachelorhood. Indeed, men complain that women are healthier and outlive them because of this ready source of orally ingested strength. (In this sense, a wife is like a boy-fellator.) Vaginal sex is generally believed to contribute neither growth nor strength to a woman; instead, indirectly, a man's semen creates and strengthens fetus and infant.

Finally, the concept of spirituality applies unequally to direct sexual transactions. No transmission of spirit familiars occurs between males and females. None is imparted to one's wife; she is simply one source of the transmission of soul and familiars to one's offspring. Again, men believe that only sons inherit the father's familiars (either indirectly, through semen via the mother, or directly, through cult ceremonies that call forth one's father's familiars after his death). A daughter's familiars come only from her mother, but her soul is linked (the notion is vague) to her father and his clan territory, though not irrevocably.[13] Moreover, there is absolutely no sense that a boy-fellator acquires his familiars from any bachelor-fellated; but the idea is neither here nor there, since Sambia never consider the possibility.[14] Conceptually, though, we should underline that their folk model of spiritual transmission keeps familiars discreetly in clans and firmly embedded in the man's procreative role. Here we see a firm separation between spiritually and sexuality, on the levels both of ideology and of social action. The division between spiritual and material reproduction in marriage is especially notable (see Tuzin 1982).

There is one other notion, which we may define as spiritual, that involves direct homoerotic transactions: *kwolaalyuwaku*, a highly secret, multivalent ritual concept referring to "masculine decorations and ritual paraphernalia," which also doubles as a ritual secret pseudonym for semen.[15] It is also close to *kweiaalyu-waku*, meaning, "sun's white grease," an alternate for cassowary fat *[kaiouwugu moonugu].*) The semantic referent of the semen aspect is esoteric, yet it clearly signifies a collective semen pool. This pool is perceived as the semen contained in the bodies of all men living within neighboring hamlets: it therefore reflects the ritual cult and the confederacy. The idea is that boys have access to this pool, which they can tap into through homosexual insemination, strengthening themselves. Symbolically, then, *kwolaalyuwaku* is a metaphor for the men's collective sense of manliness and their intergenerational transmission of semen in secret and political ways.

But on the individual level, the concept is bi-directional. I was long skeptical of certain men's statements that it strengthened themselves to inseminate many boys. How could this be? Men argue that just as a boy draws strength from numerous men, who deposit their semen in his reserve for future use, so men are kept healthy by having their semen safely "contained" in many boys, who are likened to a sort of magical string of semen depositories for one's substance, spread throughout society. Should a man or any of his semen recipients get sick, other recipients remain strong and healthy. And since recipients harbor parts of one's semen (strength) inside them, so, too, one is kept healthy (in sympathetic/contagious magical thought). A woman lacks this protection: she is not a cult initiate, and her semen comes from only one man, her husband. Nor is a man likewise protected by inseminating women or creating children: the concept is not extended beyond homoerotic contacts. Thus, semen not only bestows but also maintains strength, the only evidence known to me that directly explains why homoerotic insemination is felt to be less depleting than that of heterosexuality. In this ritual sense, boy-inseminating practices are placed within a spiritual framework and are opposed to heterosexuality and marriage.

All the above sexual contacts concern normatively appropriate semen transactions between donors and recipients. Illicit heteroerotic transactions (which includes all premarital intercourse and extramarital adultery) reveal the social boundary of ideas about exclusive jural claims over a man's semen. All adultery is severely condemned; a man may use violence against a wife suspected of it. Therefore, it is hidden until discovered, when the spouses fight. If a husband is accused of adultery or of wanting to take a second wife, the fight is called *kweikoonmulu*, literally "semen fight." Semen fights entail dreadful cursing and brawls. This adultery can be seen as "stealing another woman's semen," though it involves much more, of course. Accusations of a wife's adultery (which is rarer, for Sambia treat adulterous women harshly) also concern semen in two ways: fears that a husband's penis has been contaminated by intercourse with his wife's vagina after sex with another man (thought to bring him sickness), and questions about the wife's lover's semen contributions to a future child. In sum, adultery reveals that marriage bestows the right of exclusive spousal control over semen and insemination exchange as scarce resources.

What are the social effects of these direct sexual transactions on group relationships? Let us examine the most general latent and manifest functions of sexual contacts in the same generation. First, semen flow mirrors marriage transactions between groups. Semen may only be normatively transacted between persons of groups who can intermarry; that is, homoerotic contact is forbidden with matrilineal kin and clansmen. The same clan that donates a wife thus has clansmen who are appropriate homoerotic partners (cf. Kelly 1976). Affines of the same generation (e.g., brothers-in-law) are especially appropriate homoerotic contacts. The paradigm of this affinal homoerotic bond would be a young man who marries a younger woman and who can inseminate her younger initiate brother, either consanguineal or classificatory wife's brother (see Serpenti 1984; and Sørum 1984). This man inseminates his wife to make her grow and to strengthen her, and to procreate, and may (along with his fellow clansmen) inseminate her younger brother for erotic play, the effect of which is to help a boy grow and to strengthen him. These sexual transactions would define a man and his clan as semen donors, while his wife and brother-in-law

would be recipients. Yet ego's clan is also a wife recipient from his younger homoerotic partner's donor clan. This set of social transactions is common in Sambia life.

Second, marital/sexual bonds tend to create closer political ties between unrelated groups. Sambia generally engage in marriage and boy-inseminating practices with propinquitous groups in the same confederacy. One does not receive or give semen to intertribal enemies. Affinal ties, in particular, create closer political affiliations for mutual defense between and within hamlets. Affinal ties also establish marriage contractual obligations and sentimental bonds that persist into the next generation, influencing alignments among hamlets.

Third, semen metaphorically defines political power: inseminators are more powerful than recipients in virtually every sense. All male persons eventually serve as both direct semen donors and as recipients. All females are always direct recipients or indirect donors—to their offspring—whereas males constitute a category of both direct givers and takers. And their sexual status, of course, flip-flops during the male life cycle. Symbolically, I think, Sambia define the administration of semen as a masculine act, whereas the taking in of semen makes the recipient into an object of desire. One of the manifest functions of the secrecy of homoerotic fellatio is to hide from women the shame men feel at having earlier performed in this feminine way (Herdt 1981: chapter 8). A latent function of homoerotic secrecy is to rationalize and disguise men's use of boys as a sexual outlet. By the same token, the ritual secret of insemination growth and strength unites all males as a category against all females. This social link, which also mystifies the nature of male-female relationships, politically reinforces male power and thereby perpetuates the men's ritual cult.

INDIRECT SEMEN TRANSACTIONS

The mode of social transaction in indirect semen transactions is based on the symbolic principle that semen is transmitted to someone whose body transforms it into something else useful to a third party. The paradigm is the nuclear family triad: father-mother-child. The alternative form of indirect insemination views men as replenishing their semen from tree sap, which their bodies turn into semen: tree-man-semen recipient. Having already described direct sexual contacts, I can easily outline these semen transformations.

We have seen that sexual intercourse between spouses involves all the cultural meanings of semen value except spirituality. Now when we examine the effects of a woman's husband's semen on her prospective infant, the woman's role as transformer is clarified at two developmental points. First, to repeat, her orally ingested semen is transformed into breast milk. This milk is stored for the infant's nourishment after birth. Subsequent semen from vaginal intercourse is stored and transformed in the woman, converted by her womb into fetal tissue, as we saw. Both the intrauterine formation of the child and its postnatal breast-feeding are indirect products of the father's semen.

In this type of indirect transaction there is a subtle application of cultural beliefs to action. Erotic play occurs between the spouses, leading to procreation, but the concept is not extended to the transformative outcome, since the father never has sexual intercourse with his offspring. Indeed the paradigm of sex as work suggests that woman, as wife/mother, is the means of production men need to effect children's adult reproductive competence. Semen is indispensable for reproduction, yet so is a woman's body (breasts and womb). Moreover, no matter how much the men attempt to claim procreation as solely of their production, a wife is vital for social reproduction. She not only gives birth but also nourishes and cares for heirs, transforming semen into the strength of clans. She also transmits her husband's spirit familiars to sons and her own to daughters. Both parents contribute to the child's personhood or thought, but men believe only they produce its soul. Following weaning, a girl is believed to mature on her own, but a boy needs more semen for growth and strength. Thus, a boy indirectly taps the semen pool of his father through homoerotic contacts with other men who substitute, in his father's place, as ritual semen donors, motivated out of sexual play. The sexual cycle is completed when this son becomes an inseminator, and his sister is traded for his wife, sister and brother having reached sexual maturity.

The other form of indirect transaction consists in men's ingesting the white tree saps. It may seem odd, here, to juxtapose this secret ritual practice with reproduction. But Sambi male ideology treats tree-sap ingestion as a part of the whole adult cycle of reproduction; and, in my experience, men directly associate tree-sap drinking as a normal and regular link in a chain of psychosexual activities that are as much a part of everyday life as their own eroticism. Drinking tree sap is not actually taught until a man's last initiation, when he is a new father. Thereafter, men regularly ingest it but always in abundance after sexual intercourse with their wives. Men are thus preserving their biologic maleness (semen) and restoring their strength. Not erotic play, growth, or procreation as cultural ideas is applied to contacts with trees. Drinking tree sap simply regenerates semen and preserves health against depletion. So this ritual practice may be considered a defensive tactic—and the more so because it is secret—yet it is more than that.

Drinking tree sap also has a latent creative function: creating new semen that flows into the societal pool of semen. Sambia men do not view it this way: to them, drinking tree sap merely replaces what they have personally lost. But, besides that, they see their society as a closed system, its resources limited for reasons I shall not here detail. Suffice it to say that their religion is animistic and their ethos dominated by warrior values that recognize adulthood as a personal achievement that is, nonetheless, carefully nurtured through a strict ritual system regulating people, marriage, sexuality, and semen. This view is predicated on a cyclical model of time (see Leach 1961); seasonal movements, ceremonies, and customary transactions unfold in the round. Sambia do not recognize that their population is now expanding or that the concomitant stress on their resources (means of production) may be increasing. Nonetheless, men believe that they expend semen and that they get more from trees. Let us now consider this view for their use of the concept of spirituality.

The trees from which men acquire sap are on clan territory. The land itself is one's main material inheritance from previous generations; it is held in agnatic corporate estate, though men own specific tracts of it, from which they exploit resources (game, pandanus nuts, milk-sap trees). Land is coveted and defended against other groups; it is central to a clan's residential and territorial organization. It is also guarded by clan spirits. Ritual practices, too, are a social heritage, customs valued in themselves and for group identity, having been handed down from previous generations. It seems obvious, therefore, that the social ideology of trees provisioning new semen through the bodies of clansmen is a latent function of the regeneration of patrilineality.

Patrifiliation thus provides land and trees, ritual practices, and the social personae needed to transform tree sap into semen. Tree sap without an adult male body is just tree sap. The male body—the product of a long process of procreation with women and homoerotic insemination from men, of magical ritual treatment making it fertile and procreatively potent—is the instrument that regenerates society. Tree sap maintains maleness and masculine personhood. It regenerates one's clan, its patriline and hamlet-based warriorhood, and thus the community itself. These social identities are conceptually placed, in time and space, through concentric social networks based on a magical notion of successive degrees of purest patrilineal substance. Hence, male ideology claims that father, son, and clansmen are of one semen substance, one common origin place, one residential location—all elements of genealogical ancestry that fans out to embrace a pool of spirit familiars and ancestral spirits, the semen sustaining all. Whether the trees are seen as beginning or finishing this process is beside the point: Sambia have a cyclic view of their system that makes tree sap pivotal in a greater chain of being. What is the nature of semen value in this whole system?

DELAYED EXCHANGE

The final category of indirect semen transactions concerns exchanges across generations between groups. This subject is very complex indeed, so I shall merely sketch the contours of the system of intergroup relationships. What do groups give and receive? And do their exchanges of semen balance out across time?

The key principle of delayed exchange is that groups who exchange women also exchange semen through homoerotic contacts. Group A takes a woman from group B. They become affines. Their initiated males of different cohorts at different life-cycle stages engage in homoerotic intercourse both ways (giving and receiving semen). Children of groups A and B become matrilateral kin in the following generation. In delayed-exchange (infant betrothal or bride-service) marriage, group A later returns a woman to group B. In direct exchange (sister exchange) they will not. Marriage between generation 2 of these groups is frowned on, except in the case of delayed-exchange infant betrothal to father's sister's daughter, that is, a daughter of group A goes back to group B. Yet actual father's sister's daughter marriage (addressed as "sister" by her mother's brother's son) is also disliked; more commonly this woman is traded for another woman from a different group. Homoerotic contacts between generation 2 are also forbidden. In effect, generation 2 shares ties of blood and semen: boys of group A were formed from the blood of a woman of group B, and their body tissue came from their father, some of whose own semen may have come from males of group B. These boys (of group A) must turn to a third, unrelated group, to take both a wife and semen.

What do groups A and B exchange? Group A gets a woman as garden producer and maker of babies. She produces heirs to perpetuate group A. Group B gets food gifts and a promise of a return woman (possibly her daughter) in the next generation. Boys of group A get semen from bachelors of group B and vice versa. Homoerotic insemination ensures masculinization and adult reproductive competence. Boys of groups A and B may receive ritual sponsors from each other's group (in purest form, mother's brother). This man is the boy's guardian and teacher in sexual matters (remember, they are forbidden to have sex). So each group provides boys of the other group with semen and sexual tutorship. In generation 1, a man may copulate with both his wife and her younger brother. The man gets a wife and another homoerotic transitional sexual outlet. His wife and her younger brother both receive semen—growth, strength. And the younger brother (or, if not himself, his sons or clansmen) will eventually receive a return wife, the brother-in-law's daughter, which the latter's semen created and nourished.

What does intermarriage do to social relationships? First, marriage transforms groups from unrelated enemies to less hostile affines. Where homoerotic practices occur with groups who are politically hostile, and between which warfare and masculine competition are common, marriage places affines in a set of productive relationships where none existed before. Second, they exchange women as resources. It is in the wife-givers' best interests to ensure that the marriage is productive in every way, so that they receive a woman in return. Marital sex for procreation is productive social work; it outweighs erotic play in homoerotic contacts and results in social sanctions against adultery and barrenness. Third, women and semen thus become circulating commodities. Unrelated groups exchange semen, on both sides, with the wife-donors getting a wife out of the bargain. The initiated boys of both groups require semen to complete their personhood, while the men need wives as sexual outlets and procreators to step out of the transitional stage of homoeroticism into the adult stage of marriage and family. Semen, therefore, though a crucial commodity, is secondary to women as a commodity: without wives men cannot attain full personhood. Even though semen is needed to attain manhood and it

strengthens the new warrior recruits a village requires to protect and expand itself, this warriorhood goes for naught unless women are available for the group's economic and biologic reproduction.

Finally, the value of semen as instigator of social reproduction at both the individual and group levels pits males against one another in symmetric competition. This competition takes two forms, intragroup and intergroup transactions (Forge 1972). The one is intrahamlet individualized competition for homoerotically procured semen in order to grow and have first pick of wives needed for reproduction later. Here, boys as age mates try to outperform one another in a contest to achieve maturity first. (In fact, older brothers encourage their juniors toward this end.) The other competition is between hamlets and, in a wider sense, between a confederacy of intramarrying hamlets vis-à-vis the other confederacies of Sambia society. Men aspire to make their confederacy outdo others in war and overall productivity. Hamlets also act together to find women for their bachelors so as to produce more children—potential warriors and females for the marriage trade—compared with other groups. A race is on; its outcome is social reproduction. Conflicts within hamlets erupt over men competing with one another for wives and resources. Fights with peers over women in other hamlets also occur, sometimes precipitating warfare. But intrahamlet competition is overshadowed by the normative stress on achieving social maturity in concert with the best interests of one's own village group. Ultimately, social survival requires competing neighbors too, for they provide women and semen, and are the best defense—strength in numbers—against enemies elsewhere.

SUMMARY

The creation and regulation of semen, through a variety of structural transactions, and as measured by their valuations from several points of view, are pivotal to the production of Sambia sexual culture. What may seem esoteric, vulgar, and trivial now seems complex and symbolically significant in understanding how the Sambia construe sociality, the body, and their own folk concepts of sexuality in the structure of social relations and modes of production. Erotics belongs to this symbolic field and cannot be understood, either subjectively or objectively, except in relation to the meaningfulness of this field over time.

Until recently anthropology ignored erotics and its meanings, especially in constructing comparative models of social organization and culture. Even heteroerotic activities have, in general, scarcely been studied, and the meaning of the temporal and symbolic structuring of heterosexuality has not been accorded much analytic value beyond the vague category "sexual antagonism," which has been implicitly used to support whatever explanatory model an author advanced (Herdt and Poole 1982). The fluids of sexual and reproductive acts—semen, blood, and milk—have been too narrowly studied as entities or artifacts in exchange, or as parts of the growth process in reference only to individual development or societal functioning. They have been interpreted less often as symbolic objects and commodities, expressed through concepts and social transactions, whereby the natives reproduce the identities of persons, social roles, clans, and intergroup relationships across generations. Here, Marilyn Strathern's (1988) work is foundational and has changed the field.

Past analyses of semen and blood as culturally constructed concepts in New Guinea belief systems, for instance, reveal this structural-functional emphasis. These fluids have long been viewed as important in native notions of sexual temperament and gender. . . . The great interest in procreation beliefs shown, first by Malinowski (1913) among Aborigines, and then in Trobriand descent ideology (Malinowski 1929, 1954), illustrates this importance. Writers questioned whether natives were ignorant of procreation and what such purported ignorance of conception meant (Ashley-Montagu 1937; and see Bettelheim 1955; Leach 1966; Spiro 1968). Denial of semen valuation in kinship and rit-

ual dogma belongs to a broader cultural discourse on social regeneration and reproduction (Weiner 1978, 1980).

In New Guinea Highlands studies, since Read's (1951, 1954) work, ethnographers have noted blood and semen as cultural signs of the body, sex, and gender. Accounts of the norms of sexual contacts, dogmas about conception, sterility, and reproductive competence, and ideas about exchange of menstrual blood and semen between people as patrilineal kin and affines all illustrate how ethnographers functionally related body fluids to sociosexual relationships and the positioning of people in networks of social groups. . . . Preoccupation with the exchange of sexual fluids between groups addressed Western individualist concerns with "discrete acts of giving and receiving" (Weiner 1980:71; cf., e.g., A. Strathern 1969, 1972). Classical social theory has gone beyond exchange constructs, or structural models that view body treatment merely as reflections of society's divisions and boundaries (Douglas 1966), to interpret semen, blood, and other entities as the culturally valued materials out of which gender and reproductivity are symbolically perpetuated (Herdt 1981; Meigs 1976; M. Strathern 1988; Weiner 1980).

With the Sambia, we are dealing with people whose cultural systems use sexual relationships and fluids as objects and commodities to recreate social order in successive generations, for these are among the scarcest and most vital resources in this process. Semen and other body fluids are not just things that are: they have a value beyond themselves for extending one's personhood—that is, existence—beyond the present. No doubt many experiences of these material things (e.g., fluids, sex, and others' bodies) entail this transcendent attitude. Sambia spiritual concepts speak to this issue directly, just as the conflict between sex as work and sex as play addresses it indirectly. "Religion is an art of making sense out of experience, and like any other art, say, poetry, it must be taken symbolically, not literally," Firth (1981:596) has said, a view germane to the ritual meanings of semen.

The social fact of semen for Sambia is that it is a scarce resource that circulates through time. Its material and phenomenological attributes make it usable as commodity that can be consumed, stored, and given away. Its perceived use-value derives from the fact that (1) semen can be "contained" indefinitely in bodies and (2) then be seemingly passed, from person to person, without changing its essence or efficacy; (3) it represents an investment of labor (food, care, procreation of children) acquired through direct individual sexual transaction or indirect transformation (semen into milk), which can be given or received; (4) in being transmitted semen extends its transformative value to make the recipient more reproductively and socially competent; (5) these recipients, in turn, will produce more wealth and future individuals, who will fill productive roles and fill out social groups; and (6) by so doing, semen transactions recreate social links between the living and the dead, the worldly and the spiritual realms, between ego and others, and between the divisions of the society.

In Sambia imagination, individuals are born and die, but semen flows through them (along with blood) to recreate society. Individuals pass on. Growth as an aspect of these individuals dies with them. But strength persists: in the form of bones and skin tissue in offspring; in spirit familiars; in ghosts and spirits; and in the deceased's bones, which after death may be used for sorcery. Erotic play passes on too, but is useless except insofar as it has effected growth, strength, and procreation. Sex as work is far more productive, if less exciting: family and heirs result. In this model, a woman's body as sexual-procreative property belongs to her husband as much as his semen belongs only to her. Her blood, after marriage, belongs to his clan, through his offspring, which must be paid for in birth ceremonies. Both fluids are necessary for procreation, but it is semen that men own and control best. The natural fact that semen can be drunk (passed on) like any drinkable fluid sustains the view that it is a circulating, valuable, unchanging resource that must be, nonetheless, internally transformed in certain ways by certain persons to achieve certain ends.

The most powerful social fact of boy insemination is that it may only occur between poten-

tial enemies who may become affines (generation 1) and then kin (generation 2). Semen transactions not only define who is related and in what salient ways, but homoerotic contacts predicate the partners' relationship as prospective affines in their generation, which makes their children matrilateral kin in their own. Structurally, social ties based on blood and semen should not be mixed via sexual relationships: semen relates non-kin, who in turn, through women as links, have descendants sharing semen and blood. (A male ego may receive semen from his brother-in-law, whose children, that is the ego's sister's children, possess her husband's semen and her blood.) Ties of semen and blood (via women traded) flow in the same direction. The seeming exception is marriage to actual (not classificatory) father's sister's daughter, a marriage Sambia frown on. Such marriages are acceptable only when this woman cannot be traded for another, but in these rare marriages spouses share no blood, though they may indirectly share semen via their fathers' homoerotic contacts with each other's groups. Thus, the cultural principle not to mix blood and semen is contravened, and people resist such marriages. In general, this cultural linkage (blood and semen) makes heteroerotic relationships more socially important and multiplex than homoerotic contacts. Both men and women, their bodies and fluids, are needed to achieve biologic and social reproduction in this model (cf. Lévi-Strauss 1949; see Pettit 1977:70–72).

The practice of boy-inseminating rites is embedded in a cyclical tradition of semen transactions that made one's mother and father and will define one's own future relationships with boys and women. Identities follow from this semen flow. The tempo of such an ancient practice is to be found not only in this or that day's contacts but also in the last generation and the next. The system sets rigid constraints, but individuals and groups follow strategies around broad time posts to maximize the value of themselves and their resources. Sambia sexual culture, in this model of cyclical time, does not forget who gave and who received semen.

NOTES

1. Confederacy here marks the same social unit as "parish" and "subtribe" in other New Guineast typologies.

2. These cultural categories cross-cut various symbolic domains and social arenas, such as taboo, ritual, food sharing, myth, etc. One certainly could abstract from action and rhetoric the normative and metaphoric operations of these categories (see Wagner 1972, 1975). As I indicate below, sexual interaction is a conscious, though not always marked, frame for acting and speaking among Sambia, but I cannot here provide a description of all its manifestations.

3. See Herdt (1981) for conceptual models. This chapter considers mainly the male viewpoint, and it is not meant to be an exhaustive cultural analysis.

4. Sambia tend to treat and think of semen as an energy force, in individuals and society, that may be compared, by direct analogy, to Freud's concept of libido. The analogy is apt in several ways: This energy force circulates through others (e.g., as subjects), who may be taken in (e.g., as objects) via semen or its equivalents (mother's milk), and it can be dammed up or released—the imagery of the hydraulic model is apt (but cf. Heider [1976:78–79], who thinks otherwise). If these terms were translated into Freudian lingo, Federn (1952) would contrast subject-libido (energy available to self qua subject) and object-libido (energy available for investment in objects). Technically, I think, semen as a symbol among Sambia is used narcissistically (object libido invested in ego is narcissistic libido) in self-other interactions.

5. My use of the terms "commodity" and "fetishization" is not a homology with Marx's usage, which was tied, of course, to the specific analysis of capitalist production, characterized by the production of commodities that emerge in a market economy. By analogy, though, these terms are useful for my analysis. Marx argued that the results of human activity transform resources into items of use-value, which are assigned an exchange value by society; the worker's time is overshadowed by the supreme importance attached to the commodity, a process through which the capitalist extracts surplus labor as profit. The Sambia, however, acknowledge semen as a result of social relationships of production (e.g., as marriage bonds), and they tend also to stress the importance of semen as a fluid that can transform resources into more useful reproductive items or characteristics (e.g., babies, warrior strength). Nonetheless, the way that men value semen as a circulating commodity has a mystifying effect on these social relationships of production: They deny women's essential part in the reproductive process and claim that final biologic development in boys is achieved only through insemination. This mystification of the total reproductive process thus enables men to extract from others the resources needed to sustain and expand themselves and their clans and to control the related scarce resources in relation to women.

Finally, I do not imply by use of these terms that other Melanesian groups, or even all societies with ritualized homoeroticism, use semen as a key resource in the same way as Sambia or that they value it as a commodity in their systems of circulation in order to reproduce social entities. Elements or fluids such as semen and blood clearly have variable significance in Melanesian societies; our separable analyses of them must, in a sense, renegotiate their meaning in each cultural system.

6. By comparison, Sambia men do not use *duvono* in reference to what we would call "masturbation," which is not an explicit category in the Sambia language (the neo-Melanesian term for which means "peeling away the glans from penis"). Genital rubbing, in the limited sense (not necessarily erotic) of stimulation of the genitals, occurs. I have seen children do it, boys sometimes do it to bachelors (to produce erections for fellatio), and men sometimes report doing it to themselves in preparation for coitus with their wives. But what they mean is self-stimulation without ejaculation. This conceptual distinction is important and should not be misunderstood: spilling one's seed not only makes no sense to Sambia; it does not seem erotically exciting for them. Their fantasy life and erotic scripting have no place for it.

7. There is no marked category for erotic play as such, but the English term "pleasure," as in sexual pleasure, would be an appropriate gloss. It is signified in ideology and social intercourse by *chemonyi*, "orgasm," and several conditions of sexual excitement (e.g., erection). "Sexual" has a wide range of physical and social connotations in English; erotic, however, refers specifically to that which stimulates sexual desire and arousal, so I prefer "erotic" in this context.

8. All sexual contacts are symbolically defined by the norm of penetration and ejaculation into an insertee's mouth (initiate or woman) or vagina, insemination resulting from (the belief that) the full seminal emission ingested/absorbed by the recipient's body (mouth or vagina as entrance).

9. Oral heterosexual contacts indirectly help procreation; see below under section on growth.

10. *Monjapi'u* is shortened by men from *pinu pungooglumonjapi.*

11. Sambia have invented an art we could call semenology: they are fascinated with the forms, textures, and tastes of semen, which they discuss frequently, like wine tasters. Among boys, a fellated's penis size is not accorded much importance, whereas his seminal fluid, amount of flow, etc., is. (Privately and unconsciously, though, penis size is sometimes important.) Among women, the situation seems the reverse: a man's penis size (and sexual prowess) is important—women prefer men with big penises—whereas semenology is less significant, or so say men.

12. Sexual behavior in the imagery of dreams is viewed as erotic play: wet dreams are pleasurable but wasteful erotic play with spirits, who may wish to harm the dreamer. Breast-feeding, even though women say they experience *imbimboogu*, is never conceived of as erotic play by women, as far as I know, though breast-feeding is apparently a common image and form of scripting for men's erotic daydreams (vis-à-vis fellatio performed on them).

13. However, there is ambiguity here, since a woman who lives in another hamlet (her husband's) long enough becomes after death a ghost or hamlet spirit who may haunt there rather than return to her natal hamlet or clan territory. Even so, the souls of females are not a subject in which men place much interest.

14. Cf. the Great Papuan Plateau societies, especially Kaluli (Schieffelin 1976:127–28; 1982), which have institutionalized such beliefs about homosexual insemination (see also Kelly 1976; Sørum 1984). On the individual level, Sambia boys report fantasies and beliefs that make it clear that identification is a part of their homoerotic experience, including, for instance, notions that incorporating a fellated's semen may influence his personality traits.

15. *Kwol* marks male; *aalyu*, water; *waku*, a type of strong betel nut and a cover term for certain decorations. Sometimes the term is shortened to the secret name, *kweiwaku*, which men use explicitly to refer to "the semen of all men."

BIBLIOGRAPHY

Ashley-Montagu, M. F. 1937–38. "The Origin of Subincision in Australia." *Oceania* 8: 193–207.

Barth, F. 1975. *Ritual and Knowledge among the Baktaman of New Guinea.* New Haven: Yale University Press.

Bettelheim, B. 1955. *Symbolic Wounds, Puberty Rites, and the Envious Male.* New York: Collier Books.

Faithorn, Elizabeth. 1975. "The Concept of Pollution among the Kafe of Papua New Guinea," in *Toward an Anthropology of Women*, ed. R. R. Reiter, 127–40. New York: Monthly Review Press.

Federn, Paul. 1952. *Ego Psychology and the Psychoses.* New York: Basics.

Firth, R. 1981. "Spiritual Aroma: Religion and Politics." *American Anthropologist* 83: 582–605.

Forge, A. 1972. "The Golden Fleece." *Man* 7: 527–40.

Gell, A. 1975. *Metamorphosis of the Cassowaries.* London: Athlone.

Godelier, M. 1986. *The Production of Great Men.* Cambridge: Cambridge University Press.

Heider, K. 1976. "Dani Sexuality: A Low Energy System." *Man* 11: 188–201.

Herdt, G. 1977. "The Shaman's 'Calling' among the Sambia of New Guinea." *Journal of Societé des Oceanistes* 56–57: 153–67.

———. 1981. *Guardians of the Flutes: Idioms of Masculinity.* New York: McGraw-Hill.

———, ed. 1982. *Rituals of Manhood: Male Initiation in Papua New Guinea.* Berkeley: University of California Press.

———. 1984a. "Ritualized Homosexual Behavior in the Male Cults of Melanesia, 1862–1983: An Introduction," in *Ritualized Homosexuality in Melanesia*, ed. G. Herdt, pp. 1–81. Berkeley: University of California Press.

———, ed. 1984b. *Ritualized Homosexuality in Melanesia.* Berkeley: University of California Press.

———. 1987a. *The Sambia: Ritual and Gender in New Guinea.* New York: Holt, Rinehart, and Winston.

———. 1987b. "Transitional Objects in Sambia Initiation Rites." *Ethos* 15: 40–57.

———. 1989a. "Introduction: Gay and Lesbian Youth, Emergent Identities, and Cultural Scenes at Home and Abroad," in *Gay and Lesbian Youth*, ed. G. Herdt, pp. 1–42. New York: Haworth.

———. 1989b. "Self and Culture: Contexts of Religious Experience in Melanesia," in *The Religious Imagination in New Guinea*, ed. G. Herdt and M. Stephens, pp. 15–40. New Brunswick, NJ: Rutgers University Press.

———, ed. 1992. *Gay Culture in America.* Boston: Beacon Press.

———. 1993. Introduction to *Ritualized Homosexuality in Melanesia.* Rev. ed. Berkeley: University of California Press.

———. 1994. "Introduction: Third Sexes and Third Genders," in *Third Sex, Third Gender:*

Beyond Sexual Dimorphism in Culture and History, ed. G. Herdt, pp. 21–84. New York: Zone.

———. 1997a. *Same Sex, Different Cultures: Perspectives on Gay and Lesbian Lives*. New York: Westview Press.

———. 1997b. "Sexual Cultures and Population Movement: Implications for AIDS/STDs," in *Sexual Cultures and Migrations in the Era of AIDS*, ed. G. Herdt, pp. 3–22. New York: Oxford University Press.

Herdt, G., and F. J. P. Poole. 1982. "Sexual Antagonism: The Intellectual History of a Concept in the Anthropology of Melanesia," in *Sexual Antagonism, Gender, and Social Change in Papua New Guinea*, ed. F. J. P. Poole and G. Herdt. Special issue of *Social Analysis* 12: 3–28.

Herdt, G., and R. J. Stoller. 1985. "Sakulambei—A Hermaphrodite's Secret: An Example of Clinical Ethnography." *Psychoanalytic Study of Society* 11: 117–58.

———. 1990. *Intimate Communications: Erotics and the Study of Culture*. New York: Columbia University Press.

Kelly, R. C. 1976. "Witchcraft and Sexual Relations: An Exploration in the Social and Semantic Implications of a Structure of Belief," in *Man and Woman in the New Guinea Highlands*, ed. P. Brown and G. Buchbinder, pp. 36–53. Washington, DC: American Anthropological Association.

Langness, L. L. 1967. "Sexual Antagonism in the New Guinea Highlands: A Bena Bena Example." *Oceania* 37 (3): 161–77.

Leach, E. R. 1961. "Two Essays concerning the Symbolic Representation of Time," in *Rethinking Anthropology*, pp. 124–36. London: Athlone Press.

———. 1966. "Virgin Birth." *Proceedings: Royal Anthropological Institute* (1965), pp. 39–50.

Lévi-Strauss, C. 1949. *Les Structures elementaires de la parent*. Paris: Presses Universitaires de France.

Malinowski, B. 1913. *The Family among the Australian Aborigines*. London: University of London Press.

———. 1922. *Argonauts of the Western Pacific*. New York: E. P. Dutton.

———. 1927. *Sex and Repression in Savage Society*. Cleveland: Meridian.

———. 1929. *The Sexual Life of Savages in Northwestern Melanesia*. New York: Harcourt, Brace, and World.

———. 1954. *Magic, Science and Religion and Other Essays*. Garden City, NY: Anchor.

Marx, K. 1977. "The Fetishism of Commodities and the Secret Therof," in *Symbolic Anthropology: A Reader in the Study of Symbols and Meanings*, ed. J. L. Golgin et al., pp. 245–53. New York: Columbia University Press.

Mead, M. 1927. *Coming of Age in Samoa*. New York: William Morrow.

———. 1930. *Growing up in New Guinea*. New York: Dell.

———. 1935. *Sex and Temperament in Three Primitive Societies*. New York: Dutton.

———. 1949. *Male and Female: A Study of the Sexes in a Changing World*. New York: William Morrow.

———. 1956. *New Lives for Old: Cultural Transformation—Manus, 1928–1953*. New York: William Morrow.

———. 1961. "Cultural Determinants of Sexual Behavior," in *Sex and Internal Secretions*, ed. W. C. Young, pp. 1433–79. Baltimore: Williams and Williams.

Meggitt, M. I. 1964. "Male-Female Relationships in the Highlands of Australian New Guinea," in *New Guinea: The Central Highlands*, ed. J. B. Watson. Special issue of *American Anthropologist* 66, pt. 2 (4): 204–24.

———. 1977. *Blood Is Their Argument*. Palo Alto, CA: Mayfield.

Meigs, A. S. 1976. "Male Pregnancy and the Reduction of Sexual Opposition in a New Guinea Highlands Society." *Ethnology* 15 (4): 393–407.

———. 1984. *Food, Sex, and Pollution: A New Guinea Religion*. New Brunswick, NJ: Rutgers University Press.

Pettit, P. 1977. *The Concept of Structuralism: A Critical Analysis*. Berkeley: University of California Press.

Read, K. E. 1951. "The Gahuku-Gama of the Central Highlands. *South Pacific* 5 (8): 154–64.

———. 1952. "Nama Cult of the Central Highlands, New Guinea." *Oceania* 23 (1): 1–25.

———. 1954. "Cultures and the Central Highlands, New Guinea." *Southwestern Journal of Anthropology* 10 (1): 1–43.

Schieffelin, E. L. 1976. *The Sorrow of the Lonely and the Burning of the Dancers*. New York: St. Martin's Press.

Serpenti, L. M. 1965. *Cultivators in the Swamps: Social Structure and Horticulture in New Guinea*. Assen: Van Gorcum.

Serum, A. 1984. "Growth and Decay: Bedamini Notions of Sexuality," in *Ritualized Homosexuality in Melanesia*, ed. G. Herdt, pp. 337–61. Berkeley: University of California Press.

Spiro, M. E. 1965. "Religious Systems as Culturally Constituted Defense Mechanisms," in *Context and Meaning in Cultural Anthropology*, pp. 100–113.

———. 1968. "Virgin Birth Parthenogenesis, and Physicological Paternity: An Essay on Cultural Interpretation." *Man* 3: 242–61.

Strathern, A. J. 1969. "Descent and Alliance in the New Guinea Highlands: Some Problems of Comparison." *Proceedings of the Royal Anthropological Institute* (1968), pp. 37–52.

———. 1972. *One Father, One Blood.* Canberra: Australian National University Press.

Strathern, M. 1972. *Women in Between.* London: Seminar Press.

———. 1979. "The Self in Self-Decoration." *Oceania* 49: 224–57.

———. 1988. *The Gender of the Gift.* Berkeley: University of California Press.

Tuzin, D. 1982. "Ritual Violence among the Ilahita Arapesh: The Dynamics of Moral and Religious Uncertainty," in *Rituals of Manhood: Male Initiation in Papua New Guinea,* ed. G. Herdt, pp. 321–55. Berkeley: University of California Press.

Wagner, R. 1972. *Habu: The Innovation of Meaning in Daribi Religion.* Chicago: University of Chicago Press.

Weiner, A. 1978. "The Reproductive Model in Trobriand Society," in *Trade and Exchange in Oceania and Australia,* ed. J. Specht and J. P. White. Special issue of *Mankind* 11: 175–86.

———. 1980. "Reproduction: A Replacement for Reciprocity." *American Ethnologist* 7: 71–85.

Williams, F. E. 1930. *Orokaiva Society.* Oxford: Oxford University Press.

———. 1936a. *Papuans of the Trans-Fly.* Oxford: Clarendon Press.

24
Culture and Women's Sexualities

Evelyn Blackwood
Purdue University

Anthropological studies of women's same-sex relations in non-Western societies provide an important source for theorizing women's sexuality because they allow us to go beyond a narrow focus on Western cultures and concepts. Looking at studies from groups other than the dominant societies of Europe and America, I explore the diversity of women's sexualities and the sociocultural factors that produce sexual beliefs and practices. This article argues that sexual practices take their meaning from particular cultures and their beliefs about the self and the world. Cultural systems of gender, in particular, construct different sexual beliefs and practices for men and women. I conclude the article by suggesting some broad patterns at work in the production of women's sexualities across cultures.

Source: Culture and Women's Sexualities by Evelyn Blackwood. *Journal of Social Issues*, Vol. 56, No. 2, 2000, pp. 223–238. © 2000 The Society for the Psychological Study of Social Issues. Correspondence concerning this article should be addressed to Evelyn Blackwood, Department of Sociology and Anthropology, Stone Hall, Purdue University, West Lafayette, IN 47907 [e-mail: blackwood@sri.soc.purdue.edu].

This article explores women's sexuality from a cultural anthropology perspective. Anthropological evidence constitutes an important source for theorizing women's sexuality because it allows us to go beyond a sometimes narrow focus on the sexual categories of the dominant White societies of Europe and America (these groups will be glossed as "Western"). From a Western viewpoint, sexuality constitutes an essential or core attribute of identity; individuals are said to have fixed sexual identities or orientations. Sexuality as it is understood in the United States and Europe, however, often bears little resemblance to sexual relationships and practices across cultures. By looking at cultural evidence from ethnic groups and countries other than the dominant White societies of Europe and America, I will explore the richness and diversity of women's sexualities and the sociocultural factors that constitute those sexualities.

The perspective I take in this article follows social construction theory, which argues that sexuality depends on the cultural context for its meaning. Although Freud saw human sexuality as a precultural given that must be controlled or regulated by society, social construction theorists argue that sexuality itself is a social product (Caplan, 1987; Foucault, 1978; Padgug, 1979; Rubin, 1975). There are a variety of strands of social construction theory; the differences lie mainly in the extent to which culture is thought to produce sexuality (Vance, 1989). The strong constructionist view holds that a general sexual potential is constructed into particular desires, meanings, and behaviors by culture. A weaker view states that culture shapes or constrains the form sexuality takes but "natural" desires set the baseline of sexuality. In my view social processes do not act as constraints to a "natural" sexuality but actually produce sexualities through discourses of desire, religion, gender, and so on. This view argues that sexual acts, or what appears to be sexual, take their meaning from particular cultures and their beliefs about the self and the world. It is these beliefs or ideologies that anthropologists investigate to understand the meaning of sexuality. Sexual meanings are produced through any number of factors, including ideologies of religion, ethnicity, class, gender, family, and reproduction, as well as the material and social conditions of everyday life. These factors provide the context for the production of sexual relationships, desires, and longings.

In this article I first take a number of case studies of women's same-sex relations in ethnic groups and countries other than the dominant White societies of Europe and America to illustrate the sociocultural factors that produce sexual beliefs and practices. Then I explore how cultural systems of gender construct different sexual beliefs and practices for men and women. In the third section I use two detailed examples of female sexualities, one from Suriname and one from West Sumatra, to argue that sexuality is neither a static category nor a fixed identity. I conclude by exploring some broad patterns at work in the production of women's sexualities across cultures.

Although many of the examples presented in this article involve women whom Americans might identify as "lesbians," I do not use

that term generally. The term "lesbian" in the United States commonly refers to a woman whose primary sexual object choice is other women. When applied cross-culturally, "lesbian" invokes an essential linkage among practices whose connections may be tenuous at best (for further discussion of this point, see Wieringa & Blackwood, 1999). Since the term does not work in all cases across cultures, I use the term "same-sex relations" to refer to erotic relations or practices between women.

CULTURAL CONTEXTS OF SEXUALITY

Female same-sex sexuality has been noted in a number of colonized groups, postcolonial states, and sovereign countries since the beginning of European imperialism (Blackwood, 1986b; Blackwood & Wieringa, 1999). Case studies of women's same-sex relations illuminate the particular sociocultural processes that construct sexuality. I consider three different types of relations—intimate friendship, erotic ritual practice, and adolescent sex play—that represent both the varieties of sexualities as well as the complexities of the social processes involved.

Intimate Friendships

A study done in Lesotho, a small country surrounded by the nation of South Africa, documents intimate friendships between schoolgirls called "mummy-baby" relationships (Gay, 1986). Mummy-baby relations are institutionalized friendships between younger and older girls and women that became popular throughout much of Black southern Africa starting in the 1950s (Blacking, 1978). Prior to this time in rural communities, young women were educated at puberty in initiation schools run by women. Each initiate was appointed a "mother," an older girl who helped her "child" through initiation. This practice established strong networks between two age sets of women, ties that were maintained through visits and exchanges of gifts for many years (Blacking, 1978). Because of missionary efforts to stop this form of education, the schools are now virtually abandoned. Young women now attend public or boarding schools in neighboring towns or urban areas. Yet the bonds between initiates serve as a cultural model for the mummy-baby relations of contemporary schoolgirls and young women.

In the mummy-baby relationship, two young women start a relationship by arranging private encounters and exchanging love letters and gifts. The older girl, who becomes the mummy, might already have a boyfriend or other babies, while the younger one, the baby, is allowed to have only one mummy. The mummies are sources of guidance and "advice on sex and protection from aggressively courting young men" (Gay, 1986, p. 104) and appropriate partners in one's first romantic or sexual encounters. For girls who become mummies and babies to each other, their relationship is part of the romantic drama of growing up and learning the pleasures and responsibilities of relationships. They view their relationship as an affair or romance; hugging, kissing, and sexual relations are part of it. As they become older, they may in turn become mummies to their own babies or start to have their own boyfriends. For Lesotho women, the intensity of mummy-baby relations usually ends with marriage, when their attention is turned toward domestic responsibilities, but many women maintain the bonds of friendship with other women after marriage. Consequently, these relationships provide important emotional and economic ties for women within rural communities (Gay, 1986).

Mummy-baby relationships are constructed from a number of received cultural sources. The first source is the initiation school, where young girls received training for adult sexual practices and learned the importance of older girls and women as sources of friendship and social connection. In a culture where it is taboo for a mother to talk about sexuality with a daughter, older girls in initiation schools and now "mummies" are the culturally sanctioned source for this information. The second source comes from ideologies of sexuality. Although the Roman Catholic Church insists on virginity for Lesotho girls, within indigenous beliefs "female sensuality is both encouraged and

restrained, but it is never denied" (Gay, 1986, p. 101). Young women's practice of lengthening the labia is seen as a way to make themselves "hotter." Their experiences with other girls teach them to develop and manage their own sexual feelings.

A third factor in the construction of mummy-baby relationships is the *motsoalle* (special friend), a special affective and gift exchange partnership practiced by women of an earlier generation in rural Lesotho (Kendall, 1999). In the past both married women and men had sexual partners others than their spouses (Nthunya, 1997). These cultural practices reflected an ideology of sexuality that sees women as agents of their own sexuality. These special friendships were long-term, loving, and erotic relationships that coexisted with heterosexual marriage. One women, Nthunya (1997), who had a *motsoalle* relationship, was a poor, rural farmer most of her life. When she married her husband, she moved to his family home. She worked on their farm, raising sheep and growing maize. Her husband was often away on road construction or other wage labor jobs. Together they had six children. She describes her relationship with her female *motsoalle*:

> It's like when a man chooses you for a wife, it's because he wants to share the blankets with you. The woman chooses you the same way, but she doesn't want to share the blankets. She wants love only. When a woman loves another woman, you see, she can love her with a whole heart. (Nthunya, 1997, p. 69)

Such relationships were publicly celebrated by gift-giving and feasting that involved the whole community. For the feast, a sheep was slaughtered, gifts were exchanged, and neighbors and kin from throughout the village came to eat, drink, and dance. The ritual feast was a public, validation of the commitment the two women made to each other. A relationship with a *motsoalle* was neither an alternative nor a threat to marriage. According to Nthunya, her husband and her *motsoalle's* husband were both supportive of their relationship. Nthunya (1997, p. 72) said, "In the old days friendship was very beautiful—men friends and women friends. Friendship was as important as marriage. Now this custom is gone; everything is changing."

The poverty of Lesotho and the migration of husbands have often been used as explanations for women's intimate friendships. Such explanations assume that women love each other only when they are deprived of heterosexual outlets. The above case, however, shows the importance of other sociocultural factors in women's same-sex desires. Sexuality for women of Lesotho is constructed through the institution of women's friendships, the cultural tradition of age mates, and the cultural ideology of sexuality in which women have sexual agency. Consequently, close emotional and intimate bonds between women are seen as a natural part of growing up and an important source of social ties in adulthood.

Intimate friendships for both sexes are quite common in cultures of sub-Saharan Africa. The institution of bond friendships among Azande women of central Africa (located in the countries of Sudan and the Republic of Zaire), for example, relied on cultural patterns similar to those of the south. At the time that this institution was first noted in the 1930s (Evans-Pritchard, 1970), Azande society was composed of several kingdoms with noble and commoner classes. As in Lesotho, descent was traced through men, and children belonged to the husband's lineage. Men were allowed to marry several wives; each wife had her own dwelling in her husband's compound. The marital relationship was organized around economics, with the wife providing labor on her husband's land and receiving her own land to cultivate as well. Women maintained important trade relations to sell the produce that they grew. Exchange relations established across the village improved not only their economic resources but also their social connections and the numbers of people they could count on. Within this context Azande women looked to bond friendship as an important means to develop and broaden their networks (Blackwood, 1986a).

Bond friendships were formal relationships of exchange and service between two women. The relationship was established by holding a formal ceremony called *bagburu*, in which the two women exchanged small gifts, then divided a corn cob in half, each one taking a half to plant in her own garden. Bond friendships were not only exchange relationships; they established close emotional and sometimes erotic relationships between women. Unfortunately, most of what is known about *bagburu* relationships comes from Azande men and reflects their own fears and fantasies about their wives (Evans-Pritchard, 1970). Azande wives had to ask permission from their husbands to begin a *bagburu* relationship. The men believed that some women who were bond friends had sexual relations together. Husbands tried to discourage their wives from developing sexual attachments, although they rarely refused to give permission for the relationship itself. Evans-Pritchard reports little information about sexual practices between bond friends, but a story of two women's lovemaking after performing *bagburu* suggests that such behavior was not considered unusual (Evans-Pritchard, 1970, p. 1431). In this case the importance of social and trade networks with other women supports a construction of women's sexuality as something for them to explore and enjoy within and outside of marriage.

Erotic Ritual Practices

The homoerotic ritual practices of aboriginal Australian women constitute another case that resists a Western framework of sexual identities. Prior to colonization, Australian aborigines were seminomadic, egalitarian hunter-gatherers who lived in small camps. Their complex kinship system defined potential marriage partners as well as extramarital relations for both women and men (Roheim, 1933).

Young girls were initiated into their adult roles at first menstruation through a process of training and ritual that produced a girl's social identity. Adult women taught adolescent girls about sexuality and sexual magic through initiation ceremonies. These ceremonies conveyed messages about the configuration of tribal land, kinship categories, and proper social action;

they also included homoerotic movements or performances between the women and the initiates. Earlier anthropologists, who seemed reluctant to discuss this aspect of ritual performances, described the movements of the women dancers as sexually suggestive, leading to so-called simulated intercourse. According to Kaberry (1939), the intent of this action was to ensure heterosexual success (getting or keeping a husband or male lover). More recent interpretations (Povinelli, 1992) suggest that these ceremonies include homoerotic "digging" (*yedabetj*). For the performers, "digging" constitutes erotic play that initiates young women into the complex social and kin categories of their adult lives (Povinelli, 1992). For Australian aboriginal groups, the social processes that produce erotic ritual play include both a cultural ideology in which women have sexual agency and a belief in the power of ritual to influence and control human action.

Adolescent Sex Play

Adolescent heterosexual play is well documented for many cultures. Its practice is closely tied to ideas about childhood, sexuality, and virginity. In societies such as the !Kung San of the Kalahari Desert of southern Africa, children and adolescents engage in both heterosexual and homosexual play. Due to colonization, few !Kung now live their nomadic hunter-gatherer lifestyle, but one !Kung woman, Nisa, has recounted a life history that sheds light on these adolescent sexual practices (Shostak, 1983).

The egalitarian !Kung lived in small communities of kin that moved with the rains and availability of food. Families had few possessions. The adult couple shared a small grass dwelling with their children. In such close quarters they waited until their children fell asleep before they engaged in sex. Adults insisted that they disapproved of childhood sex play (to disapproving missionaries, perhaps), but when children played at the things their parents did, it included sexual experimentation. Nisa recounted how she watched older girls play sexually with each other and then did the same with her girlfriends as she approached adolescence. As girls got older,

they played sexually with the boys, although Nisa describes herself as initially reluctant to do so. All the young girls Nisa knew later married men. In this case marriage does not become the only adult locus of sexuality, since, according to Nisa, both men and women have sexual relations with partners other than their spouses.

The !Kung have constructed an adolescent phase of sexual experimentation that includes both same-sex and other-sex partners. This construction of sexuality is related to several sociocultural factors, including ideologies of gender, family, and childhood. Lacking any significant property or inheritance concerns vested in marriage, !Kung gender ideology is egalitarian. For !Kung families, neither marriage partner has exclusive sexual rights over the other. !Kung view adolescence as a time to learn sexual feelings and desires. All these factors combine to produce adolescence as a sexual "learning" period that precedes heterosexual marriage. In this case sexuality between young women is constructed as a part of sexual exploration.

The preceding section has described both the variety and complexity of sexuality in ethnic groups and countries other than the dominant White societies of Europe and America. As the cases show, a number of sociocultural processes construct sexuality, including initiation practices, institutions of women's friendships, the importance of social networks and cultural traditions of age mates, as well as ideologies of gender, religion, marriage, and family. These processes give sexuality its meaning and provide the context through which it is constructed.

CONSTRUCTING MEN'S AND WOMEN'S SEXUALITIES

In this section I consider how gender ideologies, the cultural set of practices and beliefs about men and women and their relations to each other, construct men's and women's sexualities differently. Because gender includes beliefs about sexual behavior, it is one of the primary crucibles within which sexuality is produced. Sexualities are informed by and embedded in conceptions of gender; that is, they are embedded in gender ideologies that enable and structure differential practices for women and men. In the following examples I examine the way gender ideologies produce very different constructions of men's and women's sexualities. I use examples from the Sambia of Papua New Guinea and from patriarchal China to show the ways in which sexual ideologies for women in these cultures are quite distinct from those for men. The differences in sexual ideologies produce very different sexual practices for women and men.

Among the Sambia of Papua New Guinea, femininity is seen as inherent, an attribute that girls are born with. In contrast, masculinity is understood as something that boys lack and must acquire as they grow up. While ritual practices ensure that young boys acquire masculinity, no rituals are necessary for girls to acquire femininity. This gender ideology encodes very different ideas about the sexuality of men and women. Boys must acquire masculinity ritually by ingesting the semen of adult men (Herdt, 1981). According to Western categories, such practices would be considered "homosexual." In this Papuan New Guinea culture, however, insemination rituals are not seen as homosexual behavior but rather as ritual measures to ensure the proper development of masculine traits and reproductive competence. Once properly inseminated and achieving their full masculinity, these young men are ready for heterosexual marriage. This ritual practice is explicitly linked to notions of the efficacy of fluids for human development (Elliston, 1995). From all accounts, young girls do not engage in ritual "homosexual" practices because they already possess the necessary substances for femininity. But although girls' sexual development is unmarked, their bodily fluids are seen as sexually dangerous and polluting to men, resulting in a negative view of women's sexuality, which must be strictly circumscribed by ritual taboos. In this case, ideas about men's and women's attributes lead to very different conceptualizations of their sexuality, men needing "homosexual" insemination and women seen as polluting and dangerous.

Another example of cultural differences in men's and women's sexualities comes from patriarchal China. In 19th-century China, women were quickly married off to a husband and were expected to be subservient and sexually faithful. In contrast, men were entitled to control wives and family property and were allowed a number of wives as well as other sexual partners. Marriage for many women in patriarchal China was an oppressive institution. Because of the importance of reproducing the patrilineage and maintaining ancestor worship, arranged marriages were the norm; oftentimes the young couple did not meet before they were married. The new wife went to live in the household of her husband and was at first considered little more than a servant under the strict supervision of her mother-in-law. In the province of Guangdon, marriage presented an especially frightening prospect, since women not only married out of their village but in many cases into enemy territory (Sankar, 1986).

Following the development of silk production in Guangdon province in south China, the practice of marriage resistance and the creation of sisterhoods arose (Sankar, 1986; Topley, 1975). With the development of the silk factories in Guangdon in the mid-1800s, many young unmarried women went to work in the silk factories, earning money for themselves as well as their families. Because they were able to earn their own income, some of these women postponed marriage indefinitely. Women who refused to marry took a public vow to remain unwed and not to engage in sexual relations with men. This vow established their adult status, freeing their parents from any obligation to arrange a marriage and securing their rights to ancestor worship in their natal houses (Sankar, 1986). Sisterhoods of six to eight women each were formed, with such names as "Golden Orchid Association" or "Association for Mutual Admiration." The sisters lived in cooperative houses called "vegetarian halls" or "spinsters' halls," where they established joint funds to be used for holidays, emergencies, and their future retirement or death (Honig, 1985; Sankar, 1986). Sisters also formed sexual relationships with each other.

"Larger sisterhoods may have contained several couples or ménage à trois" (Sankar, 1986). After the victory of the Red Army in 1949, the sisterhoods were banned as "feudal remnants" and many sisters fled to Malaysia, Singapore, Hong Kong, and Taiwan.

These sisterhoods were not simply a reaction to oppressive marriage conditions. Several other sociocultural factors were important in the development of the sisterhoods, including the institution of girls' houses, beliefs about ancestors, and sibling marriage order. First, it was the custom in this region for the kin group to build girls' houses for their adolescent daughters (Topley, 1975). Sleeping and eating in these houses, girls became close friends and confidants. Second, in patrilineal China, one's deceased parents must be given offerings regularly. Deceased wives are honored by their husband's family; unmarried or spinster women would have no one to honor them after they died. Women past the age of marriage were given a spinster ceremony through which they attained adult status and the right to have a house built for them where their kin could remember them after they died. Third, since younger sisters and brothers must wait until their elder siblings are married, the spinster ceremony allowed these siblings the right to marry. In addition to unique economic conditions, these factors contributed to the development of marriage resistance and sisterhoods in Guangdon China.

In the cases of the Chinese sisterhoods and the Papua New Guinea Sambia, cultural gender ideologies constructed different sexual practices for men and women. In the Sambia case a cultural practice rooted in an ideology of gender antagonism and the efficacy of bodily fluids legitimated particular insemination practices between men and boys, while creating women as inherently gendered and without need of adolescent homosexuality. In China patriarchal institutions created women's sexuality as subordinate to men's desires, while constructing men's sexuality more broadly to include the practice of taking male consorts, particularly among upper-class men and royalty (Ng, 1989). In China, the control of women's sex-uality produced public resistance by women to oppressive marital and economic conditions, leading to the establishment of separatist sisterhoods.

In these cases, gender ideologies create different sexual roles, behaviors, meanings, and desires for women and men. Consequently, men and women in these cultures see themselves differently as sexual actors. For Sambian men, their sexuality must be developed in adolescence through insemination practices and sustained in adult life by strict ritual taboos. In contrast, Sambian women are constantly reminded that contact with their sexual organs and fluids is debilitating and even dangerous to men, resulting in limited heterosexual contacts. Historically in patriarchal China, men's desires were constructed broadly, whereas women's sexual experiences were strictly limited to their roles as wives or concubines to men.

From these cases it is clear that gender ideologies are critical to the production of men's and women's sexualities. Such ideologies work to produce very different sets of ideas about what men and women desire. By establishing certain ideas about who and what men and women are, gender ideologies create different possibilities for men's or women's understanding of their desires and their access to other sexual partners.

DECONSTRUCTING SEXUAL IDENTITIES

Studies of sexuality in Europe and America tend to take for granted the fixity of sexual object choice and sexual identity. Categories of homosexual, heterosexual, and bisexual, which are routinely used to define study populations, however, turn out to have little cross-cultural reliability. I now discuss two cases of female same-sex relations to highlight the problems with these Western sexual and gender categories. I explore cases from Suriname and West Sumatra in which women appear to be "lesbian" or "bisexual," but in fact their own understanding of their sexuality is quite different from the way it is constructed in the West.

The Mati Work

Erotic attachments between Creole women in the postcolonial state of Suriname, South America, pose a number of problems for Western categories of sexuality. The *mati* work is a widespread institution among Creole working-class women in the city of Paramaribo, Suriname (Wekker, 1999). Creoles, the second largest population group in Suriname, are the descendants of slaves brought from Africa, living mostly in urban areas. *Mati*, although by no means a monolithic category, are women who have sexual relationships with men and with women; they may have a relationship with a man and a woman occurring at the same time or one at a time. While some *mati*, especially older women who have borne and raised their children, do not have sex with men anymore, younger *mati* have a variety of arrangements with men, such as marriage, concubinage, or a visiting relationship. Women's relationships with women mostly take the form of visiting relationships, although a minority of female couples and their children live together in one household. These varied arrangements are made possible by the circumstance that most working-class Creole women own or rent their own houses and are single heads of households (Wekker, 1999).

The Creole concepts of self and sexuality are found in the framework of the Afro-Surinamese folk religion, called *Winti*. Unlike the Western version of the self as "unitary, authentic, bounded, static, trans-situational," the self in an Afro-Surinamese working-class universe is conceptualized as "multiplicitous, malleable, dynamic, and contextually salient" (Wekker, 1999, p. 125). *Winti* religion pervades virtually all aspects of life, from before birth to beyond death. Within this framework both men and women are thought to be composed of male and female *winti*, gods. Both men and women are deemed full sexual beings with their own desires and possibilities of acting on these desires. Sexual fulfillment is important, but the gender of one's object choice is considered less important. According to one 84-year-old *mati*, who had relationships with men and bore a number of children, the "apples of her eye" throughout her long life were women:

> I never wanted to marry or "be in association with a man." My "soul"/"I" did not want to be under a man. Some women are like that. I am somebody who was not greedy on a man, my "soul," "I," wanted to be with women. It is your "soul" that makes you so. (Wekker, 1999, p. 125)

A *mati* is conceptualized as a woman, part of whose "I" desires and is sexually active with other women. Since the "I" is multiply and openly conceived, it is not necessary to claim a "truest, most authentic kernel of the self," a fixed "identity" that is attracted to other women. Rather, *mati* work is seen as a particularly pleasing and joyous activity, not as an identity (Wekker, 1999).

Surinamese *mati* (and Lesotho *motsoalle*) do not see themselves as lesbians or bisexuals; they have sex with each other, but their relations with men, including husbands and boyfriends, are also part of their sexuality. This case reflects the multiple sociocultural factors that produce the *mati* work. According to Wekker (1999), sexuality in this postcolonial working-class cultural nexus is multiply constructed through colonial discourses and Afro-Surinamese ideas about the self, sexuality, gender, and religion. But *mati* work is neither a sexual identity nor a distinct category of persons. It is encompassed by an ideology of sexuality in which men and women are seen as sexual beings whose sexuality is fluid and multiple.

Tombois in West Sumatra

One final example that complicates the Western categories of gender and sexuality comes from my own work on *tombois* among the Minangkabau in West Sumatra, Indonesia (Blackwood, 1998). The term *tomboi* (derived from the English word "tomboy") is used for a female acting in the manner of men (female here refers to physical sex of body, not gender). Although *tombois* are female, they see themselves as men who are attracted to normatively gendered women. In this overview I briefly explain the cultural factors that produce the *tomboi* identity and how this identity complicates any simple understandings of gender or sexuality.

Tombois pride themselves on doing things like Minangkabau men. They play *koa*, a card game like poker, which is perceived as a men's game. They smoke as men do; rural women rarely take up smoking. They go out alone, especially at night, which is men's prerogative. Like men, they drive motorcycles; women ride behind (women do drive motorcycles, but in a mixed couple the man always drives).

Tombois construct their desire for and relationships with women on a model of Minangkabau masculinity. The statement they often make is that their lovers are all feminine women. These women adhere to the codes of femininity assigned to female bodies. Female couples call each other *mami* and *papi*, and refer to other couples as *cowok* and *cewek*, Indonesian words that have the connotation of "guy" and "girl." Their use of gendered terms reflects *tombois'* understanding of themselves as situated within the category "man" (*laki-laki*).

Certain key social processes (cultural ideologies) in West Sumatra are involved in the production of the *tomboi* identity. The first of these is a gender ideology that constructs two genders as mutually exclusive; the second is a kinship ideology that situates women as producers and reproducers of their lineages. The Minangkabau have a matrilineal form of kinship in which inheritance and property pass from mothers to daughters. They are also devoutly Islamic. Typical of many Islamic cultures, the Minangkabau believe that men and women have different natures. Men are said to be more aggressive and brave than women are. Boys are admonished not to cry: Crying is what girls do. Women are expected to be modest and respectful, especially young, unmarried women. This gender ideology constructs differences in rights and privileges between men and women without, however, constituting men as superior (see Blackwood, 2000).

In the context of a rural kin-based society, heterosexual marriages are the key to the maintenance of a vital network of kin and in-laws. For Minangkabau women the continuation of this kinship network through marriage and children is critical to their own standing and influence both in their kin groups and in the community. Because daughters are essential to the continuation of the lineage, elders carefully monitor young women to ensure that they marry and marry well. Daughters are not just reproducers, however; they are also the leaders of the next generation of kin. Consequently, there are no acceptable fantasies of femininity or female bodies in rural villages that do not include marriage and motherhood.

The restrictive definitions and expectations of masculinity and femininity attached to male and female bodies help produce gender transgressions in the form of the *tombois*. One *tomboi* played too rough and enjoyed boys' activities when little, and was called *bujang gadis*, a term that meant "boy-girl." Identified as masculine by others, *tombois* make sense of their own gender behavior as being that of a man. Because their behavior falls outside the bounds of proper femininity, *tombois* deny their female bodies and produce the only other gender recognized in this two-gender system, the masculine gender. The persuasiveness of the dominant gender ideology circulating in West Sumatra means that other expressions of womanhood are unimaginable if they blur the prescribed lines between women and men. Consequently, some masculine females appropriate the masculine gender because it is the most persuasive model available.

But a transnational lesbian and gay discourse circulating in Indonesia primarily through national gay organizations and newsletters complicates *tomboi* identity. First organized in the early 1980s, these predominantly urban groups have nurtured a small but growing nationwide community of gays and lesbians (Boellstorff, 2000). In the process they have fostered development of a new gay identity for Indonesians, which, although not the same as that of gay Europeans and Americans, shares with them the idea of a sexual identity distinct from gender identity.

The infusion of transnational gay discourse into the lives of *tombois* and their partners presents new cultural models of sexuality. Moving between urban and rural areas, these individuals confront urban gay and lesbian identities that they negotiate and claim in hybrid ways. Identity for *tombois* in West Sumatra at this point is a mix of local, national, and transnational identities. If their identity growing up was produced by local cultural processes that emphasized mutually exclusive genders and a gender-based model of sexuality, their movement between cities and rural areas means *tombois* are exposed to other models of sexuality and gender identity. They have used these identities to construct a new sense of themselves as *tombois* and *lesbis*.

These cases illustrate the way gender as well as sexuality is culturally produced. Rather than occupying a fixed category of gender or sexuality, *tombois* do not fit into any single Western category, being neither clearly lesbian, butch (a masculine lesbian), transgender, woman, or man. For their part, *mati* women do not claim an unchanging identity as lesbians, but rather an unchanging, joyous sexuality which includes both men and women partners. The different experiences and transformations over time substantiate a view of sexuality as the product of complex social processes.

THE SOCIAL PRODUCTION OF SEXUALITIES

My discussion of the cultural processes that construct sexualities is based on a small but growing number of case studies of women's same-sex relations cross-culturally. The lack of availability of adequate information makes systematic comparison difficult. One survey found reports of female same-sex practices in 95 indigenous cultures (Blackwood, 1984), but no comprehensive world survey has been conducted to date. The difficulties of coding the various types of behavior documented even in this short article raise other problems for statistical analyses. Despite the problems of formulating comparative analyses, some consistencies appear among the cases that allow for generalization about the social processes at work.

Anthropological and historical records suggest that in indigenous cultures it is rare to find a segregated community of women involved in affective or erotic relationships with each other. Rather what appears in different times and conditions is a range of sexualities that do not fall easily into Western binaries of heterosexual or homosexual. These diverse sexualities, which include intimate friendships between adult married women, adolescent sex play, and ritual same-sex practices, change over time in response to a broad range of cultural factors.

The broader patterns that appear in the cultural construction of sexuality can be connected to different types of gender ideologies, kinship systems, and class societies. Earlier attempts at comparative theories suggested that where men have greater control over women, or in societies stratified by class and gender, women's same-sex practices are subject to more oppression than men's (Rubin, 1975) or limited to clandestine relations or marginalized groups (Blackwood, 1986a). Both these suggestions rely on the "constraint" theory of sexuality by implying that without serious controls over them, women's same-sex relations would appear much more often.

In an effort to rework these earlier theories with a stronger constructionist approach, I want to emphasize the way culture produces ideas about sexuality. For instance, in strict patrilineal class societies the importance of inheritance and property rights for men requires that women be sexually active only with their husbands. This requirement is forcefully articulated in a discourse that aligns women's sexuality with reproduction and men's desires. Thus, good women save themselves for and desire only their husbands. Other options may be imaginable, since men are known to have other heterosexual and even homosexual contacts, but the harsh consequences for women in most cases foreclose any thought of going beyond the permissible. I do not mean that women's "natural" same-sex desire is thereby repressed, but rather that the experience and understanding of such an expression of sexuality as desirable or significant is foreclosed.

In contrast to the constraints placed on women's sexuality in patrilineal societies, women in gender-egalitarian, nonclass soci-

eties, such as the !Kung and Australian aborigines, participate in a range of adolescent
and ritual same-sex practices. These societies
have marriage requirements and prohibitions
on certain forms of sexual relations. Yet lacking property relations or expectations about
rights of access found in strict patrilineal societies and dovetailing with the importance of
women's social bonds and their agency within
the community, these cultures produce an
ideology of sexuality as something powerful,
diverse, enjoyable, and explorable. This is not
to say that all nonclass societies will produce
multiple sexualities. In some societies same-
sex relations are said to be culturally unintelligible. The important point is that many
sociocultural factors work together to produce sexual meanings; it is nearly impossible to predict which ones will produce
particular forms of sexuality.

The way sexuality is constructed, the ideology of what is "natural"—for instance, who
is considered more sexually aggressive or in
need of more sex—has everything to do with
concepts of gender, selfhood, kinship (inheritance and property rights), and marriage,
among others. The cases presented here challenge the common assumption in Europe
and the United States that sexuality and sexual identity comprise stable, coherent categories. The case studies show the importance
of the cultural context in constructing sexuality; what needs to be investigated more fully
is the way sexuality is constructed in particular contexts, historical eras, and cultural
domains. Careful ethnographic analysis of
sexual practices will continue to be important
in efforts to deepen our understanding of
women's sexualities.

REFERENCES

Blacking, J. (1978). Uses of the kinship idiom in friendships at some Venda and Zulu schools. In J. Argyle & E. Preston-Whyte (eds.), *Social System and Tradition in Southern Africa* (pp. 101–117). Cape Town, South Africa: Oxford University Press.

Blackwood, E. (1984). *Cross-cultural dimensions of lesbian relations.* Unpublished master's thesis, San Francisco State University, San Francisco, CA.

———. (1986a). Breaking the mirror: The con-struction of lesbianism and the anthropologi-cal discourse in homosexuality. In E. Blackwood (ed.), *The Many Faces of Homosexuality: Anthro-pological Approaches to Homosexual Behavior* (pp. 1–17). New York: Harrington Park Press.

———. (1986b). *The Many Faces of Homosexuality: Anthropological Approaches to Homosexual Behav-ior.* New York: Haworth.

———. (1998). Tombois in West Sumatra: Con-structing masculinity and erotic desire. *Cultural Anthropology, 13*(4), 491–521.

———. (2000). *Webs of Power: Women, Kin and Com-munity in a Sumatran Village.* Lanham, MD: Rowman and Littlefield.

Blackwood, E., & Wieringa, S. E. (eds.). (1999). *Female Desires: Same-Sex Relations and Transgen-der Practices Across Cultures.* New York: Columbia University Press.

Boellstorff, T. (2000). The gay archipelago: Post-colonial sexual subjectivities in Indonesia. Unpublished doctoral dissertation, Stanford University, Stanford, CA.

Caplan, P. (ed.). (1987). *The Cultural Construction of Sexuality.* London: Tavistock.

Elliston, D. (1995). Erotic anthropology: "Ritual-ized homosexuality" in Melanesia and beyond. *American Ethnologist, 22*(4), 848–867.

Evans-Pritchard, E. E. (1970). Sexual inversion among the Azande. *American Anthropologist, 72,* 1428–1434.

Foucault, M. (1978). *History of Sexuality. Vol. 1: An Introduction.* New York: Pantheon.

Gay, J. (1986). "Mummies and babies" and friends and lovers in Lesotho. In E. Blackwood (ed.), *The Many Faces of Homosexuality: Anthropologi-cal Approaches to Homosexual Behavior* (pp. 97–116). New York: Harrington Park Press.

Herdt, G. (1981). *Guardians of the Flute.* New York: McGraw-Hill.

Honig, E. (1985). Burning incense, pledging sis-terhood: Communities of women workers in the Shanghai cotton mills, 1919–1949. *Signs: Journal of Women in Culture and Society, 10*(4), 700–714.

Kaberry, P. (1939). *Aboriginal Woman, Sacred and Profane.* London: Routledge.

Kendall. (1999). Women in Lesotho and the (Western) construction of homophobia. In E. Blackwood & S. E. Wieringa (eds.), *Female Desires: Same-Sex Relations and Transgender Prac-tices Across Cultures* (pp. 157–178). New York: Columbia University Press.

Ng, V. W. (1989). Homosexuality and the state in late Imperial China. In M. Duberman, M. Vici-nus, & G. J. Chauncey (eds.), *Hidden from History:*

Reclaiming the Gay and Lesbian Past (pp. 76–89). New York: Meridian Books.

Nthunya, M. M. (1997). *Singing Away the Hunger: The Autobiography of an African Woman.* Bloomington: Indiana University Press.

Padgug, R. A. (1979). Sexual matters: On conceptualizing sexuality in history. *Radical History Review, 20,* 3–23.

Povinelli, B. (1992, November). Blood, sex, and power: "Pitjawagaitj"/menstruation ceremonies and land politics in Aboriginal Northern Australia. Paper presented at the 91st Annual Meeting of the American Anthropological Association, San Francisco.

Roheim, G. (1933). Women and their life in Central Australia. *Journal of the Royal Anthropological Institute of Great Britain and Ireland, 63,* 207–265.

Rubin, G. (1975). The traffic in women: Notes on the political economy of sex. In R. Rapp (ed.), *Towards an Anthropology of Women* (pp. 157–211). New York: Monthly Review Press.

Sankar, A. (1986). Sisters and brothers, lovers and enemies: Marriage resistance in Southern Kwangtung. In E. Blackwood (ed.), *The Many Faces of Homosexuality: Anthropological Approaches to Homosexual Behavior* (pp. 69–83). New York: Harrington Park Press.

Shostak, M. (1983). *Nisa: The Life and Words of a !Kung Woman.* New York: Vintage Books.

Topley, M. (1975). Marriage resistance in rural Kwangtung. In M. Wolf & R. Witke (eds.), *Women in Chinese Society* (pp. 57–88). Stanford: CA: Stanford University Press.

Vance, C. S. (1989). Social construction theory: Problems in the history of sexuality. In *Homosexuality, which Homosexuality?* (pp. 13–35). London: GMP.

Wekker, G. (1999). "What's identity got to do with it?" Rethinking identity in light of the mati work in Suriname. In E. Blackwood & S. E. Wieringa (eds.), *Female Desires: Same-Sex Relations and Transgender Practices Across Cultures* (pp. 119–138). New York: Columbia University Press.

Wieringa, S. E., & Blackwood, E. (1999). Introduction. In E. Blackwood & S. E. Wieringa (eds.), *Female Desires: Same-Sex Relations and Transgender Practices Across Cultures* (pp. 1–38). New York: Columbia University Press.

25
Redirecting Sexual Orientation
Techniques and Justifications

Timothy F. Murphy
University of Illinois College of Medicine

This essay reviews efforts to alter sexual orienta-tion using behavioral, psychodynamic, hormonal, pharmaceutical and surgical methods. The essay also examines various justifications offered for such therapy and shows how these have changed as a pathological interpretation of homoeroticism has been abandoned. While such therapy was once jus-tified in language of psychopathology, some current justifications for conversion therapy now treat the matter of therapy as a matter of personal choice and do not invoke the language of pathology at all. That a formal medical rejection of a psychopatho-logical categorization of homoeroticism has not alto-gether eliminated efforts to redirect sexual orientation suggests that it is ultimately a moral and not medical devaluation of homoeroticism that at bottom drives continuing efforts to control and redirect sexual orientation.

Source: Redirecting sexual orientation: Tech-niques and justifications, by Timothy F. Murphy. *Journal of Sex Research*, Vol. 29, No. 4, pp. 501–523, November 1992. © 1992 Timothy F. Murphy. Requests for reprints should be sent to Timothy F. Murphy, Ph.D., Department of Medical Education m/c 591, University of Illinois College of Medi-cine, Chicago IL 60612.

KEY WORDS: *homoeroticism, sexual orienta-tion, therapy.*

The love of men and women for persons of their own sex has been for many the source of abiding joy, and yet this same form of eros has elicited moral condemnation, criminal sanc-tion, and religious invective. It has also been the object of attempted medical control at least since the coining of the term "homosexuality" by Hungarian writer Karl Maria Kertbeny in 1869 (Herzer, 1985/86). Various forms of reori-entation therapy have tried to reorient persons from a homoerotic to a heteroerotic orienta-tion. In technique, these therapies have ranged from threats of beating (Allen, 1958, p. 85) to brain surgery. The therapies have been both voluntary and involuntary. This essay reviews some of the many techniques that have been used as instruments of sexual reorientation. The methods of therapy are described with regard to their technique and the under-standing of homoeroticism that is thought to justify them. Many past attempts at reorienta-tion presupposed a pathological interpretation which put homoeroticism on a par with other conditions warranting medical treatment. Such a view might also have been buttressed by moral or religious interpretations of the undesirability of homoeroticism. While such views have not altogether disappeared, a number of contemporary theorists of sexual reorientation therapy, by contrast, now invoke individual choice alone as the justification for the legitimacy of reorientation therapy. Such justifications thereby make no ostensible judgment on the medical, moral or religious standing of homoeroticism. Nevertheless, there remain certain common moral presuppositions about homoeroticism which continue to unite past techniques with their contemporary counterparts no matter what specific techniques or justifications are offered.

BEHAVIORAL THERAPY

The extinction of homoerotic desires and behaviors has been pursued through a wide range of techniques. Some of the earliest forms of reorientation looked to redirect sexual orientation by effecting behavioral changes. Exercise and activities out-of-doors have often been a recommended pathway to the cure of a whole host of human ills (Money, 1985). It is not surprising that this view would be extended to homoeroticism as well. In the United States in 1892, for example, Graeme M. Hammond reported the case of a 24-year-old man suffering from sexual attraction for members of his own sex. The young man had been able to remain sexually continent to that point in his life but feared he would not be able to do so much longer and would end up committing "acts which were naturally abhorrent to him." Observing that nothing was so antagonistic to sexual appetite as physical fatigue, Dr. Hammond wrote, "I have found nothing more serviceable than the bicycle to accomplish this object." In addition to certain unnamed medications, Hammond therefore prescribed severe and fatiguing bicycle riding and found that the man's sexual appetite was thereby abolished (Hammond, 1892). Dr. Hammond had pursued this course of action because the young man suffered from "sexual abnormality."

By direct contrast to the view that homoeroticism was to be resisted through robust living, others saw homoeroticism as the consequence of urban burdens on the nervous system. Rest treatment was consequently counselled in the hope that such rest would restore the sexual equilibrium of heterosexuality (Katz, 1983, pp. 185–187).

Some physicians counselled men worried by homoerotic desires and behaviors to visit women prostitutes, there presumably to avoid the sexual temptations of men and to familiarize themselves with pleasures possible with women. German sexologist Albert Moll claimed to have "cured" some of his patients in this manner (Bullough, 1989). In summarizing several approaches to reorientation therapy, Havelock Ellis noted that in the course of hypnotic therapy, Albert von Schreck Notzing counselled frequent visits to brothels, the latter being advisable after consuming large amounts of alcohol (Ellis & Symonds, 1897). Ellis himself was skeptical not only about the success of this particular technique; he was in fact profoundly skeptical about all forms of reorientation. He found the use of prostitutes particularly odious, saying that it usually ended in backsliding where it did not also end in sexually transmitted disease and the birth of degenerate children. "For my own part," he said, "I frankly confess that the remedy seems to me worse than the disease" (Ellis & Symonds, 1897, pp. 142 ff.). He thought a brothel could scarcely be a desirable method of treatment because it invited further disgust with women (Ellis & Symonds, 1897).

Writing under the pseudonym of Heinz Heger, a survivor of World War II concentration camps has left his own recollections of Nazi attempts to use prostitutes to cure men imprisoned for violations of paragraph 175, the statute against homoeroticism. Among other techniques attempted, a brothel was installed in Flossenburg in 1943 on the orders of *SS Reichsfuhrer* Heinrich Himmler. Male inmates wearing the pink triangles that marked their sexual "crime" were ordered to weekly visits with Jewish and gypsy women brought from other camps for this purpose (Plant, 1986). The sexual performance of the inmates was observed through peepholes. If inmates appeared able to perform sexually with the women, they were judged fit to serve in the Dirlewanger penal divisions on the front, there to face the hostilities of Russian partisans (Heger, 1980). Of his own experiences in the compulsory brothel visits, Heger notes that the forced aspect of the brothels made the circumstances highly unpleasant for both the men and the women, and he believes the experience had the ironic effect of reinforcing his homoeroticism (Heger, 1980).

Perhaps aware of the possible reinforcement of homoerotic dispositions or for reasons of scruples against fornication or adultery, some advocates of reorientation counselled against using prostitutes. Instead, they held out the pursuit of virtuous women and the prospect of marriage as the route by which to discover the rewards of heteroeroticism (Katz, 1983). It was only respectable women after all who were worth pursuing and in whom a man could find abiding joy; women prostitutes by definition lacked admirable qualities. Marriage has itself therefore sometimes been pursued by some, men and women alike, as a means of overcoming homoeroticism. Magnus Hirschfeld's examination of 500 men found that 83 of them had married in order to rid themselves of their homoerotic passions, among other reasons (Anonymous, 1956). In our own very recent times, Bell and Weinberg report that significant percentages of their self-identified homosexual subjects had been married: 20% of 575 white homosexual males, 13% of black homosexual males, 35% of white homosexual females, and 47% of black homosexual females; some had even been married two or more times (Bell & Weinberg, 1978). That same study also made it clear that some men sought marriage as a way by which to overcome homoeroticism though for unknown reasons none of the women in the study reported having married for that same reason (Bell & Weinberg, 1978). The number of persons who have sought refuge in marriage in order to escape homoerotic desires or their reasons for thinking that marriage could do this is, of course, ultimately unknowable. It is also unknown how people who seek change through marriage conceive of their homoeroticism (i.e., as a burden from God, a disease, a psychological maladaptation, etc.). Nevertheless, in the Bell and Weinberg studies, roughly a quarter of their respondents did report thinking their homoeroticism was an emotional disorder (Bell & Weinberg, 1978). It would not be surprising if some of these people were among those who sought its remedy in marriage.

Whatever its lures, there is widespread caution in the literature against the expectation that marriage will succeed in sexual reorientation, and this caution comes even from those who are otherwise entirely in favor of reorientation therapy, even from those utterly opposed to homoeroticism (Buckley, 1959). In Magnus Hirschfeld's view, the marriage of a homosexual was highly undesirable for another reason. Seeing homoeroticism as a strategy of nature for bringing degenerate stock to an end, he believed the children of "homosexuals" to be mostly of inferior mentality and a threat to racial hygiene (Anonymous, 1956). Schwartz and Masters (1984) point out that marriage partners may in fact perpetuate unwanted sexual response patterns. For example, insofar as wives attempt to protect their husbands from emotional stress, they may help them avoid the very incentives successful reorientation requires. They may, that is, accept and protect the husband's homoeroticism and thus prove an impediment to its conquest.

The counsel of pursuing women nevertheless has its own contemporary forms in therapy for men. Sex with women was sometimes counselled as an adjunct to therapy: "There is only one way that the homosexual can overcome his phobia and learn to have heterosexual intercourse, and that way is in bed with a woman" (Ovesey, 1965). Other therapists have not been so eager to rush men into bed with women without otherwise inciting attraction to females. In orgasmic reconditioning, for example, sexual orientation is first redirected by changing the object of masturbation fantasies. On the view that most sexual deviations are conditioned through masturbation fantasies, the "client" (no longer the "patient") is educated in sexuality generally and told how orgasmic reconditioning will change his sexual responses. The client is advised to masturbate in ways to which he is habituated but then in the moments just before climax to shift his attention to the desired sexual object, that is to pictures of women. Over time, the client will generalize his association of orgasm with such pictures to actual women. Thus was one twenty-seven-year-old male law student reportedly able to escape his homoerotic desires (Marquis, 1970).

Though there are other dimensions to their therapy program, familiarity and confidence in sexual performance capabilities form the centerpiece of the contemporary Masters and Johnson reorientation program for men. In this "sensate focus" program, after enhancing his skills in conversation, eye contact, relaxation, and the like, a man is expected to live in isolation with a woman of his choosing for two weeks for the purposes of sexual exploration, experimentation, and performance. It is the special function of the woman to encourage heterosexual behavior, resist homoerotic behavior, and expose and neutralize fears and discomforts as they arise in the course of sexual exploration. This program does not invoke the language of disorder, mental illness or abnormality in order to justify this therapy. On the contrary, homoeroticism is said to be a "viable lifestyle" (Schwartz & Masters, 1984). The justification of reorientation focuses on respecting the wishes of certain individuals who would rather have sexual desires and behaviors other than the ones they do.

Behavioral reorientation has not only focused on discovering the rewards of heteroeroticism. It has also attempted to drive persons from homoeroticism by making it repulsive and intolerable. Electrical aversion therapy, or "Faradic therapy" as it was once called, has seen many variants. Typically, these therapies involve the administration of low-level electrical shocks in conjunction with slides of nude males (Clark, 1965; Kohlenberg, 1974). Subjects are shocked for responding sexually to arousing images and rewarded (by the absence of shock) for sexual responsivity to images of the opposite sex, and this relief in conjunction with other incentives is expected to reinforce heterosexual desire. Two researchers even offered detailed plans of a simple electroshock device which patients could use at home at times of their own choosing (McGuire & Vallance, 1964).

Electroshock has also been used in a much more aggressive way. Certain persons, typically but not only criminal sex offenders, have been electrically shocked until they exhibit grand mal convulsions (Owensby, 1940). In *The Punishment Cure*, Stephen J. Sansweet (1975) surveyed a number of the ways in which electroshock and other forms of aversive therapy have been used to extinguish homoeroticism. Subjects have been required to sniff various repulsive substances (ammonium sulfide, butyric acid, aromatic ammonia) during homoerotic fantasies. Other subjects have been deprived of fluids and at the same time been given strong diuretics which induce the desire to urinate. They are told that they may have something to drink only if they show physiological sexual responses to slides of nude females. Chemical aversion therapy has also been used to induce convulsions in the hope of sexual reorientation (Thompson, 1949).

There has also been aversion therapy of a less overtly harsh kind. Aversive therapy by covert sensitization uses mental imaging as a means to change sexual orientation. For example, a man wishing to change his homoerotic orientation will be encouraged to visualize repulsive homoerotic encounters (sexual advances, for example, from a repulsive man) in the context of anxiety-inducing circumstances (while police officers are watching). The man will gradually develop aversive reactions to all homoerotic desires and cues. Parallel imagery will associate women with positive images. Covert conditioning therapists defend this practice without a pathological definition of homoeroticism. Instead, they define as dysfunction only those behaviors which a client wishes to change (Cautela & Kearney, 1986).

What all these techniques seem to share is the view if only certain behaviors are followed and reinforced, then sexual responsivity will flow into predictable and desired channels. Unfortunately, it is not so clear that desire, especially sexual desire, follows behavior in this docile fashion. Many researchers, therefore, have sought to act more directly on the desires themselves.

PSYCHODYNAMIC INTERVENTIONS

Many reorientation therapies have aimed at dissolving specific fears, reducing anxieties, bringing certain sexual desires from latency, even altering sexual fantasy and stimulus-response patterns. These forms of reorientation typically understand homoerotic desire and behavior in adults to be the consequence of some experience during psychosexual development. Moreover, the expression of homoeroticism in adult life was typically held by many researchers to be an undesirable eroticism whose undesirability is cast variously in the language of pathology or maladaptation. Though he does not believe it is *easily* or *entirely* reversible, Judd Marmor, for example, holds that homosexuality is a potentially reversible condition because it is the consequence of psychic adaptation (Marmor, 1965, 1980). But psychodynamic understandings of homoeroticism do not necessarily invoke the language of pathology or maladaptation in order to justify reorientation efforts. Some recent justifications merely appeal to the preference of men and women who would like to rid themselves of homoerotic traits and do not invoke the language of pathology or psychological dysfunction. The goal in either circumstance, though, is a psychodynamic intervention capable of recovering or inaugurating heteroerotic desire.

Any number of forms of psychotherapy have been enlisted in the attempt to extinguish homoeroticism in both adults and adolescents. These techniques have taken various forms depending on the understanding of the human mind and its ability to be influenced. Some theorists advocated, for example, the mental equivalent of physical exercise. This has taken such forms as the severe study of abstract subjects like mathematics, science, literature and "sociology from the evolutionary viewpoint" (Kiernan, 1910). Hypnosis was put to the same use. In the late 1960s, for example, professional National Football League player David Kopay underwent a course of hypnotherapy to eliminate his homoeroticism, at a cost of $1,500. His doctor said, "We can cure this in no time at all" (Kopay & Young, 1977). More recently, Martin Duberman has told in *Cures* of his own long involvement in ultimately futile therapy in trying to conquer his homoerotic desire (Duberman, 1991).

One of the most theoretically articulate foundations for reorientation is to be found in the history of psychoanalysis, especially American psychoanalysis. Freud himself held the view that homoeroticism in adults was not necessarily any grave psychic or social disability, and he did not generally advocate reorientation. He did, nevertheless, see homoeroticism as inferior sexuality (Murphy, 1984) and thought that reorientation might be possible for some even if it is unclear whether he thought such therapy was possible through psychoanalysis alone (Murphy, n.d.). Many of those in Freud's wake, however, advanced the view that homoeroticism *is* a psychological disorder.

Sandor Rado was one of the chief advocates of such a view since he saw homoeroticism as adaptational behavior driven by anxiety (Ruse, 1988). The goal of therapy, therefore, would be to reverse underlying adaptational disorders of which homoeroticism was typically but one symptom (Mayerson & Lief, 1965). Edmund Bergler believed that male "homosexuals" were simply men frightened by women, unconsciously so, fleeing in their panic to a more familiar sexual terrain. He denied any biological basis for homoeroticism and saw it as a simple neurotic conflict, but not only by reason of homoeroticism: "The homosexual's whole personality is neurotically sick" (Bergler, 1982). He claimed to have conducted hundreds of successful reorientations in men, this by helping the client to gain insight as to the nature and origins of his fear of women and to overcome that fear. Successful therapy could be accomplished through three appointments a week, across one to two years time, though he reported some success in as little as 10 months.

Bieber and his psychoanalytic colleagues are today well known advocates of the view that homoeroticism is pathological in the sense that it is held to be incompatible with a reasonably happy life (Bieber, 1965; Bieber et al., 1962). Bieber has said: "Repetitive behavior in adult life between same-sex members is always pathological. It is never normal. There is no such thing as homosexuality being a normal sexual variant" (Departments of Psychiatry and Neurology, 1975). Bieber and those who followed him are also committed to the possibility and success of reorientation: " . . . with the possible exception of effeminate transvestites, one cannot say of any homosexual that he cannot shift to heterosexuality" (Bieber, 1965). Indeed, Bieber's 1962 study regarding the capacity of long-term psychoanalysis to change sexual reorientation is probably the single-most frequently cited study in any discussion of sexual reorientation. In that study, he claimed that after five years follow-up of many more years of psychoanalysis, one-third of 100 male homosexual subjects had become exclusively heterosexual (Bieber, 1976). The treatment itself involved that long course of self-examination and interpretation that is the hallmark of psychoanalysis.

Fantasy satiation is yet another form of therapy put to the use of eradicating homoerotic desire. This technique involves bombarding a subject with images and language that he or she finds sexually arousing to the point of utter satiation. As part of their technique of reorientation, for example, the Masters and Johnson program requires that a man vocalize his homoerotic fantasies on tape for thirty minutes each day for a period of up to several months. "In short order, the homosexual fantasy theme becomes boring and no longer has the power to elicit response. The man begins to wonder why he found the experience compelling" (Schwartz & Masters, 1984). Thus sated, the individual is free to explore other heteroerotic pleasures. Fantasy satiation has been used both in programs where homoeroticism has been characterized as abnormality and where it has not.

The rites of religion have also been employed in reorientation. Such approaches typically stress recognition of the sinfulness of homoeroticism, the resolution to overcome that and all other sinful traits, and resolution to strive toward union with God. Religious techniques of reorientation may or may not characterize homoeroticism as a pathological condition, but it is clearly understood as an undesirable moral condition. Pattison and Pattison (1980) interviewed eleven of thirty men (of an original subject group of 300) reportedly converted from homoerotic to heteroerotic disposition. These eleven men are reported to have demonstrated a profound shift in sexual orientation and attributed that shift to religious growth. The men identified themselves as religious, were active in religious services, found homoeroticism immoral, believed homoeroticism to be a psychological maldevelopment, regretted their homoeroticism, and wanted to give it up for religious reasons. In addition to Bible group study (which offered them the opportunity for interpersonal experience, behavioral rehearsal, opportunity for acceptance and the like), these men also had religious conversion or re-dedication experiences. By their own reports, they grew into heterosexuality, and out of homoeroticism, as they grew into Christian spirituality.

It is not surprising that as various forms of psychotherapy have arisen, they have been tested with respect to their potential for sexual reorientation. As mentioned above, hypnotic suggestion has been put to the use of reorientation though there was debate over its effectiveness against the various "acquired" and "congenital" forms of homoeroticism (Ellis & Symonds, 1897; Katz, 1983). Often in conjunction with other forms of therapy, assertiveness training and primal screaming (Kronemeyer, 1980) have been put to the service of reorientation. Where homoeroticism was held to be the result of a failed *aesthetic* interpretation of the world, correction and instruction in the beauty and worth of the world were purported to have the result of showing "homosexuals" the attractiveness not only of the world but also the beauty of the opposite sex (Kronemeyer, 1980).

Most psychotherapeutic approaches to reorientation have seen homoeroticism as an evil of one kind or another. In the course of describing reorientation techniques, some authors do not even explain why homoeroticism should be eliminated. That is, *they take it for granted* and *assume that their audience also shares the same view* that homoeroticism should be extinguished. In many of these cases, homoeroticism is conceived as a psychological disorder which, where it is not prevented, may be treated with the entire psychological arsenal which is brought against other mental disorders. This is not to say, of course, that all persons with homoerotic dispositions were treated or even identified as subjects for treatment. Then, as now, the treatment of such persons will always remain confined to those who for one or another reason become known to therapists. In some cases, subjects were brought by the courts; others came at the insistence of parents; others came for their own reasons.

DRUG AND HORMONE THERAPY

While there were many therapists who put their hopes for a cure of homoeroticism in the realignment of the psyche, others put their hopes in more direct biological interventions. Such interventions were undertaken on the view that sexual orientation was either directly or indirectly the result of some biological function, that homoeroticism was the result of a biological disorder. Indeed, many of the early sexologists held homoeroticism to be a heritable degenerative condition. It is not surprising that such thinking led to the medical pursuit of its cure.

Denslow Lewis (1899) went to considerable extremes to eradicate lesbianism, which he thought a matter of "pernicious practices" and he found to be a malady of the monied classes. "The poor, hard-working girl is not addicted to this vice. The struggle for life exhausts her capabilities." It is the idle woman who falls into this pernicious practice: "The girl brought up in luxury develops a sexual hyperesthesia which is fostered by the pleasures of modern society" and thereby falls into these "irregular and detrimental practices." Lewis reported finding an "overdue hyperemia" in such cases which responded to the application of a cocaine solution and "the exhibition of saline cathartics." Beyond this, he prescribed "bromides, sometimes com-

bined with cannabis indica. At other times, calomel and salines are given for a time and followed by pyrophosphate of iron." He also sometimes gave strychnine by hypodermic injection. He reports that in fifteen of eighteen cases, there were satisfactory results; these women in time became proper wives, and thirteen also became mothers. Of the failures, two never experienced any gratification during the sexual act, but they both became mothers nevertheless. The last patient became insane and was committed to an asylum.

Not all the attempts to secure sexual orientation change claimed successes. One American physician found that his attempt "to alter continuous, voluntary, passive homosexuality in males through the administration of animal organ extracts, such as orchitic substance adrenin, pituitary extract, and the like, has been uniformly disappointing" (Oberndorf, 1929). It is not surprising that this physician was disappointed; he after all understood homoeroticism to be a disease process *and* he thought all people to be homoerotic to a limited degree.

A 1940 report claimed that the administration of metrazol was capable of liberating the fixation of libidinal development responsible for homoerotic dispositions and making psychosexual energy free once more to flow through regular physiological channels (Owensby, 1940). This report was made without any long-term follow-up, but the remissions of homoerotic desire in both males and females were said to be the largest number reported. In this study, men and women from the ages of nineteen to thirty-four were treated with metrazol, inducing grand mal convulsions up to fifteen times per person. In one case, though nine treatments seemed to have eliminated all homoerotic desire from a man, he was subsequently convulsed six more times in order to, additionally, eliminate all feminine traits from him as well.

The discovery of hormones and their influence on various aspects of human life was not old before certain practitioners began to investigate how sexual orientation might be altered by hormonal interventions. From late 1880 onward, the psychological consequences of hormones were investigated with a number of reports on the uses of such therapy for the treatment of homosexual persons. These therapies involved both androgens and estrogens. In the former case, homoeroticism was hypothesized to be the consequence of androgen deprivation. Consequently, homosexual men were treated with testosterone. Researcher Karl Freund injected men with testosterone while they watched sexually explicit movies featuring women (see Sansweet, 1975). Researches were ultimately disappointed to discover, though, that testosterone could not alone redirect sexual orientation (Sands, 1954). On the contrary, it appeared often enough to heighten the sex drive without changing its basic nature (Glass & Johnson, 1944).

This failure led other researchers to treat homosexual men with estrogens, this on the hypothesis that such treatment would at least minimize the urgency of abnormal sexual expression. Experimental reorientation in this regard was often carried out on persons convicted of sexual offenses. The 1948 Criminal Justice Act in Britain even called for the development of such techniques to treat sexual offenders in preference to the alternatives of castration and sterilization that were the ordinary recourse of the courts at that time. A report by Golla and Hodges (1949) suggests that estrogen therapy was largely successful in treating a group of thirteen such men: "In all cases the treatment has been completely successful in abolishing libido." Its effects were reported as more quick-acting than castration, non-mutilating, non-destructive of sexual power for those later judged fit to be removed from therapy, and it affected equally both normal and abnormal sexual urges. On the other hand, such therapy was not without its ill effects either: gynecomastia (the development of breast tissue), darkened nipples, nausea, and weight gain (Sands, 1954). More significantly, the therapy did not seem able after all to change sexual orientation (Hemphill et al., 1958).

Perhaps the most famous person to receive court-ordered estrogen therapy was British mathematician Alan Turing who was not only instrumental in the development of computers but who was also responsible for many of the British successes in decoding German intelligence during World War II (Hodges, 1983). After the war, Turing pled "guilty" to having had consensual sex with a 19-year-old man. The judge ordered him sentenced to a year of probation during which time he was to be treated by a course of "organotherapy," that is, estrogen therapy. Turing understood this treatment to be aimed at reducing his sexual urge, not at redirecting his sexual orientation about which he had little if any regret. Indeed, he wrote in a letter that he expected to "return to normal" when the treatment was over. In fact, he developed a certain amount of gynecomastia and though the treatment did for a time make him impotent, it did not prevent him from seeking further sexual adventures when he visited Scandinavia (Hodges, 1983).

In our own time, treatment with Depo-Provera, an antiandrogen currently used on certain criminal sex offenders does seem to diminish sexual desire, this by reducing the male hormones circulating in the bloodstream (Money, 1988). It does not, however, appear to be capable of changing the direction of sexual orientation (American Academy of Pediatrics, 1985/86).

Sometimes, drug therapy was used in conjunction with other forms of therapy (Oswald, 1962). One report detailed the case of a forty-year-old university graduate with an IQ of 133, a former Army officer who had been fired from his job as an executive with an oil company for reasons related to his homosexuality (James, 1962). "He felt that the cornerstone of his problem was his homoeroticism, and that all available treatment for this condition had failed to help him." The "stilbestrol" given to this man during a course of psychotherapy left him impotent but with an increased sexual drive unaltered in direction. The man was subsequently isolated in a darkened room without food or drink for 30-hour periods. He was given emetic doses of apomorphine by injection at 2-hour intervals, followed by two ounces of brandy. At the point of nausea, photographs of nude and nearly nude men were spotlighted in the room. He was encouraged to verbalize his sexual fantasies. During the experience of his nausea, a therapist explained that the origins of homoerotic desire were to be found in the absence or failures of the father. The consequences of homoeroticism for his life were detailed in slow and graphic terms, reminding him of all the tribulations it had brought him. The noise of vomiting was played on a tape. This course of treatment was repeated after a respite of 24 hours. The man was awakened from sleep with congratulations for success in his newfound heterosexuality. During the treatment sessions, the photographs of men were gradually replaced with similar photos of women, and the man was given testosterone injections. When he felt any sexual excitement, he was told to retire to his room and listen to a sexy female vocalist on the record player (presumably to encourage masturbation). This man is reported to have thus changed his sexual orientation and be heterosexual in all aspects. Other benefits from therapy were reported as well: the man was able to write several short stories and a full-length novel during the twenty-week follow up period!

SURGERY

The scalpel has also been put to use against homoeroticism. Castration has its own history in the attempt to suppress homoeroticism and other forms of sexual abnormality. In one report, twenty-seven men and five women were castrated in the attempt to alter various forms of "sexual abnormality," including homoeroticism. Following surgery, it was found that the libido was diminished in more or less every case, and five outright cures of perverse sexual practices were claimed. In consequence of these results, the report concluded: "The operation is indicated in cases of persistent exhibitionism, rape, and homosexuality" (Anonymous, 1929).

The Nazis also investigated the cure of homoeroticism through castration. Lured by promises of release, some inmates accepted castration only to find themselves sent out of the camps to dangerous military posts (Heger, 1980). The Danish physician Carl Vaernet and German physician Gerhard Schiedlausky conducted castrations on inmates to effect a cure. After castration, eighteen men (possibly more) were injected with huge doses of male hormones to see if they began to evince any heterosexual interest. These "experiments" were ill-conducted, and some deaths apparently occurred (Plant, 1986). By reason of faults in design and shabby documentation, these castration studies bear little resemblance if any to acceptable scientific experimentation.

Castration as a means of altering sexual orientation, however, fell out of favor as empirical evidence showed that castration did not have any effect in altering sexual orientation (Bremer, 1959) though it certainly diminished sexual drive and prompted the castrate body type with changes in skin, hair, and fat distribution. There were psychic consequences, too: the perceived sense of loss, emotional regret, sense of difference from others, and embitterment either at the castration itself or its failure to deliver expected results in change of sexual orientation. In addition to its psychological consequences, castration also carried risks of somatic morbidity and mortality. One study concluded that thirteen percent of 244 males experienced illness or death as a result of their castration (Bremer, 1959).

Where there was not eagerness to remove testicles, some physicians nevertheless sought to transplant them. Various forms of experimentation occurred here. One researcher apparently implanted the testicles of a sexually normal man into the abdominal wall of a "passive homosexual" after removing that man's own testicles. The researcher reported that after a few weeks, both psychic and bodily alterations toward heterosexuality had occurred (Karlinsky, 1989). The genitalia of women also became objects of surgical interest. Denslow Lewis, mentioned above, reported finding clitoris abnormalities in lesbians. He therefore performed certain surgeries to control what he called their hyperesthesia. In one case, he even amputated the clitoris entirely because it was "hypertrophied" and excessively sensitive (Lewis, 1899).

Other interventions have been carried out on other body parts as well: cauterizations of the neck, lower back and loins (Oberndorf, 1929) and clitoridectomies (Katz, 1983). There have even been reports of lobotomies carried out in the hope of extinguishing homoerotic drives (Kronemeyer, 1980). In the 1970s, a brain operation involving the destruction of certain areas of the diencephalon was carried out on seventy-four men (and one woman) considered sexually abnormal by reason of their involvement in rape, exhibitionism, sadomasochism, or hypersexuality, or sexual relations with boys (Schmidt & Schorsch, 1981). The surgery team reported the improvement or cure of the sexual deviations in sixty-five of the seventy-five patients such that thirty-six of the thirty-nine prisoners involved and seven of the eight involuntarily hospitalized patients were freed. By 1981, this surgery had been abandoned by the surgeons themselves.

SKEPTICS

There have always been skeptics about the possibility of reorientation, and this is true no matter whether the skeptics thought homoeroticism was a pathology or not, whether they thought it congenital or not (Rosanoff, 1929). Various review articles have drawn attention to the difficulty of finding confirmation of successful reorientation (Hemphill, et al., 1958; Saghir & Robbins, 1973). *The Wolfenden Report*, which recommended that certain sexual relations be decriminalized in Great Britain, concluded that a case of reorientation had never been fully confirmed (Wolfenden Report, 1963). Indeed, that report also concluded that homoeroticism was not by itself prima facie evidence of disease. A 1955 report by the British Medical Association, while holding homoeroticism to be a serious social illness indicative of a collapse in personal and national responsibility, nevertheless concluded that there is no panacea to cure homoeroticism: "It must be admitted with regret that some of the advice given to homosexuals in the name of treatment is often useless, simply defeatist, or grossly unethical." The report concludes that success is rare in the case of "essential" "homosexuals," but there can be degrees of success in certain forms of treatment. But even then, the report notes, not all men or women need or are amenable to treatment (British Medical Association, 1955). The difficulty of reorientation

led some, including William C. Menninger, to put homoeroticism in the class of incurable conditions (Menninger, 1948).

When asked to invite one of his successful "cures" into an independent study for evaluation, Bieber could think of only one person who would be appropriate; but since he was on unfriendly terms with the man, he was unable to contact him (Tripp, 1975). Neither is Charles Socarides, who himself holds strong views regarding the pathology of homoeroticism, hopeful about the prospect for successful reorientation (Socarides, 1978).

At the present time, it is unclear whether there is any known treatment of homoeroticism in the sense that there is a reliable, replicated method offering a "cure" or reorientation to randomly selected groups. Virtually every study mentioned above failed to establish any control mechanism for the intervention being tested. It is thus impossible to tell whether the "successes" reported belong to the charm of the therapist or to the technique, were the result of psychosexual developmental changes occurring for reasons unrelated to the therapy, were the consequence of the psychologically powerful placebo effect or lasted (Murphy, 1991). One study that did utilize a scientific control found that a psychotherapeutic program of reorientation had no demonstrable benefit (Curran & Parr, 1957). In many cases, moreover, the subjects under study had bisexual histories, and it is therefore unclear whether the interventions were in fact replacing homoerotic dispositions with heteroerotic ones or resolving a conflict between competing, already existent erotic interests (Money, 1988). And certainly, since these studies lack long-term follow-ups, it is unclear that the success of reorientation is any enduring one. At a five-year follow-up study, the Masters and Johnson program reported a failure rate of 28.4 percent (Schwartz & Masters, 1984). To what extent that rate changed and increased over time is unknown.

These observations do not, of course, rule out the possibility of the development of a successful, empirically confirmed treatment. Even the skeptics acknowledge this possibility. *The Oxford Textbook of Psychiatry*, for example, offers a skeptical view of successful reorientation by observing that aversion therapy can suppress homoerotic mental imagery (which is not the same as altering sexual orientation) but that there is no convincing evidence that psychoanalysis (Bieber notwithstanding) or psychotherapy has worthwhile effects (Gelder et al., 1983). That textbook nevertheless goes on to say that it may occasionally be appropriate to attempt to modify homoerotic impulses and behaviors. In its pessimism regarding the availability of cure and its concomitant willingness to entertain the prospect for general success, its counsel is continuous with that found in numerous discussions about sexual reorientation. It is interesting to note, however, that this same text does not offer a single word on how this modification ought to be carried out.

CONCLUSIONS

Vern Bullough dates the beginning of the medicalization of homoeroticism with the work of German physician Carl Westphal (1833–1890) who believed "contrary sexual feeling" to be mostly a congenital condition (Bullough, 1989). For many of the early sexologists, part of the incentive to discover a biological basis for homoeroticism (it being a separate question whether it was also a disorder) was to shield persons from harsh criminal judgments which assumed the voluntary nature of homoeroticism. In many cases, the development of reorientation techniques followed developments in scientific progress elsewhere. The widespread availability of electricity, for example, invited experimentation for its biomedical applications. The discovery of hormones offered researchers new pathways for understanding and altering human traits. The availability of new drugs also invited speculation regarding their applicability to controlling sexual orientation. Many of the reorientation techniques described here were abandoned as their limits became clear, especially as it became clear that sexual orientation appears to be a deeply ingrained, biologically grounded, and cortically organized value system (Tripp, 1975) that is not tractable to any simple, single intervention.

The medical profession's understanding of homoeroticism has had a varied history since the work of Westphal. Its official views on homoeroticism have indeed changed a number of times, for a number of reasons, (Bayer, 1987) as evidenced by the fluid status of homoeroticism within orthodox psychiatry's diagnostic nomenclature. In the United States, in 1952 when it first drew up its diagnostic nomenclature, the American Psychiatric Association (APA) classified homosexuality as a sociopathic personality disturbance (American Psychiatric Association, 1952). In 1967, the APA removed homosexuality from the category of sociopathic personality disturbances but retained it as a mental disorder (American Psychiatric Association, 1968). In 1973, the Board of Trustees of the APA removed homosexuality per se from its nomenclature, and a 1974 vote for the membership upheld this decision. The APA did at that time retain, however, "ego-dystonic homosexuality" as a category for those persons who suffered by reason of their homosexual desires and behaviors (American Psychiatric Association, 1980). In 1984, even that classification was eliminated after further deliberation (Bayer, 1987). All that remains in current APA nomenclature relevant to homoeroticism is "sexual orientation distress," the suffering associated with an unwanted sexual orientation (American Psychiatric Association, 1987). But this classification does not single out homosexuality as the only manifestation of such suffering; the disorder theoretically applies to heterosexual orientation as well. It follows, as John Money frequently points out, that according to official nomenclature, homoeroticism is not a diagnosis: "Today the fact of an erotic encounter or partnership between two people of the same genital anatomy is not considered pathological, nor a sickness" (Money, 1980).

That medicine could come to such a conclusion was the result of a combination of factors, social and scientific. Although it is not my purpose to consider the history of disputes about the "pathology" of homoeroticism, a history covered in some detail in Bayer's work (1987), it is perhaps worth pointing out that in the United States, the work of Evelyn Hooker had significant influence in challenging the necessary connection between homoeroticism and pathology. Her work showed, for example, that Rorschach judges could not distinguish the test results of homosexual men from heterosexual men when presented in matched pairs, suggesting of course that homosexual men were not therefore obviously pathological (Hooker, 1957). Not only did her work show that there is no single pattern of "homosexual adjustment," but she also understood it to suggest that homoerotic forms are as varied as those in heteroeroticism, that homoeroticism may be a deviation within the normal psychological range, and that there is no reason to think that homoeroticism by itself could disorder the entire person. Even though she herself did not reject conversion therapy as conceptually or morally illegitimate (National Institute of Mental Health, 1972), she was among the first to point out the degree to which the "pathology" of homoeroticism might belong to its social circumstances rather than to its inherent psychological features (see Hooker, 1958, 1959). Because of empirical work like hers, it became increasingly difficult to maintain a "scientific" defense of the theory of homoerotic pathology especially as it became clearer that the origins of homoerotic "pathology" and distress were functions of society rather than traits of homoeroticism itself.

According to the social and professional standards of a number of nations, however, homoeroticism per se remains a pathological state or psychological disorder. Indeed, even in the United States, despite the formal action of the APA, many psychiatrists continue to believe that homoeroticism is a serious psychic disorder (Anonymous, 1977; Kaplan, 1983). Some even hold the view that involuntary treatment is appropriate (Davis & Wilson, 1973). Such views, of course, continue to encourage the experimental pursuit and use of reorientation techniques.

Yet even among those who see homoeroticism as part of the natural variability of human sexuality, reorientation continues to be defended and researched. As against the view that reorientation therapy is a response to pathology, reorientation therapy is now defended as a matter belonging to the domain of individual conscience: if a person would like to have a sexual orientation other than the one he or she does have, then therapy ought to be pursued and provided. Sex-

ual orientation is thus no different from the other products consumers may find on the shelves of medical practitioners.

Ellie T. Sturgis and Henry E. Adams have argued this way: "The decision concerning the modification of sexual orientation should be based on the life circumstances and values of the individual rather than the value systems of the therapists" (Sturgis & Adams, 1978). Abnormality or disordered states are not a necessary prerequisite for therapy, they go on to say. The elimination of reorientation therapy programs, as called for by Gerald C. Davison (1976), would, in their view fail to respect the sexual values (as against the actual sexual preferences) of individuals. Denial of reorientation therapy, they say, might even be a violation of patients' rights to seek treatment and the clinicians' right to treat (Sturgis & Adams, 1978).

Warren J. Gadpaille has concluded that a refusal to honor requests for reorientation (or refusal to refer patients when one is unable to honor such a request) serves a "prohomosexual" ideology which "is no more medically ethical than forcing treatment designed to produce unwanted change to heterosexuality" (Gadpaille, 1981; Kaplan, 1983). Joseph R. Cautela and Albert J. Kearney, in delineating their program of covert conditioning say that "From both an ethical and a practical point of view, it is our contention that the decision of whether or not to change an individual's sexual orientation must be made by the client rather than by society at large or subgroups of that culture" (Cautela & Kearney, 1986). They thus completely bypass as unnecessary the question of the pathological status of homoerotic desires and behaviors and leave the matter to personal preference.

What differentiates contemporary approaches to reorientation therapy from their predecessors, therefore, is that they do not usually avail themselves of the language of disease, disorder, and cure (Halleck, 1976; Sansweet, 1975). They speak instead of wishes and preferences, of rights and duties. While there are still those who interpret homoeroticism as pathological or otherwise fundamentally disordered, most of their professional colleagues maintain that reorientation is a legitimate goal of therapy even if homoeroticism is no pathology, psychological disorder, or even any necessary disability in social life.

This view obviously respects and protects individuals from unwanted medical therapy, but it also raises an interesting moral question. It is a matter of debate, that is, whether a person can come to seek reorientation in a way that is properly called "voluntary." Stephen L. Halleck, for example, has said that by reason of the considerable pressures from parents, spouses, and the law, by reason of years of struggle with self-loathing, by reason of fatigue in facing daily indignities, by reason of the powerful feelings of deprivation of acceptance, marriage, and family, he doubts that men and women requesting reorientation do so in a truly voluntary way (Halleck, 1976). If this view is true, it would appear that "treating" the "homosexual" would still be a form of blaming the victim, i.e., treating the person who suffers rather than ameliorating those social forces which devalue homoeroticism.

One way of seeing the way in which social forces shape the nature of and interest in reorientation therapy is to note that historically the vast majority of reorientation programs have been carried out on men. But what would account for this asymmetry if female and male homoeroticism were equally judged pathological? What would account for this asymmetry especially when it does not appear that women are less likely than men to consider trying to give up their homoeroticism (Bell & Weinberg, 1978)? On the face of it, reorientation programs should be equally concerned with both men and women. Perhaps part of the reason that they have not been is the judgment that men have more to lose by their homoerotic lives than do women. Perhaps part of the reason is that the lives of men are valued more in any case. That there is an historical asymmetry in the nature of research and therapy between men and women is to suggest, of course, that the reorientation therapy has been shaped by pervasive and often unconscious social forces. And once again, one confronts the question of the extent to which the "voluntary" pursuit of reorientation might be coercively motivated, especially for men.

X-ray treatment, douches, anaphrodisiacs, and various forms of hydrotherapy have all been put to use in the program against homoeroticism (Katz, 1983; Kronemeyer, 1980). The imagination with which reorientation has been thus far pursued suggests that new techniques offering control over the nature of human lives will continue to be investigated for their potential to alter the direction of sexual orientation. It is no surprise, then, that a book on acupuncture even takes up the subject (Warren & Fischman, 1978). Though the justifications of reorientation may have changed, therapy will be pursued so long as there continue to be forces which impute inferiority to homoeroticism. Without a judgment of the devaluation of homoeroticism, after all, what incentive would there be to alter sexual orientation? Those same forces which attach devaluation to homoeroticism as impediments to dignity in personal identity, as liabilities in social and religious advantage are ultimately, therefore, the incentives to both the theory and practice of reorientation therapy. It matters not, therefore, how one expresses those devaluations: as disease, disorders, psychopathologies, unwanted stress, or as personal, social and familial limitations. There would be no reorientation techniques where there was no interpretation that homoeroticism is an inferior state, an interpretation that in many ways continues to be medically defined, criminally enforced, socially sanctioned, and religiously justified. And it is in this moral interpretation, more than in the reigning medical theory of the day, that all programs of sexual reorientation have their common origins and justifications.

REFERENCES

Allen, C. (1958). Homosexuality: Its nature, causation and treatment. In C. Berg & C. Allen (eds.), *The Problem of Homosexuality*, pp. 13–109. New York: Citadel.

American Academy of Pediatrics. (1985/86). Homosexuality. *American Academy of Pediatrics—Pediatric Update* [lesson/audiorecording 6].

American Psychiatric Association. (1952). *Diagnostic and Statistical Manual: Mental Disorders.* Washington, DC: American Psychiatric Association.

———. (1968). *Diagnostic and Statistical Manual: Mental Disorders,* 2nd ed. Washington, DC: American Psychiatric Association.

———. (1980). *Diagnostic and Statistical Manual: Mental Disorders DSM-III*. Washington, DC: American Psychiatric Association.

———. (1987). *Diagnostic and Statistical Manual: Mental Disorders DSM-IIIR*. Washington, DC: American Psychiatric Association.

Anonymous. (1929). Results of castration in sexual abnormalities. *The Urologic and Cutaneous Review, 22*, 351.

Anonymous. (1956). *Sexual Anomalies. The Origin, Nature and Treatment of Sexual Disorders. A Summary of the Work of Magnus Hirschfeld.* New York: Emerson.

Anonymous. (1977). Sexual survey #4: Current thinking on homosexuality. *Medical Aspects of Human Sexuality, 11*, 110–111.

Bayer, R. (1987). *Homosexuality and American Psychiatry*, 2nd ed. Princeton: Princeton University Press.

Bell, A. P., & Weinberg, M. S. (1978). *Homosexualities.* New York: Simon and Schuster.

Bergler, E. (1982). *Counterfeit Sex*, 2nd ed. New York: Grune and Stratton.

Bieber, I. (1965). Clinical aspects of male inversion. In J. Marmor (ed.), *Sexual Inversion*, pp. 248–267. New York: Basic Books, 1965.

———. (1976). A discussion of "Homosexuality: The ethical challenge." *Journal of Consulting and Clinical Psychology, 44*, 163–166.

Bieber, I., Dain, H. J., Dince, P. R., Drellich, M. G., Grand, H. G., Bundlach, R. H., Kremer, M. W., Rifkin, A. H., Wilbert, C. B., & Bieber, T. B. (1962). *Homosexuality: A Psychoanalytic Study.* New York: Basic Books.

Bremer, J. (1959). *Asexualization.* New York: Macmillan.

British Medical Association. (1955). *Homosexuality and Prostitution.* London: British Medical Association.

Buckley, M. J. (1959). *Morality and the Homosexual.* Westminster, MD: Newman Press.

Bullough, V. (1989). The physician and research into human sexual behavior in nineteenth-century Germany. *Bulletin of the History of Medicine, 63*, 247–267.

Cautela, J., & Kearney, A. J. (1986). *The Covert Conditioning Handbook.* New York: Springer, 1986.

Clark, D. F. (1965). A note on avoidance conditioning techniques in sexual disorders. *Behaviour Research and Therapy, 3*, 203–206.

Curran, D., & Parr, D. (1957). Homosexuality: An analysis of 100 male cases seen in private practice. *British Medical Journal, 1*, 797–801.

Davis, G. C., & Wilson, T. G. (1973). Attitudes of behavior therapists toward homosexuality. *Behavior Therapy, 4*, 686–696.

Davison, G. C. (1976). Homosexuality: The ethical challenge. *Journal of Consulting and Clinical Psychology, 44*, 157–162.

Departments of Psychiatry and Neurology, Columbia University, College of Physicians and Surgeons and New York Psychiatric Institute. (1975). *Male Homosexuality* [videorecording].

Duberman, M. (1991). *Cures, A Gay Man's Odyssey.* New York: Dutton.

Ellis, H., & Symonds, J. A. (1975 [originally published in 1897]). *Sexual Inversion.* New York: Arno.

Gadpaille, W. J. (1981). Understanding the varieties of homosexual behavior. In H. I. Lief (ed.), *Sexual Problems in Medical Practice*, pp. 71–83. Chicago: American Medical Association.

Gelder, M., Gath, D., & Mayou, R. (1983). *Oxford Textbook of Psychiatry.* Oxford: Oxford University Press.

Glass, S. J., & Johnson, R. (1944). Limitations and complications of organotherapy in male homosexuality. *Journal of Clinical Endocrinology, 4*, 540–544.

Golla, F. L., & Hodges, R. S. (1949). Hormone treatment of the sexual offender. *Lancet, 1*, 1006–1007.

Halleck, S. L. (1976). Another response to "Homosexuality: The ethical challenge." *Journal of Consulting and Clinical Psychology, 44*, 167–170.

Hammond, G. M. (1892). The bicycle treatment in the treatment of nervous diseases. *Journal of Nervous and Mental Disease, VIII* [Vol. XIX in the 1986 reprint], 34–46.

Heger, H. (1980). *The Men with the Pink Triangle.* Boston: Alyson, 1980.

Hemphill, R. E., Leitch, A., & Stuart, J. R. (1958). A factual study of male homosexuality. *British Medical Journal, 1*, 1317–1322.

Herzer, M. (1985–1986). Kertbeny and nameless love. *Journal of Homosexuality, 12*, 1–26.

Hodges, A. (1983). *Alan Turing: The enigma.* New York: Simon and Schuster.

Hooker, E. (1957). The adjustment of the male overt homosexual. *Journal of Projective Techniques, 21*, 18–31.

———. (1958). Male homosexuality in the Rorschach. *Journal of Projective Techniques, 22*, 33–54.

———. (1959). What is a criterion? *Journal of Projective Techniques, 23*, 278–281.

James, B. (1962). Case of homosexuality treated by aversion therapy. *British Medical Journal, 1*, 768–770.

Kaplan, H. S. (1983). *The Evaluation of Sexual Disorders.* New York: Brunner/Mazel.

Karlinsky, S. (1989). Russia's gay literature and culture: The impact of the October revolution. *Christopher Street, 12*, 18–36. [Note 27 on p. 34

should read: M. Serreisky, "Gomoseksualizm" in *Bol'shai Meditsinskaia Entsiklopediaa*, ed. P. A. Semasko (Moscow, 1929), vol. 7, columns 668–72.]

Katz, J. N. (1983). *Gay/Lesbian Almanac*. New York: Harper and Row.

Kiernan, J. G. (1910). A medico-legal phase of autoeroticism in women. *Alienist and Neurologist, XXXI*, 329–338.

Kohlenberg, R. J. (1974). Treatment of a homosexual pedophiliac using in vivo desensitization. *Journal of Abnormal Psychology, 83*, 192–195.

Kopay, D., & Young, P. D. (1977). *The David Kopay Story*. New York: Arbor House.

Kronemeyer, R. (1980). *Overcoming Homosexuality*. New York: Macmillan, 1980.

Lewis, D. (1983 [originally 1899]). The gynecologic consideration of the sexual act. *Journal of the American Medical Association, 250*, 222–227.

Marmor, J. (1965). Introduction. In J. Marmor (ed.), *Sexual Inversion*, pp. 1–23. New York: Basic Books.

———. (1980). Clinical aspects of male homosexuality. In J. Marmor (ed.), *Homosexual Behavior: A Modern Reappraisal*, pp. 267–279. New York: Basic Books.

Marquis, J. N. (1970). Orgasmic reconditioning: Changing sexual object choice through controlling masturbation fantasies. *Journal of Behavior Therapy and Experimental Psychiatry, 1*, 263–271.

Mayerson, P., & Lief, H. I. (1965). Psychotherapy of homosexuals: A follow-up study of nineteen cases. In J. Marmor (ed.), *Sexual Inversion*, pp. 302–344. New York: Basic.

McGuire, R. J., & Vallance, M. (1964). Aversion therapy by electric shock: A simple technique. *British Medical Journal, 1*, 151–153.

Menninger, W. C. (1948). *Psychiatry in a Troubled World*. New York: Macmillan.

Money, J. (1980). *Love and Love Sickness*. Baltimore: Johns Hopkins University Press.

———. (1985). *The Destroying Angel*. Buffalo: Prometheus.

———. (1988). *Gay, Straight, and In-between*. New York: Oxford, 1988.

Murphy, T. F. (1984). "Freud reconsidered: Bisexuality, homosexuality and moral judgment," *Journal of Homosexuality, 9*, 65–78.

———. (1991). The ethics of conversion therapy. *Bioethics, 5*, 123–138.

———. (n.d.). Freud and conversion therapy. *Journal of Homosexuality* (forthcoming).

National Institute of Mental Health Task Force on Homosexuality. (1972). *Final Report and Background Papers*. Washington, DC: Department of Health, Education and Welfare.

Oberndorf, C. P. (1929). Diverse forms of homosexuality. *The Urologic and Cutaneous Review, 33*, 518–523.

Oswald, I. (1962). Induction of illusory and hallucinatory voices with consideration of behavior therapy. *Journal of Mental Science, 108*, 196–212.

Ovesey, L. (1965). Pseudohomosexuality and homosexuality in men: Psychodynamics as a guide to treatment. In J. Marmor (ed.), *Sexual Inversion*, pp. 211–222. New York: Basic.

Owensby, N. (1940). Homosexuality and lesbianism treated with metrazol. *Journal of Nervous and Mental Disease, 92*, 65–66.

Pattison, E. M., & Pattison, M. L. (1980). "Ex-gays": religiously mediated change in homosexuals. *American Journal of Psychiatry, 137*, 1553–1562.

Plant, R. (1986). *The Pink Triangle*. New York: Henry Holt.

Rosanoff, A. (1929). Human sexuality, normal and abnormal from a psychiatric standpoint. *The Urologic and Cutaneous Review, 33*, 523–530.

Ruse, M. (1988). *Homosexuality, a Philosophical Perspective*. Oxford: Basil Blackwell.

Saghir, M. T., & Robbins, E. (1973). *Male and Female Homosexuality*. Baltimore: Williams and Williams.

Sands, D. E. (1954). Further studies on endocrine treatment in adolescence and early adult life. *Journal of Mental Science, 100*, 211–219.

Sansweet, R. J. (1975). *The Punishment Cure*. New York: Mason/Charter.

Schmidt, G., & Schorsch, E. (1981). Psychosurgery of sexually deviant patients: Review and analysis of new empirical findings. *Archives of Sexual Behavior, 10*, 301–323.

Schwartz, M. F., & Masters, W. H. (1984). The Masters and Johnson treatment program for dissatisfied homosexual men. *American Journal of Psychiatry, 141*, 173–181.

Socarides, C. (1978) *Homosexuality*. New York: Aronson.

Sturgis, E. T., & Adams, H. E. (1978). The right to treatment: Issues in the treatment of homosexuality. *Journal of Consulting and Clinical Psychology, 46*, 165–169.

Thompson, G. N. (1949). Electroshock and other therapeutic considerations in sexual psychotherapy. *Journal of Nervous and Mental Disease, 109*, 531–539.

Tripp, C. A. (1975). *The Homosexual Matrix*. New York: McGraw-Hill.

Warren, F. Z., & Fischman, W. I. (1978). *Sexual Acupuncture*. New York: Dutton.

The Wolfenden Report. (1963). *Report of the Committee on Homosexual Offenses and Prostitution*. New York: Stein and Day.

PART TEN

INTERNATIONAL ENCOUNTERS
SEXUALITIES IN THE GLOBAL VILLAGE

READINGS IN THIS PART

INTRODUCTION TO SUBJECT AND READINGS

The wide usage of the term *global village* implies that the world is becoming a smaller place. We can connect and interact with each other more easily than ever before. Affordable and far-reaching air travel allows us to meet people in the once remote corners of the earth. Telephones and the Internet allow us to establish and/or maintain long-distance relationships. On one hand, we have the ability to expand our cultural and personal horizons. On the other hand, the "we/us" that I have used four times in this paragraph refers primarily to people from the first world. Most people in the world will never leave their native countries because poverty and/or visa restrictions preclude luxuries such as vacations. Instead they host tourists, hoping to benefit financially from the vast travel industry.

One commodity that poorer countries offer to tourists is sex. The following excerpt is from *www.pleasuretours.com*'s website. I have omitted the nude and semi-nude photographs and the more explicit descriptions about what is available to the sex tourist while visiting Thailand and the Philippines.

Would you like to be in a city where you can easily get simple, straightforward satisfaction?

How long has it been since you've gotten just as much sex as you wanted? Would you enjoy having a slender, giggling, affectionate escort . . . Do you need an innocent in need of seduction or a raw nymphomaniac whore? Do you like it nice or nasty?

You go home with hot memories to last a lifetime . . . or until you come back for more.

An internet search of "sex tourism" using the AltaVista search engine yielded 15,591 hits. Not all of these hits were actual sex tourism operators, but it is clear that there is no shortage of travel agencies promising "sexual adventures" with women in South East Asia, Thailand, Russia, Eastern Europe, Central America, South America, Japan, and the Philippines.

A survey of the first one hundred internet hits revealed the following results:

Agencies offering the services of women to men = 32
Agencies offering the services of men to women = 0

An occasional site boasted services for couples—yet in each case the assumption was that a couple was looking for a second woman to complete their ménage-à-trois.

Not surprisingly, most research on sex as a tourist commodity has focused on men traveling to third world countries to be serviced by women. Deborah Pruitt and Suzanne LaFont's article, *For Love and Money: Romance Tourism in Jamaica*, examines the dynamics of women traveling to foreign locals and engaging in sexual relations with men. They have termed the intimate relations female tourists have with local men *romance tourism*. This distinguishes it from *sex tourism*. There is some gray area in trying to define the relationships that local people have with tourists. Not all tourist woman/local man sexual interactions involve romance, while some tourist man/local woman surely do. The point is although tourist/host relationships come in all shapes and sizes, most sex tourism, in terms of professional sex workers, involves female sex workers and male tourists. As indicated by the Internet survey of websites, this form of travel for sex is more formalized and widespread.

Whether we are discussing sex or romance tourism, one fact remains—it is overwhelmingly first world men and women who travel and have intimate relations with women and men in impoverished or developing nations. Drawing on their ethnographic data from Jamaica, Pruitt and LaFont reveal that although gender is an important aspect of these intercultural couplings, such interactions are also about power. Their article explores the subtle discourse of gender, sexualities, and power that come into play when monied first world women meet the macho ideology of poor third world men.

Jo Doezema's article, *Forced to Choose: Beyond the Voluntary v. Forced Prostitution Dichotomy*, analyzes another gendered discourse, one that divides prostitutes into whores (voluntary sex workers) and victims (women who have been coerced or forced into the sex trade). The victim/whore dichotomy is a commonly held distinction regarding sex workers.

In my classes I show a documentary that features interviews with well-dressed, articulate prostitutes extolling the merits of the Internet. By attracting customers online, these savvy prostitutes are able to eliminate the need for a pimp and can stay off the street. Many of my students see these women as successful entrepreneurs. Yet when discussing sex tourism, these same students tend to view third world sex workers as victims. It is important to analyze, as Doezema does, the layers of assumptions about socioeconomic class, agency, protectionism, and civil rights surrounding the issue. She argues that we must distinguish between the efforts to stop the exploitation of prostitutes and the legal victimization of prostitutes themselves. Trafficking in women does exist, poor women are recruited with promises of well-paying jobs only to be imprisoned in brothels. This scenario, however, represents a very small percentage of sex workers. As Doezema points out, prostitutes, because they engage in an illegal activity, are often doubly victimized. They have nowhere to turn when they are abused by their johns, their pimps, or the police. She argues that inhibiting and limiting the rights of sex workers in the name of protection is not progress; instead it denies their agency and violates their human rights.

Although there have been World Whores' Congresses and a Whores' Bill of Rights has been drafted, prostitutes are poorly organized and remain a marginalized group fighting multiple levels of discrimination. Despite the myth, prostitution is not the oldest profession; it is, however, widespread and shows no signs of waning. As we become a global village and civil and human rights are more widely recognized, the debate about prostitution may move to the mainstream. For now it is still undercover in the United States, but Doezema's article offers insights into this complex issue and helps us understand the dialogue that is occurring in the wider arena.

TERMS AND CONCEPTS

abolitionist

commodification of Rastafarianism

COYOTE - Call Off Your Tired Old
    Ethics

eurocentrism

exotic Other

gender scripts

pandering

regulationist

romance tourism

sex tourism

sex workers

trafficking in women

white slave trade

CRITICAL THINKING AND QUESTIONS TO CONSIDER

1. According to Pruitt and LaFont, in what ways does romance tourism differ from sex tourism?

2. What are some of the major differences in the gender scripts of Western women and Jamaican men? What are the accompanying agendas that each person brings to the romance tourism encounter?

3. Pruitt and LaFont discussed "exotic Other" and "authenticity." What do these terms mean and how do they relate to each other?

4. Why does Doezema criticize the "voluntary" versus "force" dichotomy used in antiprostitution arguments?

5. Describe the three stands on prostitution—abolitionist, regulationist, and supporters of sex workers' rights—presented in Doezema's article.

FURTHER READINGS

de Albuquerque, Klaus. 1999. In search of the Big Bamboo. *Transition* 77, *www.cofc.edu/~klausda/bamboo.htm*

Doezema, Jo. 1999. Loose women or lost women? The re-emergence of the myth of "white slavery" in contemporary discourses of 'trafficking in women.' Paper presented at the ISA Convention, Washington, D.C. *www.walnut.org/csis/papers/doezema-loose.html/*

Kempadoo, Kamala. (ed.). 1999. *Sun, Sex, and Gold: Tourism and Sex Work in the Caribbean*, New York: Rowman & Littlefield Publishers, Inc.

Kempadoo, Kamala, and Jo Doezema (eds.). 1998. *Global Sex Workers: Rights, Resistance, and Redefinition.* New York: Routledge.

Lagnam, David J. 1994. *Crossing the Line: Legislating Morality and the Mann Act.* Chicago: University of Chicago Press.

Rubin, Gayle. 1975. The traffic in women: Notes on the political economy of sex. In *Towards an Anthropology of Women.* Edited by Rayna R. Reiter. New York: Monthly Review Press, pp. 157–210.

Rajan, Rajeshwari Sunder. 1999. The prostitution question(s): Female agency, sexuality and work . . . *re/production*, Vol.2., *www.hsph.harvard.edu/organizations/healthnet/SAsia/repro2/Prostitution_Questions.html*

Robinson, Laurie Nicole. 1998. The globalization of female child prostitution. *Indiana University Law School*, Vol. 4, no1. *www.law.indiana.edu/glsj/vol5/robinson.html*

Roffman, Rachel M. 1997. The forced prostitution of girls into the child sex tourism industry. *New England International and Comparative Law Annual*, Vol.3. *http://www.nesl.edu/annual/vol3/childsex.htm*

Seabrook, Jeremy. 1997. *Travels in the Skin Trade: Tourism and the Sex Industry.* London: Pluto Press.
———. 2000. *No Hiding Place: Child Sex Tourism and the Role of Extra-Territorial Legislation.* New York: Zed Book, Ltd.

Weitzer, Ronald. 2000. *Sex for Sale: Prostitution, Pornography, and the Sex Industry.* New York: Routledge.

RELATED WEBSITES

Bibliography on Trafficking in Women and Sex Tourism
www.vifu.de/students/vartti/Literature.html

COYOTE—An organization that provides assistance and works towards increased rights for sex workers
www.walnut.org/csis/groups/coyote

ICPR International Committee for the Prostitutes' Rights
www.walnet.org.csis/groups/icpr_charter.html

Preda Foundation Inc. (People's Recovery, Empowerment and Development Assistance Foundation)—Reports, News, Articles on Sex Tourism
www.preda.org/research/sextourism.html

Coalition Against Trafficking in Women
www.catwinternational.org/catw.htm

Trafficking Directory—Annotated Guide to Internet Resources on Trafficking in Women
www.yorku.ca/iwrp/trafficking_directory.htm

26
For Love and Money
Romance Tourism in Jamaica

Deborah Pruitt
Laney College

Suzanne LaFont
The City University of New York, Kingsborough Community College

Abstract: Contesting the constraints of conventional gender identity, many Euro-American women travelers to Jamaica pursue romantic affairs with local men. By elaborating on features from their gender repertoire, men articulate the women tourists' idealizations of local culture and masculinity, transforming their identity in order to appeal to the women and capitalize on the tourism trade. The disparity in economic status between partners in these relationships creates an opportunity for women to traffic in men. This situation illuminates the links between economic status and dominance in gender relations and contradicts conventional notions of male hegemony. Power in these relationships is shifting and situational, playing off traditional gender repertoires, as well as the immediate circumstances of finance and cultural capital. **Keywords**: romance tourism, gender identity, gender and power, Jamaica.

Source: Reprinted from *Annals of Tourism Research*, Vol. 22, Deborah Pruitt and Suzanne LaFont, For love and money: Romance tourism in Jamaica, 422–440, 1995, with permission from Elsevier Science.

INTRODUCTION

This study examines the negotiation of gender identity as foreign tourist women engage local men in Jamaica in emotional and intimate relationships, a process at once global and personal. While tourism research has investigated the relationships between male tourists and "host" women, commonly referred to as "sex tourism" (Bacchetta 1988; Cincone 1988; Hoblen, Horlemann and Pfafflin 1983; Lea 1988; Seager and Olsen 1986; Thitsa 1982; Thruong 1990), the relations of female tourists and local men have received decidedly less attention (Manning 1982). Yet, these relations present a rich opportunity for understanding the reproduction and transformation of gender and power as the women and men engaging in these relationships experiment with new identities and gender roles.

With new economic power, many Euro-American women are seeking an identity beyond the confines of the traditional gender scripts offered in their cultures. Conventional notions of gender are contested daily, challenged publicly through the media, and questioned privately as men and women struggle with negotiating new roles. With the ease and popularity offered by mass tourism, part of this negotiation is being conducted around the world as women travel independently of men. Free from their own society's constraints, female tourists have the opportunity to explore new gender behavior.

In turn, the local men who associate with tourists, in many ways, enter into a new tourism culture and distance themselves from their society's normative authority. These men are also free to explore new gender roles while they pursue social and economic mobility and the freedom to experience a new kind of intimate relationship.

The term *romance tourism* is used to distinguish these relationships from those of sex tourism. Rather than a simple role reversal, the fact that it is women rather than men traveling in pursuit of relationships is central to their nature. Gender is constitutive of the relationship, not ancillary to it. The purpose here is not to debate whether these men are prostitutes, but rather to convey the distinctive meaning these relationships hold for the partners and to acknowledge their definition of the situation. It is significant that neither actor considers their interaction to be prostitution, even while others may label it so. The actors place an emphasis on courtship rather than the exchange of sex for money.

These liaisons are constructed through a discourse of romance and long-term relationship, an emotional involvement usually not present in sex tourism. While both parties may share the ideal of a sustained relationship, the meanings this holds differ for each of them. However, the framework of romance serves both parties as they seek to maximize the benefits derived from this tourism relationship.

Whereas sex tourism serves to perpetuate gender roles and reinforce power relations of male dominance and female subordination, romance tourism in Jamaica provides an arena for change. By drawing on their respective traditional gender models as well as their imaginings and idealizations of each other and new possibilities, the partners in these relationships explore new avenues for negotiating femaleness and maleness. Each of them is engaged in manipulating and expanding their gender repertoires. This takes place within the context of the historical political relationships between their respective societies so that the couple must navigate the dual dominance hierarchies of culture and gender (Dubisch 1995).

Cross-cultural studies of gender have contributed to dispelling myths of biological determination and sexual universals, demonstrating that gender and sexual identity are invested with meaning by society (Leacock 1981, Mead 1935, Ortner and Whitehead 1981, Strathern 1980). Complex social and cultural processes of the construction of gender are revealed when binary views of gender roles are abandoned. Gender identities are not constant but must continually be reasserted and redefined in different contexts, often involving "refusals, reinterpretations or partial acceptances of the dominant themes" (Conway 1989:23). Normative roles and identities are not merely passively accepted, rather they are often challenged and contested. The challenge to the authority of received traditions to define the scope of culturally appropriate forms of male and female behavior is enhanced through contact between members of different cultures. Tourism is a primary agent of that contact and in its very nature involves breaking the continuity of social and cultural norms. This necessarily includes gender and cultural scripts for gender specific behavior. Thus, the personal relationships established in the tourism arena allow for the analysis of gender behavioral potential and how that potential is mediated by individual reinterpretations of gender ideologies as well as global forces of race and economics.

This ethnography evolved from research by the authors on the cultural impact of tourism and gender and power in Jamaica, based on their five cumulative years of field-work between 1989 through 1992. The methodology included participant observation, in-depth interviews, and quantitative analysis. The observations from countless hours spent in formal and informal tourism settings while living in a small town and villages surrounded by tourism activity forms the backbone of this study. Ethnographic interviews of key informants selected on the basis of their representativeness were conducted after 18 months in the field. Moreover, the authors' own experiences as foreign women in Jamaica provide important insight into the expectations and treatment of foreign women. The significance of the dynamics of tourism and gender identity became apparent from living in the tourism shadow and observing changes over time as the government increasingly set the course of the nation's economic future on the sights of the next planeload of tourists.

Foreign women on the arms of local men in the resort areas of Jamaica is a regular part of the landscape, just as it has become common in other parts of the Caribbean (Manning 1982). Furthermore, hundreds of men have "gone foreign" with women who were vacationing in the small-scale tourism center in which one author lived for two years. Virtually all of the young men who sought their livelihood from informal tourism work during that period have gone to foreign countries with their tourist girlfriends at least once in the three years since that time. Many of them are still living in Europe and all of them have ongoing relationships with foreign women. In this small-scale society, sufficient numbers of young men are involved in this activity that it is widely discussed and has recently become an issue for the media and the government-industry complex. It has been institutionalized to the point that the label "rent-a-dread" has been coined to refer to the men who get involved with foreign women. There are t-shirts, postcards, and cartoons making jokes about them for tourist consumption. Popular songs also comment on these relationships. Romance tourism liaisons are sufficiently common to encourage at least one American tour operator to consider creating a promotional brochure complete with pictures of men available as companions so she could broker the relationships from the United States before the women leave home. German women embark on these ventures frequently enough that an expression has developed in Germany that "The men go to Thailand and the women go to Jamaica."

ROMANCE TOURISM

Travel has always offered a unique opportunity for self-discovery and potential transformation. Face-to-face contact with the Other and its concomitant challenges to culturally received conceptions and beliefs inevitably involves a confrontation with one's self *qua* self. While historically the purview of men and a "medium of peculiarly male fantasies of transformation and self-realization" (Leed 1991:275), travel now serves as a medium of female self-realization. However, contrary to Leed's conclusion that the increase in numbers of women traveling with the spread of mass tourism marks the end of the "genderization of mobility and of journeying as a purely masculine or masculinizing activity" (1991:275), travel has become part of the gendering activity of women as they seek to expand their gender repertoires to incorporate practices traditionally reserved for men and thereby integrate the conventionally masculine with the feminine.

Insofar as travel has historically constituted an activity primarily of men, the journeys of women have always represented an attempt to break the "boundaries of convention and traditional feminine restraints" (Robinson 1990:6). This function of travel has simply escalated as challenges to gender roles have increased and travel has become a more accessible avenue for exploring new territory of the self. The tourism industry has responded with specialized tours for women. For example, advertisements for "adventure" travel invite women to develop a "new outdoor style" through the "empowering experience" of traveling "free of traditional gender roles and expectations" (Bond 1992).

As Western women seek to construct new identities, their spirit of adventure is often expressed by more than just a new outdoor style. Continually expanding the boundaries of the feminine requires perpetually new experiences, including a new kind of romance. As a dominant theme in Western cultures, romance serves to "construct feminine subjectivity in terms of a significant other, the boyfriend" (Christian-Smith 1990:28). This has come to include women traveling in pursuit of sex and romance with local men.

Whereas women consort with local men in countless tourism destinations throughout the world, the scale of romance tourism in Jamaica is a consequence of unique features of Jamaican culture, most specifically as the roots of the international reggae counterculture and its role in attracting tourists to Jamaica. Since the 1960s and the burgeoning of adventurous travel and the 1970s as Jamaican reggae music began spreading across the world, tourists became more closely involved with local people, including picking up local men (the particular role of reggae music is discussed later).

The women who engage local men in romantic relationships span the full range of nationalities, ages, social and economic backgrounds represented by tourists to Jamaica. The relationships are most often, though not always, cross-racial as well as cross-cultural in that the vast majority of tourists would be classified as white while the majority of the Jamaican population is of African descent. The duration of their stay is extended, lasting anywhere from a few weeks to a few months, and many of these women are repeat visitors (Pruitt 1993). However, European women who often travel for periods of two to three months and come from countries with more relaxed immigration practices than those in North America are more likely to take local men back home with them. The women are seeking an "enriching" travel experience. They shun exclusive resorts in favor of locally owned guest houses, frequent local hang-outs and socialize with the local people.

The desire for the "cultural" experience which the tourist woman seeks, coupled with prolonged exposure to local society demonstrates a readiness to embrace, however superficially, the local culture. This contrasts with the sexual liaisons of sex tourism. The local man is not merely a sexual object, but rather the woman's personal cultural broker. He serves to ease her experience in the society and provide her with increased access to the local culture.

Touring Romance

A foreign woman in Jamaica is assumed to be on vacation. If she is without a male companion, the commonly held belief is that she wants or needs a local man to increase her pleasure. This belief is due, in part, to Jamaican notions of companionship and pleasure along with generalized assumptions about what tourist women are seeking from their holidays, based largely on the frequency with which Jamaicans have observed foreign women get involved with local men. This has resulted in what one local writer has called "the sexualization of routine encounters between a female tourist and a local Jamaican male" (Henry 1980). Thus, foreign women are frequently inundated with offers from local men for companionship and a "bodyguard." One Canadian woman told the authors, "Guys at home are so confused, they don't approach women directly very much. But you come down here [Jamaica] and the men are dropping out of the trees like mangoes." The result is that many women unexpectedly find themselves accepting the flattering offers they receive from men. This might be the opportunity for the tourist to indulge in fantasies and explore a new aspect of herself by engaging in behavior that she would never allow herself at home. Adding to the allure of the vacation romance in Jamaica are Caribbean cultural ideals of attractiveness. Light skin, straight hair and caucasian facial features are highly valued, and women who are considered overweight in their own cultures are appreciated by many Jamaican men. Thus, foreign women who may not satisfy standards of beauty at home find themselves the object of amorous attention by appealing local men.

Other women travel seeking companionship. The woman might hope for the companionship of her boyfriend year after year as she returns to Jamaica, as many do. The authors became acquainted with dozens of Western women who return to Jamaica each year to visit their boyfriends. Relationships are maintained through letters, phone calls, and gifts of money and consumer goods. Unsatisfied with relationships or the lack thereof at home, some women travel with the hope of finding their ideal mate and staying in Jamaica or returning home with a partner. These women often express a frustration with the men from their own cultures as inattentive, preoccupied with career, unemotional or confused about their role (Pruitt 1993). They are lured by the possibility of having a child and establishing a family. Their romanticized notions of the alternative available from a local man interact with their similarly romanticized notions of helping him escape poverty and fuels the intensity and rapid pace of the relationship.

Most Western tourist women in Jamaica are confronted with economic hardship that is different or absent from their daily reality at home. "Third World poverty" is often perceived as noble in contrast to the slums or ghettos with which the tourist may be familiar. Rural shacks may appear quaint, whereas ghettos are frightening. Reactions to their perceptions of poverty range from guilt and pity to ideals of helping, which often bring people together despite striking social differences. This leads many foreigners to fraternize with individuals of dramatically different social status in a way that is less threatening than at home. They develop a rapport and attempt to cross the boundaries established by social inequality.

Racial, educational and economic differences that constrain tourist women at home are often diminished or ignored as part of the necessity of having a "freeing" experience. Thus, a rural, African-Caribbean man with little education and scant livelihood is often the companion of a foreign professional woman many years his senior. When necessary, the women provide the finances for the man of their choice to accompany them to dinner, stage shows, discos or trips around the island. In the light of obvious poverty, she frequently views her financial contribution to the relationship as relatively insignificant.

These women are able to explore more dominant roles in the tourism relationship. The economic and social status the women enjoy provides them with a security and independence that translates into power and control in the relationship. Some of the women enjoy the control they have in these relationships and express a preference for keeping a man dependent on them (Pruitt 1993). This ensures that he will be fully available to meet her needs and will not become distracted or otherwise occupied like the men in her society from whom she has sought an alternative.

The Caribbean man, who highly values proficiency at "sweet talk" (Abrahams 1983, Wilson 1973), finds that his gender script for romancing women connects with her desire for romance. Ardent declarations of love, praises of beauty, and the like, which are a common part of a Jamaican man's repertoire, are seen as refreshing or passionate by the foreign woman who does not understand the culture. In the words of a Jamaican woman who runs a small guest house, the men "appeal to her emotions with flattery and compliments and do things for her to make her stay in Jamaica easier and more pleasant. They appeal to her sensual side saying . . . if you come to Jamaica and never sleep with a Rastaman, the true, natural man of Jamaica, you never really experience Jamaica and yourself."

The courtship serves those women who are seeking either a "forbidden" experience or their relationship ideal, or are struggling with expectations of propriety from their native cultures wherein sex is linked to love. She responds from her cultural script, assuming that both of them hold the same ideals for intimacy. Furthermore, the romantic theme is central to Western consumption practices based on "a complex pattern of hedonistic behavior, the majority of which occurs in the imagination of the consumer" (C. Campbell 1987:89). This pattern of consumption also lies at the heart of tourism and the relationships thereby established. The men are successful at elaborating on the tourist's imagination and thus offering the promise of realization of her dreams.

Love and Money

The men hold their own ideals about the potential for emotional intimacy in relationships with foreign women. Many believe foreign women to be more tender and emotional than Jamaican women and imagine that they can experience an emotional and sexual intimacy in these relationships that is lacking in their lives, particularly as they are increasingly rejected by local women for their activities with foreigners.

Those men who desire a broader experience than that available in their immediate situation believe that a relationship with a foreign woman could also provide them with a way out of their limited circumstances. It has proven to be a successful strategy for many young men who seek opportunities and prosperity unavailable in the local society. The hope for economic benefits intertwines with emotional longing and fuels the men's romantic ideals for a relationship with a foreign woman.

Most of the men involved with female tourists can be seen as taking advantage of one of the few opportunities available to them. They generally come from that group of rural young people with little education and few social and economic prospects. The deprivation of opportunity in rural areas has led many young men to seek their livelihood directly from tourists (commonly referred to as "hustling") by taking the role of guide or informal entrepreneur in the hopes of obtaining a few of the dollars tourists often spend liberally. A steady flow of these young men who want to get out of rural areas move into the tourism developments and seek ways to make their living "hustling the tourists."

In those regions where it is concentrated, tourism dominates the economy and has been billed as "The Answer" to Jamaica's economic future (Pruitt 1993). Yet, uneducated and unskilled young men living near resort areas are effectively cut off from formal jobs in the tourism industry. The prevalence of romance tourism has meant that increasing numbers of young men routinely view a relationship with a foreign woman as a meaningful opportunity for them to capture the love and money they desire. It is not uncommon to hear young men who come into the tourism areas from deep rural villages talk about their interest in "experiencing a white woman." The following is an excerpt from field notes.

. . . It was a slow day, not may tourists were in town and none had ventured to Sunrise Beach that day. The guys were chatting about how slow things were.

"Nothing's going on. No money is flowing." Scoogie complained.

"That's right. Nothing is happening around here. I just want to get me a white-woman and get out of here. Go to America and make a real money," said Driver.

"Yeah, you have to link up with a white-woman and get her to fall in love with you if you want a break. . . ." "Yeah man, you have to hook up with a white-woman. I mean look at Decker, Jah Red, Collin, even Punkie. All gone foreign just since this year," said Scoogie. . . ." (Pruitt 1993:147).

The ability to earn a prosperous living has significance for the young Jamaican man far beyond basic needs for survival. Brodber describes the "pressure to establish one's maleness through the abilities to disperse cash" (1989:69). The Jamaican man's aspirations to the status of a "big" man (Whitehead 1992) involves money in each of the three elements—moral character, respectability and reputation—which comprise that status. Evaluations of moral character are based in part on a man's generosity. Expectations of respectability include maintaining a household, while the reputation factor central to achieving status as a "big" man is based partially on virility displayed by sexual conquests and fathering many children (Handwerker 1989, Smith 1956, Wilson 1973).

LaFont describes the expectations most Jamaican women hold of financial remuneration from men in exchange for sex and domestic duties by the woman with the result that "much of their [men's] role fulfillment is dependent on job opportunities and the economy" (1992:196). "No money, no talk" is a common expression in Jamaica. Here, the word "talk" refers to intimate relations between a man and a woman. Women expect that a man with whom they are having an intimate relationship will contribute financial support and that he will display an ability and willingness to do so early in the courtship. Thus, the road to women and reputation that verifies a young Jamaican male's manhood, and the status that follows, is constrained for the man with uncertain income opportunities.

In contrast, while his finances are important in his native culture, relations with foreign women do not depend on his ability to provide income. Her interests in him are not predominantly financial. Thus, he is able to acquire the desirable "reputation" of being successful with women without the financial outlay necessary in his own culture. This empowers the men's relations with foreign women while at the same time changing his experience of power and dominance.

While tourism acts as a catalyst for these men to manipulate gender identity as a strategy for economic access, it also places them in a subordinate role to women, which is in conflict with their own gender ideals of male dominance. The independence and power the foreign woman enjoys from her financial means yields a control in the relationship that is inappropriate for Jamaican male aspirations. He chafes against her seemingly dominant position because despite the discussions of male marginality (Smith 1956) and matrifocality (Gonzalez 1970), which refer to men's relationship within the domestic domain, his desire to be dominant in gender relations is intense. To maintain his reputation and avoid the appearance that the woman controls him, the Jamaican man without economic means continually seeks new ways to exhibit his dominion over women. During the tourist woman's holiday in Jamaica, the man has the power of local knowledge. He can control much of his female companion's circumstances in Jamaica, generally without her awareness. He actively stands as buffer between her and others who might influence her; he makes it clear that he "controls that thing" and a hands-off message is relayed to the other male hustlers. This, along with controlling the car she has rented and getting her to buy him material goods all exhibit his dominion over her.

In order to compete in his community for the status associated with a reputation for success with women, young men play off the features of masculinity available in their culture that have the greatest appeal to foreign women. For most foreign women these are associated with the male Rasta.

The Rasta Appeal

The connection a Western woman develops with a Jamaican man is generally based on her idealizations of his embodiment of manhood, idealizations fueled by the discourse of hegemonic relations constructed through "race" in which the exotic and the erotic are intertwined (Said 1978). The exotic Other has been constructed as more passionate, more emotional, more natural, and sexually tempting. Stereotypes of black men and their sexuality, of non-Western peoples, and real differences between the tourists' cultures and Jamaican culture promote the belief that Jamaican men represent the archetypal masculine. This is augmented by the men's displays of machismo drawn from their cultural gender scripts. These beliefs are held by Western women considered black as well as white, though black women may not be adhering to stereotypes of black men in general, but rather the black man who stands closer to his African heritage, in this case embodied in the Rasta identity. Though by no means exclusively, those men with dreadlocks who are assumed to be Rastafarian receive substantially more attention from foreign women than do Jamaican men without locks. Dreadlocks, "locks" or "dreads," are the result of letting hair grow naturally without cutting or combing.

In Jamaica, dreadlocks developed as a symbol of the spiritually based Rastafarian culture of resistance. Since the 1930s, they have represented "stepping out" of the dominant cultural and social system that enslaved the African and continues to denigrate that identity. Dreadlocks are symbolic of the strength of the lion, and signify pride in African heritage and represent strength, anything that is fearful. As such, dreadlocks represent a power source for the Rastafarian. They also symbolize a commitment to a natural way of life, unmediated by Western standards and vanities. Dreadlocks are but one element of a system of symbols that includes a distinctive use of the Jamaican language, images of the lion, and displaying and wearing of the colors of red, gold, and green. Each of them are a "reflection of a form of resistance, linking these symbols to some concrete struggle among African peoples" (H. Campbell 1987:95).

Reggae music developed in this same manner as an expression of the Rastafarian spirituality and as a vehicle for spreading the message of resistance with an exhortation to the international community to "live up" to standards of interracial justice and peace. The penchant foreign women have for men with dreadlocks is fueled by the mystique associated with the dreadlock singers of the international reggae music culture who project an image of the Rastaman as a confident, naturally powerful, and especially virile man. During the late 1970s, Rastafarian musician Bob Marley was the first to achieve international recognition and subsequently succeeded in capturing the attention of countercultural people across the world. Reggae music, dreadlocks, and Rastafari became synonymous for much of the international community so that, following the model of Marley's success, reggae musicians increasingly grew their hair in locks and adopted the presentation of the powerful Rasta "lion." Through the years, the music has attracted millions of Westerners disaffected by their own cultures' systems of inequality and materialism, and enticed them to Jamaica. The pilgrimage to the roots of Rasta resistance climaxes each year in July with the music festival called Reggae Sunsplash.

Whether due to an agreement with the Rasta political philosophy and a desire to demonstrate lack of prejudice, or an attraction to the powerful masculinity projected by the Rastas, or both, men who assume the Rastafarian identity have proven to be particularly popular with the female European and American tourists with a lust for the exotic. Since the 70s, young men living in the tourism areas who grew their hair in dreadlocks have attracted special attention from foreigners in general and women in particular. Therefore, those men interested in trading with foreigners, whether selling handicrafts, or marijuana (associated with Rastas and an important tourism commodity), or generally acting as companions to ease the way for foreigners through the largely informal society, have increasingly styled themselves as Rastafarian. They "locks" their hair, speak in the Rasta dialect, and develop a presentation that expresses the Rastafarian emphasis on simplicity and living in harmony with nature, in effect, constructing a "staged authenticity" (MacCannell 1973). The man with locks picks up and elaborates on aspects of the stereotype of the exotic Other, enhancing the contrast between himself and Western men, thereby strengthening his appeal to the tourist women.

In turn, because these men with locks have increased contact with tourists, they become familiar with the foreign cultures, perhaps learning to speak a little German or developing an expertise for guessing what types of experiences the specific tourists are seeking. Hence, they become more accessible to the foreigner. Those foreigners in search of an authenticity associated with nonindustrialized society (Cohen 1979; MacCannell 1976) are attracted to the Rasta images and impressions of unity associated with them. The Jamaica Tourist Board has recently reinforced these impressions by using images of dreadlock musicians singing Bob Marley's song "One Love" in the 1991 television advertisement for Jamaica.

Leed describes travel as a "stripping away of the subjectivity rooted in language and custom, allowing travelers to become acquainted with a common nature, fate, and identity that persist beneath the diversity of cultural types and ideals" (1991:218). That motivation for travel intersects in Jamaica with the philosophy of Rastafari, which has at its foundation an emphasis on that common identity and unity of spirit. The dread who approaches the tourist appears to offer travelers to Jamaica just that experience of "oneness."

A Rasta identity is attractive to the Jamaican man involved in the tourist hustle because it provides a model of masculinity that is not dependent upon disbursing cash. Rather, it developed around an articulation of the forces which prohibit the African-Jamaican man from achieving economic success. No one expects a Rastaman to be rich. He traditionally emerged from the ghettos of Kingston, and eventually took to the airwaves and concert stages to spread the Rasta message of African liberation. This is the chord Rasta has struck with thousands of men in Jamaica and throughout the African Diaspora, whether rural or urban, that is, its capacity to represent his experience and provide a definition of manhood in Afrocentric terms, thereby providing an alternative to the dominant ideology that places Eurocentric achievement of occupational success and money at the center of the status system. The political philosophy that developed out of the Rastafarian movement of the 1930s through the 1970s included in its critique of the system of oppression of Africans the manner in which the African man's identity is obscured by the Eurocentric ideology of gender and race. The Rastas went on to develop a response by articulating an identity that affirms the black man's dignity and provides a language of opposition to a social system that denies his experience and seeks to obliterate his reality.

Local Consequences

While Rastafari appeals to many rural and urban young men, those who hustle tourists also see the opportunity for parlaying that identity into an opportunity to secure his fantasy of an emotional relationship and perhaps a more comfortable way of life. Furthermore, such relationships offer the young man with no economic means the avenue to the status associated with success with women, particularly among his new peer group of other hustlers.

Those men who circulate through the tourist spots—those who work with tourists and those who hope for the opportunity to talk to one—become the community that accords status and prestige to the young men whose ambitions are frustrated by a system of inequality. This peer group becomes increasingly significant for the hustler as locals shun him for dealing with foreigners and he faces the generalized and institutionalized discrimination of those with dreadlocks.

While gaining reputation for success with women, the hustler forfeits the respect of the larger community. Anyone who chooses to spend much time with foreigners is subject to criticism and censure from the broader community for being "too much with white people." These men then become embroiled in a further opposition to cultural norms that hold that a man is not supposed to take money from a woman and are subject to persecution and shaming from others in the community. Locals ignore the nuances of the romance tourism relationship and consider the men prostitutes who are too lazy and irresponsible to work for a living. They are resented by many locals who work hard for measly wages while they watch the hustlers living luxuriously with tourist women.

The hustler's claim to be Rastafarian is viewed as superficial as he appropriates Rasta symbols for personal gain, yielding to the individualism of Eurocentric culture and failing to enter the spirituality of Rastafari, which repudiates material accumulation and participation in the system of exploitative lifestyles. His internalization of the material ethic that Rasta rejects and his willingness to achieve it by trading in his sexuality with foreign women places him in opposition to the Rastafarian critique of the political economy of Western Civilization.

Young men who sport dreadlocks while living among tourists have created ambiguity around the Rastafarian identity and the meaning of dreadlocks. As stated earlier, the term *rent-a-dread* evolved in Jamaica to refer to those men who are said to locks their hair in order to appeal to women tourists. When asked how one identifies a rent-a-dread, most locals will say something similar to, "Rasta is known by his works, his livity [manner of living]. If you see the guy around with a different white woman every week or so, then he is a rent-a-dread." The man responds from his cultural gender script for courting multiple women and, by professing his love for his companion will distinguish himself from a prostitute.

The hustler draws on the language of resistance of the Rastafarian culture to generate a response to his critics. He criticizes non-Rastas for not repudiating the dominant system and ideology by becoming Rasta. The internal contradiction in this position reflects the ambivalence and multiple realities these men confront daily. Criticism from Rastas presents a more formidable challenge for the tourist hustler. His response will usually consist of an argument that Rasta means "One Love," and that Rasta does not subscribe to racial or color discriminations.

What the tourist generally does not understand is the context of origin of her particular "dread." Anyone with dreadlocks represents Rastafari for many foreigners who are unaware of its unique history and culture, or who fail to see its symbols as signifiers rather than the thing itself and who have had contact only with those who hustle tourists and claim the identity. Whereas to "locks" one's hair was formerly a dramatic declaration of opposition to the Western system of exploitation, it now can mark an intention to maximize one's position within that system. Nurturing this possibility requires making the most of the opportunities available so that some men maintain relationships with numerous women from different countries for years until one comes through with an airline ticket, or perhaps makes the decision to move to Jamaica herself and set up a household with her boyfriend.

Beyond Romance

Those who make a commitment to the romance tourism relationship find that romance turns the corner down the path of the hard work of getting along day after day in an intimate relationship between two people whose ideals and expectations have been formed in different cultures. If the women stay in Jamaica or take their boyfriends home with them, typecasts break down to personalities in the minutiae of everyday life. The relationship that extends beyond the casual vacation romance often loses its bloom and leads to disappointment and conflict. The fact that each partner has come to the relationship with a different agenda becomes more apparent as the economic dependency within the relationship becomes more evident.

The women, ignoring or ignorant of the conflicting purposes arising from such disparity of financial means, education, and exposure, are initially unaware of many of the dynamics underlying their relationships. Those who seek their ideal relationships eventually often feel used and disappointed by their partners who likely do not share their Western ideals of sexual equality. The following remarks by a German woman to her Jamaican boyfriend illustrates this attitude. "I came to meet you half-way to help you but you are still caught up in the resentment of the past between blacks and whites and you are not ready to meet me half-way."

Cast in the role of financial provider, the women may become enmeshed in an exchange relationship that did not define their initial impulses. These women often face insecurities about the man's commitment to her, fearing he might get involved with another woman who is in a better financial position to take care of him. Furthermore, if the woman decides to remain in Jamaica, unless she is independently wealthy, she may lose the financial advantages she brought to the relationship or grow weary of the economic demands placed on her. She will also learn that her "Rasta's" alienation within the community extends to her.

The challenges become even greater if the relationship moves to the tourist's country of origin where the man has little of the cultural capital needed to achieve the success he desires in Western society. The rural Jamaican man with little formal education is ill-prepared for the demands of making a living in the postindustrial society. With the man's role as culture-broker and tour guide no longer necessary, educational, age and racial differences which seemed inconsequential in the host country are magnified. His ability to contribute to the relationship in many ways has been diminished, and his difficulty in acculturation, learning the language and bureaucratic systems, as well as making a living, place further strains on the relationship. His "natural" persona may seem incongruous with the demands of life in the "artificial" North, and he will be judged by her family and friends without, or perhaps because of, his exotic backdrop. Furthermore, by traveling to the woman's country, the man loses what independence he had in his homeland and he leaves the peer group that verifies his exploits and provides him with reputation and status. Thus, he simultaneously loses the cultural rewards for his deeds while entering a greater dependency on the woman.

The economic relationship conjoined with an emotional one sometimes backfires on the man. While the relationship between a local man and a tourist woman may at first involve a substantial element of economic venture for the man, it also springs from his desire for his ideal emotional relationship with a "tender" woman. It is an intimate relationship involving all the inevitable issues of identity, connection, and power, compounded in this case by racial issues, cultural differences, and economic dependency. Unlike the sex/money prostitutes, the Jamaican male hustler whose own culture idealizes romantic love may be caught in his own emotional web. Emotional attachments develop; hopes and desires are at work. While the man may be seeking a way out through a foreign woman, he is also vulnerable to being a mere instrument in her search for authenticity.

Tourist women often seem fickle, turning from one man, met early in their stay in Jamaica, to another man they later meet and find more desirable. These Jamaican men must cope with the insecurity of the status of one who represents an ideal type. The premise of the initial attraction is often feigned. To the extent that he has modeled himself to match an ideal, the relationship is not based on her choice of him in particular.

Many of the men describe feeling used by foreign women, only important to them so long as the desire for an exotic liaison lasts, or merely the instrument for her to have a "brown baby" to display her liberal ideas. The instances of children from these liaisons are noticeable but not easily quantified. The men are subject to being left behind as the woman returns home or moves on to new adventures. One interviewee expresses this sentiment succinctly, "I don't like the influence of tourism and being chased by white women. I realize that I can be used by these women. They go home and after a few months you are nothing. You never hear from them again." One of the authors heard a man say to his foreign girlfriend, "You are too emancipated. You think because you have money and education you can come down here, buy everything and control man. But it can't work that way." When these resentments build, it is not uncommon for the man to resort to a common feature of his gender script for control over a woman and react with violence against the woman. This widespread use of the threat of violence by Jamaican men to maintain dominance is expressed in these lyrics of a popular song in Jamaica.

Me, me, no woman can rule me.
Now me is a man and me have me woman.
But if she try to rule me, me have contention.
She could get a broke foot and get a broke hand.
And me rule she, she no rule me.
If me tell her say A, she can't tell me B.
And if me lift up me hand you know she feel it
   (Shabba Ranks, 1990).

Relationship between the tourist and local resident is generally based on stereotypes, each having preconceived but not well formulated notions about the other and often dealing with each other not only as types, but as objects (Nash 1980). Over time, the subjectivity of the partners overwhelms the simple objectified models each hold of the other. The disappointment from the failure of stereotypes to deliver their promise intrudes. The women often become dissatisfied with a partner with different ideas about loyalty and fidelity and who proves to aspire to the deluxe life-style that she believed him to refute as a Rastaman. The Jamaican who assumes that all tourists are wealthy may be disillusioned when he discovers that the object of his attentions is spending money freely in order to have a special vacation but is neither rich nor extravagant once the holiday is over.

CONCLUSION

Dissatisfied with the confines of cultural norms and expectations, people are willing, even eager, to experiment with and rewrite gender scripts. The constraining and sacrificial (Gilmore 1990) nature of gender ideologies invites response and resistance. Tourism creates a social space ripe with possibilities for change through the interplay between conventional scripts and new ideas. In a unique conjunction of need, hope, and desire, the romance relationships between tourist women and local men serve to transform traditional gender roles across cultural boundaries, creating power relations distinctive from those existing in either native society.

In that gender identity is a relational construct, the Western women who seek to break from conventional roles require a different kind of relationship with men in order to realize a new gender identity. Yet, these women who seek more control in defining their relationship are simultaneously drawn to conventional notions of masculinity. Ideas about masculine power are central to the women's attraction to local men, in particular the "natural" Rasta. The women's own gender scripts include a sense of appropriateness of the dominant male from a dualistic conception of man/woman constructed on hierarchical power relations. The farther the women push the boundary of feminine conduct to incorporate qualities conventionally defined as masculine, the more they confront internalized ideas about masculine power. The need for contrast through which to construct their identity draws them to the aspect of masculinity most closely associated with dominance, partially reproducing the dichotomy of gender from their cultural scripts. The women are drawn to the strength, the potency of the masculine even as they experiment with the power they acquire through financial superiority.

Though not motivated by the search for a new gender identity per se, the men in these relationships manipulate their identity by expanding on features from their own cultural repertoire. However, the demands of the role they have adopted put them in contradiction with their gender ideals. Euro-American women bring economic superiority and ideas of female liberation that interact in complex ways with Jamaican men's tolerance of female economic independence, a tradition in their own culture (Mintz 1981, Roberts and Sinclair 1978, Safa 1986). Despite Jamaican women's economic independence, the predominance of female-headed households and notions of matrifocality, (Gonzalez, 1970, SES 1989) men are perceived to be dominant in Jamaican culture (Brody 1981, LaFont 1992, Moses 1981, Powell 1986). The Jamaican man's tolerance of female economic independence differs significantly from the subordinate position the man has entered into with the "affluent" tourist woman. While their cultural script includes a model for the independence of women, the Jamaican woman does not control the man's opportunities for economic success. However, the men involved in romance tourism are faced with new gendered power relations in which the women control access to the financial success the men want.

While both individuals have the capacity to exert their influence over the relationship in a given circumstance, the woman possesses the disproportionate power to define the situation and the Other himself. Such a situated, contextual analysis (Rhode 1990) as presented here verifies that "it is in these contexts of inequities of wealth and power that one finds transformations of the native self" that incorporate the "evaluation of the West" (Bruner 1991:247). The potential for that transformation and the extent of its accommodation to Western fantasies and expectations is exhibited by these men as they manipulate their identity to fit the tourist's desire for a "natural" man. The consequence of the tourists' power is the commodification of Rastafarian culture and gender itself. Thus, romance recapitulates the patriarchal structure of tourism (Enloe 1989) by reproducing the dominance relation in the encounter wherein tourism functions to fulfill desires of the tourist by subordinating local culture and interests even while the women seek to challenge patriarchal power.

This situation serves to illuminate the significance of economic status for dominance and refutes conventional notions of male hegemony. Control of economic resources provides either gender the opportunity for dominance, for holding little regard for the Other's experience, needs and feelings. Rather than the purview of men, dominance is rooted in various attributes such as economic power, physical strength, and personality characteristics that may reside with the man or the woman. Gender studies have shown that gender is not sex-linked. This study contributes to a reconception of gender (Keller 1989) by further disentangling power and dominance from sex (Ortner 1983).

The dynamics of these relationships also demonstrate that dominance and power are not static, but are shifting and situational, constantly negotiated and contested. As the partners in these relationships play off traditional social and gender repertoires, as well as the immediate circumstances of finance and cultural capital, the power in the relationship fluctuates between them "in relation to opposed sets of cultural values and established social boundaries" (Conway, Bourque and Scott 1989:29).

Travel offers new opportunities for women to liberate themselves from patriarchal authority relations and redefine "woman." People might celebrate as women break free of conventional constraints and gain power over their lives. However, the personal nature of these relationships may at first mask the social and historical dynamics of racial and economic hegemony embedded in them. Those social and economic inequities as well as beliefs and stereotypes each partner holds about the Other work to construct a relationship uncomfortably similar to the power relationship between the partners' respective societies. The agency has shifted from the characteristic nation-state and its transnational corporations to the intimately personal arena. Breaking taboos and challenging tradition open uncharted territories of social relations. The outcome is never certain and carries with it the possibility of reproducing much of what is being challenged.

ACKNOWLEDGMENTS

Although it is not possible to name them, the authors wish to acknowledge the numerous men and women in Jamaica whose kind assistance made this article possible. Winsome Anderson made invaluable suggestions on an earlier draft.

REFERENCES

Abrahams, Roger D. 1983. *The Man-of-Words in the West Indies.* Baltimore: Johns Hopkins University Press.

Anderson, Patricia. 1986. Conclusion: Women in the Caribbean. *Social and Economic Studies* 35:291–325.

Baccheta, Paola. 1988. Indian women fight against sex tourism. *Off Our Backs* (January):12.

Bond, Marybeth. 1992. For Women Only. *justGO!* 2(2):13.

Brodber, Erna. 1989. Socio-cultural change in Jamaica. In *Jamaica in Independence*, R. Nettleford, ed., pp. 55–74. Kingston: Heinemann Caribbean.

Brody, Eugene. 1981. *Sex, contraception, and motherhood in Jamaica.* Cambridge: Harvard University Press.

Bruner, Edward M. 1991. Transformation of self in tourism. *Annals of Tourism Research* 18: 238–250.

Campbell, Colin. 1987. *The Romantic Ethic and the Spirit of Modern Consumerism.* London: Blackwell.

Campbell, Horace. 1987. *Rasta and Resistance.* Trenton: Africa World Press.

Christian-Smith, Linda. 1990. *Becoming a Woman Through Romance.* New York: Routledge.

Cincone, Lillian. 1988. *The Role of Development in the Exploitation of Southeast Asian Women: Sex Tourism in Thailand.* New York: Women's International Resource Exchange.

Cohen, Erik. 1979. A phenomenology of tourist experiences. *Sociology* 13: 179–201.

Conway, Jill K., Susan C. Bourque, and Joan W. Scott. 1989. *Learning about Women: Gender, Politics and Power.* Ann Arbor: University of Michigan Press.

Dubisch, Jill. 1995. Lovers in the field: Sex, dominance, and the female anthropologist. In *Taboo: Sex, Identity and Erotic Subjectivity in Anthropological Fieldwork*, D. Kulick and M. Willson, eds. New York: Routledge.

Enloe, Cynthia H. 1989. *Bananas, Beaches and Bases: Making Feminist Sense of International Politics.* London: Pandora.

Gilmore, David G. 1990. *Manhood in the Making: Cultural Concepts of Masculinity.* New Haven: Yale University Press.

Gonzales, Nancie L. Solien. 1970. Towards a definition of matrifocality. In *Afro-American Anthropology*, John Szwed and Norman Whitton, eds., pp. 231–243. New York: The Free Press.

Handwerker, W. Penn. 1989. *Women's Power and Social Revolution: Fertility Transition in the West Indies.* Newbury Park: Sage Publications.

Henry, Ben. 1988. The sexualization of tourism in Jamaica. *The Star* (September 3).

Holden, Peter, Jurgen Horlemann, and Georg Friedrich Pfafflin. 1983. *Tourism, Prostitution and Development.* Bangkok: Ecumenical Coalition on Third World Tourism.

Keller, Evelyn Fox. 1989. Women scientist and feminist critics of science. In *Learning About Women,* J. Conway, Bourque and Scott, ed., pp. 77–91. Ann Arbor: University of Michigan Press.

LaFont, Suzanne. 1992. Baby-mothers and baby-fathers: Conflict and family court use in Kingston, Jamaica. Ph.D. dissertation. Yale University.

Lea, John. 1988. *Tourism and Development in the Third World.* New York: Routledge.

Leacock, Eleanor Burke. 1981. *Myths of Male Dominance.* New York: Monthly Review Press.

Leed, Eric J. 1991. *The Mind of the Traveler.* New York: Basic Books.

MacCannell, Dean. 1973. Staged authenticity: Arrangements of social space in tourist settings. *American Journal of Sociology* 79: 589–603.

———. 1976. *The Tourist, a New Theory of the Leisure Class.* New York: Shocken.

Manning, Frank E. 1982. The Caribbean experience. *Cultural Survival Quarterly* 6(3): 13–14.

Matthews, Harry G. 1977. Radicals and third world tourism. *Annals of Tourism Research* 5: 20–29.

Mead, Margaret. 1935. *Sex and Temperment in Three Primitive Societies.* New York: William Morrow.

Mintz, Sidney. 1981. Economic role and cultural tradition. In *The Black Woman Cross-Culturally,* Filomina Chioma Steady, ed., pp. 515–534. Cambridge: Schenkman.

Moses, Yolanda T. 1981. Female status, the family and male dominance in West Indian community. In *The Black Woman Cross-Culturally,* Filomina Chioma Steady, ed., pp. 499–513. Cambridge: Schenkman.

Nash, Dennison. 1981. Tourism as an anthropological subject. *Current Anthropology* 22(5): 461–481.

Ortner, Sherry B. 1983. The founding of the first Sherpa nunnery and the problem of "women" as an analytic category. In *Feminist Re-visions: What Has Been and Might Be.* Vivian Patraka and Louise Tilly, eds., pp. 98–134. Ann Arbor: Women's Studies Program, University of Michigan.

Ortner, Sherry B., and Harriet Whitehead. 1981. *Sexual Meanings: The Cultural Construction of Gender and Sexuality.* Cambridge: Cambridge University Press.

Powell, Dorian. 1986. Caribbean women and their response to familial experiences. *Social and Economic Studies* 35(2): 83–130.

Pruitt, Deborah J. 1993. "Foreign mind": Tourism, identity and development in Jamaica. Ph.D. dissertation. University of California at Berkeley.

Rhode, Deborah L. 1990. *Theoretical Perspectives on Sexual Difference.* New Haven: Yale University Press.

Robinson, Jane. 1990. *Wayward Women: A Guide to Women Travellers.* New York: Oxford University Press.

Roberts, George W., and Sonja A. Sinclair. 1978. *Women in Jamaica: Patterns of Reproduction and Family.* New York: KTO Press.

Safa, Helen I. 1986. Economic Autonomy and Sexual Equality in Caribbean Society. *Social and Economic Studies* 35(3): 1–22.

Said, Edward W. 1978. *Orientalism.* New York: Pantheon Books.

Seager, Joni, and Ann Olsen. 1986. *Women in the World: An International Atlas.* New York: Simon and Schuster.

SES. 1989. *Social and Economic Survey.* Kingston: Statistical Institute of Jamaica.

Smith, Raymond T. 1956. *The Negro Family in British Guiana: Family Structure and Social Status in the Villages.* London: Lowe and Brydon.

Strathern, Marilyn. 1980. Culture in a netbag: The manufacture of a subdiscipline in anthropology. *Man* 16: 665–668.

Thitas, Khin. 1982. Providence and prostitution. In *International Reports: Women and Society.* London: Change.

Truong, Thanh-Dam. 1990. *Sex, Money & Morality: Prostitution and Tourism in Southeast Asia.* Atlantic Highlands: Zed Books.

Whitehead, Tony L. 1992. Expressions of masculinity in a Jamaican sugartown: Implications for family planning programs. In *Gender Constructs and Social Issues,* Whitehead and Reid, eds., pp. 103–141. Urbana: University of Illinois Press.

Wilson, Peter J. 1973. *Crab Antics: The Social Anthropology of English-Speaking Negro Societies of the Caribbean.* New Haven, CT: Yale University Press.

27

Forced to Choose
Beyond the Voluntary v. Forced Prostitution Dichotomy

Jo Doezema
University of Sussex

INTRODUCTION

At the 1995 United Nations Fourth World Conference on Women in Beijing, I and other delegates from the Network of Sex Work Projects (NSWP) and the Global Alliance Against Trafficking in Women (GAATW) lobbied to ensure that every mention of prostitution as a form of violence against women in the final conference document would be prefaced by the word "forced."[1] Because sex workers' human rights were not mentioned in the draft document, it was impossible to introduce this concept at the Conference. The best we could do was "damage limitation;" keeping abolitionist language out of the final document. Ironically, I found myself lobbying for a recognition of the distinction between voluntary

prostitution and forced prostitution, a distinction I and other sex worker activists had come to realize had been subverted in such a way that it had become a new justification for denying sex workers their human rights.

Does this mean that I deny that some women in the sex industry work in slavery-like conditions or that I deny that it is possible to choose prostitution as a profession? It does not. It means that I argue that the voluntary/forced dichotomy is the wrong theoretical framework with which to analyze the experience of sex workers. The necessity to critically examine the form this theory is taking is all the more pressing now that it is replacing abolitionism as the dominant model of prostitution at the international level.

In this chapter I examine the rise to prominence of the "voluntary" versus "forced" model of sex worker experience, and the implications and consequences of this rise for sex workers' rights. In the first section, I give a short history of feminist attempts to get prostitution on the international political agenda. Second, an examination of relevant international instruments demonstrates that the voluntary/forced dichotomy is replacing the abolitionist model of prostitution. Finally, I seek to show that this dichotomy has become another way of denying sex workers their human rights.

PROSTITUTION AND INTERNATIONAL POLITICS

A Brief History

Early attempts to deal with prostitution internationally were heavily influenced by nineteenth-century feminist activism. It was women like Josephine Butler who first brought the issue of the "white slave trade" to international attention, via a campaign to protect morals of both men and women. The feminist campaign, founded by Butler, began with attempts to repeal the Contagious Diseases Acts in Britain.[2] Under the acts, any woman identified as a "common prostitute" was forced to undergo a fortnightly internal examination. Infected women were interned in specially designated hospital wards, "pseudo-medical prisons for whores."[3]

Feminists in the repeal movement were ambivalent in their attitudes to prostitutes. They recognized a commonality of interests with prostitutes, realizing that the Acts were a threat to the civil liberties of all women. Because any woman could be identified on the word of a police officer as a "common prostitute," any woman, especially a working-class woman, on her own in a certain area at a certain time could be detained and forced to submit to an internal examination. On the other hand, prostitution was seen as "the great social evil," and prostitutes as victims of male vice, who needed to be rescued. Thus, controlling male vice was seen as the key to ending prostitution. Regulation of prostitution was condemned as an official licensing of male vice.

After the repeal of the Acts in 1883, the focus of the campaign shifted from the rejection of government attempts to monitor sexuality to the promotion of repressive measures designed to end vice. The agenda of the social purity movement was dominated by the mirages of white slave trade and child prostitution. This campaign was helped enormously by sensationalist journalists who seized on the titillating tales of deflowered innocence. According to Nicky Roberts, "The typical story involves white adolescent girls who were drugged and abducted by sinister immigrant procurers, waking up to find themselves captive in some infernal foreign brothel, where they were subject to the pornographic whims of sadistic, non-white pimps and brothel-masters."[4] Research indicates that most of the "trafficking victims" were actually prostitutes migrating, like thousands of others, in hope of finding a better life. Roberts notes that, by this stage in the repeal movement, the image of the prostitute had to be "pitched to appeal to the charitable reflexes of middle class Christians" who by then provided the main body of support for the campaign.[5] She calls the results of the social purity campaign "catastrophic" for prostitutes. Although the Contagious Disease Acts were finally repealed in 1886, in many places their regime was continued under a different name, with purity activists now patrolling the streets instead of the police.[6]

The movement for social purity had success in the US and the continent as well as in Britain. By the turn of the century, most of the existing regulatory systems in Europe and the United States had ended, and international efforts had begun to target the "white slave trade." In the five years before the end of the nineteenth century, three international conferences on the prevention of trafficking in women were held.[7] In the early years of the century, two international instruments concerning the trade were created.[8] The League of Nations adopted two conventions dealing with the traffic in women and children.[9] In 1949, the UN adopted the Convention for the Suppression of the Traffic in Persons and the Exploitation of the Prostitution of Others, which combined and superseded the earlier agreements.

Current Approaches

After the 1949 Convention was adopted, both feminist and international concern for prostitution and the traffic in women abated for a time. But since the middle of the 1980s, there has been a new wave of feminist-backed campaigning against trafficking in women, child prostitution and sex tourism. Campaign efforts have succeeded in putting prostitution back at the top of the international agenda.

Prostitution has been a deeply contentious issue for feminists. Women's bodies have been the site of women's oppression: "Female subordination runs so deep that it is still viewed as inevitable . . . rather than as a politically contracted reality. . . . The physical territory of this struggle is women's bodies. The importance of control over women can be seen in the intensity of resistance to laws and social changes that put control of women's bodies in women's hands."[10] Not that feminists agree as to what "control of women's bodies in women's hands" means. Shannon Bell observes that the prostitute body has been a site of struggle for feminists because "The prostitute body is a terrain on which feminists contest sexuality, desire, and the writing of the female body."[11]

The modern anti-trafficking campaign is split along ideological lines on views of prostitution. The fundamental difference of opinion concerns the question of whether or not a person can choose prostitution as a profession. Some feminists argue that all prostitution constitutes a human rights violation. The strongest advocate of this "neo-abolitionist" view internationally is the Coalition Against Trafficking in Women (CATW), founded by Kathleen Barry. Their "Convention on the Elimination of All Forms of Sexual Exploitation of Women," defines prostitution as a form of sexual exploitation just like rape, genital mutilation, incest and battering.[12] Sexual exploitation is defined as "a practice by which women are sexually subjugated through abuse of women's sexuality and/or violation of physical integrity as a means of achieving power and domination including gratification, financial gain, advancement."[13] Prostitution is explicitly named as a violation of women's human rights, and is also held responsible for "subordinating women as a group."[14]

The distinction between free and forced prostitution was developed by the prostitutes' rights movement in response to feminists (and others) who saw all prostitution as abusive.[15] The World Charter for Prostitutes Rights (1985) states "Decriminalize all aspects of adult prostitution resulting from individual decision."[16] This distinction was included in the analysis of some anti-trafficking organizations, such as the Global Alliance Against Trafficking in Women (GAATW) based in Thailand. The GAATW objects to international instruments for "disregarding the will of adult persons engaged in prostitution" and demand that instruments to combat trafficking be "based on respect for human rights, specifically the right of all persons to self determination."[17] Traffic in persons and forced prostitution are "manifestations of violence against women and the rejection of these practices, which are a violation of the right to self determination, must hold within itself the respect for the self determination of adult persons who are voluntarily engaged in prostitution."[18]

CHANGING THE DOMINANT DISCOURSE

The abolitionist viewpoint has defined the terms of the international discourse on prostitution for almost 100 years. This discourse is being challenged by those who see sex work as a legitimate occupation. An examination of relevant UN instruments shows that there has been a shift away from mechanisms based on abolitionist ideology and towards an approach that respects the right to self-determination. This trend is most evident in those UN instruments dealing specifically with women's human rights and violence against women.

The watershed for the shift can be located in the mid-1980s.[19] Before then, UN instruments were abolitionist in character. Since that time, the majority make a distinction between voluntary and forced prostitution. Prostitution is dealt with in many different UN bodies; it is beyond the scope of this chapter to examine them all. Rather, I will focus on key documents and the work of the main bodies to illustrate the shift towards a new discourse.

Abolitionist Instruments

The Preamble to the 1949 Convention for the Suppression of Traffic in Persons and of the Exploitation of the Prostitution of Others states that "prostitution and . . . traffic in persons for the purposes of prostitution are incompatible with the dignity and worth of the human person. . . ." The convention has come under attack from both "sides" in the anti-trafficking debate. There is fundamental disagreement about the ideological approach of the convention. An examination of this disagreement is useful for the light it sheds on the issue of "voluntary" and "forced" prostitution.

Modern abolitionists, ironically, criticize the Trafficking Convention for making a distinction between "voluntary" and "forced" prostitution.[20] Laura Reanda calls this distinction traditional: "A distinction has traditionally been made between prostitution as *a manner of personal choice and a form of work*, perhaps reprehensible but unavoidable, and enforced prostitution, or traffic in persons, considered a slavery-like practice to be combated by the international community. . . . This distinction was formalized in international law from the beginning of this century. . . . These instruments regard prostitution as a human rights violation only if it involves overt coercion or exploitation. They are silent, however, concerning the human rights implications of prostitution per se."[21]

This statement is misleading. The distinction between "voluntary" and "forced" prostitution, as it is currently understood, had no relevance at the time the international instruments to combat trafficking in women were drafted. For the regulationists, the prostitute was a fallen woman, whose personal pathology or inclination to vice, weakness, stupidity, and/or vanity led inevitably to life as a prostitute. Abolitionist ideology firmly fixed the prostitute as a victim. The image of the prostitute as agent, who willingly chooses her occupation, was unimaginable in either of these models. *Prostitution as a matter of personal choice and a form of work* is a concept developed by sex workers that radically contradicts both the regulationist and abolitionist versions of prostitute reality. To equate or collapse the very different analysis of the regulationists and prostitutes' rights supporters denies the radical implications of sex workers' politics.

Apart from abolitionists themselves, there is general agreement that the Trafficking Convention reflects an abolitionist viewpoint. According to the Advisory Committee on Human Rights and Foreign Policy to the Dutch Government:

> Generally speaking, the UN adopts an abolitionist approach and does not make a distinction between forced and voluntary prostitution. It regards both types as morally unacceptable. This attitude emerges forcefully from the 1949 Convention for the Suppression of Traffic in Persons and of the Exploitation of the Prostitution of Others of 1949 (*sic*) which states that prostitution violates human rights and human dignity and represents a threat to the welfare of the individual, the family and the community.[22]

Jean Fitzpatrick concurs: "The 1949 Convention does not draw an explicit distinction between coerced and voluntary prostitution and represents the then current consensus on an 'abolitionist' model."[23] The Working Group on Contemporary Forms of Slavery (WGS) is responsible for reviewing developments in the field covered by the 1949 Convention and for recommending action to be taken.[24] This body has from the beginning taken an abolitionist view, in line with the Trafficking Convention, and their attitude reflects the regular attendance of the International Abolitionist Federation at the WGS meetings.

The Convention on The Elimination of All Forms of Discrimination Against Women (CEDAW) was adopted in 1979. Article 6 deals with prostitution and trafficking in women. It uses the same wording as the 1949 convention, calling upon state parties to "take all appropriate measures . . . to suppress all forms traffic in women and the exploitation of prostitution of women." This would seem to imply that the drafters' intent was abolitionist. However, when the text was drafted, Morocco introduced an amendment to Article 6 which called for the suppression of prostitution in addition to the suppression of the exploitation of prostitution. This amendment was found unacceptable by the Netherlands and Italy, because they considered that the new element of suppression of prostitution unacceptable.[25] The amendment was rejected, thus it can be argued that Article 6 does not consider all prostitution inherently coercive.[26] The Mexico Declaration on the Equality of Women, adopted at the Second UN Conference on Women in 1975, makes no distinction between forced and voluntary prostitution: "Women all over the world should unite to eliminate violations of human rights committed against women and girls such as rape, prostitution, . . . "[27]

Toward a New Perspective

General Recommendation 19 of CEDAW (1992) on violence against women includes specific paragraphs relating to Article 6 (see above) of the Convention. It reaffirms the requirements of Article 6 for states to "suppress all forms of traffic in women and exploitation of the prostitution of others," but also states that "Poverty and unemployment force many women . . . into prostitution. Prostitutes are especially vulnerable to violence because their status, which may be unlawful, tends to marginalize them. They need the equal protection of laws against rape and other forms of violence." Though this text does not specifically distinguish between forced and voluntary prostitution, an important shift in emphasis is apparent. Rather than focusing on repressive measures to eliminate the practice of prostitution, the Committee instead focuses on the prostitute as a subject whose rights can be violated.

The first document to make a clear departure from an abolitionist view of prostitution is the Declaration on the Elimination of Violence Against Women (1993). "Violence against women shall be understood to encompass, but not be limited to, the following: Physical, sexual and psychological violence occurring within the general community, including rape, sexual abuse, sexual harassment and intimidation at work, in educational institutions and elsewhere, trafficking in women and forced prostitution."[28] Jean Fitzpatrick notes that "The Draft Declaration on Violence Against Women

includes only "trafficking in women and forced prostitution" despite notice that the 1949 convention considers all prostitution to have been compelled.[29]

The Declaration on Violence Against Women is the standard against which the activities of the international community must be measured.[30] The implicit distinction between forced and non-forced prostitution recognized by the Declaration signalled that the international community's view of prostitution had changed. Since the adoption of the Declaration, the majority of international agreements denote forced prostitution and trafficking, rather than prostitution itself, as violence against women. The Vienna Declaration and Program of Action of the 1993 World Conference on Human Rights, recognized women's rights as human rights, and urged state parties to adopt the Declaration on Violence Against Women.[31] At the Fourth World Conference on Women, Beijing 1995, the draft of the Platform for Action included abolitionist language in a number of paragraphs, but this language was not retained in the final document. The final document condemns only forced prostitution, not prostitution as such.[32]

Radhika Coomaraswamy, the UN Special Rapporteur on Violence Against Women, also distinguishes between voluntary and forced prostitution: "Some women become prostitutes through 'rational choice,' others become prostitutes as a result of coercion, deception or economic enslavement."[33] Arguably, the most convincing evidence for a displacement of the abolitionist discourse is the fact that she commissioned the GAATW to write a report on trafficking, rather than the CATW.[34]

This shift towards a new perspective on prostitution, while clearly evident, is not occurring at the same speed in all areas of the United Nations dealing with prostitution and trafficking. There is no commitment in the United Nations to an integrated and coordinated prostitution policy.[35] As a result, UN approaches are highly fragmented, with different UN instruments and bodies taking different ideological stances, and even with contradictory positions within the same body or agreement.[36] Some UN organizations, such as UNESCO and the Working Group on Contemporary Forms of Slavery, continue to argue that prostitution itself is a human rights violation.

BEYOND VOLUNTARY/FORCED

So should sex worker organizations be jumping for joy that the right to self determination is being recognized, at least implicitly, at international level? Does this mean that the United Nations and other international organizations are now going to start taking sex workers' human rights seriously, instead of cloaking moral condemnation of sex work under paternalistic "save us for our own good" rhetoric? Before we break out the party hats, we should look at how the concept of self-determination and the distinction between free and forced prostitution are interpreted and being translated into policy by NGOs, governments and intergovernmental agencies. Are the same old stereotypes and moral judgements now being expressed as loathing of forced prostitution?

Criticism of the Campaigns

The distinction between free and forced prostitution has implicitly been recognized by the international community. But international actors and agreements are rarely as vocal about promoting prostitutes rights as they are in condemning forced prostitution. No international agreement condemns the abuse of human rights of sex workers who were not "forced."

I believe that this is the result of two factors. Firstly, though the international community may be agreeing on condemning only forced prostitution as a human rights violation, this does not imply agreement on how to deal with voluntary prostitution; how it is to be defined, if it should be regulated by the state or left to the workers to organize, or even if it exists at all. In fact, it is because there is no agreement about "voluntary" prostitution in the first place that the consensus on "forced" prostitution has come into being. It can be seen as a compromise: those who, for whatever reason, wish to eliminate all prostitution can at least be satisfied that the

"worst" abuses are being dealt with and those who support self-determination are relieved that this right is not threatened.

Secondly, most organizations that acknowledge and support the right to self-determination place much more emphasis on stopping forced prostitution than on sex workers' rights. Partly this is because it is felt that this is more properly the domain of sex worker organizations. Given the fact that sex workers have long demanded the right to speak for themselves, this hesitance is somewhat justified. However, this reluctance to address sex workers' rights can also be attributed to the fact that it is easier to gain support for victims of evil traffickers than for challenging structures that violate sex workers' human rights.

The campaigning efforts of anti-trafficking groups have been instrumental in treating a climate wherein the great majority of sex work, and practically all sex work involving young men and women in developing countries is seen as abuse. Forced prostitution, child prostitution and sex tourism are linked together and made indistinguishable. In the race to produce yet more horrifying stories, and higher numbers, concern for rights loses out to hysteria over victims.

Though most of the criticism of the prostitutes rights' movement has focused on the abolitionist view of sex work, sex workers are now increasingly critical of anti-trafficking campaigners and human rights activists who distinguish between voluntary and forced prostitution, yet who place all their campaigning energy into stopping forced prostitution. They have been criticized for initiating their campaigns without consultation with sex workers and for using the same emotive language as abolitionists thus perpetuating "the stereotype of Asian sex workers as passive and exploited victims."[37] Such victimization, "has grave consequences for all sex workers as it perpetuates the old stereotype that prostitution is bad and should be abolished."[38] Others, such as Alison Murray in her contribution to this book, point out how the dichotomy between voluntary and forced prostitution creates false divisions between sex workers. The "voluntary" prostitute is a Western sex worker, seen as capable of making independent decisions about whether or not to sell sexual services, while the sex worker from a developing country is deemed unable to make this same choice: she is passive, naive, and ready prey for traffickers.[39] Potentially the most frightening division, however, created by the voluntary/forced dichotomy is that of sex workers into guilty/"voluntary" and innocent/"forced" prostitutes, which reinforces the belief that women who transgress sexual norms deserve to be punished. This division is thus a threat to the entire concept of women's human rights.

Innocent Victims

"In any given year, many thousands of young women and girls . . . are lured . . . into forced prostitution."[40] For the general public and bodies concerned with this issue, forced prostitution is very much a matter of coerced innocence. Th picture of the "duped innocent" is a pervasive and tenacious cultural myth.[41] High profile campaigns by NGOs and in the media, with their continued focus on the victim adds yet more potency to the myths. The public is convinced that huge numbers of innocent (read, sexually pure) women and children are being subjected to the perverse whims of degenerate Western men.

In the new discourse of voluntary/forced prostitution, the innocence of the victim determines which side of the dichotomy she will fall under. One of the consequences of thinking about prostitution in terms of choice and force is that it becomes necessary to show that instances of abuse are in fact "forced prostitution." In reports on trafficking, it is often stressed that the women did not "choose" to be prostitutes. Emotive words like "duped," "tricked" or "lured" are used time and time again to show that the women involved did not know what they were letting themselves in for. A good example of the standard scenario runs as follows: "Many women from Russia, Hungary, Poland and other countries in the region are tricked into prostitution in the West, where they had been promised jobs in offices, in restaurants, or as domestic servants. Instead, they find themselves locked up in a brothel, their papers are taken away and their earnings are kept back to repay their 'debts.'"[42]

Human Rights Watch, who did a study of Burmese women and girls trafficked into Thailand, conclude that the "combination of debt-bondage and illegal confinement renders the employment of the Burmese women and girls tantamount to forced labor, which is prohibited under international law."[43] However, the researchers found it necessary to state that only four of the twenty-nine women they interviewed knew they were going to be prostitutes.[44] It is hard to see what relevance this has: surely debt bondage and illegal confinement amount to slavery, whether or not there was initial agreement to work as a prostitute. Still, the innocence of the victim is seen to be of primary importance.

Other reports of "forced prostitution" focus on the aspect of poverty. "Susie is the face of contemporary poverty. That her job as a debt-bonded sex worker is the best economic option available to her is a metaphor for most of the world's women, whose grinding impoverishment in the Third World is accelerating."[45] This "poverty as force" approach has been criticized for its underlying racist and classist implications; even those who would accept "voluntary" prostitution, on the part of well-off Western women, refuse to respect the choice of a woman from a developing country.[46] On the one hand, this shows an underlying rejection of prostitution as a profession—no "normal" woman would choose the work unless "forced" by poverty. On the other, equating poverty with "force" is, like the focus on deceit, a way of establishing the innocence of "trafficked victims" and thus their eligibility for human rights protection.

A third way "innocence" is established is by focusing on the youth of the "victim" as children are assumed to be sexless and thus beyond "guilt."[47] Campaign pamphlet titles like "The Rape of the Innocents" and sickening stories of child abuse galvanize public opinion and get donations.[48] Tellingly, the distinctions between child and adult are blurred so as to include as many as possible in the category of unquestionable innocents. According to a United Nations report on trafficking in Burma "With the growth of sex tourism and the commercial sex trade in neighboring countries of the region, child abuse and exploitation has assumed a new form: sexual trafficking of children across international borders . . . the number of Myanmar [Burma] girls working in Thai brothels has been conservatively estimated at between 20,000 to 30,000, with approximately 10,000 new recruits brought in yearly. *The majority are between 12 and 25 years old.*"[49]

Reality: So What's Going On?

When subjected to scrutiny, the image of the "trafficking" victim turns out to be a figment of neo-Victorian imaginations. Just as the turn of the century obsession with the "white slave trade" turned out to be based on actual prostitute migration, the Dutch Foundation Against Trafficking in Women (STV) and the GAATW, in their report on trafficking to the UN Special Rapporteur on Violence against Women, conclude that slavery-like conditions in sex work are primarily problems for those already working in the sex trade: thus for prostitutes who migrate.[50] But the campaign juggernaut remains unaffected by fact. From the Arab sheik's harem slave to the village girl chained to her bed in the brothels of Bangkok, the image of the defiled innocent has a particular fascination.[51] It is reminiscent of sentiment expressed during a meeting of anti-white slave trade activists at the turn of the century. The women present were exhorted by the speaker to "Remember, ladies . . . 'it is more important to be aroused than to be accurate. Apathy is more of a crime than exaggeration in dealing with this subject.'"[52]

Parallels between the two movements are easily drawn. As a symbol, the "white slave" personified conservative moral fears of women's sexuality and economic independence, and of the growing power of the working class, and reflected racist stereotypes. The nineteenth-century sex slave was a white woman, victim of the animal lusts of the dark races. In the modern myth, the racism has changed focus: "passive," unemancipated women from the developing world are the new sex slaves.

A number of today's campaigns have become a platform for reactionary and paternalistic voices, advocating a rigid sexual morality under the guise of protecting women, and incorporating racist and classist perceptions in their analysis of the sex industry in developing countries. This is particularly the case when campaigners actually succeed in getting governments to do something about "trafficking," for then the focus shifts from women's rights to a hysterical and paranoid reaction to women's increasing sexual autonomy, the "breakdown of the family" and migration. Often, "trafficking" is used by states to initiate and justify restrictive policies.[53] There are still many governments with moral objections to prostitution. At the international level, however, most are politically savvy enough to cloak moral indignation in terms of "victimization of women."

If it is recognized that the majority of those in the sex-industry who end up in debt-bondage or slavery-like conditions were *already* working as sex workers, it is impossible to avoid the conclusion that it is prostitutes whose human rights are being violated on a massive scale. Of course this is unpalatable to the international community: it is one thing to save innocent victims of forced prostitution, quite another to argue that prostitutes deserve rights. It is not only governments who prefer saving innocent women to giving rights to guilty ones. Most feminist discourse on trafficking limits itself to the fight against "forced prostitution," the "voluntary" prostitute is not condemned—she is ignored.

Many governments place the distinction between "guilty" and "innocent" women at the heart of their legislation on prostitution and trafficking. In Germany, the penalty for trafficking is reduced in cases where the victim knew she was going to be a prostitute or when deceit was used on a person who is "not far from being a prostitute."[54] In Columbia, the use of violence to force a person into prostitution is only prohibited in cases where the woman concerned is "of undisputed virtue."[55] Other countries, including Uganda, Canada, Japan, Brazil and El Salvador, have similar provisions.[56] But even in those countries where "the virtue of the woman is not mentioned as an explicit criterion in law," it still "implicitly or explicitly plays a crucial role in the interpretation and enforcement of the law."[57] In the Netherlands, for example, police will refuse to investigate complaints of trafficking by women who continue working as prostitutes. "Supposedly there is no victim: she wanted it all the time, at least, that is what they can conclude from the fact that the woman is willing to work again in prostitution after having filed charges."[58]

Because feminists are undecided about whether or not "voluntary" prostitution exists or how it should be dealt with, their analysis of forced prostitution reinforces rather than challenges stereotypical views of female sexuality. For example, Human Rights Watch Women's Rights Project, in their report on global human rights abuses of women, states that it "takes no position on prostitution per se. However, we strongly condemn laws and official policies and practices that fail to distinguish between prostitutes and victims of forced trafficking."[59]

Focusing on forced prostitution provides a way out for those who are unwilling to admit that the issues raised by the prostitutes' rights movement have to be faced. Governments do not have to be challenged about their treatment of voluntary prostitutes, i.e., "While we recognize the right of governments to make and enforce laws that regulate national borders, they must distinguish between those who purposefully violate immigration laws and others who are victims of forced prostitution."[60] The report is not clear about how a prostitute is to be distinguished from a victim of trafficking. In order for a "victim" to be eligible for the protection recommended by Human Rights Watch, she wold have to prove her innocence, i.e. that she didn't know she was going to be a prostitute. This bears a frightening resemblance to rape trials, in which a victim's chastity status will determine the severity of the crime.

The peculiarities of viewing sex work through the distorting lens of the voluntary/forced dichotomy cause what are clearly abuses of sex workers' rights to be condemned as examples of forced prostitution. Human Rights Watch reports that women in India who are arrested for prostitution are sent to "protective homes" where "inmates complained of grave mistreatment, including branding with hot irons, rapes, and sexual assaults. Almost all inmates were suffering from malnutrition. Many also had skin diseases and tuberculo-

sis."[61] Yet, in the face of this horrific abuse of sex workers' human rights, the best Human Rights Watch can do is reiterate that "victims of trafficking" should be treated differently from prostitutes. Sex workers who are imprisoned and detained, subjected to cruel and degrading mistreatment, who suffer violence at the hands of the state or by private individuals with the state's support, are disqualified from human rights considerations if their status is "voluntary." This is the voluntary/forced dichotomy taken to its extreme and logical conclusion. Human rights organizations and bodies in the United Nations seem content to let governments trample on the rights of sex workers, as long as the morals of "innocent" women are protected.

CONCLUSION

The distinction between "voluntary" and "forced" prostitution has largely replaced the abolitionist model of prostitution in international discourse. This would seem to imply a recognition of the right to self-determination. However, this dichotomy creates divisions between sex workers. The most frightening division created by the voluntary/forced dichotomy is that it reproduces the whore/madonna division within the category "prostitute." Thus, the madonna is the "forced prostitute"—the child, the victim of trafficking; she who, by virtue of her victim status, is exonerated from sexual wrong-doing. The "whore" is the voluntary prostitute: because of her transgression, she deserves whatever she gets. The distinction between voluntary and forced prostitution, a radical and resistive attack on previous discourses that constructed all prostitutes as victims and/or deviants, has been co-opted and inverted, and incorporated to reinforce systems that abuse sex workers rights.

The campaign for sex workers' rights began with challenging the myths surrounding prostitution and women's sexuality. Claiming that prostitution could be a choice was a major step. Yet now, as old myths are being given new impetus under the guise of accepting choice, it is time to reconsider the usefulness of "choice" versus "force" as the model of sex workers' experience.

NOTES

1. The Beijing Declaration and Platform for Action, 1995.

2. These acts, passed in 1864, 1866, and 1869, targeted prostitutes in an attempt to control the spread of venereal disease. See Judith Walkowitz, *Prostitution and Victorian Society: Women, Class and the State* (Cambridge: Cambridge University Press, 1982).

3. Nicky Roberts, *Whores in History: Prostitution in Western Society* (London: HarperCollins, 1992) 248.

4. Ibid., p. 252. It is startling how little this "standard story" has changed in the intervening 100 years: accounts very similar to this are reported in today's media.

5. Ibid., p. 252.

6. Ibid., p. 258.

7. See Lenke Fereh, "Forced Prostitution and Traffic in Persons," in Marieke Klap, Yvonne Klerk and Jacqueline Smith, eds., *Combating Traffic in Persons: Proceedings of the Conference on Traffic In Persons* (Utrecht: IMS, Netherlands Institute of Human Rights, 1995) 68.

8. The International Agreement for the Suppression of the White Slave Traffic, Paris (1904), and the International Convention for the Suppression of the White Slave Traffic (1910).

9. The International Convention to Combat the Traffic in Women and Children (1921) and the International Convention for the Suppression of the Traffic in Women of Full Age (1933). Nicky Roberts links the League's concern with the traffick in women with the re-opening, after World War I, of actual international migration networks and routes used by prostitutes (279).

10. Charlotte Bunch, "Transforming Human Rights from a Feminist Perspective," in Julie Peters and Andrea Wolper, eds., *Women's Rights as Human Rights–International Feminist Perspectives* (London: Routledge, 1996) 15.

11. Shannon Bell, *Reading, Writing and Rewriting the Prostitute Body* (Bloomington: Indiana University Press, 1994) 73.

12. Developed as a replacement for the United Nations 1949 Convention For the Suppression of the Traffic in Persons and of the Exploitation of the Prostitution of Others by The Coalition Against Trafficking in Women (CATW). (Draft) Convention on the Elimination of All Forms of Sexual Exploitation of Women, 1993 Art. 2(b).

13. CATW: (Draft) Convention on the Elimination of All Forms of Sexual Exploitation of Women, 1993 Art. I.

14. Ibid.

15. For a history of the development of sex worker politics to 1986, see Gail Pheterson, ed., *A Vindication of the Rights of Whores* (Washington; The Seal Press, 1989) 3–30.

16. International Committee for Prostitutes Rights, printed in Pheterson, 1989, 40–42.

17. GAATW/STV, "A Proposal to Replace the Convention for the Suppression of the Traffic in Persons and of the Exploitation of the Prostitution of Others," Utrecht, 1994, par 11.2 and. par 111.1, emphasis added.

18. Ibid., par.111.1.

19. This was also the time when the international movement for sex workers' rights reached its peak of organization, with two international conferences held in 1985 and 1986. For documentation of these conferences, see Gail Pheterson, ed., *A Vindication of the Rights of Whores* (Washington: Seal Press, 1989).

20. See Laura Reanda, "Prostitution as a Human Rights Question, Problems and Prospects of United Nations Action," *Human Rights Quarterly* 13 (1991) 209–211, and UNESCO/CATW, "The Penn State Report," 1–2. Pennsylvania, 1992.

21. Reanda, 1991, p. 202, emphasis added.

22. "The Traffic in Persons Report" of the Advisory Committee on Human Rights and Foreign Policy, (The Hague 1992) 16.

23. Jean Fitzpatrick. "Using International Human Rights Norms to Combat Violence Against Women," in Rebecca J. Cook, ed., *Human Rights of Women: National and International Perspectives* (Philadelphia: University of Pennsylvania Press, 1994), p. 552. See also Yvonne Klerk, "Definition of Traffic in Persons," in Klap et al., and Alice M. Miller, "United Nations and Related International Action in the Area of Migration and Traffic in Women," in the *Report of the International Workshop on International Migration and Traffic in Women* (Chiangmai: The Foundation for Women, 1994) 13.

24. The WGS was established in 1974 by the Sub-Commission on Prevention of Discrimination and Protection of Minorities of the UN Human Rights Commission.

25. See Lars Adam Rehof, *Guide to the Travaux Preparatoire of the United Nations Convention on the Elimination of all Forms of Discrimination Against Women* (Dordrecht: Martinus Nijhoff/Kluwer, 1993) 91.

26. This conclusion is supported by R. Haverman and J. C. Hes in "Vrouwenhandel en Exploitatie van Prostitutie," A. W. Heringa et. al., eds., *Het Vrouwenverdrag: Een beeld van een Verdrag* (Antwerpen and Amersfoort: MAKLU, 1994).

27. Declaration of Mexico on the Equality of Women, UN 1975, par. 28 34.

28. Declaration of Mexico on the Equality of Women, UN 1975, Art. 2.

29. Fitzpatrick, 1994, p. 552.

30. Maria Hartle, "Traffic in Women as a Form of Violence Against Women," in Klap et al., eds., *Combating Traffic in Persons: Proceedings of the Conference on Traffic in Persons* (Utrecht: IMS, Netherlands Institute of Human Rights, 1995).

31. The Vienna Declaration and Program of Action, par. 38.

32. Draft Platform For Action (A/CONF.177 .1, 24 May 1995) notably paragraphs 122, 131d, 225; and the Beijing Declaration and Platform for Action, paragraphs 123, 131d, 224.

33. UN EICN 411995142.

34. Marjan Wijers and Lin Lap-Chew, *Trafficking in Women. Forced Labor and Slavery-like Practices in Marriage. Domestic Labor and Prostitution* (Utrecht: The Foundation against Trafficking in Women and the Global Alliance Against Trafficking in Women, 1996), 198.

35. Miller, 1991, p. 1.

36. The above instruments are not all inherently consistent in that several call upon states to ratify the abolitionist Trafficking Convention. However, in calling for the elimination of only "forced prostitution and trafficking" rather than prostitution itself, an implicit recognition of the right to self-determination is evident.

37. See "A Joint Statement of Policy," by the Prostitutes' Rights Organization for Sex Workers; the Sex Workers Outreach Project; Workers in Sex Employment in the ACT; Self-help for Queensland Workers in the Sex Industry; The Support, Information, Education, Referral Association of Western Australia; The South Australian Sex Industry Network; The Prostitutes Association of South Australia; The Prostitute Association Northern Territory for Health, Education, Referrals; Cybelle, Sex Worker Organization Tasmania; Sydney Sexual Health Center, Sydney Hospital; The Queer and Esoteric Workers Union and representatives of Asian sex working communities in New South Wales (1996) 3.

38. Ibid., 3.

39. See also Jo Doezema, "Choice in Prostitution," in *Changing Faces of Prostitution* (Helsinki: UnioniThe League of Finnish Feminists, 1995).

40. *The Human Rights Watch Global Report on Women's Human Rights* (New York: Human Rights Watch, 1995) 196.

41. Roberts, p. 253.

42. Tasha David, *Worlds Apart, Women and the Global Economy* (Brussels: International Confederation of Free Trade Unions, 1996) 43.

43. *Human Rights Watch*, 1995, p. 213.

44. Ibid., p. 210.

45. Angela Matheson, "Trafficking in Asian Sex Workers," *Green Left Weekly* (26 October 1994) 1.

46. See J. Doezema, "Sex Worker Delegation to the Beijing Conference," in Network of Sex Works Projects internal communication, Amsterdam, March 1995, and Alison Murray's contribution to this book. Abject poverty is not usually the primary reason for women to choose sex work or to migrate as a sex worker. Apart from the obvious fact that not all poor women chose to become prostitutes, research shows that there are other important considerations motivating someone's choice to do sex work. See, in this book, Kamala Kempadoo's chapter on the Dutch Caribbean and the research from COIN in the Dominican Republic.

47. In her contribution to this book, Heather Montgomery challenges some of the myths surrounding "child prostitution." See also Maggie Black, "Home Truths," *New Internationalist* (February 1994), 11–13, and Alison Murray, forthcoming, "On Bondage, Peers and Queers: Sexual Subcultures, Sex Workers and AIDS Discourses in the Asia-Pacific."

48. For example, see Ron O'Grady, *The Rape of the Innocent, End Child Prostitution in Asian Tourism* (Bangkok: ECPAT, 1994).

49. *Children and Women in Myanmar: A Situation Analysis* (UNICEF 1995) 38, emphasis added.

50. Marjan Wijers and Lin Lap-Chew, *Trafficking in Women. Forced Labor and Slavery-like Practices in Marriage. Domestic Labor and Prostitution*, (Utrecht: The Foundation against Trafficking in Women and the Global Alliance Against Trafficking in Women, 1996), 198.

51. This fascination has an erotic element: at an 1885 demonstration in London in the wake of a sensational article about the white slave trade "street vendors shifted record numbers of the pornographic magazine *The Devil*." See Roberts, 1992.

52. Roberts, 1992, p. 264.

53. Wijers and Lap-Chew, pp. 111–152.

54. Ibid., p. 126.

55. Ibid., p. 128.

56. Ibid., pp. 126–130.

57. Ibid., p. 153.

58. Marga de Boer, *Traffic in Women: Policy in Focus* (Utrecht: Willem Pompe Institute for Criminal Law, 1994), p. 29.

59. *Human Rights Watch*, 1995, p. 198.

60. Ibid., p. 200.

61. Ibid., p. 253.

◈ PART ELEVEN ◈

THE RIGHT TO SAY NO, THE RIGHT TO SAY YES
GENDER, SEXUALITIES, AND SELF-DETERMINATION

READINGS IN THIS PART

INTRODUCTION TO SUBJECT AND READINGS

Sufiya Huseini, a 35-year-old Nigerian divorcee, has been sentenced to death by stoning. In Nigeria, engaging in unmarried sex, even after a divorce is considered adultery and punishable by death. Huseini became pregnant after her divorce, undisputable proof of unmarried sexual activity. The court is now waiting for her to wean the infant before her sentence will be carried out, leaving the child an orphan. In another Nigerian town, a seventeen-year-old girl was given 100 lashes in public for the crime of premarital sex.[1] Such severe penalties are not necessarily isolated incidents. Equality Now is an organization that tracks gender inequality and human rights abuses. Their latest report included the following examples of gendered injustice:

• Uruguay—Article 116, Extinction of Crime by Marriage states that "Marriage between the offender and the offended extinguishes the crime or the punishment where appropriate, in the case of rape, violent indecent assault, statutory rape or abduction."

- India—Section 375, Exception to rape. "Sexual intercourse by a man with his own wife, the wife not being under the age of sixteen years of age is not rape."
- Nigeria, Section 55, Correction of Child, Pupil, Servant or Wife—"Nothing is an offence which does not amount to the infliction of grievous hurt upon any persons which is done: (d) by a husband for the purpose of correcting his wife . . . "
- Morocco, Article 418—"Murder, injury and beating are excusable if they are committed by a husband on his wife as well as the accomplice at the moment in which he surprises them in the act of adultery."
- Syria, Article 548—"1. He who catches his wife or one of his ascendants, descendants or sister committing adultery or illegitimate sexual acts with another and he killed or injured one or both of them benefits from an exemption of penalty. 2. He who catches his wife or one of his ascendants, descendants or sister in a "suspicious" state with another benefits from a reduction penalty."[2]

These blatant examples of legal gender discrimination attest to the power of the laws. They prove beyond a shadow of a doubt that there is a strong relationship between sexual/gender ideology and civil and human rights. An examination of sex laws involves questioning some of the core beliefs of a society. Sexual ideologies are shaped by a culture's morés and philosophies, determining the right of the state to regulate the sexual behavior. Societies regulate pornography, age of consent, prostitution, reproductive rights, gay and lesbian rights, marriage, adultery and divorce, sodomy, incest, and rape. Human rights, women's rights, gay rights are all either protected or violated when states regulate sexual behavior.

Douglas Jehl discusses honor killings in Jordan in the article, *Arab Honor's Price: A Woman's Blood.* If an unmarried Jordanian woman engages in sexual activity, her family is dishonored, but if a family member kills the woman, the family's honor is restored. There is no more poignant example of gendered sexualities than the value placed on female chastity in Arab culture. Honor killings are reported in Jordan, Egypt, Syria, Lebanon, Yemen, Iraq, the Palestinian territories, and among Israeli Arabs. The message is clear, "If you stray, you die."

What appears to be a shocking disregard for women's human rights is guarded as a cultural right, and attempts to reform the laws or discourage honor killings are perceived as immoral intervention from Western culture. How women's status shape and constrain their freedom is a hotly contested issue. While many Westerners view the burqa as an obvious affront to women's freedom, many Arabs, including Arab women, would view a Victoria's Secret fashion show as the degrading result of Western liberalization. What kind of freedom induces seminaked anorexic women to publically flaunt surgically augmented breasts?

The next article deals with another kind of sexual freedom. The freedom to say no. *Women: Wives, Mothers, Daughters* by Chris Beyrer discusses how Thai women's health is negatively impacted because of male dominance. In Thailand, as in many other countries, there is a double standard of sexual behavior for women and men. Women are supposed to be faithful, subservient wives. Men, on the other hand, are allowed, if not expected, to visit sex workers. As Beyrer notes, "Sex workers are for sexual pleasure, wives for producing heirs." Culturally, Thai wives are supposed to be passive sex partners who are eager to bear children. Therefore, although their husbands engage in high-risk sexual behavior, they are reluctant to ask them to use condoms. There have been so many AIDS deaths, that the gender/sexuality status quo is changing.

Beyrer discusses the surprising, unexpected shifts in the Thai gender/sexuality system due to the AIDS epidemic.

Negotiating Sex and Gender in the Attorney General's Commission on Pornography by Carole S. Vance may, at first, seem out-of-place in this section. But her article, like the other two, exposes the gendered nature of the law. The United States regulates/criminalizes the following behaviors: Rape and sexual assault, age of consent, age for marriage, sodomy, public nudity, public indecency, fornication, adultery, incest, bigamy, bestiality, necrophilia, prostitution, pandering, pimping, obscene communications, voyeurism, possession of obscene materials.

Vance's article deals with legislating obscenity and pornography. Protection or censorship? Through different periods of history, the writings of Confucius, Venus de Milo, the theories of Darwin, *The Adventures of Huckleberry Finn*, and songs by John Lennon and Bob Dylan have all been censored. Who decides what is obscene? In the United States, a special commission was appointed in 1985 to explore the social impact of sexually explicit images and texts on the American public. Vance analyzes the way the Meese Commission approached the issue of pornography. She demonstrates how the conservative agenda of banning pornography was aided by feminists. Because some feminists believe that all pornography is degrading to women, they support a total ban. Other feminists argue that there is a fine line between pornography and erotica. Banning pornography to protect women inhibits women's sexualities and treats women like children who need special protection because of their "weaker" status. This article, which has become a classic, warns that censorship can make for strange bedfellows.

The fundamental issue regarding the regulations of gender and sexualities is the tension between the rights of the individual versus protection of the individual. The justification of sexual regulations has usually been tied to the issue of victimization. However, morality lurks in the shadows of sexual legislation which is too often a conservative agenda dressed up in protectionist clothing.

TERMS AND CONCEPTS

anti-pornography feminist	honor killings
child prostitution/pornography	human rights
civil liberties	obscenity laws
female chastity	serial monogamy
fundamentalists	

CRITICAL THINKING AND QUESTIONS TO CONSIDER

1. List some of the ways in which the Arab world's concept of honor impacts Arab women's sexualities.
2. According to Beyrer, how did most HIV positive Thai women contract the disease? What type of behavior puts them at the most risk?
3. The HIV/AIDS epidemic has changed Thai women's sexual behavior. Describe the unexpected changes in Thai gender relations.
4. Describe the cultural, economic, and political factors contributing to the high percentages of infants being born HIV positive in the Third World.

5. According to Vance, why did the Meese Commission appropriate anti-porn feminist rhetoric in its campaign against porn?
6. Censorship comes down to a struggle between civil liberties and protectionism. What was the Meese Commission trying to protect? How did their agenda differ from that of the anti-porn feminists?
7. Drawing on Doezema's (from the previous part) and Vance's articles, explain how and why prostitution and pornography has divided feminists.

NOTES

1. Dowden, Richard, Death by Stoning, *The New York Times*, 1–27–2002.
2. These facts are listed on the Equality Now website, *www.equalitynow.org*

FURTHER READINGS

Beyrer, Chris. 1998. *War in the Blood: Sex, Politics and AIDS in Southeast Asia*. New York: Zed Books, Ltd.

Cook, Rebecca (ed.). 1994. *Human Rights of Women: National and International Perspectives*. Philadelphia: University of Pennsylvania Press.

Cornell, Drucilla (ed.). 2000. *Feminism and Pornography*. New York: Oxford University Press.

Fineman, Martha Albertson, and Nancy Sweet Thomadsen (eds.). 1991. *At the Boundaries of Law: Feminism and Legal Theory*. New York: Routledge.

Frank, Martina W., and Heidi M. Brauer, et. al. 1999. Virginity examinations in Turkey: Role of forensic physicians in controlling female sexuality. *The Journal of the American Medical Association*, Vol. 282, pp. 485–490.

Gruen, Lori, and George E. Panichas (eds.). 1997. *Sex, Morality and the Law*. New York: Routledge.

Kinsman, Gary. 1996. *The Regulation of Desire: Homo and Hetero Sexualities*. Cheektowago: Black Rose Books.

Nussbaum, Martha C. 1999. *Sex and Social Justice*. New York: Oxford University Press.

Parker, Richard, Regina Maria Barbosa, and Peter Aggleton (eds.). 2000. *Framing the Sexual Subject: The Politics of Gender, Sexuality, and Power*. Berkeley: University of California.

Segal, Lynne, and Mary McIntosh (eds.). 1992. *Sex Exposed: Sexuality and the Pornography Debate*. London: Virago Press.

Stone, Linda, and Caroline James. 1995. Dowry, bride-burning, and female power in India. *Women's Studies International Forum* 18 (2): 125–135.

Vance, Carole S. (ed.). 1984. *Pleasure and Danger: Exploring Female Sexuality*. New York: Routledge.

RELATED WEBSITES

Amfar—The American Foundation for AIDS Research
   www.amfar.org

Equality Now—Organization working for the promotion and protection of the human rights of women around the world
   www.equalitynow.org

International Laws (regarding sexual rights)
   www.world/legal.html

JAMA HIV/AIDS—The Journal of the American Medical Association HIV/AIDS Resource Center
> *www.ama-assn.org/special/hiv/hivhome.htm*

Lambda—Legal and Education Fund—Organization supporting the civil rights of lesbians, gay men, and people with HIV/AIDS
> *www.lambdalegal.org*

National Coalition Against Censorship
> *www.ncac.org*

Sexuality and Law: Legal Essays (Cambridge University)
> *www.cam.ac.uk/ESSAYS/sexual.htm*

Sexuality, Gender, and the Law: National and International (University of Chicago)
> *www.lib.uchicago.edu/~llou/sexkaw.html*

UNAIDS—Joint United Nations Programme on HIV/AIDS
> *www.unaids.org*

28

Arab Honor's Price
A Woman's Blood

Douglas Jehl

The New York Times

RESAIFAH, Jordan—It took six years for the al-Goul family to hunt down their daughter Basma.

She had run away with a man, afraid for her life after her husband suspected her of infidelity. Her husband divorced her and, in hiding, she married the other man. But back in this overcrowded, largely Palestinian village, where a woman's chastity is everyone's business, the contempt for her family kept spreading.

"We were the most prominent family, with the best reputation," said Um Tayseer, the mother. "Then we were disgraced. Even my brother and his family stopped talking to us. No one would even visit us. They would say only, 'You have to kill.'"

Um Tayseer went looking for Basma, carrying a gun. In the end, it was Basma's 16-year-old brother, just 10 when she ran away, who pulled the trigger.

"Now we can walk with our heads held high," said Amal, her 18-year-old sister.

What is **honor**? Abeer Allam, a young Egyptian journalist, remembered how it was explained by a high-school biology teacher as he sketched the female reproductive system and pointed out the entrance to the vagina.

"This is where the family **honor** lies!" the teacher declared, as Allam remembers it.

More than pride, more than honesty, more than anything a man might do, female chastity is seen in the **Arab** world as an indelible line, the boundary between respect and shame. An unchaste woman, it is sometimes said, is worse than a murderer, affecting not just one victim, but her family and her tribe.

It is an unforgiving logic, and its product, for centuries and now, has been murder—the killings of girls and women by their relatives, to cleanse **honor** that has been soiled.

Across the **Arab** world, in Jordan, Egypt, Syria, Lebanon, Yemen, the Palestinian territories and among Israeli Arabs, a new generation of activists has quietly begun to battle these **honor** killings, an enduring wave of attacks prompted by sexual conduct that is sometimes only imagined.

In Jordan, home to the most candid talk about the issue, the Government under King Abdullah has promised to join in the fight, following the example set by the late King Hussein and Queen Noor, who helped to lift a lid on public discussion of the killings. At a conference in Jordan in early June, delegates from the region were asked to develop ways to respond "sensitively to the situation in countries of concern." But those engaged in the battle say it would be hard to exaggerate the magnitude of the opposition they face.

Across today's **Arab** world, modernizers may be wrangling with traditionalists, and secularists with Islamists, but a nationalism overlain by Islam remains a powerful political force. Even leaders like the late King Hussein and Egypt's President, Hosni Mubarak, long entrenched, have had to balance pro-Western outlooks against the risk of being seen as the instruments of outsiders.

Activists trying to call attention to **honor** killings say they face a similar challenge from those who portray their campaign as an assault on **Arab** ways. "They accuse me of trying to make the country promiscuous," said Asma Khader, a Jordanian lawyer who is a leader in efforts to tighten the laws against **honor** killing.

Even in places like Resaifah, a largely Palestinian village of noisy streets and dirt alleyways 45 minutes from Jordan's capital, Amman, contempt for **honor** killing can be heard. "If you spit, does it come back clean?" said Sheik Ali al-Auteh, 57, a tribal leader, mocking the idea that **honor** could be cleansed with blood.

"A guy who kills might think that dishonor goes away," said his daughter, Yousra, 17. "But when he walks past, people will say, 'There goes the guy who killed his daughter.'"

THE CODE: BROAD ACCEPTANCE OF TRIBAL JUSTICE

Yet the stories told by the al-Goul family and others, including killers and women who were attacked by their families, suggest a broad acceptance of an unwritten code, one that sees the unchaste woman as a threat. As long as they can remember, girls like Amal al-Goul say, their brothers warned them: If you stray, you die.

And when a woman like Basma al-Goul is thought to have crossed the line, her family is ostracized, with her eight sisters deemed unmarriageable by the neighbors, and her five brothers confronted with taunts in the street. It was after other boys questioned his manhood, saying that Basma should be dead, the family said, that Mahmoud al-Goul ran to shoot his sister down.

"Before my sister was killed," Amal, the 18-year-old said, "I had to walk with my eyes to the ground."

Most often, the killings occur among the poorer and less educated, particularly in **Arab** tribal societies like Jordan's and the Palestinians, with long traditions of self-administered justice. The killings are rare among the educated and urbane.

But even among those upper classes, it is rare to hear condemnation of the killings. Across **Arab** society, a bride is expected to be a virgin, and other people's justice is not a subject for polite company.

In dozens of conversations in the **Arab** world in recent months, lawyers, laborers, clerics, cooks, physicians and politicians said most often that, personally, they could not condone **honor** killing. But most also said they felt the tug of traditions that could lead a man to kill, and some suggested that they would be inclined to act on them.

"I would do what I have to do," said Bassam al-Hadid, a Jordanian with an American doctorate who spent 12 years as a hospital administrator in the United States, when asked whether he would kill a daughter who had sex outside marriage.

Even some victims of the attacks said they deserved their fate. "He shouldn't have let me live," said Roweida, 17, who was shot three times by her father after she confessed to an adulterous affair, and, along with dozens of girls with similar stories, is being held for her own protection in a Jordanian prison. "A girl who commits a sin deserves to die."

THE SYSTEM: BUILT-IN EMPATHY FOR THE KILLER

Among all **Arab** countries, only Jordan publishes what are considered credible crime statistics, so the extent of **honor** killing is difficult to gauge. Often the killings are hushed up, experts say, and disguised as accidental deaths. And, most often, the killings occur outside the big cities, far from government scrutiny.

Except in Jordan, government officials tend to treat the issue as taboo, at least in response to queries from foreign journalists.

But the statistics show that **honor** killings regularly claim 25 lives a year in Jordan alone, about one in four homicides in a country of just four million people, according to Jordanian officials.

In Egypt, which last reported crime statistics in 1995, a Government report counted 52 **honor** killings out of 819 slayings. In Yemen, with a population of 16 million, Mohammed Ba Obaid, who heads the department of Women's Studies in Sanaa University, said his surveys found that more than 400 women were killed for reasons of **honor** in 1997, the last year for which research is complete.

"The culture does not allow any other choice for males," said Dr. Obaid, who attended the recent conference in Jordan and called the figures "very alarming."

The killings are also known in Lebanon, Syria, Iraq and other Persian Gulf countries, and among Arabs in Israel, the West Bank and Gaza. The experts say it would be safe to estimate that the number of **Arab** women killed for reasons of **honor** amounts to hundreds each year.

But in most countries, activists and human-rights groups say, most killers receive light punishment, when they are prosecuted at all. **Arab** judges, who are almost always male, are generally allowed great latitude in sentencing, and most tend to see **honor** as a circumstance akin to self-defense.

"Nobody can really want to kill his wife or daughter or sister," said Mohammed Ajjarmeh, chief judge of the High Criminal Court in Jordan. "But sometimes circumstances force him to do this. Sometimes, it's society that forces

him to do this, because the people won't forget. Sometimes, there are two victims—the murdered and the murderer."

That sense of empathy is built into judicial procedures.

An explicit exemption in Jordanian law, for example, allows a man who kills a female relative surprised in an act of adultery or fornication to be judged "not guilty" of murder. Another loophole sought out by most defendants allows leniency for those who can persuade the court that their sense of lost **honor** caused them to act in an uncontrollable rage.

A Jordanian found guilty in an **honor** killing can be sentenced to as little as six months of prison. If the killing is ruled to be premeditated, the minimum penalty is a year. No similar forgiveness is offered to a woman who kills, even if the circumstances are the same.

Those are the laws that Jordan's Government has signaled that it intends to toughen. But, in an indication of the depth of opposition in place around the region, the speaker of the lower house of Parliament, Abul-Hadi al-Majali, and the District Attorney of Amman, Tawfiq al-Quaisi, said in interviews that they opposed the effort.

"There is an internalized belief that the woman is the one responsible for shame, because she could have resisted the seduction," said Zahra Sharabiti, a Jordanian lawyer who specializes in defending those accused of **honor** killings. In Egypt and in Jordan, convicted killers who opened their doors warily to a Western stranger soon spoke with a defiant pride about the justice they administered and received.

"We do not consider this murder," said Wafik Abu Abseh, a 22-year-old Jordanian woodcutter, as his mother, brother and sisters nodded in agreement. "It was like cutting off a finger."

Last June, Abu Abseh killed his sister, bashing her over the head with a paving stone when he found her with a man. He spent just four months in prison.

Marzouk Abdel Rahim, a Cairo tile maker, stabbed his 25-year-old daughter to death at her boyfriend's house in 1997, then chopped off her head.

He also said he had no regrets. "**Honor** is more precious than my own flesh and blood," said Abdel Rahim, who was released after two months.

In fact, **honor** is so precious that it is not unusual, experts say, for a victim to be slain on the basis of rumor alone. As often as not, said Dr. Hani Jahshan, the deputy medical examiner of Jordan, his autopsy of a woman slain for reasons of **honor** will find that her hymen is intact.

In Jordan, premarital sex is a criminal offense, regarded as equal to adultery, while a girl under 18 who engages in consensual sex is deemed to have been raped. A woman cannot leave home without the permission of her family, and an unmarried woman who becomes pregnant is not merely a criminal, but, by law, her child is taken away at birth to be raised in an orphanage.

Dr. Jahshan's duties include examining girls and women taken into custody and accused of involvement in breaking sex laws. His findings are reported to the police and prosecutors, not to the girls' families. But three times already, girls he examined alive have been returned to him dead.

The most recent was a 17-year-old girl arrested as a runaway this spring. Her father had heard that the girl and her 16-year-old sister had been in restaurants with men. Dr. Jahshan found that the girl was a virgin, and she was ordered released by the authorities, who first obtained assurances from her family that she would be safe.

But two weeks later, the girl was back on his table, killed, along with her sister, by her father and two brothers, who could not believe that they were innocent.

"Working here is very difficult," Dr. Jahshan said, as he showed forensic photographs of the bruised, burned, battered or punctured bodies of the young women who have come to him as corpses. "We have to solve this problem."

Honor killings are not exclusively an **Arab** phenomenon. They are known in India, Pakistan and Turkey, among other places, particularly among poor, rural Muslims. Many Arabs complain that attention to their society's portion of the problem reflects a Western tendency to see them as backward.

"When a Western man kills his lover or wife, the crime is called a crime of passion," said Mohammed Haj Yahya, an **Arab**-Israeli sociologist at Hebrew University in Jerusalem who is active in efforts to combat **honor** killings. "But when it happens in **Arab** societies, it is called a family **honor** killing, and we are viewed as barbarous." Still, the prevailing tendency in the **Arab** world has been to leave the phenomenon unexplored. In Egypt, Lebanon, Syria, the West Bank and other places where **honor** killings take place, newspapers rarely mention such killings.

THE FERVOR: ISLAM'S TEACHINGS AND CHASTITY

When an American news magazine wrote earlier this year about the killings in Jordan, its Egyptian counterpart, Rose al-Youssef, issued a loud defense, saying that the notion that such a "brutal custom" was still being practiced was a product of foreigners' imaginations.

But what distinguishes honor killings in the Arab world is that they are seen less as crimes of passion than as inherently just. "Women are largely looked upon as bodies owned and protected by the husband, by the father, by the brother or even other relatives," said Salwa Bakr, a novelist who is Egypt's most prominent feminist writer.

In many Arab countries, judges see honor killings as a circumstance akin to self-defense. Ayman, 38, in jail in Amman, Jordan, for killing his sister over her sexual relationship with a man, said he expected a sentence of less than a year.

"And these crimes are committed under the pretext that these men are defending not only their honor, but society's morality."

Abu Abseh, the Jordanian who killed his sister with a paving stone, was doing more. He was administering God's law, he said. "We are Muslims," Abu Abseh's older brother said, "and in our religion, she had to be executed." That is certainly a misunderstanding of Islam, Islamic scholars say, but it is not an uncommon one.

As a result of a fundamentalist fervor that has touched much of the Arab world in the last two decades, Islamic faith has come to be worn more and more often as a badge of honor. Sometimes, it as a badge less earned than invoked, for purposes that do not always have a basis in the Koran.

"These crimes are occurring because of ignorance of Islam—by the women who commit these un-Islamic acts, but also by the men who kill them," said Abul Menem Abu Zant, a prominent Islamic leader in Jordan.

For women, and for men, Islam does put a premium on chastity, and it prescribes harsh punishments for sexual misconduct—death for adultery, flogging for fornication. But Islam also teaches that religious authorities, not family members, be the judges, and that any punishment be deferred until a considered judgment is reached.

Islamic teachings caution further against false accusations. Only repeated confessions from the accused or the testimony of four male witnesses are seen as conclusive evidence of sexual misconduct. "Treat your women well, and be kind to them," the Prophet Mohammed is recorded as saying.

But Islam has always coexisted and, in some practices, become intertwined with older Arab traditions. One pre-Islamic Arab custom still prevalent in Mohammed's time was known as almaoudeh—the practice, explicitly condemned in the Koran, of burying baby daughters alive so that they would not later cause the family shame.

The era that preceded Islam's arrival in the 7th century is now known to Muslims as Al Jahiliya, or the Age of Ignorance. But its traditions of harsh justice, rendered in verse by the 10th-century poet Al Motanabi ("Your utmost honor will not be cleansed, until blood is spilled," he wrote) have survived in Arab folklore and culture.

Even today, Arab Christian as well as Muslim men are often advised on their wedding night, only half in jest, to "slaughter the cat." The phrase is a reference to a tale in which a groom brutally beheads a kitten in the bedchamber before having sex with his virgin bride. If she strays, the man tells her, she will suffer the cat's fate.

Honor killings are not committed by Arab Muslims alone. Arab Christians are a small minority today in places like Egypt, Jordan, and the Palestinian territories, but they account for a proportionate share of those killings, experts say.

It is among Arab tribes, whose centuries of intermarriage have created powerful bonds, that traditional notions of honor may be most enduring. Even in modern urban life, in places like Jordan, many people identify most strongly with a tribe, so that the conduct of one reflects on all.

"When a man's daughter does a wrong, he cannot sit amongst men," Banjes al-Hadid, a member of Jordan's Parliament and a prominent tribal leader, told a visitor to his home, atop Amman's highest hill.

"He will be ostracized. They will not even give him coffee. Who would like to kill his wife or daughter? But if he does not, in a village or among a tribe, they will look down on him."

Some people, like Sheik Abu Zant, the Islamic leader, argue that stricter allegiance to Islam is the answer. They note that honor killing, by most accounts, is far less common in Islamic countries like Saudi Arabia and Iran, which have imposed strict Islamic law and where premarital sex, sometimes, is indeed punished by lashing, and adultery by death.

If Jordan were to follow that example, Sheik Abu Zant said, fathers, brothers and sons would be less inclined to carry out the honor killings that some now justify as taking Islamic law into their own hands.

But a broader consensus holds that a better solution is silence, when it comes to sexual misconduct. "You have to cover it up," said Sheik Hadid. "If no one knows what happened, everyone will be more secure."

One option pursued by some young Arab women is surgery. On her wedding night, an Arab bride is expected to bleed. A woman who does not can expect to be hauled to a gynecologist by her husband, who would demand to be told whether she had truly been a virgin.

THE SOLUTIONS: PROPOSALS OF SHARIA AND OF SILENCE

For women who have had premarital sex, a way to avoid discovery is known as hymen restoration. As long as the woman's sexual experience has been limited, gynecologists say, the surgical procedure is simple and inexpensive—a stitching together of what remains of the hymen, usually a few days before the wedding, so that it will tear again during intercourse.

In Egypt, Jordan, and most other Arab countries, the procedure is illegal, because it is seen as defrauding the husband. But it is also widely practiced.

"What's important is saving the woman's life," said a Jordanian gynecologist who asked not to be identified.

Banjes al-Hadid, a member of Jordan's Parliament and a prominent tribal leader, supports honor killing.

But the more traditional Arab way to cover up is through a kind of shotgun marriage that keeps honor intact. Tribal leaders in Jordan, who serve with the blessing of the Government, say they act as intermediaries many dozens of times a year, sometimes at the request of young women, and sometimes by their families, in the hope of legitimizing a union before it becomes fodder for gossip.

If the male partner is reluctant, Sheik Hadid said, he makes a powerful plea: "Do you want her parents to kill her? Do you want her to die?" And as cruel as it may sound, Sheik Hadid said, he tries to arrange marriages between the sexual partners even in cases of violent rape. "It might not be her fault," he said, "but as I see it, the girl has no other choice."

Until the Egyptian Parliament acted in April, that thinking was built into Egyptian law, with the statute that promised a pardon to any rapist who agreed to marry his victim. One attempt to change that statute failed last December, and the usually compliant Parliament did not finally acquiesce until Mubarak ordered it repealed by decree.

And even now, some Egyptian legal scholars argue that old provision should be restored. "Executing or putting a rapist in jail does not help anyone," said Mustafa Ewis, a senior lawyer in Cairo's Legal Resource Research Center, which describes itself as a human-rights advocacy group. "But if he marries the victim, then it helps both of them,

giving them a chance to start fresh and to protect the girl from social stigma."

The attitude is repellent to people like Fawziya Abdel Sattar, a leading law professor and former member of the Egyptian Parliament who was active in pressing for the change. "Instead of punishing the rapist, the law gave him back his victim to re-rape her, legally this time," Ms. Abdel Sattar said.

Still, once the specter of shame begins to loom, some families come to see killing as the only choice. In March, the family of Amal, a 17-year-old Jordanian, discovered that she was pregnant. She told them she had been raped in December by a friend of her father's, who was staying in the family home. Her sister-in-law sold her gold jewelry to pay for an abortion.

But the doctor refused to perform the procedure, which is illegal in Jordan. And so instead, Amal said, her father decided to use the money to buy a gun.

The next day, he sent her mother and younger siblings from the house, closed the windows and curtains, then turned the music loud. As Amal lay on a mattress in her room, the father and her 22-year-old brother took turns with the revolver, shooting her eight times and leaving her for dead.

Amal's brother is still in jail, but her father is already free on bail. And Amal, now bullet-scarred and six months pregnant, is also in jail, with much less hope of swift release.

Officially, she is being held for her protection.

Her father, brother and her cousins all still want to kill her. But she is also a prisoner of her culture, and of a paternalistic Jordanian law that allows a woman to be released only to a close male relative.

Among the 40 or so other Jordanian women caught with Amal in a similar limbo, prison officials say, many have been in custody for years—one since 1990.

Some activists have begun to conclude that their only escape from honor's thrall may be to leave Jordan forever, through complicated arrangements that require the help of foster families abroad. "They should be considered social refugees," said Ms. Khader, the Jordanian lawyer.

29

Women
Wives, Mothers, Daughters

Chris Beyrer
Johns Hopkins University

The basic strategy for the prevention of sexual transmission of HIV has comprised three messages: reduce the number of your sex partners (toward monogamy, if possible); use condoms every time you have penetrative intercourse; promptly treat all sexually transmitted diseases (STDs) and reduce (with condoms and partner reduction) your risk of acquiring new STDs. This strategy grew out of prevention efforts by and for gay men, with the 'sex negative' input of bodies like the US Centers for Disease Control (CDC), which was mandated to include promotion of monogamy in its messages. And it has worked, albeit with varying degrees of success. This triple approach has also had some utility for sexually active heterosexual adults and adolescents, largely in the West, and for sex workers and their clients in many countries. For people with multiple sex partners by

Source: Women: Wives, mothers, daughters, by Chris Beyrer in *War in the Blood: Sex, Politics and AIDS in Southeast Asia.* New York: Zed Books Ltd:, 1998, pp. 119–127. © 1998 Chris Beyrer. Used with permission of the author.

choice, HIV risks can be sharply reduced by adhering to consistent condom use and STD treatment.

Now imagine yourself a young married woman, in Thailand or Cambodia, Burma or Malaysia. You have only one sex partner, your husband. He is your sexual life. Your risks are his risks. You may or may not know what they are. You may or may not be able to ask. 'Reducing the number of sex partners' means not having sex with him, and thus, not at all. This is not an option for many women, no matter what their husband's behavior entails. It would mean giving up having children, an option very few women can accept, particularly among the rural poor, still the vast majority of Asians, for whom the focus of life itself is the family. 'Use condoms for penetrative sex.' Why? Why introduce condoms into your marriage? Condoms again represent your husband's risks, and again imply reduced fertility. Using them acknowledges that he *has* risks, has other partners, goes to brothels or has a mistress or sleeps with men or injects drugs. And *he* has to put the condom on, has to accept the need to protect you from his behavior. (Thai men, for example, usually report using condoms with sex workers to protect themselves, recognizing their own risk. The acknowledgement that as a user of commercial sex services they could spread HIV to others is unusual.) 'Reduce the risk of STDs' is another ambiguous message for most women. If they get gonorrhea, or syphilis, it is, again, their husband's behavior that is at issue. What can a woman do about reducing her partner's risks for STDS, or his need for treatment? To speak of these issues is to suggest infidelity. This can be frightening. It can be deadly.

If this scenario seems an unlikely or uncommon one, it may be because we're used to thinking of HIV in terms of 'high-risk sex'. Anal intercourse aside, there is no higher-risk sexual activity for HIV than trying to conceive a child. It requires regular unprotected intercourse, the exchange of just those fluids that carry and transmit HIV. Death and life in one ejaculate, a parasitic mechanism of 'fearful symmetry'. Wives outnumber sex workers by many orders of magnitude in all of the countries in this study. Probably in every society. By far the most common risk factor for HIV among women in Thailand is marriage, the having of one male partner. This is already true in India, in Burma, and in much of Africa. How else can we explain the report of the Myanmar National AIDS Program that 175,000 pregnant women in Burma were already HIV-infected by 1995? These are not addicts, or 'loose women', or sex workers, though a small minority may be. These are women whose HIV exposure comes from just the behaviors their society most strongly supports: marriage, conception, giving birth to children.

We have very little to offer women in this situation, the bulk of people now most at risk worldwide. The male condom is problematic. It is strongly associated with prostitutes, 'risky' sex and 'risky' partners, mistrust, and sex without love or commitment. A married woman in Malaysia or Thailand would probably be mortified to buy one. The female condom may be an improvement, but it is expensive, still requires male consent for use,

shows outside the vulva, and requires that a woman be willing to insert it. Many Asian women are psychologically unable to touch themselves internally. Many have never had a gynecological examination. *Our Bodies, Ourselves* has not been translated into Shan, or Lao, or Punjabi.

Looking at another gynecological disease may help to illustrate these challenges. Cervical cancer in women is a growing problem worldwide. It has been linked to another sexually transmitted agent, HPV, the human papilloma virus, which can cause genital warts in men and women. Women with only one lifetime sex partner are exposed to HPV by that partner. But HPV is tricky, like HIV. HPV-infected men often have no symptoms, although when they do, the warty lesions of penile HPV are unmistakable. In Thai they are called 'Nok Kai' the cock's comb, which they do somewhat resemble, and are one of the few STDs with such a precise folk translation. Cervical cancer is unusual among gynecologic cancers in that we have a cheap and effective screening test, the Pap smear, for early detection. Caught in the first stages, this is a curable disease. Despite the relative ease and low cost of Pap smears, they are rarely done in developing countries. Most cervical cancer in Thailand, the only Southeast Asian country for which we have reasonable data, is found in later, less treatable stages, or at incurable ones. Pap smears are not done routinely because pelvic examinations are not done routinely. Sex workers get pelvic examinations to look for STDs. Housewives and mothers do not. It should not come as a surprise to find that cervical cancer is the leading cause of cancer death among Thai women—all women, not just sex workers.

When we think of protecting women from HIV, now an incurable infection, this reality has to be kept in mind. Limitations on women's health care in much of Asia have already led to a serious failure of prevention for a common and potentially curable disease. HIV will be no easier to prevent than cervical cancer. And, while both diseases are sufficient to kill a woman, their interaction is even more deadly. HIV-infected women progress to cervical cancer more quickly than women without HIV, and HIV-positive women are more likely to infect their sex partners with HPV, since the wart virus can grow without the hindrances of a healthy immune system. The viruses accelerate each other, a phenomenon Dr. Judy Wasserheit of the CDC has called 'epidemiologic synergy'. (This synergy has also led to an increase in the number of cases of a previously rare disease, carcinoma of the anus, among men infected with both HIV and anal HPV.)

HIV exposes women's vulnerability to male sexual behavior. What can women do about it? How will women in Southeast Asia respond?

About 60 women meet each week at a Buddhist temple in Doi Saket district, Chiang Mai Province. Doi Saket was once a rural area, with a small country town and a number of farming villages. Urban sprawl has brought Doi Saket's farmers into the growing suburban economy; land has been sold for subdivisions; many villagers commute to work in the city; young people leave Doi Saket early, for schooling and for work. These changes have brought some prosperity, but not without costs. The cash economy, and men and women leaving villages for work, have loosened social structures, separated families, changed women's lives. This period of social change, unfortunately, made Doi Saket, and other communities like it, fertile ground for HIV. All of the women who meet at the temple are AIDS widows. Many are themselves infected; most are now single mothers. Despite the fact that nearly all of the women in the widows' group were farmers' wives infected by their husbands, community prejudice and discrimination against them and their children has been intense. It was this social ostracism that first brought the group together. They approached the government, who helped them to get support from an Australian donor agency. With the money, the widows of Doi Saket have set up a co-operative, making handicrafts to support themselves and their children. The Abbot of the district's central *wat*, who has taken a lead in supporting people with HIV infection, offered the temple grounds for their projects. This is not an HIV prevention program, it is perhaps too late for early interventions here, but it is a way for women to survive the loss of their husbands, to deal with discrimination, and to build solidarity with each other.

The women of a similar community, also in the suburban ring of Chiang Mai, San Sai District, have used another approach. So many young men were dying in San Sai that the community opted for a moratorium on marriage until it was clear which young men would survive the disastrous HIV epidemic in the district. (Between one in five and one in four young men have died, or will die, if spread stopped tomorrow.) This is probably not going to work, but it represents an incredible change in the social structure of San Sai's villages. Local women know what may happen when they marry—HIV infection—and are opting, at least for the short term, for not marrying rather than risk exposure.

Women's attitudes toward prospective partners are changing as well. In a study among female factory workers in northern Thailand, young women reported that they strongly favored men who did not visit sex workers, and that the sexual history of their potential partners was an important criterion for marriage. This is a sharp change from the attitudes of their mothers' generation, for whom visits to sex workers were often preferred over husbands having mistresses. These were women whose fathers and older brothers traditionally took their adolescent boys to brothels to begin their sexual lives.

The most far-reaching change is a paradoxical one. Young Thai women are increasingly having sex before marriage. The formal term for this emerging pattern is 'serial monogamy'. In serial monogamy, people tend to have only one partner at a time, a steady monogamous partner. But the first, or second, or third partner might not be the one chosen for marriage. Serial monogamy is trial and error, learning, while engaged in sexual relationships, what one wants and is prepared to give to a marriage. This requires contraception, and an awareness on the part of both partners that neither is likely to be a virgin at marriage. It requires empowerment of young women and a sea-change for men, who must go from a 'virgin or whore' conception of female sexuality to a partnership with an 'equally experienced and adult' woman.

A striking finding among Thai soldiers was that while condom use was increasing sharply in the early 1990s, and the use of prostitutes steadily declining, the age at first intercourse among these men fell through the same period (from about 16.5 years to 16.1), and the number of men who reported having girlfriends with whom they were sexually active rose. The number of men who reported having had a girlfriend as their first sex partner (not a sex worker) more than doubled between 1991 and 1995. In other words, young Thai men were still having sex, but they were losing virginity and having sexual relationships with female peers, not sex workers. Does this mean that these 'AIDS era' young men may establish sexually satisfying lives with their wives? That prostitution will decline due to a fall in demand?

Many Islamic societies believe that sexual desire is a female problem. Women's genitals must be mutilated to prevent them from developing insatiable and uncontrollable craving. Men are seen as much less physical, more spiritual; if men were not constantly aroused by licentious women they would spend their waking hours contemplating the divine. *The Perfumed Garden*, the classical Arabic erotic text, is a paean to women's 'itchy vulvas', their libidinous urges, and the great lengths to which men must go in order to restrain their women. Other cultures have seen this very differently. In Thai culture wives traditionally do not enjoy or initiate sex, and do not have orgasms. Sex workers are for sexual pleasure, wives for producing heirs. A Western colleague and social researcher has done some fascinating work on young women working in factories (women make up about 70% of Thailand's factory workers). But it was with her Thai research colleagues that she became intimate enough to encounter the sexual conservatism of middle- and upper-class married Thai women of a certain age. She had her research group to her house for tea near the completion of their project. The subject of sex within their marriages came up. Every one of these women was shocked when my friend mentioned that she and her husband had a

satisfying sexual relationship. What did she mean? That her husband was satisfied? No, she explained, she meant that she was satisfied; her husband was a generous partner. She had orgasms. *Orgasms*?! Impossible. Women couldn't have orgasms. How could they ejaculate? The Westerner insisted that women did have orgasms, and there was considerable scientific evidence to prove it. (The Thais present were all educators, physicians, or pharmacists.) When she maintained that she enjoyed sex, the consensus was that there was something very wrong with her. One colleague suggested therapy, while another thought she should take up meditation, to calm her over-aroused senses.

But the daughters of these women might tell you a very different story, one that has been profoundly affected by AIDS. Sexual equality (serial monogamy for both partners until a good match is found) may seem an unlikely outcome of the HIV epidemic in Thailand, but it is increasingly being practiced by young women who want to be a part of their husbands' erotic lives, not just dutiful and sexless mothers of children, who want to know their husbands' and their own risks, and want protection. And their husbands come from a new generation of young men, who have had their sexual debut with a girlfriend, not in a brothel.

This may sound like a change for the better. And perhaps it will be, in the long term, a partial solution to the related problems of the sex trade and sexually unfulfilling marriages. But it is having another consequence. The large pool of young men infected with HIV during the Thai boom (a similar situation prevails in Burma and Cambodia, where the booms continue) is now marrying. Young women in these countries are selecting partners with at least a 10% chance of having HIV. In the upper classes of these societies, the odds will be much lower. For women from San Sai, or Doi Saket, or Phnom Penh or the Shan States, they will be higher. Antenatal care clinics, where women go for pregnancy testing and care, have become HIV-testing sites throughout the region. Malaysia carried out a study in pregnant women in the early 1990s, but the results have been deemed too sensitive to release. The HIV rate among pregnant women in Keng Tung, one of the larger Shan State towns, was over 10% in 1995. In Payao province, northern Thailand, it is over 18%—roughly one in five babies in this farming community is being born to a mother with HIV infection. AZT, which has recently been shown to be remarkably effective in preventing HIV transmission from mother to infant, is unavailable in Laos, Burma, Cambodia, much of Thailand, Vietnam, and Yunnan. It is available in Malaysia, though how much it is used is unknown.

The study that showed the efficacy of AZT (zidovudine) in pregnancy was called ACTG 076. In the study, HIV-infected women were randomized to two groups: half the women received AZT and half placebo. The regimen was a complex one: oral AZT for the mother in the last three months of pregnancy, intravenous AZT during labor, oral AZT for the infant for six weeks after birth. In women who did not get AZT the HIV infection rate among their babies was a predictable 25%. Among the treated mothers and babies, it was 7%, a striking and statistically significant difference. *It worked*. This study was funded by US taxpayers, through the National Institutes of Health. AZT remains an expensive drug, despite the fact that its manufacturer, the British company Burroughs Wellcome, has already made profits from its sales of the order of US $275 million per year in the early 1990s, with it was one of the few licensed agents.[1] It remains so expensive as to be unavailable to the people who now need it most—pregnant women in the developing world, who give birth to 95% of the babies at risk of HIV infection. (Average developing-country expenditures on health are about US $2 per person per year, the retail cost of about two AZT tablets in the US.) If you looked for a clearer case in which First World economic considerations cause suffering in Third World settings you could find no more pernicious example than the exorbitant cost of AZT. If you have ever cared for a baby born with HIV infection, and watched its short, painful life ebb away, you know that there is no language too strong to describe this injustice. We know we can save hundreds of thousands of babies

from this fate, but we cannot make the pharmaceutical industry yield on costs. If they don't yield, perhaps Asia's entrepreneurs, who have managed to copy so many other items the West has to offer, will copy AZT as well. If fifty-cent Madonna CDs can get to Vientiane, and ten-dollar Rolex watches sell in Chiang Mai, why not 'bootleg' AZT?

There are other, less radical, solutions as well. The regimen of 076, AZT in three formulations, might be simplified, and costs reduced. Studies jointly funded by the US and Thai governments are under way to look at alternative regimens for AZT in pregnancy. Perhaps the doses for new-born babies are unnecessary, or the intravenous infusion during labor not needed; if we could get the beneficial effect of AZT with a minimal dose at the right time, the drug might be affordable in some countries where it is unavailable now. But for the others? AIDS care in Burma is extra rice, Tylenol, and prayer. If AZT were free it would remain almost impossible to deliver, given the current state of health care under SLORC.

For AZT to be effective in pregnancy on a population level, HIV testing would have to be made widely available, and offered to all women at risk. If discrimination is not addressed, the increased HIV testing necessary to prevent HIV in infants could have disastrous effects. A whole generation of children born HIV-negative but to infected mothers will grow up under a cloud. Who will educate and support them? How will the societies in which they live cope with their manifold needs? This is a question of immense importance for Thailand, Burma, and Cambodia, which will have large numbers of AIDS orphans for at least another generation. It is a reality which makes the problems of AIDS among gay men look easy.

There were three of us in the car: myself, my Thai partner S, and his older sister, Khun O, a teacher. S shares a house with his sister, her husband, and their two pre-teenage children. We were on our way to visit a Buddhist shrine in a limestone cave north of Chiang Mai, a place of pilgrimage. S and Khun O are both devout Christians, members of the Church of Christ in Thailand. They were taking me to the cave, but for them both it was a place of historical, not religious, significance. The conversation was mostly about the US—Khun O had just returned from a school trip with her students. Then we started talking about my work, and about the HIV problem in Thailand. I went into a long monologue on the current challenge: how to protect married women, the difficulty of condom use in marriage, the relative ease of dealing with commercial sex compared to dealing with sex in the home. The car became uncomfortably silent. I sensed I had overstepped the bounds of propriety, and by going on about Thai men's sexual behavior in the abstract, had insulted my friends. It was a relief to get to the cave. Khun O didn't want to join us on the long steep climb into the shrine; S and I went on alone. In the cave, I apologized to S. He stopped me cold:

'No, Chris. My sister couldn't tell you what's happening to her. I was waiting for her to tell you, but she can't. My brother-in-law has taken a minor wife. She thinks he's also going with other women, but she's not sure. She wants him back. We are very against divorce, you know? But she's very afraid. She wants me to go with her to get tested. Maybe in Bangkok. I told her I think he needs to get tested. But how to say?'

NOTE

1. For a detailed history of this controversial drug and its costs, see Randy Shilts's brilliant polemic, *And the Band Played On*.

REFERENCES

Anon., 'Bringing AZT to Poor Countries', *Science*, Vol. 269, No. 4, 1995, pp. 624–5.

Burton, R. (trans.), in A. H. Walton (ed.,), *The Perfumed Garden of the Shaykh Nefzawi*, Gramercy Publishing Co., New York, 1964.

Brown, T., W. Sittitrai, S. Vanichseni et al., The recent epidemiology of HIV and AIDS in Thailand, *AIDS*, Vol. 8 (suppl. 2), 1994, pp. S131 41.

Connor, E. M., R. S. Sperling, R. Gelbert et al., 'Reduction of maternal–infant transmission of human immunodeficiency virus type I with zidovudine treatment', *New England Journal of Medicine*, Vol. 331, 1994, pp. 1173–80.

Elias, C., Sexually Transmitted Diseases and the Reproductive Health of Women in Developing Countries, The Population Council, Working Paper 5, 1991.

Fleming, P. S., Access to Treatments in Developing Countries, address at the 11th International Conference on AIDS, Vancouver, 1996.

Nelson, K. E., D. D. Celentano, S. Eiumtrakul, D. R. Hoover, C. Beyrer et al., Changes in sexual behavior and a decline in HIV infection among young men in Thailand, *New England Journal of Medicine*, Vol. 335, 1996, pp. 279–303.

Wasserheit, J., Epidemiologic Synergy: Interrelationships between Human Immunodeficiency Virus Infection and Other Sexually Transmitted Diseases, *Sexually Transmitted Diseases*, Vol. 19, 1991, pp. 62–4.

For a thorough discussion of heterosexual transmission of HIV, see also I. De Vincenzi (for the European Study Group on Heterosexual Transmission of HIV), A longitudinal study of human immunodeficiency virus transmission by heterosexual partners, *New England Journal of Medicine*, Vol. 331, 1994, pp. 341–6.

30

Negotiating Sex and Gender in the Attorney General's Commission on Pornography

Carole S. Vance

Columbia University

Larry Madigan began his testimony in the Miami federal courthouse. Dark-haired, slight, and dressed in his best suit, he fingered his testimony nervously before he was recognized by the chair. The podium and microphone at which he stood were placed at the front of the auditorium, so when the thirty-eight-year-old looked up from his typed statement, he saw only the members of the Attorney General's Commission on Pornography. They sat on the raised dais, surrounded by staff aides, federal marshals, the court stenographer, and flags of Florida and the United States. Behind him sat the audience, respectfully arrayed on dark and immovable wood benches that matched the wood paneling which enveloped the room.

"At age 12," he began earnestly, "I was a typical, normal, healthy boy and my life was filled with normal activities and hobbies." But "all the trouble began a few months later," when he found a deck of "hard core" pornographic playing cards, depicting penetration, fellatio, and cunnilingus. "These porno cards highly aroused me and gave me a desire I never had before," he said. Soon after finding these cards, his behavior changed: he began masturbating, attempted to catch glimpses of partially dressed neighbor women, and surreptitiously tried to steal *Playboy* magazines from the local newsstand. His chronicle went on for several minutes.

"By the age of 16, after a steady diet of *Playboy, Penthouse, Scandinavian Children,* perverted paperback books and sexology magazines, I had to see a doctor for neuralgia of the prostate." His addiction worsened in his twenties, when he began watching pornographic videos. He went on to "promiscuous sex" with "two different women," but eventually found Christ. He concluded, "I strongly believe that all that has happened to me can be traced back to the finding of those porno cards. If it weren't for my faith in God and the forgiveness in Jesus Christ, I would now

Source: Negotiating sex and gender in the Attorney General's Commission on Pornography, by Carole S. Vance, in *Uncertain Terms*, edited by Faye Ginsburg and Anna Lowenhaupt Tsing. Boston, MA: Beacon Press, 1990, pp. 118–134. © 1990 Carole S. Vance. Used with permission of the author.

possibly be a pervert, an alcoholic, or dead. I am a victim of pornography."[1]

The audience sat in attentive silence. No one laughed. Only a few cynical reporters sitting next to me quietly elbowed each other and rolled their eyes, although their stories in the next day's papers would contain respectful accounts of Mr. Madigan's remarks and those of his therapist, Dr. Simon Miranda, who testified as an expert witness that many of his patients were being treated for mental problems brought on by pornography.

The Attorney General's Commission on Pornography, a federal investigatory commission appointed in May 1985 by then-Attorney General Edwin Meese III, orchestrated an imaginative attack on pornography and obscenity. The chief targets of its campaign appeared to be sexually explicit images. These were dangerous, according to the logic of the commission, because they might encourage sexual desires or acts. The commission's public hearings in six U.S. cities during 1985 and 1986, lengthy executive sessions, and an almost 2000 page report[2] constitute an extended rumination on pornography and the power of visual imagery. Its ninety-two recommendations for strict legislation and law enforcement, backed by a substantial federal, state, and local apparatus already in place, pose a serious threat to free expression. Read at another level, however, the commission's agenda on pornography stands as a proxy for a more comprehensive program about gender and sexuality, both actively contested domains where diverse constituencies struggle over definitions, law, policy, and cultural meanings.

To enter a Meese Commission hearing was to enter a public theater of sexuality and gender, where cultural symbols—many dating from the late nineteenth century—were manipulated with uncanny intuition: the specter of uncontrolled lust, social disintegration, male desire, and female sexual vulnerability shadowed the hearings. The commission's goal was to implement a traditional conservative agenda on sexually explicit images and texts: vigorous enforcement of existing obscenity laws coupled with the passage of draconian new legislation.[3] To that end, the commission, dominated by a conservative majority, effectively controlled the witness list, evidence, and fact-finding procedures in obvious ways that were widely criticized for their bias.[4] But the true genius of the Meese Commission lay in its ability to appropriate terms and rhetoric, to deploy visual images and create a compelling interpretive frame, and to intensify a climate of sexual shame that made dissent from the commission's viewpoint almost impossible. The power of the commission's symbolic politics is shown by the response of both spectators and journalists to Larry Madigan's testimony, as well as by the inability of dissenting commission witnesses who opposed further restriction to unpack and thus counter the panel's subterranean linguistic and visual ploys.

Convened during Ronald Reagan's second term, the commission paid a political debt to conservatives and fundamentalists who had been clamoring for action on social issues, particularly pornography, throughout his term of office. Pornographic images were symbols of what moral conservatives wanted to control: sex for pleasure, sex outside the regulated boundaries of marriage and procreation. Sexually explicit images are dangerous, conservatives believe, because they have the power to spark fantasy, incite lust, and provoke action. What more effective way to stop sexual immorality and excess, they reasoned, than to curtail sexual desire and pleasure at its source—in the imagination. However, the widespread liberalization in sexual behavior and attitudes in the last century coupled with the increased availability of sexually explicit material since the 1970s made the conservative mission a difficult, though not impossible, task.[5] The commission utilized all available tools, both symbolic and procedural.

PROCEDURES AND BIAS

Appointed to find "new ways to control the problem of pornography," the panel was chaired by Henry Hudson, a vigorous anti-vice prosecutor from Arlington, Virginia, who had been commended by President Reagan for closing down every adult bookstore in his district. Hudson was assisted by his staff of vice cops and attorneys and by executive director Alan Sears, who had a reputation in the U.S. Attorney's Office in Kentucky as a tough opponent of obscenity.[6] Prior to convening, seven of the 11 commissioners had taken public stands opposing pornography and supporting obscenity law as a means to control it. These seven included a fundamentalist broadcaster, several public officials, a priest, and a law professor who had argued that sexually explicit expression was undeserving of First Amendment protection because it was less like speech and more like dildos.[7] The smaller number of moderates sometimes tempered the staff's conservative zeal, but their efforts were modest and not always effective.

The conservative bias continued for 14 months, throughout the panel's more than 300 hours of public hearings in six U.S. cities and lengthy executive sessions, which I observed.[8] The list of witnesses was tightly controlled: 77% supported greater control, if not elimination, of sexually explicit material. Heavily represented were law-enforcement officers and members of vice squads (68 of 208 witnesses), politicians and spokespersons for conservative anti-pornography groups like Citizens for Decency through Law and the National Federation for Decency. Great efforts were made to find "victims of pornography" to testify,[9] but those reporting positive experiences were largely absent. Witnesses were treated unevenly, depending on whether the point of view they expressed facilitated the commission's ends. There were several glaring procedural irregularities, including the panel's attempt to withhold drafts and working documents from the public and its effort to name major corporations such as Time, Inc., Southland, CBS, Coca-Cola, and K-Mart as "distributors of pornography" in the final report, repeating unsubstantiated allegations made by Rev. Donald Wildmon, executive director of the National Federation for Decency. These irregularities led to several lawsuits against the commission.

The barest notions of fair play were routinely ignored in gathering evidence. Any negative statement about pornographic images, no matter how outlandish, was accepted as true. Anecdotal testimony that pornography was responsible for divorce, extramarital sex, child abuse, homosexuality, and excessive masturbation was entered as "evidence" and appears as supporting documentation in the final report's footnotes.

GENDER NEGOTIATIONS

The commission's unswerving support for aggressive obscenity law enforcement bore the indelible stamp of the right wing constituency that brought the panel into existence. Its influence was also evident in the belief of many commissioners and witnesses that pornography leads to immorality, lust, and sin. But the commission's staff and the Justice Department correctly perceived that an unabashedly conservative position would not be persuasive outside the right wing. For the commission's agenda to succeed, the attack on sexually explicit material had to be modernized by couching it in more contemporary arguments, arguments drawn chiefly from anti-pornography feminism and social science. So the preeminent harm that pornography was said to cause was not sin and immorality, but violence and the degradation of women.

To the extent that the world views and underlying ideologies of anti-pornography feminism and social science are deeply different from those of fundamentalism, the commission's experiment at merging or overlaying these discourses was far from simple. In general, the commission fared much better in its attempt to incorporate the language and testimony of anti-pornography feminists than that of social scientists. The cooptation of anti-pornography feminism was both implausible and brilliantly executed.

Implausible, because the panel's chair, Henry Hudson, and its executive director, Alan Sears, along with the other conservative members, were no feminists. Hudson usually addressed the four female commissioners as "ladies." He transmuted the term used by feminist anti-pornography groups, "the degradation of women," into the "degradation of femininity," which conjured up visions of Victorian womanhood dragged from the pedestal into a muddy gutter. Beyond language, conservative panelists consistently opposed proposals that feminists universally support—for sex education or school-based programs to inform children about sexual abuse, for example. Conservative members objected to sex abuse programs for children, contending that such instruction prompted children to make hysterical and unwarranted accusations against male relatives. In addition, panelists rejected the recommendations of feminist prostitutes' rights groups like COYOTE and the U.S. Prostitutes Collective,[10] preferring increased arrests and punishment for women (though not their male customers) to decriminalization and better regulation of abusive working conditions. More comically, conservative panelists tried to push through a "vibrator bill," a model statute that would ban as obscene "any device designed or marketed as useful primarily for the stimulation of human genital organs." The three moderate female commission members became incredulous and upset, when they realized that such a law would ban vibrators.

During the course of the public hearings, conservative and fundamentalist witnesses made clear that they regarded the feminist movement as a major cause of the family breakdown and social disruption which they observed during the past twenty years. Feminists advocated divorce, abortion, access to birth control, day care, single motherhood, sexual permissiveness, lesbian and gay rights, working mothers—all undesirable developments that diminished the importance of family and marriage. Conservatives and fundamentalists were clear in their allegiance to a traditional moral agenda: sex belonged in marriage and nowhere else. Pornography was damaging because it promoted and advertised lust, sex "with no consequences," and "irresponsible" sex.

Anti-pornography feminists, in their writing and activism dating from approximately 1977, saw the damage of pornography in different terms, though other feminists (and I include myself in this group) objected to their

analysis for uncritically incorporating many conservative elements of late nineteenth-century sexual culture.[11] Nevertheless, the anti-pornography feminist critique made several points which differed sharply from those made by conservatives. They argued that most, if not all, pornography was sexist (rather than immoral). It socialized men to be dominating and women to be victimized. Moreover, pornographic imagery lead to actual sexual violence against women, and it constituted a particularly effective form of anti-woman propaganda. At various times, anti-pornography feminists have proposed different remedial strategies ranging from educational programs and consciousness-raising to restriction and censorship of sexually explicit material through so-called civil rights anti-pornography legislation first drafted in 1983. But a consistent theme throughout anti-pornography feminism, as in most feminism, was intense opposition to and fervent critique of gender inequality, male domination, and patriarchal institutions, including the family, marriage, and heterosexuality.

The conflict between basic premises of conservative and anti-pornography feminist analyses is obvious. Nevertheless, the commission cleverly used anti-pornography feminist terms and concepts as well as witnesses to their own advantage in selective ways, helped not infrequently by anti-pornography leaders and groups themselves. Anti-pornography feminist witnesses eagerly testified before the commission and cast their personal experiences of incest, childhood sexual abuse, rape and sexual coercion in terms of the "harms" and "degradation" caused by pornography. Anti-pornography feminist witnesses, of course, did not voice complaints about divorce, masturbation, or homosexuality, which ideologically give feminists no cause for protest, but they failed to comment on the great divide that separated their complaints from those of fundamentalists, a divide dwarfed only by the even larger distance between their respective political programs. Indeed, some prominent anti-pornography feminists were willing to understate and most to avoid mentioning in their testimony their support for those cranky feminist demands so offensive to conservative ears: abortion, birth control, and lesbian and gay rights. Only one feminist anti-pornography group, Feminists Against Pornography from Washington, D.C., refused to tailor its testimony to please conservative members and attacked the Reagan administration for its savage cutbacks on programs and services for women.[12] Their testimony was soon cut off on the grounds of inadequate time, though other anti-pornography groups and spokespersons, including Andrea Dworkin, Catharine MacKinnon, and Women Against Pornography (New York) would be permitted to testify at great length.

In the context of the hearing, the notion that pornography "degrades" women proved to be a particularly helpful unifying term, floating in and out of fundamentalist as well as anti-pornography feminist testimony. By the second public hearing, "degrading" had become a true crossover term—used by moral majoritarians, vice cops, and aggressive prosecutors, as well as anti-pornography feminists. Speakers didn't notice, or chose not to, that the term "degradation" had very different meanings in each community. For anti-pornography feminists, pornography degrades women when it depicts or glorifies sexist sex: images that put men's pleasure first or suggest that women's lot in life is to serve men. For fundamentalists, "degrading" was freely applied to all images of sexual behavior that might be considered immoral, since in the conservative world view immorality degraded the individual and society. "Degrading" was freely applied to visual images that portrayed homosexuality, masturbation, and even consensual heterosexual sex. Even images of morally approved marital sexuality were judged "degrading," since public viewing of what should be a private experience degraded the couple and the sanctity of marriage. These terms provided by anti-pornography feminists—"degrading," "violence against women," and "offensive to women" (though conservatives couldn't resist adding the phrase "and children")—were eagerly adopted by the panel and proved particularly useful in giving it and its findings the gloss of modernity and some semblance of concern with human rights.

Although the commission happily assimilated the rhetoric of anti-pornography feminists, it decisively rejected their remedies. Conservative men pronounced the testimony of Andrea Dworkin "eloquent" and "moving" and insisted on including her statement in the final report, special treatment given no other witness. But anti-pornography feminists had argued against obscenity laws, saying they reflected a moralistic and anti-sexual tradition which could only harm women. Instead, they favored ordinances, such as those developed for Minneapolis and Indianapolis by Dworkin and MacKinnon,[13] which would outlaw pornography as a violation of women's civil rights. The commission never seriously entertained the idea that obscenity laws should be repealed; given its conservative constituency and agenda, it couldn't have.

The commission's report summarily rejected Minneapolis-style ordinances. These had been "properly held unconstitutional" by a recent Supreme Court decision, the panel agreed, because they infringed on speech protected under the First Amendment. But the panel cleverly, if disingenuously, argued that traditional obscenity law could be used against violent and degrading material in a manner "largely consistent with what this ordinance attempts to do," ignoring anti-pornography feminists' vociferous rejection of obscenity laws. The panel recommended that obscenity laws be further strengthened by adding civil damages to the existing criminal penalties. This constitutes a major defeat for anti-pornography feminists. But unlike social scientists who protested loudly over the commission's misuse of their testimony, the anti-pornography feminists have not acknowledged the panel's distortion. Instead, they commended the panel for recognizing the harm of pornography and continued to denounce obscenity law,[14] without coming to grips with the panel's commitment to that approach.

Even more startling were MacKinnon's and Dworkin's statements to the press that the commission "has recommended to Congress the civil rights legislation women have sought,"[15] and this comment by Dorchen Leidholdt, founder of Women Against Pornography: "I'm not embarrassed at being in agreement with Ed Meese."[16] Over the course of the hearings, it seems that each group strategized how best to use the other. However, the vast power and resources of the federal government, backed by a strong fundamentalist movement, made it almost inevitable that the Meese commission would benefit far more in this exchange than anti-pornography feminists.

The commission attempted another major appropriation of feminist issues by recasting the problem of violence against women. Since the backlash against feminism began in the mid-1970s, conservative groups most decisively rejected feminist critiques of violence in the family, particularly assertions about the prevalence of marital rape, incest, and child sexual abuse. Such sexual violence was rare, they countered, and only exaggerated by feminists because they were "man-haters" and "lesbians" who wanted to destroy the family. Accordingly, conservatives consistently opposed public funding for social services directed at these problems: rape hotlines, shelters for abused wives, programs to identify and counsel child victims of incest. Such programs would destroy the integrity of the family, particularly the authority of the father, conservatives believed.

The commission hearings document a startling reversal in the conservative discourse on sexual violence. Conservative witnesses now claimed there is an epidemic of sexual violence directed at women and children, even in the family. Unlike the feminist analysis, which points to inequality, patriarchy, and women's powerlessness as root causes, the conservative analysis singles out pornography and its attendant sexual liberalization as the responsible agents. Men are, in a sense, victims as well, since once their lust is aroused, they are increasingly unable to refrain from sexual aggression. It is clear that the conservative about-face seeks to respond to a rising tide of concern among even right wing women about the issues of violence and abuse, while at the same time seeking to contain it by providing an alternative narrative: the appropriate solution lies in controlling pornography, not challenging male domination; pornography victimizes men, not just women. In that regard, it is striking that the victim witnesses provided by anti-pornography feminist groups were all female, whereas those provided by conservatives included many men.

Ironically, the conservative analysis ultimately blames feminism for violence against women. To the extent that feminists supported a more permissive sexual climate, including freer sexual expression, and undermined marriage as the only appropriate place for sex and procreation, they promoted an atmosphere favorable to violence against women. The commission's symbolic and rhetorical transformations were skillful. The panel not only appropriated anti-pornography feminist language to modernize a conservative agenda and make it more palatable to the mainstream public, but it also used issues of male violence successfully raised by feminists to argue that the only reliable protection for women was to be found in returning to the family and patriarchal protection.

THE PLEASURES OF LOOKING

The commission's campaign against sexually explicit images was filled with paradox. Professing belief in the most naive and literalist theories of representation, the commissioners nevertheless shrewdly used visual images during the hearings to establish "truth" and manipulate the feelings of the audience. Arguing that pornography had a singular and universal meaning that was evident to any viewer, the commission staff worked hard to exclude any perspective but its own. Insisting that sexually explicit images had great authority, the commissioners framed pornography so that it had more power in the hearing than it could ever have in the real world. Denying that subjectivity and context matter in the interpretation of any image, they created a well-crafted context that denied there was a context.

The foremost goal of the commission was to establish "the truth" about pornography, that is, to characterize and describe the sexually explicit material that was said to be in need of regulation. Pornographic images were shown during all public hearings, as witnesses and staff members alike illustrated their remarks with explicit, fleshy, often full-color images of sex. The reticence to view this material that one might have anticipated on the part of fundamentalists and conservatives was nowhere to be seen. The commission capitalized on the realistic representational form of still photos and movie and video clips, stating that the purpose of viewing these images was to inform the public and themselves about "what pornography was really like." Viewing was carefully orchestrated, and a great deal of staff time went toward organizing the logistics and techniques of viewing. Far from being a casual or minor enterprise, the selection and showing of sexually explicit images constituted one of the commission's major interventions.

The structure of viewing was an inversion of the typical context for viewing pornography. Normally private, this was public, with slides presented in federal courthouse chambers before hundreds of spectators in the light of day. The viewing of pornography, usually an individualistic and libidinally anarchic practice, was here organized by the state—the Department of Justice, to be exact. The ordinary purpose in viewing, sexual pleasure and masturbation, was ostensibly absent, replaced instead by dutiful scrutiny and the pleasures of condemnation.

These pleasures were intense. The atmosphere throughout the hearings was one of excited repression: witnesses alternated between chronicling the negative effects of pornography and making sensationalized presentations of "it." Taking a lead from feminist anti-pornography groups, everyone had a slide show: the F.B.I., the U.S. Customs Service, the U.S. Postal Service and sundry vice squads. At every "lights out," spectators would rush to one side of the room to see the screen, which was angled toward the commissioners. Were the hearing room a ship, we would have capsized many times.

Alan Sears, the executive director, told the commissioners with a grin that he hoped to include some "good stuff" in their final report, and its two volumes and 1,960 pages

faithfully reflect the censors' fascination with the thing they love to hate. It lists in alphabetical order the titles of material found in sixteen adult bookstores in six cities: 2,370 films, 725 books and 2,325 magazines, beginning with *A Cock Between Friends* and ending with *69 Lesbians Munching*. A detailed plot summary is given for the book, *The Tying Up of Rebecca*, along with descriptions of sex aids advertised in the books, their cost, and how to order them.

The commission viewed a disproportionate amount of atypical material, which even moderate commissioners criticized as "extremely violent and degrading."[17] To make themselves sound contemporary and secular, conservatives needed to establish that pornography was violent rather than immoral and, contradicting social science evidence, that this violence was increasing.[18] It was important for the panel to insist that the images presented were "typical" and "average" pornography, but typical pornography—glossy, mainstream porn magazines directed at heterosexual men—does not feature much violence, as the commission's own research (soon quickly suppressed) confirmed.[19] The slide shows, however, did not present many carefully airbrushed photos of perfect females or the largely heterosexual gyrations (typically depicting intercourse and oral sex) found even in the most hard-core adult bookstores. The commission concentrated on atypical material, produced for private use or for small, special interest segments of the market or confiscated in the course of prosecutions. The slides featured behavior which the staff believed to be especially shocking: homosexuality, excrement, urination, child pornography, bestiality (with over 20 different types of animals, including chickens and elephants), and especially sadomasochism (SM).

The commission relied on the realism of photography to amplify the notion that the body of material shown was accurate, and, therefore, they implied, representative. The staff also skillfully mixed atypical and marginal material with pictorials from *Playboy* and *Penthouse*, rarely making a distinction between types of publications or types of markets. The desired fiction was that all pornography was the same. Many have commented on the way all photographic images are read as fact or truth, because the images are realistic. This general phenomenon is true for pornographic images as well, but it is intensified when the viewer is confronted by images of sexually explicit acts which he or she has little experience viewing (or doing) in real life. Shock, discomfort, fascination, repulsion, and arousal all operate to make the image have an enormous impact and seem undeniably real.

The action depicted was understood as realistic, not fantastic or staged for the purposes of producing an erotic picture. Thus, images that played with themes of surrender or domination were read as actually coerced. A nude woman holding a machine gun was clearly dangerous, a panelist noted, because the gun could go off (an interpretation not, perhaps, inaccurate for the psychoanalytically inclined reader). Images of obviously adult men and women dressed in exaggerated fashions of high school students were called child pornography.

Sadomasochistic pornography had an especially strategic use in establishing that sexually explicit imagery was "violent." The intervention was effective, since few (even liberal critics) have been willing to examine the construction of SM in the panel's argument. Commissioners saw a great deal of SM pornography and found it deeply upsetting, as did the audience. Photographs included images of women tied up, gagged, or being "disciplined." Viewers were unfamiliar with the conventions of SM sexual behavior and had no access to the codes participants use to read these images. The panel provided the frame: SM was non-consensual sex that inflicted force and violence on unwilling victims. Virtually any claim could be made against SM pornography, and, by extension, SM behavior, which remains a highly stigmatized and relatively invisible sexuality. As was the case with homosexuality until recently, invisibility reinforces stigma, and stigma reinforces invisibility in a circular manner.

The redundant viewing and narration of SM images reinforced several points useful to the commission—pornography depicted violence against women and promoted male domination. An active editorial hand was at work, however, to remove reverse images of female domination and male submission; these images never appeared, though they constitute a significant portion of SM imagery. Amusingly, SM pornography elicited hearty condemnation of "male dominance," the only sphere in which conservative men were moved to critique it throughout the course of the hearing.

The commission called no witnesses to discuss the nature of SM, either professional experts or typical participants.[20] Given the atmosphere, it was not surprising that no one defended it. Indeed, producers of more softcore pornography joined in the condemnation, perhaps hoping to direct the commission's ire to groups and acts more stigmatized than themselves.[21] The commission ignored a small but increasing body of literature that documents important features of SM sexual behavior, namely consent and safety. Typically, the conventions we use to decipher ordinary images are suspended when it comes to SM images. When we see science fiction movies, for example, we do not leave the theater believing that the special effects were real or that the performers were injured making the films. But the commissioners assumed that images of domination and submission were both real and coerced.

In addition, such literalist interpretations were evident in the repeated assertions that all types of sexual images had a direct effect on behavior. The idea that sexual images could be used and remain on a fantasy level was foreign to the commission, as was the possibility that individuals might use fantasy to engage with dangerous or frightening feelings without wanting to experience them in real life. This lack of recognition is consistent with fundamentalist distrust and puzzlement about the imagination and the symbolic realm, which seem to have no autonomous existence; for fundamentalists, imagination and behavior are closely linked. If good thoughts lead to good behavior, a sure way to eliminate bad behavior was to police bad thoughts.

The voice-over for the visual segments was singular and uniform, which served to obliterate the actual diversity of people's response to pornography. But sexually explicit material is a contested ground precisely *because* subjectivity matters. An image that is erotic to one individual is revolting to a second and ridiculous to a third. The object of contestation *is* meaning. Age, gender, race, class, sexual preference, erotic experience, and personal history all form the grid through which sexual images are received and interpreted. The commission worked hard to eliminate diversity from its hearings and to substitute instead its own authoritative, often uncontested, frequently male monologue.

It is startling to realize how many of the Meese Commission's techniques were pioneered by anti-pornography feminists between 1977–1984. Claiming that pornography was sexist and promoted violence against women, anti-pornography feminists had an authoritative voice-over, too, though for theorists Andrea Dworkin and Catharine MacKinnon and groups like Women Against Pornography, the monologic voice was, of course, female. Although anti-pornography feminists disagreed with fundamentalist moral assumptions and contested, rather than approved, male authority, they carved out new territory with slide shows depicting allegedly horrific sexual images, a technique the commission heartily adopted. Anti-pornography feminists relied on victim testimony and preferred anecdotes to data. They, too, shared a literalist interpretive frame and used SM images to prove that pornography was violent.

The Meese Commission was skilled in its ability to use photographic images to establish the so-called truth and to provide an almost invisible interpretive frame that compelled agreement with its agenda. The commission's true gift, however, lay in its ability to create an emotional atmosphere in the hearings that facilitated acceptance of the commission's world view. Its strategic use of images was a crucial component of this emotional management. Because the power of this emotional climate fades in the published text, it is not obvious to most readers of the commission's report. Yet it was and is a force to be reckoned with, both in the commission and, more broadly, in all public debates about sexuality, especially those that involve the right wing.

RITUALS OF SEXUAL SHAME

An important aspect of the commission's work was the ritual airing and affirmation of sexual shame in a public setting. The panel relentlessly created an atmosphere of unacknowledged sexual arousal and fear. The large amount of pornography shown, ostensibly to educate and repel, was nevertheless arousing. The range and diversity of images provided something for virtually everyone, and the concentration on taboo, kinky, and harder-to-obtain material added to the charge. Part of the audience's discomfort may have come from the unfamiliarity of seeing sexually explicit images in public, not private, settings, and in the company of others not there for the express purpose of sexual arousal. But a larger part must have come from the problem of experiencing sexual arousal in an atmosphere where it is condemned. The commission's lesson was a complex one, but it taught the importance of managing and hiding sexual arousal and pleasure in public, while it reinforced secrecy, hypocrisy, and shame. Unacknowledged sexual feelings, though, did not disappear but developed into a whirlwind of mute, repressed emotion that the Meese Commission channeled toward its own purpose.

Sexual shaming was also embedded in the interrogatory practices of the chair. Witnesses appearing before the commission were treated in a highly uneven manner. Commissioners accepted virtually any claim made by anti-pornography witnesses as true, while those who opposed restriction of sexually explicit speech were often met with rudeness and hostility. The panelists asked social scientist Edward Donnerstein if pornographers had tried to influence his research findings or threatened his life. They asked actress Colleen Dewhurst, testifying for Actor's Equity about the dangers of censorship in the theater, if persons convicted of obscenity belonged to the union, and if the union was influenced by organized crime. They questioned her at length about the group's position on child pornography.

Sexual shame was also ritualized in how witnesses spoke about their personal experiences with images. "Victims of pornography" told in lurid detail of their use of pornography and eventual decline into masturbation, sexual addiction, and incest. Some testified anonymously, shadowy apparitions behind translucent screens. Their first-person accounts, sometimes written by the commission's staff,[22] featured a great elaboration of the sexual damage caused by visual images. To counter these accounts there was nothing but silence: descriptions of visual and sexual pleasure were absent. The commission's chair even noted the lack and was fond of asking journalists if they had ever come across individuals with positive experiences with pornography. The investigatory staff had tried to identify such people to testify, he said, but had been unable to find any. Hudson importuned reporters to please send such individuals his way. A female commissioner helpfully suggested that she knew of acquaintances, "normal married couples living in suburban New Jersey," who occasionally looked at magazines or rented X-rated videos with no apparent ill effects. But she doubted they would be willing to testify about their sexual pleasure in a federal courthouse, with their remarks transcribed by the court stenographer and their photos probably published in the next day's paper as "porn-users."

Though few witnesses chose to expose themselves to the commission's intimidation through visual images, the tactics used are illustrated in the differential treatment of two female witnesses, former *Playboy* Playmate Micki Garcia and former *Penthouse* Pet of the Year Dottie Meyer. Garcia accused Playboy Enterprises and Hugh Hefner of encouraging drug use, murder, and rape (as well as abortion, bisexuality, and cosmetic surgery) in the Playboy mansion. Her life was endangered by her testimony, she claimed. Despite the serious nature of some of these charges and the lack of any supporting evidence, her testimony was received without question.[23] Meyer, on the other hand, testified that her association with *Penthouse* had been professionally and personally beneficial. At the conclusion of her testimony, the lights dramatically dimmed and large blowups of several *Penthouse* pictorials were flashed on the screen; with

rapid-fire questions the chair demanded that she explain sexual images he found particularly objectionable. Another male commissioner, prepared by the staff with copies of Meyer's nine-year-old centerfold, began to pepper her with hectoring questions about her sexual life: Was it true she was preoccupied with sex? Liked sex in cars and alleyways? Had a collection of vibrators? Liked rough-and-tumble sex?[24] The female commissioners were silent. His sexist cross-examination was reminiscent of that directed at a rape victim, discredited and made vulnerable by any admission or image of her own sexuality. Suddenly, Dottie Meyer was on trial, publicly humiliated because she dared to present herself as unrepentantly sexual, not a victimized woman.

The ferocious attack on Dottie Meyer—and by extension on any display of women's sexual pleasure in the pubic sphere—is emblematic of the agenda of conservatives and fundamentalists on women's sexuality. Although they presented their program under the guise of feminist language and concerns, their abiding goal was to reestablish control by restricting women—and their desires—within ever-shrinking boundaries of the private and the domestic. The falsity of the panel's seemingly feminist rhetoric was highlighted by the moment when a lone woman speaking of her own sexual pleasure was seen as a greater threat than all the male "victims" of pornography who had assaulted and abused women. The conspicuous absence of any discourse that addressed women's definitions of their own sexual pleasures, that enlarged rather than constricted the domain of their public speech or action, unmasked this agenda. Unmasked, too, was the commission's primary aim: not to increase the safe space for women, but to narrow what can be seen, spoken about, imagined, and—they hope—done. The invisibility and subordination of female sexual pleasure in the commission's hearings is a strait-jacket which conservatives and fundamentalists would like to extend to the entire culture. Feminist language, disembodied from feminist principles and programs, was used to advance the idea that men, women, and society could be protected only through the suppression of female desire. In the face of false patriarchal protections embedded in shame and silence, feminists need to assert their entitlement to public speech, variety, safety, and bodily and visual pleasures.

NOTES

1. Attorney General's Commission on Pornography, Miami transcript, public hearing, November 21, 1985.

2. Attorney General's Commission on Pornography, *Final Report*, 2 vols. (Washington, D.C.: U.S. Government Printing Office, July 1986).

3. See *Final Report*, pp. 433–458, for a complete list of the panel's recommendations. These include mandating high fines and long jail sentences for obscenity convictions, appointing a federal task force to coordinate prosecutions nationwide, developing a computer data bank to collect information on individuals suspected of producing pornography, and using punitive RICO legislation (the Racketeer Influenced and Corrupt Organizations Act, originally developed to fight organized crime) to confiscate the personal property of anyone convicted of the "conspiracy" of producing pornography. For sexually explicit material outside the range of legal prosecution, the commission recommended that citizen activist groups target and remove material in their communities which they find "dangerous or offensive or immoral."

4. For a detailed critique of procedural irregularities, see Barry Lynn, *Polluting the Censorship Debate: A Summary and Critique of the Attorney General's Commission on Pornography* (Washington, D.C.: American Civil Liberties Union, 1986).

5. For changes in sexual patterns in the last century, see (for England) Jeffrey Weeks, *Sex, Politics and Society: The Regulation of Sexuality Since 1800* (New York: Longman, 1981) and (for America) John D'Emilio and Estelle B. Freedman, *Intimate Matters* (New York: Harper and Row, 1988). For a history of pornography, see Walter Kendrick, *The Secret Museum* (New York: Viking, 1987).

6. Sears went on to become the executive director of Citizens for Decency through Law, a major conservative antipornography group. (The group has since changed its name to the Children's Legal Foundation.)

7. Attorney Frederick Schauer argued that sexually explicit expression which was arousing was less like speech and more like "rubber, plastic, or leather sex aids." See "Speech and 'Speech'—Obscenity and 'Obscenity': An Exercise in the Interpretation of Constitutional Language," *Georgetown Law Journal* 67(1979), 899–923, especially pp. 922–923.

8. My analysis is based on direct observation of the commission's public hearings and executive sessions, supplemented by interviews with participants. All the commission's executive sessions were open to the public, following the provision of sunshine laws governing federal advisory commissions. Commissioners were specifically prohibited from discussing commission business or engaging in any informal deliberations outside of public view.

Public hearings were organized around preselected topics in six cities: Washington, D.C. (general), Chicago (law enforcement), Houston (social science), Los Angeles (production and distribution), Miami (child pornography), and New York (organized crime). Each public hearing typically lasted two full days. Commission executive sessions were held in each city in conjunction with the public hearings, usually for two extra days. Additional work sessions occurred in Washington, D.C. and Scottsdale, Arizona.

9. Victims of pornography, as described in the *Final Report*, included "Sharon, formerly married to a medical professional who is an avid consumer of pornography," "Bill, convicted of the sexual molestation of two adolescent females," "Dan, former Consumer of Pornography (sic)," "Evelyn, Mother and homemaker, Wisconsin, formerly married to an avid consumer of pornography," and "Mary Steinman, sexual abuse victim."

10. Los Angeles transcript, public hearing, October 17, 1985.

11. Major works of antipornography feminism include Andrea Dworkin, *Pornography: Men Possessing Women* (New York: G. P. Putnam, 1979); Susan Griffin, *Pornography and Silence: Culture's Revenge Against Nature* (New York: Harper and Row, 1981); Laura Lederer, ed., *Take Back the Night* (New York: William Morrow, 1980); Catharine A. MacKinnon, "Pornography, Civil Rights, and Speech," *Harvard Civil Rights-Civil Liberties Law Review*, vol. 20 (Cambridge: Harvard University, 1985), 1–70.

Opinion within feminism about pornography was, in fact, quite diverse, and it soon became apparent that the antipornography view was not hegemonic. For other views, see Carole S. Vance, ed., *Pleasure and Danger: Exploring Female Sexuality* (New York: Routledge & Kegan Paul, 1984); Varda Burstyn, ed., *Women Against Censorship* (Vancouver: Douglas & McIntyre, 1985) and Kate Ellis et al., eds., *Caught Looking: Feminism, Pornography, and Censorship* (New York: Caught Looking, Inc., 1986).

12. Washington, D.C. transcript, public hearing, June 20, 1985.

13. For the version passed in Indianapolis, see Indianapolis, Ind., code section 16–3 (q) (1984); and Andrea Dworkin, "Against the Male Flood: Censorship, Pornography, and Equality," *Harvard Women's Law Journal* 9 (1985): 1–19. For a critique, see Lisa Duggan, Nan Hunter, and Carole S. Vance, "False Promises: Feminist Antipornography Legislation in the U.S.," in *Women Against Censorship*, ed. Varda Burstyn (Toronto: Douglas & McIntyre, 1985), 130–151.

14. Women Against Pornography press conference, July 9, 1986, New York.

15. Statement of Catharine A. MacKinnon and Andrea Dworkin, July 9, 1986, New York, distributed at a press conference organized by Women Against Pornography following the release of the Meese commission's *Final Report*.

16. David Firestone, "Battle Joined by Reluctant Allies," *Newsday*, July 10, 1986, p. 5.

17. Statement of commissioners Judith Becker and Ellen Levine, *Final Report*, p. 199. In addition, they wrote: "We do not even know whether or not what the Commission viewed during the course of the year reflected the nature of most of the pornographic and obscene material in the market; nor do we know if the materials shown us mirror the taste of the majority of consumers of pornography."

18. Recent empirical evidence does not support the often-repeated assertion that violence in pornography is increasing. In their review of the literature, social scientists Edward Donnerstein, Daniel Linz, and Steven Penrod conclude, "at least for now, we cannot legitimately conclude that pornography has become more violent since the time of the 1970 obscenity and pornography commission" (in *The Question of Pornography: Research Findings and Policy Implications* [New York: The Free Press, 1987], 91).

19. The only original research conducted by the commission examined images found in the April 1986 issues of best-selling men's magazines (*Cheri, Chic, Club, Gallery, Genesis, High Society, Hustler, Oui, Penthouse, Playboy, Swank*). The study found that "images of force, violence, or weapons" constituted less than 1 percent of all images (0.6%), hardly substantiating the commission's claim that violent imagery in pornography was common. Although the results of this study are reported in the draft, they were excised from the final report.

20. For recent work on SM, see Michael A. Rosen, *Sexual Magic: The S/M Photographs* (San Francisco: Shaynew Press, 1986); Geoff Mains, *Urban Aboriginals* (San Francisco: Gay Sunshine Press, 1984); Samois, ed., *Coming to Power*, 2nd ed. (Boston: Alyson Press, 1982); Gini Graham Scott, *Dominant Women, Submissive Men* (New York: Praeger, 1983); Thomas Weinberg and G. P. Levi Kamel, *S and M: Studies in Sadomasochism* (Buffalo: Prometheus Books, 1983); Gerald and Caroline Greene, *S-M: The Last Taboo* (New York: Grove Press, 1974).

21. The proclivity of mildly stigmatized groups to join in the scapegoating of more stigmatized groups is explained by Gayle Rubin in her discussion of sexual hierarchy (Gayle Rubin, "Thinking Sex: Notes for a Radical Theory of the Politics of Sexuality" in *Pleasure and Danger: Exploring Female Sexuality*, ed. Carole S. Vance [Boston: Routledge & Kegan Paul, 1984], 267–319.)

22. Statement of Alan Sears, executive director (Washington, D.C. transcript, June 18, 1985).

23. Los Angeles transcript, public hearing, October 17, 1985.

24. New York City transcript, public hearing, January 22, 1986.

♦ PART TWELVE ♦

THE FUTURE OF SEXUALITIES

READINGS IN THIS PART

INTRODUCTION TO THE SUBJECT AND READINGS

When contemplating the future of sexualities, cyberspace stands out as an obvious place for sexual innovations. After all, the web has developed a reputation for its sexual content and the potential for sexual exploration from the privacy of your own home seems immense. In order to gauge just how many sites relate to our discussion, I conducted a few online searches.[1] On January 23, 2002, a search for the word "sex" garnered over 17 million hits. The word "love" produced about the same number of hits as sex, whereas the word "technology," by comparison, yielded over 37 million hits. "Cybersex" is apparently a much less popular word and, together with "cyber-sex," generated only 110,000 hits. Not surprisingly, "celibacy" yielded only 34,256 hits. To put all these numbers in perspective, a search for "chopped liver" mustered more than 5,000 hits.

The amount of sexual material on the web inspired the Communications Decency Act (CDA) that was enacted 1996. The purpose of the act was to make Internet providers responsible for web content. For example, if a picture depicting a child engaged in sexual activity was found on a website accessed through AOL, AOL would be legally responsible. The implications, consequences, and complications were enormous and shortly after it was passed, the CDA was declared unconstitutional by the United States Supreme Court (1997).

Despite this victory, the role of cyberspace in sexual innovation remains to be seen. Andy Miah, in his article *.../Cybersex/no_gender/no_sexuality/no_body.html,* explores the issues raised by cybersex relationships. He notes that there has been a great deal of speculation concerning the potential of cyber-relations. There are those who envision the web as an emotionally and morally liberating environment that allows individuals to transcend sexism, ageism, and racism and experiment with gender, nontraditional behaviors, and nontraditional partners. The web offers almost unlimited virtual possibilities in the privacy of your own home. Miah argues that as more of our lives are conducted online, the boundaries of real and virtual are changing and blurring. The web provides a new environment that allows us to explore our sexualities in innovative and unconventional ways. However, if we pursue sexual possibilities in cyberspace, we may find ourselves confronted with moral quagmires we never dreamt possible. For example, do we need to redefine fidelity? If your partner takes on an online lover, is she or he being unfaithful? Can rape take place in a chat room?

As noted above, one of the sexual possibilities that can be explored on the web is celibacy. The small number of online hits generated by the word celibacy falsely implies disinterest. Nothing could be further from the truth. In 1996 Congress approved $50 million in funding for abstinence-only sex education programs. In the article *An Orgy of Abstinence,* Sharon Lerner critiques the abstinence movement among young people in the United States. She notes that the Welfare Reform Law, where the abstinence education program is housed, must teach that "sexual activity outside of marriage is likely to have harmful psychological and physical effects." Under these programs, abstinence is not being introduced as one option, it is being promoted as the only option, excluding information about safe sex and contraception. It is no less than a fight over the sexualities of our youth, with two factions dividing politicians, educators, and parents. Lerner interviews teens and offers insights and data on teen celibacy, a feature of a movement that hopes to affect the future of sexualities.

The fight over teen morality is not new. Historically, there has been an ongoing battle for the moral and social control of sexualities and gender. Jeffery Weeks, in his article *An Unfinished Revolution: Sexuality in the 20th Century,* points out that for the past two hundred years politicians and the religious figures have been lamenting about the decline of morality. The concerns and arguments sound surprisingly similar to today's discourse on sexualities. Weeks argues that sexual change has addressed boundaries; between women and men and between normal and perversity. Lines have been drawn, and the two "camps" that emerged a long time ago continue to exist today. We can summarize their basic differences:

Sexual Liberal	*Moral Conservative*
seeks change, sees old order as inhibiting	sees moral decline, seeks to preserve old order
end discrimination against gays and gender	men are dominant, gays are unnatural
values personal fulfillment and freedom	value family values and religious teachings

When all is said and done, the future of gender and sexualities are tied into the future of politics, economics and even war. In the aftermath of September 11th, reports began circulating almost immediately about a shift in gender ideology in the United States. Men, inspired by the respect and admiration gained by firefighters and policepersons, are reputedly going to be more macho hereafter. Masculinity is making a comeback as strong men make the world safe for women. Although uniformed women lost their lives on 9-11, the gendering of our heros is proof of Jeffery Weeks' assertion that, although the 20th century experienced a sexual/gender revolution, that revolution remains unfinished.

In times of trouble (Weeks refers to the AIDS epidemic, and I would add fear of terrorism), we become nostalgic, seeking a return to order and harmony. But the golden ages that we seek are largely mythical. Regarding sexualities and gender, it is difficult to identify a period in which there was no discrimination and/or persecution. Weeks notes, and I am sure we will all agree, that in terms of tolerance and humanity, we still have a long way to go.

TERMS AND CONCEPTS

sexual abstinence	postmodern consciousness
born-again virginity	premarital sex
celibacy	the secularization of sex
cyberdating	sexual liberalization
cybersex	virtual relationships
deconstructionism	voyeurism
moral absolutism	

CRITICAL THINKING AND QUESTIONS TO CONSIDER

1. The Welfare Reform Bill, which includes funding for abstinence, is supposed to promote the belief that "sexual activity outside of marriage is likely to have harmful psychology and physical affects." What are the consequences, pro and con, of this message?
2. According to the National Abstinence Clearinghouse, what behavior indicates the first stage of "sexual addiction"? And why is this behavior seen as dangerous?
3. Drawing on Miah's article, discuss how e.porn undermines some of the ethical objections created by "traditional" pornography?
4. Rheingold, as quoted in Miah asks: "Is disembodiment the ultimate sexual revolution. . . . ?" What does he mean? In what ways does/will cybersexualities allow us to broaden our sexual horizons? What new moral and ethical challenges does/will cybersex present?
5. Compare, as Weeks does, the moral issues of the 1800s with those of the 1900s.
6. Describe the three trends in sexuality that Weeks discusses in his article. How have things changed since this article was written?

NOTE

1. All of the search results were generated by Altavista's search engine.

FURTHER READINGS

Abbot, Elizabeth. 2001. *A History of Celibacy.* New York: Da Capo Press.

Bell, Sandra, and Elisa Sobo (eds.). 2001. *Celibacy, Culture, and Society: The Anthropology of Sexual Abstinence.* Madison: University of Wisconsin Press.

Califia, Pat. 1994. *Public Sex: The Culture of Radical Sex.* San Francisco: Cleis Press, Inc.

Cooper, Alvin, et al. 1999. Sexuality on the Internet: From sexual exploration to pathological expression. *Professional Psychology: Research and Practice,* Vol. 30, No.2: 154–164.

Enloe, Cynthia. 2001. *Bananas, Beaches and Bases: Making Feminist Sense of International Politics.* Berkeley: University of California.

Ginsburg, Faye, and Rayna Rapp (eds.). 1995. *Conceiving the New World Order: The Global Politics of Reproduction.* Berkeley: University of California Press.

Hirshman, Linda R., and Jame E. Larson. 1998. *Hard Bargains: The Politics of Sex.* New York: Oxford Press.

Hitt, Jack. 2000. The second sexual revolution. *The New York Times Magazine,* 2–20–2000.

O'Toole, Laurence J. 2000. *Pornocopia: Porn, Sex, Technology and Desire.* London: Serpent's Tail.

Weeks, Jeffery. 1993. *Sexuality and Its Discontents: Meaning, Myths and Modern Sexualities.* New York: Routledge.

———. 1995. *Invented Moralities: Sexual Values in an Age of Uncertainty.* New York: Columbia University Press.

Witmer, Diane F. 1997. Risky business: Why people feel safe in sexually explicit on-line communication. *JCMC,* Vol. 2: 4.

RELATED WEBSITES

Cyborgasms by Robin B. Hamman, University of Essex, UK
www.socio.demon.co.uk/Cyborogasms.html

Human Rights Watch—Electronic Privacy Information Center
www.epic.org/free_speech/intl/hrw_report_5_96.html

Network and Net Play, Vol 2, Issue 4 - Journal of Computer-Mediated Communication
http://jcmc.huji.ac.il/vol2/issue4/abstracts.html

Privacy and Human Rights: An International Survey of Privacy Laws and Practice
www.gilc.org/privacy/survey/intor.html

Sexuality and Cyberspace, Women and Performance, Issue 17
www.echonyc.com/~women/Issue17/index.html

◇ 31
…/Cybersex/no_gender/ no_sexuality/no_body.html

Andy Miah

University of Paisley, Scotland,
andymiah@hotmail.com

<i want to close my eyes>
  <i think of kissing you and I> <want to close my eyes>
<…yes>
  <I was thinking it… you were writing it>
  <i want to close my eyes and see you>
<…no words are enough>
  <i want to open them and see you> <i hate words> <I am condemned to depend on them> <i would like you to know it all without me saying it> <but feel it as strongly as if you were reading it> <i'd like you to be able to read it on me straight away>
<i want you> <right now>
  <i want to become the screen, the paper> <i hate interfaces> <i want you too>
<you can be my lap top. my hands are there>
  <now. the butterflies are getting aggressive too> <i want to be your laptop. where am i?> <hold me closer> <hold me closer.> <let me feel you>
<my hands will not leave you, ever>
  <touch me> <more>

<you are there. it is close>
  <i am so alone here>
<i am close>
  <where are you?>
<I want you beneath me> <you are> <i am above you,> <you can feel my breath>
  <I feel it>
<it is … too much>
  <on my neck> <on my breasts>
<i want to kiss your lips, so much, all over,>
  <you say forever>
<forever>
  <your lips are still saying it>
<and where are you> <do your lips move with mine>
  <where are you letting me to be> <my lips are inside yours>
<I am persuading you>
  <now is my turn to have you inside me>
<i am breathing too much. it is…> <i am <i am>
  <it is never enough> <i am too> <these hands …. til when are they going to keep writing?> <how far> <how far are we going to get?>
<i cannot stop> <how far. it is not possible to see an end> <gosh, you have to go soon. i don't want out of this>
  <i could be here all night> <but yes i have to go soon>

<stay> <stay> <with me> <tonight> <i need more nights with you> <always with u>
  <i am trembling> <i will get out of her shaking all over>
<i want to touch your hand> <i want to feel it around me>
  <i want to embrace you> <touch your hair> <kiss your eyes>
<around my waist, my back>
  <hear your heart>
<oh my god..this is so incredible>
  <i know, it is> <i am getting lost into this>
<you make me incredibly hot> <i have never felt so strongly whilst with a machine>
  <i am breathing deeply> <those machines … they are not machines any more>
<are you really there… I want you to use your hands.> <I want to touch you where I cannot>
  <how can they be??>
<I want to feel you. feel your softness.> <feel that you are ready for me>
  <how can they still be machines after all what they are experiencing through us?> <i am so ready for you, my love> <i am ready. i want you> i really want you> <i will be unable to sleep wanting you> <i must leave>
<i want to touch you. you know where.>
  <how am i going to??>
<No, do not go>

(25 October, 2000)

Cybersex and cyberdating bring into focus what constitutes human relationships and how one should conduct interactions when online. It forces a question about what is important in human relationships. In so doing, cybersex presents a form of engagement that challenges conventional understandings of sex as a fundamentally bodily engagement with others. The text-based interaction above took place between real people and, if one is to accept that it was sincere, real emotions were behind the words. The lack of physical closeness does not lessen the importance of what has been felt in this conversation. If another person is being felt, or simply perceived, then it cannot help but be real. What matters is the sincerity of the gesture, which is not dependent upon actual physical contact. Perhaps the best approximation is to consider that cybersexual encounters combine more traditional examples such as telephone sex or let-

ter writing, neither of which would be claimed as lacking meaning and realness.[1]

Although there is no clear consensus, it is sufficient to describe cyberspace as the context for information communication that exists as an electronic, virtual entity within computers. Within academic discourses, inquiries about cyberspace have focused on how it impacts upon social barriers and ways of constructing identity (Cairncross, 1997; Castells, 1997; Jones, 1997; Turkle, 1995). However, curiosity about virtual relationships seemed to reach a mainstream audience through the cinematic production *You've Got Mail* (1999). At a similar time, countless television-based documentaries were telling the story of couples who fell in love on the cyber-highway and had even arranged marriages before meeting each other in person. Amidst these cultural products have emerged contested views about whether relationships based upon virtual correspondences can be fulfilling and whether they alter the way in which people relate to each other.

The ideas presented here give reason for considering the efficacy of what takes place within cyberspatial environments. Cyberspace is suggested as being a unique location for personal expression and freedom that *does* impact upon human experiences. Specifically, cybersex is argued as sufficiently 'real' and meaningful, and virtual *only* in the sense that it is mediated by technology. Even the physical aspects of sex are becoming increasingly sophisticated with the development of teledildonic technology, which allows the users to strap-on appropriate electronic equipment and feel physical stimuli being directed from somebody at a remote location. As the name suggests, teledildonics combines the use of sex toys, such as vibrators, with telecommunications. Thus, two people wearing such equipment control the amount and location of stimulation felt by the other person through computer software.

Currently, it is unclear what can be said about online relationships, though examples of cybersex bring into question whether physical proximity is important at all. To understand this context and the challenges it raises for understanding sexuality, this paper is structured to reveal aspects of cybersexual relationships that problematise the construction and understanding of gender, sexuality, and the body.

WHEREFORE ART THOU ROMEO?

Cybersex can take place in a number of contexts that blur the boundaries of pornography, voyeurism, and romance. The futuristic and immersing experiences described in the cinematic production, *The Lawnmower Man* (1992), are becoming more aligned with current technology. In the movie, the two central characters don their virtual reality suits and enter into a cyberworld where they experience a feeling of their bodies as being fluid, weightless, and entangled in physical embrace. For the viewer, its visual representation is described by two human-like forms in a brightly coloured fantasy world that resonates beauty and affection. Yet, the most accessible opportunities to experience cybersex are through conventional computer interfaces that utilise computer-mediated communication (CMC) systems. These are best known and most widely used through such protocols as the World Wide Web, which is host to (and overwhelmed by) a wide range of sexual environments.

Not surprisingly, the web offers many opportunities to engage with sex through electronic pornography (e.porn). One of the more interesting possibilities offered by real-time e.porn is the use of camera technology to allow a viewer to enter into the day-to-day life of somebody. In this case, the website host lures the voyeuristic browser into a situation where they would be willing to pay money to peek into the lives of others; a kind of pornographic *Truman Show* (1998). Yet, the objects of our "affection" are very aware of their being observed and, often, the emphasis is not on sex. With continually up-dated cameras (web-cams) placed all around the host's house, the user is able to observe a person washing-up, sleeping, watching television, bathing and having sex.

Beyond pornography, the opportunity to form romantic or sexual relationships can be found in many locations on the web. Most commonly, this entails the use of text-based interactions in chat-rooms or messenger service software. Chat-rooms are, literally, virtual places where individuals at different places in the world can meet through computers in a social environment comparable to a night club or restaurant. It is a place where multiple interactions are possible, with discussions taking place in text format between two or more people. In such locations it is also possible to have private or public conversations by moving around the virtual environment into private rooms and so on. Whilst an understanding of these environments is developing, there are some central characteristics of these contexts that are worth noting.[2]

A chat-room or personal interaction online can be a fictional or an honest experience in the sense of revealing sincere aspects of one's personality. Particularly in virtual spaces where fictional games are being played by its users, the presentation and naming of oneself tends to be fictional, where a name is ascribed to one's own character. A similar claim can be made about virtual social environments where one might go to meet people or make new friends. It is not uncommon for users to adopt a different name or fictional characteristics of their identity in regard to such things as personal appearance or personal beliefs. However, there also exist chat-rooms where members are required to be truthful about identity and where membership is not granted until checks are conducted to confirm identity. In some contexts adopting a fictional identity does not take place, particularly where the meeting is between a well-established group of friends. An example of a conversation between two people, whose names are not given for reasons of privacy, proceeded as follows.

<so are we gonna have cybersex or what??>
　　<yes, let's go for cybersex> <it will be good.
　　Especially with everybody around>
<well. ok. you start!. ("let's go for cybersex" - i am laughing). don't forget protection> <activate your virus software>
　　<indeed> <fine so...<what are you wearing?>
　　<....and I want quick cybersex!!!>
　　　　　　　　　　　　　　　(December 15, 2000)[3]

Developing relationships in chat-rooms can have an appeal of anonymity, where one can discard any inhibitions related to physical appearance, gender, sexuality, race, disability, or age. Indeed, Markham (1998: 35) describes how using a pseudonym can provide a "sense of freedom in a dislocated place where one can be anyone or anything simply by describing oneself through words and names." Thus, cyberspace can offer the opportunity to mix fantasy with reality and to reject whichever is less pleasing. As Tamblyn (1997: 42) claims,

> . . . the Internet traffics in the encouragement of its users' utopian fantasies about accessing the power to spin out proliferating identities. Multiple personas of whatever gender, sexual preference, age, race, and ethnicity seek virtual relationships with other designer identities.
>
> Chat-rooms allow for the free construction of identities and offer an eject button if ever things get a little unpleasant. It allows individuals who would not usually tolerate one another to interact and converse without having any basis to assert any social prejudice that they might normally hold, whether in relation to, for examples, sexuality, gender, class, or ethnicity. It offers a limitless opportunity for engaging with marginal fetish tastes that can accommodate all sexualities.

However, it is in such descriptions that one also realises the contradiction of this utopian technology that promotes difference in some contexts and flattens it in others. Cybersex can provide a context for liberating individuals from the burden of prejudice, though can also reduce people to fictional personae, where difference is dealt with by its removal. Cybersex can challenge sexualised stereotypes, though at times, amplify and reinforce them through simply replicating social norms. The negative aspect of this double-edge is reinforced by recent research that suggests cyberspace offers nothing revolutionary as a means for challenging stereotypes. Such research claims that the utopian aspirations of cyberspace, where individuals are liberated from social conventions and norms, are not reflective of what is actually taking place in cyberspace (Terry and Calvert, 1997). As

Morse (1997) argues, "virtual worlds do not necessarily or even commonly reveal interactions that transcend gender or cross culture" (p. 27).

Indeed, the artificiality of chat-room environments is reinforced by Wakeford (1997: 53), claiming that "electronic networks are constructed and experienced as male territory, and not a place within which anyone would voluntarily wish to display/reveal female identity." Thus, the very claims that were given earlier about how name changing can be emancipatory, would also seem to reflect an imperative derived from sexual difference. Consequently, early cyberspace discourse that sought to reveal the web as a utopian social location seems no longer persuasive, even if cyberspace could have been a medium for the transgressing of norms (Wakeford, 1999). In its most extreme interpretation, Strehovec (1997: paragraph 2) claims that

> . . . cyberspace is less and less a portent of messianic escape; it has become a colonised and 'McDonald's-ised' field for enforcing the technototalitarianism, web fascism, machismo, and tribalism of new, distinctively yuppified elites.

In turn, this realisation has rendered a refocusing of attention in cyberspatial theorising onto the experiential effects of engaging with others through a computer. If it cannot be claimed that social stereotypes collapse in cyberspace, then, at least, they can adopt new ways of being for those engaged with it.

SEXUAL DISRUPTION: .../no_gender/no_sexuality

These examples of cybersex and cyberspatial relationships provoke mixed reactions. From one perspective, e.porn is difficult to locate because it crosses the boundaries of other kinds of sexual engagement, such as personal relationships and prostitution. For example, in many cases of e.porn, the user often engages with the person that is producing the website, even building some degree of personal relationship.[4] Thus, the person by whom the user is being aroused is often also the person that owns the site and with whom they would communicate to arrange subscriptions and so on. Thus, the interaction with the subject of the pornography is also the person that the user engages with on levels other than simply the physical titillation.[5] However, e.porn that really does challenge conventional boundaries is also part of a larger network of pornographic websites where many others do very little that is different from more familiar examples of pornography.

This ambiguity renders it unclear whether pornography can be interpreted using the conventional moral discourse surrounding it (Kizza, 1996). Claims about pornography because it is exploitative are less persuasive for e.porn. Increasingly, e.porn involves individuals who are not working for a living, not being exploited and who have arranged the website portal independent of any coercive production process. Thus the context does not generate the same kinds of moral dilemma for the customer in terms of taking advantage of another human being (although, such cases can also be found online).

At most, one can object to e.porn on the basic premise that any kind of objectification is unacceptable. However, this would underestimate the level of interaction that can take place within e.porn. Indeed, the example of web-cam sites illustrates that the medium is not necessarily valued for it being specifically or exclusively about physical gratification. Rather, the concept of companionship more accurately describes the attraction, as the browser is afforded a continuity with the life of the person or persons being viewed. Moreover, the reduction of glossy covers to amateur, real-life images of people who have not augmented their bodies to fit a sexual stereotype allows a sense of e.porn as being much more real. One is left feeling more sympathy than contempt for the e.porn consumer.

E.porn does not necessarily provoke any clear sense of objectification premised upon stereotypical gender distinctions. The web is saturated with pornography to such an extent that it makes nonsense out of previous target audience markets. Inevitably and, perhaps, unfortunately, the phrase *if you can think of it,*

it's probably online is quite appropriate in describing what can be found on the web. Thus, such a phrase as *sexual preference* has less utility in cyberspace, since the multiplication of preferences renders the business of categorisation somewhat redundant. The relatively static terms of homosexuality, lesbian, gay, bisexual, and heterosexual are impoverished in comparison to such terms as fetish, bondage, cartoons, group, stories, latinas, or upskirts. Although there are gateways to e.porn websites distinguished by conventional terms denoting sexual preference, increasingly, this method of demarcating interests is less relevant and portals offer access to all tastes to ensure utility. Sexual preference is thus, one category of many other kinds of taste. In itself, this is interesting for it reflects a shift away from sexualities to taste cultures.[6]

(RE)CONSTRUCTING SEXUALITY: no_body

The possibilities for different interactions problematises whether one can treat cyber-spatial relationships in the same way as their non-cyberspatial counterparts. Indeed, this question is part of a broader discourse about how events within cyberspace relate to life outside of it (Parks and Floyd, 1996; Mnookin, 1996). In this sense, the importance of cyber-sexual interactions is also reflected in the way that it challenges the importance of *being there*. The significance of this is recognised by Rheingold (1991: 351) where he states that,

> The secondary social effects of technosex are potentially revolutionary. If technology enables you to experience erotic frissons or deep physical, social, emotional communion with another person with no possibility of pregnancy or sexually transmitted disease, what then of conventional morality, and what of the social rituals and cultural codes that exist solely to enforce that morality? Is disembodiment the ultimate sexual revolution and/or the first step toward abandoning our body?

The consequences of interactions in cyberspace are illustrated by the disturbing case of virtual rape, which took place in a Multi-user

Object-Oriented (MOO) community in 1993. This context is comparable to that which has been previously described, where the environment is created by text-based descriptions and formed by the members of the community that are online. In this particular location, LambdaMOO, the incident was widely publicised and has been argued as being the event that turned a "database into a society" (Dibbell, title of paper, 1993 cited in MacKinnon, 1997).

The violation entailed one member of the community (the violator) taking control of another person's persona and violating the character sexually, in this case, in the presence of all other users. It would be easy to trivialise the act and argue that it is just a group of people having fun playing a game and that what happens to the character is not really what happens to the person. However, this kind of environment blurs fantasy and reality, people are there with different motivations, some playing out fantasies, others meeting with friends and having "real" conversations. As MacKinnon (1988: paragraph 51) describes,

> Many of the personae inhabiting LambdaMOO are permanent or semi-permanent members of its virtual community. They have established for themselves relationships and reputation. Their existence matters to their respective users, and accordingly, they abide by the existing collection of norms, mores, and guidelines known as netiquette.

To argue that cyberspace is a created, artificial, and unreal environment, begs the question as to whether anything at all that takes place in cyberspace is real. It is argued by MacKinnon (1998) that, whilst it can be questioned whether the LambdaMOO incident did constitute rape, there is no doubt that "the current iteration of rape as constructed in LambdaMOO poses serious, real consequences for users of virtual reality." Moreover, the physical component itself cannot be taken as a necessary condition of identifying something as rape. Indeed, the emphasis that is placed upon violations of a physical nature, can be critiqued as underestimating the significant psychological impact of rape (Turkle, 1995).

This lack of importance attributed to the body leads to a more persuasive case for arguing cybersex as problematising its associated meanings. As previously identified, it is doubtful that social stereotypes about gender and sexuality are being replaced. At most, it would seem that they are challenged and altered in some contexts of cyberspace. In contrast, the disappearance of the body in cyberspace (Hayles, 1999) provokes a blurring of the virtual and non-virtual that creates conflicts of understanding. It is not clear how one reconciles this blurring with traditional concepts related to romantic relationships, for example, fidelity. Would it constitute adultery or simply titillation if one were to engage in an affair with a real person in cyberspace?

Imagine a person in any chat-room, chatting (by writing) with strangers about something and nothing. The person is drawn to one individual in particular (or more if it helps) and finds themselves talking about loves and life, embarrassing moments, and other inconsequential matters. After some casual flirting, the discussion evolves when the other person asks 'what are you wearing?' or something equally leading or suggestive. Very soon, they are explaining how arousing the conversation is being. To clarify the circumstances, nearly nothing is known about the identity of the other person or, indeed, whether they are making a joke out of the situation. The person might be quite different in age, perhaps even a minor. Consequently, if one engages with this individual in a sexual manner, then one may be acting contrary to one's perceived sexuality and social values.

Returning to the immediate problem of whether the affair would be adulterous, it must be asked what are the salient characteristics that make adultery morally problematic? Whilst it might be a cliché to say that it is the physical act of sex (or a more diluted form of it) that is problematic, it is suggested here that the act itself is less of a problem than the mental state of intimacy that is achieved between two (or more) people. Upon such a premise, sex with a prostitute, for example, would be less problematic than the meeting of minds that can take place in cyberspace. It is the intimacy experienced between the people involved that is important, indeed, perhaps whether they are in love.

The example serves to reinforce the need to approach relationships differently when they are cyberspatial. If being faithful is a matter of physical acts, then cybersex offers little threat and what threat it does pose may be construed as simply a sophisticated form of pornography. However, if being faithful is about ensuring one's romantic interactions are with one person and one person only, then cybersex can pose a threat to remaining faithful to one's partner. Either way, there does seem a need to draw boundaries within this categorisation that derives from the possibility of cybersex. As Kanitscheider (1999) argues "we need a redefinition of jealousy, or rather a bifurcation of the semantics of the concept, one concerning natural and one concerning virtual persons."

Although this analysis is not exhaustive of these issues, cybersex and cyberdating offer an environment that allows one to form different attitudes towards morality in the context of sexual and romantic relationships; where prostitution meets pornography and where fidelity meets fantasy. Moreover, though Kitchin (1998) considers that cyberspace entails a reconfiguration of the body, the stronger case is suggested here that cybersex marginalises the body's role.

CONCLUSION

It has been argued that the impact of cybersex on the construction of gender, sexuality, and the body must be directed at the experiential quality of liberation that can be felt by CMC users. Such feelings can, at least, reconstruct notions of sexuality, though the aspirations for transcending them are less clear. The kinds of sexual experiences that are found through CMCs permit a unique approach to understanding lifestyle and identity that cannot be treated in a familiar manner. Within cyberspace, not only are the spatial and temporal barriers distorted; so too are interpersonal ones. At the same time, new social barriers and challenges emerge in relation to how one gains access to, interacts, and understands other people in these new environments.

It may be argued that I have avoided any discussion about *real* cybersex. I have made passing reference to the technology of teledildonics and based most of my claims upon a text-based interpretation of cybersex. Hopefully, the reasons for this will be self evident. The title of the paper endeavours to show how cybersex can render some central concepts relating to sex vacuous, in particular gender, sexuality, and the body. It has been claimed that cybersex can distort these concepts, liberate them from their normative understandings, and inevitably make them nonsensical. The importance of the body is reconfigured and that cybersex reaffirms the importance of the mind in sexual interactions.

The example of text-based cybersex might seem a relatively tame basis upon which to claim that there is anything particularly revolutionary about sex through a computer. However, the importance of this example is far greater than any form of cybersex mediated through teledildonics, since it implies a sharper separation of the experience from the body. This dislocation is reinforced by the real effects of acts like virtual rape. This is not to say that people are entirely without their own bodies when engaging with cybersex. Indeed, it is not uncommon for people to masturbate whilst engaged in an online chat. Yet, it is in this sense that the implied meaning of my title "*no body*" is clear.

Cybersex, with or without teledildonics, can be an isolating activity and can become a product for consumption simply because there is no one else in the same room. Thus, cybersex presents the user with a contradiction: the provision of exciting and new experiences without the need for a physical other, at the same time as being rendered spatially isolated from any other person. As Lamborn Wilson (1996: 224) so comedically writes in his analogising of cybersex with phonesex, it is but "a poor parodic rendering of the phone company's slogan, 'Reach out and touch someone,' which is so sadly, so finally, what we *cannot* do in cyberspace."

NOTES

1. It is difficult to gauge the temporal relationships of the words; textual, real-time interactions also introduce a further difference in conversing with somebody. Due to the entire conversation being recorded while the participants type, there is no possibility for mis-hearing or forgetting something. It is possible to get backwards in a conversation whilst it is still taking place, since the entire communication is recorded on the screen as it is written. As such, text-based relationships introduce a dimension that is not feasible to achieve in other contexts.

2. This dialogue and subsequent ones took place between the same two people through an electronic messenger service. For reasons of privacy, the names of the participants are not given. Pseudonyms are also omitted to avoid any unnecessary contextualising of the participants' identities.

3. It is important to recognise that an understanding of these contexts is evolving still within an academic discourse that is only very recently beginning to take seriously the concept of virtual communities and the value of ethnographic research into such sub-cultures (Markham, 1998; Ward, 1999).

4. The term "consumer" does not seem particularly accurate here though neither does "user" as it could be seen to imply the unwarranted connotation as objectifying the other person. However, it is used here in a similar way to its use in general in computer speak, where user simply means the person on the end of the computer.

5. Support for this idea is found in Kibby and Costello (2001) who claim that the presentation and re-presentation of sex entertainment is blurring the respective roles of the spectacle and the spectator.

6. Although it might be argued possible to ascribe specific kinds of taste to any particular sexual preference, the absence of any clear link serves to provide a way of accessing pornography without such associations being made.

REFERENCES

Cairncross, F. (1997). *The Death of Distance: How the Communications Revolution will Change our Lives.* London: The Orion Publishing Group Ltd.

Castells, M. (1997). *The Information Age: Economy, Society and Culture: Volume II: The Power of Identity.* Oxford: Blackwell.Kanitscheider

Ephron, N. (1998). *You've Got Mail* [Film]. Hollywood: Warner Brothers.

Fodor, J. L. (1996). Human Values in the Computer Revolution, pp. 256–266. In Kizza, J. M. (ed.) *Social & Ethical Effects of the Computer Revolution.* London: McFarland & Company, Inc.

Hayles, N. K. (1999). *How We Became Posthuman.* London: University of Chicago Press.

Jones, S. G. (ed.) (1997). *Virtual Culture: Identity and Communication in CyberSociety.* London: Sage.

Kanitscheider, B. (1999). Humans and future communication systems, *Techné: Society for Philosophy & Technology (4, 2), http://scholar.lib.vt.edu/ejournals/SPT/v4_n3html/KANITSCH.html* [June, 1999].

Kibby, M., and Costello, B. (2001). Between the image and the act: Interactive sex entertainment on the Internet. *Sexualities, 4*(3), pp. 353–369.

Kitchin, R. (1998). *Cyberspace: The World in Wires.* Chichester: John Wiley & Sons.

Kizza, J. M. (1996). *Social & Ethical Effects of the Computer Revolution.* London: McFarland & Company, Inc.

Lamborn Wilson, P. (1996). Boundary violations. In S. Aronowitz, B. Martinsons, and M. Menser, (eds.) *Technoscience and Cyberculture.* London: Routledge, pp. 221–229.

Leonard, B. (Dir.) (1992). *The Lawnmower Man* [Film]: Ben Jade Films Inc.

MacKinnon, R. (1997). Virtual rape. *Journal of Computer Mediated Communication, 2:4, http://www.ascusc.org/jcmc/vol2/issue4/mackinnon.html,* [Accessed; June, 1999].

Markham, A. N. (1998). *Life Online.* London: AltaMita Press.

Miah, A. (2000). Virtually nothing: Re-evaluating the significance of cyberspace, *Leisure Studies 19 (3),* 211–225.

Mnookin, J. L. (1996). Virtual(ly) law: The emergence of law in LambdaMOO, *Journal of Computer Mediated Communication (2, 1), http://www.ascusc.org/jcmc/vol2/issue1/lambda.html* [Accessed; June, 1999].

Morse, M. (1997). Virtually female: Body and code. In J. Terry, and M. Calvert (eds.) *Processed Lives: Gender and Technology in Everyday Life.* London and New York: Routledge, pp. 23–35.

Parks, M. R., and K. Floyd (1996). Making Friends in Cyberspace, *Journal of Mediated Communication, 1:4, http://jcmc.huji.ac.il/vol1/issue4/parks.html* [Accessed; June, 1999].

Rheingold, H. (1991). *Virtual Reality.* London: Manderin.

Strehovec, J. (1997, June 26). 'The Web as an instrument of power and a realm of freedom: A report from Ljubljana, Slovenia, *CTHEORY http://www.ctheory.com/a49.html*

Tamblyn, C. (1997). Remote Control: the electronic transference. In J. Terry, and M. Calvert (eds.) *Processed Lives: Gender and Technology in Everyday Life.* London and New York: Routledge, pp. 41–46.

Terry, J., and M. Calvert (eds) (1997). *Processed lives: Gender and technology in everyday life,* London and New York: Routledge.

The Truman Show (1998). P. Weir, Dir. Paramount Pictures.

Turkle, S. (1995). *Life on the Screen: Identity in the Age of the Internet.* London: Weidenfeld and Nicolson.

Ward, K. J. (1999). Cyber-ethnography and the emergence of the virtually new community. *Journal of Information Technology,* (*14, 1*), pp. 95–105.

Wakeford, N. (1999). Gender and the landscapes of computing in an Internet café. In M. Crang, P. Crang, and J. May (eds.), *Virtual Geographies: Bodies, Space and Relations.* London: Routledge, pp. 178–201.

32

An Orgy of Abstinence

Sharon Lerner

Renée is going out with Ronald. Anyone can deduce this from the "Renée 'N' Ronald" hearts she has doodled on her notepad alongside a few crucifixes. But still. As Dirk Been, a handsome, 25-year-old former *Survivor* contestant, climbs onstage at the world's largest abstinence conference (a three-day Miami extravaganza that ended last Saturday), Renée, a 14-year-old from nearby Miami Springs, quietly slips her retainer out of her mouth. There is something about the moment—maybe the sheer thrill of having 500 teenagers crammed into a hotel ballroom to celebrate celibacy, or maybe the way Been moves through them, wearing an appealing smirk—that makes a girl want to free her teeth of plastic and wires. So, as the lanky Been mounts the stage, Renée drops the unsightly retainer, still wet with spit, into her elegant black clutch, with its "Condoms Don't Protect the Heart" sticker pasted near the clasp.

Any movement needs sex appeal, especially one targeted at teenagers. And Been, an aspiring actor whose Web site lists his favorite pastime as dating, offers just the right mix of touched-by-television allure and benign hunkiness to lead the youth rally at "Abstinence: Taking the World by Storm." The National Abstinence Clearinghouse, the nation's largest abstinence group, which has seen its membership blossom from 500 to more than 7500 in the past four years, has gathered kids from Florida to Brazil to take in Been's chaste charms.

These are boom times for the abstinence movement. The "just say no" approach—which began on, and still encompasses, the fringes of the religious right—is now graced with government support as never before. Five years ago, in a little-known provision of the Welfare Reform Bill, conservatives in Congress set aside almost half a billion dollars in state and federal funding for programs that attempt to steer kids away from sex—and avoid any positive mention of birth control. Now, with an enthusiastically pro-abstinence administration in place, the former outsiders are gaining ground in the battle for teenage loins. In 1999, 29 percent of high schools surveyed were already promoting abstinence to the exclusion of information about contraception—a number that continues to rise as the no-sex movement surges forward.

"I've been a virgin all my life," begins Been, as the crowd launches into another round of hooting and screams. Even though he was voted off the island after only three episodes, Been is the kind of guy who knows how to see the bright side. ("I thank God every day for the opportunity to be a part of *Survivor,*" he says solemnly at one point.) Optimism—that a worthy marriage partner will eventually come along, say, or that a wayward bus won't strike before that happens—comes in handy when committing to a sex-free life. So does the ability to withstand a little taunting, which Been admits he's gotten along the way from classmates, teammates, strangers, and even the president of CBS, whom he met in the pre-*Survivor* weeding process.

Indeed, Been seems to think his unwavering commitment to premarital chastity—and his resistance to the temptress CBS producers put in his midst—had something to do with the brevity of his reality-television stint. But abstinence, he ventures, is worth the unpopularity. Holding out for his future bride, Been suggests, is even sexy. "I can't wait to tell that person this is something I saved for her," he says, shaking his head slowly as if audience members can't possibly understand just how much he looks forward to that moment.

You might say the abstinence movement has gotten lucky. The idea of confining sex to marriage is hardly new, of course. But these days, right-to-lifers, religious educators, and people in the pro-marriage movement are coalescing around an updated idea that chastity is the very salvation of society. According to many in Miami, it was teaching about birth control that sparked the sexual revolution.

Indeed, abstinence proponents seem to blame sex education more than premarital sex itself for four decades of increases in teen pregnancy, sexually transmitted disease, open homosexuality, street crime—and even for the existence of Monica Lewinsky (whose name

elicits much tongue clucking here). The reversal they're hoping for is no less sweeping: a social purification through "character education" (as opposed to sex education). Pedagogical weapons include courses such as "Sex Respect" and "Everyone Is NOT Doing It," as well as literature like *I Kissed Dating Goodbye* and "Hang On to Your Hormones."

The Welfare Reform Law specified that programs receiving abstinence-only funds must teach, among other lessons, that "sexual activity outside of marriage is likely to have harmful psychological and physical effects." Such abstinence-till-marriage programs are also only allowed to discuss birth control in the context of its failures. (If the subject comes up at all, the main message must be that the only safe way to avoid sexually transmitted disease and pregnancy is not to have sex.)

With $17 million in new federal abstinence grants awarded just two weeks ago (many of them to groups represented at the conference) and an additional $30 million on its way next year, spirits at the Miami Inter-Continental Hotel are high. There are other demonstrations of official affection: A representative of the Human Resources and Services Administration is on hand to guide those interested in applying for additional federal grant money. Longtime abstinence supporter Wade Horn, whom President Bush just appointed assistant secretary of the HRSA, gives the keynote speech at the awards banquet. And Bush himself, who oversaw the biggest state abstinence education budget nationwide as governor of Texas, issued a personal welcome letter to every conferencegoer. ("Abstinence is not just about saying 'no'—it's about saying yes to a happier, healthier future," writes the president.)

As for the looming question of whether the 1996 abstinence-education bill will be reauthorized when it expires in 2002, "I don't think we need to be too worried about that," said one smiling attendee.

Still, the idea of unequivocally telling kids to avoid sex—and shielding them from information about contraception—is very much embattled. Abstinence-till-marriage promoters are up against the overwhelming majority of both adults and teens, who see the "just say no" approach as antiquated and unrealistic. In survey after survey, parents say they support both encouraging abstinence and teaching about birth control, an approach most at the Miami conference regard as a dangerously mixed message. In June, a coalition of groups including Planned Parenthood, the American Civil Liberties Union, People for the American Way, and Americans United for Separation of Church and State called for the withdrawal of all federal funding from abstinence-only education in public schools. And Surgeon General David Satcher, a Clinton appointee, recently issued a report calling for sex education that includes information about contraception.

Perhaps the biggest challenges for the abstinence movement come from within, though, as the teens at the center of this sexuality battle try to work out the sticky logistics of remaining chaste. Even Been, purity poster-boy of the moment, sometimes finds himself at odds with the official abstinence message. The particular bone of contention that comes up in one interview is masturbation, specifically whether Been thinks it's possible to indulge and still consider oneself abstinent. After pausing to think about the question, Been decides that it is: "As a man" and "as a physical being" and "having all these hormones," he finds the practice "only natural."

This is not the Clearinghouse's official position on masturbation, as president Leslee Unruh, who was sitting in on the interview, is quick to point out. She cites the organization's "Abstinence Survival Kit," which says that "sexual self-stimulation" may "eventually leave the person unable to respond sexually to a real person." In other words, masturbators may become so addicted to this self-sex, they might not be able to enjoy the real thing with their spouses once they find them. "It's the first stage of sexual addiction," warns Unruh.

So what can teens do without straying from the path of purity? Beth and her friend Mary have both given this question considerable thought. Wearing matching glittery sweaters with "Pet Your Dog, Not Your Date" stickers affixed to them, the two ninth-graders from Homestead, Florida, have come to the conference already armed with a strong commit-

ment to abstinence. At 14, Beth has decided that she should court, rather than date, which means she hangs out with the boy in question only when they're with either of their families. When she turns 16, the two will officially start dating, though they'll only meet in public places. Mary, who's also 14, only goes on group dates. "I wouldn't want to put a boy in that kind of situation," she explains of her decision not to date one-on-one.

Perhaps their choices seem severe, but not to them. Both of Beth's two older sisters became teen mothers, one getting pregnant when she was just 15. Mary, too, has seen the toll of reckless teen sex up close. One of her friends got pregnant in seventh grade. "She missed a ton of class," Mary says sadly. Indeed, even while the teen pregnancy rate has reached record lows—between 1991 and 2000, the birthrate among 15- to 17-year-old girls dropped by a whopping 29 percent—more than 40 percent of girls still get pregnant before they exit the teen years.

Even more are having sex, of course. About 50 percent of ninth- through 12th-grade students have lost their virginity, a figure that has become the half-empty, half-full glass of sex education. While abstinence supporters tend to worry about guarding the remaining virgins, those in the sex education camp focus on the kids who have sex—and need to know about how to protect themselves against pregnancy and disease. So deep is the divide, the mere mention of the names Planned Parenthood or SIECUS, the New York City-based nonprofit that promotes sex education including contraception, elicits hisses in some conference rooms here.

While both sides claim the scientific high ground, citing studies that support their programs, the true complexity of the competing approaches is often flattened out by this partisan rancor. Abstinence supporters tend to latch onto only one part of a recent report by a Yale University researcher, for instance, touting the finding that kids who took chastity pledges were more likely to begin having sex later, while downplaying another finding: When those teens did eventually have sex, they were less likely to use birth control. Similarly, some on the other side have taken Satcher's recent report on sex education as a dismissal of abstinence-only education, though the surgeon general concluded not that such education doesn't work, but that there isn't yet convincing evidence that it does.

It's unlikely that that evidence will be coming soon. Many abstinence folks are opposed to the surveys researchers want to use to evaluate federally funded programs because they include specific questions about sex. "Questions plant ideas," warns Peter Brandt, director of issues-response for the conservative Christian group Focus on the Family. "Individuals involved with condom programs shouldn't have a role in evaluating abstinence programs," he argues. "And who cares what those people think, anyway?"

Religious zeal seems to tinge Brandt's angry comments—and, indeed, has helped fuel the entire war over teen sexuality. While there are plenty of good reasons to discourage sexual activity—not the least being the possible ineffectiveness of condoms against some sexually transmitted diseases, such as HPV—the sex education debate inevitably circles back to values on which Americans disagree. Although the Abstinence Clearinghouse is secular, and federal money comes with the stipulation that recipients can't proselytize, religious groups, including Reverend Sun Myung Moon's Unification Church, abound at the conference. Exhibitors sell an array of religious items, including "purity crosses" and "Bod 4 God" bumper stickers.

For the religious groups that have received taxpayer dollars—and there are many, including Mid-South Christian Ministries in West Memphis, Arkansas; Roseland Christian Health Ministries in Chicago; and the Catholic Archdiocese of New York, which received the largest chunk of New York State's abstinence money—the challenge is conveying their message without violating government restrictions or alienating nonbelievers.

One Christian educator, Peggy Hartshorn, devotes much of her talk to this delicate matter. Hartshorn is president of Heartbeat, a chain of so-called crisis pregnancy centers, which offer pregnancy tests and counsel young women who test positive not to have abortions. If the test comes back negative,

Hartshorn seizes the moment to encourage "born-again virginity," which she tells her clients is "God's plan for their sexuality." For those crisis pregnancy centers that have landed federal funding—and a remarkable number have—Hartshorn instead recommends more generically inspirational messages, such as "This is the first day of the rest of your life." According to Hartshorn, though, the reference to God bolsters the argument.

Even the strongest message sometimes falls short, of course. Among those leaving the rally on Thursday was a 14-year-old named David. Like the others in his group, David was wearing a "Virgin Territory" T-shirt and had received his "Don't Be a Sucker! (You're Worth Waiting For)" lollipop upon exiting. But when asked if he could imagine being a virgin at 25, like Dirk Been, David shook his head no. What about getting through college? Again, no. High school? David looked both ways, narrowed his eyes, and again shook his head. Then, lollipop in hand, he went off to join his friends, who were happily jostling and elbowing each other as the adults looked on worriedly.

SIDEBAR: GRAHAM CRACKERS AND OTHER CHASTITY DEVICES

These days, kids can choose from a variety of items to help them abstain. Available at the conference were ATM—abstinence-till-marriage—cards (expiration date: wedding day); chastity rings (to be replaced only with a wedding band); "Don't Play With Fire" abstinence candles; and "No Trespassing" underwear. Here, a sampling of some devices used to squelch sex in times past.

The chastity belt: It began in medieval times as a simple cord worn around the waist to symbolize sexual purity. Only later were metal, locks, and keys added to guard both men and women from sex.

Bundling: In the late 18th century, many families used material barriers to prevent premarital sex. Some courting couples were allowed to spend the night in the same bed (usually the man had traveled some distance for the visit), but they slept fully clothed and separated by a wooden "bundling board."

Circumcision: In the 1880s, when the practice was still rare in this country, Dr. Henry Hanchett recommended circumcision as a way of minimizing stimulation that "can ignite animal passions."

The Graham cracker: In a 1834 lecture on chastity, health reformer Sylvester Graham recommended cold baths and bland food—including a cracker he made for that purpose—as means of staving off sexual excitement.

The Kellogg approach: Meanwhile, another culinary innovator, John Harvey Kellogg (as in the breakfast cereal), recommended tying together young boys' hands and covering their genitals with metal cages to prevent masturbation. For women, Kellogg recommended applying carbolic acid to the clitoris.

33

An Unfinished Revolution
Sexuality in the 20th Century

Jeffrey Weeks
South Bank University, London

What do we mean when we write about 'sexuality'? Sexuality pervades the air we breathe, but we still lack a common language for speaking about it. It is a topic which we can all say something about, and on which we are all in one way or another 'experts', but that, somehow, increases rather than decreases our confusions: sexuality, it seems, has so many 'truths' that we are left with a cacophony of noise, and precious little good sense. There has been an ever expanding explosion of discourse around sexuality in the past century, and the volume seems unlikely to diminish in the near future. Yet it is a subject which arouses the greatest anxieties and controversies, and increasingly has become a front-line of divisive political controversy and moral debate.

This is because the sexual touches on so many disparate areas of individual and social existence. When we think of sexuality we think of a number of things. We think of reproduction, which has traditionally been seen as the main justification of sexual activity, and with which western cultures at least have historically been most preoccupied. We think of relationships, of which marriage is the socially sanctioned, but far from being the only, form. We think of erotic activities and of fantasy, of intimacy and warmth, of love and pleasure. We relate it to our sense of self and to our collective belongings, to identity, personal and political. But we also think of sin and danger, violence and disease.

Nothing is straightforward when we try to think or speak of sexuality. It is both the most private and personal of activities, and the most public. We still often speak of it in whispers, while it is all the time shouting at us from bill-boards, newspapers, radio and television, pulpits, the streets. Our own voices compete with, or may even be, those of priests and politicians, medics and militants, and all too many, many more.

So anyone rash enough to try to analyse its social forms, or predict what shape the kalei-

Source: An unfinished revolution: Sexuality in the 20th century, by Jeffrey Weeks in *Pleasure Principles*, Victoria Harwood et al., (eds.). London: Lawrence & Wishart, 1993, pp. 1–19. © 1993 Jeffery Weeks. Used with permission of the publisher.

doscope will next take, is treading on very dangerous ice. There are so many conflicting elements at play. For sex, despite its immediacy, is very much a cultural and a historical phenomenon. Whatever we like to think we are not entirely free agents in this matter, any more than we are of anything else. Our choices are real and important, but they are also constrained by a very long and complex history and intricate power relations, which tell us, amongst other things, what is natural or unnatural, good or bad, permissible or impermissible. If there is a 'crisis of sexuality' today, it is because many of the fixed points which we think we need to guide us through the maze have been pulled down or obscured; and because the language of sexuality is muddied by a long and often painful history.

If there is a confusion about values and attitudes, that should not surprise us, nor should we imagine it is anything unique to us. We can find in the history of the past two hundred years or so almost all the themes that preoccupy us now, and similar laments about the decline of morals and a confusion of values.[1] Two hundred years ago, in the wake of the French Revolution, one of the formative moments of modern Europe, we find middle-class evangelists worried about the state of morality in Britain: they saw, or believed they saw, a dissolute, amoral aristocracy, a feckless, overbreeding working class. Surely, these moralists felt, we would end up like the French, drowned in chaos and blood, unless we all learned the importance of 'respectability', what became 'Victorian values'.

Some of the implications of these Victorian values became clearer a generation later as the poverty and disease of the new industrial towns began to confront policy makers. Just as today some conservative commentators seek to blame social ills on the existence of one parent families, so in the 1840s and 50s individual behaviour was blamed for what were transparently social ills. The result was a renewed effort to moralise the masses into the image of their masters, an effort which by and large failed. The mores of the working classes may have been different from those of the middle class, but, as historians are now discovering, they were no less 'moral'.

Then take sex-related disease. Today our experience of sex is shadowed by the HIV/AIDS epidemic. In the nineteenth century the most feared scourge was syphilis, and we can find in the response to this, ominous pre-echoes of our modern reaction. In the 1860s a series of measures, the Contagious Diseases Acts, sought to control the spread of syphilis by enforcing compulsory examinations of those who were suspected of being prostitutes. The model for the acts were allegedly measures to control cattle. The result was inevitable: the intimidation of large numbers of women, growing hostility to state regulation, a radical movement of resistance, and no obvious impact on the incidence of the disease. Many of the more extreme measures proposed in the 1980s to control the spread of HIV—compulsory testing, detention of those suspected of spreading the disease— were prefigured a hundred years before.

As another example, let's take sexual abuse of children. Today we worry rightly about child sex abuse. But sexual abuse of children was raised in the 1830s in the context of debates about the impact of children working in the factories and mines; in the 1870s, in the report, no less, of the Prince of Wales's Royal Commission on Housing, in the context of housing overcrowding and the danger of incest; and in the 1880s, as a result of the panic about the 'white slave trade', when the age of consent for girls was raised eventually from 13 to 16. It takes different forms at different times, but abuse of children is not a new discovery, any more than our confusions and hesitations in confronting it are new.

The history of birth control reveals a similar pattern. Although the roots of the birth control movement are many and various, and its practice in many forms is probably as old as sexuality, its preoccupations over the past 100 years have been remarkably constant: how to balance the need for social regulation of the population with the rights of parents and of individual women to control their own fertility. When the National Birth Control Council, the immediate predecessor for the Family Planning Association, was set up in 1930 it brought together a number of groups, some of which were deeply shaped by eugenicist ideas, preoccupied with the planned breeding of the best. One of the great fears of the time was that as the population declined, so the balance of the population would shift to those who were least 'fit' to bear the burdens of modern life. Today we are more concerned with the threat of overpopulation in the Third World, or of the implications of artificial insemination or extra-uterine conception, but the same anxieties and fears still intrude: we worry about who should breed, and under what conditions and whose control, as much as why. We do not like apparently the idea of sexuality being uncontrolled and unplanned, a matter of choice rather than social obligation.

Finally, there's the question of sexual identity. It is easy for us today to assume that the sexual categories and identities we work within, pre-eminently those of heterosexual and homosexual, are fixed and eternal, corresponding to essential differences transmitted (who knows how?) from the dawn of time. It is now clear, however, that these distinctions were only formulated in a recognisably modern form in the closing years of the nineteenth century, the result of a complex process whereby the norm of heterosexuality was established and reinforced by the drawing of boundaries between it and its dangerous other, homosexuality. This in turn was intricately related to the reformulation of gender relations, so that sexual and gender identities were locked together: manhood, in particular, was defined by refusing the temptation of homosexuality. The developments of the current century have made possible the emergence of strong and vibrant lesbian and gay identities that have challenged the heterosexual norm, just as social change and the rise of contemporary feminism have undermined the hierarchies of gender, but the point that I want to underline is that the nineteenth century, like the present, was haunted by the spectre of homosexuality. There is a nice historical symmetry in the fact that just over a hundred years after the Criminal Law Amendment Act of 1885 made all forms of male homosexuality illegal, the 'promotion of homosexuality' by local authorities was banned (through what became known as 'Clause 28'). Circumstances change, and so do laws; but a fear of homosexuality apparently remains.[2]

We can, in other words, see in the fairly recent history of sexuality, many problems, dilemmas and anxieties remarkably similar to our own. They revolve essentially around boundaries, between men and women, adults and children, 'normal' and 'perverse' sexuality, between orthodox and unorthodox lifestyles and identities, between health and disease. I offer these examples not to suggest that nothing ever changes; on the contrary, I hope to show that there have been profound changes in attitudes towards sexuality. My intention, rather, is to warn against that facile history which looks back to a 'golden age' when somehow everything was better, more fixed and certain, than it is today. It wasn't, and we are not going to be able to deal with the challenges of the close of this century if we seek a return to the largely mythical, supposedly wholesome values of the last.

Nostalgia for a golden age of order and harmony is one danger when thinking of sexuality. There is another temptation as we approach the end of the millennium, to identify with that sense of an ending which seems to characterize the closing of a century, to reconstruct a *fin de siècle* mood which sees the uncertainty of our own age of anxiety as being the same as that of the most famous *fin* of all, that of the late nineteenth century. Rather than regretting a better past, this mood wallows in the 'sexual anarchy' which some contemporary commentators saw as characterizing the ending of the last century.[3] This in turn fits into a postmodern consciousness which in its most deconstructive mood celebrates the impossibility of a master, legitimizing discourse for sexuality, glories in heterogeneity, the return of the repressed of sexuality, the *bouleversement* of all values, and the subversive power of the perverse.

This opens up challenging perspectives for thinking about sexuality anew. This is especially the case as a new scholarship undermines the dominant myths and meanings that emerged in the late nineteenth century.[4] As hallowed traditions crumble, we are being forced to raise questions of value: by what criteria, and by whose sanction, can we say that this activity, desire, style, way of life, is better or worse, more or less ethically valid, than any other. If the Gods are dead, or dying, or the secular myths of History and Science lie discredited before us, is anything permitted? Postmodernist writing has been effective in tearing apart for scrutiny and critique many of our taken-for-granted beliefs. It has been less effective in elaborating alternative values. I shall return to this issue later.

I want now to look at certain key trends which seem to me to underlie the changes we have experienced over the past century, and whose consequences look set to dominate the 1990s. I identify these as, first, the secularisation of sex, an inadequate term which does, nonetheless, pinpoint some key changes; second, a liberalisation of attitudes, which has reshaped both the law and social attitudes; and third, the challenge of diversity, perhaps the key change to which everything else is secondary. Finally, I want to look at the future of all three in the context of the current crisis around HIV disease and AIDS. I am not going to offer predictions, because nothing is predictable in the world of sexuality; nor do I wish to suggest a blueprint for a new ethics: blueprints are what have so often led us astray. But I shall try to offer a framework for understanding what too often seems like a meaningless flux.

THE SECULARISATION OF SEX

First of all let's look at what I am calling the secularisation of sex. By this I mean the progressive detachment of sexual values from religious values—even for many of the religious. This has a long history, but perhaps the key feature was the process, beginning in the mid nineteenth century, whereby the initiative for judging sexuality passed from the churches to the agents of social and mental hygiene, primarily in the medical profession. Science promised to prop up, or replace, religion in explaining or legitimizing sexual behaviour. Already by the end of the century, some feminist and other critics were arguing that doctors were the new priesthood, imposing their new (overwhelmingly masculine) imperatives on the bodies of women.

Since then, the arbiters of sexual values have tended to be increasingly doctors, sexologists, psychologists, social workers, even politicians, rather than priests.

This is, of course, an unfinished revolution, as all those who have campaigned for birth control, sex education, the rights of sexual minorities or the right of sexual choice know very well. You can still be labelled as both immoral and sick, sinful and diseased, all at the same time, if you offend the norms. Nor have the churches of various kinds given up the struggle. It is only a few years since the British Chief Rabbi welcomed the 'swinging of the pendulum' back to traditional values (though as I have suggested, that tradition was itself pretty confused).[5] Elsewhere in the world, as well as in this country, we have seen what W. H. Auden called the 'fashionable madmen' attempting to assert the links between religious fundamentalism and a particular (restricted) type of sexual behaviour, and these attitudes have had many local successes to their credit. The Republican Party convention in the USA in 1992, to quote just one recent example, managed to impose on the party an extremely conservative moral agenda; opposing abortion, campaigning against the recognition of homosexual rights and affirming the merits of 'family values'.[6]

Yet it seems that despite all the huffing and puffing, the anguished debates and the like, the process of secularisation has gone too far to reverse fundamentally, as the spectacular electoral failure of the Republicans in 1992 suggests. Even in the most traditional of churches, such as the Roman Catholic, perhaps the majority of the faithful (and a significant minority of its own priesthood, apparently) ignore the Pope's injunctions against birth control, and in the USA we see openly gay Catholic priests and lesbian nuns. The fevered efforts of religious traditionalists to turn back the tide testifies, I would argue, as much to the success of secularisation as to the power of religion.

But at the same time as the power of religion is undermined, so the claims of a scientific morality have been subverted. The early sexologists, men (usually men) such as

Richard von Krafft-Ebing, Havelock Ellis, Magnus Hirschfeld, even Freud, believed that what they were doing was to put the laws of sexuality onto a scientific basis, to provide a rational basis for sex reform: 'through science to justice', proclaimed Hirschfeld in Germany before his library and legacy were piled on the Nazi book-burning pyre.[7] Today we are a little more sceptical of the claims of science to guide us through the moral maze. Many of those labelled and categorized by the early science of sex (women as the 'dark continent', homosexuals as a biological aberration) have resisted the labels, and developed their own definitions in a sort of grass roots sexology which plays with and subverts inherited descriptions.

The significance of all this is profound, because what it does is to take responsibility for sexual behaviour away from external sources of authority and to place it squarely on to the individual. This introduces into the debate on sexuality a contingency that is, for many, troubling and enfeebling. But it is important to recognise that this sense of contingency is not just confined to the domain of sexuality. On the contrary, the existence of a dual consciousness, of the necessity, but difficulty and pain, of individual choice, can be seen as a key element of our late modern sense of self. As the 'juggernaut of modernity', in Anthony Gidden's phrase, gathers momentum, dissolving all certainties and transforming all fixed identities and relationships, so the sense of the contingency of self, its provisional placing in a changing world, a narrative quest for partial unity rather than a fixed attribute of essential being, becomes paramount.[8] In the twentieth century the Enlightenment belief in the constitutive individual, Man (and it was usually male) as the measure of all things, has been severely challenged: by Freud's discovery of the dynamic unconscious, by the recognition of cultural and sexual diversity, by the challenges of feminism and lesbian and gay politics, by the historical and deconstructive turns in the social sciences, by the experiences of fragmentation which for many characterizes late or post-modernity. In all these contexts sexuality becomes problematized, dethroned from its position of being a determining essence. Yet at the same time, as if by a necessary reflex, sexuality becomes a source of meaning, of social and political placing, and of individual sense of self.

This of course poses many problems, and is probably the main focus of anxiety about sexuality today. The public debates about sexuality since the 1960s, including those around the so-called 'permissive reforms' of the law on abortion, homosexuality, divorce, censorship and birth control, far from being a licence to do what you want, were actually about finding the right balance between private pleasures and public policy, between freedom and regulation. In other ways, the rise of the caring professions, the pressure on organisations like Relate (the National Marriage Guidance Council), and the proliferation of experts and therapies of various sorts, indicate the difficulties of relying on ourselves alone. But the conclusion we must draw from this secularisation seems to me inescapable: today we see sexual matters as essentially about individual choice. The debate is about the legitimate limits of choice, not about the legitimacy of choice itself.

LIBERALISATION OF ATTITUDES

This is closely related to the second trend I have identified, the growing liberalisation of attitudes over the past generation. By this I mean the gradual abandonment of authoritarian or absolutist values, and a growing stress on individual decision-taking about sexuality. People are generally more accepting today of birth control, abortion, pre-marital sex, co-habitation before or instead of marriage, divorce, and homosexuality than ever they were in that supposed haven of the 'sexual revolution', the 1960s. And despite its espousal of Victorian values, and a certain closing of space around a number of key issues, this liberalisation continued to grow, perhaps even increase during the Thatcher years, and is likely to continue during the 1990s.[9]

Here are a few examples. About 50 per cent of single women lived with a man before marriage by the end of the 1980s, compared to 7 per cent in 1970, and over triple the figure when Mrs. Thatcher took office in 1979. The proportion of children born outside marriage rose from 12 per cent in 1980 to 25 per cent in 1988. For women under 20, the figure is much higher: around 82 per cent in the north-west and north of England. Britain now has one of the highest divorce rates in Europe, over 150,000 a year in the 1980s, and 4 out of 10 marriages, it is projected, will end in divorce in the 1990s.[10]

Then there is the touchstone issue of abortion, a highly contested issue throughout much of the west (it was, for example, one of the issues that threatened to hold up German unification in 1990, because of the conservative fear in west Germany of the liberal laws in the east), and a highly divisive issue in the USA. Despite strenuous efforts since the law was liberalised in Britain in the 1960s to reduce the time during which termination is permitted, all have failed, not only because a majority of MPs were resistant or because of the campaigns of pressure groups, for example, the National Abortion Campaign, but because access to abortion had become the wish of the majority of the population. I am sure that abortion will continue to be a key moral issue, but it is difficult to believe that there will be a consensus in Britain in the near future for restrictive change.

These examples suggest to me that there has been a crucial long-term shift in the way we see sexual activity and relationships. I would be cautious about calling it a revolution. In many ways it is startlingly like a reversion to much earlier, pre-'Victorian values' mores, with a high rate of formal illegitimacy, toleration of certain forms of pre-marital sex, and a relatively late age of marriage. This is accompanied, however, by a new explicitness in talking about sex which magnifies and dramatises the impact of the transformations that have taken place.

There is, however, an ambiguity in this continuing liberalisation, which underlines the limits of the changes that have taken place, and this is seen most clearly in relation to homosexuality. According to opinion surveys, there was a continuing liberalisation in attitudes towards homosexuality from the late

1960s into the early 1980s, then a shuddering set back, which has only recently, according to the survey *British Social Attitudes*, been partially reversed. So while in 1983, 62 per cent censured homosexual relationships, by 1987, in the wake of the AIDS panic, this had risen to 74 per cent of those interviewed. Public hostility was even sharper when asked their attitudes to lesbians and gay men having the right to adopt children. In 1987, 86 per cent would forbid lesbians adopting children, and 93 per cent gay men. A Gallup Poll shortly after the Clause 28 controversy in late 1987, early 1988, confirmed a deep seated hostility: 60 per cent thought that homosexuality should not be considered an accepted lifestyle, compared with 34 per cent who did approve—though perhaps significantly for the coming decade, 50 per cent of those under 35 were accepting.[11] What seems to be happening is a greater acceptance of the fact of homosexuality ('live and let live') whilst there remains an ingrained refusal to see it as of equal validity with heterosexuality.

There is a sharp paradox in attitudes towards homosexuality. While prosecutions for 'homosexual offences' reached a height in the late 1980s only previously attained in 1954, before legislation, suggesting an increased police interest in the issue, while the popular press pursued people suspected of homosexual tendencies fervently, and while the incidence of 'queer-bashing' increased dramatically, there were abundant signs of a more general growth of the homosexual community. Social facilities continued to expand, gay characters appeared in soap operas on television, people spoke more easily about homosexuality than ever before. The prosecutions, 'queer-bashings', and Clause 28 can be seen as distorted responses to real changes taking place in attitudes to non-heterosexual behaviour. It is not too much of an exaggeration to say that Mrs. Thatcher, despite her rhetoric and actions, presided over the biggest expansion of the lesbian and gay community in its history.

This is in line with the wider point I am making: there seems to be a long-term shift both in beliefs and behaviours taking place which governments have only a limited power to effect. They can toughen laws, pursue errant fathers, condemn the 'promotion of homosexuality' and the like. They can contribute to the sum total of human misery. But they cannot force people to behave in ways that they don't want to.

This is, in part at least, recognized in the new legal framework that reached its apogee in the liberal reforms of the 1960s, but which still, if inadequately, shapes legal responses. The liberalization of the legal framework that followed the Wolfenden report on homosexuality and prostitution in 1957 signalled an abandonment of legal absolutism, that is a view of the law which saw it as embodying the moral norms of society. Instead, the new approach relied on a clear distinction between the role of the law, to uphold generally acceptable standards of public behaviour, and the domain of morals, increasingly seen as a matter of private choice (the 'Wolfenden strategy').[12] In practice this meant allowing, in the famous phrase, 'consenting adults in private' to pursue their personal ends without interference so long as the public were not unduly frightened. The actual implementation of the new legal framework was less clear cut, however. For example, abortion on demand was tempered by the need for medical authorization of abortions. The rights of homosexuals was restricted by narrow interpretations of 'consent' (which could be given only by those over 21, not at all in Scotland or Northern Ireland until a decade later, and never in the armed forces), and of 'privacy' (which was not recognized if more than two people were present, or potentially present). Regulation was changed, but not abandoned; the locus of control shifted. A form of sexual pluralism was recognized, but it was not fully legitimized. Yet it provided a space which has allowed sexual autonomy to grow. During the 1970s and 1980s there were various challenges to this legal compromise, especially with regard to pornography; but despite a harsher climate and a closing of space for social experimentation, the framework held, even under a political regime committed to moral conservatism. Clause 28 is again a test case. Although its intention was restrictive and punitive, it was still clearly within the framework of the Wolfenden strategy. It did not propose making homosexuality illegal, intending instead to prevent 'promotion'. Of course, by doing that, the government's intervention gave unprecedented publicity to homosexuality, and helped to forge a stronger sense of identity and community amongst lesbians and gay men than ever before.[13] But that is one of the paradoxes of legal involvement in sexual lives. The unintended consequences are often more important than the intended. The liberal legal experiment attempted as much to regulate as to free individuals, but its consequences have been to institutionalize a form of tolerance of diversity and choice. That tolerance falls far short of full acceptance of difference, as the case of homosexuality underlines. Nevertheless, it highlights my central point: legal and moral absolutism are fading as the guidelines of policy, but the alternatives have still to be fully worked out.

To close this discussion of what I have called liberalisation, I want to pin-point two further historic shifts that underlie some of the patterns I have mentioned. The first is the changing balance of relations between men and women. This is most obvious in the taken-for-granted assumption today that women have their own sexual needs and desires, with as much claim to satisfying them as men. This has been a long revolution since the nineteenth century, and one that is not clear cut or unproblematic. Some feminist historians have suggested that what has happened is a sexualisation of the female body on male terms, and for the servicing of men. Against this it is important to remember the struggles of women themselves for sexual autonomy and freedom of choice.[14]

Beyond this is a more profound questioning of the power relations between women and men, the result of both of feminism and the changing role of women in the economy and society. Despite ups and downs in the path to full equality, there is no doubt that this represents a radical transformation of relationships, whose effects in the next decade are impossible to underestimate. We have already seen its impact in, amongst other things, the changing agenda on rape and sexual violence and a new concern with the sexual abuse of children, in all of which questions of power are to the fore.

The second shift that must be recognised is the growing recognition of the fact of sexual diversity. I have mentioned homosexuality, and the contradictory responses it evokes. But it is clear today that there is a much greater variety of beliefs, identities and relationships than our moral codes allow. The truth is that people's sexual needs and desires do not fit easily into the neat categories and moral systems we build to describe and contain them.

Both these shifts are critical elements in the third major trend I want to outline: the challenge of diversity.

THE CHALLENGE OF DIVERSITY

The heart of the challenge is this: we increasingly have to accept the fact of diversity. We know that people have different needs and desires, that they live in different types of households and have various sorts of relationships. But we are reluctant to accept the norm of diversity: that is, we still seek to judge people as if there were a common moral standard by which they should live. I believe that one of the key issues of the 1990s will be precisely the attempt to move from recognition to normalisation of diversity.

The constant laments about the impact of permissiveness and the evocation of 'Victorian values' during the 1980s suggested that the key changes we have noted—the rise of illegitimacy, the rising divorce figures, the new presence of homosexuality, etc.—indicated a drastic decline of moral standards, a disintegration of old values, leading to a threat to the very existence of the family. Interestingly, more recently, there has been a dawning recognition that something else is afoot: not so much a collapse of morals, as a change in their form, not so much a decline of the family, as the rise of different sorts of families. Angela Rumbold, when briefly the minister for the family in the late 1980s, suggested that these facts were beginning to filter through into government thinking.[15] The point was made more sharply by the then Leader of the Opposition, Neil Kinnock, in a speech in 1990: 'Anyone concerned about the future of the family', he said, 'should understand that in our generation the family is changing, it is not collapsing'.[16] Those who regarded the rise of the non-traditional family as evidence of social delinquency, he went on, showed not only prejudice but impracticality in the face of the problems accompanying change.

Behind such statements is a growing body of social research which has traced the shifts in the domestic patterns which frame sexual behaviour. In many ways, we are still deeply familial in our behaviour patterns. Although the age of marriage has crept up in recent years, most people still get married. Though there has been a recent decline, a high proportion of divorced people re-marry. And even though there is a growing percentage of children born outside marriage, they are more often than not born into marriage-like relationships. A majority of 'illegitimate births' are jointly registered by both parents. Although we are more tolerant of pre-marital sex, we remain very censorious of extra-marital sex. And the majority, as we have seen, still disapprove of homosexual relationships, and the adoption of children by lesbians and gay men. We remain, in the words of the sociologist David Clark, deeply 'Wedlocked'.[17]

Yet these overall figures conceal a great deal of variety. A survey by National Opinion Polls for the *Independent* showed that the traditional view of the family was held by only a minority, while the under-35's have a 'radically different view of family life to that of their parents' generation'. These different views of the under-35s include a more relaxed attitude to both partners working, joint rearing of children, and a more tolerant attitude (though still only amongst about a third of those polled) to homosexual adoptions.[18]

But beyond such generational shifts is a growing recognition that the word 'family' covers a multitude of forms. In the early 1980s the family sociologists Rhona and Robert Rappoport distinguished five types of family diversity: by internal organisation of the family; as a result of cultural factors such as race and ethnicity, religious and other factors; class differences in family life; changes over the life-course; and differing patterns by generation. Others have listed different types of 'families', ranging from non-married cohabitation to single parenthood, from 'commuter-marriages' to lesbian and gay relationships.[19] As we know, the latter were labelled 'pretended family relationships' in the Local Government Act of 1988, but once you broaden the definition of the family to include non-traditional forms, it is difficult to know what you can legitimately exclude.

The point I am making is that sexual activity, and committed sexual-emotional relationships, take place today in a number of more or less long term settings, and have given rise to a range of patterns of domestic organisation. We have not yet sorted out, however, the implications of this for policy or ideology. We know, for example, that many women choose single-parenthood. We also know that more often than not single-parenthood is associated with poverty. The Conservative government in 1990 announced proposals for making errant fathers contribute to the rearing of children, presumably as one sort of response to poverty. But little thought has been given to the implications of that response to the question of choice.[20] More often than not we continue to pay lip-service to individual freedom while being punitive to those who exercise it.

These are difficult issues, but ones which, I believe, will dominate the social agenda in the 1990s. They are likely to shift us away from a moral politics which relies on *a priori* positions towards one which looks at needs and how they can be satisfied. Put another way, we are likely to see less and less emphasis on moral absolutes and an increasing willingness to live with moral diversity.

THE IMPACTS OF AIDS

Finally, I want to look at an experience which has fed into the moral absolutism of the 1980s, threatened to create a sort of backlash against sexual liberalism, and has had a tragic effect on the lives of many people—the impact of the health crisis associated with HIV disease, and AIDS.

The response to HIV has been coloured by the fact that it has been seen as a disease, in the west at least, of the marginal and the execrated. In America and Britain—but not, it must be said, in all European countries—largely, it has so far affected gay men and intravenous drug users, the so called 'guilty victims' compared to supposedly 'innocent victims' such as haemophiliacs. It was only when it seemed that HIV was likely to seep through into the heterosexual community that governments in the USA and Britain displayed any urgency on the matter. The British government's launch into urgent action at the end of 1986 was precipitated by the U.S. Surgeon-General's report on the danger of a heterosexual epidemic earlier that year. A tailing off in urgency followed in 1989 after reports circulated that rumours of a heterosexual threat were much exaggerated. It seems that urgency is not required if only unpopular minorities are at risk.[21]

But, and it should not need saying, we are complacent about the risks of HIV and AIDS at our peril. In Africa and other parts of the developing world millions are at risk. In the USA well over 100,000 people have been diagnosed with AIDS, more than half are dead. HIV disease is the largest single cause of premature death amongst men and women in cities like New York. It is estimated that one in four American families have already been personally affected. In Britain at the time of writing nearly 6,500 have been diagnosed with AIDS, some 4,000 are dead. And the most recent figures are ominous. AIDS cases amongst heterosexuals are now rising faster than amongst any other category. The figures amongst heterosexuals are still very small in Britain, about the same as they were amongst homosexual men in 1984. But that itself indicates the dangers.[22]

The problem is that the population as a whole seems pretty resistant to warnings about these dangers. The gay community quite early on learnt the need for safer-sex techniques, and the avoidance of high-risk activities. The results were seen in a drop of Sexually Transmitted Disease (STD) infections amongst gay men in the late 1980s, and a slowing down of the expected rate of increase of infection. But there is no similar evidence for a widespread adoption of safer sex amongst heterosexuals. Recent STD figures suggest, moreover, a dangerous increase again of infections. In one London hospital, gonorrhoea infections rose by almost 100 per cent between 1988 and 1990. It seems that people are becoming complacent about the dangers.[23]

This suggests that the doom-laden warnings that have characterised much of the public education on AIDS are not effective. Equally ineffective, however, were the calls for a re-moralisation of behaviour that we heard in the 1980s. There was certainly, as we have seen, a renewed hostility towards homosexuality, and this had very unpleasant effects. A recent *British Social Attitudes* survey indicated that there has been a slight decline in the tendency to see AIDS in moral terms, though there remains strong support for statements that certain sexual practices are morally wrong.[24] Yet there is overwhelming evidence that this does not stop people doing them. What such moralism does do, however, is prevent the full dissemination of knowledge about risk activities and safer-sex techniques.

That moralism is not surprising, however, because the HIV/AIDS crisis dramatizes many of the uncertainties and ambiguities that are shaping sexual mores at the end of this century. It feeds into that sense of an end of an era which I have already noted as an important component of our culture at the present. It dramatizes the existence of sexual and cultural diversity. It underlines the absence of a consensus concerning what is ethically valid and invalid, acceptable or unacceptable, right and wrong. People with HIV and AIDS have had to endure stigma because our culture has been unable to come to terms with the changes that have transformed sexual life in the twentieth century.

I have suggested in this chapter that sexual behaviour and sexual beliefs are being shaped and re-shaped by a number of long-term trends: secularisation, liberalisation, and the growth of social and moral diversity. During the 1980s, under the impact both of political forces and of AIDS, a number of these trends seemed to be on the point of going into reverse. But it is already looking as if these were blips rather than fundamental shifts. If this is so, then we need to adjust to these trends in our thinking about sexuality. It's time, I suggest, that our moral systems begin to move closer to what we actually do and are, rather than what inherited traditions say we should do and be. If that were to happen we would, I believe, see the development not only of a more humane and tolerant culture, but one that was also more responsible and healthier in facing the challenges of this particular *fin de siècle*.

NOTES

1. Further details for the examples given can be found in Jeffrey Weeks, *Sex, Politics and Society: The Regulation of Sexuality since 1800*, 2nd edition, Longman, Harlow 1989.

2. On homosexuality see the title essay in David M. Halperin, *One Hundred Years of Homosexuality, and Other Essays on Greek Love,*, Routledge, New York and London 1990; Eve Kosovsky Sedgwick, *Epistemology of the Closet*, University of California Press, Berkeley and Los Angeles 1990; and the essays in Jeffrey Weeks, *Against Nature: Essays on History, Sexuality and Identity*, Rivers Oram Press, London 1991.

3. On this theme, see Elaine Showalter, *Sexual Anarchy: Gender and Culture at the Fin de Siècle*, Bloomsbury, London 1991.

4. On the 'sexual tradition', see Jeffrey Weeks, *Sexuality and its Discontents: Meanings, Myths and Modern Sexualities*, Routledge, London and New York 1985.

5. Interview with Sir Immanual Jakobovits, *Independent*, 27 November 1987.

6. See coverage of the 1992 convention in the newspapers of August 1992.

7. See Weeks, *Sexuality and its Discontents*, chapter 4; and Jeffrey Weeks, *Sexuality*, Ellis Horwood/Tavistock, Chichester and London 1986, chapter 6.

8. On this theme see Anthony Giddens, *The Transformation of Intimacy, Sexuality, Love and Eroticism in Modern Societies*, Polity Press, Cambridge 1992.

9. On the Thatcher years see Martin Durham, *Sex and Politics: The Family and Morality in the Thatcher Years*, Macmillan, Basingstoke 1991.

10. See, for example, Roger Jowell, Sharon Witherspoon, Lindsay Brook (eds.), *British Social Attitudes—the 7th Report*, Gower, Aldershot 1990;

Regional Trends 25, HMSO, London 1990; *Family Change and Future Policy*, Family Policy Studies Centre, London 1990; *Key Population and Vital Statistics 1989*, HMSO, London 1990; *Population Trends 61*, HMSO, London 1990; *Single Person Households—Single Living, Diverse Lifestyles 1992*, Mintel International Group, London 1992, quoted in *The Times*, 15 September 1992.

11. Roger Jowell et al. (eds.). *British Social Attitudes. The 5th Report*, Gower, Aldershot 1988; Gallop Poll reported in the *Sunday Telegraph*, 5 June 1988.

12. On the Wolfenden strategy and its implications see Jeffrey Weeks, *Coming Out: Homosexual Politics in Britain from the Nineteenth Century to the Present*, 2nd edition, Quartet Books, London 1990, chapter 15; Weeks, *Sex, Politics and Society*, chapter 12.

13. Stephen Jeffery-Poulter, *Peers, Queers and Commons: The Struggle for Gay Law Reform from 1950 to the Present*, Routledge, London and New York 1991, chapter 11; Antony Grey, *Quest for Justice: Towards Homosexual Emancipation*, Sinclair-Stevenson, London 1992, pp. 233–5: Jeffrey Weeks, 'Pretended Family Relationships', chapter 8 in Jeffrey Weeks, *Against Nature: Essays on History, Sexuality and Identity*, Rivers Oram Press, London 1991.

14. See for example, Sheila Jeffreys, *Anti-climax*, Pandora, London 1991 for an argument about the limitations of liberalization. For an alternative feminist argument see the two books by Lynne Segal, *Is the Future Female? Troubled Thoughts on Contemporary Feminism*, Virago, London 1987, and *Slow Motion, Changing Masculinities, Changing Men*, Virago, London 1990.

15. Patrick Wintour, 'Changing attitudes shake family values', *Guardian*, 9 October 1990; Judy Jones, 'Minister urges need to target resources', *Independent*, 22 October 1990.

16. Jack O'Sullivan, 'Labour stakes claim to be party for community care', *Independent*, 21 September 1990; news report of Kinnock's speech, *Guardian*, 21 September 1990.

17. David Clark and Douglas Haldane, *Wedlocked?*, Polity Press, Cambridge 1990.

18. Peter Kellner, 'Traditional view of family "held by minority of people"', *Independent*, 21 September 1990.

19. Robert and Rhona Rapoport, 'British Families in Transition', in R. N. Rapoport, M. P. Fogarty and R. Rapoport (eds.), *Families in Britain*, Routledge and Kegan Paul, London 1982. See the discussion of this theme in Weeks, 'Pretended Family Relationships', op cit.

20. For the effects of that policy see Sally Malcolm-Smith, 'Single mothers harassed to name absent fathers', *Observer*, 22 September 1991.

21. 'AIDS: the intellectual agenda', chapter 7 in Weeks, *Against Nature*; Virginia Berridge and Philip Strong, 'AIDS policies in the UK: a preliminary analysis', in Elizabeth Fee and Daniel Fox, *AIDS: Contemporary History*, University of California Press, Berkeley 1991.

22. For up to date figures see *WorldAIDS*, Panos Institute, London, continuing.

23. For a commentary on changing figures see Graham Hart, Mary Boulton, Ray Fitzpatrick, John McLean and Jill Dawson '"Relapse" to unsafe sexual behaviour amongst gay men: a critique of recent behavioural HIV/AIDS research', *Sociology of Health and Illness: A Journal of Medical Sociology*, volume 14, no 2, June 1992, pp. 216–32.

24. Roger Jowell, Sharon Witherspoon and Linday Brook (eds.), *British Social Attitudes—the 7th Report*, Gower, Aldershot 1991; see chapter by Kaye Wellings and Jane Wadsworth.

GLOSSARY

asceticism   The principles and practices of extreme austerity and self-denial.

adolescence   The period of physical and psychological development that begins with puberty and ends with adulthood.

affine   Kinship relations established through marriages rather than birth, e.g., in-laws.

androgyne   The blending or uniting of male and female attributes.

anthropology   The holistic study of hominid and human societies, past and present.

asexual   Without sex or without sexuality.

autoerotism   Sexual satisfaction obtained without others, as by masturbation.

berdaches   A widespread gender variance known among Native American cultures, berdaches, depending on the culture, could be male or female. *Also see* two-spirits.

binary fission   Asexual reproduction that occurs by a cell's ability to split itself in half.

binary gender model   The gender model that categorizes humans as either male or female. This model dominates the Western world and leaves little room for gender variance.

biological imperative   A principle or instinct that compels certain behaviors relating to, caused by, or affecting survival or life.

biopower   Medical knowledge that enables physicians to control human biology, for example, the ability to create/change the sex of the human body.

bipedal   In humans, the ability to walk upright on two legs.

bisexual   The state of being sexually attracted to both genders.

bonobo chimpanzees   The non-human primate (Pan paniscus) of north-central Congo who along with common chimpanzees are genetically our closest relative.

bridewealth (bride price, bride service)   The transfer of goods and/or services from the groom's family to the bride's family.

canon law   An ecclesiastical law established by a church council.

celibacy   The condition of being unmarried especially by religious vows (in common usage it implies someone who does not engage in sexual intercourse).

chromosomes   The DNA-containing cells which are responsible for the determination and transmission of hereditary characteristics.

civil liberties   Fundamental individual rights, such as freedom of speech and religion, protected by law against unwarranted governmental or other interference.

coming out   A western term used to describe the process by which a person who is attracted to the same gender makes their desire known to friends and family.

common law   A system of laws that originated from England based on custom and cultural morés.

conjugal   Relating to marriage or the relationship of spouses.

consanguineal   Of the same lineage or origin or having a common ancestor.

concealed ovulation   The fertile period, so obvious in other female animals, is hidden in the human female.

concealed sex   A term sometimes used to describe private sex, one of the hallmarks of human sexual behavior.

concubine   A woman who resides with a man without being married to him.

congenital   Relating to a condition that is present at birth, as a result of either heredity or environmental influences.

consensual sex   Voluntary, mutually desired sexual contact.

constructionism (sexual)   The belief that sexuality and our ideas about sexuality are created and shaped by society. Constructionists are interested in power and how the power structures of our society are replicated and reflected in sexual relationships and sexual norms.

control group   Scientists often study how a particular condition or factor influences an outcome. The use of two groups of subjects in such a scientific experiment, the group that is exposed to the condition or factor (such as a drug) is called the experimental group, while the other group, which provides a basis for comparison, is called the control group.

coitus   Sexual intercourse between a man and woman.

copulate/copulation   To engage in intercourse/intercourse.

COYOTE (Call Off Your Old Tired Ethics)   A organization that works for the rights of sex workers and provides various programs to assist sex workers.

cross-cultural research   The exploration of cultural variation by using ethnographic data from many cultures.

cross-dressing   To dress in the clothes characteristic of the other gender.

cultural influence model   The idea that biological theories provided neutral truths about human needs and that human variation occurs because socialization influences how these biological needs are met.

cultural relativism/relativity   The principle that cultural traits are best understood in the context of the cultural system in which they occur.

culture   Learned patterns of thought and behavior that are shared by a particular social group.

cunnilingus   Oral to female genitalia sexual contact.

cyberdating   A romance/courting relationship established and maintained through online contact.

cybersex   Sexual interaction or arousal arising from online contacts or websites.

developmental system theory (DST)   A way of understanding human development that transcends the nature/nurture debate and focuses on the interrelationships of the body and mind.

deviance   Behavior that violates the rules, morés, or norms of society.

dharma   The Hinduism and Buddhism principle of individual obligation with respect to caste, social custom, civil law, and sacred law.

diagnostic nomenclature   Medical terminology designating a name, symptoms, and treatment for a psychological or physical condition.

dichotomies   The division of something into two usually contradictory/opposite parts or opinions.

discourse analysis   The study of the interrelationship of information, messages, and communication in society.

dowry   The transfer of goods and/or services from the bride's family to the groom's family.

egalitarian   Social and economic equality.

ejaculation   Discharge of semen.

Ellis, Havelock   (English 1859–1939) Psychologist and writer known for Studies in the Psychology of Sex (seven volumes, 1897–1928). Believed that sex is not a sin and that morality and religion had twisted and deformed our ideas about sex. Progressive in his ideas about homosexuality, women's sexuality, and masturbation.

embryo   An organism in the early stages of development before birth.

empirical research   Scientific investigation or inquiry derived from observations or experiments and verifiable or provable using the scientific method.

enculturation   *See* socialization.

endogamy   A marriage rule or custom which encourages members to marry within their group.

essentialism   The theory that the essential properties of an object can be distinguished from those that are accidental to it.

estrus   The phase of the female mammalian cycle when females encourage copulation.

ethnocentrism   The assumption that one's own ethnic group's way of life is superior to other groups.

ethnography   A detailed description of a culture based on data drawn from fieldwork.

eurocentrism   Valuing or granting primacy to European culture and values.

evolution   The process of change in the genes or culture of a species or group over time.

evolutionary biology   The branch of evolutionary science that focuses on the origin and of living organisms.

exhibitionism   The compulsive act or practice of exposing one's genitals in public.

exogamy   A marriage rule or custom which encourages members to marry outside of their group.

fellatio   Oral to male genitalia sexual contact.

fetish   Excessive or obsessive attraction or attachment for something.

fieldwork   The method of research which involves long-term residence with the people being studied.

fornicate/fornication   Sexual intercourse between a woman and a man who are not married to each other (interestingly, this word probably comes from the term used to describe vaulted underground dwellings in ancient Rome which housed poor people and prostitutes).

foraging   Hunting and gathering as a subsistence strategy.

Foucault, Michel   (French 1926–1984) French philosopher, who attempted to show that the basic ideas which people normally take to be truths about human nature and society change over time. *The History of Sexuality, Volume I: An Introduction* was influential and important in revealing how society constructs sexual ideologies.

Freud, Sigmund   (Austrian, 1856–1939) Physician and founder of psychoanalysis. His theories, influenced twentieth-century thought. Popularized the idea that the brain is the largest sex organ.

fundamentalism   Belief in the rigid adherence to religious texts and principles, often accompanied by intolerance of the views of others.

gay   A western term to describe a man who erotically prefers the same gender.

gender   The learned ideas and behaviors relating to masculinity and femininity.

gender dysphoria   The medical term to describe a perceived mismatch of a person's biological sex and their gender identity. Such an individual may be labeled transgendered or transsexual.

gender scripts   The roles related to gender that are written (created) by society. The idea is that much of gender behavior is performance and these scripts provide models and guidelines for behavior.

gender variance   Cultural expressions of more than two genders.

genitalia   The reproductive organs, especially the external sex organs.

heterosexual   The state of being sexually attracted to the other sex/gender.

hijras   An institutionalized East Indian male gender/sex variance, often referred to as a third gender.

Hirchfield, Magnus   (German, 1869–1935) Gay researcher and activist; interested in sex in general, not just deviance. Established the Institute of Sexual Science with over 20,000 books and 35,000 pictures, which were destroyed by the Nazis in 1933.

holism   Analyzing or studying something by looking at its role in the bigger picture and its interdependency on the phenomena in that picture.

hominid   An erect bipedal primate; humans and their extinct ancestors.

homoerotic   Attraction and/or desire for the same gender/sex.

homophobia   Having fear of homosexuals or homosexuality.

homosexual   Being sexually attracted or engaging in sexual relations with members of one's own gender.

human rights   The basic rights and freedoms to which all humans are entitled, often held to include the right to life and liberty, freedom of thought and expression, and equality before the law.

human universal   A trait or behavior found in all human cultures.

hypothesis   A tentative assumption about the relationship between specific variable or phenomena.

ideology   The beliefs, values, and ideals of an individual or group.

impotent   Incapable of sexual intercourse.

incest   A sexual union between two persons who are so closely related that their marriage is forbidden by custom.

indigenous   The original or native population of a particular region or environment.

infanticide   Killing a baby soon after birth.

infidelity   Lack of loyalty or an unfaithful act.

inherent   Existing as an essential or intrinsic characteristic.

insemination   To put or inject semen into something.

intersexed   Biologically having sexual characteristics intermediate of those of typically male and typically female.

intromission   When used in a "sex" sense, this is the term to refer the penis being inside the vagina.

kathoey   A gender/sex variance in Thailand, originally related to hermaphroditism but in contemporary usage the term refers primarily to transgendered males.

Kinsey, Alfred   (American, 1894–1956) Biologist noted for his studies of human sexuality, published as *Sexual Behavior in the Human Male* (1948) and *Sexual Behavior in the Human Female* (1953). Exposed the hypocrisy in U.S. sexual mores, believed that a good sex life is an important part of health.

kinship   A network of culturally recognized relationships among individuals.

Krafft-Ebing, Richard von   (Austrian, 1840–1902) Clinical researcher who documented sexual deviance. Published *Psychopathia Sexualis* in 1886. Believed that sex is an animal instinct and that the church and society must control and contain it.

lactation   The production of milk by the mammary glands (breast feeding).

lascivious   Characterized by lust, lewdness, or lechery.

lesbian   A western term to describe a woman who erotically prefers the same gender—a woman homosexual.

levirate   The practice by which a man is expected to marry the wife or wives of a deceased brother.

libidinous plasticity   The idea that the human sexual drive is malleable, that it is capable of being shaped or formed.

libido   A term used to refer to an inherent sexual energy or sex drive.

mahu   A male sex/gender variance in some Polynesian cultures.

menarche   The first menstrual period, usually occurring during puberty.

menstrual huts   Found in many different cultures, menstrual huts are separate dwellings where women reside during their menses.

masochism   Deriving sexual gratification from being physically or emotionally abused. Krafft-Ebing popularized the term in reference to an Australian novelist, Sacher-Masoch, whose hero in *Venus in Furs* was tortured by a dominant woman.

Masters, William   (gynecologist) **and Virginia Johnson**   (psychologist) (Americans) Researched the physiological aspects of sex. Published *Human Sexual Response* in 1966. Helped to define sexual pleasure and desire are normal; that should be socially accepted as an important part of life.

maternity   The state of being a mother, biologically or socially.

matriarchy   A form of social organization in which power and authority are vested in the women.

matrilineal   Descent traced through the female line.

matrilocal   A post-marital residence custom by which newlyweds live with or near the bride's family.

molly   A term to refer to men in eighteenth-century England who cross-dressed and engaged in same-sex sexual behavior.

morés   (mor-rays) Strongly held norms with moral and ethical significance.

natural selection   The primary force of evolution that causes changes in gene frequencies for environmentally adaptive traits.

neolithic   The new stone age, marked by the adoption of agriculture, starting about 10,000 years ago.

nocturnal emission   Ejaculation while sleeping, commonly referred to as "wet dreams."

norms   Standards of behavior characteristics of a particular society.

obscenity   Something, such as a word, act, or expression, that is considered to be indecent or lewd.

onanism   Masturbation, originates from Onan, son of Judah in the Bible's book of Genesis.

origin myth   A story found in most cultures that explains the creation and population of the world.

ovulation   The part of the menstrual cycle in which the egg (ovum) is released and fertilization can occur.

paleolithic   The old stone age, before agriculture.

pandering   Recruiting persons into the profession of prostitution.

paradigm   A model or set of assumptions, concepts, and values that constitute a way of viewing reality.

paternity   The state of being a father, biologically or socially.

patriarchy   A form of social organization in which power and authority are vested in the men.

patrilineal   Descent traced through the male line.

patrilocal   A post-marital residence custom by which newlyweds live with or near the groom's family.

patrivirilocal   The kinship rules of patrilineal descent (land, etc., passed through the father's side of the family) and post-marriage residence with or near the husband's family.

pederasty   A term used to describe homoerotic relationships in ancient Greece between older and younger males.

pedophile   A person who is sexually attracted to or engages in sex with children.

phallic   Pertaining to or resembling a penis.

phallocentrism   A term to refer to theories, research, etc., that granted primacy to the penis or the male perspective.

pheromones   A chemical secreted by animals that influences, often attracting, members of the opposite sex.

polyandry   A form of marriage in which women have more than one husband at the same time.

polygamy   A term for marriage in which men or women have more than one marriage partner simultaneously.

polygyny   A form of marriage in which men have more than one wife.

post-operative transsexual   A person who has completed the hormonal and genital male to female or female to male transformation.

postpartum   The period of time immediately following childbirth.

precultural   The notion of a human before "nurture." A purely biological being.

prehistoric   The time before written records.

pre-operative transsexual   A person who identifies with another gender but has not yet undergone a surgical transformation.

primate modeling   Using nonhuman primates as models in order to understand behavioral or biological processes that are difficult or impossible to study in humans.

primatology   A branch of biological anthropology that studies nonhuman primates.

protohuman   A term used to refer to various extinct hominids or other primates that resemble modern humans.

prurient   Overly or obsessively interested in sex, sexuality, and sexual behavior.

psychodynamic   The interaction of various conscious and unconscious psychological or emotional processes.

psychopathology   The study of the origin, development, and manifestations of psychological or behavioral disorders.

psychosexual   Psychological development that pertains to sexuality and sexual behavior.

puberty   The stage of maturation in which an individual becomes physiologically capable of reproduction.

puritanical   Originating from the Puritan religion, the word has come to mean strict morality relating to social and sexual pleasures.

queer theory   A theory/movement that involves deconstructing our ideas about gender and sexual identity, challenging heteronormality and heterosexism. Envisioning a world where gender and sexual identity are open and fluid, and labeling is constraining and destructive.

religion   Attitudes, beliefs, and practices related to supernatural powers.

reproductive success   A variable which refers to an individual's overall achievement in reproduction of their own genes (through direct offspring or kin).

rites of passage   Rituals that mark important changes in individual status or social position.

ritual   A set of acts following a sequence established by tradition.

romance tourism   A term used to describe sexual/love affairs that foreign women engage in with local men while on vacation. *Also see* sex tourism.

sadhin   A female sex/gender variant in India, a role associated with asceticism and virginity.

sadism   Taking pleasure in inflicting pain on others (*also see* masochism). The word sadism comes from reference to Marquis de Sade who is infamous for his sadistic sexual exploits.

sadomasochism (S&M)   Deriving sexual gratification from inflicting or submitting to physical or emotional abuse; when a sadist and a masochist come together for mutual pain/pleasure role playing.

same-gender sexual behavior   Engaging in sex acts with someone of your own gender (socially or culturally feminine or masculine)—not necessarily the same as same-sex sexual behavior.

same-sex sexual behavior   Engaging in sex acts with someone of your own sex (biologically male or female)—not necessarily the same as same-gender sexual behavior.

sanctions   Negative or positive responses to individual or group behavior.

scientific theory   A testable, correctable explanation of observable phenomena that yields new information.

serial monogamy   More than one marriage, one at a time.

sex   1. The property or quality by which organisms are classified according to their reproductive functions. 2. Sexual interaction.

sex role   Learned social activities and expectations made on the basis of gender.

sex tourism   Traveling with the intent to engage in sexual activity with sex workers.

sexual abstinence   The act or practice of refraining sexual activity.

sexual dimorphism   Marked difference in size and form of the sexes.

sexual identity   Identifying with and/or embracing a particular sexual orientation, i.e., homosexuality or heterosexuality.

sexual inversion   An old term to describe homosexuality/transgenderism. As implied, inversion means a change in "normal" sexual/gender order.

sexual orientation   A sexual preference/desire for members of one's own or other gender, homosexuality or heterosexuality.

sexual reassignment   To have one's sex/gender changed, usually through surgery, male to female or female to male.

sexual reorientation   Attempting to change a person's sexual orientation.

sexual selection   A Darwinian adjunct of natural selection relating to evolutionary changes that are the result of heightened reproductive success due to characteristics found desirable by the other sex.

sex workers   Women and men who make money working in the sex industry, including prostitutes, strippers, professional pornography workers, deliverers of phone sex, and Internet sex providers.

shaman   Religious practitioner who goes into trance state to communicate with the spirit world for the benefit of the community.

social control   Practices that induce members of a society to conform to norms.

socialization   Enculturation, the process by which culture is learned.

social stratification   Hierarchical levels of society based on access to resources and/or power.

sociobiology   The systematic study of how biology affects social behavior.

sodomy   Oral and/or anal sexual contact.

somatic   Relating to or affecting the physical body as opposed to mental or spiritual factors.

status   Position in a social system that is characterized by certain rights and obligations.

subculture   The culture of a subgroup of a society that has its own ideas, values, and beliefs.

taboo/tabu   A supernaturally forbidden act as defined by a culture.

theoretical perspective   Examination or analyses of something from a specific theoretical point of view.

third genders   A gender identity available in many cultures that is neither male or female.

trans-cultural   Across and/or beyond cultures.

transgendered   Persons whose expression of gender is outside the current cultural expectations or norms.

trans-historical   Across and/or beyond historical time frames.

transnational   Reaching beyond or transcending national boundaries.

transsexual   A person who surgically alters their genitals in order to change their sexual identity.

transvestite   A person who wears clothing that is appropriate to the other sex; cross-dressing.

travesti   Transgendered Brazilian men who alter their bodies with silicone and hormones to achieve a woman's physique but retain their male genitalia.

tribadism   An old word from French used to refer to lesbianism.

two-spirits   A pan-Native American lesbian/gay identity that embraces traditional ideas of spirituality.

virtual relationships   Interpersonal contact that occurs in cyberspace.

voyeurism   Deriving sexual gratification from observing (sometimes secretly) the nudity or sexual acts of others.

Western culture   A generic term referring to the common beliefs, values, and traditions of Europeans and their descendants.

world view   The particular way in which a society constructs ideas of space, time, social relationships, and the meaning of life.

xaniths   A gender variance available to transgendered males in Oman.

A LIST OF JOURNALS
FOR THE STUDY
OF GENDER, SEXUALITY,
AND CULTURE

Some of the listed journals are available free online, others require an electronic subscription, still others are only available in hardcopy but subscription information is available online. Many offer free sample issues.

This is not meant to be an exhaustive list of journals. If you know of a journal that should be included on this list please email the journal's information to constructingsexualities@hotmail.com

Annual Review of Sex Research   An integrative and interdisciplinary review.
   www.ssc.wisc.edu/ssss/annual_review.htm

Archives of Sexual Behavior   Offers full articles and book reviews online.
   http://ipsapp008.lwwonline.com

Canadian Queer Studies   Seeks to publicize scholarly and creative work on topics concerning queer aspects of Canada.
   www.englilsh.upenn/CFP/archive/Gender-Studies/0060.html

The Electronic Journal of Human Sexuality   A publication of the Institute for Advanced Study of Human Sexuality
   www.ejha.org

GLQ: Gay and Lesbian Quarterly   An interdisciplinary journal of lesbian and gay studies
   http://muse.jhu.edu/journals/journal_of_lesbian_and_gay_studies

Genders   Presents innovative work in the arts, humanities, and social theories.
   www.genders.org

Journal of History of Sexuality   About the history of sexuality in all its expressions, recognizing various differences of class, culture, gender, race, and sexual orientation.
   http://ftp.utexas.edu/utpress/journals/jhs.html

The Journal of Human Sexuality   Offers articles on issues related to the biological, psychological, historical, theological, and social aspects of sexuality.
> *www.leaderu.com/jhs*

The Journal of Sex Research   A publication of the Society for the Scientific Study of Sexuality.
> *www.ssc.wisc.edu/ssss/jsr2001toc.htm*

International Journal of Sexuality and Gender Studies   (formerly called the *Journal of Gay, Lesbian, and Bisexual Identity*)   A progressive, interdisciplinary journal.
> *www.english.upen.edu/CFP/archive/Gender-Studies/0027.html*

The National Journal of Sexual Orientation Law   Online law journal devoted to legal issues affecting lesbians, gay men and bisexuals.
> *www.ibiblio.org/gaylaw/*

Re/productions   Seeks to expand conceptions of public health to include the social conditions re/producing "health."
> *www.hsph.harvard.edu/organizations/healthnet/SAsian/ejournals/ejournals.html*

Sex Roles: A Journal of Research   Publishes original research articles and theoretical papers concerned with the underlying process and consequences of gender role socialization, perceptions, and attitudes.
> *http://ipsapp008.lwwonline.com*

Sexual Abuse: A Journal of Research and Treatment   Published by the Association of the Treatment of Sexual Abusers
> *http://ipsapp008.lwwonline.com*

Sexualities   An international journal providing a forum for debate and discussion on the changing nature of the social organization of human sexual experience.
> *www.sageltd.co.uk/journals/details/j0065.html*

Sexuality and Culture   An interdisciplinary journal analyzing of ethical, cultural, psychological, social, and political issues related to sexual relationships and sexual behavior.
> *www.englilsh.upenn/CFP/archive/Gender-Studies/0019.html*

Sexuality and Disability   Publishes articles relating to issues on sexuality and disability.
> *http://ipsapp008.lwwonline.com*

Studies in Gender and Sexuality   A journal dedicated to promoting dialogues about sexuality and gender about clinicians, researchers, and theorists.
> *www.analyticpress.com/sgs.html*

Women and Performance: A Journal of Feminist Theory
> *www.womenandperformance.org*

SEXUALITY, GENDER, AND CULTURE BIBLIOGRAPHY

This bibliography is nowhere near an exhaustive list of all the readings relating to sexualities, gender, and culture. I have concentrated on newer works while also including some classics. In addition to these readings, see the list of journals.

Abbot, Elizabeth. 2001. *A History of Celibacy*. New York: Da Capo Press.

Abramson, Paul R., and Steven D. Pinkerton (eds.). 1995. *Sexual Nature, Sexual Culture*. Chicago: University of Chicago Press.

Alison, Jolly. 1999. *Lucy's Legacy: Sex and Intelligence in Human Evolution*. Cambridge: Harvard University Press.

Angier, Natalie. 1999. Men, women, sex and Darwin. In *The New York Times Magazine*, 2–21–99: 48–53.

———. 1999. *Woman: An Intimate Geography*. New York: Anchor Books.

Atkins, Dawn (ed.). 1998. *Looking Queer*. Binghamton, NY: Haworth Press.

Bagemihl, Bruce. 2000. *Biological Exuberance: Animal Sexuality and Natural Diversity*. New York: St. Martin's Press.

Barale, Michele Aina, Henry Abelove, and David M. Halperin (eds.). 1993. *The Lesbian and Gay Studies Reader*. New York: Routledge.

Barrecay, Regina (ed.). 1995. *Desire and Imagination: Classic Essays in Sexuality*. New York: Plume.

Bataille, George. 1962. *Erotism: Death and Sensuality*. New York: Walker and Company.

Bell, Sandra, and Elisa Sobo (eds.). 2001. *Celibacy, Culture, and Society: The Anthropology of Sexual Abstinence*. Madison: University of Wisconsin Press.

Bernstein, Dennis, and Leslie Kean. 1998. Ethnic Cleansing: Rape as a Weapon of War in Burma. *The Nation Editorial*, 5–31–98.

Beyrer, Chris. 1998. *War in the Blood: Sex, Politics and AIDS in Southeast Asia*. New York: Zed Books, Ltd.

Blackwood, Evelyn. 1984. Sexuality and gender in certain Native American tribes: The case of cross-gender females. *Signs: Journal of Women in Culture and Society*, Vol. 10, no 11, pp. 27–42.

———. 1986. Breaking the Mirror: The Construction of Lesbianism and the Anthropological Discourse on Homosexuality. In *The Many Faces of Homosexuality*, pp. 1–18, edited by Evelyn Blackwood. New York: Harrington Park Press.

Blackwood, Evelyn, and Saskia E. Wieringa (eds.). 1998. *Female Desires: Same-Sex Relations and Transgendered Practices Across Cultures.* New York: Columbia University Press.

Bland, Lucy, and Laura Doan (eds.). 1998. *Sexology Uncensored: The Documents of Sexual Science.* Chicago: The University of Chicago Press.

———. 1998. *Sexology in Culture: Labelling Bodies and Desires.* Chicago: The University of Chicago Press.

Bledsoe, Caroline H., and Gilles Pison (eds.). 1994. *Nuptiality in Sub-Saharan Africa: Contemporary Anthropological and Demographic Perspectives.* New York: Oxford University Press.

Bolin, Anne. 1987. *In Search of Eve: Transsexual Rites of Passage.* Westport, CT: Greenwood Publishing Group.

Bolin, Anne, and Patricia Whelehan. 1999. *Perspectives on Human Sexuality.* Albany: State University of New York Press.

Bonvillain, Nancy. 2001. *Women and Men: Cultural Constructs of Gender.* Upper Saddle River, NJ: Prentice Hall.

Bornstein, Kate. 1994. *Gender Outlaw: On Men, Women and the Rest of Us.* New York: Routledge.

Boswell, John. 1994. *Same-Sex Unions in Premodern Europe.* New York: Villard Books.

Bremmer, Jan (ed.). 1991. *From Sappho to De Sade: Moments in the History of Sexuality.* New York: Routledge.

Bretschneider, Peter. 1995. *Polygyny: A Cross-Cultural Study.* Philadelphia, PA: Coronet Books.

Brettell, Caroline B., and Carolyn F. Sargent (eds.). 2001. *Gender in Cross-Cultural Perspective.* Upper Saddle River, NJ: Prentice Hall.

Brophy, Julia, and Carol Smart (eds.). 1985. *Women in Law: Explorations in Law, Family and Sexuality.* New York: Routledge.

Brown, Donald E. 1990. The Penis Pen: An Unsolved Problem in the Relations Between the Sexes in Borneo. In *Female and Male in Borneo,* edited by V. Sutlive, The Borneo Research Council, pp. 435–454.

Brundage, James A. 1987. *Law, Sex, and Christian Society in Medieval Europe.* Chicago: University of Chicago Press.

Bullough, Bonnie, Vern L. Bullough, and James Elias (eds.). 1997. *Gender Blending.* Amherst, NY: Prometheus Books.

Bullough, Vern L. 1994. *Science in the Bedroom: A History of Sex Research.* New York: Basic Books.

Bullough, Vern L., and Bonnie Bullough. 1995. *Sexual Attitudes: Myths and Realities.* New York: Prometheus Books.

Bulter, Judith. 1990. *Gender Trouble: Feminism and the Subversion of Identity.* New York: Routledge.

Buss, David M., and Neil M. Malamuth (eds.). 1996. *Sex, Power, Conflict: Evolutionary and Feminist Perspectives.* New York: Oxford University Press.

Califia, Pat. 1994. *Public Sex: The Culture of Radical Sex.* San Francisco, CA: Cleis Press, Inc.

Caplan, Pat (ed.). 1987. *The Cultural Construction of Sexuality.* New York: Routledge.

Chase, Cheryl. 1998. Hermaphrodites with attitude. *GLQ,* 4:2 :189–211.

Colapinto, John. 2001. *As Nature Made Him: The Boy Who was Raised as a Girl.* New York: Harper Trade.

Comfort, Alex (ed.). 1972. *The Joy of Sex: A Gourmet Guide to Lovemaking.* New York: Fireside Books.

Cook, Rebecca (ed.). 1994. *Human Rights of Women: National and International Perspectives.* Philadelphia: University of Pennsylvania Press.

Cooper, Alvin, et al. 1999. Sexuality on the Internet: From sexual exploration to pathological expression. *Professional Psychology: Research and Practice,* Vol. 30, No. 2:154–164.

Cornell, Drucilla (ed.). 2000. *Feminism and Pornography.* New York: Oxford University Press.

Crocker, William and Jean. 1994. *The Canela: Bonding through Kinship, Ritual, and Sex.* New York: Harcourt Brace College Publishers: New York.

Croutier, Alev Lythe. 1998. *Harem: The World Beyond the Veil.* New York: Abbeville Press.

Dahlberg, Frances (ed.). 1981. *Woman the Gatherer.* New Haven: Yale University Press.

Daly, Mary. 1978. *Gyn/Ecology: The Metaethics of Radical Feminism.* Boston: Beacon Press.

Davis, D. L., and R. G. Whitten. 1987. The Cross-Cultural Study of Human Sexuality. *Annual Review of Anthropology,* 16: 69–98.

de Alburquerque, Klaus. 1999. In Search of the Big Bamboo. *Transition 77, www.cofc.edu/ ~klausda/bamboo.htm*

DeMeo, James. 1989. The geography of genital mutilation. In *Truth Seeker,* July/August pp. 9–13.

D'Emilio, John, and Estelle B. Watson. 1988. *Intimate Matters: A History of Sexuality in America.* Chicago: University of Chicago Press.

Dening, Sarah. 1996. *The Mythology of Sex.* New York: MacMillan.

Denny, Dallas (ed.). 1997. *Current Concepts in Transgender Identity.* New York: Garland Publishing.

de Waal, Frans, and Frans Lanting. 1997. *Bonobo: The Forgotten Ape.* Berkeley: University of California Press.

Diamond, Jared. 1997. *Why is Sex Fun: The Evolution of Human Sexuality.* New York: Basic Books.

Dirie, Waris, and Cathleen Miller. 1998. *Desert Flower: The Extraordinary Journey of a Desert Nomad.* New York: William Morrow & Company.

Donahue, Emma. 1995. *Passions Between Women: British Lesbian Culture 1668–1801.* New York: Harper Collins.

Dorkenoo, Efua. 1996. *Cutting the Rose: Female Genital Mutilation: The Practice and Its Prevention.* Auckland: Paul & Co Publishers Consortium.

Dove, Kenneth J. 1989. *Greek Homosexuality.* Cambridge, MA: Harvard University Press.

Doezema, Jo. 1998. Forced to choose: Beyond the voluntary v. forced prostitution dichotomy. In *Global Sex Workers: Rights, Resistance, and Redefinition,* edited by Kamala Kempadoo and Jo Doezema. New York: Routledge, pp. 34–50.

———. 1999. Loose Women or Lost Women? The re-emergence of the myth of 'white slavery' in contemporary discourses of 'trafficking in women.' Paper presented at the ISA Convention, Washington, D.C. *www.walnut.org/csis/papers/doezema-loose.html*

Dreger, Alice (ed.). 1999. *Intersex in the Age of Ethics.* Hagerstown, MD: University Publishing Group.

———. 2000. *Hermaphrodites and the Medical Invention of Sex.* Cambridge, MA: Harvard University Press.

Dworkin, Andrea. 1981. *Pornography: Men Possessing Women.* London: The Women's Press.

Ehrenreich, Barbara, Elizabeth Hess, and Gloria Jacobs. 1987. *Re-Making Love: The Feminization of Sex.* Garden City, NY: Anchor Press.

Ellison, Deborah A. 1995. Erotic anthropology: "Ritualized homosexuality" in Melanesia and beyond. *American Ethnologist* 22(4):848–867.

Enloe, Cynthia. 2001. *Bananas, Beaches and Bases: Making Feminist Sense of International Politics.* Berkeley: University of California.

Eskridge, William N., Jr., and Nan D. Hunter. 1997. *Sexuality, Gender, and the Law.* University Casebook Series. Westbury, NY: The Foundation Press.

Evans-Pritchard, E. E. 1970. Sexual Inversion among the Azande. *American Anthropologist,* (72), pp. 1428–1434.

Faderman, Lillian. 1991. *Odd Girls and Twilight Lovers: A History of Lesbian Life in Twentieth-Century America.* New York: Penguin Books.

Fausto-Sterling, Anne. 1985. *Myth of Gender: Biological Theories about Women and Men.* New York: Basic Books.

———. 1989. Life in the XY corral. *Women's Studies International Forum,* 12(3).

———. 1993. The five sexes: Why male and female are not enough. *The Sciences* (33)2, pp. 20–24.

———. 1999. *Sexing the Body: How Biologist Construct Human Sexuality.* New York: Basic Books.

———. 2000. The five sexes, revisited. *The Sciences,* July/August, pp. 19–23.

Fineman, Martha Albertson, and Nancy Sweet Thomadsen (eds.). 1991. *At the Boundaries of Law: Feminism and Legal Theory.* New York: Routledge.

Fisher, Helen. 1992. *Anatomy of Love: A Natural History of Adultery, Monogamy and Divorce.* New York: Simon & Schuster.

Fone, Byrne. 2000. *Homophobia: A History.* New York: Metropolitan Books.

Ford, Clellan S., and Frank A. Beach. 1951. *Patterns of Sexual Behavior.* New York: Harper & Brothers.

Foucault, Michel. 1978. *The History of Sexuality, Volume I: An Introduction.* New York: Random Books.

Fout, John C. (ed.). 1992. *Forbidden History: The State, Society and the Regulation of Sexuality in Modern Europe.* Chicago: University of Chicago Press.

Fradenburg, Louise, and Carla Feccero (eds.). 1996. *Premodern Sexualities.* New York: Routledge Press.

Francouer, Robert T. (ed.). 1997. *The International Encyclopedia of Sexuality,* Vol. 1–3. New York: Continuum Publishing.

Frank, Martina W., and Heidi M. Brauer, et al. 1999. Virginity examinations in Turkey: Role of forensic physicians in controlling female sexuality. *The Journal of the American Medical Association,* Vol. 282, pp. 485–490.

Frayser, Suzanne G. 1985. *Varieties of Sexual Experience.* New Haven: Human Relations Area Files.

Friedl, Ernestine. 1994. Sex the invisible. *American Anthropologist* 96(4):833–844.

Garber, Marjorie. 1992. *Vested Interests: Cross-Dressing and Cultural Anxiety.* New York: Routledge.

Gay, Judith. 1985. "Mummies and babies" and friends and lovers in Lesotho. *Journal of Homosexuality* 2(3):97–116.

Giddens, Anthony. 1992. *The Transformation of Intimacy: Sexuality, Love & Erotism in Modern Societies.* Stanford: Stanford University Press.

Ginsburg, Faye, and Anna Lowenhaupt Tsing (eds.). 1990. *Uncertain Terms: Negotiating Gender in American Culture.* Boston: Beacon.

Ginsburg, Faye, and Rayna Rapp (eds.). 1995. *Conceiving the New World Order: The Global Politics of Reproduction.* Berkeley: University of California Press.

Gollaher, David L. 2000. *Circumcision: A History of the World's Most Controversial Surgery.* New York: Basic Books.

Gough, E. Kathleen. 1959. The Nayars and the definitions of marriage. *Journal of the Royal Anthropological Institute,* 89, pp. 23–34.

Graber, Robert Bates. 1981. A psychocultural theory of male genital mutilation. *Journal of Psychoanalytic Anthropology,* 4(4):413–434.

Greene, Beverly. 2000. African American lesbian and bisexual women. *Journal of Social Issues,* 56:239–249.

Greenberg, David F. 1985. Why was the Berdache ridiculed? *Journal of Homosexuality,* Vol. 11, pp. 179–189.

Gregersen, Edgar. 1996. *The World of Human Sexuality: Behaviors, Customs, and Beliefs.* New York: Irvington Press.

Gregor, Thomas. 1985. *Anxious Pleasures: The Sexual Lives of an Amazonian People.* Chicago: University of Chicago Press.

———. 1995. Sexuality and the experience of love. In *Sexual Nature, Sexual Culture,* edited by Paul R. Abramson and Steven D. Pinkerton. Chicago: University of Chicago Press, pp. 330–350.

Gruen, Lori, and George E. Panichas (eds.). 1997. *Sex, Morality and the Law.* New York: Routledge.

Gruenbaum, Ellen. 2000. *The Female Circumcision Controversy: An Anthropological Perspective.* Philadelphia: University of Pennsylvania Press.

Gutiérrez, Ramón A. 1991. *When Jesus Came, the Corn Mothers Went Away: Marriage, Sexuality and Power in New Mexico, 1500–1846.* Stanford: Stanford University Press.

Hallett, Judith P., and Marilyn B. Skinner (eds.). 1997. *Roman Sexualities.* Princeton, NJ: Princeton University Press.

Harding, Jennifer. 1998. *Sex Acts: Practices of Femininity and Masculinity*. London: Sage Publications.

Harrington, Charles. 1968. Sexual differentiation in socialization and some male genital mutilations. *American Anthropologist*, 70: 951–956.

Hatfield, Elaine, and Richard L. Rapson. 1996. *Love and Sex: Cross-Cultural Perspectives*. Boston: Allyn and Bacon.

Hegarty, Peter, and Cheryl Chase. 2000. Intersex activism, feminism, and psychology: Opening a dialogue on theory, research, and clinical practice. *Feminism & Psychology* 10: 117–132.

Heider, Karl G. 1977. Dani sexuality: A low energy system. *Man NS*, 11(2): 188–201.

Hekma, Gert. 1991. A history of sexology: Social and historical aspects of sexuality. In *From Sappho to De Sade: Moments in the History of Sexuality*. Jan Bremmer, ed. New York: Routledge.

Herdt, Gilbert H. 1990. Mistaken identity: 5-Alpha reductase hermaphroditism and biological reductionism. *American Anthropologist* 92(2): 433–446.

———. 1997. *Same Sex, Different Cultures: Gays and Lesbians Across Cultures*. New York: Westview Press.

———. 1999. *Sambia Sexual Culture: Essays from the Field*. Chicago: University of Chicago Press.

Herdt, Gilbert H. (ed.). 1984. *Ritualized Homosexuality in Melanesia*. Berkeley: University of California Press.

———. 1996. *Third Sex, Third Gender: Beyond Sexual Dimorphism in Culture and History*. New York: Zone Books.

Hinsch, Bret. 1990. *Passions of the Cut Sleeve: The Male Homosexual Tradition in China*. Berkeley: University of California Press.

Hirshman, Linda R., and Jame E. Larson. 1998. *Hard Bargains: The Politics of Sex*. New York: Oxford.

Hitt, Jack. 2000. The second sexual revolution. *The New York Times Magazine*, 2–20–2000.

Hogan, Steve, and Lee Hudson. 1998. *Completely Queer: The Gay and Lesbian Encyclopedia*. New York: Henry Holt and Company.

Hrdy, Sarah Blaffer. 1999. *Mother Nature: Maternal Instincts and How They Shape the Human Species*. New York: Ballantine Books.

Jacobs, Sue-Ellen, Wesley Thomas, and Sabine Lang (eds.). 1997. *Two-Spirited People*. Chicago: University of Chicago Press.

Jehl, Douglas. 1999. Arab honor's price: A woman's blood. *The New York Times*, 6–20.

Jolly, Alison. 1999. *Lucy's Legacy: Sex and Intelligence in Human Evolution*. Cambridge, MA: Harvard University Press.

Katz, Jonathan Ned. 1995. *The Invention of Heterosexuality*. New York: Plume.

Keen, Lisa, and Suzanne B. Goldberg. 1998. *Strangers to the Law: Gay People on Trial*. Ann Arbor: University Press.

Kempadoo, Kamala. (ed.). 1999. *Sun, Sex, and Gold: Tourism and Sex Work in the Caribbean*. New York: Rowman & Littlefield Publishers, Inc.

Kempadoo, Kamala, and Jo Doezema (eds.). 1998. *Global Sex Workers: Rights, Resistance, and Redefinition*. New York: Routledge.

Kenyetta, Jomo. 1962. *Facing Mt. Kenya*. New York: Random House.

Kessler, Susan J. 1990. The medical construction of gender: Case management of intersexed infants. *Signs: Journal of Women in Culture and Society*, Vol. 16, No. 1, pp. 3–26.

———. 1998. *Lessons from the Intersexed*. Piscataway, NJ: Rutgers University Press.

Kessler, Suzanne, and Wendy McKenna. 1978. *Gender: An Ethnomethodological Approach*. Chicago: University of Chicago Press.

———. 2000. Who put the "trans" in transgender? Gender theory and everyday life. *The International Journal of Transgenderism*, Vol. 4, no. 3, July-September.

Kinsey, Alfred C., Wardell B. Pomeroy, and Clyde E. Martin. 1948. *Sexual Behavior in the Human Male*. Philadelphia: W. B. Saunders Company.

Kinsey, Alfred C., Wardell B. Pomeroy, and Clyde E. Martin. 1953. *Sexual Behavior in the Human Female*. Philadelphia: W. B. Saunders Company.

Kinsman, Gary. 1996. *The Regulation of Desire: Homo and Hetero Sexualities*. Cheektowago: Black Rose Books.

Kon, Igor. 1995. *The Sexual Revolution in Russia*. New York: The Free Press.

Kulick, Don. 1997. The gender of Brazilian transgendered prostitutes. *American Anthropologist* 99(3): 574–585.

———. 1998. *Travesti: Sex, Gender, and Culture among Brazilian Transgendered Prostitutes*. Chicago: University of Chicago Press.

Lacan, Jacques and the école freudienne. 1985. *Feminine Sexuality*. New York: Pantheon.

LaFont, Suzanne, and Deborah Pruitt. 1995. For love and money: Romance tourism in Jamaica. *Annals of Tourism Research* 22: 422–440.

LaFont, Suzanne. 2001. Very straight sex: The development of sexual mores in Jamaica. *Journal of Colonialism and Colonial History* 3(2).

———. 2000. Gender wars in Jamaica. *Identities: Global Studies in Culture and Power* 7(2).

Lagnam, David J. 1994. *Crossing the Line: Legislating Morality and the Mann Act*. Chicago: University of Chicago Press.

Lancaster, Roger N., and Micaela di Leonardo. 1997. *The Gender/Sexuality Reader: Culture, History, Political Economy*. New York: Routledge.

Lang, Sabine. 1999. Lesbians, men-women and two-spirits: Homosexuality and gender in Native American cultures. In *Same-Sex Relations and Female Desires*, edited by Evelyn Blackwood and Saskia E. Wieringa. New York: Columbia University Press, pp. 91–116.

Laumann, Edward O., John H. Gagnon, Robert T. Michael, and Stuart Michaels. 1994. *The Social Organization of Sexuality: Sexual Practices in the United States*. Chicago: University of Chicago Press.

Leacock, Eleanor Burke (ed.). 1981. *Myths of Male Dominance: Collected Articles on Women Cross-Culturally*. New York: The Monthly Review.

LeMoncheck, Linda. 1997. *Loose Women and Lecherous Men: A Feminist Philosophy of Sex*. New York: Oxford.

LeVay, Simon. 1993. *The Sexual Brain*. Cambridge, MA: The MIT Press.

Levi-Strauss, Claude. 1971. *The Elementary Structures of Kinship*. New York: Beacon Press.

Lewin, Bo, et al. 1996. *Sex in Sweden: On the Swedish Sexual Life*. Stockholm: The National Institute of Public Health.

Lighthouse-Klein, Hanny. 1989. *Prisoners of Ritual: An Odyssey into Female Genital Circumcision in Africa*. New York: Harrington Park Press.

Low, Bobbi S. 2000. *Why Sex Matters: A Darwinian Look at Human Behavior*. Princeton, NJ: Princeton University Press.

Love, Brenda. 1992. *The Encyclopedia of Unusual Sex Practices*. Barricade Books.

Luhmann, Niklas. 1986. *Love as Passion: The Codification of Intimacy*. Stanford: Stanford University Press.

MacHover Reinisch, June. 1991. *The Kinsey Institute New Report of Sex: What You Must Know to be Sexually Literate*, Vol. I. New York: St. Martin's Press.

MacKinnon, Catherine. 1987. *Feminism Unmodified*. Cambridge, MA: Harvard University Press.

———. 2001. *Sex Equality*. University Casebook Studies. New York: Foundation Press.

Maines, Rachel P. 1999. *The Technology of Orgasm: Hysteria, the Vibrator, and Women's Sexual Satisfaction*. Baltimore: Johns Hopkins University Press.

Malinowski, Bronislaw. 1927. *Sex and Repression in Savage Society*. New York: Meridian Books.

———. 1929. *The Sexual Life of Savages in North-Western Melanesia*. pp. 44–64, new edition 1987, Boston: Beacon Press.

———. 1962. *Sex, Culture, and Myth*. New York: Harcourt, Brace & World, Inc.

Margulis, Lynn, and Dorian Sagan. 1991. *Mystery Dance: On the Evolution of Human Sexuality*. New York: Summit Books.

Marshall, Donald S., and Robert C. Suggs (eds.). 1971. *Human Sexual Behavior: Variations in the Ethnographic Spectrum.* New York: Basic Books.

Master, William H., and Virginia E. Johnson. 1966. *Human Sexual Response.* Boston: Little Brown.

Matzer, Andrew. 2001. *O Au No Keia: Voices from Hawaii's Mahu and Transgender Communities.* Philadelphia, PA: Xlibris Corporation.

Mead, Margaret. 1935. *Sex and Temperament in Three Primitive Societies.* New York: William Morrow and Company.

———. 1949. *Male and Female: A Study of Sexes in a Changing World.* New York: William Morrow and Company.

Michael, Robert T., John H. Gagnon, Edward O. Laumann, and Gina Kolata. 1994. *Sex in America: A Definitive Survey.* Boston: Warner Books.

Miller, Suzanne. 2000. When sex 'needs' to be fixed. *World and I,* September 2000 Vol. 15: 9, pp. 148–155.

Millet, Kate. 1970. *Sexual Politics.* New York: Doubleday.

Montagu, Ashley. 1968. *The Natural Superiority of Women.* New York: Macmillan Books.

Murphy, Timothy F. 1992. Redirecting sexual orientation: Techniques and justifications. *The Journal of Sex Research,* Vol. 29, No. 4, pp. 501–523.

———. 1994. *Ethics in an Epidemic: Aids, Morality, and Culture.* Berkeley: University of California Press.

———. 1999. *Gay Science: Between Men~Between Women: Lesbian and Gay Studies.* New York: Columbia University Press.

Murray, Stephen O. 2000. *Homosexualities.* Chicago: University of Chicago.

Murray, Stephen O. (ed.). 1995. *Latin American Homosexualities.* Albuquerque: University of New Mexico Press.

———, and Will Roscoe (eds.). 1997. *Islamic Homosexualities: Culture, History, and Literature.* New York: New York University Press.

———. 2001. *From Boy-Wives and Female Husbands: Studies in African Homosexualities.* New York: St. Martin's Press.

Namaste, Viviane K. 2000. *Invisible Lives: The Erasure of Transsexual and Transgendered People.* Chicago: University of Chicago Press.

Nanda, Serena. 1999. *Neither Man nor Woman: The Hijras of India.* New York: Wadsworth Publishing.

———. 2000. *Gender Diversity: Crosscultural Variations.* Prospect Heights, IL: Waveland Press, Inc.

Newton, Esther. 1972. *Mother Camp: Female Impersonators in America.* Chicago: University of Chicago.

Nussbaum, Emily. 2000. A question of gender. *Discover,* January 2000 Vol. 2: 1, pp. 92–98.

Nussbaum, Martha C. 1999. *Sex and Social Justice.* New York: Oxford University Press.

Ortner, Sherry B., and Harriet Whitehead (eds.). 1981. *Sexual Meanings: The Cultural Construction of Gender and Sexuality.* New York: Cambridge University Press.

Ortner, Sherry B. 1996. *Making Gender: The Politics and Erotics of Culture.* Boston: Beacon Press.

O'Toole, Laurence J. 2000. *Pornocopia: Porn, Sex, Technology and Desire.* London: Serpent's Tail.

Parker, Richard, and Peter Aggleton. 1999. *Culture, Society and Sexuality: A Reader.* Philadelphia: University College London Press.

Parker, Richard, Regina Maria Barbosa, and Peter Aggleton (eds.). 2000. *Framing the Sexual Subject: The Politics of Gender, Sexuality, and Power.* Berkeley: University of California.

Parker, Richard. 1998. *Beneath the Equator: Male Homosexuality and Emerging Gay Community.* New York: Routledge.

Paternosto, Silvan. 1998. *In the Land of God and Man: Confronting Our Sexual Culture.* New York: E. P. Dutton.

Patron, Eugene J. 1995. Heart of Lavender: In Search of Gay Africa." *Harvard Gay and Lesbian Review,* Fall 1995. *www.fordham.edu/halsall/pwh/patron-africhomo.html*

Paul, Elizabeth L. (ed.). 2000. *Taking Sides: Clashing Views on Controversial Issues in Sex and Gender.* Guilford, CT: Dushin/McGraw-Hill.

Phillips, Kim M., and Barry Reay (eds.). 2002. *Sexualities in History: A Reader.* New York: Routledge.

Pomeroy, Wardell B. 1972. *Dr. Kinsey and the Institute for Sex Research.* New York: Signet.

Posner, Richard A., and Katherine B. Silbaugh. 1996. *A Guide to America's Sex Laws.* Chicago: University of Chicago Press.

Rahman, Anika, and Nahid Toubia (eds.). 2000. *Female Genital Mutilation: A Guide to Laws and Policies Worldwide.* London: Zed Books.

Rajan, Rajeshwari Sunder. 1999. The prostitution question(s): Female agency, sexuality and work. *re/production,* Vol. 2., *www.hsph.harvard.edu/organizations/healthnet/SAsia/repro2/Prostitution_Questions.html*

Reiter, Rayna R. (ed.). 1975. *Towards an Anthropology of Women.* New York: Monthly Review Press.

Rhode, Deborah L. 1990. *Theoretical Perspectives of Sexual Difference.* New Haven: Yale University Press.

Rich, Adrienne. 1986. Compulsory heterosexuality and lesbian existence. In *Blood, Bread and Poetry: Selected Prose 1979–1985.* New York: W. W. Norton & Company, pp. 23–75.

Ridley, Matt. 1993. *The Red Queen: Sex and the Evolution of Human Nature.* New York: Penguin Books.

Robinson, Jennifer. 1998. *Takarazuka: Sexual Politics and Popular Culture in Modern Japan.* Berkeley: University of California Press.

Robinson, Laurie Nicole. 1998. The globalization of female child prostitution. *Indiana University Law School,* Vol. 4, no. 1. *www.law.indiana.edu/glsj/vol5/robinson.html*

Roffman, Rachel M. 1997. The forced prostitution of girls into the child sex tourism industry. *New England International and Comparative Law Annual,* Vol. 3. *http://www.nesl.edu/annual/vol3/childsex.htm*

Roper, Lyndal. 1994. *Oedipus and the Devil: Witchcraft, Sexuality and Religion in Early Modern Europe.* New York: Routledge.

Rosaldo, Michelle Zimbalist, and Louise Lamphere (eds.). 1974. *Woman, Culture, and Society.* Stanford: Stanford University Press.

Roscoe, Will. 1992. *The Zuni Man-Woman.* Albuquerque: University of New Mexico Press.

Roscoe, Will (ed.). 2000. *The Changing Ones: Third and Fourth Genders in Native North American.* New York: St. Martin's Press.

Ruan, Fang Fu. 1991. *Sex in China: Studies in Sexology in Chinese Culture.* New York: Plenum Press.

Rubin, Gayle. 1975. The traffic in women: Notes on the political economy of sex. In *Towards an Anthropology of Women,* edited by Rayna R. Reiter. New York: Monthly Review Press, pp. 157–210.

Saitoti, Tepilit Ole. 1986. *The Worlds of a Maasai Warrior: An Autobiography.* Berkeley: University of California Press.

Schuler, Sidney R. 1987. *Other Side of Polyandry: Property, Stratification, and Non-Marriage in the Nepal Himalayas.* New York: Westville Press.

Schwartz, Pepper, and Virginia Rutter. 2000. *The Gender of Sexuality.* Walnut Creek, CA: AltaMira Press.

Seabrook, Jeremy. 1997. *Travels in the Skin Trade: Tourism and the Sex Industry.* London: Pluto Press.

———. 2000. *No Hiding Place: Child Sex Tourism and the Role of Extra-Territorial Legislation.* New York: Zed Book, Ltd.

Seidman, Steven. 1997. *Difference Trouble: Queering social theory and sexual politics.* New York: Cambridge University Press.

Shell-Duncan, Bettina, and Ylva Hernlund (eds.). 2001. *Female 'Circumcision' in Africa: Culture, Controversy, and Change.* Boulder, CO: Lynne Rienner Publishers.

Shostak, Marjorie. 1981. *Nisa: The Life and Words of a !Kung Woman.* New York: Vintage Books.

Singer, Philip, and Daniel E. Desole. 1967. The Australian subincision ceremony reconsidered: Vaginal envy or kangaroo bifid penis envy. *American Anthropologist,* 69:355–358.

Small, Meredith F. 1996. *What's Love Got to Do with It?: The Evolution of Human Mating.* New York: Bantam Doubleday Dell Publishing Group.

Smuts, Barbara. 1987. What Are Friends For? *Natural History,* 9(2): 15–21.

Spencer, Colin. 1995. *Homosexuality in History.* London: Harcourt Brace & Company.

Stern, Pamela R., and Richard G. Condon. 1995. A good spouse is hard to find: Marriage, spouse exchange and infatuation among the Copper Inuit. In *Romantic Passion,* edited by William Jankowiak. New York: Columbia University Press, pp. 196–218.

Stone, Linda, and Caroline James. 1995. Dowry, bride-burning, and female power in India. *Women's Studies International Forum* 18(2): 125–135.

Strathern, Marilyn. 1994. *The Gender of the Gift.* Berkeley: University of California Press.

———. 1995. *The Women in Between: Female Roles in a Male World: Mount Hagen, New Guinea.* London: Rowman & Littlefield Publishers.

Suggs, David N., and Andrew W. Miracle (eds.). 1993. *Culture and Human Sexuality.* Pacific Grove, CA: Brooks/Cole Publishing Company.

Sullivan, Andrew (ed.). 1997. *Same-Sex Marriage: Pro and Con.* New York: Vintage Books.

Tannahill, Reay. 1992. *Sex in History.* Blue Ridge Summit, PA: Scarborough House.

Taylor, Timothy. 1996. *The Prehistory of Sex: Four Million Years of Human Sexual Culture.* New York: Bantam Books.

Tong, Rosemarie. 1984. *Women, Sex, and the Law.* New Jersey: Rowman & Allanheld Publishers.

Torgovnick, Marianna. 1997. *Primitive Passion: Men, Women and the Quest for Ecstacy.* New York: Knopf Press.

Trawick, Margaret. 1992. *Notes on Love in a Tamil Family.* Berkeley: University of California Press.

Trumbach, Randolph. 1998. *Sex and the Gender Revolution: Heterosexuality and the Third Gender in Enlightenment London,* Vol. 1. Chicago: University of Chicago Press.

Van Wagner, Richard S. 1989. *Mormon Polygamy: A History.* Salt Lake City: Signature Books.

Vance, S. Carole. 1990. Negotiating sex and gender in the Attorney General's Commission on pornography. In *Uncertain Terms,* edited by Faye Ginsburg and Anna Lowenhaupt Tsing. Boston: Beacon Press, pp. 118–134.

———. 1991. Anthropology rediscovers sexuality: A theoretical comment. *Social Science and Medicine,* 33(8)875–884.

Vance, Carole S. (ed.). 1984. *Pleasure and Danger: Exploring Female Sexuality.* New York: Routledge.

Vanita, Ruth. 2001. *Queering India: Same-Sex Love and Eroticism in Indian Culture and Society.* New York: Routledge.

Watson, Virginia Drew. 1997. *Anyan's Story: A New Guinea Woman in Two Worlds.* Seattle: University of Washington Press.

Weatherford, Jack McLiver. 1986. *Porn Row: An Insider Look at the Sex-for-sale District of a Major American City.* New York: Arbor House.

Weeks, Jeffery. 1993. An Unfinished Revolution: Sexuality in the 20th Century. In *Pleasure Principles,* Victoria Harwood et al. London: Lawrence & Wishart, pp. 1–19.

———. 1993. *Sexuality and Its Discontents: Meaning, Myths and Modern Sexualities.* New York: Routledge.

———. 1995. *Invented Moralities: Sexual Values in an Age of Uncertainty.* New York: Columbia University Press.

Weeks, Jeffery, Jan Willem Duyvendak, and Judith Schuyf (eds.). 2000. *Gay and Lesbian Studies.* London: Sage Publications.

Weitzer, Ronald. 2000. *Sex for Sale: Prostitution, Pornography, and the Sex Industry.* New York: Routledge.

Westheimer, Ruth K., and Jonathan Mark. 1995. *Heavenly Sex: Sexuality in the Jewish Tradition.* New York: New York University Press.

Weston Kath. 1993. Lesbian gay studies in the house of anthropology. *Annual Review of Anthropology,* Vol. 22, pp. 339–67.

————. 1998. *Long Slow Burn: Sexuality and Social Science.* New York: Routledge.

Wilchins, Riki Anne. 1997. *Read My Lips,* Ithaca, NY: Firebrand Books.

Williams, Walter L. 1986. *The Spirit and the Flesh.* Boston: Beacon Press.

Wolf, Arthur P. 1968. Adopt a daughter-in-law, marry a sister: A Chinese solution to the problem of the incest taboo. *American Anthropologist* 70: 5, pp. 864–874.

Wrangham, Richard W. 1993. The evolution of sexuality in chimpanzees and bonobos. *Human Nature* 4(1): 47–79.

Young, Antonia. 1999. *Women Who Become Men: Albanian Swore Virgins.* Berg Publishers.